Westminster
DICTIONARY
of THEOLOGICAL
TERMS

Westminster
DICTIONARY
of
THEOLOGICAL
TERMS

DONALD K. McKIM

Westminster John Knox Press
Louisville, Kentucky

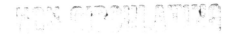

© 1996 Donald K. McKim

Book design by Jennifer K. Cox
Cover design by Kim Wohlenhaus

First edition

Published by Westminster John Knox Press
Louisville, Kentucky

This book is printed on acid-free paper that meets the American National Standards Institute Z39.48 standard. ∞

PRINTED IN THE UNITED STATES OF AMERICA

96 97 98 99 00 01 02 03 04 05 — 10 9 8 7 6 5 4 3 2 1

Library of Congress Cataloging-in-Publication Data

McKim, Donald K.
    Westminster dictionary of theological terms / Donald K. McKim — 1st ed.
       p.   cm.
    Includes bibliographical references.
    ISBN 0-664-22089-4 (cloth)
    ISBN 0-664-25511-6 (paper)

    1. Theology—Dictionaries.   I. Title.
BR95.M378   1996
230'.03—dc20   96-21588

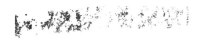

Foreword

Words are the building blocks for Christian theology. Through long centuries, Christian theological reflection has been expressed in words. Vocabularies have been built. Events have happened and words to describe them have been coined. The Christian church has worshiped, educated, and preached. It has passed on a tradition of faith. Theological movements have been born and have flourished, and some have died. Ecclesiastical bodies have functioned in history. Christians have sought spiritual growth and carried out ministries. The church has studied the Scriptures and adopted ethical stances. All this, and more, has happened. And words have been crucial to all these developments.

A number of years teaching in theological seminaries has convinced me of the need for a volume that defines words which are important theological terms. A number of specialized dictionaries and encyclopedias are available to offer extended treatments of vocabularies for particular fields, for example, Bible, theology, church history, and worship. These are crucial resources. Yet today's theological vocabularies are wide-ranging and technical. Specialized works cannot attempt to be extensive. So there is also need for a wider, synthetic work that gives short, identifying definitions over a more comprehensive range of theological disciplines. This dictionary seeks to meet such a need.

The *Westminster Dictionary of Theological Terms* provides a short, one-to-three-sentence definition of theological terms from some twenty-one theological disciplines. The more than 5,500 terms here are drawn from the following areas: Bible, American church history, church government, general church history, ethics, evangelicalism, feminist theology, fundamentalism, general religion, liberation theology, liturgical theology, Lutheran theology, ministry, philosophical theology, Protestant theology, Reformed theology, Roman Catholic theology, social-scientific terms, spirituality, theology, Wesleyan theology, and worship. While the volume is not "deep," in the sense of delving into intricate theological discussions, it is "broad" in covering a wide waterfront in short compass. My hope is that this type of resource will fill an important niche in the theological literature while providing easy access to an expanse of theological terms.

A survey of the areas listed will indicate that I have construed "theological terms" rather widely. This list extends beyond a traditional, formal description of theology in terms of subdisciplines such as biblical, constructive, dogmatic, fundamental, historical, and systematic theology. Instead, I have wanted to ask of each area: what terms are used as vocabulary in the field; what is their importance; and, most significant: what are their theological meanings? Major events in church history, biblical terms, philosophical movements, social-scientific terminology, and objects used in worship are examples of the types of terms included that extend beyond the traditional theological confines. But my hope is for this volume to acquaint readers with likely terms they will encounter as they read in a wide variety of theological sources.

I have not included here as entries proper names of persons or (except in rare instances) titles of books. These would have needed new dictionaries in themselves. The primary focus is on what a term means in the Christian theological tradition. In some cases, this significance is not directly drawn, or is alluded to generally. For some terms in general religion or philosophical theology no focused allusion to Christian theology is made. Yet I have seen these to be of enough widespread importance to include them, while at the same time not making this book a dictionary of "religion." The terms are defined on their own, and I have tried not to make any definitions sound pejorative. At some points it does need to be indicated, however, whether the term or the view is used widely in Christian theology or narrowly by a designated group or movement.

Also, it will be apparent at times that not all the uses or definitions of a term will be listed. The reason for this in some cases will be ignorance; in others, it is because my self-imposed space constraints have meant I have needed to mention only the most important ways the term is employed. The etymologies included will usually reflect Latin, Greek, or Hebrew derivations. Often the Greek and Hebrew will indicate the most important usage in Old and New Testament texts.

This book could not have been written without the help of a number of people. I would like to thank the following persons for their support and suggestions of additions to my initial word lists in the areas of their special competence: Gabriel Fackre, Andover Newton Theological Seminary; Joseph A. Favazza, Rhodes College; Janet Fishburn, Drew University Graduate School; Christine E. Gudorf, Florida International University; Steve Harper, A Foundation for Theological Education; Catherine T. R. MacDonald, the Presbytery of Boston; Ralph W. Quere, Wartburg Theological Seminary; Peter H. Van Ness, Union Theological Seminary in New York; and James F. White, University of Notre Dame. These colleagues have been tremendously helpful and I am grateful to them. Responsibility for the final word lists and for the definitions is my own.

Also to be thanked is Rich Cook, my student assistant at Memphis Theological Seminary. He has aided this endeavor through proofreading and has been a lively conversation partner in encouraging me to dream about possibilities for multimedia resources in theological education. Carla S. Hubbard also assisted in proofreading.

This work owes its genesis to Davis Perkins, President & Publisher of Presbyterian Publishing Corporation. Davis approached me with the offer to work on this volume and for that I am very glad. He has been a strong and patient supporter through the writing process when other duties have slowed my progress. But he has remained a firm friend. He and the staff at Westminster John Knox, including Managing Editor Stephanie Egnotovich, deserve special thanks. Production Editor Carl Helmich has been careful, meticulous, and most helpful.

My own family—LindaJo, Stephen, and Karl—deserve the most thanks of all. They bear with me through all the zigs and zags of our lives together and with their love support me during times of writing and in all else. To them I express my deepest gratitude for all the joys we share.

This book is dedicated to the Faculty and Staff of Memphis Theological Seminary, 1993–96. As Dean, I am most grateful for their work. These dedicated ecumenical colleagues have been wonderfully supportive friends who are deeply committed to the theological education this volume hopes to enhance. For the gracefulness, I am thankful.

Through much of this work I have been, unexpectedly, boosted by the music of

Michael Doucet & Beausoleil. Garrison Keillor called Beausoleil the "greatest Cajun band in the world." Until I saw them in concert, I'd never been drawn to this type of music. But, Amazingly, they provided the most wonderful background for defining theological terms!

One of my favorites from the past is Dr. Samuel Johnson (1709–84) "Dictionary Johnson," the great English lexicographer, produced his monumental *Dictionary of the English Language* (1755) after nine years of work. His portrait, sketched by my wife, has gazed directly down on me at my home computer. Now his famous definition of a lexicographer has taken on a very personal meaning: "Lexicographer. A writer of dictionaries, a harmless drudge. . . ."

Yet I hope the outcome of these labors will take away some "drudgery" from theological work. Karl Barth considered theology "the joyful science." So it is! The following is offered to all those interested in Christian theology, everywhere. May they understand what they read—all the words, the "building blocks"—and in understanding find for themselves the joys of doing theology.

D.K.M.

Memphis, Tennessee
Lent 1996

a cappella (Ital. "according to chapel") Choir or congregational singing without musical accompaniment.

A cruce salus (Lat. "Salvation comes from the cross") Affirmation that God's plan for human salvation focuses on Jesus' death on the cross.

a posteriori Latin term referring to thought or knowledge that is based on, or arises after, experience.

a priori Latin term referring to thought or knowledge arising from a concept or principle that precedes empirical verification, or that occurs independently of experience.

a se (Lat. "[existing] of itself") A philosophical concept applied to God as the only entirely independent and self-sustaining being.

abandon (Fr. "relinquishment," "surrender") Term used by some 17th-century French writers for the willing acceptance of God's providence and one's obedient cooperation with it.

abba Aramaic term for "father," used by Jesus in addressing God and connoting intimacy (Mark 14:36; cf. Rom. 8:15–16; Gal. 4:6).

abbess (Lat. *abbatissa,* feminine form of *abbas,* "abbot") Female superior who oversees a nunnery.

abbey (Lat. *abbatia,* from *abbas,* "abbot") A monastery or nunnery that houses a society of persons who are separated from the secular world or who work in the world. Also, a church connected with a monastery.

abbot (From Gr. and Lat. *abbas,* from Aramaic *abba,* "father") Superior in charge of a monastic community in certain religious orders.

Abecedarians Followers of Nicholas Storch (d. 1525), who believed that all knowledge prevented religious understanding, even knowledge of the alphabet.

abjuration (Lat. *abjurare,* "to deny an oath") A formal renunciation of what is recognized as false, such as heresy, sin, or false doctrine.

ablutions (Lat. *ablutio,* "cleansing") In the Roman Catholic tradition, ritual washing of the chalice and other objects with wine and water prior to the Eucharist. Also the washing of the fingers and chalice after the Eucharist has been received. The term is no longer used, but the rituals remain.

Abolitionism Reform movement in 19th-century America that sought the abolition of the slave trade and emancipation of all slaves.

abomination of desolation A term used by Jesus in Matt. 24:15 and Mark 13:14 (KJV; see Dan. 11:31; 12:11). It is seen either as "Antichrist," a sign or act of the Antichrist figure, or as idolatry.

abortion The removal of a fetus from the mother's womb. Regarded variously in Christian ethical traditions: by some, as justified in certain circumstances; by others, as murder.

absolute (Lat. *absolutus,* from *absolvere,* "to set free") That which exists in and of itself with no dependence. A philosophical description of God.

absolute idealism Philosophical view of G.W.F. Hegel (1770–1831) in which all reality is perceived as the expression of an absolute idea.

absoluteness of Christianity An affirmation of the Christian faith that God's

1

full and final revelation is given to the world in Jesus Christ.

absolutes, moral   In ethics, the rules that are to be observed in all situations, regardless of contexts, and with no exceptions.

absolution   (From Lat. *absolvere,* "to set free") The formal act of pronouncing forgiveness of sins. In Roman Catholic theology, the formula the priest uses in the sacrament of reconciliation (formerly penance), usually "I absolve you." In Eastern churches it is "May God forgive you."

absolutions of the dead   Medieval service after a Requiem Mass consisting of prayers for the dead.

absolutism   The establishment of one element, text, person, ideology, or reality as supreme in relation to all else. Also, the understanding of the absolute or ultimate reality as existing independently and unconditionally.

abstinence   (From Lat. *abstinentia,* "self-restraint") Voluntarily forgoing a certain practice or appetite, e.g., doing without certain foods, usually for a spiritual or devotional purpose. The term is also used to designate fasting and sometimes for refraining specifically from alcoholic beverages.

absurd   In existentialist writings, an expression of the meaninglessness of human life and activities.

abuna   Derived from "our father." The patriarch of the Ethiopian Church.

abuse   In ethics, the mistreatment of other persons, particularly the perversion or misuse of the opportunities to care for others, such as one's spouse, children, or elderly relatives.

abyss   A term frequently used in the theology of Paul Tillich (1886–1965) to indicate the "depth of the divine life, its inexhaustible and ineffable character" (*Systematic Theology,* 1:156).

Acacian schism (484–519)   Temporary schism between Rome and Constantinople (482–519) during the patriarchate of

Acacius (471–489) over the concern that the Constantinopolitan patriarchs were leaning toward Monophysitism and were thus not in accord with the teachings of the Council of Chalcedon (451) on the person of Jesus Christ.

academies, dissenting   *See* dissenting academies

acceptilation   (Lat. *acceptilatio,* "a formal discharging from a debt") A term from Roman law indicating a verbal release from an obligation. It was used by medieval theologians to describe God's acceptance of the death of Jesus Christ as the satisfaction of the penalty for human sin.

accident   Term used by Thomistic philosophy and theology for that which concurs or accedes to a substance and perfects it. Accidents determine the way a substance is perceived—as, for example, shape, size, and color determine how a chair is perceived. They are the outward appearance.

accidie   (Gr. *akēdeia,* Lat. *acedia,* "negligence") The neglecting of duties to God and others due to an inner turmoil.

accommodation   (From Lat. *accommodatio,* "adjusting one thing to another") Theologians trained in classical rhetoric (Origen, Chrysostom, Augustine, and Calvin) used this idea to indicate God's condescension in revelation. God communicated in ways adjusted to limited human capacities.

accountability, age of   The age at which one is considered to be responsible for the rightness or wrongness of one's own actions.

Acemetae   (Gr. *akoimētai,* "sleepless ones") Name for a group of monks who supported the Council of Chalcedon (451) against the Monophysites. They stressed poverty, withdrawal from society, and perpetual liturgical adoration.

acolyte   (Gr. *akolouthos,* "follower") A nonordained person who assists in a worship service by performing actions such as carrying a cross or lighting candles.

acosmism (Gr. *a*, "no, not"; *cosmos*, "created order") A philosophical view that denies the existence of the physical world and claims that only the absolute spirit of which the world is the expression is real. Associated with Baruch Spinoza (1632–77).

acrostic Arrangement of words, lines, or verses to form a word, phrase, or alphabetical sequence where key letters or syllables are found in certain positions. Alphabetic sequences occur in Psalms 9, 10, 25, 34, 37, and 119. A Christian example is *ichthys*, formed from the initial letters of the Greek word for "fish," and standing for "Jesus Christ God's Son Savior."

act (From Lat. *agere*, "to do") The deed that is done by an agent.

act of faith (Lat. *actus fidei*) Term used by post-Reformation Lutheran and Reformed theologians to describe the actualizing of faith in which the intellect and will appropriate the object of faith (*obiectum fidei*), referring either to the Scriptures or to Jesus Christ.

act of trust (Lat. *actus fiduciae*) Term used by post-Reformation theologians to describe the actualization of trust, which means the apprehension by the will of the truth of Jesus Christ.

act of union (Lat. *actus unionis*) Term used by post-Reformation theologians to describe the personal union of the two natures—divine and human—in Jesus Christ.

action (Lat. *actio*) Term used for the eucharistic prayer in the Mass, which in Roman Catholic theology constitutes the sacrificial action of Christ's death.

acts of a human (Lat. *acti hominis*) Acts done by a person that are not specifically human in character, such as instinctive reactions like sleeping when tired. The term is distinguished from "human acts" (Lat. *acti humani*) in Roman Catholic moral theology.

Acts of the Martyrs Accounts in the early church of the actions and deaths of Christian martyrs.

actual sin *See* sin, actual

actualism A philosophical view which holds that the act of thinking is the "pure act" that creates the world of human experience. It is associated with Giovanni Gentile (1875–1944) as the subjective extreme of the idealism of G.W.F. Hegel (1770–1831).

actuality Term from Aristotelian metaphysics denoting the realization of potentiality. In the thought of Thomas Aquinas (1225–74), God is pure actuality, for there is no change in God from potentiality to actuality as there is in finite beings.

actus purus (Lat. "pure act") Medieval philosophical definition of God signifying absolute, eternal, unlimited perfection.

A.D. *See: anno Domini*

ad fontes (Lat. "to the sources") A watchword of Renaissance Humanist scholars. They urged a return to the original sources of the Greek and Roman classics, the Scriptures, and the writings of early Christian theologians. This approach influenced Protestant Reformers such as John Calvin (1509–64).

ad majorem Dei gloriam (Lat. "for the greater glory of God") Motto of the Society of Jesus (Jesuits).

Adam (Heb. *ha'adam*, "the man," "humanity") The biblical accounts (Gen. 1) consider the first human to be a male, made from the earth (Gen. 1:26–27; 2:7), who received the "breath of life" from God and was created in God's image.

Adam, last Designation for Jesus Christ, who represents the new humanity in contrast to "the first man, Adam" (1 Cor. 15:45).

Adamites Small sect in the early church period that sought to return to the innocence of the Garden of Eden by practicing nudity.

adherents (From Lat. *adhaerere*, "to cling to") A term used by churches following a presbyterial order of church government to describe those who attend church worship regularly and participate in the church's life but who are not official members.

adiaphora (Gr. "things indifferent") Elements of faith regarded as neither commanded nor forbidden in Scripture and thus on which liberty of conscience may be exercised (see Rom. 14:17; 1 Cor. 6:12; 8:8; Gal. 5:6). It was a controversy in relation to the Augsburg Interim (1548) which led to Article 10 of the Formula of Concord (1577).

adiaphorists Those who believed certain Christian practices were adiaphora. Also, some Protestants who tolerated certain Roman Catholic practices as adiaphora for the sake of Christian unity.

adjuration (From Lat. *adjurare,* "to bind earnestly") Solemn invocation of the name of God or a holy person or thing (Matt. 26:63).

administrative commission In certain forms of church government, a group charged with taking over the administrative duties of an institution or church. It may be formed for a number of reasons, but usually to provide a better responsibility or stability for a situation.

administrative review A form of ecclesiastical assessment in which the administrative actions and practices of a church body are examined.

admonition, pastoral (From Gr. *nouthesia,* "counsel," "warning," "instruction") A theme in classical pastoral care literature for the duty of a pastoral guide to offer correction, give advice, and instruct others out of the love of Christ (Rom. 15:14; Col. 3:16; 1 Thess. 5:14).

Adonai (Heb. *'adonay,* "Lord") A term for the God of the Hebrews, used as a substitute for "Yahweh" (Jehovah). The Hebrews considered Yahweh to be God's true name but would not pronounce it because they considered it too holy.

adoption (Gr. *huiothesia*) Reception of a sinner into the familial relationship of a child to God as parent through Jesus Christ by the work of the Holy Spirit (Rom. 8:15, 23; Gal. 4:5; Eph. 1:5).

adoptionism/adoptianism (From Lat. *adoptare,* "to adopt") A view of Jesus Christ that sees him as a human who was adopted or chosen by God to be elevated into being God's divine Son or a member of the Trinity.

adoration (Lat. *adorare,* "to pray to," "to adore") The true worship of God in recognizing God alone as ultimate Lord.

adoration of the cross A part of Good Friday services in some Roman Catholic churches in which the priest uncovers the cross of Jesus Christ, which is adored by the people who approach it in reverence, kneel, kiss, and sing hymns to it.

adoration of the Magi *See* Magi

adoration of the shepherds In Christian art, the portrayal of shepherds giving reverence to the Christ child in the manger in the presence of Mary and Joseph (Luke 2:15–20).

adorn (Lat. *adornare,* "to embellish") To enhance a religious object by beautifying, decorating, or imbuing it with more dignity.

adultery Sexual intercourse between a married person and someone to whom that person is not married. Forbidden in the Ten Commandments (Ex. 20:14; cf. Matt. 5:27–30).

advent (Lat. *adventus,* "coming") In reference to Christ, the first advent is his incarnation; the second is his future second coming. Also used for the first season of the Christian year, Advent, in which the coming of Jesus Christ is anticipated.

Advent star A custom from eastern Germany (1850) of hanging an illuminated star during the period from the first Sunday of Advent until Epiphany. It symbolizes the star guiding the Magi (Matt. 2), the majesty of the Creator God who made all stars (Gen. 1:16a), and Christ the "bright and morning star" (Rev. 22:16).

Advent wreath A wreath made with pine branches or other materials with four candles that are lit during the four weeks of the Advent season. A center or Christ candle is lit on Christmas Eve or Christmas Day. A short ceremony is often used for the lighting of the candles in churches or homes.

Adventism Belief in the second coming of Jesus Christ. Also a reference to the Seventh-day Adventist denomination.

advocate (Gr. *paraklētos*, "intercessor," "comforter," "advocate") Description of the Holy Spirit (John 14:16, 26; 15:26; 16:7) and of Jesus Christ (1 John 2:1). In Roman Catholic canon law, an approved expert who safeguards a party's rights in a canonical process.

aeon (Gr. *aiōn*, "age," "epoch") In the New Testament, the present evil age (Gal. 1:4) is contrasted with the age to come, which constitutes the kingdom or reign of God (Heb. 6:5).

aesthetics (From Gr. *aisthēsis*, "sensation") The full domain of the sensible or that which can be known by the senses. More specifically, a distinct field of philosophy that deals with interpretations of beauty and of art.

aetiology *See* etiology

affection (Gr. *diathesis*, Lat. *affectio*, "a state of feeling") Passion or desire as an emotional state or tendency. The term is used to indicate, ethically and theologically, one's dispositions.

affective prayer The orientation of a prayer in which one seeks to unite one's will more directly to God's. It engages one's emotions or feelings in loving and positive ways.

affective spirituality The devotion of love toward God inspired by God's tender regard for humanity in Jesus Christ.

affinity A term used in moral theology to describe the condition created by the marriage relationship.

affirmation Term used by some groups, such as Quakers, in place of an "oath" (which they reject on biblical grounds; Matt. 5:33ff.) to indicate the truthfulness of their statements.

affliction (Lat. *tentatio*, "trial," "temptation") Those elements of temptation or difficulty which are seen as means by which one's Christian life may be strengthened in faith and obedience.

affusion/infusion (Lat. *affundere*, "to pour out") A mode of baptism in which water is poured on one's head.

African liberation theology Movements for freedom and liberation among African peoples stemming from a theological belief that God's will is for the people to be freed from oppression.

African-American religion The religious beliefs, practices, and ethos of African Americans. Visible expressions are in African-American Christian churches and among the church members.

Africentric (Afrocentric) theology The construction of Christian theology using the resources and cultural contexts of Africa, rather than of Europe or North America. It is of particular significance to African-American theologians.

afterlife Condition after the cessation of physical life. Often a reference to final destinies, traditionally associated in Christianity with heaven or hell.

agape (Gr. *agapē*, "love") The self-giving love seen supremely in God's love for the world (John 3:16) and as a mark of the Christian life (1 Cor. 13). Also a fellowship meal (love feast) in the early church held in conjunction with or separate from the Lord's Supper.

agapic Having the qualities of "agape" love, as God's love expressed in Jesus Christ, and the love of humans for God and for each other.

agathology (From Gr. *agathos*, "good") Theological study into the nature of the good.

Agde, Council of (506) A council held in the south of France that dealt with clerical celibacy, the age for ordination, the relation of a bishop and a diocesan synod, church property, public peace, and religious obligations.

age, canonical   The age at which, according to Roman Catholic canon law, one may enter into a church office, undertake a special duty, or receive certain privileges.

age, this   Biblical description of the present, earthly state of existence (2 Cor. 4:4; Eph. 6:12).

Age of Faith, the   Designation sometimes used to describe the medieval period (c. 1000–1500) in the Western world because of the dominance of the Roman Catholic Church and thus of the Christian faith as a spiritual, political, and intellectual force.

age of reason   The age at which children are considered to be accountable for their decisions about right and wrong and thus for their actions. Historically, a designation used for the 18th century in the Western world, when the philosophy of rationalism, stressing the powers of the human mind and reason, was a dominant force.

age to come   *See* aeon

ageism   Discrimination against and stereotyping of people because they are older.

agenda   (Lat. "things to be performed") A term used by some 17th-century English theologians to distinguish matters of religious practice from those of religious belief (*credenda*).

aggiornamento   (Ital. "renewal," "bringing up to date") A term used to describe the reforms of the Second Vatican Council (1962–65) in the Roman Catholic Church. They called for a new openness in the church to the world, toward other Christian churches, and to non-Christian religions.

Agnoetae   (From Gr. "*agnoeō*," "to be ignorant of") A 4th-century sect that taught God's omniscience extends only to the present. A 6th-century Monophysite sect that, on the basis of Mark 13:32, attributed ignorance to the human soul of Christ.

agnostic   (From Gr. *a*, "not," and *gnōstikos*, "one who has knowledge of") One who doubts the existence of God in the belief that truth about God's existence and the spiritual world can neither be proved nor disproved. It confines valid knowledge to sense or empirically verifiable experience.

agnosticism   (From Gr. *agnōstos*, "unknown") The view that it is not possible to have any certain knowledge beyond ordinary experience, so that one cannot know whether or not God exists.

Agnus Dei   (Lat. "Lamb of God") An image for Jesus Christ (John 1:29). Used in the service of the Mass and as an anthem in the form of a prayer: "Lamb of God, you take away the sin of the world, have mercy on us."

agony, Christ's   A reference to the sufferings of Jesus endured as he anticipated his impending death by crucifixion.

agrapha   (Gr. "unwritten sayings") Sayings attributed to Jesus that circulated as traditions during the period of the early church. Also those sayings attributed to Jesus found outside the canonical Gospels.

Agricolan   Pertaining to Johann Agricola (c. 1449–1566), who disputed with Melanchthon and Luther by arguing that the law of God is not necessary to bring a sinner to repentance (antinomianism).

aisle   (From Lat. *ala* and Fr. *aile,* "wing") A lateral division on either side of the nave in a church.

alb   (From Lat. *alba,* "white") A white vestment worn by a minister at the Eucharist.

Albigensians   Heretical sect from 12th-century France that denied the true humanity of Jesus Christ, his crucifixion, and his resurrection.

Alcoholics Anonymous   A self-help group (founded 1934) of those who are recovering alcoholics and who meet regularly to support each other in trying to control their alcoholism through the use of spiritual principles such as faith in a higher power, confession, and restitution.

Alexandria, school of *See* catechetical schools

Alexandrian theology Theology arising from Alexandria in the 3d to 5th centuries, associated with Clement, Origen, Athanasius, and Cyril. Influenced by Platonism, it stressed the allegorical interpretation of Scripture and tended to emphasize the divinity of Jesus.

alien immersion A term used by Baptists, particularly in the southern United States, to refer to baptism by immersion administered by non-Baptists.

alienation (Lat. *alienare,* "to estrange") Estrangement. Often used as an image for the results of sin in which separation from God, others, and self is experienced.

aliturgical days Days of fasting and penance on which the Eucharist may not be celebrated. The Roman Catholic Church has two such days (Good Friday and Holy Saturday), the Eastern Orthodox churches have many more.

All Saints' Day The church feast on November 1 to celebrate Christian saints, known and unknown. The evening prior is "All Hallows Eve" (Halloween).

All Souls' Day The feast on November 2, the day after All Saints' Day, to commemorate the "souls" of all Christians who have died.

allegiance, oath of A pledge to the king required of clergy in the Church of England by an act of 1868.

allegorical sense of Scripture The interpretation of Scripture by use of allegory in which passages are seen to have a hidden, spiritual meaning beyond the literal reading. One of the four medieval "senses of Scripture."

allegory (Gr. *allēgoria,* "description of one thing under the image of another") Communication of meaning by assigning a nonliteral meaning to elements or images in a story. As an extended metaphor, each element in a narrative serves as a symbol of meanings outside the narrative.

alleluia *See* hallelujah

alleosis (alloiosis) (Lat., from Gr. *alloiōsis,* "exchange," "interchange") A rhetorical figure in which one thing is referred to in terms of, or by means of, another. Used by Huldrych Zwingli (1484–1531) in his Christology and doctrine of the Lord's Supper to signify the use of one nature of Christ to speak of the other nature.

Almighty, the Designation for God as unlimited and as the all-powerful sovereign Lord of all.

alms (From Gr. *eleēmosynē,* "mercy") Refers to charitable gifts, the presentation of which became part of worship during the early church period.

alms dish A slotted chest used in medieval English churches to collect alms for the poor.

almsgiving (Gr. *eleēmosynē,* "charity," "mercy") The act of giving to those in need as an expression of Christian love. It was commanded by Jesus (Luke 18:22) and practiced by the early church (Acts 9:36; 24:17).

Alogi (Gr. *a,* "no," and *logos,* "word") Second-century sect in western Asia Minor led by Gaius, which denied the divinity of the "Logos" (Jesus Christ), perhaps to protect the "oneness" of God.

Alpha and Omega (A and O) The first and last letters of the Greek alphabet (A and Ω) used in the Bible to indicate God's eternal nature (Rev. 1:8; 21:6).

already/not yet The view of some New Testament scholars, according to which Jesus taught that the kingdom (reign) of God was "already" here in his own life and ministry, but is "not yet" fully here and will not be until his second coming or Parousia.

altar (Gr. *thysiastērion;* Lat. *altare,* "high place") The raised place on which sacrifices were offered in the Old Testament period. In many churches, a raised table as the place where the bread and wine of the Eucharist are consecrated.

altar, stripping of the   Ceremonial removal of ornaments, candles, and cloths from the altar when the Eucharist is ended or on Maundy Thursday. Symbolically it was a reminder of the stripping of Jesus' body of its clothing at the time of his crucifixion.

altar, washing of the   Early Christian practice of preparing the altar for the Easter celebration by washing it at the conclusion of the Maundy Thursday worship service. It is now observed only at St. Peter's in Rome and is done with a mixture of wine and water.

altar call   The practice of inviting persons at the close of a worship service to gather at the altar in the church to confess their sins and make a personal profession of faith in Jesus Christ as their Savior.

altar fellowship   Term used in Lutheranism to designate participation in Holy Communion.

altar lights   Candles placed on altars in Christian churches on either side of the cross.

altar prayers   Prayers by those who come to the altar or Communion rail at the front of the church. They are often offered in a kneeling position.

altar rail   A rail around the Communion table, established originally to protect the table from the irreverent but later used as a support for those who knelt while receiving Holy Communion. Also called Communion rail.

Altar Society (Altar Guild)   A group of persons in a parish (usually women) who care for the altar and the sanctuary area around it. Other names in the Roman Catholic tradition are "Rosary and Altar Society" or "Tabernacle Society."

altruism   (From Lat. *alter,* "another") Commitment to serving the needs of others, either from explicitly Christian convictions or as an expression of another philosophy of life.

Alumbrados   A 16th-century Spanish mystical sect stressing direct communion with God. Also known as Illuminati ("enlightened").

Amana Society   Small communal sect strongly influenced by Pietism that emigrated to America in the 19th century and settled in Amana, Iowa.

amanuensis   (Lat.) Term for one who writes on behalf of another (a secretary). Some letters of Paul indicate that a person was used in this way (see Rom. 16: 22; 2 Thess. 3:17).

ambiguity   The pluralism and change in the contemporary world that affect Christian theology by forcing it to deal with multiple options and to recognize the presence of multiple value systems and multiple interpretations of experience.

ambo (ambon)   (Gr. *ambōn,* "raised edge," "rim") A structure, often surrounded by a parapet and stairs, from which the reading of the Gospel was done at medieval eucharistic worship services.

Ambrosian Rite   A non-Roman rite, used in the province of Milan, that survives in the Roman Catholic Church.

Ambrosians   Sixteenth-century Anabaptist sect, led by Ambrosius, which believed that God's direct revelation rendered priestly mediation or interpretation unnecessary (see John 1:9).

ambulatory   (Lat. *ambulare,* "to walk") A passageway for processions around the back of the high altar. Also a covered walkway outside a church.

amen   (From Heb. "firm," "established"; adverbial use: "certainly," "assuredly") Used biblically to acknowledge the validity of a saying and its reliability. Liturgically its sense is "so be it," proclaiming faith and assent. Some sayings of Jesus begin with the term (John 1:51; 6:26, 32).

American Standard Version of the Bible (ASV, 1901)   An interdenominational English translation of the Bible that modified a similar English Revised Version (1881–85) and became popular in many American Sunday school publications during the early 20th century. It is marked by the use of "Jehovah" for "Lord" in the Old Testament.

Americanism A 19th-century controversy within the Roman Catholic Church over the degree to which traditional Roman Catholic policies could be adapted for a specifically American setting. It was condemned by Pope Leo XIII in his apostolic letter *Testem Benevolentiae* in 1899.

amice (Lat. *amictus,* "that which is wrapped around") A neckerchief and hood worn along with the alb by those ministers presiding at a service of the Eucharist.

amillennialism A view first suggested by Augustine that the "thousand years" of Christ's reign (Rev. 20:4ff.) should be interpreted symbolically rather than literally.

Amish North American Christian group with 17th-century Swiss Mennonite roots. Amish live simple, agrarian lives, rejecting modern elements, dress uniformly in plain clothing, practice footwashing, and will not participate in state functions.

amoral That which is neither moral or immoral. Persons considered amoral are believed to be unable to distinguish right from wrong and thus to have no sense of moral responsibility.

Amplified Bible, The **(1958, 1965)** An English translation of the Bible that features many words given expanded meanings within parentheses, brackets, or italics. The Old Testament was prepared by Frances E. Siewert (1958) and the New Testament was produced by a committee.

Amsterdam Assembly (1948) The constituting meeting for the World Council of Churches in Amsterdam, the Netherlands.

Amsterdam Conference (1983) A historic gathering of 4,000 participants from 133 nations to discuss the church's evangelistic task.

Amyraldianism The theological system of Moïse Amyrald (1596–1664), which modified orthodox Calvinism's teachings on God's eternal decrees in favor of a decree of universal redemption with no decree for reprobation.

Anabaptists (From Gr. *ana,* "again," and *baptein,* "to dip in water") Those who advocated rebaptism in certain instances. Most prominently, then 16th-century reformers who renounced infant baptism, stressed the literal reading of Scripture, and supported the separation of church and state.

anacephalaeosis *See* recapitulation

anagogical sense of Scripture The interpretation of Scripture according to anagoge (Gr. *anagōgē,* "a leading up"), which saw scriptural passages as having a mystical, moral, or spiritual application beyond the literal interpretation. One of the four medieval "senses of Scripture," associated with Peter Lombard and Thomas Aquinas.

anakephalaiōsis *See* recapitulation

analogia entis *See* analogy of being

analogia fidei *See* analogy of faith

analogical predication An attempt by Thomas Aquinas (1225–74) to indicate a resolution for the paradox of how finite minds can have knowledge of the true nature of the infinite God, namely, by the use of analogy, in which it is recognized that humans can understand characteristics of God, albeit on a much smaller scale.

analogue The earthly reality corresponding analogously to the person or condition to which it points (e.g., the kingdom or kingship of God).

analogy (Gr. *analogos,* "proportionate") The use of likeness or proportionateness to relate one known thing to another that is unknown. Aquinas used analogy to indicate how the same qualities could be ascribed to God (who is infinite) and humans (who are finite).

analogy, way of (Lat. *via analogiae*) The way of attributing characteristics to

God based on the concept of proportionality or similarity of relationships. It was developed fully in the thought of Thomas Aquinas (1225–74).

analogy of being (Lat. *analogia entis*) According to Thomas Aquinas (1225–74), the relationship between God as creator and humans as creatures ("analogy of being") establishes the legitimacy of using "analogy" as a way for finite humans to be able to speak of the infinite God.

analogy of faith (Lat. *analogia fidei*) The Protestant principle that individual doctrines are to be understood in light of the whole understanding of Christian faith, that obscure passages of Scripture are to be understood in light of clearer portions, and the Old Testament in light of the New Testament (Rom. 12:6).

analogy of Scripture Protestant belief that since Scripture has an ultimate unity because it is inspired by God, a Scripture passage may be understood more fully as it is studied in conjunction with other passages.

analysis fidei (Lat. "analysis of faith") Term used in Roman Catholic theology for the theological investigation of the faith.

analytic statement In philosophical analysis, a statement that gains its truth by virtue of the words it contains.

analytical philosophy *See* philosophy, analytical

anamnesis (Gr. *anamnēsis,* "memorial," "remembrance") Used liturgically to recognize the presence of the person or event commemorated and in the Lord's Supper service. As the prayer following the consecration of the elements it "recalls" the sacrificial death of Jesus Christ (1 Cor. 11:24, 25).

anaphora (Gr. "offering") Used liturgically to describe the eucharistic prayer or prayer of consecration of the elements used in the Eucharist.

anastasis (Gr. "resurrection") Term for the raising of Jesus Christ from the dead by the power of God (Acts 2:31; 1 Peter 1:3; 3:21).

anathema (Gr. "accursed"; Heb. *ḥerem,* "placed under a ban") Term of strongest denunciation used by church bodies against heretical doctrines. In the Roman Catholic Church it is a formula for excommunication.

anchor-cross, marine In Christian art, a symbol for the Christian faith expressed as a cross in the form of a marine anchor (Heb. 6:19–20). It represents hope.

anchorite/anchoress (From Lat. *anachoreta,* Gr. *anachōrētēs,* "one who withdraws") Synonymous with "hermit." A term used to designate one who chooses to renounce the world and lives a solitary existence devoted to prayer, contemplation, and penance.

Ancient of Days (Heb. "advanced in days") Term for God (Dan. 7:9, 13, 22) connoting the image of an old and wise judge who rules over the world.

Ancyra (Angora, Ankara) Site in Asia Minor (present-day Turkey) where two Christian synods met; one dealt with the "lapsed" (314); the other, as a council of Semi-Arians (358), rejected extreme Arianism. It taught that the Father and Son were of "like" substance (Gr. *homoiousios*), rather than of "same" substance (Gr. *homoousios*).

Andover controversy Theological controversy in 19th-century America at Andover Theological Seminary in which "Progressive Orthodoxy" sought to gain dominance over traditional Calvinism. At issue was whether one has an opportunity after death to respond to the gospel ("future probation"). The view that this opportunity existed was called the Andover Theory.

Andover Theory *See* Andover controversy

androcentrism (From Gr. *andro-,* "male," and *kentrikos,* "of the center") Male-centeredness of a culture as based on male value norms. Feminist theologies see traditional theology as being rooted in androcentric and patriarchal cultures.

androgyny (Based on Gr. *andro-*, "male," and *gyn-*, "female") A psychological and psychic mixing of traditional masculine and feminine virtues.

Anfechtungen (Ger. "trials," "temptations," "doubt") A term associated with the quest of Martin Luther (1483–1546) to find a "gracious God." Luther was assaulted by fear and anxieties. These spiritual conflicts he saw as warfare with the devil.

angel (Gr. *angelos*, "messenger") Scriptural term for heavenly beings who praise and serve God. They are variously portrayed in Scripture as announcing a child's birth and destiny (Gen. 16:11; Luke 1:11–20), interceding with God (Gen. 22:11), executing judgment (2 Sam. 24:16), etc.

angel of the Lord Appearance of a messenger of God in the Old Testament, identified at points with God (Gen. 16:13; Judg. 6:14), while also distinguished from God at other times (Ex. 23:23; 32:34). The angel Gabriel (Luke 1:19) and other messengers appear in this role in the New Testament (Matt. 1:20; 2:19; Luke 2:9).

angelic hymn (Lat. *hymnus angelicus*) Another name for the Gloria in Excelsis sung by the angelic host at the birth of Jesus Christ (Luke 2:14).

angelology Study of the doctrine of angels.

angelophanies Physical appearing by angels on special occasions.

angels, evil Demons who oppose the will of God.

angels, holy A term for those angels who have not fallen into sin and who serve God in heaven.

angels of the churches The seven angels of the seven churches in Ephesus, Smyrna, Pergamum, Thyatira, Sardis, Philadelphia, and Laodicea listed in Rev. 1—3.

Angelus A prayer or devotion commemorating the announcement by the angel Gabriel to Mary that she would bear a son who would be the "Son of God" (Luke 1:26–38). In Roman Catholic devotional practice it is recited at 6 A.M., noon, and 6 P.M. The Latin begins: "Angelus Domini nuntiavit Mariae."

Anglican One who is a member of the Anglican Communion.

Anglican Communion The Church of England in a fellowship relation with Anglican churches throughout the world, i.e., churches that trace their origins to the Church of England.

Anglicanism The theological movement and churches originating directly or indirectly from the Church of England.

Anglo-Catholicism Anglicanism with highly developed liturgical practices and strong affinities for Roman Catholicism. It emphasizes the Church of England's historical continuity with medieval Catholicism and interprets church doctrine in ways that are consistent with Roman Catholic teachings.

angst (Ger. "anxiety," "dread," "terror") A term associated with Søren Kierkegaard (1813–55) denoting the sense that as one contemplates one's own existence in relation to impending death and the vast universe, one is filled with anxiety and dread.

Anhomoeans (Gr. *anomoios*, "unlike") Early Christians who believed Jesus Christ was unlike God and thus not of the same substance (Gr. *homoousios*) as taught by the early church councils.

anhypostasia (Gr. *anypostasia*, "not a 'person' on its own") Belief that the Second Person of the Trinity took on an impersonal or generic nature in the incarnation, rather than the humanity of a specific individual.

anima In Jungian psychology, the female soul.

Anima Christi (Lat. "soul of Christ") Famous prayer of Ignatius Loyola (1491–1556) that begins, "Soul of Christ, be my sanctification; Body of Christ, be my salvation."

Anima naturaliter christiana Latin phrase of Tertullian (c. 160-c. 220), "The soul is naturally Christian" (*Apologeticum* 17.6), meaning that each soul is endowed with a knowledge of God and that this knowledge can never be completely obliterated.

animal rationale (Lat., "rational animal") The definition of a human being by theologians such as Athanasius, John of Damascus, and Vladimir Soloviev, who believed human rational capacity corresponds to or participates in the divine mind.

animism (Lat. *anima*, "soul") Religious belief and practice relating to spiritual beings that sees natural objects as possessing spiritual life and values.

Anknüpfungspunkt *See* point of contact

annates (Lat. *annata*, from *annus*, "year") The first year's revenue derived from an ecclesiastical benefice and paid to the papal curia during medieval times.

annihilationism (Lat. *annihilare*, "to reduce to nothing") The belief that those not believing in Jesus Christ will be directly obliterated by God because of their sin.

anno Domini (**A.D.**) (Lat. "in the year of the Lord") The calendar reform carried out by Dionysius Exiguus (6th century) established A.D. to designate years beginning from the supposed year of the birth of Jesus Christ.

announcements Statements made during a service of worship concerning events or concerns that are important to the worshiping congregation.

annual conference A yearly assembly of an ecclesiastical body. In Methodist churches, the annual convocation that serves as a basic governing body.

annulment (From Lat. *nullus*, "none") Official ecclesiastical declaration that a contract (usually of marriage) is invalid.

annunciation (of the Virgin Mary) The announcement by the angel Gabriel that Mary would bear a son who would be the "Son of God" (Luke 1:26–38). Some churches celebrate this event on March 25.

anointing (Lat. *inunguere*, "to anoint") Pouring, spreading, or rubbing holy oil upon persons to consecrate or set them apart for service or devotion. In Israel, priests (Ex. 29:1–9) and kings (1 Sam. 10:1–8; 16:13) called "the Lord's anointed" (1 Sam. 24:6; Heb. *mashiah*) were anointed.

anointing of the sick, sacrament of the The procedure of anointing the sick and praying for their recovery (James 5:14–16). It became the Roman Catholic sacrament of extreme unction (Lat. "last anointing") in the Middle Ages when applied to those facing death. Now it is practiced as anointing with oil and prayers for health.

Anomoeans (Anomoians) (From Gr. *anomoios*, "unlike," "dissimilar") Extreme group in the 4th-century Arian controversy who taught that the Father and the Son had "dissimilar" natures. Also known as Aetians, Eunomians, and Exoucontians. The view was condemned in A.D. 381 at the Council of Constantinople.

anonymous Christians/Christianity The view of the Roman Catholic theologian Karl Rahner (1904–84) which holds to the possibility that salvation may be granted to many persons who are not visibly identified as Christians or members of a church. It affirms a universality of grace and God as giver of salvation in Christ.

ante Christum (Lat. "before Christ") Also written as B.C., the term designates the time before the birth of Jesus Christ.

antechapel The part of a chapel on the western side of the area occupied by the choir as distinct from the area occupied by the congregation.

antecommunion (From Lat. *ante*, "before") The first part of a Lord's Supper service. It is also called "proanaphora," "synaxis," or "foremass."

antediluvium (From Lat. *ante,* "before," and *diluvium,* "flood") A term for the materials in the book of Genesis that are recorded prior to the flood that covered the earth in the story of Noah (Gen. 6—8).

antelapsarian(ism) *See* supralapsarianism

antependium (Lat. "hanging before") The liturgical covering that "hangs before" or is on the front of an altar.

anthem (From Lat. *antiphona,* "sung responses") The sacred music sung by a choir in worship.

anthropic revelation (From Gr. *anthrōpos,* "human") The view that revelation is given in human form.

anthropocentrism (Gr. *anthrōpos,* "human"; *kentrikos,* "of the center") The view that humans and their values constitute the central fact of the universe. Humanity can be considered autonomous of any divine being as in the saying of Protagoras (5th century B.C.) that "man is the measure of all things."

anthropology, theological The doctrine of humanity, which views humans in terms of their relationships to God. It includes critical reflection on issues such as the origin, purpose, and destiny of humankind in light of Christian theological understandings.

anthropology of religion (Gr. *anthrōpos,* "human") The study of religion in relation to the lived significance of religious ideas, experiences, and institutions. It adduces general concepts about the roles that religion plays in human existence.

anthropomorphism (From Gr. *anthrōpos,* "human," *morphē,* "form") The attribution of a human quality to God, such as "eyes," "hands," or "arms." It uses analogous and metaphorical language (see Gen. 3:8; Ps. 18:15).

anthropopathism (From Gr. *anthropopatheia*) The view that God has human emotions. Biblical writers at points speak in this way (Hos. 1:6–7; 8:5).

anthroposophy (Gr. "wisdom about humanity") Philosophical view that one may escape the material world through discovery of truths within human beings. Derived from the philosophy of Rudolf Steiner (1861–1925).

Antiburghers Eighteenth-century seceders from the Church of Scotland who refused to take the "Burgess Oath," which named the church as "the true religion."

antichrist (From Gr. *anti,* "against," and *Christos,* "Christ") The spirit of opposition to Christ, sometimes personified (1 John 2:18, 22; 4:3; 2 John 7) who appears in relation to apocalyptic events in the last times.

anticlericalism Opposition, by those either inside or outside the church, to the role or power of clergy.

antidoron (Gr. "instead of the gift") Name for blessed bread distributed to worshipers at the conclusion of the eucharistic service in the Byzantine Rite.

antifoundationalism A philosophical view which denies that there are certain "first principles" or standards for rationality that can provide a basis or foundation for the discovery of truth and the ascertaining of certain knowledge. It is thus opposed to "foundationalism."

antilegomena Books about which there was once dispute as to whether or not they should be in the New Testament.

antimetaphysical Opposed to an understanding of reality on the basis of metaphysics.

antinomianism (From Gr. *anti,* "against," and *nomos,* "law") The view that there is no need for the law of God in the Christian life (Rom. 3:8; 6:15). It has appeared periodically throughout church history.

antinomy (From Lat. *antinomia,* "conflict of laws") The opposition of two conclusions that are contradictory. Thus, a paradox or pair of opposites, as in the philosophical thesis "God is the cause of all things" and the antithesis "I have freedom."

Antioch, Council of (341)   The first of a number of 4th-century councils in which attempts were made to replace the Nicene theology. It produced four creeds, all intended to supplant the Nicene Creed, and twenty-five disciplinary canons.

Antioch, Councils of   Church councils held in Antioch in A.D. 268, 325, 341, and 375.

Antioch, school of   Theological trends developing from Antioch during the early Christian centuries characterized by concern for the literal rather than the allegorical sense of the text of Scripture and the perfect humanity of Jesus Christ. Its school of interpretation contrasted with that of Alexandria.

Antiochene theology   Theology associated with Antioch in Syria and 4th- and 5th-century theologians such as Marcellus of Ancyra, John Chrysostom, Theodore of Mopsuestia, and Nestorius that emphasized the humanity of Jesus in distinction from Alexandrian theology, which emphasized his divinity.

antipaedobaptism   *See* believers' baptism

antiphon   (From Gr. *antiphonos*, "responsive") A short chant sung in connection with a psalm in worship, or the psalmody where two sides of a choir respond alternately to each other.

antiphonal   (From Gr. *antiphonos*, "sung response") The division of chants by different voices or groups of voices. Often used as a way of singing or chanting the psalms in Christian worship.

antipope   A figure who opposes and claims to supersede the bishop of Rome as pope. A number of antipopes have been rejected by the Roman Catholic Church through the centuries.

anti-Semitism   Opposition or hatred of Jews. It may take the form of discrimination, arrest, or extermination.

antisupernaturalism   Rejection of belief in the divine activity in the earthly realm.

antisupersessionism   The view that the Christian church has not "superseded" the Jews as the exclusive people of God. It is in contrast to supersessionism.

antithesis   (From Gr. *antitithenai*, "to set against") That which opposes or contrasts. In the thought of the philosopher G.W.F. Hegel (1770–1831), the counter to an initial "thesis" then later joined at a higher level as a "synthesis."

antitrinitarianism   Rejection of the doctrine of the Trinity.

antitype   In biblical interpretation, the reality to which a "type" points.

Antonians   The name of communities throughout church history claiming descent from Anthony of Egypt (c. 251–356).

anxiety   *See* angst

anxious bench   *See* mourners' bench

apartheid   The extreme legalized racial segregation that has been practiced in South Africa. The term means "apartness." It is assumed that racial groups must be separate since they are inherently different. This also assumes the racial superiority of some and inferiority of others.

apatheia   Greek term indicating the impassibility or absence of passions in God. In humans, it is the mastering of passions.

Aphthartodocetists   (From Gr. *aphthartos*, "imperishable") A Monophysite sect from the first half of the 6th century, founded by Julian of Halicarnassus, which regarded Christ's body as impassible, immortal, and imperishable from the moment of his conception.

apocalypse   (Gr. *apokalypsis*, "revelation," "disclosure," "unveiling") The final "revealing" of divine mysteries. It is a type of revelatory literature. The book of Revelation is also called the Apocalypse.

apocalyptic, New Testament   Portions of the New Testament that describe the end of the world. The book of Revelation with its symbolic forms and visions is a major example.

apocalyptic, Old Testament Portions of the Old Testament featuring symbolic forms or visions and pointing toward the future, marked especially by the theme of judgment. In the Old Testament, the book of Daniel is an example.

apocalyptic literature (From Gr. *apokalyptein*, "to uncover," "to reveal") The genre of (biblical) literature that portrays the end of the world and of human history.

apocalypticism (Gr. *apokalyptein*, "to uncover," "to reveal") Concern for the end of the world.

apocatastasis (Gr. *apokatastasis*, "restoration") Biblical picture of the final restoration of all things (1 Cor. 15:24–28; 2 Peter 3:13). Some believe this includes universal salvation. It is associated with Origen (c. 185–c. 254) who believed all would be restored to a loving unity with God.

Apocrypha, New Testament (Gr. *apokryphos*, "hidden") Early Christian books from the 2d century that were not accepted by the church into the canon of Scripture.

Apocrypha, Old Testament (Gr. *apokryphos*, "hidden") Writings from the intertestamental period included in the Greek translation of the Old Testament (Septuagint) but not included in the Hebrew Bible. The Roman Catholic Church has received these as canonical Scripture; Protestant churches have not.

apocryphal gospels *See* gospels, apocryphal

Apollinarianism The view of Apollinarius (c. 310–c. 390) that Christ did not assume full human nature but that in the incarnation the divine Logos took the place of the human soul or psyche. It sought to maintain the unity of the person of Jesus Christ as the one incarnate nature of the divine Logos.

apologetics (Gr. *apologētikos*, "suitable for defense") The endeavor to provide a reasoned account for the grounds of believing in the Christian faith.

apologist One who advocates for a particular viewpoint, specifically for the Christian faith.

apologist, Christian One who advocates for the Christian message. The term was applied to 2d- and 3d-century theologians who defended the Christian faith in the Greek world.

apology (Gr. *apologia*, "speaking in defense of," "justification") A reasoned defense of a particular view.

apophatic statements (Gr. *apophasis*, "denial") Negative statements about God. These contrast or negate God, attributing to God human or creaturely limitations and imperfections.

apophatic theology (From Gr. *apophasis*, "denial") The belief that human categories are not capable of conceptualizing God.

apophatic way, the (From Gr. *apophasis*, "denial") A way of theological inquiry into the knowledge of God that proceeds by negations or saying what God is not.

aporetics (From Gr. *aporos*, "impassable," "difficult") The philosophical method that seeks to unravel problems (aporias) into their strands and to present clear-cut issues, usually antinomies, to enable an assessment of the pros and cons of different apparent solutions.

apostasy (Gr. *apostasis*, "rebellion"; Lat. *apostasia*, "abandonment") Falling away from or renouncing the Christian faith.

apostil *See* postil

apostle (Gr. *apostolos*, "one who is sent") One sent to act on the authority of another. Refers to the earliest, closest followers of Jesus (Matt. 10:2–4).

apostles, the twelve The twelve persons Jesus chose to be his closest followers. Also "twelve disciples" (Peter, Andrew,

James, John, Philip, Bartholomew, Matthew, Thomas, James the son of Alphaeus, Simon the Zealot, Judas the son of James, and Judas Iscariot). See Matt. 10:1–4; Mark 3:13–19; Luke 6:12–16.

Apostles' Creed Early (probably 8th-century) summary of Christian belief with three articles devoted to God, Jesus Christ, and the Holy Spirit and traditionally ascribed to the twelve apostles. Arising from the 2d-century Roman Creed, it was probably recited at baptism. It is the major creed used in Western churches.

apostolate (Lat. *apostolatus,* "apostleship") The office, mission or actions of an apostle, particularly the apostles of Jesus. In the Roman Catholic tradition, ordination is seen as the means by which members of the church hierarchy enter into the apostolate.

apostolic age The early period of the Christian church from approximately A.D. 30–90, when the apostles of Jesus were still alive.

apostolic blessing The papal blessing pronounced at the conclusion of the Mass on special occasions.

Apostolic Canons Rules for clerical life written as an anonymous document in the 4th century. They include a list of the books of the Bible.

apostolic college A term in the Roman Catholic tradition for the transmission of Jesus' authority through Peter as the first pope and through subsequent popes as the successors of the apostles (Matt. 10:1ff.; 16:18–20; Luke 22:29; John 21:15ff.).

apostolic constitution A papal document presented in solemn form with a legal content dealing with issues of faith, doctrine, or discipline that are important for the universal church, or a specific diocese.

Apostolic Constitutions Collection of eight books on church law that probably originated in late-4th-century Syria but that were supposedly compiled by Jesus' apostles and passed on to the church through Clement of Rome. Includes 85 rules of the *Apostolic Canons.* Condemned by the Trullan Synod (692).

apostolic delegate A papal representative to a country that does not have any other diplomatic relations with the Vatican. Also, a papal representative to international conferences or councils.

Apostolic Fathers Early Christian theologians of the first half of the 2d century who were thought to have historical ties with the apostles. They provide an early witness to developing Christianity.

Apostolic See A church believed to have been founded by an apostle. Most specifically used for the church of Rome.

apostolic succession The belief that there is an episcopal succession of events and persons going back to the twelve apostles of Jesus. Properly ordained bishops convey God's grace through this succession by the laying on of hands. It is considered crucial for ministry by the Roman Catholic, Eastern, and Anglican Churches.

apostolicity Having the authority and sanction of the apostles. It is often used as a mark of the church (Eph. 2:19ff.) to indicate the essential continuity of the church with apostolic teaching.

Apostolicum, the A European designation for the Apostles' Creed.

apotheosis (Gr. *apo,* "completion," and *theos,* "God") The glorification or deification of someone as God during the person's life or after death.

apparitions (visions) Psychical experiences in which invisible and inaudible objects or persons become perceptible to the senses in a supernatural manner. The most frequent example, in Roman Catholic devotion, is of the Virgin Mary. Contemporary claims of apparitions are checked by bishops.

apparitor Term for an officer chosen by an ecclesiastical judge to summon persons to appear and to carry out court orders. Also called "summoner" in ancient times.

appeals (From Lat. *appellare,* "to entreat") Applications for reconsideration of a decision in an ecclesiastical case from a lower judicial authority to a higher one.

appearance A traditional philosophical term for that which stands in contrast to reality.

appointive powers The right to choose those who will serve in various ecclesiastical positions.

appropriation (Lat. *appropriare,* "to appropriate") Designating to one Person of the Trinity an attribute that belongs to the whole Godhead.

approximation Term used by Søren Kierkegaard (1813–55) to describe the process of knowing objective or scientific (nonexistential) truth. It is always relative and unfinished.

apse (Lat. *apsis (absis),* "arch," "vault") Architectural term for a semicircular structured enclosed by a half-dome roof and used as the standard sanctuary form for early Christian basilicas.

Aquarians (Aquarii) (Lat. from *aqua,* "water") Extreme ascetics in the 4th century who used water rather than wine in the Eucharist.

Aramaic A language related to Hebrew. Parts of the Old Testament are in Aramaic (Ezra 4:8–6:18; 7:12–26; Dan. 2:4–7:28). It was the spoken language of Jesus. New Testament Aramaic phrases are found in Mark 5:41 and 7:34.

archaeology, biblical The scientific study of biblical history, cultures, and peoples through examination of artifacts, inscriptions, and other remains. These studies help in the understanding of biblical texts.

archangel (Gr. *archangelos*) A chief angel in the hierarchy of angels (1 Thess. 4:16; Jude 9).

archbishop (Gr. *archiepiskopos,* "principal bishop") A chief bishop for an area of the church called an archdiocese.

More administrative responsibility is usually given for the office in the Roman Catholic Church.

archdeacon (Gr. *archidiakonos*) A member of the senior clergy given specific legal and administrative duties by a bishop. Also, the primary deacon in a Byzantine monastery.

archdiocese A diocese presided over by an archbishop. It is centered in a principal city of the province.

archimandrite (from Gr. *archimandrites,* "ruler of a fold") Formerly used, especially in Eastern Orthodoxy, to designate the head of a monastery or group of monasteries. Today often used as an honorific title for a member of a monastic order.

architecture, church The design and construction of churches. Both theological and practical aims may be in mind as church structures are envisioned architecturally.

archpriest (Gr. *archipresbyteros*) A designation of preeminence among priests, sometimes connected in the Roman Catholic Church with special duties. In Eastern churches it is an honorary title.

Areopagus (Gr. "Mars' Hill") The sacred meeting place in ancient Athens where the apostle Paul preached to the Athenians (Acts 17:19).

argument from silence An argument made without specific evidence on the basis that there is no direct evidence.

argument of convergence Proof of a proposition through demonstrating that it is supported by several independent considerations, thus giving it certainty or probability.

arguments for the existence of God Rational arguments believed by some to be logically valid ways of proving that a God exists. Traditionally these arguments have included the causal, cosmological, ontological, moral, and teleological.

Arianism The teaching of the 4th-century theologian Arius (c. 256–336) that Jesus is the highest created being but does not share the same substance as God the Father (Gr. *heterousios*, "different substance"). It was declared heretical by the Council of Nicaea (325).

aridity   (Lat. *aridus*, "dry") Term used in spiritual theology to denote periods in which regular devotion in prayer is difficult for physical or spiritual reasons.

Aristotelianism   The teachings of Aristotle (384–322 B.C.) which provided a philosophical framework for Christian theology at points, such as in medieval Catholicism and post-Reformation Protestantism. Stress is on facts and substances, as well as causality, reasoning, and logic.

ark   (Heb. *'aron, tebah*) A vessel or chest. Biblical arks include Noah's ark (Gen. 6—9) and the Ark of the Covenant (Josh. 3—8).

Ark of the Covenant   The chest carried by the Hebrews that contained the tablets of the law. It was lost from history after the time of Nebuchadnezzar's destruction of Jerusalem (586 B.C.).

Arles, Synods of   Series of fifteen synods held in Arles in southeastern France during the early church period from 314, which dealt with the Donatist schism, through 1263, in which the teachings of Joachim of Fiore were condemned.

Armageddon   (Gr., from Heb.) A mountain of Megiddo in Palestine (Harmagedon) portrayed as the place where a final battle between God and the forces of evil occurs (Rev. 16:16). Some interpret this as a literal occurrence while others see it as a symbol of the ultimate triumph of God over all evil.

Armenian Church   The church in Armenia, which adopted Christianity in the early 4th century.

Arminianism   The teaching of James Arminius (1560–1609), which conflicted with Calvinism, particularly on issues of human sinfulness, predestination, and whether or not salvation can be lost. It stressed human response to the gospel, conditional election, unlimited atonement, and resistible grace.

Armstrongism   Movement founded in 1933 by Herbert W. Armstrong that emphasized biblical prophecy, British Israelitism, and the observance of Jewish feasts. It led to the founding of the Worldwide Church of God and the widely distributed magazine *The Plain Truth.*

ars moriendi   (Lat. "the art of dying") A type of book, widely used during the Middle Ages, that provided spiritual instructions for preparing to die.

ars praedicandi   (Lat. "the art of preaching") A type of book produced by 13th- and 14th-century friars to give instruction on how to preach.

art, Christian   Art that portrays Christian themes as expressions of the biblical faith.

article of faith   A specific doctrinal statement that is believed, or an entire creed or confession.

Articles of Religion   Twenty-five articles of belief dating from 1784 that constitute the doctrinal standards of the United Methodist Church. They were prepared by John Wesley (1703–91) on the basis of the Thirty-nine Articles of the Church of England.

Articles of War   Required document for signature by every new soldier in the Salvation Army renouncing the use of alcohol, drugs, bad language, and unbecoming behavior and demanding total commitment to the "salvation war."

articuli fidei fundamentales   (Lat. "fundamental articles of faith") Essential doctrines of the Christian faith.

articuli fidei mixti   (Lat. "mixed articles of faith") Doctrines considered to be derived from both the natural and supernatural (revealed) knowledge of God. An example is the doctrine that God is Creator.

articuli fidei puri   (Lat. "pure articles of faith") Doctrines derived on the basis of

God's supernatural revelation, such as the doctrine of God as Trinity.

Ascension Day   The day commemorating the ascension of Jesus into heaven from the Mount of Olives (Acts 1:3–11), celebrated in the church on the fortieth day after Easter, a Thursday.

ascension of Jesus   The departure of Jesus from earth to heaven marking the end of his postresurrection appearances to his disciples (Acts 1:3, 9).

ascetical theology   The attempt to gain Christian perfection through the ordinary ways of life as assisted by God's grace. Its origins as a discipline are in medieval Roman Catholic writers, with later important treatises written by Ignatius Loyola (1491–1556) and Francis de Sales (1567–1622).

asceticism   (Gr. *askēsis,* "exercise," "renunciation") Forms of discipline that include renouncing desires or pleasures for the purpose of doing God's will.

aseity   *See* God, aseity of

Ash Wednesday   The first day of Lent, forty weekdays before Easter. The practice of placing ashes on the forehead symbolizes repentance and contrition.

ashes   Biblical symbol of purification (Num. 19:9; Heb. 9:13) and penitence (Jonah 3:6; Luke 10:13). They have been used in Christian rites through the centuries. They come from the burning of the palms used on Palm Sunday. The Christian use is rooted in Jewish practice.

Asian theology   Theological understandings developed by Asians to indicate the relevancy of the Christian gospel to Asian cultures.

Asperges   (Lat. *aspergere,* "to sprinkle") First Latin word of the "Thou Shalt Purge" antiphon in a Roman Catholic Mass. The priest sprinkles the congregation with holy water while the choir sings, "Thou shalt purge me with hyssop, and I shall be clean" (Ps. 51:7; cf. Ex. 12:22; Lev. 14:51).

aspersion   (Lat. *aspersio,* "sprinkling") Mode of baptism in which the candi-

date's head is sprinkled with water while the Trinitarian formula is said.

aspirant   One who seeks to enter a religious vocation. The term has been used within the Roman Catholic tradition.

Assemblies of God   *See* Pentecostalism

assembly   (Fr. *assembler,* Lat. *assimulare,* "to assemble") A liturgical term for the congregation or community that has come together for worship. It is rooted in the Heb. *kahal,* a term indicating both the divine call to the faithful to gather, and the community that responds (Gr. *ekklēsia*).

assent   (Lat. *assensus,* "assent," "spiritual acknowledgment") Term indicating the intellectual aspect of faith in which one acknowledges the truth of faith.

assistant pastor   A pastor who assists another (often "senior") pastor with the ministerial duties of a church.

associate pastor   A pastor who assists another (often "senior") pastor with the ministerial duties of a church. Sometimes regarded as the same as "assistant pastor." Some polities distinguish between the two. In others, "assistant pastor" is not used.

association   A group of local churches in an area or region having a working relationship with each other. The term is used for denominational groupings in some instances. In others it may be an ecumenical network.

assumption   (Lat. *assumptio,* "a taking, receiving") Refers to the bodily ascension of someone to heaven. In the biblical tradition, Enoch (Gen. 5:24) and Elijah (2 Kings 2:11) were said to have left earth in this way.

Assumption Day   The commemoration of the death of the Virgin Mary, celebrated on August 15.

Assumption of the Blessed Virgin Mary   Roman Catholic dogma that the Virgin Mary was taken, body and soul, into heaven and thus did not die. It was promulgated by Pope Pius XII in 1950 and is celebrated liturgically on August 15.

assumptus-homo theology A type of Christology that regards the incarnation as an elevation (Lat. *assumptio*) of humanity rather than an abasement or self-emptying of God. It also views the human being Jesus Christ as "someone" distinct from the Son of God, a view condemned by the Roman Catholic magisterium (1951).

assurance of pardon In corporate worship, the declaration that the sin of the congregation is forgiven on the basis of God's promises to forgive sin in Jesus Christ (1 John 1:9).

assurance of salvation Divinely given confidence that one has truly received salvation.

astrology (Gr. and Lat. *astrologia*, "knowledge of the stars") The study of the ways by which stars and planets influence human decisions and destinies. Regarded by most today as not compatible with the Christian faith (Rom. 8:38; Col. 1:16; 2:8, 20).

ASV *See* American Standard Version

asylum, right of (sanctuary) (Gr. *asylon*, from *a*, "without," and *sylē*, "right of seizure"; Lat. *asylum*) A medieval practice whereby a criminal who had fled for refuge in a church could not be removed.

Athanasian Creed Fifth-century creed traditionally ascribed to Athanasius (d. 373) and commonly called the "Quicunque Vult" (Lat. "Whosoever will") from its opening words. It expounds orthodox Christian views of the Trinity and the incarnation, warning that these beliefs are indispensable for salvation.

Athanasianism Views based on the writings of Athanasius (c. 293–373), bishop of Alexandria, who vigorously defended the teachings of the Council of Nicaea (325) that Jesus Christ was eternally divine and fully God ("of the same substance," Gr. *homoousios*). He contended against Arianism.

athanatism (From Gr. *a*, "not," and *thanatos*, "death") The view that the soul in some form survives in some place after death. Belief in immortality. Opposite of "thanatism."

atheism (From Gr. *a*, "not," and *theos*, "God") Denial of the existence and reality of a god.

atheism, Christian Theological movement in the 1960s that argued that the experience of the transcendent was no longer part of contemporary experience and thus "God is dead."

atonement (From English "at" and "one") The death of Jesus Christ on the cross, which effects salvation as the reestablishment of the relationship between God and sinners.

Atonement, Day of (Heb. *Yom Kippur*) Day on which the high priest offered a sacrifice of atonement for the forgiveness of Israel's sins (Lev. 16).

atonement, extent of The theological issue of whether the death of Jesus Christ on the cross was intended to procure salvation for a limited number (the elect) or, more generally, for all people. Variations on these two basic views are also found.

atonement, limited In Reformed theology, the view that the death of Jesus Christ was intended to benefit only God's elect. Also called particular atonement.

atonement, particular *See* atonement, limited

atonement, theories (models) of Different theological descriptions of the ways by which the death of Jesus Christ on the cross effects an "atonement" or bringing together of God and humanity. The Christian church has never stated only one, definitive view or theory of how the death of Jesus Christ effects salvation.

atonement, universal The view that the atoning death of Jesus Christ was intended for the whole world without regard to whether or not one is "elect." Also called unlimited atonement.

atonement, unlimited   *See* atonement, universal

atonement, vicarious   (Lat. *vicarius,* "substituted") The view that Jesus Christ died on behalf of sinners (Rom. 5:6; 1 Cor. 8:11; Gal. 1:4) by "taking their place" on the cross. In some views, he received the judgment or wrath or death that sinners rightly deserve.

atrium   Entrance or forecourt of a basilica, often open in the center and surrounded by covered colonnades.

attributes, communication of   *See* communication of attributes

attributes of God   Characteristics or qualities of God that constitute God's very being.

attributes of God, absolute   Attributes of God considered to be independent of any relationships between God and created objects or beings.

attributes of God, communicable those attributes of God considered to have corresponding characteristics in human beings.

attributes of God, emanant (transitive) Those attributes of God which operate outside God's nature and have effects within the creation. An example is God's mercy.

attributes of God, immanent (intransitive)   Those attributes of God which remain within God's own nature, such as God's existence as a spirit.

attributes of God, incommunicable Those attributes of God for which there is no corresponding attribute in humans such as perfection, omnipotence, and omniscience.

attributes of God, moral   Attributes of God pertaining to God's righteous relationships to humans.

attributes of God, natural   Attributes of God without regard to humans such as God's power and knowledge.

attributes of God, relative   *See* attributes of God, transitive

attributes of God, transitive   Attributes of God involving God's relationship to creation. Also called relative attributes of God.

attrition   (Lat. *attritio,* "a rubbing against") In Roman Catholic theology, the sorrow for sin that comes from a fear of punishment or repulsion at what sin is rather than from a love of God. This is contrasted to "contrition."

Auburn Affirmation (1924)   A statement, signed by 1,274 ministers in the Presbyterian Church U.S.A., that objected to the requirement that Presbyterian ministers subscribe to five "fundamental" doctrines as "essential and necessary articles of faith."

Auburn Declaration (1837)   A theological statement issued by "New School" American Presbyterians that affirmed their faithfulness to traditional Presbyterian doctrinal standards and eventually led to the reunion of the "Old School" and "New School" parties (1868).

Audiani   A 4th-century sect, founded by Audius (a layperson), that separated from the church because of its belief that the clergy were too secularized.

audience, papal (pontifical)   A reception granted by the pope to those visiting Rome or to officials conducting business with the papal office.

audientes   (Lat. "hearers") The first stage of the catechumenate in the early church.

Aufklärung **(the Enlightenment)**   (Ger. "enlightenment") General movement found in 18th-century Germany that stressed the dominant powers of human reasoning to arrive at truth.

Augsburg, Interim of (1548)   A temporary religious agreement (until 1552) between Protestants and Roman Catholics in Germany drawn up by the order of the emperor Charles V. It was rejected by both Protestants and Catholics because of the parts of it which they could not accept.

Augsburg, Peace of (1555) The religious agreement in Germany, enacted into civil law, by which the official religion in each territory was determined by whether the ruler was Roman Catholic or Protestant. The slogan was (Lat.) *Cuius regio, eius religio,* "The religion of the region shall be that of the ruler."

Augsburg Confession (1530) (Lat. *Confessio Augustana*) Lutheran confession of faith written by Philip Melanchthon (1497–1560) and presented to the emperor Charles V that defined Lutheran doctrine (21 articles) and indicated seven abuses which Martin Luther (1483–1546) perceived in the Roman Catholic Church.

Augsburg Confession, Apology for the (1537) The response to a Roman Catholic reply to the Augsburg Confession, written by Philip Melanchthon. It was accepted by Lutheran churches as an authoritative interpretation or commentary on the confession. It is included in the *Book of Concord* (1580).

Augustine, Rule of St. A rule for the religious life attributed partially to Augustine of Hippo (354–430). It emphasized a life lived in love, community, obedience, and service. It was approved as a rule of the church at the Fourth Lateran Council (1215).

Augustinian theodicy The explanation of evil as part of the creation which is necessary in order for creation's greater good to be possible. Formulated by Augustine (354–430).

Augustinianism Views that emerged from the teachings of Augustine (354–430) about such matters as sin, salvation, predestination, human freedom, God's grace, and the church. It gives primacy to the will and love over the intellect and knowledge. It stresses human depravity and inability for salvation.

Augustinians The Order of Hermits of St. Augustine (O.S.A.). It is a mendicant order linked spiritually to Augustine of Hippo (354–430) that was organized in the 13th century. The order originated to study Scripture, church teaching, and Augustine's writings. It has stressed education and missions.

aumbry (ambry) (Lat. *armarium,* "a cupboard," "a safe") A cabinet or safe in which elements consecrated for Holy Communion are stored for distribution to the sick, and where oils blessed by bishops were kept.

aureole (Lat. *aureolus,* "golden") The gold background in religious pictures, signifying glory. Distinct from the halo or nimbus, which surrounds only the head.

auricular confession (Lat. *auricula,* "the ear") A private confession of sins to a priest. In the Roman Catholic tradition, it became part of the sacrament of penance, later renamed the sacrament of reconciliation.

authentic existence Term used in existentialist theology to indicate a way of life that asserts personal individuality and freedom as expressions of the decision of faith.

authority The power or right to command belief, action, and obedience.

authority, ecclesiastical The right of a church body or duly constituted church leaders to exercise power and decision-making for the church, its ordained ministers and members.

authority, historical The Bible's reliability in relating historical events or in recording what was normative for biblical people.

authority, normative Authority that is binding in terms of beliefs or actions.

authority, religious The power to influence belief and action through the free decision of those who are willing to adhere to certain ways of religious understanding. Historically, church, Scripture, religious experience, and reason have been channels of authority for Christians.

Authorized Version of the Bible (1611) The "King James Version" (KJV). English Bible translation authorized by King

James I of England, which because of its beauty and rhythms has profoundly influenced Western English-speaking Christianity.

auto-da-fé (Portuguese, "act of faith") Public ceremony in which the sentences for those brought before the Inquisition as sinners and heretics were read. It took place in southern France, Italy, Spain, and Portugal until the middle of the 18th century.

autobasileia (Gr. "self-kingdom") A term used by Origen (c. 185–c. 254) and other early Christian theologians to describe the kingdom or reign of God as found in Jesus Christ himself (Mark 1:15; Luke 17:21).

autocephalous churches (Gr. *autokephalos*, "himself/itself the head") Early church term for bishops who were under no ecclesiastical authority, particularly those in Eastern churches. Today they are in communion with other Eastern Orthodox churches but appoint their own primate or highest-ranking bishop.

autonomy (Gr. *autonomia*, "self-law") Philosophical principle that an object is totally self-sufficient and is dependent on nothing external for its existence.

autopistic faith (Gr. *auto-*, "self, same," and *pistis*, "faith") A faith that is in need of no sanctioning authority or experience to authenticate it. In Christian theology, the faith engendered by God's revelation made known by the Holy Spirit.

autotheism (Gr. *autos*, "self," and *theos*, "God") A contrasting view to the Christian doctrine of the Trinity that states that Jesus was God himself and existed in and by himself, not by means of a Father.

autotheos (Gr. *autos*, "self" or "same," and *theos*, "God") The view that Jesus contained his own status as a God-figure and was thus completely distinct from God the Father and the Holy Spirit.

autousia (Gr. *autos*, "self" or "same," and *ousia*, "essence") The view that Jesus contained his own essence as God, distinguishing him from God the Father and the Holy Spirit.

auxiliary bishop In the Roman Catholic Church, a bishop appointed by the Holy See at the request of a diocesan bishop for the purpose of assisting with duties.

auxiliary saints (Lat. *auxilium*, "assistance") Fourteen saints venerated on feast days in the Roman Catholic tradition for their efficacious prayers on behalf of those in human need.

AV *See* Authorized Version

Ave Maria (Lat. "Hail Mary") Prayer to Mary in Roman Catholic practice: "Holy Mary, Mother of God, pray for us sinners now and at the hour of our death." It is based on the angel's words to Mary at the annunciation and Elizabeth's greeting to Mary (Luke 1:28, 42).

Averroism The philosophical system of the Spanish Muslim Averroës (1126–98), a commentator on Aristotle. His view of "double truth," according to which there may be some things that are true philosophically but not true theologically according to the Catholic faith, was condemned.

Avignon schism *See* Babylonian Captivity

awakening Term for the revival or renewal of a church community to a stronger vitality in worship and mission.

awe Feelings of wonder and amazement, fear, dread, and reverence associated with experiencing the presence of the divine.

axiology (From Gr. *axios*, "worthy," "value," and *logos*, "study") In ethics, the theory of values by which right and wrong actions are determined in light of their values, ends, consequences, or motives.

axiom (Gr. *axiōma*, Lat. *axioma*, "statement") A statement that requires no proof and that thus serves as a premise or basis for arguments. In Christian belief, "God exists" would be an axiom.

Azusa Street revival (1906) The revival on Azusa Street in Los Angeles that became the founding event of modern Pentecostalism.

Azymites Eastern church designation for Western churches in the schism of 1054 deriving from the West's use of unleavened bread (Gr. *ta azyma*) in the Eucharist. Also (Lat.) *Infermentarii*.

B

Baal Semitic term for "owner," "husband," "lord." A Canaanite god that became prominent as the god of virility and fertility, against whose worship the Israelite literature warned (Judg. 8:33; 1 Kings 18:21; 2 Kings 17:16; Jer. 7:9).

Babel, tower of Story (Gen. 11:1–9) of the tower erected by people who spoke one language. Because of the desire to reach up to heaven—and thus show that the people could do whatever they wished—it was destroyed by God, with the result that people were scattered and many languages arose.

Babylonian Captivity (Avignon schism) Period between 1309 and 1377 when popes lived in Avignon, France, due to the political situation. The term, which referred to the Jews' captivity in ancient Babylon (586 B.C.), was used by Luther in the 16th century to describe the Roman Catholic Church's "captivity" to the papacy and need for gospel liberation.

backsliding The diminishing of one's Christian commitment. The term is particularly used in the Arminian and Holiness traditions and not in the Calvinist and Reformed tradition.

Baconian The philosophical tradition arising from the works of Francis Bacon (1561–1626). As an empiricist he held that the basic principles of all things can be derived by induction from human experience. This had key implica-

tions for 19th-century approaches to biblical interpretation.

Baianism Views of the Flemish Roman Catholic theologian Michael Baius (1513–89) emphasizing original sin as a habitually corrupt desire transmitted genetically instead of as a lack of grace. Redemption is recovery of original innocence by letting love rule one's heart. This view was condemned in 1567.

baldachino (From Ital. *Baldacco*, "Baghdad," from which fine cloth came) A fabric hung over an altar as a canopy and a sign of honor. Also "tester." When the canopy is of wood, stone, or metal resting on four columns it is a "ciborium."

Baltimore Catechism (1884) Roman Catholic catechism from the Third Plenary Council of bishops of U.S. dioceses of the Roman Catholic Church held in Baltimore. It was approved by Cardinal James Gibbons on April 6, 1885, as the official text from which children were to be instructed in religion. It was the standard in the United States until Vatican II.

Banezianism A doctrine of grace, based on the teachings of Thomas Aquinas (1225–74) and named for Domingo Bañez (1528–1604), that sought to explain how God gives both an act and the freedom to choose an act.

banners, processional Flags with sacred symbols used for processions and display within churches.

banns of marriage   The reading in public worship of the names of those who will be married in the church. It is primarily practiced in countries with a state church.

banquet, messianic   *See* marriage feast of the Lamb

baptism   (Gr. *baptizein,* "to dip in water") Initiation into the Christian faith through a worship ceremony in which water is applied by sprinkling (aspersion), pouring (affusion), or immersion while the Trinitarian formula is spoken. Regarded as a sacrament by most churches.

baptism, adult   The practice of baptizing adults who make a profession of their Christian faith.

baptism, believers'   Baptism administered only to those who make a conscious profession of Christian faith and who have reached an age of accountability (adulthood). This practice is found in Baptist and other traditions.

baptism, infant   The administration of baptism to infants. In Roman Catholicism it is seen as necessary for salvation. In the Reformed tradition it is a sign of God's covenant of grace. Baptism is usually by sprinkling, with Christian parents, sponsors and/or a Christian congregation present.

baptism, Jesus'   The baptism administered to Jesus by John the Baptist (Matt. 3:13–17; Mark 1:9–11; Luke 3:21–22). It is celebrated in the church year on the first Sunday after Epiphany in most Protestant churches and on the day following Epiphany (when Epiphany is observed on Sunday) in U.S. Roman Catholic churches.

baptism, John's   The baptism administered by John the Baptist in the Jordan River prior to John's baptism of Jesus (Matt. 3:1–12; Mark 1:1–8; Luke 3:1–18; John 1:24–28).

baptism, lay   Administration of baptism by someone who is not ordained by a church body. In the Roman Catholic tradition, an emergency baptism may be performed by a nonordained person, such as a nurse when a person is near to death.

baptism, modes of   The manner in which baptism is administered. Main modes of baptism are immersion (dipping or plunging), pouring (affusion), and sprinkling (aspersion).

baptism for the dead   The practice of baptizing a living person on behalf of a dead person. It has been found among Marcionites, Novatianists, and Mormons.

baptism of blood, the   Term for belief that martyrdom was an equivalent of baptism for those who had not been previously baptized but who died for the Christian faith. It is so regarded in the Roman Catholic tradition. It is only a sacrament by analogy, being "like" the sacrament of baptism.

baptism of desire   The view of some Roman Catholic theologians that those who seek the highest elements of their own religions in seeking God are perceived by God as receiving the equivalent of a water baptism. Such seeking is considered a substitute for baptism for adults of goodwill who never accept Christ as savior.

baptism of Jesus   The baptism administered to Jesus by John the Baptist in the Jordan River linked in the Gospel accounts with his anointing by the Spirit and the declaration of his "sonship" (Matt. 3:13–17; Mark 1:9–11; Luke 3:21–22; cf. John 1:29–34).

baptism of the Holy Spirit   Blessing promised by John the Baptist as accompanying Jesus' ministry (Mark 1:8), which is seen at Pentecost as a fulfillment of Joel's prophecy (Acts 2:16–21; Joel 2:28–32). Many believe all Christians receive this baptism (1 Cor. 12:13); some that it is a special act.

baptismal font   *See* font, baptismal

baptismal formula   The words used when Christian baptism is administered. The historic formula is Trinitarian in form: "I baptize you in the name of the Father, and of the Son, and of the Holy Spirit." This formula provides a common unity so that all Christian bodies may recognize baptisms.

baptismal regeneration   The belief that salvation is conferred through baptism (see John 3:5; Titus 3:5). This view has been prominent in Roman Catholicism and Lutheranism.

baptismal renewal   Services at which those who have been baptized renew the vows their parents took for them if they were baptized as infants, or the vows they took at their baptism if they were baptized as adults.

baptismal service   A service of worship in which baptism is administered.

baptismal vows   The promises made by parents for a child at the time of infant baptism or the promises made by an adult at the time of his or her baptism.

Baptist tradition, the   Recognizable beginnings date to 16th-century Anabaptism, English Puritanism, and later to 17th-century Separatism. Its emphases have included believers' baptism, the authority of the Bible, freedom to worship, the primacy of conscience, and baptism by immersion.

baptistery   (From Gr. *baptistērion,* "bathing place") Area that surrounds a baptismal font, where baptism is administered. May also refer to a large, pool-size font where baptism by immersion is administered.

Baptists   Churches and denominations that reject infant baptism and practice believers' baptism, usually by immersion. The churches are usually congregational in church government.

barbe   (Fr. "uncle," lit. "the bearded") Term of respect used by Waldensians for their pastors.

Barebone's Parliament (1653)   Satiric name for English Parliament nominated by Oliver Cromwell (1599–1658) that consisted of 140 "godly men" and whose number included Praise-God Barebone

(c. 1596–1679). Despite its zeal, the parliament accomplished little.

Barmen, Theological Declaration of (1934)   Declaration of faith by the German Evangelical Church (the Confessing Church, "Bekennende Kirche") on May 29–31, 1934, opposing Nazi ideology and proclaiming the supreme Lordship of Jesus Christ as "the one Word of God which we have to hear and which we have to trust and obey."

Barthian/Barthianism   Designation for those whose theology follows the views of the Swiss Reformed theologian Karl Barth (1886–1968). Barth emphasized God's Word in Jesus Christ, Scripture, and preaching. He rejected natural theology. His work was christocentric, stressing the triumph of God's grace.

base communities/basic Christian communities   (Span. *comunidades eclesiales de base*) Small lay Roman Catholic communities found among the urban poor and in isolated rural areas of Latin America. They are allied with liberation theology for evangelization and social action. They function with or without clergy.

Basel, Confession of (1534)   A twelve-article confession of the Reformed faith written by John Oecolampadius (1472–1531) and Oswald Myconius (1488–1552) adopted by the citizens of Basel. It represented a middle view between Luther and Zwingli, particularly on the Lord's Supper.

Basel, Council of (1431–49)   A general council of the Roman Catholic Church that dealt with issues of papal supremacy, high tax demands, the Turkish threat to Christendom, and the followers of John Huss (c. 1372–1415). Conciliarism predominated at the council, though only for a short while afterward.

Basil, Rule of St.   Two works of Basil the Great (d. 379) that were parts of his ascetical theology and that because of their spiritual merit and the ecclesial authority of Basil became highly influential in Eastern and Western monasticism.

basileia (Gr. "kingdom") The reign of God at the climax of history when judgment is rendered and a new aeon established. The present kingdom is established in the life and work of Jesus Christ (Mark 1:15).

basilica (Gr. *basilikē,* "royal portico," "court") Early type of church building that was rectangular in shape with an apse at one end, columns extending the length of the nave, and narthex at the other end. It is also now a title of honor bestowed by the pope on certain churches.

Bassendyne Bible, The (1576, 1579) The earliest English edition of the Bible to be published in Scotland (New Testament, 1576; whole Bible, 1579). It was licensed to be printed by Thomas Bassendyne (d. 1577).

bath qol (Heb. "daughter of a voice") Term used in Rabbinic theology for a voice from heaven that communicated the divine will, connected also with significant events in the life of Jesus (Mark 1:11; 9:7; John 12:28) and in the early church (Acts 9:4; 10:13).

B.C. (Lat. "before Christ") A term designating the time before the birth of Jesus Christ.

B.C.E. "Before the Common Era." A way of designating the years before the birth of Christ without making specific reference to Christ. Years after this calendar dividing point may be designated C.E. ("Common Era").

beadle The attendant to the minister in Scottish Presbyterianism who may care for the church building and carry the Bible into the sanctuary for the worship service.

beads (Middle English *bede,* from Old English *bed, gebed,* "prayer") Small spherical objects used in the Roman Catholic tradition in the recitation of the Rosary for counting.

beast, mark of the *See* mark of the beast

beatific vision (From Lat. *beatificare,* "to make happy") In Roman Catholic theology, the direct, joyful perception of God by angels and saints after death (Matt. 5:8; 1 Cor. 13:12; Rev. 21:4).

beatification (From Lat. *beatificare,* "to make happy") In the Roman Catholic Church, the second step toward sainthood, in which the pope permits a faithful Christian who has died to be venerated.

beatitude (Lat. *beatitudo,* "blessing," "blessedness") In Roman Catholic understanding, the total ultimate perfection of the whole person who has been blessed by grace.

Beatitudes, the Teachings of Jesus in the Sermon on the Mount regarding the lives and dispositions of his followers (Matt. 5:3–12; Luke 6:20–22).

Beelzebub A god of the Philistines (2 Kings 1:2) and name given by Jews in New Testament times to the "prince of demons" (Matt. 12:24).

begotten "Fathered by" or "derived from." Used in the Authorized Version (KJV) as a translation of (Gr.) *monogenēs,* "only-begotten," in reference to God's Son, Jesus Christ (John 1:14, 18; 3:16, 18; Heb. 11:17; 1 John 4:9).

being (Lat. *ens*) The most basic characteristic or property of all things that exist, their reality, essence or "whatness."

being, analogy of (Lat. *analogia entis*) The assumption of a likeness ("analogy") between infinite and finite being making it possible to argue for the existence of God on the basis of limited, human phenomena. It is associated with the Thomist tradition.

being/becoming A basic philosophical question is, which is more basic: being or becoming? Responses relate to views of how God, history, human nature, and nonhuman nature are conceived. Contemporary process philosophy and theology stress "becoming" over classical views of "being" as primary.

Belgic Confession (1561) A thirty-seven-article statement of faith composed by Calvinistic Dutch Protestants who sought religious toleration from Philip IV. After revision at the Synod of Dort (1619) it became the primary confession of Reformed churches in the Low Countries.

belief   A common synonym for "faith" in the Christian context with the emphasis usually falling on trust in the truth of that which one believes. This also implies the transcending of "doubt" and is a claim to a kind of knowledge.

belief system   The total structure and content of that which is held to be true religiously or philosophically.

believer   One who subscribes to the teachings of a religion, particularly the Christian faith.

believers' baptism   *See* baptism, believers'

believers' church   Term used in the free church tradition to describe the church as the gathering of those who are genuinely converted to Christ (regenerate) and fully committed to living the Christian life.

bells   (Old English) Bells have been used in Christian worship since at least the 6th century. Large bells summon worshipers to worship services. Smaller bells have been used in the Mass and at funerals, and have sometimes been attached to clerical vestments.

Benedicamus Domino   (Lat. "Let us praise the Lord") A liturgical formula used in the Roman Catholic Mass with the response "Thanks be to God" (*Deo gratias*).

Benedict, Rule of St.   A rule for the religious life associated with Benedict of Nursia (c. 480–547). It combines spiritual doctrine and practical actions. It became the primary basis for monastic practice up to the present time. Emphases are on prayer, work, liturgy, and works of charity.

Benedictine order   (O.S.B.) A group of monasteries adhering to the Order of St. Benedict. They are presided over by a primate in Rome. The order emerged

from the rule of life adopted by Benedict of Nursia (c. 480–547). Focuses are on the common life, prayer and study, liturgy, and service.

benediction   (Lat. *benedictio*, "blessing") A blessing that is spoken at the close of a worship service. In the Roman Catholic tradition, a term for a service of exposition and adoration of the Blessed Sacrament. It concludes with a blessing of the people with the Eucharist.

Benedictus (Dominus Deus)   (Lat. "Blessed be the Lord, the God of Israel") The Song of Zechariah (Luke 1:68–79), often used liturgically in morning prayer services for its reference to "the dawn from on high" (1:78).

Benedictus Qui Venit   (Lat. "Blessed is he who comes in the name of the Lord," Matt. 21:9) Formula found in ancient liturgies.

benefice   (Lat. *beneficus*, "beneficent") The benefits related to an ecclesiastical office such as income or property. These may be attached to the office itself or accrue through the performance of ecclesiastical duties.

benefit of clergy   The medieval practice of trying clergy (and persons who could read) in an ecclesiastical instead of a secular court. It often resulted in lighter penalties or the perversion of justice and also granted legal exemptions and privileges. It has disappeared in legal codes.

benevolence of God   *See* God, benevolence of

Bereshith   (Heb. "In the beginning") The Hebrew name for the book of Genesis.

Berne, Ten Theses of (1528)   Ten theological theses in defense of Reformed theology drawn up by two Swiss pastors and revised by Zwingli in response to a set of seven theses propounded by Johann Eck (1486–1543). They led to the Swiss Reformation.

Bethel   (Heb. "house of God") A significant biblical location 11 miles north of Jerusalem where Abraham built an altar

(Gen. 12:8) and Jacob had a dream (Gen. 28:19; 35:1–7).

Bethlehem (Heb. "house of bread") The native city of King David (1 Sam. 17:12) and birthplace of Jesus (Matt. 2:1).

betrothal (From Middle English *betrouthe*) The promise of future marriage between two people, sometimes accompanied by religious ceremonies.

beyondness, dimensional Term used by Søren Kierkegaard (1813–55) to convey God's transcendence in being "beyond" the created world and in another dimension of reality from that in which humans exist.

Bible (Gr. *biblia*, "[the] books") The canonical writings accepted as normative for a religious faith. In Christianity, the Old Testament (Hebrew Scriptures) and the New Testament comprise the Bible. Theologically, the Bible is acknowledged in the church as a revelation from God.

Bible, authority of the Recognition of the Bible's status and function as providing a source and norm for such elements as belief, conduct, and the experience of God.

Bible, canon of the *See* canon of Scripture

Bible, inerrancy of the A way of expressing a commitment to the belief that the Bible contains no "errors" of any sort and is completely truthful on all matters on which it teaches such as history, science, and biology. Some equate "inerrancy"and "infallibility" while others do not.

Bible, infallibility of the Commitment to a belief that the Bible is completely trustworthy as a guide to salvation and the life of faith and will not fail to accomplish its purpose. Some equate "inerrancy" and "infallibility"; others do not. For those who do not, infallibility does not necessarily entail inerrancy

Bible, inspiration of the (Gr. *theopneustos,* "God-breathed"; Lat. *inspirare,* "to breathe in") Belief that God is the source behind biblical writings and acted through the Holy Spirit with the biblical writers (and editors) to communicate what God wished to communicate (2 Tim. 3:16; 2 Peter 1:21).

Bible Belt Term used to describe the southern United States, where strong emphasis is placed on the Bible as an authority. A primary emphasis is often on the literal interpretation of Scripture.

Bible schools Educational institutions, particularly in the United States, devoted to the study of the English Bible and to training pastors and missionaries.

Bible societies Organizations for translating and distributing the Bible. Among the largest are the American Bible Society and the British and Foreign Bible Society, the National Bible Society of Scotland, and the Netherlands Bible Society.

Bible study The personal or communal study of the Scriptures, usually with a focus on the practical implications for contemporary living and Christian devotion.

Bible translations The rendering of the Old Testament and New Testament Scriptures, written originally in Greek and Hebrew, into a particular language.

biblical authority *See* Bible, authority of the

biblical commentary Written or oral presentations of the meaning of biblical texts. These take a variety of forms, from free-flowing narratives to minute exegetical and linguistic studies of biblical verses, phrases, or words.

Biblical Commission, Pontifical The central group charged with advising the pope on biblical study and interpretation in the Roman Catholic Church. Pope Leo XIII established it in 1902 with cardinals and their advisors. In 1971, Pope Paul VI restructured it to be composed of twenty biblical scholars.

biblical criticism (From Gr. *krinein,* "to decide") The use of methods and procedures for studying literary and historical documents applied to the Bible.

biblical interpretation   The ways of understanding the Scriptures. The methods and practices of biblical interpretation vary widely and they have taken different forms in the history of the church.

biblical realism   An imprecise term for the perspectives of scholars who combine the use of scientific critical approaches to biblical studies with a theological concern to understand Scripture as divine revelation.

biblical theology   The attempt to arrange biblical teachings or themes in a more systematic way while maintaining biblical images, frameworks, and worldviews.

biblical theology movement   A movement, strongest between 1945 and 1965, that sought to recover the theological dimensions of the Bible by stressing the unity of Scripture, God's revelation in history, the distinctive biblical mentality, and the Bible's contrast with its cultural environment.

biblicism   An unquestioning allegiance to the Bible and one's own understanding of it.

bibliolatry   A high veneration of the Scriptures to the point that, according to critics, the Bible is nearly worshiped or idolized.

bibliology   (Gr. *biblia*, "Bible," and *logos*, "study") The study of the Bible.

bibliomancy   (From Gr. *biblos*, "book," or *biblia*, "the Bible," and *manteia*, "divination") The practice of opening the Bible at random and seeking guidance through the first verse one sees.

bidding prayer   A form of prayer in which a leader invites persons to pray for particular requests. A period of silence or audible prayers may follow. The form dates to the *Apostolic Constitutions* (c. 380).

bigamy   (Lat. *bigamus*) The condition of entering into a second marriage when the spouse of the first marriage is still alive and that marriage has not been ended.

bilocation   Ability to be in two places at one time. In Christian theology, it refers to the risen, exalted Christ being in many places at once when the Lord's Supper is celebrated.

bination   (From Lat. *bini*, "two at a time") In the Roman Catholic Church, a priest's celebration of two Masses on the same day. This is forbidden except by a special dispensation from the local bishop for situations of pastoral need or a shortage of priests.

binding and loosing   In Roman Catholic understanding, the power signifying the authority Christ conferred on Peter (Matt. 16:19; 18:18) and the "disciples" (18:1).

binitarianism   The view that the Godhead consists of only the Father and Son (see Rom. 4:24; 2 Cor. 4:14; 1 Tim. 2:5–6). It was prevalent in the early church among Monarchians, some Arians, and the Pneumatomachians ("Spirit-fighters"). Today it is found in views that deny divinity to Jesus Christ or the Holy Spirit.

bioethics (biomedical ethics)   Ethical issues relating to biological matters, particularly human life. It explores ethical dimensions of technological developments in the life sciences and related fields.

biographies, spiritual   Stories of persons' lives written for the purpose of spiritual edification.

biomedical ethics   *See* bioethics

birth, new   A term to describe the new life brought by the Holy Spirit in the act of regeneration (1 Peter 1:3).

birth control   Control over the conception of children. The issue has been debated among Christians, particularly when the method of contraception is advocated. Other moral issues relate to nonmarried sexuality, governmental actions, rape, and abuse.

bishop   (Gr. *episkopos*, "overseer") In the New Testament, used synonymously with "presbyter" (Phil. 1:1). The term came to describe the chief pastor of an area with responsibility for guiding the church's work. Later, the bishop gained pastoral oversight of a specific geographical area.

bishop of Rome The primary bishop in the Roman Catholic Church, who became known as the pope.

Bishops' Bible, the (1568) A revision of the Great Bible (1539) published in England under the order of Archbishop Matthew Parker that remained the official version of the English Church until the Authorized (King James) Version was published in 1611.

Bishops' Book, the (1537) A book compiled by English bishops that explained the Ten Commandments, Lord's Prayer, Ave Maria, etc. It also considered the theological questions of justification and purgatory and the relation of the Church of England to the pope.

bishops' pastoral letter A letter written either by a bishop to the bishop's own diocese or as a group letter by several bishops to all their dioceses.

Bishops' Wars, the (1639, 1640) Two short wars between the English King Charles I and the Scots, who wanted to abolish what the king wanted to impose on them: the episcopal system of church government, the *Book of Common Prayer,* and other Anglican practices. These wars eventually led to Charles's execution.

bitheism (Lat. *bi-,* "two," and Gr. *theos,* "god") Belief in two gods.

Black Canons A name given to Augustinian canons in medieval England due to their distinguishing black habits.

Black Friars Term for the Dominican order, derived from the black mantle worn over the friars' white habits.

black letter days Festival days of lesser (mostly nonscriptural) saints that were printed in black in various pre- and post-Reformation service books and calendars. Major festivals were printed in red and were thus "red letter days."

Black Mass Popular name for a Requiem Mass, or Mass for the Dead, because of the black vestments worn by the priest. Since Vatican II, white vestments are worn by priests at funerals in the Roman Catholic Church. Also, a parody of the Mass in worship of the devil.

Black Monks A name given to Benedictine monks in medieval England due to their distinguishing black habits.

black power A term that indicated societal and ethical goals of a number of black Americans during the civil rights struggles of the 1960s in America.

black religion The beliefs and practices of black persons, particularly in the United States, as these emerged from their African heritage. The term includes more than exclusively Christianity.

Black Rubric (1552) A "Declaration on Kneeling" added to the Second Prayer Book of the English King Edward VI (Anglican Prayer Book) at the end of the Communion service. It was printed in black and indicated that kneeling at Communion did not imply belief in transubstantiation. It was deleted in 1559.

black theology A twentieth-century North American theological movement. It interprets Scripture and the Christian gospel from the context of the oppression of black people engaged in the struggle for spiritual, social, economic, and political liberation.

Blake-Pike Unity Proposal (1960) The proposal of Eugene Carson Blake (1906–84) of the United Presbyterian Church and Bishop James A. Pike (1913–69) of the Protestant Episcopal Church that a plan of union be adopted that was truly "catholic and reformed" to unite Protestant churches. COCU (Church of Christ Uniting) resulted.

blasphemy (Gr. *blasphēmia,* "curse," "vilifying") Expressing through speech or writing that which is impious, mocking, or contemptuous toward God. It was met with the death penalty in ancient Judaism (Lev. 24:16) and is warned against in the New Testament (2 Tim. 3:2; 2 Peter 2:2; Rev. 16:9, 11).

blasphemy against the Holy Spirit   *See* sin against the Holy Spirit

bless/blessing   (Heb. *berakah,* "blessing"; Old English) To praise, petition for divine favor, wish someone well, convey favor. Used biblically to describe God's actions, as in the frequent blessings that Jesus conferred on people. A closing blessing or benediction has traditionally been a feature of Christian worship.

Blessed Sacrament   Term used for the sacrament of the Eucharist and the eucharistic service itself in the Roman Catholic Church.

Blessed Virgin   *See* Mary, Virgin

blessedness   *See* beatific vision

blessing, a   A particular goodness received or given. Liturgically, it is an expression of God's graciousness and love.

blessing of children   A practice modeled on Jesus' blessing children (Matt. 18:2–5) and found particularly in Baptist churches. Parents bring their infants to the congregation to be blessed and dedicate themselves to providing a Christian upbringing for their children.

blood   Often used in the Bible to symbolize life, so that the shedding of blood refers to giving one's life.

Blood, Precious   Reference to Jesus' blood shed during his passion and death. It is associated with the wine of the Lord's Supper (Mark 14:24; John 6:54–58; 1 Cor. 10:16).

blood of Christ   The blood of Jesus shed at his crucifixion has beome a theological symbol of his atoning death effecting a new covenant, reconciliation, and salvation (Matt. 26:28; Mark 14:24; Luke 22:20; Heb. 9:11–14; John 1:7).

blue laws   Laws that restrict conduct, derived from a practice in the 18th-century New Haven, Connecticut, Puritan community of printing laws governing dress, Sabbath observance, etc., on blue paper. In the United States such laws regulating tobacco and liquor sales on Sunday were common.

bodily presence   The view that the body and blood of Jesus Christ are actually present in the bread and wine of the Lord's Supper.

bodily resurrection   *See* resurrection of the body

bodily resurrection of Christ   The belief that the resurrection body of Christ was physical and not merely a spiritual appearance.

body, mortal   The present, physical body of a person which is susceptible to death and, theologically, to the power of sin.

body of Christ   Literally refers to the physical body of Christ. The term is used in the New Testament as an image for the Christian church (1 Cor. 12:27), which is united in the one body of Christ (1 Cor. 10:16–17).

body, soul, and spirit   *See* trichotomy

body-soul dualism   A characteristic of much of the writing of Christian theologians as inheritors of the dualism found in ancient Greek philosophers. Feminist theologians, among others, have questioned its appropriateness for Christian anthropology. Emphasis on the wholeness of the person is more biblical.

Bohemian Brethren   A 15th-century religious group in Bohemia and Moravia whose principles emerged from the teachings of John Huss (c. 1372–1415). These included commitments to simple lifestyle, the Bible as the sole rule of faith, nonviolence, and Christ as sole mediator between God and humanity.

bondage, freedom from   The capacity to resist the power of sin given by the Holy Spirit through the work of regeneration and faith so that the Christian is free to serve God. Also the Christian gains freedom from God's wrath, from the law, and freedom from death (Rom. 5—8).

bondage of sin   Reference to the enslaving power of sin that affects the whole person in terms of one's relationship to God.

bondage of the will   The view that because of human sinfulness, the human will is bound to act according to its sinful nature and is therefore captive to it, unable to choose to do anything good apart from its liberation by the Holy Spirit. The issue has been a source of theological controversies.

bonum diffusivum sui   (Lat. "diffusing his goodness") Referring in Thomas Aquinas (1225–74) to God alone as the source of all "good," who diffuses goodness throughout all creation.

Book of Common Order   The liturgical service book of the Church of Scotland and of some other Presbyterian churches.

Book of Common Prayer   The official liturgical service book of Anglican churches.

Book of Confessions   A collection of eleven creeds and confessional documents from the early church, the Reformation period, and the 20th century that is the confessional standard of the Presbyterian Church (U.S.A.).

Book of Discipline   The volume containing the doctrinal and procedural standards of the United Methodist Church at all levels. It is revised every four years by the General Conference. It has its equivalent in other denominations, such as in the "Rules of Discipline" which is part of the *Book of Order* of the Presbyterian Church (U.S.A.).

book of life   Figurative term for the heavenly record of the righteous (Ps. 69:28; Mal. 3:16). In the New Testament, those in this "book" receive a place in God's ultimate kingdom (Phil. 4:3; Rev. 3:5; 21:27; cf. Luke 10:20; Heb. 12:23).

born again   *See* birth, new

born of the Spirit   *See* regeneration

bottomless pit   (From Heb. *tehom*, "the deep") Image describing the place from which the "beast" and the "antichrist" arise (1 John 2:18; Rev. 11:7; 17:8; 20:1–3).

boundary situation   (Ger. *Grenzsituation*) Term used by existentialist writers for the point of awareness where a person becomes cognizant of a transcendent dimension beyond mere existence, often at times of personal crisis.

bourgeois   A French term referring to the middle class and its values, usually associated with a pro-capitalist worldview. The desire is for individuality and material comforts, values often challenged by liberation theology.

bowing   A sign of reverence and honor (Phil. 2:10), usually done in prayer. In some traditions such as the Roman Catholic, Episcopal, and Anglican, bowing is done before the cross and at specific times in a worship service.

branch theory of the church   Description of the church by the 19th-century Oxford movement in which each major "branch" of the Christian church—Roman, Eastern, and Anglican communions—are seen as branches of Christ's true church as long as they maintain the faith and the apostolic succession of their bishops.

brazen serpent   Image erected by Moses in the wilderness. To look at it would bring healing to those bitten by serpents (Num. 21:8, 9). Mentioned in the New Testament as a "type" of Jesus Christ (John 3:14).

bread   Pervasive symbol of "life" as the common food of humanity (Luke 11:3), one of the elements used in the Eucharist (1 Cor. 10:16–17; 11:23–28), and as representative of Jesus Christ himself (John 6:35, 41–58).

bread, leavened and unleavened   Western Roman Catholic churches use unleavened bread in the Eucharist while Eastern churches (except the Armenian) typically use leavened bread.

breaking of bread   *See* Lord's Supper

Breeches Bible (1560)   Common name for the Geneva Bible derived from the term "breeches" used in the translation of Gen. 3:7.

Brethren (Dunkers)   Eighteenth-century German separatists who emigrated to the United States, called Baptist Brethren, the Fraternity of German Baptists, Dunkards, or Tunkers. They emphasized pacifism, believers' baptism (threefold immersion), foot washing, and the love feast ("agape").

Brethren of the Common Life Religious community of the 14th to 17th centuries organized in the Netherlands by Gerhard Groote (1340–84) that stressed Bible reading, personal meditation, and holiness of life. The movement influenced Thomas à Kempis (c. 1380–1471), Erasmus (1466–1536), and Luther (1483–1546).

Brethren of the Free Spirit Term used for medieval sects that claimed to be free from ecclesiastical authority and to live in the freedom of the Holy Spirit.

breviary (liturgy of the hours) (Lat. *breviarium,* "abridgment," "summary") A book containing the biblical readings, hymns, and meditative materials for daily use by Roman Catholic clergy and laity. These materials are for use during various parts of the day. Also called "the hours."

bride of Christ An image of the Christian church (Rev. 21:2, 9; 22:17) reflecting its relationship to Jesus Christ.

Brief Statement of Faith, A (1991) A contemporary confession of faith by the Presbyterian Church (U.S.A.). It is Trinitarian in structure, beginning with the Second Person of the Trinity. It uses gender-inclusive language for humans, includes male and female images for God, recognizes women's ordination, and calls for stewardship of the planet.

British Israel theory The theory that the British people are descendants of the ten lost tribes of Israel which were taken captive into Assyria (722–721 B.C.). Some who emphasize biblical prophecy propound this, including the Worldwide Church of God.

Broad Church Term for those who interpret historic Christianity in broad and more liberal ways, especially within the Church of England. Attitudes of doctrinal toleration are characteristic.

brokenness of revelation The theological recognition that divine revelation can never be received in a pure form because of human finitude and sinfulness. The concept was particularly stressed in the 20th century by Karl Barth (1886–1968) and Emil Brunner (1889–1966).

brothers, religious In the Roman Catholic tradition, male members of clerical orders or congregations of lay religious communities. They take vows of poverty, chastity, and obedience.

Brownists Sixteenth-century followers of Robert Browne (c. 1550–1633) who formed "independent" congregations in England and were thus instrumental in the beginnings of English Congregationalism.

Brunnerian The theological thought emerging from the writings of Swiss theologian Emil Brunner (1889–1966). He was influenced by Kierkegaard (1813–55) and identified with neo-orthodoxy. He was open to a "point of contact" between God and humans (against Barth) and emphasized the divine-human encounter.

Bucerian The theological thought emerging from the writings of the German theologian Martin Bucer (1491–1551). He was a Reformed theologian and played a mediating role between the Lutherans and the Reformed. He influenced Calvin and developed his own views of predestination, worship, and the Lord's Supper.

budget A projected listing of income and expenditures for an institution such as a church body. Local churches as well as other ecclesiastical bodies prepare budgets as a means of seeking to make responsible use of financial resources.

bull, papal (Lat. *bulla,* "lead seal") A written directive from the pope, formerly having attached to it the papal seal of gold or lead with engraved effigies of Sts. Peter and Paul. It deals with matters of importance for a major portion of the church.

bulletin, church   A piece distributed to worshipers with the order of worship for a church service printed on it.

bulletin board   An announcement board inside or outside a church.

Bultmannian   The theological thought emerging from the work of German New Testament scholar Rudolf Bultmann (1884–1976). He stressed the need for demythologization of biblical materials to make the (Gr.) "kerygma" meaningful for modern persons. He made a sharp distinction between history and faith.

Burghers   An 18th-century Scottish secessionist group that agreed to take an oath acknowledging agreement with the established church. Antiburghers refused to take the oath.

burial, Christian   The traditional Christian practice of placing those who are dead in the earth, a cave, or a large receptacle. It is accompanied by acts of worship and proclamation of the Christian hope of eternal life.

burial service   Worship service that includes the burial of a deceased person.

The service of interment often takes place at the grave site.

buried with Christ   A New Testament reference to Christian baptism. It points to the union of those who are baptized with Jesus Christ (Rom. 6:4).

burning bush   The scene of Moses' encounter with God who revealed the divine name and commissioned Moses to lead the liberation of God's people from Egypt (Ex. 3:2–4).

burnt offering   The most general Old Testament sacrifice for atonement or thanksgiving, designed to gain God's favor, in which the sacrificial victim was consumed on the altar (Lev. 1). It played an important part in worship.

Byzantine period   Term for the time period (4th to 14th centuries) when Byzantium (Constantinople, Istanbul) was ruled by Christian emperors.

Byzantine Rite   Liturgy of Eastern churches (Orthodox and Uniate) deriving from Byzantium (Constantinople). Sometimes called the "Greek Rite," it is rich in liturgical symbolism.

Cabala (Cabbala, Kabala, or Kabbala) (Heb. "heritage") A mystic form of Judaism that developed in the Middle Ages and practiced an esoteric method of scriptural interpretation that assigned numerical values to Hebrew letters that were then used to derive a hidden meaning from each Hebrew word.

Caeremoniale Episcoporum   Book containing the rites and ceremonies for a bishop in the Roman Catholic Church.

caesar   (Gr. *kaisar*) Latin title for Roman emperors (1st to 3d centuries A.D.), alluded to at points in the New Testament (Mark 12:14–17; John 19:12; Acts 25:8–12).

caesaropapism   Form of government in which both church and state are controlled by a civil ruler. It was the political principle for Byzantine rulers from the 5th century and was a source of contention between Rome and Constantinople that led to the schism of 1054.

Cainites   Second-century Gnostic sect that praised Cain and Judas. The first was seen as one of a number of primordial beings, the other as superior to other apostles since he knew the (Gnostic) truth about Christ.

calced   (From Lat. *calceus*, "shoe") Shod. A term for those of religious orders who wore shoes or boots. These are distinguished from the "discalced," or those who did not.

calendar, liturgical   The system of celebration, within the church, of Christian festivals and commemorations throughout the year.

Calixtines   (From Lat. *calix*, "chalice," "cup") Moderate followers of John Huss (c. 1372–1415) who urged that communicants receive both the bread and the wine during the Lord's Supper.

call (calling)   (Gr. *kaleō*, "to call"; Lat. *vocatio*, "vocation") God's summons to salvation or to a particular work of service, implying a divine selection. God called Moses (Ex. 3:4) and prophets (Jer. 1:5). Jesus called apostles (Matt. 4:21; Rom. 1:1) and others (Matt. 9:13; 22:14).

call, general   Term used by John Calvin (*Institutes* 3.24.8) to indicate the invitation God extends to all people to have faith in Jesus Christ.

call, inner   The personal call by the Holy Spirit to salvation in Jesus Christ. It was a term especially stressed by John Calvin (1509–64).

call, internal   *See* call, inner

call, outer   Term used to designate a church body's permission for one to serve in a particular form of ministry.

call, special   Term used by John Calvin (*Institutes* 3.24.8) to denote the personal call to faith in Jesus Christ by the work of the Holy Spirit.

call, the   A term for the sense that one is drawn into a particular form of mission or ministry. It is most often associated with a sense of being drawn to the ordained ministry. Many factors become involved and the sense of call occurs in many ways.

calling, effectual   *See* effectual calling

calling, external   An invitation or summons emerging through external means such as preaching, rather than a conscious, internal sense of the influence of God.

calling, special   A sense of one's being called by God to serve in a special capacity or in a certain vocation. It may be considered either a more permanent or a temporary direction for one's life.

Calvary   (Lat. *Calvaria*, "a bare skull"; Gr. *Kranion*, Aramaic *Golgotha*) A hill outside Jerusalem, used for crucifixions and shaped like a skull ("Place of a Skull," Mark 15:22), where Jesus was crucified.

Calvinian   Following the views of John Calvin (1509–64). A distinction is sometimes made between "Calvinian" and "Calvinist." The "Calvinian" emphasis is to focus on Calvin's own views rather than the theological system developed later by those who were called "Calvinists."

Calvinism   The developed and systematized teachings of John Calvin (1509–64), which spread throughout Europe and internationally from the 16th century to the present day. It is also called the Reformed tradition. Calvinism embraces both theological beliefs and a way of life.

Calvinist   One who adheres to the theological thought developed by John Calvin (1509–64) and his followers.

Calvinistic Methodism   The Presbyterian Church of Wales, which originated through 18th-century Methodist revivals. While the church is Methodist in outlook, its confession of faith is based on the Westminster Standards and it is presbyterial in government.

Cambridge Platform (1648)   Statement by New England Congregationalists on church polity drawn up at the Cambridge Synod in Massachusetts. It advocated a congregational form of church government while maintaining adherence to the Westminster Confession (1646) in doctrinal matters.

Cambridge Platonists   Seventeenth-century philosophers and theologians influenced by Neoplatonic philosophy. They advocated toleration within the church and emphasized reason as the judge of revelation.

Cameronians Seventeenth-century Scottish covenanter Presbyterians who followed the principles of Richard Cameron (c. 1648–80). They fought for religious freedom under Charles II and James VII.

Camiscards/Camiscard Wars Extremist French Protestants who revolted in 1702 against the suppression of their faith by Louis XIV. They were perhaps named for their black peasant shirts. They were defeated by the king by 1704 and repudiated by a French Reformed Church synod (1715).

camp meetings Nineteenth-century American open-air religious gatherings for worship and social contact on the frontier. They featured preaching, singing and were revivalistic in orientation.

campanile (Ital. from Lat. *campana*, a bell [made of metal produced in Campania]) A bell tower or bell steeple.

Campbellites Followers of Alexander Campbell (1788–1866), one of the founders of the Christian Church (Disciples of Christ). They practice a congregational form of church government and believers' baptism, and they celebrate the Lord's Supper each Sunday. They reject all credal statements.

campus ministries Christian ministries found on the campuses of colleges, universities, or other centers of higher education.

candle (Old English, from Lat. *candere,* "to shine") Candles are lit during liturgical services to symbolize a number of Christian beliefs. These include the divine light (1 John 1:5), purity, holiness, and the Risen Jesus Christ as the "light of the world" (John 8:12; 1:5).

Candlemas (Anglo-Saxon *candelmaesse,* "mass for the candles") Feast of the Purification of the Blessed Virgin Mary and the Presentation of Jesus in the Temple (Lev. 12:1–8; Luke 2:22ff.). The day is celebrated on February 2 and is marked by a blessing of candles and a procession symbolizing Christ as light of the world entering the Temple.

canon (Gr. *kanōn,* Lat. "rule") An ecclesiastical decree from a church council or church body. Also, ecclesiastical legislation (e.g., "canon law"); a list of sacred books ("canon of Scripture"); a list of saints; the central portion of the Mass; and a person with an ecclesiastical office such as a diocesan priest attached to a cathedral or a member of certain religious orders.

canon (hymnological) In the Eastern Orthodox Church, nine hymns of the morning office of worship (*orthros*). They originate from the singing of biblical canticles or songs.

canon, New Testament The writings relating to Jesus Christ accepted by the Christian church as the authoritative source for faith. Protestants and Roman Catholics recognize 27 New Testament books as Holy Scripture.

canon, Old Testament The writings prior to the birth of Jesus Christ accepted by the Christian church as the authoritative source of God's revelation as Scripture. Protestant churches recognize 39 and the Roman Catholic Church recognizes 46 Old Testament books as Holy Scripture. The Jewish canon includes 24 books but these appear as 39 books in modern translations.

canon law, code of Church laws concerning procedures and discipline that are considered authoritative in the Roman Catholic tradition.

canon of Scripture The biblical books constituting the Old and New Testaments and considered authoritative by the Christian church.

canon of the Mass Also called the eucharistic prayer, the term refers to the fixed liturgical formula of the Roman Catholic liturgy proclaimed by the priest after the gifts of bread and wine have been offered in the Eucharist. The central focus is the formula of consecration for the elements.

canon within the canon The recognition that theological perspectives and systems may influence biblical interpretation in ways tending to emphasize some concepts more heavily than others. This, in effect, establishes a group of Scriptures or biblical books that function more authoritatively than others.

canoness   Term from the mid-8th century for a member of a female religious community who lives under a rule of life and has taken vows of celibacy and obedience.

canonical hours   Traditional set of seven times during the day when services are to be read by monks and clergy belonging to the Roman Catholic, Orthodox, and other churches. Also called "canonical services" or "the hours."

canonization   The process by which biblical books became recognized as authoritative in the Christian church and were eventually drawn together into a collection of books. In Roman Catholic theology, the process by which someone is made a saint.

canons, the   The main body of ecclesiastical legislation in the Church of England.

canons regular   (Lat. *canonici regulares*) Canons who live under a rule, usually the Augustinian, and thus their normal designation as Augustinian Canons.

canopy, processional   An awning over the Communion elements as they are carried in processions. In the Roman Catholic Church it is used over church dignitaries as well.

cantata   (From Ital. *cantare*, "to sing") A musical form directly related to scriptural readings and performed as part of a worship service. It is to be sung, in contrast to a "sonata," which is to be played by musical instruments.

canticles   (Middle English from Lat. *canticulum*, "little song") Songs (other than psalms) or biblical poems, usually taken from Scripture and used as part of the liturgy of a church in a worship service. These would include Ex. 15:1–19; Deut. 32:1–43; Luke 1:46–55, 68–79; 2:29–32.

Canticles, book of   Another name for the Song of Solomon or Song of Songs.

cantor   (Lat. "singer," from *cantare*, "to sing") The clergy or lay person who sets the pitch and leads (usually unaccompanied) singing in a worship service. The office exists in Judaism and has existed in both Eastern and Western Christianity.

cantoris   (Lat. "the place of the cantor") Traditionally, the location of the cantor on the north side of a cathedral or church.

capital punishment   The taking of a life as the judicial punishment for a crime committed. It was carried out in Israel (Ex. 21:12–17; 22:18–20) and was experienced by early Christians. Since the 18th century, its prevalence has lessened. Its legitimacy has been much debated.

capital sins, capital virtues   (Lat. *capitalis*, "principal") The sins and virtues considered by some to be the source of other sins and virtues. Traditionally these contrasts have been: pride/humility, avarice/liberality, lust/chastity, anger/meekness, gluttony/temperance, envy/love, sloth/diligence.

capitalism   A system of organizing economic life and its means of production, beginning in 16th-century Europe after the breakdown of feudalism. It is linked by some with the rise of Protestantism, which encouraged hard work and savings. It has been critiqued as producing inequality and poverty.

Cappadocian theologians (fathers) Fourth-century theologians from Cappadocia concerned especially with establishing the doctrines of the Trinity and Christology against Arianism. They were Basil the Great of Caesarea (c. 330–79), Gregory of Nyssa (c. 335–c. 395), and Gregory of Nazianzus (c. 329–90).

captivity epistles   *See* prison epistles

cardinal   (Lat. *cardinalis*, from *cardo*, "hinge," "that on which anything depends") An evolving term that today refers to the "princes of the church" appointed by the pope. They form his council and are the group next to the pope in the Roman Catholic hierarchy. The cardinals choose the pope.

cardinal sins Roman Catholic designation for the major sins of pride, covetousness, lust, anger, gluttony, envy, and sloth. They are "cardinal" in that they are hinges (Lat. *cardo*, "hinge") on which lesser sins turn.

cardinal virtues Roman Catholic designation for the seven major virtues of faith, hope, love, justice, prudence, temperance, and fortitude. They are "cardinal" in that they are "hinges" (Lat. *cardo*, "hinge") on which lesser virtues turn.

cardiognosis (From Gr. *kardiognōsis*, "knowledge of the heart") In Roman Catholic theology the view that only God knows the condition of one's relationship with God but that this knowledge may be granted to someone as a special "charism" (gift).

care, pastoral *See* pastoral care

Carmelite order (O. Carm.) A Roman Catholic religious order founded around 1200 by penitent lay hermits on Mount Carmel near Haifa. Carmelites identified with the Virgin Mary and have a strong mystical tradition. They have looked to Elijah and balance solitude and community. Both women and men belong.

carnal (Lat. *carnalis*, from *carnis*, "flesh") That which relates to the body, usually associated with desires such as sensuality, lust, and indulgence.

carnival (Lat. *carnem levare*, "to put away meat") Traditional season of celebration immediately preceding the season of Lent.

carol (Old French from Gr. *choraulēs*, "a piper for a choral dance") A joyful song, originally sung with an accompanying circular dance, now designating a popular, more informal religious song.

Caroline divines, the Seventeenth-century theologians of the Church of England, including Lancelot Andrewes (d. 1626) and William Laud (d. 1645), who maintained high views of the importance of bishops, sacraments, and liturgy.

Cartesianism The philosophy of René Descartes (1596–1650), stressing the rational powers of the human mind to discover truth. Also called "rationalism."

Carthage, Councils of Four main groups of church councils were held at Carthage under Cyprian, Gratus, Aurelius, and Boniface from the 3d to the 6th centuries. They dealt with matters including the problem of those who "lapsed" during the Decian persecution and the rebaptism of heretics.

Carthusian order (O. Cart.) An order of women and men which has emphasized silence and solitude in the search for God in the context of a monastic community. The order was founded by Bruno (c. 1030–1101) in 1084. Members live in separate cells and take vows of silence and total renunciation of the world.

Carthusians A contemplative order of monks founded by Bruno the Carthusian (c. 1030–1101) and six others in Chartreuse, France.

cassock (Ital. *cassaca*) The basic garment of medieval persons. Now a long, ankle-length garment with narrow sleeves worn by clergy, symbolizing devotion.

cassock-alb A combination cassock and alb worn by clergy participating in the Eucharist.

casuistry (From Lat. *casus*, "case") The application of ethical rules or norms to specific instances or cases in order to guide the conscience or conduct. The tradition is found in the New Testament (Mark 2:23–28; Luke 20:20–26) and in Roman Catholicism and Protestantism in "cases of conscience."

Catabaptists (Gr. *katabaptistēs*, "against baptism") Term used in the 16th century for those who opposed the practice of infant baptism, notably the "Anabaptists."

catacombs Underground tunnels used as burial grounds in which early Christians met for worship from the 2d to the early 5th centuries. Most were in Italy, particularly Rome. They developed elaborate systems of galleries, rooms, and corridors.

catafalque (Ital. *catafalco,* "funeral canopy," from Lat. *catafalicum,* "scaffold") In general, a coffin and all that surrounds it. More specifically, the framework on which the coffin rests at a funeral.

cataphatic theology (Gr. *kataphasis,* "affirmation") A mode of theology used to describe God positively on the basis of the divine self-revelation. In contrast to "apophatic theology," the "way of negation."

Cataphrygians Another name for Montanists, referring to their origins in Phrygia.

catechesis (From Gr. *katechein,* "to teach by word of mouth") Technical term for instruction given to persons in preparation for baptism or confirmation in the Christian church (Acts 18:25; Rom. 2:18; Gal. 6:6).

catechetical schools Schools begun by early Christians to teach the faith to the young. The most prominent was begun in the second century in Alexandria. Clement of Alexandria (c. 150–220) and Origen (c. 185–c. 254) were each head of this school.

catechetics (From Gr. *katechein,* "to instruct") A term that emerged in the 20th century within the Roman Catholic tradition for the study of methods by which the Christian faith may be taught. It refers to the process of forming persons in a faith community.

catechism (Gr. *katechein,* "to instruct by word of mouth") A means of instruction, often in question-and-answer form, that conveys a summary of Christian theological beliefs.

catechist (From Gr. *katechein,* "to instruct") One who gives instruction in Christianity. The term is now often used for one who instructs children.

catechumen (Gr. *katechoumenos,* "one who is being instructed") One who is being instructed in the Christian faith, usually in preparation for church membership. The term originated in the early church with the instruction anticipating Christian baptism.

categorical imperative In the thought of Immanuel Kant (1724–1804), a moral law, given in reason, that has universal and unconditional binding force. More simply, it advocates acting in a way that one could accept as good (as a universal law) if everyone acted in that way.

catena (Lat. "chain"; Gr. *seira*) A type of biblical commentary from the 5th century onward marked by explanations of the biblical text through a "chain" of passages derived from earlier commentators. More widely, it refers to any collection of passages on a subject from various writers.

Cathari (From Gr. *katharos,* "pure") Name for various groups in church history that have emphasized purity of life. These have included Novatianists, Manichaeans, and the medieval Albigensians.

catharsis (Gr. "a cleansing") The events and processes that can cleanse and free one from impediments to union with God or true human existence.

cathedra (Gr. "a chair") The bishop's "chair" or throne in a cathedral from which official pronouncements may be made. It thus, by extension, means episcopal authority.

cathedral (From Gr. *kathedra,* Lat. *cathedra,* "chair," "throne") The church containing the "throne" or official "seat" (Lat. *sedes*) of a bishop of a diocese. Here the bishop presides over the liturgy and, by extension, the diocese.

cathedral office Form of morning and evening prayer focused on psalmody and intercession, performed daily in cathedrals and parish churches.

cathedral schools Schools established during the Middle Ages and later to educate choirboys for singing in cathedral churches. They also served as grammar schools and as a source of free education for the poor boys of a cathedral city.

catholic (Gr. *katholikos,* "universal," "general") Term used since the 2d century to designate the Christian church throughout the world. It is opposed to "sectarian," which refers to those who have separated from the worldwide church. It is a "mark" of the church along with "one," "holy," and "apostolic."

Catholic Church, Roman   *See* Roman Catholicism

catholic epistles/letters   Seven New Testament letters addressed to a general audience ("catholic"; Gr. *katholikos,* "universal") and not to specific churches. These are James, 1 and 2 Peter, 1, 2, and 3 John, and Jude.

Catholic social teachings   The body of teachings promulgated by the Roman Catholic Church and focused on political, social, and economic problems and conditions. These teachings are set forth in various papal encyclicals as well as materials from other bodies such as councils and synods.

catholic spirit   A term used by John Wesley (1703–91) to describe an approach to Christianity that stressed a unity on the essentials of Christian faith while showing toleration for those elements and practices which are nonessentials, i.e., which are not necessary for Christian salvation.

Catholic truths   (Lat. *veritates catholicae* or *doctrina catholica*) In Roman Catholic theology, all the truths the church teaches authentically but not infallibly (by which they differ from dogmas).

Catholicism, conventional Roman   Forms of Roman Catholicism that support the traditional positions promulgated at the Council of Trent (1545–63).

catholicity   (Gr. *katholikos,* "universal") Term used to designate the universal nature and spread of the Christian church.

catholicos   (Gr. "regarding the whole") Title of the heads or patriarchs of the Armenian, Georgian, and Nestorian churches. Originally the term was used for the chief bishop of a local church, who was subordinate to a patriarch.

Catholics, Old   *See* Old Catholics

causa sui   (Lat. "cause of itself") A philosophical reference to God as the being who is uncaused by any other source or power.

causality/causation   (Lat. *causa,* "that by which anything is done") A philosophical concept for that which produces something in terms of which its effects can be explained. In the Christian understanding of God and creation, God is the ultimate or final cause from whom all else emerges as "effect."

cause, first   A philosophical term referring to God as the primary and final source of the whole created universe.

C.E.   "Common Era." A term used to designate the years since the birth of Jesus Christ. It does not make the same religious claim as A.D. (Lat. *anno Domini,* the "year of the Lord"), yet it recognizes this as the common calendar dividing point in the Western world. Earlier years are designated B.C.E. ("before the Common Era").

CELAM II   *See* Medellín Conference

CELAM III   *See* Puebla Conference (1979)

celebrant   (From Lat. *celebrare,* "to fill," "celebrate") One who officiates at a service of worship. In the Roman Catholic tradition it has meant the presider at the Eucharist. Because all worshipers celebrate in worship, "presider" is now a preferred term in the Roman Catholic Church.

celebritism, Christian   The practice of exalting well-known Christians to a celebrity status.

celestial flesh Christology   A term associated with Menno Simons (1496–1561) and others who taught that Jesus did not receive his human nature from the Virgin Mary. He was born "out of" and not "from" Mary. This view sought to maintain Christ's sinlessness. John Calvin (1509–64) considered it Docetism.

celibacy (Lat. *caelebs*, "unmarried") State of being unmarried due to religious convictions.

celibacy of the clergy (Lat. *caelebs*, "unmarried") Clergy living in an unmarried state. This has been the historic requirement of the Roman Catholic Church.

cell (Lat. *cella*) A private room or apartment of a person dedicated to a religious vocation. Also used for small groups of Christians who have dedicated themselves to a purpose, often the spreading of the Christian gospel in the midst of their secular surroundings.

cell group A small group of individuals who form part of a larger institutional structure but who are gathered for a specific purpose or task. The term appears in 20th-century religious, political, and psychological contexts.

Cenaculum, the (Lat. "upper room") The "upper room" in which the Last Supper was celebrated (Mark 14:15; Luke 22:12) and where the apostles stayed at the time of Pentecost (Acts 1:13).

cenobite (Gr. *koinobios*) One who has taken religious vows and lives in community, as distinct from a hermit.

censer (Old French *encens*, "incense") A container in which incense is burned. Also "thurible" (Lev. 16:2, 12–13; Num. 4:5–8; Rev. 8:3–5).

censures (Lat. *censura*, "censor's office," "judgment") Reprimands or punishments by the church to violators of church laws. Their purposes are corrective and in some churches they may be lifted when reform has occurred. They may include excommunication, suspension, or interdiction.

ceremonial (Middle English from Lat. *caerimonia*, "sacredness," "religious rite") Prescribed actions or movements as part of a liturgical rite.

ceremonial laws In the Old Testament, laws pertaining to religious sacrifices and purification rather than moral laws.

certainty/certitude, theological (Lat. *certitudo theologica*) Also *certitudo fidei*, "the certainty of faith." Theological certainty is not something to be demonstrated or proved by certain self-evident principles. It is an absolute and infallible certainty that rests on God's revelation as received by faith.

certainty of salvation *See* assurance of salvation

CEV *See* Contemporary English Version

chaburah (From Heb. *ḥaber*, "friend") In Judaism, friends joined for a religious purpose. Some see this as a description of Jesus and his disciples, the Last Supper being a regular, common meal rather than a Passover meal (John 18:28; 19:14). Early Christians continued this practice (Acts 2:46; 20:7).

chain of being A popular metaphorical description developed during the Renaissance to express the order, unity, and completeness of the universe. God was seen at the top of the chain with decreasing levels of "being" emerging from God down to the smallest realities. Thus it was hierarchical in nature.

Chalcedon, Council of (451) Fourth ecumenical council, held at Chalcedon in Asia Minor, which reaffirmed the christological statements of Nicaea (325) and Constantinople (381). It confessed Jesus Christ as "one person with two natures," human and divine, which are united but not mixed. This became the orthodox Christian theological description of the person of Jesus Christ.

Chalcedonian Christology Teachings about the person of Christ that accord with the teachings of the Council of Chalcedon (451).

Chalcedonian Definition Teachings about the person of Jesus Christ established by the Council of Chalcedon (451). It reaffirmed the Councils of Nicaea and Constantinople and rejected the views of the Nestorians and Eutychians by asserting Jesus Christ as fully God and fully human.

Chalcedonian Formula *See* Chalcedonian Definition

Chaldean Christians Those churches descended from ancient Nestorian churches.

Chaldee An archaic term for the Aramaic language.

chalice (Lat. *calix*, "a cup") The cup used in the Lord's Supper to hold the wine, which Jesus Christ said was his blood (Mark 14:23–24; 1 Cor. 11:25).

chancel (Lat. *cancellus*, "a screen") The part of the church in which the altar or Communion table, clergy, and choir are found. A screen often separated this area from the nave in medieval times.

chancel, split A term for the front of a church sanctuary that features a pulpit on one side of the chancel and a lectern or reading stand on the other. It is a common form in church architecture.

chancellor, diocesan A bishop's chief administrative representative in diocesan matters. The person is the principal archivist of a diocesan curia and must be a notary.

chancery, papal The office in charge of papal correspondence and archives.

chant (Middle English from Lat. *cantare*, "to sing") A melody sung to unmetrical verses as a liturgical part of a worship service.

chantry (Middle English) A chapel, separate from a church or monastery, often containing a tomb of someone associated with the church or monastery. Also, the duty of a Roman Catholic priest to celebrate masses for a deceased person or persons.

chaos (Gr. "gap," "chasm") Description of the formless primal matter before God brought it to order (Gen. 1:1–5).

chapel (Middle English from Lat. *capella*, "shrine containing the cape [*cappa*] of Martin of Tours [c. 316–97]") Usually the designation for part of a church set apart as an additional area for holding religious services.

chaplain (From Lat. *cappellanus*, "custodian of St. Martin's cloak") Originally the custodian of sacred relics in a royal chapel. Now, a clergyperson who performs ministerial duties apart from a parish, often in an institution such as a college, a hospital, or the military.

chapter (Middle English from Lat. *caput*, "head") Divisions of a book, such as the Bible. Also members of a special religious group dedicated to certain purposes. It originated from the monastic practice of daily gathering to hear a chapter of the monastic rule read.

character, moral (Gr. *charaktēr*, "graving tool," or its mark) Features and traits forming a person's nature and thus a clue to moral or ethical qualities. It includes ways of acting, responses, and ways of perceiving situations. It is the enduring personality on which morality is evaluated.

character, sacramental (Gr. *charaktēr*, "distinctive mark") In Roman Catholic theology the belief that sacraments, especially baptism, confirmation, and holy orders, make an indelible imprint of divine grace in one's life. Thus these sacraments may not be repeated.

charge An address made on a special occasion, often ordinations, which may be exhortatory in nature. At a service of installation for a pastor in a new congregation a charge may be given both to the pastor and to the congregation.

charis *See* grace

charism/charismata *See* charismatic gifts

charismatic gifts (Gr. *charismata*, "gifts of grace") Gifts of grace given by God's Spirit for the upbuilding of the Christian church (1 Cor. 12:1–31, esp. 8–10).

charismatic movement A transdenominational movement originating in the 1950s that emphasizes the charismatic gifts of the Spirit, particularly "speaking in tongues" ("glossolalia"), words of wisdom, knowledge, healings, prophecy, and the interpretation of tongues (1 Cor. 12:4–11).

charismatics Term for those who have been given charismatic gifts (all Christians), but especially used for those who emphasize the spiritual gifts, often particularly "speaking in tongues" ("glossolalia").

charity (Lat. *caritas,* Gr. *agapē,* "love") Old English term for God's love and the love placed by God in human hearts. The term was frequently used in the King James Version of the Bible (1611) for "love" (see 1 Cor. 13; 1 John 4). It is the greatest of the theological virtues.

chastity (From Lat. *castus,* "clean," "pure") Sexual purity in all aspects of existence; violated by fornication and adultery. As a virtue it is to order human sexuality for its proper purpose.

chasuble (Lat. *casula,* "little house") A priest or bishop's outermost vestment worn while celebrating the Eucharist.

cheap grace Term popularized by Dietrich Bonhoeffer (1906–45) to indicate the desire to accept God's gift without the corresponding response of repentance and obedience.

Cherubicon (Gr. *cheroubikon*) "The Cherubic Hymn," sung in Eastern churches as the choir enters a worship service and signifying the presence of cherubim.

cherubim Hebrew term for supernatural beings associated with sacred contexts in the Bible (Gen. 3:24; Ezek. 10:3; Heb. 9:5).

Chicago school of theology Early 20th-century theological movement associated with the University of Chicago Divinity School representing the most radical side of liberal theology. The Chicago school stressed theological modernism and sought to legitimate religion by appealing to public, verifiable experience.

child of God *See* adoption

children of the faithful (Lat. *infantes fidelium*) Term for the offspring of believers, usually spoken of in the context of the doctrine of the covenant.

Children's Crusade (1212) A predominantly legendary account describes the march of children from France and western Germany after the Fourth Crusade (1202–4) for the purpose of recapturing Jerusalem.

children's rights The recognition that children have inherent rights even though they may themselves be incapable of articulating or defending them. They are vulnerable persons created in the image of God (Gen. 1:26–27), and ethical concern is particularly expressed to protect them and give them dignity.

chiliasm (Gr. *chilioi,* "thousand") Another name for millenarianism and the belief that Christ will return to earth for a thousand-year reign prior to the final consummation (Rev. 20:1–5).

chiliast One who adopts the view that Christ will return to earth for a thousand-year reign prior to the final consummation (Rev. 20:1–5).

Chi Rho The first two letters of the Greek XPICTOC (*Christos,* "Christ"). Used as a monogram for "Christ."

choice (Lat. "choice," "decision," "judgment") The human capacity to choose. Theologically, a choice may be a "bound choice" reflecting enslavement to the power of sin; or "free choice" on the basis of the liberation of one's will by the power of the Holy Spirit to choose the will of God.

choir (Middle English from Lat. *chorus,* "a dance") The singers who lead the congregation in singing or sing alone during public worship. In church architecture, the area of a church in which the clergy are seated.

chorale (From Ger., short for *Choralgesang,* from Lat. *cantus choralis,* "choral song") A harmonized hymn, particularly one written for organ. Also a choir or chorus.

chorbishop (*chorepiscopus*) (Gr. "country overseer" or "country bishop") A rural bishop subject to a bishop in a nearby town. The term is no longer used except as an honorary title for leading presbyters in West Syrian and Maronite churches.

chorister (Middle English) One who sings in a choir, particularly a choirboy.

choruses (From Gr. *choros,* Lat. *chorus,* "a dance") Simple "gospel songs," usually four lines long with repetitive texts or tunes so they are easily learned by rote.

chrism (Gr. *chrisma,* "anointing") The holy oil (traditionally, olive oil mixed with perfume) used sacramentally in baptism, confirmation, and ordination and at church dedications in Roman Catholic and Orthodox churches symbolizing the gifts and working of the Holy Spirit.

chrismation (Gr. *chrisma,* "anointing") In Eastern churches, the practice of anointing a newly baptized person with oil and the sign of the cross as the priest says, "The seal of the gift of the Holy Spirit." More generally, it is anointing with the holy oil of chrism.

chrismatory (Lat. *chrismatorium*) In Roman Catholic theology, a vessel in which the holy oil (chrism) is kept.

chrisom (Variant of "chrism") White robe or blanket put on one at baptism, signifying purity.

Christ (Gr. *Christos,* Heb. *mashiah,* "anointed one") Old Testament Israel anticipated a coming deliverer "anointed" by God to initiate God's rule of righteousness and peace. Early Christians saw Jesus as fulfilling this hope and designated him as "Christ" (Mark 8:29; Acts 5:42; Rom. 5:6).

Christ, active obedience of Theological description of the fulfillment of the will of God by Jesus Christ. In some theological systems it refers specifically to Christ's fulfilling of the law of God in behalf of sinners. It is complemented by his passive obedience.

Christ, advent of (Lat. *adventus,* "coming") The "coming of Christ." Used by 2d-century Christians to refer to both Jesus' birth and second coming, which the Greek New Testament refers to as the *parousia* (1 Cor. 15:23; 1 Thess. 4:15).

Christ, benefits of The theological importance of what Jesus Christ has done in his incarnation, death, resurrection, and ascension. These are personally appropriated through faith in Jesus Christ.

Christ, blood of Image referring to the death of Jesus Christ, particularly as it effects atonement and reconciliation between God and humanity (Rom. 3:25; 5:9; Eph. 1:7; Col. 1:14 KJV; 1 John 1:7).

Christ, deity of Description of Jesus Christ as being God as is God the Father. Also termed the divinity of Christ.

Christ, divinity of Description of Jesus Christ as being divine as is God the Father. Also termed the deity of Christ.

Christ, doctrine of *See* Christology

Christ, exaltation of Theological term for the resurrection and ascension of Jesus Christ to God the Father and his continuing kingly rule (Acts 2:33; Phil. 2:9; Heb. 7:26).

Christ, humanity of Description of Jesus Christ as truly a human being. Jesus' humanity was in every way like that of other persons except he did not sin (Heb. 4:15; 1 Peter 2:22).

Christ, humiliation of Theological term to describe the earthly life, suffering, death, and burial of Jesus Christ (Phil. 2:5–8). Some include the "descent into hell," mentioned in the Apostles' Creed, as part of this state. It stands in contrast to his exaltation (Phil. 2:9–11).

Christ, identification with *See* union with Christ

Christ, imitation of (Lat. *imitatio Christi*) Description in popular piety of the attempt to follow the life and teachings of Jesus Christ and live according to his example.

Christ, impeccability of A view of Jesus Christ as being unable to sin.

Christ, intercession of   Description of Jesus Christ's continuing interceding with God the Father on behalf of sinners (Rom. 8:34; Heb. 7:25).

Christ, intercessory work of   Christ's work of atonement on the cross on behalf of sinners as well as his interceding with God the Father (Heb. 7:25).

Christ, Jesus   *See* Jesus Christ

Christ, kingdom of   *See* kingdom of Christ

Christ, Kingship of   The sovereign rule of Jesus Christ over all the universe (Phil. 2:9–11; Col. 2:9–10).

Christ, Lordship of   Acknowledgment of the authority and power of Jesus Christ over the cosmos, creation, and human life, especially the lives of those who believe in him.

Christ, nature of   The indication of who Jesus Christ was and is.

Christ, offices of   The work performed by Jesus Christ in his humiliation and exaltation as prophet, priest, and king.

Christ, passive obedience of   Jesus Christ's sufferings on the cross. Some have used the term to designate his vicarious suffering that pays the penalty of sin which humans have incurred, and thus his discharging of the debt they owe to God. It complements his active obedience.

Christ, person of   Description of who Jesus Christ is. In the New Testament, descriptions of who Jesus is are accompanied by descriptions of what he did (Matt. 1:21; John 1:1, 3, 29; Heb. 1:2, 3).

Christ, preexistence of   The theological view that Jesus existed before his incarnation as the eternal second Person of the Trinity (John 1:1; Phil. 2:6–7).

Christ, preincarnate prophetic ministry of   The view that Jesus Christ ministered prior to his incarnation through the Old Testament prophets.

Christ, reign of   The kingly rule of Jesus Christ begun in his incarnation and coming to completion in the final consummation of all things.

Christ, sacrificial death of   The view that the death of Jesus Christ was a sacrifice in which he was the victim as were the sacrificial animals in the Old Testament (Heb. 9:26; 10:12).

Christ, satisfaction of   The view that Jesus Christ made "satisfaction" or expiation or payment on the cross for the sin of humanity in the sense of paying a debt to the justice or righteousness of God and thus gaining forgiveness for those who have faith but cannot provide needed satisfaction by their own merit.

Christ, second coming of   *See* second coming of Christ

Christ, two natures of   The view that Jesus Christ had both a divine and a human nature.

Christ, vicarious death of   The view that Jesus Christ's death was a death on behalf of sinners and that in his death Christ took the place of those who because of their sin deserve themselves to die (Mark 10:45).

Christ, work of   Description of the actions of Jesus Christ, focusing particularly on his death, resurrection, and ascension.

Christ event   A term for the incarnation of Jesus Christ.

Christ mysticism   Emphasis on the believer's union with Christ, inspired by the apostle Paul's frequent use of the phrase "in Christ" (2 Cor. 5:17). Some, such as Adolf Deissmann, Albert Schweitzer, and James S. Stewart have viewed this phrase as a central theme in Paul's theology.

Christ of faith   Term used by some to designate the Christ proclaimed by the early Christian church in distinction from the Jesus of history who is known through historical investigation.

Christ the King, Feast of   Church festival celebrating the sovereign reign of Jesus Christ, usually celebrated on the last Sunday prior to the beginning of Advent.

Christadelphians   ("Christ's brethren")   A 19th-century American sect that claimed to return to the beliefs and practices of the primitive disciples and that stressed the return of Jesus Christ to establish a visible earthly kingdom.

Christendom   A collective sense of Christianity itself. Also, a description of Christianity as a dominant religion.

christening   (From Anglo-Saxon *cristnian,* "to name with a Christian name") The giving of a Christian name. Also synonymous with baptism (infant).

Christian   Name applied originally in Antioch to followers of Jesus Christ (Acts 11:26) and now used to designate those who believe in Jesus Christ and seek to live in the ways he taught.

Christian beliefs   The theological content of the Christian faith. Different Christian groups and individuals vary in their specific views on a number of Christian doctrines.

Christian calendar   The important dates of the Christian year. These may include not only feasts and festivals of the Christian year but also saints' days and other commemorative events.

Christian doctrines   The teachings of the Christian faith as these have been developed and formulated by the church and its theologians through the centuries.

Christian education   (Gr. *en Christō paideia*) The education and formation of persons in the Christian church in all areas of life in light of the Christian faith.

Christian educator   One who is devoted to teaching the Christian faith, usually spoken of as working within a church or a religious setting.

Christian ethics   The teachings of Christianity on actions, motives, and behavior that is right or wrong in light of the Christian faith.

Christian experience   The personal experience of Christians in relation to their faith.

Christian feminism   Variety of views about women in relation to Christian theology, ordination, and women's participation as professionals in Christian churches. Concerns are for justice and equality, freedom from oppression, and the resistance of sexism and patriarchy.

Christian freedom   *See* freedom, Christian

Christian humanism   *See* humanism, Christian

Christian Platonism   The combining of elements of Christian theology with Platonic philosophy. At various points, different dimensions have been emphasized by Christian theologians. These include innate knowledge of God, body-soul dichotomy, concepts of the image of God, and immortality.

Christian Science (Church of Christ, Scientist)   Religious body begun by Mary Baker Eddy (1821–1910) in 1875 which teaches that only God is real and that evil has no reality. Thus matter, evil, sin, and sickness only receive the reality given them by humans. "Healing" is the spiritual understanding that disease is not real.

Christian Socialism   Movement begun in the mid-19th century that sought to apply Christian principles to politics and modern society.

Christian theology   The body of beliefs and doctrines that constitute the Christian faith. Theology has been understood as faith seeking understanding and the critical reflection on God's revelation. Various theological methods have been used with differing emphases.

Christian year   *See* church year

Christianity   The religion founded on the life, teachings, and actions of Jesus Christ.

Christianity and culture   The relationship between the Christian faith and its surrounding social settings. Differing understandings of this relationship have emerged through the centuries. These have depended both on theological commitments and the specific context in which the church has found itself.

Christianization   The process by which one or more persons or groups of persons become Christian. When used in relation to countries or cultures, a critique is that often in the past, "Christianization" has really meant "Westernization" when Western culture was made the norm for defining genuine Christianity.

Christmas   (Old English *Christes mass*) Church festival marking the birth of Jesus Christ. It is observed on December 25.

Christmas Conference (1784)   The organizing meeting leading to the formation of American Methodism. John Wesley (1703–91), ordained as an Anglican priest, recognized the ordinations of Thomas Coke (1747–1814) and Francis Asbury (1745–1816) to minister in America as independent ecclesiastical leaders.

Christocentrism   A designation for views that place Jesus Christ in a central position throughout theological systems. A frequently mentioned example of a christocentric theology is that of Karl Barth (1886–1968).

christological   Referring to the doctrine of Jesus Christ.

Christology   (From Gr. *Christos,* "anointed one," and *logos,* "study") The study of the person and work of Jesus Christ. The church's understanding of who Jesus Christ is and what he has done grew and developed through the centuries. Early church councils produced christological statements.

Christology, classical   The theological views about Jesus Christ as accepted by the various church councils of the first five centuries, particularly at Nicaea (325), Constantinople (381), and Chalcedon (451).

Christology, functional   Name for christological views that emphasize what Jesus Christ did rather than who he was.

Christology, New Testament   The views of Jesus Christ found in the various New Testament writings.

Christology, patristic   The views of Jesus Christ found among the Christian theologians of the early church.

Christology, Word-flesh   The view that in the incarnation the Second Person of the Trinity took on a human physical nature but did not possess a human soul.

Christology, Word-(hu)man   The view that in the incarnation the Second Person of the Trinity took on a full and complete human nature, except for sin.

Christology from above   Method of developing a view of Jesus Christ that begins from his preexistent nature as the Second Person of the Trinity and moves to his incarnation (John 1:1).

Christology from below   Method of developing a view of Jesus Christ that begins from his human nature as known by historical research.

Christomonism   (From *christos,* "anointed one," and *mono-,* "one") The use of Jesus Christ as the overriding, determining principle in a theological system.

christomorphic   ("Christ-shaped," from Gr. *christos,* "Christ," *morphē,* "shape") A term used to describe something that is "shaped by Christ" in the sense of Christ's influence being a predominating factor. It may be used to describe the emphases of a theological position or of a Christian's own life.

Christotokos   (Gr. "Christ-bearer") Term used by Nestorius (d. 451) for Mary, mother of Jesus, in place of Theotokos, or "God-bearer."

Christus pro me   (Lat. "Christ for me") A phrase often used by Martin Luther (1483–1546) to convey the intensely personal and profound nature of the Christian gospel and faith in Jesus Christ.

Christus Victor   (Lat. "Christ the Victor") A term for the view that in his death and resurrection Jesus Christ defeated the powers of sin and evil, winning a cosmic victory over these enemies. Associated particularly with early church views of the atonement.

church (Gr. *kyriakon,* "thing belonging to the Lord," Lat. *ecclesia,* Fr. *église,* derived from Gr. *ekklēsia,* "assembly") The community of those who profess faith in Jesus Christ. In the New Testament it is used in a limited sense for local communities and in a universal sense for all believers.

church, authority in the The ways by which the church's beliefs and practices are determined. Ultimately, all authority is God's; historically, avenues of authority have included Scripture, tradition, the experience of the Spirit, and reason.

church, biblical images of the A number of ways of describing the church found throughout the New Testament. Among prominent images are the church as body of Christ (1 Cor. 12:27), people of God (Heb. 11:25), new creation (2 Cor. 5:17), a fellowship in the Spirit (1 Cor. 3:16), and household of God (1 Peter 4:17).

church, doctrine of the The theological understanding of the nature and mission of the Christian community. It also includes consideration of the church's government and discipline, sacraments, and order.

church, holiness of the A classic mark of the church denoting the church's being "set apart" by God for the work of carrying out God's mission in the world. It may also denote the purity of the church insofar as it is recognized that this is an eschatological gift of God to be realized finally only in the future.

church, invisible *See* invisible church

church, local A community of Christian believers associated for worship and service in a specific locality.

church, mission of the The Christian church's perception of its essential task in the world. Various aspects are emphasized by different church bodies. These may include evangelization, witnessing to the Gospel, promoting peace and justice, being an alternative community, and serving others.

church, models of the A term associated with the book *Models of the Church* (1974), by the Roman Catholic theologian Avery Dulles (b. 1918), in which he outlined various theological understandings of the nature of the church: as institution, mystical communion, sacrament, herald, servant, and community of disciples.

church, particular A term to designate a specific local church congregation.

church, purity of the The ideal of a church that is as pure as Jesus Christ. It is sometimes associated with the "holiness" of the church, where holiness is related to moral purity rather than to being "set apart."

church, visible *See* visible church

church and state The issue of how the church relates to the political governing body in its cultural context.

church and state, separation of The practice in the United States of excluding civil authority from involvement in religious affairs and recognizing religious institutions as independent from government sanction or support. This has meant the nonestablishment of religion and its free exercise.

church authority In Roman Catholic theology, the sum of the powers with which the church is endowed to fulfill its mission, divided into the power of order and the power of jurisdiction.

church catholic, the A term for the universal church as it exists throughout the world.

church constitution Document delineating the governing procedures for denominations or local church bodies.

church expectant In Roman Catholic theology, a term for the faithful who undergo purification in purgatory.

church fathers, early Name given to important theologians of the early Christian church from the end of the New Testament era until approximately the 5th century. The period is also called the patristic period in reference to these theologians.

church government The system by which a local church, denomination, national or international church is governed in accord with established principles. Major forms are episcopal, congregational, and presbyterial.

church growth A term coined by Donald A. McGavran (1897–1990) to describe the Christian mission of spiritual outreach to the non-Christian persons of the world.

Church Growth movement A movement, begun by Donald A. McGavran (1897–1990) in the early 1960s, emphasizing the study of those conditions and factors that appear to help in planting churches and helping congregations grow in size.

church history The discipline that investigates and describes the history of the Christian church in its original life and thought as an entity of God's saving purposes in universal history.

church meeting Regular meeting of all members of a congregation for the purpose of conducting church business.

church membership The formal affiliation of a person with a particular local church, including both privileges and responsibilities.

church militant Term for the visible Christian church on earth, in contrast to the church triumphant, which is the church in heaven.

Church of Christ Uniting (COCU) An ecumenical movement seeking formal organic unity in some form among church denominations. It was originally called the Consultation on Church Union (COCU, 1962) and emerged from a sermon (1960) by Eugene Carson Blake (1906–84) that called for Protestant church union.

Church of England *See* Anglicanism

church of the poor A term used in liberation theologies to describe the fellowship of those in poverty and their common oppression in contrast to established and elite church bodies.

church offices Positions of official responsibility within a church body.

church order *See* order

church planting The establishment of new church congregations.

church renewal Emphasis on the recovery of vitality in the church's life and ministry. In earlier times "revival" or "awakening" were comparable terms.

church triumphant The church as the company of all those who have died and share in the reality of heaven in praise of God.

church union movements Movements, particularly in the latter half of the 20th century, that have sought to unite different Christian bodies or denominations into one body.

church universal All Christian believers in all times and places as well as the Christian church spread throughout the whole world (Gr. *katholikos*, "universal").

church year The ecclesiastical calendar of the church by which the year is marked through the seasons and holy days of the Christian faith. It begins with Advent and Christmas and proceeds through Epiphany, Lent, Holy Week, Easter, Whitsuntide (Pentecost), and Kingdomtide (Christ the King).

Churches of God A number of Christian denominations that have variants of the term in their names and that identify themselves with the Pentecostal and Holiness movements.

churchwarden One charged with protecting church property (Church of England), or one who manages the temporal affairs of a parish (Protestant Episcopal Church in the U.S.A.).

churchyard The grounds on which a church stands, often traditionally used to include a cemetery.

ciborium (Gr. *kiborion*, hollow seedcase of an Egyptian water lily and thus a drinking cup) Canopy over an altar supported by four columns ("baldachino"). Also, a vessel with a lid holding wafer bread for the Eucharist.

cincture (Lat. *cinctura,* "girdle," "belt") The cord used to tie an alb at the waist.

circuit rider Itinerant Methodist preacher on the American frontier. These preachers were in the tradition of the itinerancy of John Wesley (1703–91) and Francis Asbury (1745–1816).

circumcision Removal of the male foreskin as a sign of the covenant in Old Testament Israel (Gen. 17:9–14). It signifies membership within the Jewish community.

Circumcision, Feast of the Feast on the eighth day after Christmas (January 1), now observed in the Roman Catholic Church as the celebration of Mary, the mother of God, and in the Episcopal and Lutheran traditions as the Holy Name of Jesus. It commemorates the circumcision of Jesus (Luke 2:21).

circumincession (*circumincessio*) *See: perichoresis*

citation (Lat. *citatio*) A summons to be present before an ecclesiastical court.

city of earth (Lat. *civitatis terrena*) Portrayal by Saint Augustine (354–430), in his *City of God,* of the forces of evil in human history that seek to counter the will of God.

city of God (Lat. *civitas Dei*) The portrayal by Saint Augustine (354–430), in his book of the same name, of a human society controlled by love of God in conflict with the city of earth/the devil, or human society controlled by self-love.

civil disobedience The breaking of civil laws, usually as a protest against injustice.

civil religion The blending of general religious values, practices, rites, and symbols with those of a particular nation or political unit.

civil rights The recognition of the rights of persons in a free society. The civil rights movement in the United States (1954–66) sought equal civil rights

for African Americans and is an ongoing quest.

civitas Dei *See* city of God

clandestinity Celebration of a marriage without the knowledge of the proper authorities.

class meeting Methodist weekly gathering of small groups within congregations, begun by John Wesley (1703–1791) in 1742 for the purposes of deeper understanding of the faith, enrichment of the spiritual life, and the collection of church funds.

classical theology Reference to the theological positions developed during the first five centuries of the Christian church.

classis Governing body of some denominations in the Reformed theological tradition, composed of clergy and ruling elders, corresponding to "presbytery" in Presbyterian churches.

classism Discrimination against or favoring of persons on the basis of their social class. It becomes an ethical issue when dimensions of justice are involved. Liberation theologians and others have pointed out the prevalence of this attitude in Western, industrialized societies.

cleanness The state of purity in Hebrew ceremonial law, which indicated how one may be free from physical, moral, or ritual contamination.

clergy (Gr. *klēros,* "portion," "lot") Those designated, often by the act of ordination, to perform the services of the church and carry out specific functions. Clergy are distinct from the laity.

clergy, regular Clergy who belong to religious orders. They obligate themselves to follow the rule (Lat. *regula*) of their order.

clergy, secular In Roman Catholic theology, a term for clergy who are not associated with any specific religious order and are attached solely to a diocese.

cleric (From Lat. *clericus,* "priest") A clergyperson.

clerical collar   A stiff white collar buttoned from behind and used by clergypersons to identify themselves as such.

clericalism   (Gr. *klērikos,* "pertaining to a priest") Power and influence exercised by clergy in governmental or political arenas, and the support of such powers. Often used in a derogatory sense.

clerk   One who is responsible for keeping various kinds of records for a church body.

clerks, regular   A term for certain Roman Catholic clergy who take vows to live in community and work in certain types of active pastoral ministries.

Clermont, Council of (1095)   Church council at which Pope Urban II (1042–99) initiated the first of the Crusades against the Muslims.

clinical theology   The study of the relationships of psychic, mental, spiritual, and emotional factors as they affect a person's well-being.

cloister   (Middle English from Lat. *claustrum,* "enclosed place") An enclosed space forming the central part of a monastery or other religious building.

Cloud of Unknowing   A description of God stressing the limitations of all language and images of God and thus urging meditation only on God's presence.

Cluniac reforms   Twelfth-century reforms of liturgical and spiritual life carried out by many monasteries in southern France and Italy. They were modeled after the reforms instituted at the Abbey of Cluny, France. Efficient organization and administration were also emphasized.

coadjutor bishop   In the Roman Catholic Church, a bishop appointed to assist a diocesan bishop.

coconsecrator   An assisting bishop for the ceremony of the laying on of hands at the ordination of a bishop in the Roman Catholic Church.

COCU   *See* Church of Christ Uniting

codex   (Lat. "a book," "a writing") Sheets of vellum or papyrus laid on top of each other and sewn together to form a book. The codex replaced scrolls and is the form in which many important New Testament manuscripts are found.

Codex Iuris Canonici   *See* canon law, code of

coenobite   *See* cenobite

Cogito ergo sum   (Lat. "I think, therefore I am") The formulation by René Descartes (1596–1650) in which knowledge of the self is seen as indubitably true and becomes the starting point for all other knowledge. It forms the foundation of the philosophy of rationalism.

cognition   (From Lat. *cognoscere,* "to know") The act of knowing. Intellectual knowledge.

cohabitation   (From Lat. *cohabitare,* "to dwell together") A couple's living together, often in a sexual relationship, without being married.

coinherence   *See: perichoresis*

collect   (Middle English from Lat. *collecta,* "assembly," and *collectus,* "collected") A short set prayer for particular occasions in public worship. Also, the opening prayer of the Roman Catholic Mass.

collection   A term for the offering of money that is collected during a service of worship and used for the work of the church's mission and ministry. It emerges from early Christian practice of giving to help those in need (Acts 4:37; 11:27–30; Gal. 2:10).

collective eschatology   *See* eschatology, collective

College of Cardinals   In the Roman Catholic tradition, the body of up to 70 cardinals who elect and give advice to the pope.

collegialism   (Lat. *collegia,* "college") The view that the church and state are both purely voluntary associations where complete authority rests with the members of each group.

collegiality (Lat. *collegium*, "a body") In the Roman Catholic Church, the sense that an assembly of bishops is acting corporately as representatives of the entire church.

colonialism/colonialization The exploitation of a people by another nation for the purposes of gain. It is emphasized in liberation theology by recognizing the plight of the poor and dispossessed and the reasons for their situations as stemming from systematic exploitation by rich and powerful nations.

colors, liturgical The use of various colors for different seasons within the church year. They are violet (Advent, Lent); white (Christmas, Easter, Trinity Sunday); red (Pentecost, Holy Week); green (after Epiphany, after Pentecost); black (Good Friday, for funerals).

comfortable words, the Four biblical passages recited during Holy Communion in the Church of England to confirm the absolution of the people. They are Matt. 11:28; John 3:16; 1 Tim. 1:15; 1 John 2:1f.

Comforter (Gr. *paraklētē*, "called to the side of," "advocate") Reference to the Holy Spirit, especially in portions of John's Gospel (chaps. 14—16), where the KJV uses this translation.

coming of Christ *See* Christ, advent of

command An explicit statement of God's will. In the ethical thought of Karl Barth (1886–1968) and Emil Brunner (1889–1966), the command of God is taken as the fundamental focus of Christian ethics.

Commandments, Ten *See* Ten Commandments

commandments of God Statements by God as expressions of the divine will for people.

commandments (precepts) of the church Traditional description of five duties required of Roman Catholics: keep Sunday and holy days; attend Eucharist on these days; keep prescribed fasts; make confession of sins to a priest at least once a year; receive Holy Communion during the period of Easter.

commands of love (Lat. *praecepta caritatis*) The rules of Christian obedience and thus "Christian ethics" as distinct from the "articles of faith" (Lat. *articuli fidei*).

commands of the law (Lat. *praecepta Decalogi*) The moral law or Ten Commandments (Ex. 20).

commemoration *See* anamnesis

commendation of the Soul (Lat. *commendatio animae*) Prayers prescribed to be used for the dying.

commination (Middle English from Lat. *comminari*, "to threaten") A rite of penitence for use on Ash Wednesday in the *Book of Common Prayer* that has been in the English Prayer Book since 1549 and has been so named since the edition of 1552. It was intended to be used prior to Holy Communion.

commingling In christological formulations, the issue of whether or how Christ's divine and human natures related to each other and thus whether they were "commingled." Athanasius (d. 373) rejected the view that the two natures of Christ were commingled.

commission, ecclesiastical A selected group to carry out a specific ecclesiastical task, often relating to investigation or discipline. The group would normally have more extensive powers than a committee.

commissioner One who is selected as a delegate or representative to an ecclesiastical governing body such as a presbytery, synod, or General Assembly in presbyterian forms of church government. More generally, one who serves on an ecclesiastical commission.

commixture The mixing of bread and wine in the Eucharist to symbolize the resurrection or the unity of the body and blood of Christ. In cases where the bread is from a previous Mass, the unity of all celebrations of the sacrament may be symbolized. Also called commingling.

Common Bible (1966)   A later edition of the Revised Standard Version of the Bible.

common cup   A single cup from which everyone participating in a Communion service partakes. Some churches celebrate the Lord's Supper in this way. Others use individual cups for each communicant.

common grace   *See* grace, common

Common Prayer, Book of   Official service book of the Church of England first produced for the Anglican Church during the reign of King Edward VI (1549). It has exercised a significant influence in worship practices of many different church bodies.

Common Sense philosophy   Also "Scottish Realism." Views espoused by the Scottish philosopher Thomas Reid (1710–96) and others to refute the philosophies of David Hume (1711–76) and Immanuel Kant (1724–1804) by arguing that knowledge is by intuition and that common sense experience is reliable.

Common Worship, Book of   The first officially sanctioned collection of prayers and liturgical services in American Presbyterianism (1906). The work was influential, but was for the voluntary use of Presbyterian congregations. It was revised twice (1932, 1946) before new liturgical resources were produced.

commonplaces   (Lat. *loci communes*) A collection of basic scriptural texts and their interpretations to form a coherent system of Christian doctrine. A frequent term for such systems of doctrine in the Reformation and post-Reformation periods.

commune   (Middle English *communen,* "to share") To receive Holy Communion.

communes   Groups of Christians who live together in community as a model of life with spiritual purposes.

communes/communitarian movements (Lat. *commune,* "that which is common") A group living situation or groups that live together. Participants share expenses and resources as well as a common commitment to a philosophy or religious vision. They are often utopian groups and were found in 19th-century America and during the 1960s.

communicable attributes of God   *See* attributes of God, communicable

communicant   One who participates in the Lord's Supper service. More generally, communicants are those who are church members and are entitled to participate. The term may be used synonymously for "church members."

communicate   (From Lat. *communicare,* "to share in") To receive Holy Communion.

communicatio essentiae   (Lat. "communication of essence") Term used to indicate that the communication of the essence (Gr. *ousia,* "substance") of the Godhead proceeds from the Father to the Son and from the Father and Son to the Holy Spirit.

communicatio idiomatum   *See* communication of properties

communicatio operationum   (Lat. "sharing of operations") Term used by Lutheran theologian Martin Chemnitz (1522–86) to indicate a transference of Christ's presence (ubiquity) in the Lord's Supper from the divine to the human nature of Christ so that the symbols in the Supper contained Christ's spiritual presence.

communication of attributes   (Lat. *communicatio idiomatum*) A way of speaking theologically to indicate that what may be said of Jesus Christ in his divinity may also be said of his humanity, and vice versa. Thus, it may be said that "the Son of God died on the cross." It is a rhetorical way of indicating the mysterious nature of the incarnation.

communication of idioms   *See* communication of properties

communication of properties   (Lat. *communicatio idiomatum,* "interchange of the properties") A way to express the view that the attributes of the divine and human natures of Jesus Christ are attributes of the one person and that what can be said of Christ's divinity can be said of his humanity, and vice versa.

communio sanctorum   *See* communion of saints

communion   (Lat. *communio*) A designation for those united in a common church fellowship, tradition, or set of beliefs.

Communion, closed   The practice of restricting participation in the sacrament of the Lord's Supper to a particular group, such as to those who are in good standing in a certain denomination. It is not commonly practiced today in Christian churches.

Communion, corporate   The celebration of the Lord's Supper by a group, such as a church congregation or body. It contrasts with private Communion.

Communion, open   The practice of inviting all Christian believers, regardless of particular denominational affiliation, to participate in a celebration of the Lord's Supper.

Communion, private   The celebration of the Lord's Supper by a celebrant and a single person. It may be done when Communion is taken to those who are sick or absent from a worship service in which the Lord's Supper was celebrated. It thus contrasts with corporate Communion.

Communion (altar) bread   The bread used during a celebration of the Lord's Supper. In some Christian churches, unleavened bread is used, as in the Jewish Passover meals (Ex. 12:15).

Communion (Holy)   A frequently used term for the Lord's Supper.

Communion cup (altar wine)   A term for the wine used in celebrations of the Lord's Supper. Some churches use a single, common cup from which everyone drinks. Others use individual cups. Some use real wine, others use grape juice.

Communion in both kinds (under both species)   The reception of both the bread and wine in the Lord's Supper.

communion of saints   (Lat. *communio sanctorum*) A phrase in the Apostles' Creed with meanings ranging from participation in the sacraments, to the fellowship of present-day believers, to the fellowship of all members of the church universal in every time and place. It stresses unity in Christ (1 Cor. 12:12–13).

Communion rail   *See* altar rail

Communion Sunday   A Sunday on which the sacrament of the Lord's Supper is administered in a worship service.

Communion table   The table at the front of a church sanctuary on which the elements for the Lord's Supper, the bread and wine, are placed and from which they are administered. Some denominations, such as those in the Reformed tradition, are careful to indicate that the Communion table is not an altar.

Communion tokens   Tokens given to those who were fit to receive the Lord's Supper. In the post-Reformation period in the Church of Scotland, it was mandatory for a person to attend a preparatory worship service in which confession of sin and contrition were present in order to receive the sacrament.

Communion wafer   A thin, flat cake of (unleavened) bread used in celebrations of the Eucharist. The term is primarily associated with the sacrament in the Roman Catholic Church.

Communion ware   The materials such as plates, cups, and coverings used in connected with celebrations of the Lord's Supper.

communitarianism   Description of the common sharing of life and property among those of the early church (Acts 2:44–46), which later led some to communal living and forms of Christian socialism.

community   (Lat. *communitas*) A group with common interests, often used to describe the church. In feminist theology, relationships of sharing and warmth among individual women.

comparative study of religion The study of religion by comparisons of the various world religions.

competentes (Lat. *competere*, "to seek or strive together") Catechumens who came to the final stage in preparation for Christian baptism during the early church period. Also called *electi*, "the elect," or, in Eastern churches, *phōtisomenoi*, "illuminated," "enlightened."

compline (liturgy of the hours) (From Lat. *completorium*, "completion") The final of the traditional services of the day in the Western church. In the Eastern church it is carried out "after supper" (apodeipnon).

comprecation (From Lat. *comprecari*, "to pray to") Term for the intercessions that departed saints are said to make on behalf of the church.

compromise (From Lat. *compromissum*) In ethics, the accommodation of an ethical role in light of a context or particular situation that is given a significant weight toward arriving at a course of action. It may be a serious attempt to adapt a principle to life's circumstances.

compulsion (From *compellere*, "to compel") An interior or exterior situation making it impossible for a person to make a free decision or enact that decision.

concelebration (Lat. *com*, "together," and *celebrare*, "to frequent," "to celebrate") The participation by several priests or a bishop and a priest at the central part of the Eucharist.

Conception, Immaculate *See* Immaculate Conception of the Blessed Virgin Mary

conception, miraculous Reference to the virgin birth of Christ (Matt. 1:23).

conceptualism The philosophical view that universal concepts—such as humanity, trees, redness—exist only in the mind and, in reality, only in specific individual entities, such as in a person, a tree, shades of red. It stood between nominalism and realism and was held by Abelard (1079–1142).

concern, ultimate *See* ultimate concern

concerns In worship services, the mentioning of situations or persons whom the congregation is asked to take notice of, assist, or remember in prayer.

conciliar (Lat. *concilium*, "council") Relating to church councils such as Nicaea, Trent, and Vatican II.

conciliarism/conciliar theory In Roman Catholic theology, the belief that supreme authority in the church is with the church's general councils rather than the pope. The main conciliar movement began in the 15th century with the Council of Constance (1414–18) and the Council of Basel (1431–38).

conclave (From Lat. *cum clavis*, "with key") Term for the locked area in which cardinals meet to elect a new pope. It also describes the meeting of those cardinals.

concomitance (Lat. *concomitans*, "accompanying") In Roman Catholic theology, the view that both the body and blood of Christ are present in the Eucharist in the bread and wine.

Concord, Book of (**1580**) The doctrinal standard of Lutheranism, consisting of a collection of ancient church creeds and various Lutheran writings.

Concord, Formula of (1577) A twelve-article confession of faith written to settle theological questions that arose after the death of Martin Luther (1483–1546).

concordance (Lat. *concordantia*) An alphabetical listing of biblical words with Scripture references indicating where they occur in the Bible.

concordat (From Lat. *concordatio*, "unanimity") An agreement between civil and ecclesiastical authorities. Also agreements made specifically by popes with governmental leaders to establish the rights of Roman Catholics in an area.

concupiscence (From Lat. *con*, "with," and *cupere*, "to desire") The desire of the self for the self, which is the human tendency toward sin.

concurrence, divine (Lat. *concursus divinus*) The actions of God in working in the world in conjunction with the actions of human beings.

concursus divinus   *See* concurrence, divine

condignity   (From Lat. *condignus,* "very worthy") The theological view that supernatural grace can enable a person to merit eternal life (Lat. *gratia de condigno*). The teaching is found in medieval Scholastic theology (see Acts 10:31).

conditional baptism   The celebration of Christian baptism with the inclusion of words making the act of baptism conditional: it is baptism if the person has not previously been baptized. This may occur if there is doubt about the fact of one's baptism or if a church doubts the validity of a past action as a true Christian baptism.

conditional immortality   The view which teaches that believers in Christ receive immortality while unbelievers are annihilated and pass out of existence.

conference   Generally, a gathering of people for a specific purpose. Ecclesiastically, a governing body in Methodist polity that includes the churches of a local area or region. It is presided over by a bishop.

Confessing Church   The Protestant movement in 20th-century Germany that resisted the "German Christians," who had gained power in the Evangelical Church and supported Nazi ideology. Prominent leaders of the Confessing Church included Martin Niemöller (1892–1984) and Dietrich Bonhoeffer (1906–45).

confessio   (Lat.) The affirmation of one's Christian faith, especially in the midst of persecution or imminent death. Also, the tomb or burial place of a martyr or saint.

confession   (Middle English from Lat. *confiteri,* "to acknowledge") The act of acknowledging and articulating one's sin.

confession, prayer of   In a worship service the corporate and/or private

acknowledgment of sin against God or others in the form of a prayer.

Confession of Dositheus (1672)   The most significant contemporary confession of faith for Orthodox Christianity. It emerged from a synod presided over by the Patriarch of Jerusalem, Dositheus (1641–1707), that defined Orthodox theology against Reformation Protestantism.

confession of faith   A proclamation or statement of beliefs held by a group of Christians or individual Christians. Confessions of faith are formal standards that serve as authoritative guides to the doctrinal beliefs of a church body.

Confession of 1967   A statement of faith adopted by the United Presbyterian Church in the U.S.A. in 1967 as part of its *Book of Confessions.* Its central theme is the reconciliation of the world in Jesus Christ.

confession of sin, corporate   In public worship, the prayer of confession prayed by the congregation to acknowledge human sinfulness. It is usually followed by a declaration or assurance of pardon.

confession of sin, individual   Admission or acknowledgment of motives or behavior that is sinful either against God or against others. In Roman Catholic theology, confession is made to a priest, who indicates conditions for forgiveness.

confessional   In the Roman Catholic tradition, the place where sins are confessed to a priest and the sacrament of reconciliation (penance) is enacted.

confessional standard   The document or documents recognized by church bodies as being authoritative for belief and practice.

confessional theology   The term is primarily used for Lutheran and Reformed theologies because of their use of creeds and confessions of faith as guides to scriptural interpretation and as a basis for church beliefs.

confessionalism   The view that a church must have a confession of faith to be constituted as a church or denomination.

confessor   A person, usually a priest or clergyperson, to whom one's sins are confessed. In the early church the term referred to those who maintained a fidelity to their Christian faith in the face of persecution.

confirmation   (Lat. *confirmare,* "to make firm") The formal personal affirmation of vows of faith taken for one in baptism. In the Roman Catholic tradition (and others), it is a sacrament. In Protestantism, it is not considered a sacrament.

confirmation in grace   A technical term in scholastic theology to indicate that a person has received the gift, humanly impossible to achieve, of actual sinlessness and impeccability. In Roman Catholic tradition, Mary and Joseph, John the Baptist, and the apostles, with others, received this gift.

Confiteor   (Lat. "I confess") The formula for the confession of sins found in the Roman Catholic Mass.

congregants   Those who are part of a congregation of people, usually gathered for worship.

congregation   (From Lat. *congregare,* "to congregate," "to gather together") The people assembled for worship. Local churches are also often called congregations.

Congregation for the Doctrine of the Faith, Sacred   A congregation of the Roman Curia established by Pope Paul III (1542) for the purpose of safeguarding the Roman Catholic faith, rejecting false doctrines, and defending the church against heresy. It was originally called the Congregation of the Universal Inquisition. Pope Paul VI renamed it the Sacred Congregation for the Doctrine of the Faith (1967). Its purpose is to safeguard faith and morals.

Congregational Churches   Churches practicing a congregational form of church government, where authority is with the local congregation.

congregational form of church government   A form of church government in which governing authority is with the local congregation, which is autonomous and independent.

congregational rule of life   The communal life of a Christian congregation on a daily, weekly, monthly, and yearly basis into an ordered pattern. The church (Christian) year provides a basic structure, with additional aspects of Christian discipleship being emphasized among congregational members.

congregationalism   *See* congregational form of church government

Congregationalist   One who is a member of a communion that practices a congregational form of church government.

congruism   An attempt by 17th-century Jesuit theologians to reconcile God's purposes of grace with the freedom of the human will. In it, God gives individuals the grace they need to perform the good works God desires them to do, congruently with the most favorable foreseen circumstances.

connectional   A form of church governmental organization that stresses the relationships among the various constitutive parts. It is particularly used to describe the Methodist system of churches, circuits, districts, and annual conferences.

conscience   (Lat. *conscientia,* "knowledge with another," "knowledge within oneself") Ethically, the sense of moral awareness where practical judgments are made about right or wrong or what is one's responsibility. Theologically, it is affected by sin and may be an "erring conscience."

conscience, examination of   The process of calling to mind one's sins and failures, often in preparation for the sacrament of the Lord's Supper or the sacrament of reconciliation (penance) in the Roman Catholic tradition.

conscientious objection   Refusal to participate in military service on religious or moral grounds, chiefly due to objections to killing another person, even in war.

conscientization The process of becoming aware of one's situation, particularly of suffering and oppression by social structures, racism, or sexism. Persons may also become aware of their capacities to transform those realities as well. The term is used in various forms of liberation theologies.

consciousness raising Term used especially in feminist theology to describe the process of becoming aware of one's own repression by recognizing the validity of one's own experience. It is often abbreviated CR.

consecration (Lat. *consecratio,* from *consecrare,* "to make sacred") The setting apart of a person or object or place for a special divine use.

consecration, prayer of The prayer in the Eucharist that relates to the elements of the bread and wine. Various theological views of what occurs when this prayer is uttered are to be found.

consecration (dedication) of churches A service of worship in which special focus is given to a new church or church building as it is dedicated to carry out its ministries. The observance was modeled on King Solomon's dedication of the Temple (1 Kings 8:63).

consecration of the elements/eucharistic species In the Roman Catholic Mass, the act by which the wafer (bread) becomes the body of Jesus Christ by transubstantiation. It occurs at the moment in the eucharistic prayer when the presider recites the words of Jesus over the elements (1 Cor. 11:23–25).

consensus fidelium (Lat. "consensus of the faithful") Theological agreement as reached among persons or church bodies on doctrinal issues.

consent (Lat. *consensus,* "agreement") The willing agreement to do something. The term is used in various ethical contexts to indicate free decisions to do good or evil actions.

consent of the Fathers (Lat. *consensus patrum,* "agreement of the Fathers") The common doctrinal agreements on such doctrines as the Trinity and the person of Christ as arrived at by the theologians of the first five or six centuries.

consequentialism An ethical theory that judges rightness or wrongness of actions solely in terms of their outcomes or consequences.

conservation (Lat. *conservatio*) A part of the classical doctrine of God's providence that describes God's ongoing protection and preservation of the created order.

conservative theology A general term for theological viewpoints that seek to maintain a reverence for and connection with older, classical theological formulations.

consistent Calvinism Called variously, Edwardsianism, Hopkinsianism, and New Divinity, the term refers to the work of Samuel Hopkins (1721–1803) and Joseph Bellamy (1719–90) in developing the thought of Jonathan Edwards (1703–58) as a modification of traditional Calvinism in America.

consistory (From Lat. *consistere,* "to stand together") The governing body of local congregations consisting of the minister and ruling elders in the Reformed theological tradition. Also called the "session." In Roman Catholic theology, the cardinals meeting with the pope present.

consolations (From Lat. *consolatio,* "comforting") Term used by writers on the spiritual life to indicate the joy, peace, and encouragement coming from a recognition of God's presence.

Constance, Council of (1414–18) The sixteenth ecumenical church council, called by the antipope John XXIII (d. 1419). Its purpose was to end the Great Schism in the Roman Catholic Church, initiate church reforms, and suppress heresy.

Constantinople, First Council of (381) The church council, attended by 150

Eastern bishops, that deposed Arius (c. 250–c. 336), condemned Sabellianism and Apollinarianism, and reaffirmed the Creed of the Council of Nicaea (325). Its creed, commonly called the Nicene Creed, is actually the Niceno-Constantinopolitan Creed.

Constantinople, Second Council of (553) The fifth ecumenical church council, called by the emperor Justinian and attended by 168 bishops, nearly all from Eastern churches. It condemned Nestorianism and Origenism and declared the perpetual virginity of Mary.

Constantinople, Third Council of (680–81) Sixth ecumenical church council, called by the emperor Constantine IV. It sought to restore orthodoxy in the face of Islam's advance and condemned Monothelitism. It affirmed a divine and a human will in Jesus Christ, acting in moral unity.

constructive theology Term given to theological efforts to relate Christian theology to the contemporary world.

consubstantial (Lat. *consubstantialis*, "with or of the same nature and kind") With, or of, the same substance or being. Equivalent of Gr. *homoousios*, used in the creed of Nicaea (A.D. 325) to designate the relation of Jesus Christ to God.

consubstantiation (From Lat. *consubstantialis*, from *con-*, "with," and *substantia*, "substance") A late medieval view of the Lord's Supper. While the "substance" of the bread and wine are not changed into the body and blood of Christ, they coexist or are conjoined in union with each other: bread with body and wine with blood. The term is sometimes used to describe Lutheran views of the Lord's Supper.

consultation A gathering of people for a specific purpose. Ecclesiastically, the term may be used for a gathering of various churches or church leaders to address a specific issue or problem. It is usually ecumenical in nature.

Consultation on Church Union *See* Church of Christ Uniting

consummation (From Lat. *consummatio*) The final climax of history and full establishment of the reign or kingdom of God.

contemplation (Lat. *contemplari*, "to contemplate," "to meditate upon") The intuitive approach to God in prayer viewing God in light of the truth already known.

contemplative life (From Lat. *contemplari*, "to survey") A life devoted to prayer and to spiritual disciplines. It is sometimes contrasted to the "active" life. Medieval monks and nuns in monasteries were called contemplatives and perceived the contemplative life as primarily mystical.

contemporaneity The theological concept of being a "contemporary with Christ." All Christians, regardless of their historical time periods, receive from God the conditions for being a disciple of Jesus Christ. In the moment of decision to follow Christ, all barriers vanish and believers become contemporaries with Christ.

Contemporary English Version (CEV, 1995) An English translation of the Bible by the American Bible Society. It had accuracy as a goal but also tried to produce a text that would be easy for hearers to comprehend and that could be read without stumbling. It is described as "user-friendly" and as "lucid" and "lyrical."

contemporary theology Term for theological movements and the views of theologians that are current or have ongoing relevance from the recent past.

contemporization The attempt to state theological truths in terms readily understandable in the contemporary world.

context (From Lat. *contextus*, "a weaving together") The social location of a group or class. This shared social location according to liberation theologies is central to the theological task. What it means to do theology is inevitably interwoven with all the social dimensions of life.

contextual (From Lat. *contextere,* "to weave together") Relating to a particular setting in history, culture, or other aspects. It is recognized that theological formulations inevitably reflect a number of factors that influence them from their settings and are always "contextual."

contextual theology Theological approach that seeks to take seriously the various social settings in which the theological task is carried out. Liberation theologies particularly take context and social location seriously and begin with praxis as the first step for theological reflection.

contextualization of theology The concern for theology to arise out of and adapt to the historical, social, and cultural settings in which people live.

continence (Lat. *continere,* "to hold together" or "to repress") Abstinence from sexual intercourse, often based on a specific religious conviction.

contingency (Lat. *contingentia,* from *contingere,* "to affect," "to influence") A condition that exists when one object or being is dependent (contingent) on another and cannot exist or function in the same way without that other. The absence of a necessity.

contingency argument for God A cosmological argument for the existence of God by Thomas Aquinas (1225–74) which claims that for anything contingent to exist, there must necessarily be at least one being which is not contingent.

contingent beings Beings that have no self-existence but depend on other beings for their existence.

continuous creation *See* creation, continuous

continuum (Lat. *continuus*) A continuing or ongoing structure with interrelated parts. Philosophically or theologically, views of certain issues may relate to each other in varying ways and also stand in relationship to a larger system or structure of views or beliefs.

contraception Birth control to prevent conception. Methods vary. The Roman Catholic tradition has been opposed to any form of artificial contraception. Protestants have tended to see contraception as a God-given means toward responsible family planning and parenthood.

contradiction, law of A principle of logic indicating that a thing cannot be A and non-A at the same time and in the same way.

Contra-Remonstrants Strict Calvinists of the 17th-century Netherlands who stood against the "Remonstrants," who sought to modify Calvinism. The Contra-Remonstrants prevailed at the Synod of Dort (1618–19), which produced a set of strongly Calvinistic canons.

contrition (Lat. *contritio,* "a wearing away of something hard") The state of inner sorrow for sin and desire to confess sins. In Roman Catholic theology, true contrition includes the desire not to sin again because of one's love for God (contrasted to "attrition").

control beliefs A term used in the work of Nicholas Wolterstorff (b. 1932) for beliefs, such as belief in God or belief in scientific theories, that are not simply one belief among many but that function as a control over many other beliefs. They will affect the selection of the theories one believes in, the questions one asks, and one's behavior.

controversial theology In Roman Catholic theology a term to describe the study of theologies of other than Roman Catholicism.

convent (Lat. *conventus,* "a meeting") A community of monastic persons who live life under a superior, or the building in which they live. Commonly used for a residence of religious women who are under a superior.

conventicle (Lat. *conventus,* "assembly") A group meeting for worship or religious purposes outside of the land or country's established church.

conversation Verbal interaction. Sometimes used to describe a reader's interaction with a text.

conversion (Gr. *metanoia*, Lat. *conversio*, "turning around") One's turning or response to God's call in Jesus Christ in faith and repentance. It is profound in its effects in that it radically transforms one's heart, mind, and will.

conversion, theory of In Roman Catholic theology the theoretical explanation for the sacrificial character of the Mass and also of transubstantiation, in which it is believed that the body of Christ becomes present through the change or conversion of the bread.

conversion narratives Speeches given by those in some colonial American churches who sought full membership. In the speeches they detailed their Christian experience and particularly their experience of conversion to Jesus Christ.

convert (From Lat. *convertere*, "to turn around") To change from one religion or faith to another. Also, a person who makes such a change.

conviction of sin The sense of the reality of sin in one's life as known by the work of the Holy Spirit (John 16:8–9).

convocation (From Lat. *convocare*, "to call together") A religious assembly, often for purposes of worship or instruction.

cope (Old English from Lat. *cappa*, "a cloak") A liturgical cape or cloak worn in church processions or festival services.

Coptic Church The primary Christian church body in Egypt.

coram Deo (Lat. "in the presence of God") A term used by Martin Luther (1483–1546) and other Protestant theologians to indicate that all life is lived "before God" and thus under God's scrutiny. John Calvin (1509–64) indicated that no life area is exempt from "business with God."

Coredemptrix In traditional Roman Catholic theology, a title for Mary indicating her role as the mother of Jesus and thus in the redemption of the world.

cornerstone, Christ as (From Heb. *'eben pinnah*, Gr. *akrogoniaios*) Image of Christ in relation to the Christian church denoting him as the standard by which the church is measured or his primacy as the "keystone" or "capstone" which completes and binds the church together (Eph. 2:20; 1 Peter 2:6).

corporal (Lat. *corporale*, "pertaining to the body") A twenty-inch-square white linen cloth that is placed on the altar in Roman Catholic churches and on which the elements and vessels for the Eucharist rest for consecration.

corporate personality Term used by some Old Testament scholars to describe the idea, found particularly in the Old Testament, that the individual represents the community and that the community is "summed up" in the individual. The story of Achan illustrates how the sin of one affects the community (Josh. 7).

corporate prayer of confession Prayer recited in unison, within a worship service, in which the congregation confesses its solidarity in sin.

corporate solidarity The view that the human race is an organic whole and that the actions of one person has effects on all others. The concept is important theologically for indicating the oneness of humanity.

corporeal acts, the seven Also called the seven corporeal works of mercy. Actions derived from Jesus' parable of the last judgment (Matt. 25:31–46; cf. Isa. 58:6–10): Feed the hungry, give drink to the thirsty, give shelter to strangers, clothe the naked, visit the sick, visit prisoners, and bury the dead.

Corpus Christi, Feast of (Lat. "body of Christ") A feast celebrated in the Roman Catholic Church on the Sunday after Trinity Sunday honoring the presence of Christ in the Eucharist.

Corpus Iuris Canonici (Lat. "body of canon law") The major collection of canon law in the Roman Catholic Church prior to 1917. It included Gratian's *Decree* and collections of papal decretals.

correlation (Lat. *correlatio*) A one-to-one correspondence.

correlation, method of A way of doing theology, proposed by Paul Tillich (1886–1965), in which theology takes shape in the answers to questions raised by the surrounding culture, as being implied by human existence.

correspondence A term used in church polity to indicate a formal relationship that one church body may have with another. To "be in correspondence" means mutual recognition of various church forms such as ordinations, church memberships, etc.

corresponding member A status used in various ecclesiastical polities for the recognition by a governing body of a person from another denomination or tradition who is attending their meeting. This person is usually granted the right to speak in the meeting but not to vote.

corrupted nature Human nature as sinful due to the fall (Gen. 3; Eph. 4:22; 2 Tim. 3:8; Titus 1:15; 2 Peter 1:4, 19).

corruptible (perishable) body The present, physical body subject to death and decay (1 Cor. 15:50, 53–54).

corruption Theological description of the manifestation and the result of human sin.

cosmogony (Gr. *kosmogonia,* "creation of the world") Theory concerning the origins of the physical universe.

cosmological argument for God Argument for God's existence which proposes that since all things in the universe must have a cause, God must exist as the ultimate cause of all things.

cosmology (Lat. *cosmologia*) The study of the universe, including its origin, evolution, and overall structure. The term is also used for the worldview of a particular age. Recognition of this view is helpful for the interpretation of texts written at a certain time.

cosmos (Gr. *kosmos,* "world," "universe") The world or universe. In Christian theology, all is believed to be created by God.

cosmoscope A worldview. Associated with Calvinist thinkers who develop a philosophy of the universe based on biblical premises.

Council of Trent *See* Trent, Council of

councils, church Gatherings of representative churches to discuss important issues.

councils, ecumenical Gatherings of representatives from the ecumenical church to discuss important issues. A New Testament example is the Jerusalem Council (Acts 15). Councils were called through the early centuries of the Christian church to deliberate, especially on doctrines of the Trinity and Christology.

councils of churches Associations of church bodies to carry out common purposes or ministries.

counsel of God (Lat. *consilium Dei*) God's decision or the divine will, resting on nothing other than the essential nature of God.

counseling, pastoral The practice of offering spiritual counsel or advice from the perspective of a pastor or with the intent of fostering one's specifically Christian values and commitments.

counsels, evangelical Traditional description of the directions for life given in the example of Christ including poverty, chastity, obedience, and loving one's enemies (Matt. 19:11–12; Mark 9:35; 10:17; Luke 6:27, 35).

counsels of perfection The three obligations of poverty, chastity, and obedience taken as vows by those who enter a religious order in the Roman Catholic Church. The vows were seen as approximations of Jesus' command to be perfect (Matt. 19:21), a prescription impossible for the common Christian. Also "evangelical counsels."

Counter-Reformation/Catholic Reformation The period of church reform instituted by Roman Catholicism as a reaction to the Protestant Reformation. It extended from the early 16th to the mid-17th century and set the course for Catholic theology and practice until Vatican Council II (1962–65).

courts, ecclesiastical   The bodies that deal with judicial ecclesiastical matters in churches. They exist at various levels in church governmental structures, including those of the Roman Catholic Church, where the term "tribunal" refers to courts at all levels of the judicial system.

courts of the church   The regularly structured bodies that deal with judicial matters in churches. The term may describe bodies, such as the presbytery or synod, that deal with more than just judicial matters.

covenant   (Heb. *berith,* Gr. *diathēkē*) A formal agreement or treaty between two parties that establishes a relationship and in which obligations and mutual responsibilities may be enacted. Many biblical covenants are found, some providing only divine promises while others entail obligations.

covenant, new   *See* new covenant

covenant, old   *See* old covenant

covenant community   A theological description of Israel and the Christian church as communities that are related to God by means of various covenants.

covenant nation   A term designating Israel as the people of God who are bound by God's covenants with Abraham (Gen. 17:1–19) and at Sinai (Ex. 19—24). A relationship was established by God with the nation, which promised obedience to God's laws.

covenant of grace   (Lat. *foedus gratiae*) The relationship into which God entered to provide, by grace, the promise of salvation to sinful humanity. It extends throughout the Old Testament by means of various covenants to its final fulfillment in Jesus Christ.

covenant of redemption   Theological description of the agreement between

God the Father and God the Son to provide for the salvation of sinful humanity by Christ's death on the cross.

covenant of works   (Lat. *foedus operum*) Theological description, found in some streams of Reformed theology, to describe God's initial covenant with humanity ("Adam") before the fall into sin. A perfect relationship with God could be enjoyed if humans maintained a perfect obedience to God's law.

covenant people   A term to describe those groups with whom God has entered into a covenantal relationship, most generally a description of Israel and, after Christ, the Christian church.

covenant relationship   A relationship between God and persons or groups of persons marked either by God's unilateral promises or by mutual agreements, and marked especially by human promises for obedience to God's will.

covenant renewal   Liturgically, times and ceremonies when important covenant relationships are remembered and renewed. These include baptism (not "rebaptism") and marriage as well as vows relating to church membership or profession of faith in Jesus Christ.

covenant renewal service   A worship service found in the Methodist tradition, usually held on the first Sunday of a new calendar year. At this time, church members rededicate themselves to serving God. It began with a covenant service held by John Wesley (1703–91) on August 11, 1755.

covenant theology   A theological perspective most developed by 17th-century Reformed theologians. It focuses on the ways in which the divine-human relationship has been established by "covenants." These include God's covenant of grace and works, though this covenant is not recognized by all Reformed theologians.

covenanted communities   Communities of the Holy Spirit within the charismatic movement composed of those who are committed to a corporate lifestyle in "households," which may be either in one place or "nonresidential."

Coverdale Bible (1535) The first complete Bible published in England. It was translated by Miles Coverdale (1488–1568) based on Tyndale's translations, Luther's Bible, the Vulgate, and other sources.

covetousness An intense desire for that which does not properly belong to one but belongs to another. This desire is regarded as sinful (Ex. 20:17).

cowl (Lat. *cucullus*, "hood") A garment with a hood that is worn by monks.

creatio de novo (Lat. "creation from the new") Creation without the use of any materials that exist. The Christian doctrine of creation sees God as creating all things from nothing and thus genuinely creating, rather than refashioning what already existed.

creatio ex nihilo (Lat. "creation from nothing") The Christian view that God created all things out of "nothing" and is thus the ultimate cause and source of meaning for the whole created order.

creation The causing to exist of that which was previously nothing. In the Christian view, God is the creator and thus the source of all things (Gen. 1—3). God also continues to sustain the creation. Most theologians do not hold that a particular theory as to how God created may necessarily be derived from the biblical materials.

creation, continuous The view that creation is continually being "re-created" by God as it passes into and out of existence through each instance of time. It was associated with the Lutheran theologian Karl Heim (1874–1958).

creation, development within The view that there has been an ongoing development within the created order and thus that all elements of creation were not initially created by God in their final forms.

creation, doctrine of The Christian theological view that God is the creator

of all things and is thus their ultimate source. It does not need to entail a view as to how God accomplished creation. The doctrine points to God as the source of all, to the dependence of all things on God, and to human responsibilities to God.

creation, new A New Testament description of God's ongoing work within the present created order for its renewal and its ultimate fulfillment in a "new heaven and a new earth" (Rev. 21:1), as well as the radical newness of life for individuals who are reconciled to God through Jesus Christ (2 Cor. 5:17).

creation, theology of Theological views about the nature of creation and its prominence within a whole theological system. God as creator means all things are good, that God is the source of all, and that humans depend on God. God is beyond creation, yet involved in it. God grants freedom within creation.

creation of humanity The Christian view that God is the source of all life, particularly of human life as its creator. The biblical accounts focus on humanity as created to be in relationship with God the Creator (Gen. 1—3).

creation science The view that contemporary scientific theories and research can substantiate a reading of the creation materials of the Bible (Gen. 1—3) that interprets them as literally and historically recounting the ways by which God created the world and humanity.

creation theology The theological affirmations of God as creator of all and particularly of the earth and its resources (Gen. 1:1–2:4a; Pss. 65, 96, 98, 104).

creationism The view that God creates each individual human soul at the point of conception in the womb (opposed to traducianism). Also the doctrine of God as creator as opposed to pantheism, emanationism, and dualism. Used popularly to stand opposed to evolution. Thus it is linked with creation science.

creationism, progressive Also "microevolution." The view that God initially created the first member of each "kind" which have not "evolved" from other "kinds." The members of each "kind" have evolved or developed from each other. The view intends to emphasize creation rather than evolution.

creationist view of the origin of the soul *See* creationism

creative evolution A variety of theistic evolution that views God as working through the laws of nature as the means of evolution.

creator The one who brings into existence all things. In Christian theology, God is the sole creator of all. God is thus the one source of all and the one on whom all creation depends.

creator emeritus The view that God began the creation process but is not further involved with it. Characteristic view of 17th- and 18th-century English Deism.

creature (Lat. *creatura*) That which is created. In Christian theology, all beings owe their existence to the creative actions of God (see Gen. 1:20, 24; Ps. 104:24; Rev. 5:13).

creature, new *See* creation, new

credence (Lat. *credentia*, "belief," "trust") To give weight to an argument in terms of plausibility or truth. Also, a small side table near an altar to hold the elements for the Eucharist and other items used in a worship service.

credenda (Lat. "those things which are believed") Term for the articles of faith or those things to be believed.

Credo quia absurdum (Lat. "I believe because it is absurd") A statement of theological method emphasizing a sharp antithesis between faith and reason and assuming that those things which must be known by faith cannot be known by reason. It is associated with Tertullian (c. 160–c. 220).

Credo ut intelligam (Lat. "I believe in order that I might understand") A statement of theological method emphasizing that faith is the first step that leads to further understanding and knowledge of Christian truth. Associated with Augustine (354–430) and Anselm (c. 1033–1109). Also *fides quaerens intellectum.*

creed (Lat. *credo*, "I believe") A formal statement of belief. Christian churches from the early church period to the present have often constructed summary statements of Christian beliefs.

creed, baptismal Earliest Christian summaries of beliefs that were recited as personal affirmations of faith at the time of baptism.

creed, conciliar A creed composed by a church or ecumenical council to provide guidelines to Christian beliefs as they are understood by that body.

Creed, the A common reference to the Apostles' Creed as the most widely used creed in the Western church.

cremation (Lat. *crematus*, from *cremare*, "to burn") The burning of corpses after death. This practice is not prohibited in Christianity.

crisis (Gr. *krisis*) A point of significance that anticipates future actions. In theology, a decision in relation to Jesus Christ and the Christian gospel is seen to be a point of crisis that provides a direction for one's future life and thus is of utmost importance.

crisis theology A term for neo-orthodox or dialectical theology associated with the views of Karl Barth (1886–1968) and others. It emphasized the "crisis" (Gr. *krisis*, "separation," "judgment") between humans and God who are separated by time and eternity, human sin and divine perfection.

criteriology (From Gr. *kritērion*, "a standard") Study of the standards (criteria) applied to judge the truth or value of an issue.

critical apparatus (Lat. *apparatus criticus*) The list of manuscript readings of variations from the accepted biblical text printed in editions of the Old (Hebrew) and New (Greek) Testaments.

critical consciousness   A description of modern perceptions of reality marked by objectification, nonparticipation, and alienation, and thus "distance." It is separation of subjective consciousness from any objective realities. All values, such as good and evil, may be considered purely subjective.

critical methodology   An approach to documents (such as the Bible) that examines them in terms of evidences for genuineness, etc., not merely taking these elements without questioning.

critical realism   A theory of perception associated with some 20th-century American philosophers such as A. O. Lovejoy, George Santayana, and R. W. Sellars. It affirmed sense data as yielding "characters" to awareness that point to the article being perceived. While there is distance between the data and the object, knowledge of the former gives knowledge of the latter.

criticism, biblical   (From Gr. *krinein*, "to judge," "to discern") The study and the investigation of biblical writings through many means to understand elements such as their backgrounds, forms, history, authorship, audience, message, language, circumstances, and relation to other biblical writings.

criticism, canonical   A means of biblical criticism that studies texts according to their final form in the canonical text of Scripture and how it stands in relation to other portions of Scripture. A particular text or passage is now addressed to a universal audience and is part of many "voices" in Scripture.

criticism, comparative-religions   An approach to explaining the development of the history of the Christian faith in terms of patterns that are considered to be common in all religions.

criticism, form (*Formgeschichte*)   A means of biblical criticism that studies texts according to their "prehistory," in oral and written stages. It employs literary criticism to classify texts in their literary forms or genres. This is correlated with its "setting in life" (Ger. *Sitz im Leben*) to enhance understanding.

criticism, historical   A means of biblical criticism that studies texts according to their historical setting(s). This includes their time and place of composition, circumstances, author(s), how they came to be written, and audience(s) addressed. To reconstruct the historical situation is the main task.

criticism, literary-source   A means of biblical criticism that studies texts according to their final, finished form. The focus is on what the text itself says. This means the texts create a "world" that can be investigated in every dimension. Language study, literary style, genre, and forms are key parts.

criticism, narrative   A means of biblical interpretation that focuses on stories in the biblical literature and seeks to read these stories using insights derived from the field of modern literary criticism. The goal is to understand the stories' effects on their audiences.

criticism, redaction   A means of biblical criticism that studies texts according to the ways in which they have been edited or "redacted." Key aspects are analysis of points where editors have redacted a text or tradition, assessing the changes, and interpreting them in light of the editor's purposes.

criticism, rhetorical   A means of biblical criticism that analyzes biblical texts in relation to their distinctive properties as human discourse, focusing particularly on their artistry and arguments used by biblical writers to persuade others of the truth of their beliefs.

criticism, source   A means of biblical criticism that studies texts according to their source origins. It is a subdiscipline of historical criticism and focuses on what sources have been used in the composition of biblical texts. Notable are the JEDP (Yahwist, Elohist, Deuteronomist, and Priestly) sources identified for the Pentateuch.

criticism, structural   A means of biblical criticism that focuses on the linguistic structures of biblical texts as a means of ascertaining their "narrative grammar" and what this communicates to readers.

criticism, textual   A means of biblical criticism that studies texts according to the original wordings or forms of the texts themselves. The goal is to discover what the ancient writer actually wrote. Since no original autographs are extant, study of subsequent changes in wording is important.

critique/criticism, philosophical   (Gr. *kritikēs*, "the art of criticism") A critical examination of a philosophical or theological subject. Immanuel Kant (1724–1804) wrote famous critiques: of "pure reason" (1781), "practical reason" (1788), and "judgment" (1790).

crosier (crozier)   (Middle English from Old French *crossier*, "a staff-bearer," from *crosse*, "a bishop's cross") The staff carried by an archbishop or bishop in a procession; a symbol of the role of shepherd or pastor.

cross   (Lat. *crux*) The instrument of execution which in the Christian faith is also the means of salvation through the death of Jesus Christ on a cross (1 Cor. 1:23; 2:2; Gal. 6:14; Col. 1:20). The term is used by Jesus to indicate discipleship in following him (Matt. 10:38; Luke 9:23).

cross, adoration of the   *See* adoration of the cross

Cross, Exaltation of the Holy   A liturgical feast known as the Triumph of the Cross is celebrated in the Roman Catholic Church on September 14. In Rome, a procession precedes a veneration of the cross before Mass. In the East, the cross is venerated through elevation and blessings toward the four compass points.

cross, pectoral   (Lat. *pectoralis*, "of the breast") A cross made of precious metal that is worn by bishops and abbots on their chest and is suspended by a chain around the neck. Some Eastern priests also wear this cross.

cross, processional   A cross mounted on a pole that is carried at the beginning of a liturgical procession. It is sometimes made of precious metal and is to be carried in front of everything else in the procession. In the Roman Catholic tradition it may or may not be a crucifix.

cross, sign of the   *See* sign of the cross

Cross, Stations of the   *See* Stations of the Cross

cross, theology of the   *See* theology of the cross

crown   (Lat. *corōna*, "wreath") The headpiece of rulers signifying honor and high office. Used to signify future rewards of believers (1 Peter 5:4; Rev. 2:10). Jesus Christ, who is the "King of kings and Lord of lords" (1 Tim. 6:15; Rev. 17:14), is the one to whom the ultimate crown belongs.

crown of thorns   Part of the passion and humiliation of Jesus prior to his crucifixion, when he was mocked and scourged by Roman soldiers. The crown of thorns was to ridicule the claim that he was king of the Jews (Matt. 27:29; Mark 15:17; John 19:2).

crucifer   (From Lat. *crux*) One who carries a cross in a church procession.

crucified with Christ   The self-identification with Christ by those who believe in Jesus Christ (Gal. 2:19). It points to self-denial and sacrifice.

crucifix   (Lat. *crucifixus*, "fastened to a cross") A depiction of Jesus crucified on a cross. In the Roman Catholic tradition it is a common object of devotion.

crucifixion   Method of execution used by the Romans and to which Jesus Christ was subjected. It was regarded as shameful and was extremely brutal (Matt. 27:45–66; Mark 15:33–41; Luke 23:44–49; John 19:28–37). Theologically the church sees Christ's death as the means of salvation (1 Cor. 1:18).

cruet   (Norman French "little flask") A small glass pitcher that may contain the wine for Holy Communion or water to cleanse the chalice.

Crusades   Military campaigns led by the Western church during the period 1095–1221 to gain control of the Holy Land from the Muslims and to establish Christian rule.

crusades, evangelistic   Meetings often held by traveling evangelists for the purposes of preaching the gospel and inviting persons to make a personal decision of faith in Jesus Christ as their Savior. They are often ecumenically sponsored and have been a feature of American Protestantism in the 19th and 20th centuries.

crypt   (Gr. *krypta*, "vault") A cell or vault beneath a church used as a chapel or place for burials.

crypto-Calvinist   (From Gr. *kryptos*, "hidden," "secret") A 16th-century term for Lutherans in Germany and Scandinavia who privately espoused or were sympathetic to the beliefs of Calvinism. In France the term referred to professing Roman Catholics who were accused of secretly being Calvinists.

Cuius regio, eius religio   (Lat. "The religion of the region shall be that of the ruler") Principle adopted through the Religious Peace of Augsburg (1555) to determine the means by which a territory's religion in the Holy Roman Empire would be decided, between Roman Catholicism and Lutheranism.

cult (cultus)   (Lat. *cultus*, "devotion," "worship") The form and practice of worship or the religious rites of a people. Also, a term to designate a "sect." The term is also used to indicate adoration or devotion.

cults   Groups regarded as heretical, often marked by strong social controls.

cultural-linguistic   Description of religion as analogous to a culture or language that establishes its own meaning system through its "rules."

culture   (From Lat. *colere*, "to till," "to cultivate") Most generally, the description of all human endeavors and activities.

culture, theology of   *See* theology of culture

cuneiform   (From Lat. "wedge") The arrow-shaped characters used for the inscription of ancient Akkadian and Persian documents on clay tablets.

cup of wine   *See* Communion cup

Cur Deus homo?   (Lat. "Why [did] God [become] human?" A basic theological question relating to the doctrine of the incarnation, and, as Anselm of Canterbury (c. 1033–1109) expounded it in his book by this name (1098), also to the atonement of Jesus Christ.

curacy   (From Lat. *cura*, "care") The office, status, or authority of a curate.

curate   (Middle English from Lat. *cura*, "care") A clergyperson charged with the "care of souls." More commonly, a clergyperson who serves as an assistant in a parish under a pastor's direction.

cure of souls   A term to indicate the spiritual care that a clergyperson has for parishioners.

Curia Romana   (Lat. "Roman Curia," from *curia*, "court") The organized structure of those who assist the pope in carrying out the papal duties.

curse   An oral pronouncement for harm or evil to befall another. Sin, disease, and death are the curse on humanity because of sin (Gen. 3:16–19). It was a means of divine enforcement of the Mosaic law which violators bring upon themselves (Deut. 28:15). Ultimately accursedness ends (Rev. 22:3).

cyclical view of history   The view that certain patterns of events in history recur periodically. It was a characteristic of Greek historical thinking. A Christian view focuses on the ongoing work of God to accomplish divine purposes in and through history.

D   Designation of the "Deuteronomist" writer, whom scholars believe contributed portions of the Pentateuch, particularly those upholding monotheism and centralized worship in Jerusalem. The book of Deuteronomy is the prime example of this writing.

daily office   The times of daily prayer and worship services prescribed in the Roman Catholic Church and practiced in various ways by other Christian groups or churches.

damn   (Lat. *damnare*, "to condemn") To judge as guilty and to condemn, a prerogative that ultimately belongs only to God according to Christian theology.

damnation   The condemnation to eternal punishment, which can be pronounced only by God according to Christian theology.

damnation, eternal   The judgment rendered on those who do not accept the salvation offered by God in Jesus Christ, and their eternal separation from God (Matt. 3:12; 5:22; Mark 9:43; Luke 13:28; 2 Thess. 1:9).

dance, liturgical   The form of religious worship expressed through dancing. In Christian practice, it often takes the form of storytelling or expressional movement to explore physical dimensions of meaning in stories or give bodily shape to gratitude and joy.

Darbyites   Followers of John Nelson Darby (1800–1882), founder of the Plymouth Brethren movement. They are marked by a dispensational theology, strong interest in Bible study and missions.

Dark Ages   A phrase formerly used for the period in Western European history between the fall of Rome (5th century) and the Renaissance (16th century). The phrase was reflective of the Renaissance view that the earlier period lacked the light of classical culture.

dark night of the soul   A term used in spiritual theology to indicate periods when the sense of God's presence is absent.

darkness   A biblical symbol associated with chaos, evil, ignorance, and destruction (Gen. 1:2; John 3:19; Eph. 6:12). It represents death and the underworld (Job 17:13; Ps. 143:3; Isa. 5:30) as well as characterizing the day of the Lord (Joel 2:2; Amos 5:18).

Darwinian controversy   Nineteenth- and twentieth-century controversies in the United States over the teachings of Charles Darwin (1809–82) and the theory of evolution in relation to a literal reading of the opening chapters of the book of Genesis.

Darwinism   The theory propounded by Charles Darwin (1809–82) that all things now living have emerged through a process of evolution and natural selection from simpler forms of life. The relation of this theory to biblical accounts of God as creator has been a source of controversy.

Dasein   (Ger. "existence," "presence," "life") Term in existentialism and existential theology to indicate the type of existence that pertains to things in distinction from the existence that applies to individuals who are living an "authentic existence."

Davidic covenant   The covenant God initiated with King David in which an everlasting dynasty was granted to David and his descendants (2 Sam. 7; cf. 2 Chron. 13:5).

day hours   Traditional worship services held through the day: lauds, prime, terce, sext, none, vespers, and compline. Also called "the hours."

Day of Atonement   *See* Atonement, Day of

day of the Lord   A term associated with coming judgment in the Old Testament (Isa. 13:9; Joel 1:15; 2:11; Amos 5:20) and in the New Testament with the second coming of Jesus Christ (2 Peter 3:10).

days, last   *See* last days

deacon/deaconess   (Gr. *diakonos*, "servant"; Lat. *minister*) A church office originating from those who "served" at meals (Acts 6:1–6) and emerging in the early church with liturgical and social duties, particularly the care of the poor. Different church traditions give different roles today.

deaconess movement   (Gr. *diakonissa*, Lat. *diaconissa*) The movement of women thoroughly the history of the church to serve in diaconal functions. The work began in the early church and has taken a variety of forms. Some churches, such as the Church of England, have a deaconess office.

dead, abode of the   *See* intermediate state

dead, prayers for the   In the Roman Catholic and Orthodox traditions, petitions offered to God for blessing upon those who have died, particularly (in Roman Catholicism) for those believed to be in purgatory.

dead in Christ, the   Those who have died and had faith in Jesus Christ (1 Thess. 4:16).

Dead Sea Scrolls   Documents (c. 250 B.C.–A.D. 70) found in Judean caves (1947) that constituted the library in the Qumran community. A number of Old Testament texts, the oldest in existence, were found in addition to those documents which regulated the community's life.

dean   (Lat. *decanus*, from *decem*, "ten") Originally the title for a monk who su-

pervised ten novices, but used more generally to designate administrators of cathedrals, collegiate churches, etc., as well as specialized offices.

death   The cessation of all vital functions that sustain life. Questions of death's origins, the destiny of the dead, and rituals at the time of death are in all religious traditions. In the Christian theological context, death is also the life of sin (Rom. 5–8) that is separation from God.

death, first   Physical death as the cessation of life. It is contrasted to a "second death" which is spiritual (Rev. 2:11; 20:6).

death, second   A biblical image from the book of Revelation for the final status of those who do not receive the eternal life given by God in Jesus Christ (Rev. 2:11; 20:6; 21:8).

death of God theology   A movement in the 1960s that believed the traditional Christian view of God had lost relevance for contemporary Western culture. Christianity, proponents believed, must be radically reinterpreted for a scientific, secular society.

Decalogue   (Gr. *dekalogos*, "ten words") The Ten Commandments (Ex. 20:1–17), which express the will and law of God and deal with relations between humans and God as well as humans with each other.

decision   (From Lat. *decidere*, "to decide") An element of faith in Jesus Christ is the commitment to become a disciple, as marked by an act of surrender and commitment of one's life (Matt. 9:9; 10:38). Theologians have stressed the need for this personal decision as well as recognizing that persons may make and express their commitments in various ways.

decision for Christ   Term used by evangelical Christians to indicate one's personal acceptance of the Gospel of Jesus Christ by faith.

declaratory acts   Several sets of acts by Reformed churches at various points to clarify their attitudes toward their confessional standards. The United Presbyterian Church in Scotland (1879), the Free Church of Scotland (1892), and the Presbyterian Church in the U.S.A. (1903) passed such acts.

deconstruction/deconstructionism
Method of analysis stressing the arbitrariness, manipulation, or bias involved in the composition of texts or the construction of modes of thinking, speech, or behavior. Generally it views language as not having any transcendental meaning. It denies epistemological certainty.

decree   Official pronouncments made by authorized ecclesiastical bodies. The decree of an ecumenical council would be of the highest order.

decree, conciliar   In the Roman Catholic tradition, a doctrinal or pastoral statement that concerns a particular group of people or an important church issue. Sometimes it contains prescriptions for reform or renewal.

decree, eternal/decrees of God   (Lat. *decretum aeternum*) Expression of the will of God, particularly in Reformed scholasticism; or the ways by which God enacts the divine plan of salvation in history. Theological elements considered to be part of God's actions include election, the fall into sin, and salvation to eternal life. These are understood in differing manners by various theologians.

decretal   (Lat. *decretalis*, "depending on a decree") Letter detailing papal rulings on issues of law, especially those relating to canonical discipline in the Roman Catholic tradition.

decretalism   A feature of Reformed scholasticism that gave a prominent place to the decrees of God in constructing its theological system.

decretive will of God   (Lat. *voluntas decreti*) Term used in Protestant scholasticism to indicate the ultimate and effective will of God which underlies the will of God that is revealed to humanity. Also called the "hidden will" (*voluntas arcana*) and the "decisive will" (*voluntas decernens*).

decretum horribile   (Lat. "terrifying decree") A term associated with John Calvin (1509–64), often mistranslated as "horrible decree." It refers to God's eternal predestination as awesome and terrifying to those who do not have faith in Jesus Christ.

dedicate   (Lat. *dedicare*, "to declare," "to dedicate") To consecrate or set apart for a specific use or function. Often used in a religious context to indicate the devoting of life and energies to a specific vocation, task, or service.

dedication   (From Lat. *dedicatio*, "devotion") The formal action of making over something or someone to another. In Christian practice, the "other" is God. Liturgically, dedication may be of a church, liturgical objects, or children. Some churches hold festivals to commemorate the time when their building was dedicated.

dedication of infants   A practice, particularly in Baptist churches, of giving thanks in a service of worship for the birth of an infant and praying for the child's future. It functions in many respects in a parallel way with the practice of infant baptism in other churches.

deductive method   (From Lat. *deductio*, "a leading away") A method of reasoning that derives a conclusion from the logical and necessary consequences of the premises.

Defender of the Faith   (Lat. *Fidei Defensor*) Title used by English monarchs, originating from its conferment on Henry VIII by Pope Leo X (1521) as a reward for Henry's writings against Martin Luther (1483–1546). The pope may confer the title on those who are distinguished exponents of Roman Catholicism.

deference   (Lat. *deferre*, "to bring down") A term used in spiritual theology to indicate a completely voluntary surrender to the will of God. It indicates devotion.

definition, dogmatic   Term used to describe a church's declaration on an issue of Christian doctrine.

defrock   To deprive a person of ecclesiastical rank, duties, or functions. It is an action of a church court or judicatory.

degrees of glory   (Lat. *gradus gloriae*) A view that sees gradations in heavenly gifts as a reflection of the differences between individuals in their earthly lives. It does not imply a lesser or greater degree of blessedness or a fuller "vision of God" for some than for others (1 Cor. 15:41–42).

dehumanization   The suppression or loss of human traits that are basic to life such as creativity, dignity, freedom, love, capacity to worship. Ethically, it is a form of oppression when, explicitly or implicitly, some persons attempt to dehumanize others.

Dei gratia   (Lat. "by the grace of God") A phrase recognizing God's power in human arenas. It is often abbreviated D.G.

deicide   (From Lat. *deus*, "god," and *caedere*, "to kill") The killing of a god. In some religions an animal incarnating a deity is sacrificed.

deification   (From Lat. *deificatio*) To elevate to the position of a god. In early Eastern church theologians, an image for salvation in which through Christ believers can be made like God (2 Peter 1:4). Also, divinization.

Deism   (From Lat. *deus*, "god") A view contrasting to atheism and polytheism. It emerged in 17th- and 18th-century England. It holds that knowledge of God comes through reason rather than revelation, and that after God created the world, God has had no further involvement in it.

deity   (From Lat. *deus*, "god") A term for God or a god. Also the quality of godlikeness or divinity.

deliverance   (From Lat. *deliberare*, "to liberate") The act of being freed, liberated from a constraint. It describes the lib-

eration of Israel from Egypt (Ex. 14:13) and Israel's future glory (Ps. 14:7; Isa. 51:5; 56:1). Theologically, liberation is from the power of sin, through Jesus Christ.

deliverer   One who brings safety or salvation (Judg. 3:9, 15; 18:28). God is a deliverer of the people (2 Sam. 22:2; Pss. 70:5; 140:7). Theologically it is an aspect of the anticipation of a "messiah" in the Old Testament, which Christians see fulfilled in the work of Jesus Christ.

Deluge   (From Lat. *diluvium*, "flood") A term for the Flood that covered the earth in the story of Noah (Gen. 6—8).

demigod   (Lat. *semideus*) A being who is semidivine or a lesser god. Various strands of Gnosticism regarded Jesus Christ in this way.

demiurge   (From Gr. *demiourgos*, "crafter") A Platonic view of a god as one who crafts the world as a sculptor would shape a piece of stone or clay. Also used in Gnostic philosophical systems to describe an inferior or "lesser" being who is creator of the world, but less than a supreme god.

demon   (Gr. *daimōn*, Lat. *daemon*, "spirit") An evil spirit that works contrary to the divine will (Mark 1:34, 39).

demon possession   View that a person or being may be completely taken over or dominated by evil demons. Thus the person is not capable of voluntary action. Jesus is portrayed as exorcising demons (Matt. 8:28–34; Mark 5:1–20; Luke 8:26–39).

demonic   (From Gr. *daimōn*, Lat. *daemon*, "spirit") Possessing the evil characteristics of a demon (Rev. 16:14).

demonolatry   (From Gr. *daimōn*, "demon," and *latreia*, "worship") The worship of demons.

demonology   (From Gr. *daimōn*, Lat. *daemon*, "spirit") The study of demons.

demonstrative theology   A style of systematic theology in the Roman Catholic tradition that seeks to clarify understanding through deducing conclusions based on the laws of logic from a major and minor premise. Both premises may be a revealed truth, or the major may be revealed and the minor may be a truth of reason.

demythologize/demythologization (Ger. *Entmythologisierung*) A term associated with the New Testament scholar Rudolf Bultmann (1884–1976) which indicates his contention that interpreters must ask what biblical myths and symbols point toward and translate these into the categories of existential philosophy.

denomination (Lat. *denominatio,* from *denominare,* "to name") A distinct religious group with particularly held beliefs or practices. Numerous Christian denominations exist throughout the world.

denominational/denominationalism Referring to the various Christian religious bodies or denominations that exist as self-governing and doctrinally autonomous units.

Deo gratias (Lat. "thanks be to God") A liturgical expression used throughout worship services in Christian churches as an expression of praise and gratitude. It is often abbreviated D.G.

Deo volente (Lat. "God willing") An expression recognizing God's will, purposes, and providence in human life. It is often abbreviated D.V.

deontology/deontological (Gr. *deon,* "duty," and *logos,* "study") A term for a system of ethics in which rightness rests on adherence to certain principles without regard for outcomes or consequences. This is sometimes called an ethics of duty or moral obligation.

depatriarchalization A process associated with feminist theology in which elements of patriarchalism in the Christian tradition and Christian theology are recognized and newly approached from feminist perspectives.

dependence/dependency A state of subordination. It is recognized in feminist theology as women's dependence on men, especially in industrialized societies.

deposit of faith (Lat. *depositum fidei*) The truths which God has entrusted to the church, particularly through Jesus Christ and the apostolic tradition (1 Tim. 6:20; 2 Tim. 1:12, 14). Used particularly in Roman Catholic theology to indicate what the church must guard and propound.

deposition (From Lat. *depositio,* "a putting aside") A term to indicate the removal of one from a church office or ministerial status by an ecclesiastical body.

depravity (Lat. *depravare,* "to make corrupt") A theological term to indicate the state of sinfulness or wickedness in which humans apart from God exist and which is characteristic of the human state after the fall.

depravity, total *See* total depravity

descent into hell (Lat. *descensus ad inferos*) Statement from the Apostles' Creed referring to the belief that, in some sense, Jesus "descended" to the realm of the dead (Hades, Sheol) prior to his resurrection (1 Peter 3:19). Interpretations emphasize Christ's victory, or agony, or preaching to the dead.

descent of the Spirit Description of the coming of the Spirit to Jesus at his baptism (Mark 1:9–11) and also of the Pentecost event in which the Holy Spirit came upon the early Christians (Acts 2).

desert fathers and mothers Early Christian spiritual leaders who lived in the deserts of Egypt as an act of devotion and commitment to God. Well known are Anthony (c. 251–356), Macarius (c. 300–c. 390), Abba ("father") Moses, Abba Poemen, Ama ("mother") Sarah, and Ama Syneletia.

desertion, spiritual Term used by 17th-century English Puritans to describe periods in which God seemed far away from believers. They experienced the presence of the absence of God or the absence of the presence of God. Mystics have called it "the dark night of the soul."

design, argument from   *See* teleology

desire   (Lat. *appetitus,* "appetite," "desire") The capacity of an agent to seek its own good. In ethics, a desire may be a perverse or right desire, depending on whether or not it proceeds from sinful motivations.

despair   (Lat. *desperatio,* "hopelessness") In existential theology, the sense of anguish or despair that arises from recognition of one's finiteness. More generally, the abandonment of hope (Ps. 69:20; Eccl. 2:20).

destiny   (From Fr. *destiner,* "to destine") That which has happened or will happen to a person. Theologically the term describes the ultimacy of eternity and views of heaven and hell.

detachment   (Fr. *détachement,* "cutting off") The spiritual process of correcting one's strivings after realities other than God in order to be free and liberated for a committed relationship with God. It has been called mortification or self-denial but also may be viewed positively.

determinism   (From Lat. *determinare,* "to limit") A philosophical view that all humans and events are prescribed by the law of cause and effect so that human "freedom" is denied as a reality. In its extreme form it may be called "fatalism."

Deus a se   (Lat. "God in God's self") Referring to God's inner, mysterious nature that can never be penetrated by human reason. Contrasts with *Deus pro nobis* ("God for us") or God as God is known to humans.

Deus absconditus   (Lat. "the hidden God") Term based on Isa. 45:15, often used by Martin Luther (1483–1546) to indicate that a knowledge of God can only come through God's self-revelation, since God is "hidden" from our reason by human finitude and sin.

Deus est suum esse   (Lat. "God is God's own being") The concept associated with Thomas Aquinas (1225–74) that views God as necessary being or as the pure act of existing.

Deus ex machina   (Lat. "God from a machine") A way of entering the notion of God into an argument to answer all difficulties and end discussion.

Deus pro nobis   (Lat. "God for us") Description of God as revealed to humans and God's relation to them as known through revelation and reason (in contrast to *Deus a se*). Also a description of God's work in salvation through the atonement of Jesus Christ.

Deus revelatus   (Lat. "the revealed God") The God who is revealed and known in Jesus Christ, as contrasted to the "hidden God" (*Deus absconditus*) who cannot be humanly perceived.

Deus vult   (Lat. "God wills it") A phrase with which Pope Urban II inspired the First Crusade to recover the Holy Land from the Muslims (1095).

deuterocanonical books   (Lat. "second canon") Books in the Greek (Septuagint) translation of the Old Testament but not in the Hebrew canon. The term is used in Roman Catholicism to describe those Old Testament books which are not in the biblical canon used by Protestantism. Protestants call them the Apocrypha.

Deutero-Isaiah   The name assigned by biblical scholars to the unknown author of chaps. 40–55 of the Old Testament book of Isaiah.

Deuteronomic History   The name given by Old Testament scholars to the books of Joshua, Judges, Samuel, and Kings with Deuteronomy as a preface. A unified history is presented, with the same editorial views of obedience to divine commands leading to success, and disobedience leading to disaster, being found throughout. Some scholars limit the term Deuteronomic to the book of Deuteronomy and use "Deuteronomistic" for the History through 2 Kings.

Deuteronomic theology   The theology expressed in the book of Deuteronomy as a perspective on the development of the Jewish Torah. It stresses the place of obedience to God's law as leading to "life" while disobedience brings disaster and death (Deut. 30:19).

Deutsche Christen   *See* German Christians

development in fruition   The theological idea, propounded by John Baillie (1886–1960), that saints in heaven will not progress beyond their perfected state but will continue to exercise that perfection.

development of doctrine   The recognition that Christian doctrine as a whole and individual Christian doctrines emerge through historical periods of time toward their formulations. They are influenced by contemporary cultural contexts as well as other more specifically theological factors.

development within creation   *See* creation, development within

devil   *See* Satan

devil ransom   Image derived from an early theory of the atonement. It was suggested that Satan had become the proper owner of sinful humanity but that God, in love, sent Jesus to "ransom" humankind from the power of Satan, who lost humankind through Christ's death and resurrection.

devil ransom theory   Part of an early theory of the atonement which said that Christ paid a ransom to Satan of his own life as the price for the liberation of sinful humanity (Mark 10:45; Rom. 3:24; 1 Peter 1:18–19).

devil's advocate   Popular term for an official in the Roman Catholic Church who is to bring forth any unfavorable information or ask difficult questions in the process of having a deceased person declared "blessed" (beatification) or a "saint" (canonization).

Devotio Moderna   (Lat. "modern devotion") A medieval form of devotion which emphasized devotion to the Eucharist, meditation on Christ's humanity, and the imitation of the virtues of Christ. Exemplified in the work of Thomas à Kempis (c. 1380–1471).

devotion   (From Lat. *devovere*, "to vow") Commitment to the ways and will of God expressed through the Christian life and its practices.

devotional literature   A wide variety of materials that aim to enhance the living of the Christian life in commitment to God's will and ways.

devotions, liturgical   The religious acts including festivals and rituals which express feelings toward God through worship.

devotions, personal   The practice of Bible reading, prayer, and meditation as acts of private worship.

diaconal ministries   Forms of mission and service carried out either formally or informally by "deacons." Historically these have been primarily forms of social ministry, including a strong concern for the care of the poor and those in need. The element of "service" is the main focus.

diaconicum   (Gr. *diakonikon*, "pertaining to a deacon") In Greek and Eastern churches a small room overseen by deacons in which necessary items for worship services are kept. Similar to the "vestry" in Western churches.

dialectic   (Gr. *dialektos*, "discourse," "debate") Reasoning method whereby a conclusion emerges from the tension between two opposing positions. In history, the force that moves through historical conflicts toward culmination.

dialectic, Hegelian   View of G.W.F. Hegel (1770–1831) about the rational process of reality wherein the movement of both "object" and "subject" unite in the movement of the whole and evolve toward a final union of all in absolute spirit.

dialectical materialism   Marxist view of history which holds that material forces are determinative and that progress occurs through continuing conflict and resolution, moving toward a classless society.

dialectical theology   A theological movement, associated with Karl Barth

(1886–1968) and others in their earlier periods, stressing the paradoxical nature of divine truth. Thus is God both grace and judgment. Also called crisis theology and neo-orthodox theology.

dialectics (Gr. *dialektos*, "discourse," "debate") Term used by G.W.F. Hegel (1770–1831) to indicate the logical pattern that thought must follow. The main steps are thesis, antithesis, and synthesis.

dialogue (Gr. *dialogos*, Lat. *dialogus*, "conversation") The process of conversation, especially as representatives of differing religious traditions talk and learn from each other. Formal interfaith dialogues are often held among different church bodies.

Diaspora (Gr. "a scattering") Term for Jews living outside Palestine after the Babylonian exile (586 B.C.) and at other times. More generally, the religion and culture of any particular group apart from its native land. Also called Dispersion.

Diatessaron (Gr. "through four") An edition of the four Gospels that set them in a continuous narrative. It was compiled by Tatian (c. 160) and constituted a "harmony of the Gospels."

dichotomism (From Gr. *dichotomia*, "division into two") A view of humanity that sees a person as constituted by two elements, usually material and spiritual—such as body and soul.

dichotomy (Gr. *dichtomia*, "division into two") A division into two parts, usually to define a philosophical or theological perspective. Dichotomies such as body-soul, theoretical-practical, real-ideal have been characteristic of the Western philosophical and theological traditions.

dictation theory of biblical inspiration *See* inspiration, dictation theory of

Didache (Gr. "teaching") The teaching about the Christian faith conveyed to new converts. Also the name of an early Christian manual on the Christian life and church practice (c. A.D. 100).

Dieu avec nous (Fr. "God with us") A French expression recognizing God's presence in human life.

digamy (From Gr. and Lat. *digamia*, "a marrying twice") A second marriage when a first marriage has ended with the death of one of the partners. Contrasted with "bigamy," which refers to one being married to two persons at one time.

Diggers A 17th-century English communal group led by Gerrard Winstanley (1609–52). They believed true freedom came with the free enjoyment of the earth. They espoused pantheism as well as radical social, religious, and political views. Their name came from their "digging" of the earth.

dignity, human (From Lat. *dignitas*, "worthiness," "merit") The view that all human life has an intrinsic worth. Theologically, it is grounded in humans as created in God's image (Gen. 1:26–27). In the ethics of Immanuel Kant (1724–1804), dignity means persons are to be treated as ends rather than means.

dimensional beyondness A term used by Søren Kierkegaard (1813–55) to indicate God's transcendence being not simply as removed spatially from the creation but that God dwells in a completely different realm of reality which is beyond time and space.

Ding-an-sich, das (Ger. "the thing-in-itself") A philosophical term used by Immanuel Kant (1724–1804) to indicate real objects insofar as their structure and reality are apprehended by a subject who stands in relation to them.

diocese (Gr. *dioikēsis*, "housekeeping," "province," "administrative unit") A territorial unit under the oversight of a bishop. Called "eparchy" in the Eastern church.

diophysite (From Gr. *di-*, "twofold," and *physis*, "nature") A theological term for the view that two natures, divine and human, were present together in Jesus Christ.

dipolar theism   *See* theism, dipolar

diptych   (Lat. *diptycha,* "two-leaved tablet") A pair of hinged clay or wax tablets used in the early church period to record the names of Christians who had died and were to be remembered in prayers. More generally, a list of names for prayers of intercession or thanksgiving.

direction, spiritual   Guidance toward a life of deeper devotion and commitment to God gained through prayer and often the counsel of someone who is regarded as having a gift for helping others on their spiritual journeys.

directions, liturgical   The descriptions of the arrangements and procedures for a service of worship.

directory   (Lat. *directorius,* "guiding") A book which gives instructions for the ordering and practicing of Christian worship.

dirge   (Lat. *dirige,* "direct") Traditional name for the Office of the Dead, derived from the opening Latin words in Ps. 5:8: "Dirige Domine Deus meus in conspectu tuo viam meam" ("Direct, O Lord my God, my way in thy sight").

discalced   (From Lat. *calceus,* "shoe") Unshod. A term for those of religious orders who did not wear shoes or boots. These are distinguished from the "calced," or those who did.

discernment   (Fr. *discernement*) The process of assessing and evaluating, particularly in relation to trying to determine God's will in a particular situation or for one's life direction.

discernment of spirits   Evaluating what is said by prophets (1 Cor. 14:29), or the presence or absence of God, or an evil spirit, when making decisions (Rom. 12:2; 1 Cor. 2:14–15).

disciple   (Lat. *discipulus,* "learner") One who follows and learns from another as a pupil. Old Testament prophets had disciples (Isa. 8:16), as did John the Baptist and the Pharisees (Matt. 9:14; Mark 2:18). It is used specifically for those who follow Jesus Christ (Matt. 5:1; Luke 6:13; Acts 11:26).

disciples, Jesus' twelve   The twelve followers whom Jesus Christ called to himself (Matt. 10:1–4; Luke 6:13–16). Also called "apostles" (Matt. 10:2).

discipleship of equals   A phrase emphasized by Elisabeth Schüssler Fiorenza to indicate the radically inclusive actions of Jesus in sharing his ministry with women as well as men in a nonhierarchical, liberating, and "democratic" vision of "G-d's *basileia*" ("commonwealth," "alternative world").

discipline   (Lat. *disciplina,* from *discipulus,* "disciple") The rules and practices of a religious order or tradition.

discipline, book of   A manual or directory that prescribes the rites, governance, or activities of a church body.

Discipline, Books of (1560, 1581)   Two documents of Scottish Presbyterianism declaring the church's uniformity on various doctrinal and ministerial matters and, in the Second Book, defining also the specific principles of Scottish Presbyterian church government.

discipline, church   The church's regulation of conduct among its clergy and members through counsel, correction, and, at times, censure or excommunication.

discipline of the secret   (Lat. *disciplina arcani*) Early church practice of withholding knowledge of certain doctrines from pagans and from those who were being instructed in the faith in preparation for baptism to guard against misunderstandings and misrepresentations.

disciplines, spiritual   Religious practices that are expressions of devotion to God. In Judaism, these include giving, prayer, and fasting. In Christianity, a number of individual and corporate disciplines are carried out. These include worship, meditation, study, solitude, service, fellowship, and confession.

discipling   The process of assisting others in the Christian faith to become and continue to be "disciples" of Jesus Christ.

discourse theory   A theory of understanding language in which language is a signifying process that constructs reality rather than represents reality. Feminist and liberation theologies recognize that discourse (language) can oppress or liberate.

discrimination   (Lat. *discriminatio*) Unjust or preferential treatment of individuals or a group, often on the basis of social class, gender, race, nationality, or religion.

disembodied state   A person's status between the time of death and the resurrection of the body according to some theological views.

disinterested love   A concept of medieval spirituality which claimed that even if there was no heaven and one's soul was in hell, the love of God in itself would be its own reward. The view was condemned in a papal bull in 1699.

dismissal   (From Lat. *dimissus,* "sent away") The liturgical practice of sending forth worshipers at the conclusion of a worship service. It is usually marked by a charge to the congregation and/or a benediction.

dispensation   (Lat. *dispendere,* "to weigh out," "to dispense") The means by which God relates to people, as through covenants and thus the "old" and "new" dispensations. Also, the administration of sacraments, or the exemption from an obligation or ecclesiastical regulation.

dispensation of grace   A reference to the new covenant in Jesus Christ (1 Cor. 11:23–25).

dispensation of innocence   In Dispensationalism, the period in which God dealt with Adam and Eve prior to the fall into sin (Gen. 3).

dispensation of law   In Dispensationalism, the period of God's dealing with humanity from the time in which the law was given at Mount Sinai (Ex. 20) until the New Testament period.

Dispensationalism   A view of God's activities in history expounded in *The Scofield Reference Bible* and traced to John Nelson Darby (1800–1882). Each dispen-

sation is a different time period in which humans are tested in responding to God's will. Seven dispensations cover creation to judgment.

Dispersion   *See* Diaspora

disposition   (Lat. *dispositio,* "direction") In ethics, the state or attitude of a thing that is necessary before a characteristic or action emerges. It is related to intention and is a component in assessing moral dimensions.

disposition of faith   (Lat. *habitus fidei*) The capacity, given by God, of sinful humans to have faith.

disposition of grace   (Lat. *habitus gratiae*) God's gift to a human so that God's grace becomes part of the person's nature. This functions as God's justifying or sanctifying grace.

disputation   (From Lat. *disputatio*) An ecclesiastical debate or controversy.

dissent   A judgment that disagrees with official church teaching or practice. Differing forms of dissent are found in various traditions. Dissent may be individual, by groups, or public and organized. In some cases it is a formal procedure to be pursued in ecclesiastical courts.

Dissenters   Those who withdrew from the national church (Anglican) of England on the basis of conscience during the 16th to 19th centuries. The term includes Congregationalists, Presbyterians, Baptists, and Roman Catholics.

dissenting academies   Educational institutions begun in post-Restoration England (17th century) to train those who would not subscribe to the established state (Anglican) church. These "Independents" were called "Nonconformists."

dissident   (From Lat. *dissidere,* "to disagree") A person or a church group that leaves an already established body of Christian believers.

dissolution   Term for the action of ecclesiastical bodies in ending a relationship, such as that between a pastor and congregation, or a marriage. It is also used for the disbanding of a local congregation.

dissolution of monasteries (1536, 1539–40) The suppression of monasteries by King Henry VIII of England in an attempt to raise money and to solidify his claim to royal supremacy over the church.

distinguishing of spirits *See* discernment of spirits

distribution of the elements A term for the administration of the elements, i.e., bread and wine, to worshipers in a Communion service.

distributive justice One of the three recognized major forms of justice: commutative, distributive, and social. Distributive justice is concerned with the allocation of social resources, wealth, and power.

district In the Methodist system of church government, a subunit of the Annual Conference organized to carry out conference programs and presided over by a district superintendent.

district superintendent An appointed Methodist minister who presides over a district and has various administrative powers.

ditheism (Gr. *dis*, "double," and *theos*, "God") Belief in the existence of two gods struggling for supremacy. One is usually good, the other, evil.

divination (Lat. *divinatio*, from *divinare*, "to foresee," "to predict") Attempt to gain supernatural knowledge, often by the means of omens or the occult.

divine (Lat. *divinus*) Pertaining to the supreme force or power in the universe or "God."

divine afflatus (From Lat. "to breathe," "to blow on") The inspiration by God through which some form of knowledge such as insight, wisdom, or prophecy is imparted.

divine attributes *See* attributes of God

divine decrees *See* decrees, eternal/decrees of God

divine healing God's work in bringing about human healing, usually regarded as the healing of physical problems.

divine law Term used to describe God's governance of the universe. It is understood as the law God has made known through divine revelation. Thomas Aquinas (1225–74) developed the concept. It is divided into the Mosaic law and the law given by Jesus, particulary in the Sermon on the Mount.

divine monarchy The view that God the Father is the primary member of the Trinity and is the ontological source of the Son and Spirit. Called Monarchianism and seen as heretical in the early Christian church.

divine names The names of God made known by God's self-revelation in the Scriptures.

divine office, the (Middle English from Lat. *officium*, "performance of a responsibility") The church's daily prayers or "canonical hours" observed as morning and evening prayer with compline and the "little hours." Also called "the hours."

divine presence *See* presence, divine

divine right of kings The view that the power to rule and make laws resides solely with the king. Originally found in Byzantium, the view was propagated by the later Stuart monarchs in 17th-century England.

divine service A term for a service of public worship.

divinitatis sensus *See* sense of divinity

divinity (From Lat. *divinus*, "divine") God or godlike. A term sometimes used as a synonym for "theology."

divinization (Gr. *theōsis*) The view of Eastern theologians that sees salvation as the penetration of the human condition by the divine energies (2 Peter 1:4), beginning a process of uniting human and divine that is completed only with the resurrection of the dead. Also deification.

divorce (Lat. *divortium*, "a separation") The legal dissolving of a valid marriage. Attitudes about divorce vary among different Christian churches and groups.

Docetism (Gr. *dokein*, "to seem") Belief that Jesus only "seemed" or appeared to have a human body and to be a human person. The view was found during the period of the early church among Gnostics, who saw materiality as evil. It was condemned by Ignatius of Antioch (c. 35–c. 107).

doctors, scholastic Term for significant theological teachers and others in the medieval period.

doctors of the church In Roman Catholic theology, a list of some thirty theologians who have been prominent and exemplary through the history of the church. They have been officially recognized by the pope or an ecumenical council and canonized.

doctrinal freedom The freedom of Roman Catholic schools and theologians to believe and teach within the church's doctrinal limits.

doctrinal preaching The preaching of sermons that have the explication of Christian doctrines as a primary focus.

doctrinal theology The body of theological discussion that deals with Christian doctrines or the teachings of the church.

doctrine (Lat. *doctrina*, from *docere*, "to teach") That which is taught and believed to be true by a church. In various ways churches sanction their official teachings or doctrines.

doctrine, development of *See* development of doctrine

documentary hypothesis Theory that the first five books of the Old Testament (Genesis–Deuteronomy) were composed through four traditions from different periods of Israel's tradition. They are identified as J (Yahwist), E (Elohist), D (Deuteronomist), and P (Priestly Code), known as JEDP.

dogma (Gr. *dogma*, "that which seems to one," "an opinion") A teaching or doctrine which has received an official church status as truth. In the Roman Catholic Church it has status as a definitive or infallible church teaching.

dogmatic facts In Roman Catholic theology, those facts that are not deduced directly from divine revelation but that are necessary for the preservation of the church's faith. Examples would be the legitimacy of a pope or the ecumenical character of a church council.

dogmatic theology Theological reflection on the beliefs of the Christian community, primarily though not exclusively through the study of Christian creeds and confessions of faith.

dogmatics (Gr. *dogma*, "dogma," from *dokein*, "to think," "to appear") The formal study of the Christian faith which presents its beliefs and doctrines in an organized and systematic way.

dogmatism (From Gr. *dogmatizein*, "to lay down a decree"; Lat. *dogmatismus*) A decidedly stated and expressed opinion, many times unwarranted or without a foundation.

doing theology A term for the process of carrying out theological reflection, articulation, and action.

dolors of Mary, the seven *See* sorrows of Mary, the seven

dom (From Lat. *dominus*, "master") A title for monks in certain religious orders, particularly the Benedictine, Carthusian, and Cistercian.

dome (From Lat. *domus*, "house") The large semicircular spherical ceiling or roof of a church. Often it is decorated or painted to represent heaven or the cosmos.

domestic church A term used in the "Dogmatic Constitution on the Church" (1964) of the Second Vatican Council and other Roman Catholic writings to refer to the Christian family as the most basic unit of the Christian church. It suggests that the community of faith is found in the home.

domination (Lat. *dominatio*, "rule," "dominion") The power held by one group or individual over another group or individual. Feminist theology relates this to male domination of women.

dominical injunctions (Lat. *dominus,* "master," "Lord") The wishes or commands of God or Jesus. The "dominical sacraments" are said to be baptism and the Lord's Supper, since these originated directly from commands of Jesus himself (Matt. 28:16–20; 1 Cor. 11:24–25).

Dominican order The Order of Preachers (O.P.) founded by Dominic de Guzman (1216) to share in the ministry of the Word, to preach and teach the gospel. The priests and brothers share a life of contemplation of God through liturgical worship, private prayer, and Scripture study.

dominion, having A reference to Gen. 1:28 where humans were to have dominion over creation as they recognized that all has come from God (Gen. 1:29–30). Some see this as constituting the image of God in humanity (Gen. 1:26–27).

Dominus vobiscum "The Lord be with you" as a liturgical greeting in worship services. The response is "And with your spirit" (Lat. *Et cum spiritu tuo*). A revised text in the Roman Catholic Mass is "And also with you."

Donation of Constantine An 8th-century forgery of a document proporting to show that Constantine the Great (c. 280–337) gave Pope Sylvester I (314–35) and his successors both spiritual power over other leaders and spiritual and temporal power over Rome and the Western Empire.

Donatism North African separatist movement begun by Donatus (d. 355). He objected to permitting Christians who had "lapsed" in their faith, by turning over Scriptures when persecuted, to be reinstated in the church. He did not want "traditors" (traitors) who were clergy to preside at the Eucharist.

donum superadditum (Lat. "super-added gift") In Roman Catholic theology, the gifts humans lost at the fall into sin as restored and added by God to human nature. In medieval theology, the "likeness of God" (*donum superadditum*) was lost through sin while the "image of God" was not affected by sin.

doomsday philosophy The view that history will have a climactic and disastrous end.

Dooyeweerdian Following the teachings of Herman Dooyeweerd (1894–1977), a Dutch Reformed philosopher and theologian who posited a complex philosophical system of autonomous "spheres" that collectively helped form a Christian "worldview."

Dormition of the Virgin Feast celebrating the falling asleep (Lat. *dormitio,* Gr. *koimēsis*) of the Virgin Mary, observed on August 15 in Orthodox churches and corresponding to the Feast of the Assumption in Roman Catholic churches.

Dort, Canons of the Synod of The theological teachings of the Synod of Dort (1618–19). It propounded a systematized Calvinism, in opposition to Arminian views. Its five canons related to Total depravity, Unconditional election, Limited atonement, Irresistible grace, and the Perseverance of the saints (TULIP).

Dort, Synod of (1618–19) A gathering of Reformed theologians at Dort (Dordrecht) in the Netherlands to counter and condemn the teachings of Arminianism.

Dositheus, Confession of (1672) A confessional statement of the Greek Orthodox Church written chiefly by Dositheus, patriarch of Jerusalem (1669–1707), to combat Protestantism.

Douay (Douai) Bible *See* Rheims-Douay Version of the Bible

double effect In ethics, the side effects of making an ethical decision and carrying it out. These, while anticipated, may not be desired. Yet they do occur. The doctrine of double effect is often considered so that the primary criterion for morality is the intention, not the side effects.

double predestination (Lat. *praedestinatio gemina*) The view that God has freely chosen both to save some people (election) and to damn others (reprobation). It is "double" in that it recognizes both election and reprobation as divine decrees.

double procession of the Holy Spirit
The view that within the Trinity, the Holy Spirit proceeds both from the Father and the Son. This is the view of the Western church, while the Eastern church teaches a single procession. The double procession is associated with the *filioque* ("and the Son") phrase in the Niceno-Constantinopolitan Creed (381).

double standard   A practice of sanctioning or accepting certain behavior by males while condemning the same if done by females. These practices are pointed out by feminist writers as inherently sexist.

doubt, religious   (From Lat. *dubitare*, "to waver") Uncertainty, as opposed to denial, of religious truths.

dove   (Gr. *peristera*) A symbol of the Holy Spirit. In Christian art, the dove depicts the Spirit's descent during Jesus' baptism (Luke 3:22). It is also used as a sign of peace.

doxology   (Gr. *doxologia*, from *doxa*, "praise, " and *legein*, "to speak") A form of praise to God, such as "Glory be to the Father, and to the Son, and to the Holy Ghost (Spirit)."

Doxology, the   (Gr. *doxologia*, "a praising") A widespread sung response in worship, particularly among American Protestants. The text, "Praise God from whom all blessings flow . . . ," was written by Thomas Ken (1637–1711) in 1695 and is often sung to the tune "Old Hundredth."

Dragonnades   Persecutions by mounted troops ("dragoons") against French Huguenots ordered by King Louis XIV to induce the Huguenots to accept the Roman Catholic faith.

dread   Term used by Søren Kierkegaard (1813–55) and other existentialist writers. A state of precondition of sin constituted by an anxiety about one's life due to the tension between finitude and freedom. It can occur when one has the freedom to face the uncertainty of the unknown.

Dry Mass   (Lat. *missa secca*) A shortened form of the Roman Catholic Mass that omits the offertory, canon, and

Communion. It was viewed in the Middle Ages as a substitute for the Mass when the latter was not allowed for some reason.

dualism   (From Lat. *duo*, "two") Any view that is constituted by two basic or fundamental principles such as spirit and matter or good and evil. Can also refer to belief in the existence of two gods (ditheism).

dulia   (From Gr. *douleia*, "service") In Roman Catholic theology, the recognition of a saint as a model worthy to receive homage and respect is the "cult of dulia." It is distinguished from the "cult of latria," which is adoration due to God alone.

Dunkers/Dunkards/Tunkers   *See* Brethren (Dunkers)

duty   (Lat. *debere*, "to owe," "to be in debt") That which one owes to God in terms of obedience and the commitment of one's life, which also entails commitment to the church and to the care of others.

dynamic presence   The view that Jesus Christ is present in the Lord's Supper, not literally and physically, but spiritually.

Dyophysitism   (From Gr. *dyo*, "two," and *physis*, "nature") The view that Jesus Christ has two natures, a divine and a human nature, inextricably united. This position was accepted by the Council of Chalcedon (451) and the Council of Constantinople (553). It contrasts with Monophysitism.

Dyothelitism   (Gr. *dyo*, "two," and *thelein*, "to will") The view that Jesus Christ had two wills, corresponding to his two natures: divine and human. They are believed never to be in conflict and always in a moral union. This view was adopted at the Third Council of Constantinople (680–81). It contrasts with Monothelitism.

dysteleology   The view, made popular after the publication of works by Charles Darwin (1809–82) on natural selection, that nature has no obvious purpose or grand design. It contrasts with teleology.

E Designation of the Elohist writer or tradition. One of the several written traditions found in the Pentateuch. It uses "Elohim" as a name for God.

early church Term variously ascribed to the earliest period of the Christian era. It was constituted by the formation of New Testament churches. More generally, it often refers to the longer period of the early centuries of the church's existence until the Middle Ages.

earth, new The redeemed earth of the future as part of God's new universe called the "new heavens and a new earth" (2 Peter 3:13; Rev. 21:1; cf. Isa. 65:17; 66:22).

earthly body The body a human has while living on earth (1 Cor. 15:42–50).

earthly kingdom The reign of God as it is carried out on earth, often with reference to a future "millennial" rule of Christ (Rev. 20:4).

Easter (Easter Sunday) The yearly Christian festival celebrating the raising of Jesus Christ from the dead three days after his crucifixion. It is preceded by Good Friday. Easter is the first Sunday following the full moon that occurs on or after March 21. The date varies between March 22 and April 25. Theologically it celebrates the victory of Christ over death and evil as well as Christian hope.

Easter faith A term for the faith of the early church, which proclaimed the resurrection of Jesus Christ (Acts 2:32; 1 Cor. 15:20). Some contrast "Easter faith" and "Easter fact," arguing that the resurrection does not need to be "historical" but only a matter of "faith." Others contend there could be no "Easter faith" without "Easter fact."

Easter season The season of the church year extending from Easter Sunday until the festival of Pentecost, fifty days later. Its first eight days are known as the Octave of Easter. In the early church newly baptized Christians continued to receive catechetical instruction in this season.

Easter Vigil The watch held on Holy Saturday night, prior to Easter. It dates from the mid-2d century and is seen as the culmination of the entire church year. It rehearses salvation history and is marked by a service of light and Scripture readings, with the Eucharist, and may include baptism or the renewal of baptism. Also called Paschal Vigil.

Eastern Catholic churches Churches of the Eastern Orthodox tradition that having returned to Roman Catholicism continue to maintain their distinctive liturgies, canon law, and religious customs under a chief bishop (patriarch).

Eastern Orthodox Church Churches rooted in the split between Western churches and Eastern churches in 1054 and presided over by the ecumenical patriarch of Constantinople.

Eastern Orthodoxy The theological views of Eastern Orthodox churches.

Eastern religions Those religious faiths, such as Hinduism, Confucianism, Taoism, and Buddhism, which originated in Asia.

Eastern Rites (liturgies) The liturgical traditions used in Orthodox and Eastern Catholic churches. These are: Armenian, Byzantine, Coptic, Ethiopian, East (Assyro-Chaldean) Syrian, West (Antiochene) Syrian, and Maronite. They are marked by their length, use of incense, and rich use of symbols.

easy believism   Popular slogan for the view that one simply has to "believe" in order to be saved and that there is no corresponding need for a committed life of Christian discipleship.

eating (sacramental)   (Lat. *manducatio,* "eating") The practice of partaking of the Lord's Supper. Some distinguish between an outer partaking of the elements by believers and unbelievers and an inner, spiritual eating in which the benefits of the Supper are received only by believers who have faith.

EATWOT   An acronym for the Ecumenical Association of Third World Theologians. It was founded in 1976.

'ebed Yahweh   (From Heb. "servant of Yahweh [God]") An Old Testament term for all pious Israelites and especially for the figure in the "Servant Songs" of Isaiah 42, 49, 50, 52—53.

Ebionism   (Heb. *'ebyonim,* "poor people" [Matt. 5:3]) Early heretical sect of ascetic Jewish Christians. It stressed obedience to the Mosaic law and believed Jesus was not divine but became "Son of God" when the Holy Spirit descended on him at his baptism (Matt. 3:16).

Ebionites   (From Heb. *'ebyonim,* "the poor") A group of Jewish Christians who practiced an ascetic lifestyle and lived simple, communal lives, continuing for approximately 200 years after Jesus. They practiced ritual cleansings and baptisms.

Ecce homo   (Lat. "Behold the man") The Latin words of Pontius Pilate when he presented Jesus to the Jews (John 19:5). A number of paintings of Jesus' judgment by Pilate bear this title.

ecclesia (ekklesia)   (Gr. *ekklēsia,* from *ek,* "out of," and *kalein,* "to call"; Lat. *ecclesia,* "church") Those "called out," as in the ancient Greek practice of calling together citizens for a political meeting. The church is all believers in Jesus Christ through all ages.

ecclesia docens/ecclesia discens   (Lat. "the teaching church"/"the learning church") In Roman Catholic theology, the distinction between the church hierarchy ("magisterium") in whom resides teaching authority, and the body of the faithful or laity who accept the truth of the church.

ecclesia reformata sed semper reformanda   (Lat. "the church reformed, but always being reformed") A basic principle of the Protestant Reformation, echoed by Roman Catholicism in the teachings of Vatican Council II (1962–65). Reformed churches have understood the church's reformation to be in light of Scripture.

ecclesial   Relating to the Christian church.

ecclesiastic   (Gr. *ekklēsiastikos,* "preacher") A clergyperson.

ecclesiastical   (From Gr. *ekklēsia,* "assembly called out," "church") Relating to the clergy, church organizations, administration, or governance. Contrasted with "secular."

ecclesiastical separation   *See* separation, ecclesiastical

ecclesiasticism   A term of deprecation referring to an exaggerated concern with the external details of church practices and administration. Also, a point of view that is oriented only by what benefits the church as an organization.

ecclesiolatry   (From Gr. *ekklēsia,* "church," and *latreia,* "worship") A strong devotion to the church, often used in criticism to denote an excessive obedience or undue devotion to church practices.

ecclesiology   (From Gr. *ekklēsia,* "church," and "logos," "study") The study of the church as a biblical and theological topic. The New Testament presents various images of the church that the early church struggled with as it sought its self-understanding in light of the gospel and controversies.

eclectic   (Gr. *eklektikos,* from *eklegein,* "to select") Coming from diverse and varied sources. The term is used in philosophical theology to describe points of view that incorporate parts of various philosophical or theological systems.

ecoethics   An ethical approach that incorporates concern for the whole biosphere as a primary principle.

ecofeminism   A strong emphasis in feminist theology is that a concern for the environment and the integrity of creation be a mark of theological understanding and Christian praxis.

ecojustice   A perspective combining concerns of ecology and justice. It focuses on the use and care of the limited resources of earth in ways that are just and beneficial for the human community. Theologically, it is rooted in the view of a just God who calls humans to care for the environment.

ecology   (Gr. *oikologia*) The relation of human organisms to their environment. Theologically, a concern for ecology is rooted in the recognition of God as creator who calls humans to care for the earth and its resources in responsible and just ways.

economic Trinity   A view of the Trinity, propounded by Hippolytus and Tertullian, that stressed the functions ("economies") or work of the Father, Son, and Holy Spirit rather than their eternal being in relation to each other.

economics   (Gr. *oikonomikos*, Lat. *oeconomicus*, "pertaining to household management") The science of the production, distribution, and consumption of wealth. Ethical issues in economics relate to aspects of justice in the acquisition and distribution of wealth.

economy, divine   (Gr. *oikonomia*, Lat. *dispensatio*, "plan," "arrangement") God's plan for salvation and ongoing providence, which is cosmic in scope. It embraces all aspects of human existence and the universe itself.

ecstasy/ecstatic utterances   (From Gr. *ekstasis*, "standing outside oneself") The state of altered consciousness, often in relation to the divine, and the speech which issues from that condition. The

experience is found within the Christian mystical tradition.

ectene   (Gr. *ekteneia*, "earnest prayer"; cf. Acts 12:5) A short liturgical prayer in the Eastern church constructed as a litany in which a deacon offers a petition followed by the choir or congregation's reponse with the Kyrie Eleison.

Ecthesis (638)   (Gr. *ekthēsis*, "statement of faith") Formula by the emperor Heraclius that prohibited the mention of "energies" (Gr. *energeiai*) in discussion of the person of Christ. It maintained that the two natures of Christ were united in a single will (Monothelitism). It was later rejected by the Christian church.

ecumenical (oecumenical)   (Gr. *oikoumenē*, "the inhabited world") Relating to ecumenism as embracing the whole "household" of God. It thus concerns all churches and their relationships with each other as well as the relation of Christianity to other world faiths.

ecumenical councils   *See* councils, ecumenical

ecumenical creeds   Statements of faith used by the whole church. In the early church period the most notable of these were the Nicene Creed (325) and the revised and enlarged Niceno-Constantinopolitan Creed (381; now called the Nicene). The latter is used in worship today.

ecumenical ethics   The cooperation of various church bodies and Christians in ethical discussions and endeavors.

ecumenical evangelical   A term used in American religion to describe those who have evangelical emphases in their theology and who also wish to maintain an open, ecumenical stance in relation to other Christians.

ecumenical movement, modern   A widespread movement, beginning in 1910, to bring about unity among the various Christian churches. It has been marked by concerns for cooperation, mutual understanding and respect through dialogues, and common witness to the gospel in the midst of the search for unity (John 17:21).

ecumenical patriarch   Title of the patriarch of Constantinople (residing in Istanbul, Turkey) as the primate of the Eastern Orthodox Church.

ecumenical relationships   Relationships among various church bodies in which there is mutual cooperation, recognition of each other's ministries, and common participation in various activities.

ecumenics   The study and practice of ecumenism.

ecumenism   (From Gr. *oikoumenē*, "the whole inhabited world") The desire for unity among churches and believers in Jesus Christ. The concern emerges from Jesus' prayer (John 17:21). Churches attempt to find the visible unity that they confess they have theologically in Christ (1 Cor. 12:12–20).

ecumenism, early   The attempts to establish a unity among Christian churches in the early church period through authoritative doctrinal formulations.

Eden, Garden of   Description of the place in which Adam and Eve found themselves after their creation according to the biblical account (Gen. 2:8–3:24). It has also become a synonym for "paradise."

edification   (Gr. *oikodomē*, "building up") The upbuilding of Christians in the Christian church and thus the strengthening of their faith and devotion to God in Jesus Christ (Rom. 15:2; 1 Cor. 14:3; 2 Cor. 10:8; 13:10).

education, Christian   *See* Christian education

education, theological   *See* theological education

Edwardsian   Following the thought of the American philosopher and theologian Jonathan Edwards (1703–58). His New England Puritanism modified traditional Calvinism and favored "experiential religion." It was influenced by doctrines of original sin and irresistible

grace as well as by the scientific and philosophical views of Isaac Newton (1642–1727) and John Locke (1632–1704).

effectual calling   (Lat. *vocatio efficax*) In Reformed theology, God's calling to the elect with the result that they respond in faith.

efficacious grace   *See* grace, efficacious

efficacy   (From Lat. *efficax*, "effectual") The accomplishment of purpose. Often used in regard to the sacraments. The term is also applied in reference to the salvation gained through the death of Jesus Christ: Christ's death has efficacy for those who believe.

egocentricity   Understanding that begins from the self (in contrast with exocentricity).

egoism   (From Gr. *egō*, and Lat. *ego*, "I") Centering in the self. Philosophically, subjective idealism and solipsism consider self to be the only reality. Practically, self-centeredness as inordinate self-love (2 Tim. 3:2) is characteristic of sinners. Love of God is to be the primary orientation of God's people (Deut. 6:5; Matt. 22:37).

Einmaligkeit   A German term referring to the sense of absolute uniqueness in that something happens only once. Theologically it indicates God's unique revelation in Jesus Christ or some dimension of the Christ event, such as the resurrection. It stands against the view that Jesus Christ is only an example of a universal truth that can be known through human reason.

eirenicism   *See* irenicism

eisegesis   Reading meanings "into" a biblical text as opposed to "out of" a biblical text ("exegesis").

El   The generic Semitic name of "God" or "deity" and found as a common name for God in the Hebrew Bible. It signifies mysterious divine power. El was worshiped in Canaanite religions as a high god and the father of Baal. El is used as a synonym for Yahweh and combined with other forms.

elder (Gr. *presbyteros,* "presbyter," "elder") Leaders in early Christian churches with governmental oversight. The Reformed tradition distinguishes between "teaching" and "ruling" elders.

elder, ruling In the Reformed tradition, a lay church officer who is part of the body with spiritual oversight in a local church.

elder, teaching In the Reformed tradition, one who has been ordained to the office of pastor and who thus has teaching responsibilities within a local congregation.

elect (Gr. *eklektos,* "chosen") Those who are chosen by God to receive salvation (Rom. 8:33; Col. 3:12; Titus 1:1).

election (Gr. *eklogē,* Lat. *electio,* "a choice") God's choosing of a people to enjoy the benefits of salvation and to carry out God's purposes in the world (1 Thess. 1:4; 2 Peter 1:10). This doctrine has been of particular importance in Reformed theology.

election of officers The practice of ecclesiastical bodies in selecting leaders through a procedure of voting by members of a particular unit. This occurs in local congregations as well as at other levels of the church's governing structures.

electronic church A term for various means of religious broadcasting, most prominently for television programs produced by Protestant evangelists. They are often considered to constitute an experience of "church" for their audiences.

elements (Middle English from Lat. *elementum,* "rudiment") The bread and wine used in the Lord's Supper.

elevation of the Host (From Lat. *elevare,* "to lift up") In the Roman Catholic Mass, the point where the consecrated bread and then the cup are lifted up for adoration. This action follows the words of consecration.

Elizabethan Settlement (1559) The religious settlement in England in which Queen Elizabeth I (1553–1603) abolished papal power and required all to acknowledge her as "supreme governor" of the church and follow prescribed state church practices.

Elohim (Heb. `elohim,* "gods") Frequent Hebrew term for God in the Old Testament. The term is plural but was used to designate the one God of Israel. It has the effect of intensification: "God of gods," "the highest God" (Gen. 1:1). It is used in the Psalter (Pss. 42—83) and is a synonym for Yahweh, the self-revealed name of the God of Israel in other Old Testament writings.

emanant attributes *See* attributes of God, emanant

emanation(ism) (Lat. *emanare,* "to flow out from") Usually applied to a view that the universe emerged from God as its central and eternal principle as light "emanates" from the sun as its source. Opposed to *creatio ex nihilo.*

emancipation (From Lat. *emancipare,* "to declare free") Growth in freedom, expressed in liberation and feminist theologies to indicate either changes in existing societal frameworks or the transformation of social frameworks.

emancipatory historiography The recovery of past historical events, traditions, and lives of persons that provide significant models and insights for the liberation of groups or persons in the present. This may involve seeing events in a new light, reappropriating traditions, or finding new biographies.

ember days (Old English *ymbrendagas,* "recurring days") Four groups of three days (Wednesday, Friday, Saturday) observed as times of special prayers and fasting. They were formerly periods for penitence. Now prayers are for peoples' needs, for the earth's productivity, and for human labor, while public thanks is given to God.

embodiment An emphasis in feminist theology on the need for theology to focus on bodies and their basic needs for shelter, food and water, and companionship. Bodies matter. Some advocate an earthly theology with the world as God's body.

emergent evolutionism   *See* evolutionism, emergent

eminence   (Lat. *eminentia,* "a standing out," "prominence") An honorific title given to a cardinal in the Roman Catholic Church. It is preceded by the words "Your" or "His" and is joined with the formal address "Most Reverend."

eminence, method of   Method of coming to know God by elevating human characteristics that reflect God to a heightened degree.

Emmanuel/Immanuel   (Heb. "God with us") The name for a child in Isaiah's writings as a sign of God's presence and protection (Isa. 7:14; 8:8). It is seen in the Gospel of Matthew as a prophecy of the miraculous conception of Jesus Christ, who will be called "God with us" (Matt. 1:23, citing Isa. 7:14).

empirical   (From Gr. *empeirikos,* Lat. *empiricus,* "experienced") That which can be known through sense perception or experience.

empirical approach   Approach to theology that finds knowledge through sense perception or experience and uses it for theological purposes.

empirical church   The church as it exists and is experienced in human history.

empirical theology   A theological approach based on sensory experience. Also used as a term for "natural" theology.

empiricism   Philosophical view that truth is obtained through experience. Classical empiricism considers data as derived from the five senses. Radical empiricism emphasizes the relations and qualities of particular actualities as the data of bodily experience, rather than sense data.

empowerment   A term used in various liberation theologies to indicate the gaining of power and control over life by groups that have been oppressed. It is a goal that is realized only through struggles.

enchiridion   (Gr. "something to have in hand") A concise textbook. Used especially to describe Roman Catholic manuals that collect church doctrinal teachings and are used for theological study.

encounter   (From Old French *encontrer,* from *encontre,* "against") The reception of God's revelation in a personal act of confrontation. Associated particularly with the theology of Emil Brunner (1889–1966).

Encratites   (From Gr. "self-control," "continence") A 2d-century ascetic group that abstained from eating meat, drinking wine (even in the Eucharist), and marriage. Considered by some writers as heretical because of their Gnostic overtones.

encyclical   (Gr. *enkyklios,* from *en,* "in," and *kyklos,* "circle") A general ecclesiastical letter circulated among churches or persons.

encyclical letter   In Roman Catholicism, a papal encyclical is sent by the pope as a letter to all bishops to point out errors of faith in doctrine, discipline, or morals or to promote the work of the church.

end of the world   The point at which human history on earth will end. In Christian theology, this is associated with the second coming of Jesus Christ.

ends and means   Terms from ethics referring to the results of actions ("ends") and the instruments by which the results are achieved ("means"). Ends are considered to have intrinsic value; means are judged morally in relation to the ends.

endurance   (From Lat. *indurare,* "to harden," "to tolerate") The Christian's perseverance in the Christian life through all things as sustained by God's grace (Luke 21:19; Rom. 5:3–4; James 1:3–4).

energies, divine   (From Gr. *energeia,* Lat. *energia,* "activity") In Eastern Orthodoxy, a way of describing God's presence and action or God's exterior manifestation throughout the universe.

English Revised Version (ERV; 1881, 1885)   A revision of the King James Version of the Bible by British and American scholars. It was begun in 1871 and based on the best available manuscripts. The New Testament was published in 1881 and the Old Testament in 1885. The Apocrypha was published in 1898, as was a whole Bible edition.

enhypostasia / enhypostasis   (Gr. from *en*, "in," and *hypostasis*, "substance") Literally, "in-personality." The christological view from the Council of Chalcedon (451) in which the church declared that the full humanity of Christ was preserved but also included within the eternal person of the Word (Logos).

Enlightenment, the   (Ger. *Aufklärung*) A period in 18th-century Europe marked by the intellectual and philosophical conviction that truth could only be obtained through the powers of human reason, observation, and experiment.

entelechy   (Gr. *entelecheia*, Lat. *entelechia*) Philosophically, a realization or actuality as opposed to a potentiality. That which accounts for form. Theologically, scholastic theologians considered an example of entelechy to be the soul as opposed to the body.

enthronization   (Gr. *enthronizein*, Lat. *enthronizare*, "to enthrone") A description of the rite used when a bishop assumes a bishopric, or when the relics of a saint are consecrated in a church, or generally, when clergy are installed in their churches.

enthusiasm   (Gr. *enthousiasmos*, "inspiration by a god") The sense of divine inspiration or ecstasy. Also used to describe the religious fervor of groups such as early Quakers and Methodists in reaction to the formalism of established churches.

entire sanctification   A view found in the Wesleyan and Holiness traditions which teaches that a Christian can attain a freedom from sin and full sanctification or holiness in this life.

entrance, great   In the Byzantine Rite, the name for the procession of ministers who bring the bread and wine as gifts to the altar at the beginning of the eucharistic service. Theologically it prefigures the coming of Jesus Christ in the sacrament of his body and blood. Also called "major introit."

entrance, little   In the Byzantine Rite, the name for the procession of ministers who carry the book of the Gospels at the beginning of the liturgy of the Word. It is carried from the altar through the church and back to the altar again. Also called "minor introit."

entrance rites   Ceremonies or rites that mark the beginning of one's full participation in a religion. In Christianity, baptism may be considered a rite of entrance.

envy   (Gr. *phthonos*, "jealousy," Lat. *invidia*, "envy") The desire to possess what belongs to another. In the Roman Catholic tradition it is considered one of the seven deadly sins and stands as a violation of the Christian attitude of love to others.

eparch   (Gr. "ruler") In Eastern church canon law, the bishop who presides over an eparchy (diocese) in his own name. Equivalent to a diocesan bishop in the Western church.

eparchy   (Gr. "territory under rule") Eastern church term for a territory under the oversight of a bishop. Called "diocese" in the Western church.

Ephesus, Council of (431)   The third ecumenical council, which condemned Nestorianism and Pelagianism while reaffirming the unity of the person of Jesus Christ. It also declared Mary the "Mother of God" (Gr. "Theotokos").

Ephesus, Robber Synod of (449)   A church council at Ephesus that reinstated Eutyches (c. 375–454) and asserted the view that the idea of the two natures of Jesus Christ was heretical. This view was ultimately rejected by the Council of Chalcedon (A.D. 451).

epiclesis (Gr. *epiklēsis*, "invocation") The prayer offered in the Eucharist seeking the presence of the Holy Spirit. In Eastern Orthodoxy it seeks the Spirit's work to change the bread and wine into the body and blood of Jesus Christ.

Epicureanism A Greek philosophical view, patterned after Epicurus (341–270 B.C.) in which contentment is seen as the supreme good. It aims at achieving happiness through the absence of pain and anxiety. Along with Stoicism it became a very important Greek philosophical school in the Roman world.

epikeia/epieikeia (Gr. *epieikeia* "reasonableness," "equity"; Lat. *aequitas*, "equity") An act of justice that is done for the common good and for individual good, and in which the intention of the law is recognized as a higher norm than the letter of the law. It is found in Aristotle and Aquinas and opposes legalism.

Epiphany (Gr. *epiphaneia*, "manifestation") In general, an appearance of the divine. Specifically, a church festival of January 6 celebrating the visit of the Magi to Jesus as a divine "manifestation" to Gentiles (Matt. 2). Eastern churches celebrate Christ's "appearance" at his baptism.

Epiphany Sunday The Sunday between January 2 and January 8, on which the Christian church celebrates the feast of Epiphany. It recognizes the revelation of Jesus Christ to the entire world as represented by the coming of the Magi to worship the Christ child (Matt. 2).

episcopacy (Gr. *episkopos*, "overseer"; Lat. *episcopus*, "bishop") The form of church government in which bishops oversee a diocese, as in Roman Catholicism, Orthodoxy, and Anglicanism. Also, in Roman Catholicism, the highest level of the sacrament of holy orders.

episcopal church government *See* episcopacy

Episcopalian One who is a member of the Anglican Church (in England and

Scotland) or the Episcopal Church in the U.S.A.

episcopalism The view that authority in church government should reside in a body of bishops and not in a single office such as the papacy or patriarchy.

episcopate A group of bishops. Also, a bishop's term or office.

episcopi vagantes (Lat. "wandering bishops") The view that even an excommunicated bishop can continue to ordain priests because the holy orders the priest received conveyed an indelible and permanent character.

epistemological privilege A view in liberation theology that the world's poor and oppressed have a better knowledge and perception of God's truth because of their situations and because of God's special concern for the oppressed.

epistemology (From Gr. *epistēmē*, "knowledge") Study of how human knowledge is obtained, its bases, forms, and criteria.

epistemology, Reformed An approach to the study of how knowledge is obtained, led by philosophers of the Reformed theological tradition, particularly Alvin Plantinga (b. 1932) and Nicholas Wolterstorff (b. 1932). They argue that it is legitimate to include belief in God in the foundations of knowledge structures, just as one does with belief in the existence of other minds or that there has been a past.

epistle (Gr. *epistolē*, "letter," "message") Term for one of the group of "letters" found in the New Testament. Also, a reading from these biblical writings in a worship service.

equality The view that all people should share the same opportunities for human rights. Some feminist theologians see full equality of formal rights for women as a way of ending women's subjection in male-dominated societies.

equiprobabilism The view, supported in Roman Catholic moral theology, according to which it is permissible to choose an opinion in favor of liberty when two options appear to be nearly equal in probability. It was used by Alphonsus Liguori (d. 1787).

equivocal/equivocity (Lat. *aequivocus,* "two voices") Referring to two views that are equally correct. Also a philosophical description of the use of language for names; e.g., when terms carry different meanings, to say that "God is good" is not the same as to say that "Humans are good."

Erasmian humanism The humanism that emerged from the work of Desiderius Erasmus (c. 1466–1536). It sought reform and education emphasizing a return to the classical sources (*ad fontes*, "to the sources"). It stressed studies of history, language, rhetoric, and philosophy, and influenced Martin Luther (1483–1546).

Erastianism The view, argued by a Swiss professor of medicine at the University of Heidelberg, Thomas Erastus (1524–83), that the state has the right to exercise supreme authority over the church in all issues.

eristics (From Gr. *eristikos,* from *erizein,* "to strive") Term used by Emil Brunner (1889–1966) in place of "apologetics" to indicate the disputational activities of Christians in presenting the truth of God's self-revelation in Jesus Christ.

ERV *See* English Revised Version

eschatological parable A parable dealing with the end of the world (e.g., Matt. 25:31–46).

eschatology (From Gr. *eschatos,* "last," and *logos,* "study") Study of the "last things" or the end of the world. Theological dimensions include the second coming of Jesus Christ and the last judgment.

eschatology, collective Events of the end time concerning the total universe or the entire human race. They anticipate the ultimate triumph of the kingdom of Jesus Christ, when all things will be subject to him (1 Cor. 15:25; Phil. 3:21). Resurrection, judgment, and transformation of the world will occur (Rev. 21:1).

eschatology, consistent The view of Albert Schweitzer (1875–1965) and others that Jesus' teachings as a whole were thoroughly eschatological in nature. According to Schweitzer, Jesus mistakenly believed that the end of the world would occur soon.

eschatology, cosmic Study of the "last things" in relation to all the elements of the cosmos, including humans.

eschatology, futuristic The view that all the major eschatological events indicated in Scripture are still in the future. This has been the primary viewpoint of major theologians throughout the church's history.

eschatology, inaugurated A view combining futuristic and realized eschatology. The eschaton has come in the resurrection of Jesus Christ, while there are also events, such as the return of Christ and the resurrection of the dead, that are in the future. Eschatology is inaugurated, but still future.

eschatology, individual Study of the future in terms of events relating to individual persons such as death, judgment (Matt. 25:31–46), and resurrection (Phil. 3:21).

eschatology, New Testament Study of what the New Testament teaches about the future and the end of the world.

eschatology, Old Testament Study of what the Old Testament teaches about the future and the end of the world.

eschatology, realized The view, popularized by C. H. Dodd (1884–1973) and others, that New Testament eschatological passages do not have a future reference but are to be understood as being fulfilled in biblical times and especially in the life and ministry of Jesus Christ.

eschatology, symbolic The view of Paul Tillich (1886–1965) and Reinhold Niebuhr (1892–1971) that while the eschatological passages in the New Testament are to be taken seriously, they should be interpreted symbolically and not literally. They indicate that human existence can never be fulfilled within history alone.

eschatology, teleological The view that eschatological events mentioned in Scripture are not events that will occur at the conclusion of history but are events that are being carried out concurrently with human history. Thus every generation encounters an eschatological Christianity.

eschatomania Popular name given to an intensive preoccupation with the last things (eschatology).

eschaton (Gr. "the last thing") The final event of history, considered by many theologians to be the return of Jesus Christ to earth.

eschatophobia Popular description of a fear of discussing or studying the last things (eschatology).

esoteric (Gr. *esōterikos*, "inner") Referring to the secret and inner teachings and rituals of a religious group shared only by those initiated into the group.

essence (Lat. *essentia*, from *esse*, "to be." Corresponds to Gr. *ousia*, "being") That which something is as its permanent aspect, as compared to "accidents" or a particular mode of being at a certain time. In Christology, Jesus Christ has a human and a divine essence but is one person.

essence of Christianity The attempt to discover the central, fundamental, or most essential aspects of Christianity.

essence of God *See* God, being of

Essenes An ascetic, monastic Jewish sect that existed from the 2d century B.C. until the end of the 1st century A.D. in a settlement found near the Dead Sea at Qumran. They were the probable transcribers of the Dead Sea Scrolls. They were strict adherents of the Torah, communalistic, and highly organized.

Essentia nec generat nec generatur A Latin phrase used by scholastic theologians and based on Aristotelian concepts to say that "an essence can neither generate another essence nor be generated (by another essence)." It was used to deny views of the Trinity which claimed that each member was an essence that could generate or produce the others.

essential humanity Humanity as God intended humans to be in creation; in contrast to humanity after the fall into sin.

essential Trinity *See* Trinity, essential

essentialism The belief of some feminist theologians that there is a unique female nature expressed, for example, in predispositions for motherhood and female bonding. This is true even for women who do not wish to mother or affiliate with other women. Philosophically, the term refers to the view that objects can be understood by discerning their essences.

established churches Those churches that are sanctioned by governments as official "state churches."

estrangement (Lat. *extraneus*, "strange") Act of withdrawing oneself or keeping oneself at a distance. Paul Tillich (1886–1965) used the term as a description of "sin," which distances one from a right relationship with God or with others or with oneself.

eternal (Lat. *aeternus*, from *aevum*, "age") Everlasting, enduring forever. Philosophically and theologically, the claim to be eternal can only be made for God.

Eternal, the A term for God, whose being is timeless and everlasting (Ex. 3:14–15).

eternal condemnation Condemnation lasting beyond the present life and into eternity (Matt. 25:46).

eternal consequences of sin The unending results that sin brings, extending beyond the present life and into eternity, in contrast to the temporal results of sin, which end with death.

eternal damnation *See* damnation, eternal

eternal death The final and permanent separation of a sinner from God.

eternal destiny The final and permanent future state, which in Christian theology may be in heaven with God or in hell, separated from God.

eternal generation The relation of the Son to the Father in the Godhead, with the Son being "eternally begotten" or "generated" by and from God the Father.

eternal ideas The eternal universal ideas that are archetypal in God's mind and which provide the basis of certainty for all human ideas, according to the views of scholastic theologians and Augustine (354–430).

eternal life (Lat. *vita aeterna*) Present participation in God's reign and in the benefits of salvation through faith in Jesus Christ by the work of the Holy Spirit (John 3:16). After death, it is consummated by life in heaven in God's presence, which lasts forever. Also everlasting life.

eternal punishment The final and permanent punishment of the wicked after the last judgment (Matt. 25:46).

eternal redemption A phrase found in Heb. 9:12 to indicate that in contrast to Old Testament animal sacrifices, which offered only a limited effect, the death of Jesus Christ has eternal redeeming effects.

eternal security The view, espoused in Reformed theology, that those who truly believe in Jesus Christ as their Lord and Savior will never lose their salvation, due to God's ongoing power and faithfulness (John 10:28). Also called the perseverance of the saints.

eternal state *See* final state

eternal will of God An expression to designate that which God has willed from all eternity.

eternity (Lat. *aeternitas*, from *aevum*, "age") That which is distinct from time and has no beginning or end. It is an attribute that belongs only to God.

ethical code A series of prescriptions detailing what is right or wrong, and the ways in which judgments should be made.

ethical kingdom A term for God's rule over the ways in which one makes decisions and choices (ethics).

ethical naturalism The view that values and actions are grounded in biological or natural principles.

ethical purity One's strict adherence to the standards of a moral code.

ethical system, Christian Guidance for making choices and decisions, and for acting, based on Christian theological understandings.

ethical teaching Teaching that describes ways in which one should make choices and decisions and take actions.

ethics The study of human conduct, focusing particularly on attitudes and actions that are considered to be "right" or "wrong."

ethics, biblical Those views of what is right or wrong in God's sight, as derived from or found in the Bible.

ethics, Christian That which constitutes right or wrong or the formation of the moral life according to the Christian faith. It is also the academic discipline that engages in critical reflection on moral values and actions from a Christian perspective.

ethics, consequentialist view of The view that the standard by which right or wrong is to be determined is the consequences it produces.

ethics, contextual The view that human choices, decisions, and actions should be made with a high regard for the context of the particular situation. This context may be much more important than strict ethical rules in assessing what ethical actions to take. Also called situation ethics.

ethics, norms for   In the Protestant tradition, Scripture has been seen as providing the primary standard for judgment and ethical action. Revelation and reason (as it perceives the natural law) have been major norms in Roman Catholicism.

ethics, personal   The values, norms, and actions carried out in personal decisions. These are concerned with relationships in settings such as the home, work, and church, and with personal conduct. Attitudes, intentions, speech, and deeds are all part of the ethical life.

ethics, situation   *See* ethics, contextual

ethics, social   *See* social ethics

ethnicity   Having the characteristics of a particular group of people, especially a cultural group or country. Recognition of this factor can be taken into account in biblical interpretation.

ethnocentric   A way of thinking that cannot see difference. It thus universalizes all values and ideas from the experience of one's own ethnic group.

ethos   (Gr. *ēthos,* "disposition," "character") Prevailing values, ideas, and cultural expressions that define a particular time or place. These shape and are shaped by religious or theological viewpoints.

etiology   (Gr. *aitiologia,* "study of causation") The inquiry into origins in which stories are said to have been constructed as explanations for phenomena. The tower of Babel story (Gen. 11:1–9) may be said to explain why there are so many languages.

Eucharist   (Gr. *eucharistein,* "to give thanks") A term for the Lord's Supper deriving especially from Jesus' prayer of thanks for the bread and wine, which he related to his body and blood given for those he loved (Matt. 26:26–29; Mark 14:22–25; Luke 22:15–20; 1 Cor. 11:23–26).

eucharistic fast   The practice of abstaining from food and drink prior to the reception of Holy Communion.

eucharistic prayers   Prayers offered during the celebration of the Eucharist, most particularly, the great prayer of thanksgiving.

eucharistic sacrifice   The image of the offering of the sacrifice of Jesus Christ that is found in the liturgical texts of the Christian church (1 Cor. 5:7).

eucharistic theology   Theological understandings about the Eucharist or Lord's Supper. These are concerned with its nature and function, as well as with questions about the presence of Christ in the Supper, the work of the Holy Spirit, the relation of faith to the Supper, and what happens in relation to the elements.

eucharistic vestments   Vestments worn by clergy and those who participate in the Eucharist or Lord's Supper.

Euchites/Messalians   (Gr. "praying ones") Fourth-century Christian group originating in the Middle East which believed that each person's soul is attached to an evil spirit which can only be expelled by praying without ceasing. They were condemned at the Council of Ephesus (431).

euchologion   (Gr. "book of thanksgivings") A liturgical book with the full texts of the sacraments and blessings used for Eastern churches.

eudaimonism   (Gr. *eudaimonia,* "the well-being of the *daemon* [spirit]") The view that ethical decisions and actions should be based on that which will produce happiness or well-being.

eugenics   (Gr. *eugenēs,* "well-born") A term for "genetic engineering" in which, through breeding, certain characteristics or traits may be manipulated. A number of ethical issues are involved in both the elimination of defective genes and attempts to improve attributes.

eulogia   (Gr. "blessing") The blessed (but not consecrated) bread distributed after the Eucharist in Eastern churches, more commonly called "antidoron." In the Roman Catholic Church, the term "eulogia" is also used for the consecrated bread and wine. The term is also used for a blessing or holy place.

eulogy (Gr. *eulogia*, "praise") An address given at a funeral that celebrates the life of the deceased and offers "good words" on his or her behalf. Christian funeral services often seek to subordinate eulogies to the proclamation of the gospel through a sermon on Christian hope.

Eunomians *See* Arianism

Eurocentric Judging all things and valuing all things from the perspective of European experience. The term is used to indicate the dominance of this approach in theological writing and thinking in the Western world.

euthanasia (Gr. "an easy death") The termination of human life for the purpose of ending misery and suffering. It may be by action or by omission, voluntary or involuntary, direct or indirect, active or passive. It has been the source of much moral debate. Also called "mercy killing."

Eutychianism Teaching of Eutyches (c. 375–454) that Jesus had only one nature.

evangel (Gr. *euangelion*, "good news") The good news or gospel of salvation through Jesus Christ.

evangelical A term used in Europe for "Protestant." In America it has come to refer to one who stresses the need for a personal relationship with God in Jesus Christ by faith. Some who claim the term seek to define it further in terms of theological beliefs about particular issues.

evangelical churches In Europe the term refers to Protestant churches. In America the term is generally applied interdenominationally to churches that emphasize evangelism and the need for a personal relationship with God in Jesus Christ by faith.

evangelical counsels *See* counsels, evangelical

evangelical liberalism A movement within Protestant theology (1880–1930), also called "New Theology" or "progressive orthodoxy," that sought to synthesize traditional Christian doctrine

with the advances in science and culture in order to make Christianity more appealing to contemporary persons.

evangelical theology A transdenominational movement in American Protestantism that stresses the need for a personal relationship with Jesus Christ and the proclamation of the gospel (Gr. *euangelion*). It is variously defined, emphasizing biblical authority and Jesus as Savior.

evangelicalism An interdenominational movement in American Protestantism that emphasizes the spreading of the gospel through evangelism and the need for a personal relationship with God in Jesus Christ through faith. It has been marked by a more pronounced social concern than is common in fundamentalism.

evangelism (From Gr. *euangelion*, "good news") The sharing of the gospel of Jesus Christ through a variety of means.

evangelist (From Gr. *euangelion*, "good news") One who shares the gospel of Jesus Christ.

evangelistic crusades *See* crusades, evangelistic

evangelistic zeal A great enthusiasm or effort in evangelism or promulgating a particular viewpoint.

evangelists, the four Those whose names are connected to the four Gospels in the New Testament: Matthew, Mark, Luke, and John.

Eve (From Heb. *ḥawwah*, derived from *ḥayah*, "to live") In the biblical story of the creation, the first woman, created as a companion to "Adam" (Gen. 2:23).

evening prayer The evening service of the Anglican Church, equivalent to "vespers" in the Roman Catholic Church. Also called evensong.

everlasting life *See* eternal life

every member canvass A process of visiting every member or household of a church or parish for evangelical, spiritual, or stewardship purposes.

evidences of Christianity Factual data used by some theologians to argue for the truth of Christianity, usually including prophecy and miracles.

evil That which opposes the will of God. It is both personal and structured oppression that takes shape in societies. It has been defined as "the absence of good" (Augustine). Distinctions are made between physical and moral evil, natural and intrinsic evil.

evil, intrinsic (Lat. *intrinsice malum*) That which stands directly opposed to the will of God. This refers to those things which are wrong in every circumstance. The term was used by medieval theologians. Its validity is questioned by those who believe circumstances must be considered.

evil, moral Evil in the universe that affects human beings and their relationships with each other, in contrast to natural evil, which does not involve the human will. Moral evil emerges from a human will that is turned away from, or in opposition to, God's will.

evil, natural Evil in the universe that does not involve the human will, in contrast to moral evil. Natural or physical evil emerges from a disorder in creation which produces suffering and harm to those who are not responsible for its causation.

evil, problem of The difficulty in reconciling God's omnipotence and God's love with the existence of evil, or that which opposes God. This is also the issue of theodicy.

evil one Another term for Satan (see Matt. 5:37; 6:13; 13:19; John 17:15; Eph. 6:16).

evil powers A term for those forces which oppose God (see Matt. 4:1–11; John 12:31; 16:11; Eph. 2:1ff.; 6:12; 1 Peter 5:8; 1 John 3:8–10; Rev. 13:1ff.).

evil spirits Demons; powers that work in opposition to God and God's purposes (Luke 7:21; Acts 19:12–15).

evolution (Lat. *evolutio*, "an unrolling") The development of one form into another. The term is associated with the views of Charles Darwin (1809–82) concerning the means by which animal and human life came into existence and through which they became increasingly complex life forms.

evolution, naturalistic The view that evolution has proceeded purely as a matter of natural forces without any divine influence.

evolution, theistic The view that God has guided the process of evolution and used it as a means of achieving divine purposes.

evolution debate Debates over the theory of evolution as proposed by Charles Darwin (1809–82) and the question of whether evolution can be reconciled with Christianity. Those who oppose a reconciliation believe the theory is counter to a literal reading of the creation accounts in Genesis.

evolutionism, emergent The view that the evolutionary process is capable of establishing new forms of life because of the creative forces that are found within the process. Some regard these forces as natural, others as the means through which God works.

ex cathedra (Lat. "from the chair") The concept of acting by virtue of one's office. It is used most for the pope's explication of a dogma of faith or morals. This is the highest level of papal teaching.

ex lege (Lat. *ex*, "from," and *lex*, "the law") The view that sees God as beyond or outside law and thus not bound by it.

ex nihilo, creatio See: *creatio ex nihilo*

ex opere operantis (Lat. "out of [by] the work of the worker") The view that the efficacy of a sacrament depends on the spiritual goodness of the one who administers it and that the proper attitude must be present in the recipient.

ex opere operato (Lat. "from the work done") In the Roman Catholic tradition, the view that the efficacy of a sacrament depends on it being a valid sacrament and not on the spiritual goodness of the one who administers it. It seeks to emphasize a sacrament as an objective pledge of God's grace.

exaltation of Jesus Christ   Theological expression of the resurrection and ascension of Jesus Christ which constitute his victorious work (Phil. 2:9–11; Eph. 1:20; Rev. 3:21). It contrasts with the humiliation of Christ, constituted by his incarnation and his death on the cross.

exclusivism   The view that God will not grant salvation to those who do not believe in Jesus Christ or who are outside the Christian church (John 14:6; Acts 4:12).

excommunication   (Lat. *excommunicare*, "to excommunicate," "put one out of a community") Ecclesiastical sanction that cuts one off from the church and its benefits.

executive   One who is charged with various administrative responsibilities in a church governing body. In presbyterian polity, a presbytery or synod may have such a person.

exegesis   (Gr. *exēgēsis*, "interpretation," from *exēgeisthai*, "to draw out or explain") The act of interpreting or explaining the meanings of verses or passages of Scripture.

exegesis, structural   *See* criticism, structural

exegetical method   The processes used to interpret and explain the meanings of Scripture passages. Many different exegetical methods have been used through the history of the church and are to be found among contemporary biblical scholars.

exemplar causality   *See* ideas, divine

exemplarism   (Lat. *exemplarium*, "ideal model") The view that the death of Jesus Christ provides atonement by portraying Jesus as the supreme example of God's love, thus inspiring repentance and love in those who have faith in him. It is also called the "moral" or "subjective" view of atonement.

exemption   (Lat. *exemptio*, "a taking out") The granting of freedom by one's ecclesiastical superior.

existence   (From *ex*, "out of" and *sistere*, "to stand") The state of being. It is a basic philosophical term, historically contrasted with "essence." Existence is the act of existing.

existence of God, arguments for the   *See* arguments for the existence of God

existential   (Lat. *existentialis*) A philosophical term referring to that which is of ultimate importance to one's being or existence.

existential, supernatural   *See* supernatural existential

existential estrangement   In the theology of Paul Tillich (1886–1965), the condition of humans as dependent on the "ground of being" ("God") for existence and yet separated or "estranged" from the ground of being by their actions which deny their essential being ("sin").

existential humanity   The reality of the human condition as it currently exists in contrast to what God originally created humans to be.

existential state   A technical term from the philosophy of Martin Heidegger (1889–1976) denoting the "self-confrontation" of the human with one's own condition, characterized by a sense of "thrownness" and "being-in-the-world."

existential theology   Theology rooted in existential philosophy. The theologies of Paul Tillich (1886–1965), Rudolf Bultmann (1884–1976), and the early Karl Barth (1886–1968) were influenced by existential philosophy stemming from Søren Kierkegaard (1813–55), Friedrich Nietzsche (1844–1900), and Martin Heidegger (1889–1976).

existentialism, Christian   The use of categories and insights from existential philosophy within a basic Christian framework. It sees Christianity as stressing the need for personal decision and commitment to Jesus Christ by a "leap of faith" that affects one's whole existence.

existentialism/existential philosophy A philosophical movement that emerged from the emphasis of Søren Kierkegaard (1813–55) on the way to truth as found through human subjectivity and a person's participation in "reality" ("being"). It developed through Martin Heidegger (1889–1976) and influenced Rudolf Bultmann (1884–1976) in his approach to issues of the transcendence of God, faith and history, hermeneutics, the historical Jesus, and eschatology.

existenziell (existentiell) (Ger.) In existential theology, pertaining to a person's own concrete existence and experience as opposed to a formal analysis of human existence in general.

exocentricity Understanding that begins from outside the self (in contrast to egocentricity).

exodus A term for the escape from oppression in Egypt by the people of Israel through the liberating power of God, around 1200 B.C. Also Exodus, the second book of the Bible.

exomologesis (Gr. "confession") A term for the process of reconciliation in the church that includes confession of sins, satisfaction for wrongs, absolution, and restoration to the church community of one who is penitent.

exorcism (Middle English, from Gr. *exorkizein,* "to drive out an evil spirit by use of an oath") The driving out of an evil spirit. It is a form of liberation from the power of evil and was carried out in the ministry of Jesus (Luke 11:14–23) and his disciples (Acts 16:18).

exorcist (Gr. *exorkistēs,* Lat. *exorcista*) One who drives out an evil spirit by performing an exorcism.

exoteric (Gr. *exōterikos,* "outer," "exterior") Referring to the open and public presentation of beliefs for all to see; in contrast to "esoteric."

Exoucontians A group of 4th-century Arians who followed Aetius (d. c. 370) and took the view that the Son was created from "nonbeing" (Gr. *ex ouk ontōn*).

expectant, the church The church on earth awaiting the consummation of history and the final establishment of the kingdom or reign of God.

Expectation Sunday A title for the Sunday between Ascension Day and Pentecost, derived from the "expectation" of the early disciples, who looked for the coming of the Holy Spirit after Christ's ascension (Acts 1:4f.).

expediency (From Lat. *expediens,* "advantageous") Acting in a way which increases one's own advantage, often at the sacrifice of ethical principles.

experience (From Lat. *experientia,* "a trial," "proof") A state of being that is consciously affected by something. Or, the consciousness of the content of life, on the part of an individual, a group, or a community.

experience, religious Most broadly, all the ways in which individuals or groups come to an awareness of things or events that can be considered to be sacred. Christian theology has variously assessed the role of experience in theological understanding, some theologians giving it a prominent place.

experience, theology of A theology based on one's own experience rather than on an external authority.

experiential-expressivist The view that religion originates in the inner experience of the transcendent.

expiation (Lat. *expiatus,* from *ex,* "out," and *"piare,"* "to seek, appease, or purify through a sacred rite") Release from sin as well as the means by which this release is accomplished. The RSV translates the Greek (*hilastērion, hilasmos*) in relation to the work of Jesus Christ (Rom. 3:25; 1 John 2:2; 4:10).

Expiation, Day of *See* Atonement, Day of

exploitation (From Lat. *explicare,* "to set forth") Use of the experience, wealth, or skills of others without reward. Some feminist theologians argue that exploitation forms the basis of male-female social relations as characterized by patriarchy.

exposition of Scripture   (From Lat. *exponere*, "to expound") The act of interpreting the Scriptures and, usually, preaching from the Scriptures.

exposition of the Sacrament   The exhibiting of the vessel containing consecrated bread to a congregation during a eucharistic service.

expositor   (Lat. "an interpreter") One who interprets the Bible.

expository sermon   (From Lat. *expositorius*, "setting forth") A sermon that seeks to interpret and explain a passage of Scripture.

extempore prayer   (Lat. *ex*, "from," and *tempus*, "the time") Prayer that is spontaneous rather than premeditated or previously written.

external calling   *See* calling, external

external grounds   Means by which the attempt is made to justify a theological belief other than through explicitly theological means.

externalism   An emphasis on the outward practices, forms, or rites of a religion, in contrast to its deep meanings and values.

extra calvinisticum   (Lat. "the Calvinistic extra") A term used by 17th-century Lutheran theologians to describe the Reformed view that the human nature of Christ as the second Person of the Trinity was utterly transcendent during the incarnation, i.e., that the Word was never totally contained in flesh.

Extra ecclesiam nulla salus   (Lat., "Outside the church there is no salvation") A phrase, associated with Cyprian (d. 258), for the view that Christian salvation is only possible for those who are affiliated with the Christian church.

extra nos   (Lat. "outside ourselves") A term used in Protestant understandings of justification. It refers to the righteousness of Jesus Christ that is imputed to sinners through faith, which comes entirely from a source "outside" the sinner.

extrabiblical materials   Materials not found within the Scriptures or biblical writings.

extrabiblical sources   Sources independent of the Scriptures or biblical writings.

extranatural   That which is distinct from the physical universe.

extrasensory perception (ESP)   The ability of some persons to acquire knowledge in ways beyond normal human limitations. It is an ability associated with mystics, saints, and prophets. Contemporary secular interest in the phenomenon relates to the perception of a spirit world beyond space and time.

extratextual   The meaning or reference of a text, as being outside or independent of the text itself.

extreme unction   *See* anointing of the sick

extrinsicism   (Lat. *extrinsecus*, "from without," "outer") Understanding of values or attributes as coming from the external nature of an object rather than belonging to it internally.

Faith   (Gr. *pistis*, Lat. *fides*, "trust," "belief") In Christianity, belief, trust, and obedience to God as revealed in Jesus Christ. It is the means of salvation (Eph. 2:8) or eternal life (John 6:40). Faith affects all dimensions of one's existence: intellect, emotions, and will.

faith, confession of   *See* confession of faith

faith, explicit   (Lat. *fides explicita*) Faith in that of which one has knowledge. Thus, the term may be understood as referring to what one professes to believe because of what is known.

faith, gift of   The recognition that faith comes as unmerited benevolence from God's Spirit (1 Cor. 12:9) and not as a result of human efforts (Eph. 2:9).

faith, implicit   (Lat. *fides implicita*) The Roman Catholic view that one believes as true "what the church believes," even without certain knowledge. It was rejected by the Protestant Reformers as a true faith because the element of knowledge was lacking.

faith, infused   (Lat. *fides infusa*) The teaching in the Decree on Justification of the Council of Trent (1545–63) that at the moment of justification, faith is given along with hope and love. Thus the three theological virtues are simultaneously infused into a person.

faith, the   The body of Christian doctrine believed by the church and explicated in creeds and confessions of faith.

Faith and Order   International Christian conferences at Lausanne (1927) and Edinburgh (1937) that marked important steps in the growth of the ecumenical movement, culminating in the formation of the World Council of Churches (1948).

faith and reason   Traditionally seen as two means by which a knowledge of God may be gained or maintained. The relationship of faith and reason has been variously assessed throughout the history of Christian thought. Some have seen them as complementary, others as in paradox or contradiction, or with one as having priority.

faith healing   Healing that comes as a result of religious faith rather than through overt medical means. The means are often prayer and the laying on of hands (James 5:14).

faithfulness   The characteristic of being steadfastly loyal to a person or to promises. Theologically, it is a basic description of God who is perfectly faithful to all that God promises, in contrast to sinful humans who are unfaithful in their relationships and actions.

fall, effects of the   The theological results of the human fall into sin (Gen. 3), such as human guilt and the sinfulness of human nature.

fall, literal view of the   The view that a historical Adam and Eve sinned precisely as recorded in Genesis 3.

fall, premundane   The view of some early church theologians that angels fell from God's grace prior to the fall into sin by Adam and Eve. The figure of Lucifer (Satan, the devil) is considered to have led other angels in revolt against God and to have been expelled from heaven together with them.

fall, symbolic view of the   The view that the fall into sin (Gen. 3) is a theological account which explains the human condition and that its symbolic truth does not depend on its literal historicity.

fall, the   The act of Adam and Eve, as presented in Gen. 3, in which they disobeyed God and thus lost the relationship they were originally created to have with God.

fallenness of humanity   The theological condition of all people as sinners because of the fall into sin (Gen. 3).

falling away   *See* apostasy

false Christs   Those claiming to be the Christ (Matt. 24:5; Mark 13:22).

False Decretals, the   Documents containing a mixture of truth and fabrication that were used to defend the claims of the papacy. They were attributed to Isidore of Seville (c. 560–636) but were actually composed c. 850 in France. In the Middle Ages they were assumed to be genuine. They were exposed as forgeries in the mid-16th century.

false prophet   (Gr. *pseudoprophētēs*) A term introduced in the Septuagint, where the Old Testament Hebrew text negatively describes prophets who opposed God's prophets and sought to turn people away from God's will (Jer. 6:13; 26:7–8, 11, 16; 27:9; 28:1; 29:1, 8; Zech. 13:2). Tests for distinguishing true and false prophecy are given (Deut. 13:1–5; 18:15–22). Jesus warned against false prophets (Matt. 24:24; Mark 13:22; cf. 1 John 4:1–3).

familialists   *See* Family of Love

familism   *See* Family of Love

family altar   A place in the home where family devotional activities such as prayers and Bible reading are conducted.

Family of Love (Familists)   A 16th- to 17th-century group, founded by Henry Nicholas (Hendrik Niclaes), whose members were anticlerical and anti-Trinitarian in their mystical pantheistic beliefs. They were absorbed into Quakerism and other sects by the end of the 17th century.

family prayers/worship   The practice of families praying or worshiping together, usually daily. This was a feature of Puritanism, which saw the home as a miniature church.

family values   Ethical and religious convictions that support the well-being of families and promote the ideals of family life.

fast days   Days when for various reasons people refrain from eating solid food because of religious convictions or because of special spiritual concerns. Their purposes are often to enhance one's sense of the presence of God. They may also be for penance or repentance, either on a regular basis or as perceived needs arise.

fast/fasting   Abstinence from food for the purposes of religious devotion and spiritual discipline.

Fastnacht   (Ger. "fast night") A name for Shrove Tuesday, the day before Lent begins, in German-speaking places.

fatalism   (From Lat. *fatalis*, "of fate") The philosophical view that events occur as the outworking of an impersonal force and that these events cannot be changed by human decisions or actions. It is sometimes wrongly confused with the Christian doctrine of predestination.

fate   (Lat. *fatum*, "an oracle," "that ordained by the gods") Impersonal power viewed as controlling all destinies so that all ends are predetermined. Ancient philosophies such as Stoicism were marked by a strong sense of fate. Christianity focuses on God's will and not fate.

fates, the   Personified powers or destinies, a view in opposition to Christian theology.

father   (Gr. *patēr*) An image used for God (Matt. 6:9; 2 Cor. 1:2). Also a title for a priest, a monk, or others ordained in the Roman Catholic and High Anglican churches to indicate a spiritual relationship with those to whom ministry is extended.

Father, God the   The first Person of the Trinity. The one whom Jesus addressed as "Abba, Father" (Mark 14:36; cf. Rom. 8:15; Gal. 4:6) and to whom prayer is offered (Matt. 6:9) and who is in a unique relationship with Jesus Christ (Gal. 1:3; Eph. 1:2; Phil. 1:2).

Father, work of the   Actions attributed to the First Person of the Trinity. In the process of salvation this includes sending Jesus Christ (John 3:16) and the Holy Spirit (John 14:16) into the world and choosing a people to carry out divine purposes in the world (Rom. 8:28; 1 Peter 2:9). Ultimately God will draw together all things in heaven and on earth in Jesus Christ (Eph. 1:10).

father of lies   Description of Satan (John 8:44).

Fatherhood of God   The view that God is as a father to all people through the act of creation and also that God relates to Christian believers in a parental relationship.

fathers, church   *See* church fathers, early

fault   (Lat. *culpa*, "guilt," "crime") An action or state in which one has done that which is contrary to an established order of law.

fear of God (the Lord) (Lat. *timor Dei*) "Servile fear" of God is based on the threat of divine punishment. "Filial fear" recognizes God's person as one who is righteous and thus the awe and reverence which evokes the desire not to offend God. Biblically, "fear" (Heb. *yir'ah*) means "awe" (Prov. 9:10).

Feast of Fools A mock religious festival held in the Middle Ages, normally on New Year's Day. It was marked by unchristian behavior and was condemned by the Roman Catholic Church. Sometimes called the Feast of the Ass, since an ass was often brought into a church.

feasts, Christian (ecclesiastical/liturgical) Days of the church calendar commemorating important events in the life of Christ or saints or Christian people. The resurrection of Jesus Christ is celebrated on Sundays. "Movable feasts" have no fixed date (e.g., Easter), while "immovable" feasts have fixed dates (Christmas). Also called "festivals."

feasts, Old Testament Three annual Hebrew feasts (Deut. 16:16) were the feasts of Unleavened Bread (Passover), Weeks (First Fruits), and Booths (Tabernacles).

feasts of obligation In the Roman Catholic tradition, those days in which clergy and laity are obligated to hear Mass and abstain from certain forms of work.

Febronianism An 18th-century German theological movement, associated with Johann Nikolaus von Hontheim (Justinus Febronius, 1701–90), that countered the claims of papal infallibility and claimed that Roman Catholic bishops acting as a whole have more power than the pope.

federal headship The view that Adam acted as a representative of the whole human race and that through the fall into sin (Gen. 3), the whole human race now experiences the consequences of this sinful act (Rom. 5:12, 17–19).

federal theology A form of Calvinism, developed in the 17th century, that stressed the "federal headship" of Adam, who acted as a representative of all humanity in a covenant of works established by God. It is also called "covenant theology."

federated churches A term used in America for two or more churches joining in common ministry while maintaining their own denominational identities in terms of doctrinal beliefs and church governing structures.

feeling, theology of A phrase associated with Friedrich Schleiermacher (1768–1834), who focused on human feelings or experience, rather than beliefs or actions, as the place from which true theology begins.

felix culpa *See* fortunate fall

fellowship (Gr. *koinōnia*) The sense of unity, community, and participation in the lives of others that emerges among Christians and in the church from the common experience of faith in Jesus Christ (1 John 1).

fellowship with God The sense of the love relationship experienced by Christian believers (1 John 1:3).

female consciousness Recognition by women of the ways that specific class, cultural, and historical factors create societal definitions of female.

female ethic The critique of abstraction and the contention that female thinking is more concrete; stress on the values of empathy, nurturing, and caring as women's values; emphasis that "choices" are actually demands of situations.

feminism The movement that advocates for the full equality and participation of women in all aspects of society and culture. Among concerns are violence against women, racism, sexism, environmental destruction, and ways of knowing.

feminist One whose consciousness has been raised about women's oppression and the recognition of women's differences and communalities. A woman-centered perspective that advocates for women's rights and equality with men.

feminist criticism   A critical approach to reading the Bible which focuses on the political, social, and economic rights of women. Diverse goals and methods are employed, with a common recognition that all texts are gendered. This implies not only that they reflect sexual differences between males and females, but also that they involve power. Feminist criticism seeks to make clear culturally based presuppositions found in texts.

feminist theologies   The variety of theological perspectives developed to focus on the experiences, needs, and concerns of women. The differing forms emerge out of the common recognition of women's oppression. They critique patriarchy and emphasize the role of women's experience in the quest for justice and liberation.

feminization of poverty   A term used by feminist theologians and others to describe the increasingly difficult position of women in relation to dependency, limited economic status, access to land and legal autonomy, as well as other elements of poverty.

feria   (Ecclesiastical Lat. "weekday") A weekday, in contrast to a Sunday or festival day. It is a day on which there is neither an ecclesiastical feast nor a fast prescribed.

festivals, biblical   See feasts, Old Testament

festivals, ecclesiastical   See feasts, Christian

fiat creationism   The view that God brought into being all things that exist by a direct act. All things were created virtually instantaneously by God's direct working. It opposes evolutionary views or the concept of God using existing materials out of which to produce new species or organisms. Humans were thus created by a direct action of God.

Fidei Defensor   See Defender of the Faith

fideism   (From Lat. *fides*, "faith") The view that faith rather than reason (Lat. *ratio*) is the means by which Christian truth is known.

fides ex auditu   (Lat. "faith from hearing") A phrase, emphasized especially by Protestants, that stresses the primacy of Christian preaching as a means by which the Christian faith is conveyed (Rom. 10:17).

fides historica   (Lat. "historical faith") Faith that one inherits on the basis of one's tradition or through one's family. It refers to that which one may accept but which has no spiritual effects on the person.

fides qua creditur   (Lat. "faith by which [it] is believed") The actual act of faith or believing what one holds to be revealed by God.

fides quae creditur   (Lat. "faith that is believed") The content that one believes as being revealed by God.

fides quaerens intellectum   (Lat. "faith seeking understanding" or "faith preceding the intellect") The theological method stressed by Augustine (354–430) and Anselm (c. 1033–1109) in which one begins belief in faith and on the basis of that faith moves on to further understanding of Christian truth.

fiducia   (Lat. "trust") Along with assent and understanding, one of the components of faith, indicating the sense of personal trust in God (Pss. 25:2; 31:4; 2 Tim. 1:12; 1 Peter 1:21).

fiduciary   (Lat. *fiducia*, "trust") Term describing a relationship of trust with an object of faith.

Fifth Monarchy Men   Seventeenth-century English Puritan extremists who believed that the "fifth monarchy," predicted by the prophet Daniel to succeed the monarchies of Assyria, Persia, Greece, and Rome, was the kingdom of Christ, which would soon come to England.

They sought to establish it by force in 1657 and 1661.

filial   (From Lat. *filius*, "son") Term used classically to describe the relationship of Jesus Christ the Son to God the Father.

filiation   (From Lat. *filius*, "son") In the doctrine of the Trinity, the eternal relationship of God the Father to God the Son.

filioque   (Lat. "and the Son") Phrase inserted into the Niceno-Constantinopolitan Creed (381) at the Council of Toledo (589) to say that the Holy Spirit proceeds from both Father and Son ("double procession") in the Trinity. It was rejected by the Eastern church (1054) and was part of the reason for the East-West church schism.

filled with the Holy Spirit   Description of a Christian believer's life as under the direction and control of the Holy Spirit (Acts 11:24; 13:9, 52).

final body   The ultimate, resurrection body (1 Cor. 15:53–54).

final state   The ultimate state of an individual in either heaven or hell.

finalism   The philosophical view that there is purpose in the universe and that all events move toward a final end.

finite   (From Lat. *finitus*, "limited") Refers to the limitation of objects or persons, their inability to transcend the boundaries of existence.

finite God   The view of some that God's power is limited. Thus evil exists because God is not able to keep it from occurring.

finiteness, anxiety of   The view of Reinhold Niebuhr (1892–1971) that sin occurs because of the human sense of finiteness and the anxiety it engenders. Thus humans seek to find their own security in a source other than God.

finitism   (From Lat. *finitus*, "limited") Belief in a God who is limited or finite.

finitude   (From Lat. *finitus*, "limited") Condition of being finite or limited in time and space.

Finitum capax infiniti   (Lat. "The finite can contain the infinite") A phrase used by Lutheran theologians, in controversy with the Reformed, to express the view that Jesus as a finite human could express the full dimensions of God's attributes such as omnipotence and omniscience.

Finitum non capax infiniti   (Lat. "The finite cannot contain [is incapable of] the infinite") The view of Reformed theologians, maintained in controversy with Lutherans, that Jesus as a finite human did not express the full dimensions of God's attributes such as omnipotence and omniscience.

First and Last   *See* Alpha and Omega

first cause   Philosophical description of God as the uncaused being who causes all else in the universe to come into existence.

first day of the week   The Lord's Day (Sunday), on which Christians worship in celebration of the resurrection of Jesus Christ (Luke 24:1).

first death   *See* death, first

first fruits   An image drawn from harvesting and applied to Jesus Christ, who, raised from the dead by the power of God, is the one who conveys the sure promise that believers who now die will also be raised in the resurrection of the dead (1 Cor. 15:20, 23).

first mover   *See* prime mover

First Person of the Trinity   A term referring to God the Father.

first resurrection   *See* resurrection, first

firstborn of all creation   Reference to Jesus Christ (Col. 1:18; Heb. 1:6) stressing his primacy over all creation.

firstborn of (from) the dead   A description of Jesus Christ (Col. 1:18; Rev. 1:5) indicating that he is the first to be raised from the dead. The promise is that others will follow.

fish   (Gr. *ichthys*) Early symbol of Jesus Christ. The letters of this word were taken to stand for the first letters of five words describing Christ: *Iēsous* (Jesus),

Christos (Christ), *Theou* (of God), *Huios* (Son), *Sōtēr* (Savior). Thus: "Jesus Christ, Son of God, Savior."

five articles of Arminianism   Classic distinctive views of Arminianism in relation to Calvinism. They are: election based on divine foreknowledge of faith, universal atonement, salvation only by grace, grace as necessary but not irresistible, the possibility of falling from grace.

Five Mile Act (1665)   An act of English law that prohibited any Nonconformist member of the clergy from coming within five miles of his former parish or of any city or corporate town. Teaching was prohibited unless the Nonconformist promised loyalty to the established order and nonresistance.

five points of Calvinism   *See* TULIP

Five Ways, the   Five philosophical arguments propounded by Thomas Aquinas (1225–74) as logical proofs of God's existence: ontological, teleological, causal, moral, and cosmological. They are also called "theistic proofs." They have been variously assessed as being logically valid or invalid.

five wounds of Christ   The five wounds experienced by Christ during his crucifixion, on his two hands, two feet, and side.

fixed feast   A Christian holiday that is celebrated yearly on the same date (e.g., Christmas on Dec. 25).

flagellants   (Lat. *flagellare,* "to whip") Those who flagellate or harm themselves to imitate the wounds suffered by Jesus prior to his crucifixion (Matt. 26:67). In the Middle Ages they were groups who scourged themselves in a public procession in penance for their own and the world's sins.

flagellation   (Lat. *flagellum,* "whip" or "scourge") The punishment of one's body by whipping or scourging, understood by some as a form of penance and as a participation in the passion of Jesus Christ (John 19:1). Voluntary flagellation was common in the Middle Ages as penance for personal sins.

flesh   A biblical expression for human nature, used not only literally to denote the human (corporeal) body as distinct from "soul" or "spirit" but also figuratively to indicate the sinful condition of humanity apart from Jesus Christ and the Holy Spirit (Rom. 8:4–8; Gal. 5:16ff.).

flight from the world   (Lat. *fuga mundi*) An expression of a Christian attitude of rejection toward the world and toward earthly things. Desert saints adopted this stance in early times. Today it can be considered in a spiritual sense to be the rejection of common attitudes such as greed or consumerism.

flight into Egypt   A reference to the journey of Joseph, Mary, and the infant Jesus to Egypt when King Herod ordered babies to be slaughtered in searching for the child about whom the Magi told him (Matt. 2:13–23).

Flood, the   The catastrophic deluge of water that covered the earth and from which only Noah and his family and the animals were saved in the ark (Gen. 6—8). The story shows an undoing of creation and a return to primeval watery conditions (Gen. 1:2, 9) from which a new world could begin.

Florence, Council of (1438–45)   An ecumenical council of the Roman Catholic Church, held in three Italian cities, that discussed various doctrines as well as seeking reunion between Greek and Latin churches, a union quickly rejected by Greek churches. The *filioque* clause was the chief obstacle to union.

folk church   (Ger. *Volkskirche,* "people's church") A church that is coterminous with a nation. To be born in a particular country is to be a member of the particular church of that country. The concept was developed in Lutheranism, where princes decided the religious faith of their people.

folk religion   Those popular religious beliefs and practices that exist alongside or in opposition to dominant religious traditions in a society. They have often involved magic, healing, prophecy, and charismatic leaders.

folklore Term coined by William Toms (1846) as the study of customs and manners of "olden times." In general, popular learning. It is often oral, rather than written, and closely related to labor, trades, and crafts. In some societies, religious life is so inseparable from cultural existence that this popular learning is key to understanding religious faiths.

followers of the Way A designation used by Christians for themselves in the early church period when the Christian faith was referred to as "the Way" (Acts 9:2; 19:9, 23; 22:4; 24:14, 22).

font, baptismal (Lat. *fons,* "spring of water") A type of large bowl used for holding water used in baptisms. Baptismal fonts are found in churches near the door, in a baptistery, or in the sanctuary near the pulpit. They may be constructed in shapes symbolic of the sacrament of baptism.

foot washing (pedilavium) The practice of some Christians in fulfillment of Jesus' command to follow his example by washing the feet of others (John 13:14). On Maundy Thursday in the Roman Catholic tradition, the pope washes the feet of thirteen priests (or poor persons).

forbearance (Gr. *anochē,* "a holding back") Patience and self-restraint as a quality of God (Rom. 2:4; 3:25) that should mark the lives of Christians as well (Eph. 4:2; Col. 3:13).

forbidden tree In the story of the Garden of Eden, the tree of the knowledge of good and evil was a tree from which Adam and Eve were forbidden to eat (Gen. 2).

foreknowledge (Lat. *praescientia*) Knowing a thing or event before it has happened. It is applied to the God who knows all things—including their causes—prior to their occurrence in time (Ps. 139:4). As a dimension of God's omniscience, God eternally knows all things

that to humans appear to be "in the future."

foreknowledge of faith (Lat. *praevisa fidei*) The view that God knows those who will have faith, which becomes the ground or cause of their election to salvation. It is characteristic of Arminian theology.

forensic act (Lat. *forensis,* "belonging to the forum") A legal act or declaration, used in relation to "righteousness" and "justification" in Protestant theology. It indicates that God "declares" a sinner righteous or justified (not "makes" one righteous) through Jesus Christ.

foreordination (From Gr. *proorizein,* Lat. *praedestinare,* "to predestine," "to foreordain") God's ordaining or predestining what will happen in history and in relation to human salvation (Acts 4:28; Rom. 8:29–30; Eph. 1:5, 11).

forerunner One who goes before and prepares the way. The term applies particularly to the work of John the Baptist, whose ministry prepared the way for Jesus (Mark 1:3–9).

forgiveness (Gr. *aphesis,* "letting go") Pardoning or remitting an offense. It restores a good relationship with God, others, or the self after sin or alienation.

forgiveness of sins God's action in pardoning or remitting sinful offenses, which includes canceling the penalties that such acts would have merited. Forgiveness of sins comes through Jesus Christ (Col. 1:14) and is to be a mark of the Christian's life as well (Matt. 6:12–15; 18:21–35).

form (Gr. *eidos,* Lat. *forma*) Philosophical term for the visible pattern or arrangement of matter, which is distinguishable from but not separable from matter. Together, matter and form constitute "substance" (Aristotle). In Plato's thought, forms are assumed to have an independent existence from matter.

form criticism *See* criticism, form

formal cause Derived from the four causes of Aristotle (384–322 B.C., and used to account for anything that is. In the Christian doctrine of the justification of sinners, the righteousness of Jesus Christ is the formal cause, since it is that which enables justification to take place.

formal norms In ethics, the standards, rules, or laws that are to be obeyed as standards for decisions or conduct.

formal principle The source of authority or criteria to which a church appeals as the basis for its beliefs and teachings. The 16th-century Protestant Reformers considered the Bible the formal principle for Christian beliefs.

formalism A heightened concern for outward religious observances and a corresponding lack of concern for the inner or spiritual significance of the "forms." In ethics, a theory that seeks the grounds for moral action solely in the form of the moral law.

Formgeschichte *See* criticism, form

forms, Platonic In Plato's philosophy, the unchanging essence of things that exist independently of any specific instances, such as "humanness," "love," "justice."

fornication (Gr. *porneia,* Lat. *fornicatio*) Heterosexual intercourse between two unmarried persons. It has been regarded as sinful in the Scriptures and the Christian church (1 Cor. 6:13, 18; Gal. 5:19; Eph. 5:3; 1 Thess. 4:3).

fortitude (Lat. *fortitudo,* "strength") A firmness and perseverance toward righteousness associated with the fourth Beatitude (Matt. 5:6). It has been regarded as a cardinal virtue equivalent to courage. Some have seen its ultimate expression in martyrdom.

fortunate fall (Lat. *felix culpa,* "happy crime") An expression of faith in God's ultimate power to bring good out of evil. Used in ancient liturgies to celebrate God's redemption from sin through Jesus Christ.

Forty-two Articles (1553) Anglican doctrinal articles, drafted mainly by Thomas Cranmer (1489–1556), that were never enforced but became the basis for the Thirty-nine Articles (1563).

forum (Lat. "place of public assembly") A judicial tribunal in which the church exercises judicial power and may hold an ecclesiastical trial.

forum, external The church's use of ecclesiastical courts for exercising judicial power on issues affecting the church's public good.

forum, internal The Roman Catholic practice of relying on personal conscience and an individual's personal communion with God rather than on formal church law.

forum of conscience (Lat. *forum conscientiae*) Recognition of the authority of the individual conscience in making decisions.

foundation of election (Lat. *fundamentum electionis*) A term used by Reformed theologians to refer to Jesus Christ, in whom the elect are chosen by God. Arminian theologians refer to the human decision to believe in Christ as the basis of election to salvation.

foundation of faith (Lat. *fundamentum fidei*) Description of Jesus Christ, on whom faith and human salvation are based.

foundational theology In Roman Catholic theology, the synthesis of biblical, historical, dogmatic, and systematic theology that forms and is formed by spiritual theology.

foundationalism (From *fundamentum,* "groundwork") Philosophical or theological approaches affirming specific truths as bases and criteria for all other truths.

Four Causes The types of causes according to Aristotle (384–322 B.C.): material, formal, efficient, and final. These were used by Christian theologians such as Thomas Aquinas (1225–74) to attribute all things to God's ultimate causation.

Four Horsemen of the Apocalypse The images of destruction found in the book of Revelation. The four riders are Conquest, Violence, Famine, and Death, who ride upon white, red, black, and pale horses (Rev. 6:1–8).

Four Spiritual Laws   Formulation of the gospel associated with evangelical groups which teach that: (1) God loves all and has a plan for all persons; (2) all are sinful and separated from God; (3) Jesus Christ is the only one through whom sin can be forgiven; (4) each person must receive Christ as Lord and Savior by faith.

fourfold sense of Scripture   The medieval view that the Bible can be interpreted literally, morally, allegorically, and anagogically and that Scripture passages and verses may carry more than one of these senses.

fraction   (Lat. *fractio,* "a breaking") The breaking of the bread during the Eucharist as Jesus broke bread at the Last Supper (Mark 14:22; cf. Luke 22:19).

Francis, Rule of St.   A rule for the religious life composed by Francis of Assisi (1181/82–1226). It was rooted in a life of poverty, peacefulness, and gentle care for all God's creation and all people, particularly the poor.

Franciscan order   The Order of Friars Minor ("Lesser Brothers"). The order follows the rule of life from Francis of Assisi (1181/82–1226) and was approved by Pope Honorius III (1223). It sought a return to primitive Christianity, following the example of Jesus. It has emphasized ministry to the poor.

free choice   (Lat. *liberum arbitrium*) The capacity of the human will to be free from any external constraint or imposed necessity.

free churches   Churches not established by any government or supported by a government. In 17th-century England, those churches which would not adhere to the discipline and liturgical practices of the Church of England were called Nonconformist or Independent.

free will   A loose rendering of (Lat.) *liberum arbitrium.* The term seeks to de-

scribe the free choice of the will which all persons possess. Theological debates have arisen over the ways by which and the extent to which sin has affected the power to choose good over evil, and hence one's "free will."

freedom, Christian   The freedom of the Christian, on the basis of the work of Jesus Christ by the Holy Spirit, to be free from the power of sin in all its forms (John 8:36; Rom. 6:18, 22; Gal. 5:1).

freedom, human   Condition in which humans may freely choose their own behavior and situations without external coercions or oppression. Societal freedom enables human freedom to operate.

freedom of the will   *See* free choice

Freer Logion   The term for an addition to the words of Jesus in Mark 16:14. It is found in a Greek codex from the 5th century.

freethinker   One who comes to an ultimate conviction on the basis of human reason alone without regard for church tradition or biblical revelation. The term often has a distinctly anti-Christian connotation.

freewill offering   An Old Testament offering made as part of a request to God or in gratitude for God's actions (Lev. 22). The term is now used to describe a charitable donation or offerings received at regular or special worship services for particular purposes.

fresco   (Ital. "fresh") An artistic technique of painting on wet plaster, usually on a wall or ceiling. Many historic churches are so decorated.

Freudian   Concepts deriving from Sigmund Freud (1856–1939). They have been criticized, rejected, modified, and developed by feminist writers among others.

friar   (From Lat. *frater,* and Middle English *frere,* "brother") A member of a Roman Catholic order in which a vow of poverty is taken and a rule of life combining contemplation with action is adopted.

Friends, Society of   *See* Quakers

Friends of God A 14th-century group of mystics that included Johann Tauler (c. 1300–1361) and Henry Suso (1295–1366). They emphasized the transforming power of union with God.

friendship (From Middle English *frendship*) In the spiritual tradition, the relationship among Christians that enhances love of God and others. The term is used by feminist theological writers to describe a form of women's emotional bonding which is self-affirming.

frontal (Lat. *frons,* "the front," "forehead") A parament in the appropriate liturgical color covering the full front of an altar in a church.

frontier religion The religious ethos associated with the expansion into the western United States (1790–1890). It featured camp meetings, circuit-riding preachers, an emphasis on personal faith, and a sense of fellowship among isolated peoples. Methodist and Baptist groups predominated.

fruit of the Spirit A description of the ways by which the Holy Spirit works within the Christian life (Rom. 8:23; Gal. 5:22–23).

fuga mundi (Lat. "flight from the world") A type of spirituality claiming the need for one to flee from the world. It may refer to one's affections and/or literally to one's movement into the desert to be a hermit and live a solitary life, as was done by persons in the 3rd and 4th centuries.

fullness of time (Gr. *plērōma tou chronou*) Phrase from Gal. 4:4 describing the time of Jesus Christ's first coming. It is often seen as indicating God's intended time as well as the readiness of world conditions for Christ's advent.

functional analysis *See* philosophy, analytical

functional subordination The view that within the Trinity, Jesus Christ the Son voluntarily submitted himself to the will of God the Father and carried out this will in being subordinate to the Fa-

ther but without ceasing to be coequal with the Father.

functionalism The theory that all social institutions and practices have functions in maintaining the social process, so that social activities are seen as fulfilling social needs or functions. Also, the understanding of an object in terms of its purpose or function.

fundamental articles (*articuli fundamentales*) In Protestant theology, those basic doctrines which are necessary to the Christian faith, as distinguished from doctrines which are secondary or are derived from other doctrines. The fundamental articles are those without which Christianity could not exist. They are known only by God's revelation.

fundamental option A technical term in Roman Catholic theology for one's own free determination in relation to the totality of existence. One must make fundamental choices between such elements as self and God, sin and faith, or selfishness and love.

fundamental theology The study of that which is most basic to theology. Used most often in Roman Catholic theology to establish theology's basic intelligibility, using methods of philosophy, linguistics, and historical-critical studies.

fundamentalism/fundamentalist Term for an evangelicalism in 20th-century America that sought to preserve conservative Protestant views and values against liberal theology and the higher criticism of Scripture. A strong focus was on the inerrancy and literal interpretation of Scripture.

fundamentalist-modernist controversy The ideological conflict in America during the 1920s between those who wished to preserve Christianity by accommodating it to modern culture ("modernists") and those who zealously sought to preserve the faith by resisting Darwinism and emergent modern trends ("fundamentalists").

funeral/funeral service (Lat. *funeralis*) A worship service at the time of a person's death that usually commemorates the life of the deceased and proclaims the Christian hope of resurrection and eternal life.

future (Lat. *futurus,* "about to be") The history that is still to come. In Christian theology, history is understood to move toward climactic events that mark the fulfillment of God's ultimate purposes.

future body *See* final body

future kingdom The ultimate, eternal reign of God in the "kingdom" which is established by the return ("parousia") of Jesus Christ to earth.

future life The belief that some form of existence is found beyond physical life on earth. In the Christian view, the resurrection of Jesus Christ assures an eternal existence after death (1 Cor. 15:24).

future punishment The punishment administered as a result of God's future judgment.

future state *See* final state

futurism (Ital. *futurismo*) The study of the future. Also the view that biblical prophecies, and particularly those in the book of Revelation, will be fulfilled in the future.

Gallican Articles, the Four (1682) Statement by French clergy declaring the pope supreme in spiritual but not secular areas, subordinate to ecumenical councils, bound to accept certain traditional French customs, and that his judgments may be questioned. The articles were revoked by King Louis XIV (1693).

Gallican Confession (1559) French Reformed confession of faith, ratified by the La Rochelle Synod (1571), that set forth basic Protestant doctrine including a moderate form of predestination.

Gallicanism French movement begun in the 14th century that sought to diminish papal authority and increase state power over the church.

Gangra, Council of (345) A church council held at Gangra near the Black Sea. It condemned Eustathius and his false asceticism through his attacks on marriage and church attendance. The council defined true asceticism.

gap theory The belief that there is a gap of time between Gen. 1:2 and 1:3 that accounts for the geological time be-

tween God's original creative act and the subsequent re-forming of the world.

gaps, God of the Popular term to describe an appeal to God as the answer to all the mysteries in nature and the gaps in human knowledge.

Garden of Eden Scene of the creation and the environment of Adam and Eve, portrayed as the first humans (Gen. 1).

gathered church Those who meet together as an independent body of Christians seeing themselves as visible saints. This view assumes that, ecclesiologically, the church is a local congregation of believers. It is directly opposite to a hierarchical view of the church as unified under a hierarchy.

Gaudete Sunday (From Lat. "rejoice") The third Sunday of Advent. Its name is from the first word of the medieval Latin introit ("Rejoice," Phil. 4:4). It is parallel to the fourth Sunday in Lent ("Laetare") and marks a temporary break in the solemnity of the season.

Gehenna (Gr. *Geenna* from Heb. *ge' hinnom*) Reference to the valley of Hinnom outside Jerusalem, which was used as the city's garbage dump and was kept continually burning. Image used in the New Testament for hell as the place of judgment and eternal punishment after death for sinners.

Gelassenheit (Ger. "calmness," "tranquillity") A term used in German mystical theology for a letting loose of one's self. It indicates an attitude of total dependence, humility, and trust before God (Eccl. 10:4). The concept is also found in Martin Luther (1483–1546) and the Anabaptists.

Gemara (Heb. "learning") The second part of the Talmud of the Land of Israel and of the Babylonian Talmud, containing a commentary on the Mishnah (the first part of the Talmud). It was composed during the 3d to 6th centuries A.D. and provides information on Jewish history and customs of that time.

Gemeinde (Ger. "community," "corporate body," "congregation") The term most often used by Martin Luther (1483–1546) for the church (Matt. 16:18). It denotes fellowship (Gr. *koinōnia*).

Gemeinschaft German term for "community," often translated in English as "church," denoting a sense of intimacy and loyalty within the group (Acts 2:42).

gender (From Lat. *genus*, "kind," "sort") Attributes and behaviors shaped by culture to describe either males or females. Feminist writers often distinguish sex as biological and gender as behavioral.

general Term for the head of a religious order or congregation. In the Roman Catholic tradition, canon law refers to the person as the supreme moderator.

General Assembly In Presbyterian churches, the annual meeting of elected pastors and elders from each presbytery that forms the church's highest governing body.

general calling *See* call, general

general chapter A meeting of representatives of religious orders to choose new superiors and conduct business.

General Conference The highest governing body of the United Methodist Church. It meets every four years (quadrennium) to enact legislative changes in the church's governing standards, establish policies, and modify practices.

general confession A collective confession of sin prayed by a congregation in corporate worship. Also, a comprehensive confession of all sins committed.

general faith A belief in statements or propositions, as opposed to a vital Christian faith that includes trust in God as a person.

general judgment *See* last judgment

general redemption (unlimited atonement) The belief that the death of Jesus Christ on the cross was intended to provide salvation for the whole world whether or not all persons have faith in Christ. Also called unlimited atonement.

general resurrection The future resurrection of all persons.

general revelation *See* revelation, general

general superintendent A term formally used for the highest ecclesiastical office in a number of German Protestant churches.

General Synod In Lutheran churches, the highest governing body, which exercises final ecclesiastical authority.

generation of the Word/Son (From Lat. *generare*, "to generate," from *genus*, "birth") In the doctrine of the Trinity, the procession of the eternal Son from the eternal Father (John 1:14, 18; 3:16, 18).

generationism A variation of traducianism which teaches that both the soul and the body of a child are propagated by parents.

Geneva bands Two white strips that hang from the neck opening of a clerical gown. They are sometimes said to represent the law and the gospel.

Geneva Bible (1560) English translation of the Bible by English Puritans and Scots in Geneva during the Marian exile. It was the first English Bible to use verse numbers. Marginal notes that gave Reformed theological interpretations were featured. It became the most widely read English Bible. It is also called the Breeches Bible.

Geneva Catechism (1538)   Catechism for the city of Geneva written by John Calvin (1509–64) and published in French (1537) and Latin (1538) as an early expression of the Reformed faith.

Geneva gown   A black gown worn for preaching by early Reformed ministers in Geneva. It was worn to emphasize the ministry of the Word of God as opposed to ministries emphasizing the sacrificial priesthood.

genocide   (From Gr. *genos*, "race") The deliberate and systematic extermination of a race, nation, or ethnic minority. The violation of a group's basic human rights is also a form of genocide.

genre   (Fr. "kind," "sort") A genre is a particular type of literary writing. More fully, genres refer to conventional and repeatable patterns in oral and written speech. They function to faciliate interaction among persons in particular social situations. Recognition of genres is an important step in biblical interpretation.

Gentile   (From Lat. *gentilis*, "member of a people") Term used by Jews for one who is not Jewish by racial origin. In the Old Testament, "the nations" (Heb. *goyim*) is used.

genuflect/genuflection   (From Lat. *genu*, "knee," and *flectere*, "to bend") Briefly kneeling on the right knee as an act of devotion in acknowledging God's presence. It is practiced particularly in the Roman Catholic tradition upon entering or leaving a church and when passing in front of the Blessed Sacrament.

German Christians   Twentieth-century German Protestants who conformed to Nazi ideology and espoused nationalist and racist tenets. They were opposed by the Confessing Church.

Geschichte   (Ger. "history") A term used by some 20th-century German the-

ologians to denote the special actions of God in history in contrast to *Historie* as the objective facts of history.

gestures   (Lat. *gestura,* "mode of action") In worship, liturgical gestures are stylized movements by those who lead, particularly relating to the use of the hands. They are used to lead the congregation in actions (such as rising or being seated), as well as for other purposes.

Gethsemane, agony in   Jesus' suffering on the eve of his crucifixion, in the Garden where he prayed and was arrested (Matt. 26:36ff.; Mark 14:32; Luke 22:43, 44).

Ghost, Holy   In the King James Version of the Bible, the term for the Holy Spirit.

gifts, spiritual   Those abilities given by the Holy Spirit to persons in the church for the upbuilding of the church. Examples are listed in Rom. 12:6–8; 1 Cor. 12:4–11; Eph. 4:11; and 1 Peter 4:11.

gifts of the Magi   The gifts of gold, frankincense, and myrrh brought by the Magi to the infant Jesus (Matt. 2:11).

gifts of the Spirit   *See* gifts, spiritual

giving   A response of devotion to God and God's blessings. It consists of the use of one's resources for support of God's work in the world. Typically, Christian churches speak of giving one's time, talents, and "treasure" (financial resources) out of gratitude to God.

Glasites   *See* Sandemanians

Gloria   *See* doxology

Gloria in Excelsis   (Lat. "Glory in the highest") The song sung by the angels on the night of Jesus' birth (Luke 2:14). In the Roman Catholic Mass the angels' words are the opening verse of the Gloria in Excelsis.

Gloria Patri   (Lat. "Glory to the Father") An ascription of praise to the Holy Trinity: "Glory be to the Father, and to the Son, and to the Holy Spirit." Later was added: "as it was in the beginning, is now, and ever shall be, world without end. Amen." It is sung or spoken in worship services.

glorification (From Lat. *glorificare*, "to glorify") The final dimension of Christian salvation, which includes eternal life in heaven and the eternal glorifying of God.

glorification of God The praise and worship of God.

glorified body The resurrection body that will belong to those who share eternal life in heaven.

glorified with Christ The promise of sharing in Christ's heavenly glory given to those who share his sufferings on earth (Rom. 8:17).

glorious mysteries, the five In Roman Catholic theology, the third part of the Rosary commemorating the resurrection, the ascension, the descent of the Holy Spirit at Pentecost, the assumption of the Virgin Mary, and the coronation of the Virgin Mary.

glory (Lat. *gloria*) Exalted praise and honor. Glory is an attribute of God.

glory, theology of *See* theology of glory

glory of God (Lat. *gloria Dei*) The divine essence of God as absolutely resplendent and ultimately great (Rev. 21:23). The praise and honoring of God as the supreme Lord of all (1 Cor. 10:31; Phil. 2:11).

gloss (Gr. *glōssa*, "tongue," "language") A word or words added in the margins or between lines in a text to explain foreign or difficult words. More generally, a commentary on Scripture, particularly the medieval (Lat.) *glossa ordinaria*, which consisted of citations from patristic writers.

glossa ordinaria (Lat. "ordinary interpretation") The "gloss" or commentary on the Latin Vulgate, which became a significant medieval resource for interpreting Scripture. The glosses added to biblical texts were drawn from patristic writers. More than 3,000 manuscripts with such glosses exist.

glossolalia (Gr. *glōssa*, "tongue," and *lalia*, "chatter") Also known as "speaking in tongues," glossolalia denotes the utter-ing of a language unknown to the speaker that is seen as a gift from the Holy Spirit enabling one to praise and worship God (1 Cor. 14:2; cf. Acts 2:4–13).

gluttony (Lat. *gula*) One of the "seven deadly sins" as understood by medieval theologians and characterized by an inordinate indulgence in food and drink (in contrast to abstinence).

GNB *See* Good News Bible

Gnesio-Lutheranism (Gr. *gnēsios*, "true," "genuine") Those in the 16th century led by Flacius Illyricus (1520–75) who saw themselves as true followers of Martin Luther rather than of Luther's associate Philip Melanchthon (whose followers were called "Philippists").

Gnosis (Gr. *gnōsis*, "knowledge") A Greek term that gave rise to "Gnosticism" in its various forms (1 Tim. 6:20). "Secret knowledge" could free the "elect" from the limits of the world (spirit from matter, light from darkness) and enable them to return home to the kingdom of light (salvation).

Gnosticism (From Gr. *gnōsis*, "knowledge") An amorphous movement during the early church period which featured complex views that focused on the quest for secret knowledge transmitted only to the "enlightened" and marked by the view that matter is evil. Gnostics denied the humanity of Jesus.

God (Gr. *theos*, Lat. *Deus*) The supreme being who is creator and ruler of the universe (Gen. 1:1). Christians believe God is Trinity: Father, Son, and Holy Spirit, three Persons and one God. God created humans in the divine image (Gen. 1:26) and loves them in Christ (John 3:16).

God, absoluteness of The view that God alone is perfect and therefore unchanging or absolute.

God, acts of The workings of God within human history as revealed and known through the biblical accounts.

God, aseity of (Lat. *aseitas*, "self-existence") The view that God is entirely self-sufficient and not dependent upon anything else.

God, attributes of   *See* attributes of God

God, awareness of   The sense of God's reality. Theologians have variously expressed how this awareness is attained. Some have spoken of an innate knowledge of God (Calvin), a sense of "absolute dependence" (Schleiermacher), or an awareness of God's existence gained through theistic proofs (Aquinas).

God, being of   God's essence. A philosophical description of the reality of God apart from any "acts" of God. God in God's pure essential nature.

God, benevolence of   (Lat. *benevolentia Dei*, "goodwill of God") God's willing of the good as an expression of God's love (Lat. *amor Dei*).

God, breath of   God's life-giving power or spirit (Gen. 2:7). The Hebrew *ruaḥ* means both "breath" and "spirit" (Job 27:3).

God, changelessness of   The view that God's essence does not vary, and thus that God eternally exists without development.

God, children of   A biblical term that designates the theological reality of believers with God through Jesus Christ (John 1:12; Rom. 8:14–21; Gal. 3:26; 1 John 5:2).

God, consequent nature of   In the process philosophy thought of Alfred North Whitehead (1861–1947), God's activity in relation to the world and its evolutionary processes.

God, decretive will of   God's decrees or decisions which bring to pass all events.

God, dependability of   God's constant nature which enables people to believe the divine promises as trustworthy. It is expressed biblically as faithfulness (Pss. 71:22; 86:15; Lam. 3:23).

God, doctrine of   Christian beliefs and teachings about who God is and what God does. It includes God's triune nature and God's activities in creation,

redemption, and providence within the universe.

God, essence of   *See* God, being of

God, eternity of   (Lat. *aeternitas Dei*) The ongoing existence and continuance of God without beginning or ending and distinct from all change.

God, faithfulness of   (Lat. *fidelitas Dei*) God's consistency and constancy in relation to the divine promises and grace, providing a source of trusting consolation for believers (1 Cor. 1:9; 2 Cor. 1:18; 2 Thess. 3:3; Heb. 10:23; 1 John 1:9).

God, Fatherhood of   *See* Fatherhood of God

God, foreknowledge of   (From Gr. *prognōsis theou*; Lat. *praescientia Dei*) God's knowing things and events before they happen in history. An aspect of divine omniscience, it relates to human perceptions of time, since all things are known by God eternally and simultaneously, even salvation (Rom. 8:29).

God, general will of   A description of God's overall will and those things which God values as being good.

God, genuineness of   God as a living being in contrast to all idols or other objects of worship.

God, glory of   *See* glory of God

God, good pleasure of   (Lat. *beneplacitum Dei*) God's will to act freely and bring about what is good and desired by God without any influence from other sources (Eph. 1:5; Phil. 2:13).

God, goodness of   (Lat. *bonitas Dei*) The divine character which is morally good in an absolute sense and constitutes along with all the other divine attributes God's divinely perfect essence.

God, government of   (Lat. *gubernatio Dei*) An aspect of God's providence in which God governs and directs all things in the universe according to the divine will and in accord with divine purposes.

God, grace of   (From Gr. *charis,* Lat. *gratia Dei*) God's goodness toward humanity as expressed in the unmerited, undeserved favor given supremely in

Jesus Christ to bring salvation, forgiveness, and new life (Rom. 3:24; Eph. 2:5–9; 2 Thess. 2:16).

God, greatness of   God's attributes of power, knowledge, and eternity. Praise for the greatness of God is often found in Scripture (1 Chron. 16:25; Pss. 48:1; 96:4; 145:3).

God, holiness of   (Lat. *sanctitas Dei*) God's separateness from all creation as well as the divine purity and goodness in God's being and willing (Isa. 6:3; Rev. 4:8).

God, image of/divine image   (Lat. *imago Dei*) The created state of humans (Gen. 1:26–27), who were made in God's likeness and intended to enjoy the divine-human relationship. The divine image is fully seen in Jesus Christ, who is the "image of the invisible God" (Col. 1:15).

God, immanence of   God's presence and ongoing actions within the created order.

God, immateriality of   God's being as a spirit without a physical or material nature.

God, immensity of   (Lat. *immensitas Dei*, "immeasurability of God") God's freedom from all limitations of place, space, or measure.

God, immutability of   (Lat. *immutabilitas Dei*) God's freedom from all change, understood to emphasize God's changeless perfection and divine constancy.

God, impassibility of   The traditional theological view that God does not change and thus is not affected by actions that take place in the world, particularly in terms of experiencing suffering or pain. It emphasizes that God is active, rather than passive or acted upon by other agents.

God, inclusive language about   The use of both male and female images as language about God. Both types of images are found in Scripture (Luke 15:20; Isa. 49:15).

God, incomprehensibility of   God's greatness as exceeding all human capabilities ever to understand God fully.

God, independence of   God's self-sufficiency and freedom from any form of dependence on another in order to exist.

God, infinity of   (Lat. *infinitas Dei*) The limitlessness of the divine essence so that God is superior in all ways to all things (Job 11:7–10).

God, integrity of   The aspects of God's truthfulness that include God's being true (genuineness), telling the truth (veracity), and proving to be true (faithfulness).

God, interdependence of   See interdependence of God

God, invisibility of   (Lat. *invisibilitas Dei*) God as spirit (John 4:24) is thus not able to be seen unless God desires to be seen.

God, justice of   (Gr. *dikaiosynē theou*, Lat. *iustitia Dei*) God's righteousness and uprightness whereby God governs the universe in accord with God's law as an expression of God's character. Biblically, God's justice relates to God's concern for the poor and for human obedience to God's will.

God, kingdom of   See kingdom of God

God, knowledge (as an attribute) of   (Lat. *scientia Dei*) The knowledge by which God knows the divine self and all the divine works perfectly.

God, law of   See law of God

God, life of   (Lat. *vita Dei*) God as a living being in distinction from all idols or objects of worship.

God, love of   (Lat. *amor Dei*) The love created beings have for God as their Creator. Also, God's own doing of the good in grace, kindness, and care for the creation.

God, majesty of   (Lat. *maiestas Dei*) The supreme greatness and glory of God (1 Chron. 29:11; Pss. 29:4; 104:1; Isa. 33:3).

God, mercy of   (Lat. *misericordia Dei*) God's grace and compassion toward sinful creatures and special care for those in need (Ps. 119:156; Jer. 31:20; Dan. 9:9).

God, moral purity of   God's holiness and righteousness by which God is separate from all sin and evil in the created order.

God, names of   (Lat. *nomina Dei*) The biblical designations and identifications of the divine. In the Old Testament, the variety includes: Yahweh, God Most High, Everlasting God, Almighty, Mighty One, God, Lord, Lord of hosts. In the New Testament, God is also related to Jesus Christ (Rom. 15:6; Eph. 1:3; Col.1:3).

God, nature of   God's being or who God is in contrast with God's actions or what God does. Biblically, God's nature includes God as one, creator, redeemer, the source of law, just, loving, gracious, faithful, patient, merciful, giver of life and peace, sovereign, judge, righteous, truth.

God, omnipotence of   (Lat. *omnipotentia Dei*) God's ability to do all things that do not conflict with the divine will or knowledge. God's power is limited only by God's own nature and not by any external force (Job 42:2; Matt. 19:26; Luke 1:37).

God, omnipresence of   (Lat. *omnipraesentia Dei*) God as an infinite spirit being everywhere present in the cosmos (Ps. 139:7–10; Jer. 23:23–24).

God, omniscience of   (Lat. *omniscientia Dei*) God as knowing all things, all events, and all circumstances in a way that is perfect and immediate (Heb. 4:13).

God, oneness of   God as a single essence who exists as a trinity of persons: Father, Son, and Holy Spirit.

God, perfection of   God as lacking in nothing and as free of all moral imperfection.

God, persistence of   God's continuing and ongoing purposes to bring about

salvation for persons despite their sinfulness, unfaithfulness, and rejection of God's works.

God, personality of   God as a personal being who may be known and related to by humans, rather than an impersonal and unresponsive force.

God, plan of   God's will as it unfolds in history that moves toward God's ultimate purposes according to the divine good pleasure.

God, power of   God's abilities to accomplish divine purposes.

God, preceptive will of   The will of God's eternal decrees, which is the ultimate, effective, and completely mysterious will of God and is what God desires to accomplish.

God, primordial nature of   In process philosophy and theology, the designation for the unchanging essence of God.

God, righteousness of   (Lat. *iustitia Dei*) God's nature as the supreme source of all that is right, and thus as one who is able to judge what is right (Pss. 7:11; 50:6; Isa. 5:16). In the New Testament, God gives righteousness through faith in Jesus Christ, who is God's righteousness (Rom. 1:17; 3:21–31).

God, simplicity of   (Lat. *simplicitas Dei*) God as absolutely ultimate and perfect by being completely free from all composite "parts." All the attributes of God do not become added together to form God; rather, God's attributes are identical with God's essence and constitute God's oneness.

God, sovereignty of   God's ultimate Lordship and rule over the universe so that the divine will is supreme over all else (Eph. 1:11; Rev. 4:11). This will is known most fully in Jesus Christ, who expressed God's ways in self-giving service (Phil. 2:5–8).

God, Spirit of   A designation for the Holy Spirit as the third Person of the Trinity (Rom. 8:9, 14; 1 Cor. 12:3; Eph. 4:30).

God, transcendence of   God as being over and beyond the created order and superior to it in every way.

God, unity of   The oneness of God as a trinity of persons: Father, Son, and Holy Spirit.

God, veracity of   (Lat. *veritas Dei*) God as absolute truth in itself (Num. 23:19).

God, will of   (Lat. *voluntas Dei*) God's good pleasure in expressing the divine purposes. Many distinctions are made among differing aspects of "the will of God" as it is perceived and described differently. Ultimately, God is what God wills, since God works to bring about what God wills.

God, wisdom of   (Lat. *sapientia Dei*) As an attribute of God, the recognition that God always acts with total and complete knowledge and in ways that convey the divine character and its values.

God, worship of   The praise and honoring of God above all else as the supreme good in the universe (Ex. 23:25; Deut. 10:20; Pss. 22:27; 95:6).

God, wrath of   (Lat. *ira Dei*) An expression of the righteousness of God in relation to human sin and its just punishment (Rom. 1:18; 2:5; Eph. 5:6; Col. 3:6). Also called "anger" in the Scriptures (Ex. 4:14; Deut. 29:23).

God Almighty   (Heb. ʾ*El Shaddai*, "God, the one of the mountains") A Hebrew name for God (Gen. 17:1; 28:3). It is found mostly in Genesis, Exodus, and Job. After the patriarchal period it was sometimes used synonymously with "Yahweh." It points to God's power.

God as necessary being   A philosophical designation for God as the one on whom all else in the universe depends and who is totally self-sufficient. Without God, nothing would exist or be able to exist. All other beings are contingent beings and depend on God.

God as subject   An emphasis emerging from the thought of Blaise Pascal (1623–62) and Søren Kierkegaard (1813–55), and emphasized by Emil Brunner (1889–1966) and Karl Barth (1886–1968). God is known only as God wills to be known and according to the conditions God desires. Humans know God only in their subjectivity. Thus God can never be an "object," since God is totally free and not a creature who can be manipulated by humans.

God as Trinity   The divine being existing as Father, Son, and Holy Spirit according to Christian theology. They share the same divine essence (Gr. *ousia*) and are equal in power and glory. They are three "persons" yet one God.

God-breathed   (Gr. *theopneustos,* "inspired by God") A term to describe the Holy Spirit's work with those who wrote the Scriptures as well as the resulting biblical texts as the written Word of God (2 Tim. 3:16).

Goddess   A female deity figure. Some feminist theologians argue that Goddess symbols can counter the repressive patriarchy of monotheistic religions.

Godhead   The nature or essence of God as Trinity: Father, Son, and Holy Spirit.

God-(hu)man   A reference to the incarnate Jesus Christ whom the Christian church confesses as having a divine and human nature, as the second Person of the Trinity.

godliness   Displaying a God-like character (1 Tim. 2:2; 4:7–8; 6:11; 2 Peter 1:6–7).

godparent   One who sponsors a child who is being baptized and makes a statement of faith on its behalf, often also taking on responsibilities in the event of the parents' death.

God-talk   A shorthand definition of "theology."

GodWalk   An alternative shorthand term for "theology" proposed by Frederick Herzog (d. 1995) as a perspective by a liberation theologian. It indicates that theology must be grounded in the actual practices of Christian communities in particular times and places.

Gog and Magog Two powers mentioned in apocalyptic literature (Ezek. 38:2; Rev. 20:8) as being opposed to God.

golden calf An object erected for worship by the Israelites during the wilderness period. It became a source of idolatry during the time that Moses was receiving the divine law on Mount Sinai. He ordered it ground into powder and made the people drink it. The result was a plague (Ex. 32).

Golden Rule Jesus' admonition on the treatment of others: "In everything do to others as you would have them do to you" (Matt. 7:12; Luke 6:31; cf. Tobit 4:15).

Golgotha (Gr. from Heb. *gulgoleth,* "skull"; Lat. *Calvaria,* "skull," "Calvary") The "place of the skull" as the hill with a skull-like appearance outside Jerusalem where Jesus was crucified (John 19:17).

good Excellence of quality, particularly in regard to moral qualities. God is the supreme good who not only "does good" but "is good," and thus is the standard by which all grades of "goodness" are assessed.

Good Friday (Middle English from "God's Friday") The Friday of Holy Week, before Easter Sunday, commemorated in the Christian church as the day on which Jesus Christ was crucified.

good news (Gr. *euangelion*) The gospel of Jesus Christ (Mark 1:1).

Good News Bible (GNB, 1976) The translation of the Old and New Testaments "in Today's English Version" (1966, 1976), produced by the American Bible Society. It sought to render the Scriptures in simplified syntax and with a limited vocabulary.

Good Shepherd An image of Jesus Christ (John 10:11; Heb. 13:20; 1 Peter 2:25; 5:4).

good works Actions that emerge in Christians as a result of the Holy Spirit's activity. They are a response to God's grace in Christ (James 2:17ff.) and are acts of love, care, and justice that render practical service to others. Their place in the plan of salvation has been a source of disagreement.

goodness (Lat. *bonitas*) Moral excellence in relation to God. Creation and humanity have "goodness" in that they are created by God, who is the supreme Good. Their ethical actions are assessed in relation to God and the degree to which they are "like God" in doing what is genuinely good.

gospel (Gr. *euangelion,* "good news"; Anglo-Saxon *godspell,* "good story") The central message of the Christian church to the world, centered on God's provision of salvation for the world in Jesus Christ. Also Gospel, one of the first four books in the New Testament: Matthew, Mark, Luke, and John.

Gospel, Social *See* Social Gospel

gospel hymns and songs Popular religious music that emerged from 19th-century American camp meetings and revivals marked by a focus on personal religious experience and the comfort and security of Christian faith.

gospel of Christ A New Testament phrase used by the apostle Paul to designate the church's message of salvation (Rom. 15:19; 1 Cor. 9:12; Gal. 1:7; Phil. 1:27, etc.).

gospels, apocryphal Writings that circulated during the early church period but were not accepted as canonical by the Christian church. They conveyed sayings of Jesus and apocryphal stories about him. Among these are the Gospels of Thomas, Peter, Philip, Mary, Nicodemus, and the Hebrews.

Gospels, the four The first four books of the New Testament: Matthew, Mark, Luke, and John. Their subject matter is the "gospel of Jesus Christ" (Mark 1:1), the story of Jesus (Mark 13:10; 14:9). They are a distinct literary genre, each being dependent on common, as well as unique, oral and written traditions.

gourd A symbol used in Christian art for the resurrection.

governing assembly   A group that sets directions and makes decisions for a particular body of Christians or a church.

government, church   *See* church government

government, divine   An aspect of God's providence by which God directs and rules over all things according to the divine will.

goy/goyim   (Heb. "nation[s]") Jewish term for a Gentile or Gentiles. Collectively, the Jewish term for all the nations of the world, or all the Gentiles.

grace   (Gr. *charis,* Lat. *gratia,* "favor" "kindness") Unmerited favor. God's grace is extended to sinful humanity in providing salvation and forgiveness through Jesus Christ that is not deserved, and withholding the judgment that is deserved (Rom. 3:24; Eph. 1:7; Titus 2:11).

grace, actual   In Roman Catholic theology, the assistance given by God to meet a particular need or enable a particular good action. It is complemented by habitual grace in the teachings of the Council of Trent (1545–63).

grace, cheap   A phrase, associated with the writings of Dietrich Bonhoeffer (1906–45), that pointed to the acceptance of God's grace in salvation without the desire to repent of sin or live a life of obedience in Christian discipleship.

grace, common   (Lat. *gratia communis*) God's universal, nonsaving grace in which blessings are given to humanity for physical sustenance, pleasure, learning, beauty, etc., as expressions of God's goodness. It is particularly contrasted in Reformed theology with God's special or saving grace.

grace, cooperating   In Roman Catholic theology, the Holy Spirit's action to enable humans to respond to God's initial action in establishing a divine-human relationship with a person. It is also the grace that enables the ongoing living of the Christian life.

grace, covenant of   *See* covenant of grace

grace, efficacious   The grace of God that accomplishes the purpose of salvation.

grace, free   A term used by John Wesley (1703–91) to indicate that God's grace given universally is not dependent on human goodness or merit.

grace, glorifying   A term used in Wesleyan theology to indicate the final expression of sanctifying grace, which is the attainment of the perfection of love.

grace, habitual   *See* grace, sanctifying

grace, irresistible   (Lat. *gratia irresistibilis*) An emphasis of Reformed theology that God's grace is always efficacious and accomplishes its purpose in those whom God has chosen to receive salvation (the elect).

grace, justifying   A term used in Wesleyan theology to indicate the grace of God extended to those who believe in Jesus Christ and thus are justified or saved.

grace, means of   (Lat. *media gratiae*) The ways by which God's grace is extended and received by humans. In Protestant theology, the emphasis has been on the Word and Sacraments as God's instituted means of conveying the grace that leads to justification and sanctification.

grace, prevenient   (Lat. *gratia praeveniens*) The grace that "comes before" any human response to God in justification or conversion. In Reformed theology, this grace is seen as irresistible. In Arminianism and Wesleyanism the view is that God's grace is extended and persons may choose whether or not to believe in Jesus Christ. The human decisions of the faithful are responsive to and enabled by God's grace.

grace, sanctifying   In Roman Catholic theology, the grace conveyed by the sacraments embracing both "justification" and "sanctification." Also called "habitual grace." In Wesleyan theology, the grace God gives throughout the

Christian life to enable one to live as a faithful Christian disciple.

grace, saving (Lat. *gratia salvifica*) God's gracious favor for salvation on the basis of the work of Jesus Christ.

grace, special (Lat. *gratia specialis*) In Reformed theology, the grace of God given specifically to the elect, to those whom God will save, in contrast to "common grace."

grace, sufficient (Lat. *gratia sufficiens*) A reference to the belief that God's grace is fully adequate to bring salvation to those who believe. In Roman Catholic theology, a form of actual grace, which refers to the grace that is offered to humans but that does not take effect.

grace, systems of A term used by Roman Catholic theologians to indicate the various speculative systems used to understand the workings of God's grace in relation to human freedom.

grace, theology of The full theological understanding that God acts toward the world in grace, and the recognition of the range of God's gracious activities in history and in the process of Christian salvation.

grace, universal *See* universality of God's grace

grace at meals Prayers of thanksgiving said before a meal, usually as a regular devotional practice.

grace of God *See* God, grace of

graces, Christian Virtues such as love, forgiveness, humility, and patience that are expressed in the Christian life.

gradual (Middle English from Lat. *gradus*, "a step") A set of antiphons sung after the first Scripture reading in Western churches, originally sung from the steps of the altar.

Grail, Holy The cup used by Jesus Christ at the Last Supper was romanticized in medieval legends of quests for the Holy Grail, which supposedly conveyed the effects of Holy Communion on those who possessed it.

grammatico-historical exegesis The interpretation of biblical texts by focusing on their syntactical construction, cultural and historical contexts.

gratitude (From Lat. *gratitudo*) The response to God and God's blessings that is an expression of praise and devotion. In the Christian context, believers respond in gratitude for the "indescribable gift" (2 Cor. 9:15) of Jesus Christ, who is the supreme expression of God's grace.

gratuity of the kingdom A term to indicate that the kingdom (reign) of God comes as God's gift and is not earned or achieved by human action or work.

gravamen (From Lat. *gravare*, "to weigh down") A term used in the Anglican tradition for a memorial or petition in the Church of England to remedy problems or grievances.

Great Awakenings, the Two 18th-century American revivals, one occurring in the American colonies (1725–60) through the leadership of George Whitefield (1714–70) and Jonathan Edwards (1703–58). The second (beginning in 1787) was marked by various leadership and featured camp meetings.

Great Bible (1539) An English translation by Miles Coverdale (1488–1568) and Richard Grafton presented to King Henry VIII by Thomas Cromwell (c. 1485–1540), a copy of which was ordered placed in every English parish church. It was the first authorized English version.

Great Commission The command of Jesus to his disciples to go into all the world and preach the gospel, as recorded in Matt. 28:19–20. While some scholars dispute its authenticity as being Jesus' own utterance, the passage has served as a warrant for the church to spread the gospel and for Christian evangelism.

Great Schism *See* Schism, Great

greed (Lat. *avaritia*, "avarice," "greed") One of the "seven deadly sins," being the opposite of the virtue of "liberality" and representing a heightened desire for material things.

Greek, Koine (Gr. *koinē,* "common") The everyday Greek spoken at the time the New Testament was written, and thus the language of the Greek New Testament.

Greek Church In contrast to the Latin or Roman Church (Roman Catholic). A term for the Eastern or Eastern Orthodox Church.

Greek dualism A characteristic of ancient Greek philosophy to distinguish sharply between the material and the nonmaterial as comprehending all reality. The principle is carried through the system as in the contrast between body and soul. Some Christian theologies exemplify these features.

Greek fathers Early Christian theologians from the Eastern regions including John Chrysostom (c. 347–407), Athanasius (c. 293–373), and Basil the Great (330–79).

Greek metaphysics The thought of ancient Greek philosophers such as Plato and Aristotle on the nature of reality. These views have affected Christian theology at numerous points, including, for example, expressions of the dualism of "body" and "soul."

Greek Orthodox Church The national church of Greece, or more generally, a term for Eastern Orthodox churches.

Green Thursday (Lat. *dies viridium,* Ger. *Gründonnerstag*) A term for Maundy Thursday in Germany and other places. It came from the practice of giving those who confessed their sins on Ash Wednesday green branches to indicate that their penance was completed.

Gregorian calendar The calendar now used throughout the major part of the Christian world. It resulted from the calendar reform instituted by Pope Gregory XIII (1582).

Gregorian chant A historic liturgical song used in Western churches; named

for Gregory the Great, bishop of Rome (590–604), who standardized its usage.

Gregorian reform A reform movement in the church initiated by Pope Gregory VII (1073–85). It sought to free the church from secular involvement in religious affairs. Reforms focused specifically on eliminating simony (the buying and selling of church offices) and on urging celibacy for clergy.

grotto (Ital. "cavern") An artificial cavernlike structure often associated with religious experiences or sites.

ground of being A term used by Paul Tillich (1886–1965) to indicate God as the source of all reality or being.

guardian angel An angel believed by some to be assigned to watch and care for individual persons on the basis of Matt. 18:10 and Acts 12:15.

guilt (Lat. *culpa*) Theologically, the condition in which one is estranged from God because of sin, which ruptures the divine-human relationship. The experience of guilt that results from breaking a divine law can be accompanied by a sense of shame.

guilt offering Prior to the destruction of the Temple in Israel, the trespass or guilt offering was the sacrifice of a ram plus damages to the person one had wronged (Lev. 5:1–7:10).

Gutenberg Bible (1456) A Bible printed in Mainz, Germany, by Johann Gutenberg (c. 1397–1468). It was the first produced by movable type. It is also called the Mazarin Bible.

gynaesthesia Term used by Mary Daly in *Gyn/Ecology* (1978) to describe women's new forms of perception and understanding when they become feminists. This means the ability to respond holistically to the environment and perceive interrelatedness in disparate phenomena.

gyn/ecology Term used by Mary Daly in *Gyn/Ecology* (1978) to describe new "bodies" of knowlege leading to the creation of women-only collective relationships.

gynergy Term used by Emily Culpepper (1975) and adopted by Mary Daly to refer to the strength of feminist ethics in which the development of women's collective consciousness will produce new ways of determining values.

gynocentric (From Gr. *gynē*, "female," "woman") Sharing of certain kinds of women-centered beliefs and women-centered social organizations.

gynocentric vocabularies The transvaluation or creation of theological vocabularies that address the oppression of women. New terms are created that reverse negative associations and turn them into compliments. In this way, patriarchy is counteracted and a woman-centered (gyno-centered) language is created.

gynomorphic Term used by Mary Daly in *Gyn/Ecology* (1978) to describe a whole new women's language that replaces the language of patriarchy by involving women in the process of the creating of knowledge.

habit (From Lat. *habere*, "to possess") Term used in medieval Roman Catholic theology to describe a permanent characteristic or quality possessed by the "heart" and affecting the whole person. Also, a term for the traditional dress of friars, monks, nuns, and others of religious orders.

Hades Greek term used to translate Heb. "Sheol," indicating the place of those who are dead. In the New Testament it represents the place where the wicked are punished (Matt. 11:23; Luke 10:15; 16:23).

haggadah (Heb. "narrative") Those parts of Jewish scriptural interpretation by rabbis that were nonprescriptive. It contrasts with "halakah." Also, the narration of the liberation of Israel from Egypt as told during the Passover Seder meal (Ex. 13:8).

Hagiographa (Gr. "sacred writings") The third division of the Old Testament canon of Scripture that includes all books that are not part of the Law or Prophets. These are Psalms, Proverbs, Job, Ruth, Lamentations, Song of Songs, Ecclesiastes, Esther, Daniel, 1 and 2 Chronicles, Ezra, and Nehemiah. Also known as the "Writings."

hagiography/hagiology (Gr. *hagios*, "holy," and *graphein*, "to write") Literature pertaining to the lives of the Christian saints. The study of the saints and their veneration.

hagiolatry (Gr. *hagios* "holy," and *latreia*, "worship") The worship of saints or those considered to be holy persons. Also the invoking of saints as mediators with God in order to secure blessings.

hag-ography A term used by Mary Daly in *Gyn/Ecology* (1978) to describe the "living/writing" process of women's history in reestablishing the power of hags or witches.

Hail Mary (Lat. *Ave Maria*) In Roman Catholic tradition, the form of prayer addressed to the Virgin Mary, based on the greetings of the angel Gabriel (Luke 1:28) and of Elizabeth (Luke 1:42). It has been used devotionally.

hair shirt A shirt of cloth woven from hair, worn by ascetics as a sign of spiritual discipline.

halakah (Heb. "that by which one walks") The body of teaching that grew up in Jewish law that sought to apply the law to all situations of life and to give instruction. It contrasts with "haggadah."

Halfway Covenant (1662)   A form of church membership in 17th-century New England Congregationalism. Children of church adherents were allowed to be baptized, even though their parents were not full members and had not professed Christian faith. The parents were considered "halfway" members.

Hallel   (Heb. "praise") A term for Psalms 113–118 (and more generally to other groups in Psalms 104–150), sung during major Jewish festivals as expressions of praise to God. The term "hallelujah" occurs throughout.

hallelujah (alleluia)   (Heb. "[let us] praise the Lord"; Gr. *allēlouia,* Lat. *alleluia*) A religious cry of praise and joy. It is found only in the Psalms in the Hebrew Bible (Pss. 104–150) and is transliterated in the Septuagint and Vulgate. In ancient Israel it was used in the liturgical recitation of psalms as a way to encourage the congregation to participate. It became a word of great praise to God (3 Macc. 7:13; Rev. 19:1–8) and was prominent in early Christian liturgies.

hallow   (Anglo-Saxon *halig,* "holy") To consecrate, set apart, or regard as holy.

Halloween   *See* All Saints' Day

halo   (Gr. *halōs,* "circle of light around a sun or moon") Also aureole, corona, glory, nimbus. Used in Christian art to surround the heads of saints, indicating their holiness and heavenly state.

hamartia   (Gr. "missing of the mark") A biblical term for "sin" in the sense of failure, guilt, or not living according to that which is expected by God (Luke 5:21; John 16:8; Rom. 6:23; Heb. 9:28).

Hampton Court Conference (1604)   Meetings between English bishops and Puritan leaders in which King James I considered Puritan demands for church reforms as expressed in the Millenary Petition.

hands, laying on of (imposition of)   A form of blessing found in the Old Testament (Gen. 48) and used by Jesus Christ and throughout the history of the Christian church (Acts 8:18; 13:3; 19:6; 1 Tim. 4:14).

haplography   (From Gr. *haplo-,* "single," "simple," and *graphē,* "writing") The accidental omission of a letter or letter group in copying manuscripts. Some biblical manuscripts have suffered from this problem.

happy (cheerful) exchange   (Ger. *fröhlicher Wechsel*) A phrase from Martin Luther (1483–1546) used to indicate that justification occurs in the exchange of Christ's righteousness for human sin so that sinners receive a new status before God.

hardening (hardness) of heart   A term indicating human resistance to the Word or will of God (Matt. 19:8).

harmartiology   (From Gr. *harmartia,* "sin," "a missing of the mark") A theological term for the study of the doctrine of sin.

harmonistic school   Those who attempt to synthesize, and bring together into harmony, biblical passages where there appear to be discrepancies.

harrowing of hell   The defeat of Satan and evil by Jesus Christ as he descended to hell ("Hades") between his crucifixion and resurrection. A theme in medieval English religious dramas.

Hartford Appeal for Theological Affirmation (1975)   A statement signed by 18 theologians from Roman Catholic and mainline Protestant churches indicating 13 themes that in their view were characteristic of recent tendencies to accommodate the Christian faith to a secular worldview.

hate   (Heb. *sane',* Gr. *misein,* "to hate"; Lat. *odium,* "hate") Strong opposition to love as the desire for harm or evil to come upon another person. It is characteristic of sinners in relation to God (John 15:23) and toward others (Gal.

5:20). It is contrary to the love Jesus requires (Matt. 22:37–40).

Hatfield, Council of (680) An English church council that rejected Monothelitism and accepted the decrees of the first five general councils, also affirming the double procession of the Holy Spirit.

Haystack Prayer Meeting (1806) A meeting held by students at Williams College in Massachusetts, out of which grew the American overseas missionary movement and the founding of the American Board of Commissioners for Foreign Missions (1810).

healing To restore to health and thus the bringing of wholeness or soundness to all aspects of human life. Jesus healed (Matt. 14:36; Luke 6:18), as did his disciples (Luke 9:2) and later followers (Acts 4:22; 9:34; 1 Cor. 12:9).

health Well-being in multiple dimensions of life. Issues surrounding decisions about physical health are ethical concerns, while "spiritual health" has often been related to "salvation" (Lat. *salus*, "health"). In the Christian view, God's desire for human wholeness includes both physical and spiritual concerns.

heart (Heb. *leb*, Gr. *kardia*) Biblically, the center of the human person from which emotions and values arise. It may be portrayed as "devious" and "perverse" (Jer. 17:9) or "pure" (Matt. 5:8), "upright" (Ps. 32:11), and "clean" (Ps. 51:10). It is known by God (1 Sam. 16:7).

heathen *See* pagan

heaven (Anglo-Saxon *heofon*) The place beyond earth that is the abode of God. In Christian theology, it is the future eternal abode of those who receive salvation in Jesus Christ. It is portrayed as a place of blessedness, without pain or evil, distinguished by the presence of God.

heaven, new *See* new creation

heavenly Father The first Person of the Trinity, to whom Jesus prayed (Matt. 6:9).

heavenly host Angels of God (Luke 2:13).

Hebraic Relating to the Hebrew people, particularly as portrayed in the Old Testament Scriptures.

Hebrew A Jewish person. Also the language of the Jewish nation. In the Table of Nations (Gen. 10:21), the descendants of Eber, son of Shem. In the early church period, the term referred to Hebrew- or Aramaic-speaking Christians (Acts 6:1).

Hebrew psychology A term used to describe the ways that human persons were understood by the writers of the Hebrew Scriptures.

Hebrew Scriptures A term for the canonical writings that Christians refer to as the Old Testament. The Jewish canon of Hebrew Scriptures has 24 books divided among Torah (5), Prophets (8), and Writings (11), which appear in modern translations as 39 books. They form the basis for Jewish belief and life as well as being Holy Scripture for Christians.

hedonism (From Gr. *hēdonē*, "pleasure," "delight") In ethics, the view that the enjoyment of pleasure is the highest good and goal for human life and action. It may be individualistic or egoistic in teaching that each individual should act toward his or her own maximum pleasure.

Hegelianism A system of philosophical thought, based on the works of G.W.F. Hegel (1770–1831), that greatly influenced 19th-century philosophy, especially Marxism and certain systems of Christian theology. It taught that history was determined by a pattern of thesis/antithesis/synthesis.

hegemony (Gr. *hēgemonia*, "leadership") The predominant influence of one nation over another. The term is used in liberation theology to indicate the dominance of Western countries over the economies of other, underdeveloped nations. Oppression and repression of autonomy results.

hegumenos (Gr. *hēgoumenos*, "leader") A title in the Eastern church for the abbot or superior of a Byzantine monastery.

Heidelberg Catechism (1563) Confession of faith written by Reformed theologians Zacharias Ursinus (1534–83) and Caspar Olevianus (1536–87) marked by a strong accent on personal faith and practical piety. It has been one of the Reformed confessional statements most widely used throughout the world.

Heilsgeschichte (Ger. "holy history") A term used by some biblical scholars to mark the history of Israel and the subsequent Christian church as God's "salvation history" being worked out as God's plan in the midst of human history as a whole.

hell (Gr. *Geenna,* "Gehenna"; North German *hel,* "realm of the dead") In Christian theology, the place of the dead after death in which the wicked endure eternal punishment and the total absence of God (Matt. 25:46; Luke 10:15; Rev. 20:13–15). It has also been interpreted symbolically to indicate the most profound separation from God.

hell, descent into "He descended into hell" is a phrase in the Apostles' Creed, variously interpreted to indicate what Christ did between his death on the cross and his resurrection. Views include descending to "Hades" to preach the gospel or liberate captive souls. Symbolically, it refers to the spiritual torments Christ underwent, particularly on the cross.

Hellenism Greek culture and thought influential in the non-Greek world after Alexander the Great (356–323 B.C.). It pervasively affected all life from language (Greek became the international means of communication), to architecture, to modes of thought. It facilitated the spread of Christianity.

Hellenistic Pertaining to Hellenism and its influence as it related to the early Christian church and the development of early Christian theology.

Hellenistic world The Greek culture and thought that became pervasive throughout the Mediterranean areas after the time of Alexander the Great (356–323 B.C.). It was in this context that the early Christian church spread and gained converts.

Hellenization of Christianity The Greek (Hellenistic) influences on the development of early Christian thought and practice, seen particularly by some in the language and conceptual categories used by Christian theologians and in various pronouncements of church councils such as Chalcedon (451).

Helvetic Confessions (1536; 1562) Reformed confessions of faith associated with Heinrich Bullinger (1504–75) and other Swiss Reformers (First, 1536; Second, 1562) reflecting a hoped-for union between the Reformed churches and Lutheranism.

henosis (Gr. *henōsis,* "union") A term used to describe the unity of the divine and human natures of Jesus Christ.

henotheism (Gr. *henos,* "one," and *theos,* "God") The view that while there is one God who is supreme, other deities may also exist. Some see this as being a recognized view in relation to the commandment to Israel to have no other gods than Yahweh (Ex. 20:3; Deut. 5:7).

Henoticon (482) (Lat. "union") A law promulgated by the Roman emperor Zeno. It sought to settle the Monophysite controversy and was based on the Nicene Creed. Yet it did not satisfy either side and the controversy continued. Many Eastern but no Western churches accepted it.

heortology (From Gr. *heortē,* "festival") A branch of the study of liturgy focusing on the origin, history, and significance of festivals and seasons of the church year.

Heptateuch (Gr. *hepta,* "seven," and *teuchos,* "book") A term to describe the first seven books of the Old Testament, in which a unity is perceived.

heresiarch (From Gr. *hairesis,* "choice," "heresy," and *archēs,* leader) One who originates a heresy or is the founder of a heretical sect or group.

heresy (Gr. *hairesis,* "choice") A view chosen instead of the official teachings of a church. Such a view is thus regarded as wrong and potentially dangerous for faith.

heresy, christological A view that is not consistent with official church teachings or doctrines about the person of Jesus Christ.

heresy trial A formal ecclesiastical proceeding to establish the validity of charges that someone espouses or teaches what is contrary to established church theological beliefs.

heretic One who espouses a view that is not consistent with an official church teaching or doctrine.

heretics, baptism of A theological issue in the 3d century, when questions were raised as to whether those who were converted to the Christian faith from heretical sects and had already been baptized by the sect should be baptized as Christians. Church synods ruled that if the Trinitarian formula had been used, rebaptism was not necessary.

Hermeneutic, New *See* New Hermeneutic, the

hermeneutical circle A contemporary recognition in biblical interpretation that the person of the interpreter inevitably becomes part of the interpretive process. If so, then the one who interprets will find that any interpretation of the biblical texts and contexts will be affected by one's own context.

hermeneutical method A conscious way of approaching the interpretation of texts according to certain procedures.

hermeneutical question The theological question of how the ancient biblical documents can speak meaningfully to contemporary culture and experience. It also raises the question of appropriate means of interpreting the biblical materials (hermeneutics).

hermeneutical theology An approach to theology through the study of the interpretation and meaning of texts.

hermeneutics (Gr. *hermēneutikē* "interpretation") The rules one uses for searching out the meaning of writings, particularly biblical texts.

hermeneutics, sociocritical The work of interpretation that seeks to make clear ways in which texts may be used to serve self-interest or the interests of power structures that are socially and culturally dominant. Social manipulation and control as well as the service of self-interest may occur through the use of (biblical) texts.

hermeneutics of suspicion A term in liberation theology to denote the need to recognize that certain dominant forms and conclusions in biblical interpretation may be serving to reinforce forms of dominance, oppression, and agendas of power. Thus one should be suspicious of received interpretations.

Hermesianism A philosophical and theological system based on the work of Georg Hermes (1775–1831) that sought to reshape the teachings of Roman Catholicism to conform with the philosophy of Immanuel Kant (1724–1804).

hermit (From Gr. *erēmia,* "desert") One who lives in solitude (often in the desert) in withdrawal from the world out of religious convictions. Christian hermits were found in the deserts of Egypt and Palestine at the end of the 3d century.

herstory A term used particularly by feminist writers to describe women's stories. It is an alternative term to "history."

Hesychasm (Gr. *hēsychia,* "quiet") A system of mysticism spread in the Greek Orthodox Church by monks during the 14th century. It stresses elaborate ascetic exercises and emphasizes divine quietness in prayer. More generally, the contemplative tradition of Eastern Orthodoxy. It is also called Palamism for Gregory Palamas (c. 1296–1359), its principal theologian.

heterodox/heterdoxy (Gr. *heterodoxos,* from *heteros,* "other," and *doxa,* "opinion") That which is counter to or different from accepted orthodox belief in a church.

heteronomy (Gr. *heteros,* "other," and *nomos,* "law") An outside control over the state of being of an object or subject (opposite of autonomy).

heteroousios (Gr. *heteros,* "another" and *ousios,* "being") A term used in early church christological debates for the view of Arius that the Son (Christ) was of a different "substance" or "being" from God the Father. It was rejected in favor of *homoousios* ("of the same substance").

heterosexuality A sexual relationship between those of the opposite gender.

heterotopia A term used by the philosopher Michel Foucault (1926–84) to describe the postmodern universe as having no "center" or perfect "utopia." Instead, there are conglomerates of societies, smaller social units with no common standards or allegiances so that the "universe" is now the "multiverse."

heuristic theology (From Gr. *heuriskein,* "to find out") A theological approach that opens an issue or argument for further questioning.

hexaemeron (Gr. *hexaēmeron,* "[a work] of six days") Term used to describe the "six days" of creation as portrayed in Genesis 1.

Hexapla (Gr. "sixfold") An edition of the Old Testament by Origen (c. 185–254) that featured the Hebrew text, the Hebrew text transliterated into Greek characters, and four Greek versions in parallel columns. At some points, three other Greek versions were added.

Hexateuch (Gr. "six books") A term for the first six books of the Hebrew Bible, used by Julius Wellhausen (1844–1918) in 1876 as a way of indicating his belief that a single set of literary sources stands behind them.

Hicksites Followers of Elias Hicks (1748–1830), who formed the liberal faction of American Friends (Quakers).

hierarchicalism Gradations of value and worth based on cultural assumptions. According to feminist writers, these reflect male norms and are established by dominant male power in society.

hierarchy (Gr. *hierarchia,* "rule of the high priest") Organized and structured levels of ecclesiastical power and the offices that form a means of church government.

hierarchy of truths A phrase used since Vatican Council II (1962–65) in the Roman Catholic Church to recognize that various Christian doctrines are more or less important than others. A relative weighting is a helpful way of promoting or enhancing ecumenical dialogue as well as recognizing some diversities.

hierology (From Gr. *hieros,* "sacred") A body of sacred knowledge or literature.

hieromonk (Gr. *hieromonachos,* from *hieros,* "sacred," and *monachos,* "monk") In the Eastern church, a monk who is also a priest.

high altar Term for the main altar in a church.

High Church Term for the portion of the Anglican Church that emphasizes liturgy and has close affinities with Roman Catholicism.

High Mass Traditional term in Roman Catholicism for a eucharistic service sung, rather than recited, by a priest and choir.

high priest (Gr. *archiereus*) The head of the Levitical priesthood (Ex. 28). After the Babylonian exile, the high priest also became head of the Jewish state. Jesus Christ in his saving work is referred to as a high priest throughout the book of Hebrews (2:17; 3:1; 6:20; 8:1).

higher criticism A term introduced in 1881 to designate approaching the forms and sources of the biblical texts with the tools of scientific and literary-critical study in hand. It is distinguished from lower (or textual) criticism, which deals with establishing the most reliable biblical manuscripts and texts.

Higher Life theology   A form of Christian holiness popular in England and America beginning in the 19th century through best-selling books and the Keswick Convention. It stresses deliverance from sins that are apparent, continual cleansing by identifying with Christ, and the filling of the Holy Spirit.

high-priestly prayer of Jesus   The prayer of Jesus for his followers that they may be "one" (John 17).

Hillel, school of   At the time of Christ, those who followed the teachings of Rabbi Hillel and who held a more lenient interpretation of the Jewish law in opposition to the stricter views of the Shammai school.

His Holiness   A title used in the Roman Catholic Church since the 14th century solely for the pope.

historical consciousness   A recognition that ancient texts were shaped by the cultural contexts and thought forms of those who composed them. It stands in opposition to the view that contemporary forms of logic and understanding can be directly imposed on them.

historical criticism   *See* criticism, historical

historical Jesus, the   A term to describe the Jesus of Nazareth who lived in history and whose life can be studied by the methods and tools of historical research. The term is contrasted to "the Christ of faith," with some scholars emphasizing differences between the two.

historical Jesus, quest of the   Attempts by biblical scholars, beginning with Albert Schweitzer (1875–1965), to determine what the historical Jesus said and did.

historical method   The means used by historians to approach and interpret texts. They are also applicable to the interpretation of biblical texts.

historical religion   A religious system that features a linear view of time. Ancient Israel's religion is considered historical in comparison with religious systems of surrounding cultures that featured a cyclical view of time associated with Near Eastern myths.

historical theology   The study of the views of theologians, and of the Christian church, in their historical contexts.

historical-critical method   Approach to the meaning of biblical texts on the basis of what the texts meant in their earliest form and contexts.

historicism   An approach to history seeking explanations solely on the basis of the historical-critical method. The assumption is that humans are exclusively historical beings. All human ideals, ideas, and institutions have significance only in relation to the positions they occupy in place and time.

historicity   That which is accepted as being historically true because it is based on verifiable facts and accounts. Also, the human condition of being creatures in time and space and thus inevitably "historical."

Historie   German term for the "objective" study of past events in order to determine what actually happened. The term is contrasted by some theologians with *Geschichte,* i.e., *Heilsgeschichte,* or the "history of salvation" or "history from the perspective of faith."

history   (Gr. and Lat. *historia*) The events that occur within the world in space and time. A Christian perspective views these events as expressions of God's will and the outworking of God's ultimate purposes.

history, theology of   A term denoting a theological understanding of history in its beginnings, its outworkings according to God's purposes, and its ultimate ending in the reign (kingdom) of God. God is active in history, as the biblical record shows. Human events are moving toward their final climax.

history of doctrine   The evolution of the teachings or doctrinal understandings of the Christian church over periods of time.

history of dogma   The evolution of the official teachings of Christian churches over a period of time as these convey an understanding of the Christian faith as a whole.

history of religion school   (Ger. *Religionsgeschichtliche Schule*) An approach to religion that studies the historical development of the religion, particularly the phases of development through which Judaism and Christianity have passed.

Hoc est Christum cognoscere, beneficiis eius cogni   (Lat. "To know Christ is to know his benefits") A description by Philip Melanchthon (1497–1560) to indicate the personal character of the knowledge of Christ as Lord and Savior.

holiness   (From Gr. *hagios*, "set apart") In Christian spirituality, the devotion and purity of life associated with Christian discipleship, in which one lives according to God's will and exhibits that commitment in all areas of behavior.

holiness, Christian   (Gr. *hagios*, "set apart") The sanctification or Christian life of believers. It is often defined in terms of aspects of personal character or actions.

Holiness churches   Christian churches originating from 19th-century Holiness movements in America that emphasized the experiential dimensions of Christian faith.

Holiness Code   The prescriptions given by God to the people of Israel (Lev. 17—26) for the regulation of societal and personal life in accordance with God's will for the people. The laws were both theological and ethical in nature.

Holiness movements   Nineteenth-century American religious groups that sought to perpetuate Methodist views of entire sanctification and the concept of Christian perfection as understood by John Wesley (1703–91). The various streams of the movements are related to but distinct from Pentecostalism.

holiness of the church   *See* church, holiness of the

holism   (From Gr. *holos*, "whole") Emphasis of feminist writers on rejections of dualistic divisions in favor of nonexploitative, nonhierarchical and reciprocal relationships.

holistic salvation   The view that Christian salvation affects and involves the whole person in a full range of actions that are personal and corporate, spiritual and material, temporal and eternal.

holocaust   (Gr. *holokauston*, Lat. *holocaustum*) Consumed by fire. Biblically, "burnt offering" (Heb. 10:6, 8). In ethics, the Holocaust was the genocide of the Jewish people practiced by the Nazis in 20th-century Germany during World War II.

holy   (Gr. *hagios*, "set apart"; Anglo-Saxon *hal*, "well," "whole") That which is regarded as sacred or able to convey a sense of the divine. Also, that which is set apart for God's will or use or that which is godlike by being spiritually whole, well, pure, or perfect.

holy angels   *See* angels, holy

Holy Communion   *See* Lord's Supper

Holy Cross Day   The Feast of the Exaltation of the Holy Cross (September 14), honoring the cross of Jesus Christ.

holy days of obligation (holydays)   Feast days on which Roman Catholics are to attend Mass. Typically these are Christmas; Epiphany; Ascension Day; Corpus Christi; Solemnity of Mary, Mother of God; Immaculate Conception; Assumption of Mary; St. Joseph; Sts. Peter and Paul; and All Saints' Day.

Holy Family   Term for Joseph, Mary, and the infant Jesus.

Holy Father   (Lat. *Sanctissimus Pater*, "the Most Holy Father") A title for the pope.

Holy Ghost   *See* Holy Spirit

Holy Innocents   Term for those children under two years of age who were slaughtered by King Herod as he sought to destroy the child of whom the Magi told him, the infant Jesus (Matt. 2:16–

18). They are commemorated on December 28.

Holy Land   Term for the land of Palestine and its sacred locations. Israel became known as the Holy Land in the Middle Ages. Christian pilgrimages there have been made since the 4th century.

holy mutability   A term used by Karl Barth (1886–1968) to express the view that God's freedom enables God to suspend, correct, or replace God's own decrees.

Holy of Holies   The innermost portion of the Jewish Temple, into which only the high priest could enter to offer a sacrifice once a year on the Day of Atonement (Heb. 9:3).

Holy Office   *See* Congregation for the Doctrine of the Faith

Holy One of Israel   A term used for God, particularly in the writings of the prophet Isaiah (1:4; 10:20; 41:14; 43:3, etc.).

holy orders   *See* orders, major; orders, minor

Holy Place   The sanctuary of the Tabernacle in ancient Israel. It was 20 cubits long and 10 cubits in breadth and height (about 30 × 15 × 15 feet; Ex. 26:16, 18, 22–24). It contained the altar, incense, table for the showbread, and a golden lampstand. The Holy of Holies was a second room of half the length, at one end of the Holy Place.

holy places   Locations in the Holy Land that are associated with Jesus. Most popularly, the Upper Room, the Via Dolorosa (Way of the Cross), the Church of the Holy Sepulchre, and the Mount of Olives. Christian pilgrims come to these sites.

Holy Rollers   A term coined in the early 20th century for those who gave excessive emotional expression to their Christian faith, particularly Pentecostals. It is not frequently used today.

Holy Saturday   The day in Holy Week between Good Friday and Easter Sunday.

Holy Scripture(s)   *See* Scripture

Holy See   (Lat. *sancta sedes*, "holy chair") The pope's see or "seat" of authority. It refers as well to the Roman Catholic view of the pope as pastor of the universal church and the attendant rights and obligations of that office.

Holy Sepulchre   The cave tomb in Jerusalem where Jesus was buried (Luke 23:53).

Holy Shroud/Shroud of Turin   A relic at Turin, Italy (since 1578), venerated as the burial cloth of Jesus (Luke 23:53).

holy souls   A popular designation in the Roman Catholic tradition for souls who are still in purgatory and are being cleansed of the last remnants of their sins before entering heaven. The term is associated with All Souls' Day (Nov. 2).

Holy Spirit   (Heb. *ruaḥ*, Gr. *pneuma*, "spirit") The third Person of the Trinity. God the Father, God the Son, and God the Holy Spirit constitute the eternal Godhead. The Spirit inspired biblical writers, makes known the saving work of Jesus Christ, and is God as present in and with the church. The Spirit acts to incorporate all things into the life of the triune God.

Holy Spirit, baptism of the   *See* baptism of the Holy Spirit

Holy Spirit, deity/divinity of the   A description of the Holy Spirit as fully divine and thus sharing the divinity of God the Father and God the Son (Gr. *homoousios*, "of the same substance").

Holy Spirit, double procession of the   *See* double procession of the Holy Spirit

Holy Spirit, personality of the   A reference to the Holy Spirit's personhood and thus the Spirit's ability to enter into relationships with persons, instead of being a force or an impersonal principle.

Holy Spirit, single procession of the   *See* single procession of the Holy Spirit

Holy Spirit, witness of the   *See* internal testimony (witness) of the Holy Spirit

holy table   *See* altar

Holy Thursday The Thursday of Holy Week, prior to Good Friday. Also called Maundy Thursday (from *mandatum novum,* "a new commandment," John 13:34). It commemorates the Last Supper which Jesus ate with his disciples and in which he shared the bread and wine and washed his disciples' feet (Matt. 26:20–29; John 13:5).

Holy Trinity *See* Trinity, doctrine of the

holy war A war carried out and sanctioned by a religion. Often "holy wars" have been wars of religion to defend or spread a faith. The concept of holy war has been challenged as not ethically valid by those who do not believe the use of violence to be an appropriate expression of "religion." In Christian ethical thought it is criticized as not compatible with Christianity.

holy water Water blessed as a reminder of baptism. In some churches it is placed in fonts at the entrance to the church. It may be sprinkled on people and objects.

Holy Week The last week in Lent, commemorating the last week of the earthly life of Jesus. It begins with Palm Sunday and ends on Holy Saturday, prior to Easter.

Holy Writ Another name for Holy Scripture or the Bible.

Holy Year A year in which the pope grants a special plenary indulgence to those who make a pilgrimage to Rome according to certain conditions.

homage (From Lat. *homo,* "man," "vassal") The act of showing reverence and honor to God.

home missions A term used for mission work that takes place within the same country or land in which a church is located, as compared with "foreign missions."

homecoming The practice in some American churches of inviting former members and pastors of churches to return at the same time for a service of worship and time of fellowship.

homilaria (From Gr. *homilia,* "sermon") Ancient and medieval collections of sermons.

homiletical Pertaining to preaching or the study of preaching.

homiletics (From Gr. *homilētikos,* from *homilein,* "to be in company," "to converse") The theological discipline that deals with the preparation, construction, and delivery of sermons. Also, the study of preaching.

homily (Gr. *homilia,* "conversation," "discourse") A sermon given to an assembled audience.

Homoeans (From Gr. *homoios,* "like") Fourth-century group which stated that Jesus Christ is "like" the Father but denied that the Father and the Son were of the same (*homos*) substance (Gr. *ousia*) or being.

homoios (Gr. "like") Term used in christological controversies in the word *homoiousios* to say Jesus Christ was of "like" substance with the Father, rather than *homoousios,* of the "same" substance.

homoiousios (Gr. *homoios,* "like," and *ousios,* "substance") "Of like substance" was a term used in early christological debates by Arians and others who perceived Jesus Christ as "like" God the Father (*homoiousios*), but not as being of the "same" substance as God the Father (*homoousios*).

homologoumena New Testament writings that were universally recognized as canonical by the church, in comparison to "antilegomena," those about which there was dispute.

homoousios (Gr. *homos,* "same," and *ousios,* "substance") *Homoousios,* "of the same substance" was a term used in early church christological debates and adopted by church councils of Nicaea (325) and Constantinople (381) to indicate that Jesus Christ was of the same essence as God the Father. It contrasts with (Gr.) *heteroousios* and *homoiousios.*

homophobia A term coined by George Weinberg (1973) for the "irrational fear" (phobia) that some heterosexual persons have of being near a homosexual. It is used generally and specifically to denote a dislike or hatred of gay persons as well as discrimination against them.

homosexuality   (From Gr. *homos*, "same") A sexual relationship between those of the same gender.

honesty   (From Lat. *honestas*) Speaking or conveying the truth. This is both a societal (Lev. 19:36; Deut. 25:15) and a personal ethical standard (Luke 8:15; Eph. 4:15) since it is reflective of God as the God of truth.

honor   (Gr. *timē*, Lat. *honor*) Glory or respect: worship owed to God as the sovereign creator and redeemer (Ps. 96:6; Rev. 5:12–13). Also, the elevating of a person within the eyes of a community (1 Sam. 15:30; Prov. 29:23). It is also a commandment to honor parents (Ex. 20:12).

hope, Christian   The Christian anticipation of the future as the fulfillment of God's purposes based on God's covenant faithfulness and the resurrection of Jesus Christ as known by the work of the Holy Spirit in the church (Rom. 8:18–25; 1 Peter 1:3, etc.).

hope, theology of   A 20th-century form of Christian theology propounded by Jürgen Moltmann (b. 1926) that emphasizes God's future actions (eschatology) as the starting point for Christian theology so that traditional doctrines may be reinterpreted in light of God's promises and openness to the future.

Hopkinsianism   Modified form of Calvinism associated with the American Congregational minister Samuel Hopkins (1721–1803). Also called New England theology, it sought to reconcile traditional Calvinistic emphases on election and predestination with evangelism.

horologion   (Gr. "timepiece," "book of hours") A liturgical book used in the Eastern church that contains recurring portions of the ecclesiastical office to be used throughout the year.

hosanna   (Heb. "O save now!") Greek form of the Jewish cry used in the pro-

cession of the Feast of Booths (Ps. 118:25–26). In the New Testament it is associated with the triumphal entry of Jesus into Jerusalem on Palm Sunday (Matt. 21:9, 15; Mark 11:9, 10; John 12:13).

Host, consecration of the   *See* consecration of the elements

Host, sacred   (Lat. *hostia*, "sacrifice," "victim") The bread consecrated in the Roman Catholic Eucharist in the form of a wafer to become the body of Jesus Christ. Also, the bread of Communion prior to its consecration. The term recalls Christ as the paschal Lamb who is sacrificed (1 Cor. 5:7).

hosts, Lord of   (Heb. *Yahweh ṣebaʾot* [*Sabaoth*]) A frequent title for God, emphasizing God's Lordship and sovereignty over all creation and all creatures as well as God's rule in history (Ps. 89:6–8; Isa. 1:9; Rom. 9:29; James 5:4).

hours, the   Also called "canonical hours," "daily office," and "liturgy of the hours." Times when services of prayer are conducted. Traditionally these have been matins (with lauds), prime, terce, sext, none, vespers, and compline.

house church   Groups of Christian believers who meet in houses rather than in ecclesiastical structures (church buildings). They are constituted as "churches," in that they follow the practices of early Christians (Rom. 16:5; 1 Cor. 16:19; Col. 4:15; Philemon 1:2).

House of Bishops   A part of the national legislative body of the Episcopal Church in the United States in which each bishop has a vote. It chooses the presiding bishop for the church.

House of Deputies   A part of the national legislative body of the Episcopal Church in the United States in which each diocese elects clergy and lay representatives.

house of God   Term used by the Jews in the Old Testament for God's dwelling place or sanctuary in the Temple or Tabernacle. A term used by Christians for a church as a place of worship.

household baptism   A baptism administered to an entire household, as in Acts 16:33. Some see in this the likelihood that infants and children were included and this provides a basis for the practice of infant baptism.

household codes   (Ger. *Haustafeln*) New Testament passages that provide ethical instruction for various social pairings: wives and husbands, children and parents, slaves and masters (Eph. 5:22–6:9; Col. 3:18–4:1; 1 Peter 2:18–3:7). It was a form already found in Stoicism and Jewish Hellenism.

hubris   (Gr. "pride"; Lat. *superbia*) Placing too high a value on one's self or giving too much love to one's self (*amor sui*). Some theologians have regarded pride as the root of all sin since it sets the self higher than all else, including God who is, by definition, the "highest good."

Huguenots   Name for 16th- and 17th-century French Protestants. It was perhaps derived from (Ger.) *Eidgenossen* ("confederates," "conspirators"). The term was used for those who resisted the Guises (1562–94). Over 30,000 Huguenots were killed in the St. Bartholomew's Day massacre.

human acts   (Lat. *acti humani*) A term used in Roman Catholic moral theology for acts done by humans which involve the exercise of judgment and will. They contrast with "acts of a human" (Lat. *acti hominis*).

human beings   (Gr. *anthrōpos*, Lat. *homo*) The highest of God's created beings who, as created in God's image, have the capacity to be in relationship with God (Gen. 1:26–27) but who, as a result of sin (Gen. 3), stand in need of the redemption, restoration, and salvation found in Jesus Christ.

human condition   A term used to indicate the theological relationship of humanity to God as affected by sin and its results.

human effort   That which humans may do for themselves or for others, in contrast to the work that God does on behalf of humanity, particularly in relation to salvation.

human freedom   *See* freedom, human

human nature   That which constitutes the human person and is used to explain certain actions or behavior. In Christian theology, humans are seen to be sinful and separated from the loving relationship with God that God intends for them.

human rights   Those rights which humans have on the sheer basis of their humanity and not by any merit or demerit of their own. From the Christian perspective, these emerge from humanity's creation by God and God's love for humanity. They are at least minimal conditions for community life.

humanism   A philosophical or religious viewpoint that emphasizes human values, worth, and achievement. It is sometimes used in contrast to a theological viewpoint that gives God the place of supreme value.

humanism, Christian   An intellectual movement in 14th- to 16th-century Europe that sought to base education on the Greek and Latin classics, interpreted from within a Christian context. Theologically, the term indicates the high value that Christianity places on humans as created and redeemed by God.

humanity, doctrine of   The theological understandings of humankind's creation by God, sinful nature, redemption through Jesus Christ, and ultimate destiny in God's future reign (kingdom).

humanity, origin of   In Christian theology humanity is seen to have originated with the creative action of God, who established a relationship with the human race by creating humans in the divine image (Gen. 1:26, 27).

humanity of Christ   The theological view that Jesus Christ was fully human, possessing a sinless human nature.

humankind   *See* humanity, doctrine of; humanity, origin of

humiliation of Jesus Christ (Lat. *status humiliationis,* "state of humiliation") A theological term for the action of Jesus Christ as the second Person of the Trinity in becoming incarnate, suffering, and dying ignominiously on the cross to provide salvation (Phil. 2:6–8). His life and death are a prelude to his exaltation.

humility (Lat. *humilitas*) The proper valuing of one's self and proper love of one's self, in contrast to "pride."

Hutterites Sixteenth-century Anabaptist sect named for Jakob Hutter (d. 1536) They had origins in Moravia and stressed communal property ownership. They were also called the Hutterite Brethren and migrated throughout central and eastern Europe before settling on the North American prairies in the 1870s.

hylomorphism Philosophical view of Aristotle, amplified by medieval scholastic philosophers, that all physical beings are constituted by "matter" (Gr. *hylē*) and "form" (Gr. *morphē*), which together define a single entity. It is a way of understanding Roman Catholic sacramental theology.

hylotheism (Gr. *hylos* "matter," and *theos,* "God") The belief that the physical matter of the universe is divine.

hylozoism (Gr. *hylē,* "matter," and *zōē,* "life") The view that all matter is alive.

hymn (Gr. *hymnos,* "song of praise") A song of praise rendered to God. The term is used in the Septuagint to refer to the psalms and in the New Testament for Christian songs (Eph. 5:19; Col. 3:16). Hymns are used in services of Christian worship with both text and tune giving praise to God.

hymn of the month The practice of singing the same hymn during worship services for a designated period. The intention is usually to make the hymn more familiar to a congregation.

hymnal (From Gr. *hymnos,* "song of praise") A book of hymns. Hymnals may also include other liturgical aids for worship. Often denominations produce their own hymnals. There are hymnals used for interdenominational or ecumenical purposes. Also hymnbook.

hymnarium (From Gr. *hymnos,* "song of praise") Liturgical book used in the Western church with hymns for the divine office arranged according to the different rites of the liturgical year.

hymnology (From Gr. *hymnos,* "song of praise") The study of the content, nature, and history of hymns.

hypocrisy (Gr. *hypokritēs,* "actor") The outward appearance of conveying truth or righteousness that masks the inner state of mind or intention of untruth or evilness (Matt. 23:28; Mark 12:15; James 3:17).

hypostases, divine (Gr. "person") The members of the Trinity or Godhead: Father, Son, and Holy Spirit.

hypostasis (Gr. "self-subsistence," "substance") The objective essence of something (Heb. 1:3). Biblically, the term is used for confidence or assurance (Heb. 3:14; 11:1; 2 Cor. 11:17). Theologically, it was used in the early church for the three "Persons" of the Godhead, each as an individual reality.

hypostatic union Theological term denoting the union of the two natures, divine and human, in the one person Jesus Christ. It was defined at the Council of Chalcedon (451). It seeks to affirm the personal unity as well as the two natures. This reality is a divine mystery.

hypothetical universalism The theological view that Jesus Christ died for all people and that all are capable of being saved. In this view it is "hypothetically" possible that all will be saved ("universalism"), though this may not actually be so.

hypothetico-deductive An approach to knowledge that assumes a hypothesis in order to test its validity against data derived from an experiment.

Hypsistarians (From Gr. *hypsistos,* "highest") A 4th-century Cappadocian sect that would not worship God as "Father" but only as "All-Ruler and Highest."

I

I AM sayings A series of sayings by Jesus in the Gospel of John (6:51; 8:58; 10:11; 11:25; 14:6, etc.) that are seen by some as parallel to the disclosure of the divine name by God to Moses: "I AM WHO I AM" (Ex. 3:14).

icon/ikon (Gr. *eikōn*, "image") A representation of someone who is venerated, always on a flat or two-dimensional surface. Icons are used in the decoration of Eastern churches. They are to point to the eternal mysteries of the gospel.

iconoclasm (Gr. *eikōn*, "image," and *klaein*, "to break") The breaking of physical images in churches. Notably it occurred during the 8th century in the Eastern church and during the Reformation period, with the approval of some Protestant reformers.

iconoclast (Gr. *eikōn*, "image," and *klaein*, "to break") One who breaks images that depict God or Christ, usually as a protest against a perceived idolatry.

iconoclastic controversy Prolonged controversy (c. 725–842) over the veneration of icons in the Eastern Orthodox Church.

iconography The study or practice of representation through the use of images or pictures.

iconostasis (Gr. "icon stand") Screen (usually wooden) separating the sanctuary from the nave in Eastern Orthodox churches. It is covered with icons.

idealism (Gr. *idealismus*) Philosophical or metaphysical system that sees the ideas of the human mind as the fundamental means of understanding reality. The ideal is present in the real. Among theologians influenced by idealism were Pierre Teilhard de Chardin (d. 1955),

Paul Tillich (d. 1965) and Karl Rahner (d. 1984).

idealism, Berkeleian A philosophical system derived from the views of George Berkeley (1685–1753) that no material reality exists independently and apart from mental constructs or ideas. Also called "immaterialism."

idealism, Hegelian A philosophical system derived from the views of G.W.F. Hegel (1770–1831). The rational was seen as the real and the universe as containing an "absolute spirit" that is being realized through a dialectical process of thesis, antithesis, and synthesis. Also "absolute idealism."

idealism, Leibnitzian A philosophical system derived from the views of G. W. Leibniz (1646–1716), who posited the soul as a monad and argued that reality is personal and social, so that only selves or persons are real. Also called "personal idealism."

idealism, personal *See* idealism, Leibnitzian

idealist eschatology A view of the future that understands biblical apocalyptic materials to refer not to specific events but more generally to timeless truths.

ideas, divine Term used in Neo-Platonism for God's creative ideas about those beings whom God created.

ideas, Platonic The view of the Greek philosopher Plato (428–348 B.C.) that universals or pure essences exist as "ideas" and that physical realities are only copies or patterned after them.

identification with Christ *See* union with Christ

identity The sense of who or what one is. Feminist theologians point to the importance of women establishing a strong sense of their own identity so that they do not seek to derive their sense of who they are from men.

identity, law of   The principle in logic that "A is A." It is considered a basic premise for philosophical and theological reasoning.

ideology   The body of ideas from which one's thinking and approach is drawn, sometimes rigidly held and imposed. Liberation theology emphasizes the dominant role that particular political, economic, or social ideologies play in theological formulations or policies. These may be counter to the gospel.

idiomata   (Lat. "attributes," "properties of a thing") Attributes or properties of a thing that identify it in its individualness.

idol   (Gr. *eidōlon*, "image") A false god or representation of such a one that may be worshiped (Ex. 20:4).

idolatry   (Gr. *eidōlolatreia*, from *eidōlon*, "image," and *latreia* "worship") The worship of a false god or image of such, a practice prohibited by the law of God (Ex. 20:4–5). Figuratively, any obsessive concern can become an idolatry (Eph. 5:5; Col. 3:5).

ignorance   (Gr. *agnoia*, Lat. *ignorantia*) A lack of knowledge of God and God's will, seen in Scripture as sinful (Ezek. 45:20; Eph. 4:18; 1 Peter 1:14).

ignostic   A term used by Rabbi Sherman Wine in 1965 to call attention to his view that there is no empirical evidence for the existence of God.

IHS or IHC   A monogram from the first three Greek uncial letters of the name IHCOYC (*Iēsous*), "Jesus." Other explanations have been offered such as: *In Hoc Signo* ("In this sign [conquer]"); "In His Service"; *In Hoc Salus* ("In this [the cross] is salvation"; *Jesus Habemus Socium* ("We have Jesus as our Companion").

illocal presence   (Lat. *praesentia illocalis*) In scholastic theology, the presence of a finite spiritual being which cannot be placed in a defined point because it is immaterial. Yet it is limited or defined by a limit in its power and operation. Examples are souls and angels.

Illuminati   Another term for the Alumbrados. Also a term for 18th-century mystics in southern France, Rosicrucians, and some 18th-century rationalists.

illumination   (Lat. *illuminatio*) The work of the Holy Spirit in conveying to sinners the knowledge and grace of the gospel through the ministry of the Word of God. The biblical image is of being "enlightened" (Eph. 1:18; Heb. 6:4; 10:32).

illumination, spiritual   A general religious term for the light that frees the spirit from darkness and imprisonment. It was used in early Gnosticism and at other points in the Christian mystical tradition.

illuminative way   In mystical theology, the second of three stages of mystical experience between cleansing from sins ("purgative way") and mystical union with God ("unitive way"). In it, the soul is cleansed from attachment to things of sense and prepared to be spiritually illuminated or enlightened.

image of God   (Lat. *imago Dei*) The condition in which humans were created so that they might have a relationship with God (Gen. 1:26–28). Theologians have varied views of what constitutes the image theologically and the ways in which it has been affected by the fall into sin (Gen. 3).

image of God, formal   A term used by Emil Brunner (1889–1966) to designate the fact that humans are created in the image of God and retain that relationship to God, even after the fall and human sinfulness. This contrasts with the "material image of God," which refers to humanity's response to God.

image of God, functional view of the   The view that the image of God in humanity is not found in who humans are but in what they do. Humans are to "image" God.

image of God, relational view of the
The view that the image of God in humanity is grounded in the particular relationships within which humans stand. Thus it takes shape in Christian community and in the interactions of people, particularly through love.

image of God, structural or substantive view of the   The view that the image of God in humanity is inherent in persons as qualities that define their nature.

images, Christian   Art in general or, particularly, icons, which insofar as they represent spiritual realities, are intended to promote worship and devotion. They are not meant to be worshiped in themselves but to point to the proper object of worship.

images, veneration of   The giving of honor to representations of figures such as Christ, the Virgin Mary, or various saints. The practice has been of special significance in the Roman Catholic tradition.

imagination in theology   Theologians interpret the imagination as the ability of humans to construct meaning from images and concepts, and as a medium through which religious communities may be shaped through Scripture and tradition.

imago Dei   *See* image of God

imago Trinitatis   (Lat. "image of the Trinity") A term associated with the discussion by Augustine (354–430) of analogies from human experience that point to the divine Trinity, such as the human's experience of being, knowing, and willing—three dimensions of the one person.

imitation of Christ   (Lat. *imitatio Christi*) A devotional commitment to the conforming of one's life and actions to those of Jesus Christ. Also, the name of the spiritual classic promoting this devotional life by Thomas à Kempis (c. 1380–1471).

Immaculate Conception of the Blessed Virgin Mary   The view defined in the bull *Ineffabilis Deus* by Pope Pius IX (December 8, 1854) that Mary "at the very moment of her being conceived, received immunity from all stain of original sin, due to the merits of Jesus Christ the Savior of humanity." It is celebrated on December 8.

immanence of God   (Lat. *immanere*, "to remain in") The view that God is present in and with the created order. In Christian belief, God is not identified with the created order. It contrasts with transcendence.

immanent Trinity   The relationships among the three members of the Trinity—Father, Son, and Holy Spirit—in and with themselves.

immanentism   A belief in the immanence of God in the creation.

immanentist apologetics   Trends in 19th- and 20th-century French Roman Catholic theology that made humans' innate tendencies, as these are affected by divine grace and revelation, the beginning point for the exposition of the presuppositions of faith.

Immanuel   *See* Emmanuel

immersion   (Lat. *immergere*, "to dip") A method of baptism in which a person is lowered completely into standing water. It is practiced in Eastern Orthodoxy and by some Protestant churches.

immersionism   The belief in or practice of immersion as the mode of baptism. The term implies the conviction that this is the only proper method to use.

imminence of the end   The view held in the Christian church from the earliest times that the return of Christ and the end of the world may happen at any time. While the end may not be "immediate," it is always imminent.

imminent posttribulationism   The view of some Dispensationalists that the return of Jesus Christ to earth (Gr. *parousia*) may be imminent. It assumes that this return will be after a tribulation period which may be presently taking place.

immolation (From Lat. *in,* "in," and *mola,* "meal mixed with salt") A term borrowed from pagan sacrificial ritual, where the victim was first sprinkled with meal. In Roman Catholic theology, the offering of Jesus Christ in the Eucharist. More generally, and in Protestant usage, an act of sacrificial offering and thus appropriate for the death of Christ on the cross.

immortality (Lat. *in,* "not," and *mors,* "death") The condition of not being mortal and, thus, of being deathless, undying, or everlasting. Only God is inherently immortal. In Christian theology, those who receive eternal life, and thus immortality, receive it as a gift of God.

immortality, conditional The view that Adam and Eve, before their fall into sin (Gen. 3), would have had the capacity to live forever if they had obeyed God.

immunity (Lat. *immunitas*) An exemption to a civil obligation granted to a religious leader or group.

immutability, divine *See* God, immutability of

impanation (Lat. *in,* "in," and *panis* "bread") A view of Christ's presence in the Lord's Supper taught by Andreas Osiander (d. 1552), similar to consubstantiation. The elements of the Supper are believed to remain as bread and wine, but to include within themselves miraculously the body and blood of Jesus.

impassibility, divine *See* God, impassibility of

impeccability (Lat. *impeccabilitas*) Sinlessness or inability to sin. It refers to God alone, and in Christology to whether or not Christ was able to sin. The church has always held that Jesus was sinless (Heb. 4:15). Glorified saints and angels will be so enabled in the future reign of God.

impediment A term used in Roman Catholic canon law to indicate an obstacle to a valid performance of an act. An impediment may be grounded in church laws or the natural law.

imperfection (Lat. *vitium*) The condition of human sinfulness and thus of not being perfect in God's eyes.

imperialism Control of one state or country by another. In liberation theologies, the economic and ideological control of one group by another.

imperishable (Gr. *aphthartos, aphtharsia,* "imperishable," "incorruptible") Not subject to death, decay, or destruction. A term used by Paul in describing the resurrection body promised to believers (1 Cor. 15:42, 50, 52).

impersonal humanity of Christ *See* anhypostasia

impersonality *See* anhypostasia

implicit faith (Lat. *fides implicita*) In Roman Catholic theology, a faith that fully assents to a doctrine even when all the specific aspects or particulars of the doctrine are not understood. It is rejected by Protestantism as "blind faith" devoid of needed knowledge.

implicit Trinitarianism A term for those biblical passages which may indirectly point toward the doctrine of the Trinity (Matt. 28:19; 2 Cor. 13:14, RSV; Eph. 4:4–6; Titus 3:4–6, etc.).

implicit truth A truth contained within another explicit statement.

implied audience/readers An element in contemporary literary theory and in biblical interpretation that considers the nature of the audience presupposed by a narrative or story. It asks questions about the effects a story is designed to have on the audience, which, though not named, is "present" in the story insofar as the narrative is designed to do something with it.

imposition of hands *See* laying on of hands

imprecatory psalms Psalms, such as Pss. 58; 68:21–23; 109:5–19; 137:7–9, where the psalmist invokes God's curse upon the enemies of God or of Israel.

imprimatur (Lat. "let it be printed") In Roman Catholic practice, the authoritative sanction for a publication, usually by a bishop, who indicates that there is no basic objection to the work's content (*Nihil obstat*).

imputation, doctrine of (Lat. *imputatio* from *imputare*, "to reckon in") To attribute or ascribe in the sense of reckoning. The concept relates to sin, guilt, or righteousness, as when Paul indicates that through Adam's sin, death and guilt are imputed to all (Rom. 5:12–14), while through Christ's work, righteousness is "reckoned" ("imputed," KJV) to those who believe (Rom. 4:22–24; 5:15–21).

imputation of Christ's righteousness (satisfaction) (Lat. *imputatio satisfactionis Christi*) In the Protestant understanding of justification, God's action by which the righteousness of Jesus Christ is reckoned to or bestowed on the sinner (Rom. 5:17–18). This is an "alien righteousness" given as an act of God's grace apart from works and received by faith alone.

imputation of sin (guilt) (Lat. *imputatio peccati*) God's reckoning or regarding a person as a sinner on the basis of an action of another, particularly in regard to the imputation of the sin of Adam to all subsequent humanity (Rom. 5:12–14).

imputation of sin, conditional The view that the sin of Adam is imputed to subsequent humanity only when one personally sins.

imputed righteousness *See* imputation of Christ's righteousness

in Adam A term used to indicate the solidarity of the human race. It is the effect of an "original" sin as portrayed in the story of the sin of Adam in the Garden of Eden (Gen. 3). See Rom. 5:12; 1 Cor. 15:22.

in Christ (Gr. *en Christō*) A term often used by the apostle Paul to indicate the Christian believer's union with Jesus Christ and the benefits this brings for salvation (Rom. 8:1; 1 Cor. 15:18; 2 Cor. 5:17; Eph. 1:4).

in patria (Lat. "in the fatherland," i.e., "in paradise") A term to describe the place and condition of those who are blessed (Lat. *beati*) in heaven in contrast to those who are "on the way" (Lat. *in via*) or still "wanderers" on earth.

in via Those who are "on the way" or are earthly "wayfarers" (Lat. *viator*, "traveler") seeking the "city that is to come" (Heb. 13:14), in contrast to the blessed who are in heaven (Lat. *in patria*, Heb. 11:16; 12:22).

inability Theological term to describe the condition of human helplessness because of sin, so that one cannot do genuinely good things, and so that salvation must originate with God's power and not one's own. It is an emphasis in Reformed theology (Pss. 14:3; 53:3; Eph. 2:5).

inauthentic existence A term used in existential theology for the human condition of being unwilling to accept responsibility for one's own actions and existence, and thus, one's estrangement from the "ground of being" (Paul Tillich's phrase).

incardination A term in Roman Catholic canon law for the bond between a cleric and a diocese or structure for religious life. All clergy must have this type of bond and be under the supervision of a bishop or other ecclesiastical superior.

incarnate Christ Jesus Christ, the incarnation of the second Person of the Trinity, as he lived on earth and was known as Jesus of Nazareth.

incarnation (From Lat. *in*, "in," and *caro, carnis*, "flesh") The doctrine that the eternal second Person of the Trinity became a human being and "assumed flesh" in Jesus of Nazareth. Jesus Christ was the "Word made flesh" (John 1:14). The doctrine holds that Jesus was one divine person with both a divine and a human nature.

incarnation, dynamic   The view that Jesus Christ was not ontologically "God" but that the influence and power of God were operative within him to a high degree. A view of "Dynamic Monarchianism," an early Trinitarian heresy. The view is also found in some 20th-century christological formulations.

incarnational theology   A theology that affirms the incarnation of Jesus Christ as the human expression of the second Person of the Trinity. The term is also used to describe the idea that humans must represent Jesus Christ to others in the world.

incense   (Middle English, from Lat. *incendere,* "to set on fire") Fragrant smoke or the sweet odor of spices that are burning. Incense was introduced into Christian worship around A.D. 500. It is mentioned in Scripture in connection with prayer, which the smoke symbolizes (see Rev. 8:3–5).

incense, offering of   A Jewish offering made in the Tabernacle or Temple (Ex. 30:8; cf. Luke 1:10).

inclusive language   The use of language that is not gender-, race-, or ability-specific in Christian theology, worship, educational materials, and the rendering of Scripture. Language about humanity and God are particular foci so that a more accurate theological understanding may be communicated than through the use of gender-specific language when that kind of specificity is not actually meant.

inclusiveness   In matters of church government, the conscious orientation toward selecting representatives of many differing groups according to gender, age, race, ethnicity, etc., to serve in various capacities or in positions of leadership within the church.

inclusivism, religious   The view that one religion includes that which is true and able to bring salvation in other religions.

incognito, divine   A view of theologians who see divine revelation in its worldly form as always being in the context of ordinary events (indirect revelation). They teach that God's revelation in Christ must be such that there could be nothing special about the appearance of Jesus to indicate he was God in the flesh.

incommunicable attributes   *See* attributes of God, incommunicable

inculturation   Assimilation of something within a specific culture through observation, experience, and instruction. Theologically it is the process by which the gospel is adapted to a specific cultural setting.

inculturation, liturgical   The process by which liturgical forms and ways of worship emerge from the specific cultural heritage of a particular people.

incumbent   Term used in the Church of England to designate one who holds an ecclesiastical charge, such as a rector, vicar, or curate-in-charge.

indefectability   The claim of the church that by the power of the Holy Spirit it will remain ultimately faithful to the gospel and confess its faith between the times of Christ's first and second comings.

independency   A form of church government in which ultimate authority resides with individual congregations (Congregationalism). The term was used in England during the 17th and 18th centuries for Congregationalists, who were outside the Church of England.

independent churches   Churches that are not related to a specific denomination and that function in a purely congregational mode of government.

Independents   Seventeenth- and eighteenth-century adherents of the congregational form of church government (independency) as opposed to the established episcopal form of the state church in England.

indeterminism   The philosophical view that human actions are not determined by any other force than the human will.

Index of Forbidden Books   (Lat. *Index Librorum Prohibitorum,* ILP) Official list (maintained 1557–1966) of books prohibited by the Roman Catholic Church for reading or possession by its members.

Index, the *See* Index of Forbidden Books

Indian theology The construction of Christian theology using the categories and thought forms of India rather than those of western Europe.

indifference *See* adiaphora

indifferentism Living life without any important influence from one's (theoretical) belief in God. Also called "practical atheism." The term can also refer to the belief that all the differences among Christian denominations, or the differences that separate Christians from each other, are of no genuine significance.

indigenization The expression in local terms of what has come from somewhere else. This process in theology occurs when theological work is done in a given culture in a way that fully uses the intrinsic cultural forms, expressions, and resources of the culture rather than using extrinsic ones. Also called inculturation.

indigenous church A church that is native to a particular area and is controlled and structured by those who live in that place.

indigenous peoples Those peoples who are the original possessors of a land or nation and who have often been conquered or killed by oppressors who have taken over their lands. Liberation theology has emphasized the plight of indigenous peoples in many places throughout the world.

individualism Concern for the interests and rights of the self as more dominant than similar concerns for a larger group. Feminist theologians have pointed to an increase in positive values when women are able to see themselves as individuals rather than solely in relation to more powerful males.

individuality Philosophically, that which determines an entity's oneness in relation to the "general" (genus). The

Fifth Lateran Council (1512–17) established each soul's "individuality" against Averroism and the Neo-Aristotelianism which taught that humans only share one universal intellect.

induction (From Lat. *inducere*, "to lead in," "to introduce") A philosophical term for the process of reasoning that begins by experience or observation of a particular instance, which leads logically to the establishment of a general law or principle.

induction, ecclesiastical The final stage in which a person assumes an ecclesiastical office.

inductive method The use of probable inferences as a means of coming to conclusions. With theological doctrines, such as the doctrine of humanity, this approach would examine human lives and infer a teaching rather than beginning with a doctrine.

indulgences (Lat. *indulgere*, "to be indulgent," "grant a favor") In Roman Catholic theology, a pardon for temporal punishments that remain due for sin after repentance and the forgiveness of guilt. The issue was highly disputed by Martin Luther (1483–1546) during the Protestant Reformation.

indwelling (Middle English *indwellen*) A term that describes the presence of Jesus Christ or the Holy Spirit in the lives of believers. It was used by John Wycliffe (c. 1330–84) in his English translation of the Bible for (Lat.) *inhabitare.*

inequality The domination of one group by another. Feminist theologians have pointed to oppressive domination of women in patriarchal societies.

inerrancy, absolute The view that the Bible is written with full historical and scientific accuracy on all matters it affirms and thus is completely truthful.

inerrancy, doctrine of (From Lat. *inerrans*, "not wandering," "fixed") The theological conviction that the Bible is completely truthful and accurate in every respect about all it affirms.

inerrancy, harmonistic approach to The view that apparent discrepancies in various parts of the Bible can be brought into agreement ("harmony") with each other to resolve what appear to be contradictions or inaccuracies.

inerrancy, limited (From Lat. *inerrans,* "not wandering," "fixed") A view that the "inerrancy" of Scripture is restricted to certain elements, such as its theological content rather than its historical or "scientific" statements.

inerrancy of purpose (Lat. *inerrans,* "not wandering," "fixed") A way of describing the belief that the Scriptures will not fail to accomplish the divine purpose for which they were written.

infallibility (Lat. *infallibilis,* from *in,* "not," and *fallere,* "to deceive") That which will not deceive or lead to error.

infallibility, papal A dogma, adopted by the Roman Catholic Church at Vatican Council I, stating that when the pope speaks officially (*ex cathedra,* "from the chair") and according to certain conditions on matters of faith and morals, his teaching will not err.

infallibility of Scripture *See* Bible, infallibility of the

infancy gospels Apocryphal, popular stories of the birth and childhood of Jesus that were circulated in the early church period. They refer to the "hidden years" of Jesus and his family.

infant baptism *See* baptism, infant

infant Communion The practice in Eastern Orthodoxy and at some points in Roman Catholicism and other churches of giving the bread and wine of the Lord's Supper to infants.

infant salvation The view that infants who die before the age of accountability are saved by God's grace.

infidel (Lat. *infidelis,* "unfaithful") One who does not believe in the Christian faith and proclaims so.

infidelity Unfaithfulness or unbelief. Also the term may refer to the rejection of a religion or the violation of a vow, particularly in marriage.

infinite being A being not limited by anything. In Christian theology, God is perceived to be the only infinite being.

infinite qualitative distinction A phrase associated with the early writings of Karl Barth (1886–1968) and drawn from the thought of Søren Kierkegaard (1813–55). It distinguishes between God and humanity by indicating that God is infinite and holy whereas humans are finite and sinful.

infinite/infinity (Lat. *infinitus,* "boundless") That which is without limits or boundaries. Only God is truly infinite.

infralapsarianism (Lat. *infra,* "below" or "after," and *lapsus,* "fall") The view found in orthodox Lutheran and Reformed theology that in the order of God's decrees, God decreed to permit the fall of humanity into sin before decreeing to save some of humanity ("the elect").

infused knowledge A term developed in medieval theology by Alexander of Hales (c. 1185–1245) for direct knowledge given to a human or angel immediately by God. He spoke of it as a type of knowledge in Jesus.

infusion (Lat. *infundere,* "to pour into") The work of the Holy Spirit in animating new life (regeneration) through the gift of faith in Jesus Christ and by continuing to be present in the lives of believers (sanctification). Also, baptism by pouring water on the head (affusion).

ingeneracy (Lat. *ingenerare,* "to bear," "to bring forth") In Trinitarian theology, the view that God the Father uniquely possesses the quality of being ungenerated, while the Son is eternally generated and the Spirit eternally proceeds (from the Father and the Son, in Western theology).

inheritance The reception of that which one receives as an heir. Used in the Old Testament to designate Israel's reception of the promised land (Num.

34:2; Deut. 26:1; Ps. 105:11), and in the New Testament for reception of the kingdom of God given to those who are Christian believers (Matt. 25:34; Gal. 5:21; Heb. 1:14).

inheritance of Adam's sin   The view that subsequent humanity have in some way been affected by the sin of Adam (Gen. 3).

iniquity   A biblical term for sin that encompasses elements of lawlessness, injustice, unrighteousness, and wickedness (Ex. 34:7; Isa. 13:11; Matt. 23:28).

initiation   (Lat. *initiatio,* "participation") A term used in the comparative study of religion to indicate an introduction, usually by a ceremony or rite, whereby one is received into a community. In the Christian context, baptism and confirmation have been seen as initiatory rites.

initiation, Christian   (From Lat. *initiare,* "to begin") The means by which one enters into the Christian church, often referring to rites, ceremonies, teachings, and sacraments such as baptism and the Eucharist.

initium fidei   (Lat. "beginning of faith") An important theological issue concerning the way in which faith begins or the movement toward faith. The term can also mean the first act of faith. Theological controversies occur over the roles of God through the Holy Spirit and human desire or intellect.

injustice   The ethical wrong of not rendering to another that which is due. It is condemned by the biblical prophets (Isa. 58:6; Jer. 22:13; Hos. 10:13).

inner light   A term used by Quakers to indicate personal illumination that comes from their experience of God's presence and that directs their actions and lives.

inner person   A term used to indicate the sense of the transformation of the person who is redeemed in Jesus Christ, as in "inner nature" (2 Cor. 4:16), "inner being" (Eph. 3:16), "inner self" (1 Peter 3:4).

innocence   (Lat. *innocentia*) In ethical discourse, the condition of being free from any moral defect that would warrant the loss of a particular good, such as liberty due to a crime committed. It is in contrast to guilt.

Inquisition, the   An ecclesiastical court established by Pope Gregory IX in the 13th century to investigate heresy, try those suspected of heresy, and call them to repentance. The Spanish Inquisition lasted from the 15th to the 19th century.

INRI   The first letters of the Latin words inscribed over the cross of Jesus: *Iesus Nazarenus Rex Iudaeorum* ("Jesus of Nazareth, the King of the Jews"). The words were written in Hebrew, Latin, and Greek (John 19:19f.).

inscripturation   The process of God's revelation being formed as the Holy Scriptures.

insight   A mental illumination that enables one to find a solution to a problem or answer to a question. The relation of insight to theological method has been explored by the Roman Catholic theologian Bernard Lonergan (1904–85).

inspiration   (From Lat. *inspirare,* "to breathe in") That which moves humans to receive divine or supernatural truths, associated particularly with biblical writers in the writing of Scripture (2 Tim. 3:16; cf. 2 Peter 1:21).

inspiration, concursive   The view that God's power in inspiring biblical writers worked in conjunction with human personalities and did not override them, so that they wrote freely.

inspiration, dictation theory of   The view that the words of the biblical texts were suggested directly to biblical writers by the Holy Spirit and they recorded them as would a person taking dictation.

inspiration, dynamic theory of   The view that biblical writers freely chose the words they wrote in the Scriptures as they received God's guidance as to what ideas or concepts were to be recorded.

inspiration, illumination theory of The view that biblical writers received heightened powers by the work of the Holy Spirit so that they were able to write the Scriptures, without any direct influence of the Spirit on words or concepts chosen.

inspiration, intuition theory of The view that the inspiration of the Scriptures should be understood simply as a heightened sense of general religious insight.

inspiration, plenary The "full" ("plenary") inspiration of the Scriptures, in the sense that the whole Bible is inspired and not simply portions of it.

inspiration, verbal theory of The view that God through the Holy Spirit directly guided the exact words recorded by the biblical writers as they wrote the Scriptures.

inspiration of Scripture *See* Bible, inspiration of the

installation (From Lat. *installare*, "to put in place") The formal induction of a person into an ecclesiastical office.

instantaneous resurrection The view that resurrection bodies received for eternity are received at the instant of death rather than at a future "bodily resurrection."

instinct (From Lat. *instinctus*, "impulse") In ethics, the attraction toward the good that precedes a person's free decision to act.

institution, words of The words of Jesus, "This is my body . . . ," "This is my blood . . . ," as used in the celebration of the Lord's Supper (1 Cor. 11:23–26; cf. Matt. 26:26–29; Mark 14:22–25; Luke 22: 14–20).

institutional church The church in its present, historical form gathered into a fellowship and organizational structure.

institutionalized violence A term for the indirect forms of pressure that are inherent in the structures of society and thus also in human relationships. This leads to dominant society groups that have "power over" others who are the victims of these structures and the destruction they bring.

instrumental cause (Lat. *causa instrumentalis*) The means or medium that brings about a particular effect. It is distinct from "formal" and "material" causes. In "justification by faith," "faith" is the means of justification and thus its "instrumental cause."

instrumentalism The view adopted by pragmatic philosophy following John Dewey (1859–1952) that ideas are instruments to enable scientific and life problems to be resolved. Their truth or falsity is not important, since they should be useful enough to help solve human dilemmas.

insufflation (From Lat. *insufflare*, "to blow," "to breathe") The action of blowing air upon a person or thing to symbolize the Holy Spirit's actions. It arises from the Vulgate's use of the term in translating John 20:22 (*Haec cum dixisset insufflavit*). It is also associated with exorcisms.

integralism A movement in the 19th and early 20th centuries among Roman Catholics in France which opposed ecumenism and the approaches of modern biblical studies. It was denounced by Pope Benedict XV (1914) and its organizational structure "Sodalitium Pianum" suppressed (1921).

integrationist In feminist writings, the view that convincing, informing, and consciousness raising within various disciplines will transform education. Others argue for the separateness of women's studies as studies in their own right.

integrity (Lat. *integritas*, "soundness") A theological term to indicate the purity and uprightness in which humans were created in the "image of God" (Gen. 1:26–27). In ethics, adherence to moral principle and character as formed by a Christian conscience.

intention In ethics, the recognition of a conscious decision of the will to attain an end. In Roman Catholic sacramental theology, the requirement that a sacrament be administered with the explicit desire ("intention") to do what the church does (*quod facit ecclesia*) so that it may be valid.

intercession/intercessory prayer (Lat. *intercessio,* "a coming between," "intervention") Prayer offered on behalf of others (1 Tim. 2:1).

intercession of Christ (Lat. *intercessio Christi*) The work of the ascended and glorified Christ, who is "at the right hand of God," on behalf of believers (Rom. 8:34; Heb. 7:25).

intercession of the saints (Lat. *intercessio,* "intervention") The belief that saints in heaven can be called upon through prayer and are able to affect the will of God in relation to those alive. It is found particularly in Roman Catholic theology.

intercessory work of the Holy Spirit The work of the Holy Spirit for the good of believers, helping them to pray in their weakness (Rom. 8:26, 27).

intercommunion The practice of churches recognizing members of other church bodies for the purposes of permitting them to participate in the Lord's Supper.

interdependence of God A term used in process theology to indicate God's essential relationship with the world and involvement in it in contrast to an immutable and detached God.

interdict (Lat. *interdicere,* "to forbid") A term used in the Roman Catholic Church to denote an ecclesiastical forbidding of persons from participation in certain rites or sacraments yet without changing their status of being in communion with the church.

interfaith dialogue Mutual discussions for ecumenical purposes held among members of differing Christian groups or with representatives of non-Christian religions.

interfaith relations Ecumenical associations among differing religious bodies including various forms of cooperation and mutual service.

interfaith worship Joint worship by differing church bodies or by differing religious groups.

interim ethic A term from Johannes Weiss (1863–1914) and Albert Schweitzer (1875–1965), who claimed that Jesus during his life anticipated a rapid coming of the kingdom of God as a cataclysmic event. His ethical teachings were therefore meant as an intense preparation for it, since they would not be needed later.

interim pastor A pastor who provides pastoral services for a church after its pastor has left and before a new pastor begins to serve.

interiority A person's subjectivity, usually referring to capacities for self-consciousness, reflective judgment, and decision.

intermediate state The condition between one's death and one's resurrection. The term can designate views of purgatory, limbo, soul sleep, etc., as found in some theologies.

internal call *See* call, inner

internal communion The divine interrelationships among the members of the Trinity: Father, Son, and Holy Spirit.

internal grounds Evidences that lead to a conclusion as found within a concept or passage itself, in contrast to those which come from outside sources ("external grounds"). The term is particularly used in Scripture study.

internal testimony (witness) of the Holy Spirit (Lat. *testimonium internum Spiritus Sancti*) A particular emphasis in Reformed theology that stresses the work of the Holy Spirit as witnessing or testifying to Jesus Christ as Lord and Savior and to Scripture as divine revelation.

interpretation of the Bible The way in which the Bible is exegeted or understood. A number of ways of interpreting Scripture have been used in the history of the church.

interpretation of tongues, gift of In the New Testament, a spiritual gift of being able to understand and communicate what someone says in an unknown language or by "speaking in tongues" ("glossolalia," 1 Cor. 12:10, 30; 14:13, 26–28).

interreligious dialogue Discussions for mutual understanding held among differing religious bodies.

intersubjectivity The dialectical relationship between a person as subject and the object of one's research.

intertestamental period The period between the writing of the last Old Testament book (Malachi; first half of the 5th century B.C.) and the destruction of the Jerusalem Temple (A.D. 70). It was the period of postexilic Judaism. Others would designate the years from 587 B.C. to A.D. 135 as the period.

intertextuality (Fr. *intertextualité*) The transposition of one or more systems of signs into another so that new ways of communication and understanding may emerge.

intinction (Lat. *intinctio*, "a dipping in") The practice of dipping the bread into the wine as one receives the elements in the Lord's Supper.

intone To chant or recite on a single note.

intratextual *See* intertextuality

introit (Lat. *introitus*, "entrance") The opening act of worship in a worship service, often marked by music or singing by a choir.

intuition (Lat. "contemplation") Knowledge of something that comes without the use of the senses. Some consider this to be the means by which persons created in the image of God (Gen. 1:26–28) attain knowledge of God.

intuitionism (From Lat. *intueri*, "to look at") The view that mystical knowledge can be directly conveyed to the mind itself, as in a "flash of insight" which is more profound than reason or sense experience. In ethics, the view that basic moral principles or rightness are known intuitively rather than by any other discernment process.

investiture controversy (1075–1122) Part of the medieval conflicts between the pope and various emperors over control of the church. The conveying of symbols of authority (investiture) was the basis of a controversy between Pope Gregory VII (1075) and King Henry IV of England. The conflict continued until the Concordat of Worms (1122).

invincible ignorance A term in Roman Catholic moral theology that excuses sin on the basis of conditions about which one is unaware or which cannot be reasonably removed by prudent persons such as those who, because of their past history or upbringing, do not accept the church's teachings.

invisible church A term used particularly in Reformed theology with roots in the thought of Augustine (354–430) to indicate the company of those who truly believe in Jesus Christ and are the recipients of salvation (the elect), both those who are currently alive and those who have died.

invisible presence A way of describing the presence of God the Father, Son, and Holy Spirit with believers, even though unperceived by the senses.

invitation A call to prayer or to the confession of sins during a worship service. Also, an evangelistic call to receive Jesus Christ as Lord and Savior, confess one's sins, and become a Christian believer. The invitation at evangelistic services is often referred to as an altar call.

invitatories Verses recited at the beginning of a service of prayer. They usually form a prelude to the opening words of Psalm 95.

invocation (Lat. *invocatio*, "a calling upon") A prayer at the beginning of worship for God's blessing, or the use of the Trinitarian formula for the same reason.

Also, a prayer, the epiclesis, calling for the Holy Spirit's presence when the elements of the Lord's Supper are consecrated.

invocation of the Blessed Virgin Mary Prayers to the Virgin Mary.

invocation of the saints Calling upon saints in prayer, a particular practice in the Roman Catholic tradition.

inward nature One's true inner condition before God.

inwardness A concept emphasized by Søren Kierkegaard (1813–55), who maintained that Christianity must be internally, passionately, and subjectively appropriated to be genuine, and that its truth consists in its personal appropriation.

ipsissima verba (Lat. "the very words") A term for the exact words spoken by Jesus. The question is raised because the Gospel accounts appear in slightly different forms (e.g., Matt. 5:1–12; Luke 6:17, 20–23).

ipsissima vox (Lat. "the very words") The sense conveyed by the words of Jesus, rather than his exact words (Lat. *ipsissima verba*).

ipsum esse (Lat. *ipse*, "itself," and *esse*, "being") Philosophical term for God as pure being.

Irenaean theodicy An understanding of evil in relation to God along the lines of the theology of Irenaeus of Lyons (c. 130–c. 200), who believed in God's universal providential and redemptive activities.

irenicism (From Gr. *eirēnē*, "peace") Peacefulness and openness in a theological viewpoint.

Irish Articles of Religion (1615) The 104 articles of faith accepted by the Irish Episcopal Church, which leaned more strongly in the direction of Calvinism than did the Thirty-nine Articles of the Church of England (1562).

irrationalism A philosophy that does not value the place of reason. In existentialism, for example, that which stands against reason is valued highly.

irregularity In the canon law of the Roman Catholic Church, a legal obstacle or a permanent impediment that prevents the reception of holy orders or the exercise of holy orders already received.

irresistible grace (Lat. *gratia irresistibilis*) A view stressed in Reformed theology that God's grace as it works for the salvation of an individual will accomplish its purpose and will not be thwarted. It was one of the five canons of the Calvinistic Synod of Dort and part of TULIP.

isagoge (Gr. from *eisagōgein*, "to introduce") Preliminary study of the Bible in terms of its literary history prior to the study of its interpretation.

Israel The nation of Israel as descended from Jacob (Gen. 32:28), after whose twelve sons the twelve tribes of Israel were named (Gen. 49).

Israel, new A theological term for the Christian church.

Israel, restoration of The view that in the future the historic nation of Israel will be restored to a special place of prominence with God.

Israelology The study by some of the nation of Israel as a clue to biblical prophecies as they understand them.

Ite, missa est (Lat., "Go, this is the dismissal") The historic concluding formula of the Roman Catholic Mass for centuries. The most common contemporary English dismissal formula is: "The Mass is ended, go in peace."

I-thou relationship A term popularized by the Jewish theologian Martin Buber (1878–1965) in *I and Thou* (1923) and used by Christian theologians to indicate the personal nature of God's self-revelation.

itinerancy/itinerant preachers A common practice on the American frontier of ministers preaching in churches from place to place on an irregular basis. Itinerancy is also a term used to describe the system of assigned placement of ministers by bishops in Methodist traditions.

J A tradition source (Yahwist) in the Pentateuch that uses the name "Yahweh" ("Jahweh") for God. It is considered to be a Judean source from the 10th century B.C. and to have been combined with the Elohist, Deuteronomist, and Priestly sources over a long period of time to form the Pentateuch.

Jacobites Syrian Monophysite followers of Jacob Baradaeus (c. 500–578) who denied the "two natures" (divine and human) of Christ. Also, a name for many Roman Catholics who adhered to James II (Jacobus Secundus) after the 1688 Revolution in England when William and Mary came to the throne.

Jacob's ladder A dream of Jacob's in which a ladder extended from earth to heaven with angels ascending and descending (Gen. 28:12). It was a divine manifestation and was accompanied by a divine promise of land and many descendants (Gen. 28:13–15).

Jahweh *See* Yahweh

Jansenism Seventeenth-century Roman Catholic theological reform movement in which followers of Cornelius O. Jansen (1585–1638) emphasized God's irresistible grace in baptism and conversion and a rigorous morality. It was condemned by Pope Innocent X in 1653.

JB *See* Jerusalem Bible

jealousy (Heb. *qana'*, Gr. *zēloō*, "be jealous") An emotion that emerges in response to a perceived disloyalty or rivalry as hatred and envy of others.

Jehovah *See* Yahweh

Jehovah's Witnesses A sect founded by Charles Taze Russell (1852–1916), who announced that they as his followers would be the heirs of the Messianic kingdom. The "Russellites" deny the Trinity and the deity of Christ and hold strict moral views.

jeremiad A term derived from the name of the Old Testament prophet Jeremiah, the supposed writer of the book of Lamentations. It originated in Puritanism to describe a sermon that predicted woes because of the hearers' moral failures and that was designed to induce anxiety leading to repentance.

Jerusalem, new Also, heavenly Jerusalem (Heb. 12:22). The ultimate city established by the rule of Jesus Christ (Rev. 3:12; 21:2).

Jerusalem Bible (JB, 1966) The first English translation of the Bible from the original languages made by Roman Catholic scholars, appearing in both French and English editions, the latter in 1966. The second English edition (New Jerusalem Bible, 1985) avoided paraphrase more completely than the first and sought to reduce some of the preferences of English for masculine language.

Jerusalem Council Meeting of early church leaders at which it was decided that Gentile converts to Christianity did not need to keep Jewish laws or to be circumcised (Acts 15).

Jesuits (Society of Jesus) Members of the Society of Jesus founded by Ignatius Loyola (1491–1556) in 1534 and canonically established in 1540. The society focuses on teaching and Roman Catholic higher education. Its unofficial motto is "for the greater glory of God" (*ad majorem Dei gloriam*).

Jesus (Heb. *Yehoshua'*, "Yahweh is salvation") Name given to the son of Joseph and Mary who will "save his people from their sins" (Matt. 1:21).

Jesus the Christ is considered by Christians to be the promised Messiah who as God incarnate is God's self-revelation who brought salvation to the world.

Jesus, divinity of   The Christian belief that Jesus Christ was truly God and thus divine.

Jesus, historical   *See* historical Jesus

Jesus, humanity of   *See* humanity of Jesus

Jesus, name of   Veneration of the "name of Jesus," regarded as sacramental and as an effective sign of Jesus' power and presence.

Jesus Christ   Jesus of Nazareth as the Messiah and according to the Christian church the incarnate second Person of the Trinity. He was crucified on a cross and was raised from the dead by the power of God (Acts 3:15; 13:30). His followers ("Christians") worship him and seek to obey his will.

Jesus movement   An American Christian countercultural youth movement of the 1960s and 1970s that paralleled contemporary counterculturalism. It stressed among diverse groups a fervent evangelicalism and an emphasis on experience. Also called the "Jesus revolution" or "Jesus people movement."

Jesus of history, the   The portrait of Jesus of Nazareth derived from scholarly study of the Gospels using the tools of critical research. This has led some to speak of the "quest for the historical Jesus."

Jesus of Nazareth   The historical Jesus who is portrayed in the four Gospels of the New Testament as having grown up in Nazareth (Matt. 2:23; 21:11).

Jesus prayer   Prayer used in Eastern Orthodox churches since the 6th century and stressed in the Hesychast tradition: "Lord Jesus Christ, Son of God, have mercy upon me, a sinner."

Jesus Seminar   A group of biblical scholars that began meeting in 1985. Their purpose has been to examine all the sayings attributed to Jesus in the New Testament and in the documents of early Christianity in order to assess the degree of scholarly consensus about the historical authenticity of each saying.

Jesusologies   A term used particularly for 19th-century attempts to discover the "historical Jesus." These focused on the earthly life of Jesus with little consideration for the church's confession of his divinity as well as his humanity.

Jew   A term for one who is of Hebrew descent or who adheres to the Jewish faith, or both.

Jewish believers   Those of Jewish descent who have come to believe that Jesus is the Messiah (Christ).

Jewish Christianity   The Christianity found in the early period of the church among those churches whose members were primarily of Jewish background.

Jewish law   The law given to Moses as the legal standard in the nation of Israel, along with its subsequent additions and expansions by Jewish rabbis.

Jewish-Christian dialogue   Conversations between Jews and Christians with the goal of greater mutual understanding and respect.

Johannine theology   The theological perspectives found in the New Testament writings attributed to "John": the Gospel of John; 1, 2, 3 John; and the Revelation to John.

journal, spiritual   A recognition of the ways in which one's life has been guided by God, frequently recounted in written form in a spiritual autobiography.

journey, spiritual   A term used to describe the life of faith one lives throughout the years.

joy   (Lat. *gaudium*) A sense of extreme happiness and well-being related in Scripture to knowing God and God's actions and love, specifically in Jesus Christ (Neh. 8:10; Isa. 29:19; Rom. 15:13; 1 Peter 1:8).

joyful mysteries, the five   In Roman Catholic theology, the first part of the Rosary commemorating the Annunciation, Mary's visit to Elizabeth, the Nativity, the presentation of Jesus in the Temple, and the finding of Jesus in the Temple.

Jubilate   The name for the third Sunday after Easter in medieval missals, from the first word of the introit (*Jubilate Deo*, "Make a joyful noise unto God"). Also, the first (Latin) word of Ps. 100 (*Jubilate Deo*).

jubilee   The Old Testament prescription that in every fiftieth year (Lev. 25:8–55; 27:17–21; Num. 36:4), fields were to be left fallow, slaves set free, and debts canceled in remembrance that all belongs to God. Some see a reference to this in Jesus' Nazareth sermon (Luke 4:19).

Jubilee, Year of   A term used since 1300 in the Roman Catholic tradition for a Holy Year, in which the pope issues special indulgences for those who make a pilgrimage to Rome and do other religious acts.

Judaic   Pertaining to Judaism or the Jewish people.

Judaism   (Gr. *Ioudaismos;* 2 Macc. 2:21; Acts 13:43; Gal. 1:13–14) The religion and culture of the Jewish people.

Judaizers   Those in the early church who sought to impose the Jewish laws and rites on Christian believers.

Judaizing movements   Those movements throughout the history of the Christian church which have sought to mix elements of Judaism with Christianity.

Judeo-Christian tradition   A term to describe the general religious heritage of the Western world as it has been shaped and influenced by the ideals and values of Judaism and Christianity. The term has also been used as a polemical political slogan.

judgment   (Lat. *iudicium*) The evaluation of one's guilt or innocence. It is associated in the Scriptures with God's assessments of nations and people (Rom. 2:5–13; 1 Cor. 3:11–15).

judgment, day of   A New Testament term that refers to the action of God or the Messiah (or Son of Man) to redeem the righteous and punish the wicked (Matt. 10:15; 11:22, 24; 12:36; 2 Peter 2:9; 3:7; 1 John 4:17). Other equivalent terms

are "day of the Lord" (1 Thess. 5:2) and "day of Christ" (Phil. 1:10; 2:16).

judgment, final   *See* last judgment/final judgment

judgment, last   *See* last judgment/final judgment

judgment, particular   (Lat. *iudicium particulare*) The judgment of each individual at death by God.

judgment seat   (Gr. *bēma*) The place from which a judge's ruling is given. It is used in the New Testament to describe the judgment rendered by God and Christ (Rom. 14:10; 2 Cor. 5:10).

judicatory   An ecclesiastical body beyond a local church that conducts church business and/or church discipline such as, in a presbyterian system, a presbytery or classis, synod, or general assembly.

judicial authority   Ecclesiastical authority to enact church discipline.

judicial commission   A group appointed to exercise judicial authority or discipline in a particular situation or in relation to a particular member of a church body.

judicial union   A theological term used to indicate that in the Christian believer's union with Christ, the person's sin is carried by Christ while Christ's own righteousness is given to the believer.

jurisdiction   (Lat. *iurisdictio*, "administration of the law") The authority by which a church or church office holder makes decisions.

Jurisdictional Conference   An organizational body within the United Methodist Church that elects bishops for a large geographical region.

juristic view of sin   The view that sin violates God's law and is thus morally wrong, deserving punishment or satisfaction.

jus divinum   (Lat. "divine law") The law prescribed by God.

jus naturae   (Lat. "natural law") The law derived from nature.

just price   An ethical concept formulated in the Middle Ages to say that in economic transactions, a price should be sought that rewards the seller and satisfies the customer. The exchange thus should involve equivalent values to both. Thomas Aquinas (1225–74) based this on Matt. 7:12.

just wage   Payment of a wage that reflects the value of the work produced by an individual. The issue was dealt with in papal encyclicals by Pope Leo XIII (1878–1903) in *Rerum Novarum* (1891) and Pope John Paul II (1978–) in *Laborem Exercens* (1981).

just war theory   A way of morally justifying war by the theory that, despite its evils, war may be necessary and justifiable under certain conditions and within certain limitations. Conditions for entering and conducting wars are constructed. It differs from pacifism and the holy war theory.

justice   Classically, the concept of each person receiving what is due. Biblically, the emphasis is on right relationships and persons receiving a share of the resources of the society. Concern is expressed for the oppressed and their right treatment. Justice is related to love and grace.

justice, distributive   A classical distinction within the concept of justice referring to the rendering of justice to a person when that which is rendered does not come as a result of the person's having done anything wrong.

justice, retributive   A classical distinction within the concept of justice to refer to a person's receiving justice on the basis of having done something wrong. Thus a person receives what is due because of one's action.

justice, social   The recognition of the rights and obligations of individuals and a society. Full participation in the institutions and processes of society is a goal. Exclusion and marginalization become forms of social injustice.

justification   (Gr. *dikaioō*, Lat. *iustificatio*, "a reckoning or counting as righteous") God's declaring a sinful person to be "just" on the basis of the righteousness of Jesus Christ (Rom. 3:24–26; 4:25; 5:16–21). The result is God's peace (Rom. 5:1), God's Spirit (8:4), and thus "salvation."

justification by faith (Protestantism)   The theological principle, emphasized in Protestantism, that salvation comes to an individual by God's grace through faith so that to be "declared righteous," or "justified," or "saved" is on the (sole) basis of one's faith in Jesus Christ apart from any works of merit (Rom. 1:17; 3:28; 5:1).

justification by faith (Roman Catholicism)   (Lat. *iustificare*, "to justify") In Roman Catholic theology, God's making persons just or righteous and thus setting them in harmony with God through their participation in the sacraments of the Roman Catholic Church and by the gift of the Holy Spirit which is the new life principle of grace, expressed through love.

justification by grace alone   Slogan associated with 16th-century Protestantism and the view that salvation is a free gift of God's grace and cannot be earned or merited (Eph. 2:8–9).

justitia civilis   *See* righteousness, civil

Kabbala   *See* Cabala

kairos   Greek term for "time" denoting a special, significantly critical point in human history when God's will and purposes are carried out, particularly in the coming of Jesus Christ (Mark 1:15; Rom. 3:26; 1 Peter 1:10ff.).

Kairos Document (1985)   A document written by black and white pastors in South Africa (Sept. 25, 1985) that critiqued state theology and church theology in the country, one of which was idolatrous and the other ineffective in stopping apartheid. It proposed a prophetic theology, calling for conversion.

Kantian(ism) Relating to the philosophy of Immanuel Kant (1724–1804) and his followers. Kant synthesized European rationalism and British empiricism, asking what the human mind is able to know. He showed what knowledge is possible and how it is attained. Ethically, he stressed freedom and duty.

kataphatic statements (Gr. *kataphasis*) Positive statements indicating perfections directly ascribable to God in contrast to negative or apophatic statements.

kenosis (Gr. *kenōsis*, "emptying"; Lat. *exinanitio*) A theological term for the "self-emptying" of Jesus Christ in which he took the form of a slave or servant (Gr. *doulos*; Lat. *forma servi*) to accomplish the work of salvation through his death and resurrection (Phil. 2:5–11).

kenotic theology/Christology A theological approach that emphasizes the self-emptying of Jesus Christ, through which he relinquished heavenly authority to accomplish the work of salvation by his death and resurrection (Phil. 2:5–11). It thus strongly emphasizes the humanity of Jesus.

kerygma (Gr. *kērygma*, "proclamation") The content of the early Christian gospel message as proclaimed by the apostles. It centered on God's saving actions in the life, death, resurrection, and ascension of Jesus Christ (Rom. 16:25; 1 Cor. 1:21; 2:4). Faith and conversion are responses to the gospel.

kerygmatic Christ The portrait of Jesus Christ that emerges from the preaching of the early apostles in distinction from the "historical Jesus," the Jesus of Nazareth who lived as a historical person and about whom historical research can yield results.

kerygmatic theology A term associated with the New Testament scholar Rudolf Bultmann (1884–1976), who emphasized the New Testament preaching (Gr. *kērygma*) about Jesus as the Christ as the starting point for interpreting the New Testament.

Keswick movement A movement, begun in the 19th century, of evangelical Protestants in Great Britain and America stressing personal holiness. Open-air meetings were held in Keswick, England, that attracted large numbers. Keswick became a center for teaching about the victorious life in the Spirit.

Ketubim (Heb. "writings"; Gr. *hagiographa*, "sacred writings") The third division of the Hebrew Scriptures. Included are the books of Psalms, Job, Proverbs, Ruth, Song of Songs, Ecclesiastes, Lamentations, Esther, Daniel, Ezra-Nehemiah, and Chronicles.

keys, office of the The authority for binding and loosing or retaining and remitting sins. It is related to church discipline and also to the absolution granted by the priest in the Roman Catholic sacrament of reconciliation.

keys, power of the Also "keys of the kingdom." A reference to a saying of Jesus in which he spoke of granting authority (Matt. 16:19). The Roman Catholic tradition has interpreted the verse as referring to Peter's place as the primary apostle and first pope. Protestants interpret it as referring to the spiritual authority of the church.

keys of the kingdom *See* keys, power of the

Kierkegaardian Views or actions derived from the thought of the Danish philosopher Søren Kierkegaard (1813–55), sometimes called the "father of Christian existentialism." Kierkegaard linked truth to the subject who "exists" rather than to the object being considered. He emphasized the "leap of faith" as personal commitment rather than objective fact or beliefs.

killing The taking of another life, prohibited throughout the Old Testament (Gen. 9:6; Ex. 20:12) and reinforced by Jesus and the New Testament, where love is a primary ethical norm (Matt. 5:21; Rom. 13:9–10).

King, Christ as *See* Christ, Kingship of

King James Version (KJV, 1611) American name for the English version of the Bible authorized by King James I and produced by forty-seven translators, which became known as the Authorized Version and has had a very significant influence in Western literature and culture, as well as for Christian faith.

King of glory A biblical phrase emphasizing God's power and splendor (Ps. 24:7–10).

kingdom of Christ An equivalent phrase for "kingdom of God" emphasizing Christ's role as sovereign ruler (Eph. 5:5; cf. 1 Cor. 15:24).

kingdom of God God's sovereign reign and rule. God's reign was the major focus of Jesus' teaching (Matt. 6:33; Mark 1:15; Luke 6:20, etc.). Its fullness is in the future (Luke 13:29; 22:18) and yet it has also come in Jesus himself (Luke 10:9; 17:21).

kingdom of heaven An equivalent term for "kingdom of God" found in Matthew's Gospel (Matt. 3:2; 4:17; 5:3, 10, 19; etc.).

Kingdomtide As observed by some, a period of weeks in the church year that ends prior to Advent.

kings, divine right of The view that the sovereign of a nation is granted royal position and power by the direct authority of God.

King's Confession *See* Scots Confession

kirk The term used for "church" in Scottish Presbyterianism.

kiss of peace (pax) Mutual greeting by early Christians symbolizing their unity in Jesus Christ (Rom. 16:16; 1 Peter 5:14).

KJV *See* King James Version

kneel/kneeling To bend the knee in worship, humility, submission, or penitence. A traditional posture for prayer. It was required of penitents in the early church, who were called *genuflectentes.*

knowability of God God's revelation entails the possibility that God may be known. Varying views have emerged about the nature and extent of this knowability.

knowledge The organization of ideas or ways of coming to perceive realities. Philosophically, a number of views indicate the ways knowledge is obtained (epistemology).

knowledge of God Human awareness or nonawareness of who God is, what God is like, and what God requires (see Hos. 4:1; 6:6; Col. 1:10; 2 Peter 1:2). Theologically, the possibility, extent, means, and effects of a knowledge of God have been debated.

Koine (Gr. *koinē,* "common") The everyday Greek language used by inhabitants of the Roman Empire, and the language in which the New Testament was written.

koinonia (Gr. *koinōnia,* "fellowship," "participation in," "communion") The relationships experienced by Christians with God, Jesus Christ, the Holy Spirit, and among themselves in the early church (Acts 2:42–47; 1 Cor. 1:9; 2 Cor. 13:14, RSV; 1 John 1:3, 6).

Komvologion An Eastern Orthodox equivalent to the Rosary in the Roman Catholic Church, used when praying the Jesus prayer.

Kulturkampf (Ger. "culture struggle") A conflict in Germany in the 1870s, when nationalists sought to curb the power and claims of the Roman Catholic Church.

Kuyperian Relating to the work of Abraham Kuyper (1837–1920), a Dutch theologian and political leader who sought to bring his Calvinism to bear on the whole of Dutch society.

kyriarchy A term coined by Elisabeth Schüssler Fiorenza that literally means "the rule of master, lord, father, or emperor." She suggests that it replace "patriarchy" in defining the oppression experienced by women in that it points more directly to the complexities of the social systems, dominations, and subordinations women encounter.

Kyrie eleison (Gr. "Lord, have mercy") An ancient and frequently used liturgical prayer, to which the response is made, *Christe eleison* ("Christ, have mercy").

Kyrios (Gr. "Lord") The title ascribed to the exalted Jesus Christ (Phil. 2:11) in the New Testament and the translation of "Yahweh" in the Septuagint. It indicates supreme sovereignty over all creation and became a common designation for Jesus Christ (Rom. 1:7; 1 Cor. 1:7; Col. 1:3).

labarum Term for a military standard, especially that of the emperor Constantine, which bore a monogram composed of the first two Greek letters in the Greek word for "Christ," X (chi) and P (rho), intersecting. It became widely used as a Christian symbol.

labor (Lat. "work") Issues of choices relating to labor are ethical in nature. Among other dimensions are the dignity of labor, the right to labor, just compensation for labor, and the use of labor. In Christian perspective, one's "vocation" may be associated with one's labor.

Laborare est orare (Lat. "To work is to pray") An ancient Christian motto indicating the interrelationship of labor and devotion to God.

ladder, spiritual A term in Christian spiritual theology that points to human progress toward finding union with God. It has been variously conceived: as a ladder of love, virtues, or contemplation; or as relating to the Virgin Mary, the cross, or Jesus Christ.

Laetare Sunday (From Lat. "rejoice") The fourth Sunday in Lent. Also called Refreshment Sunday. Its name is from the first word of the medieval Latin introit ("Rejoice," Isa. 66:10). It is parallel to the third Sunday of Advent (Gaudete Sunday). Each is midway through the season and represents a brief lessening of the solemnity of the days.

laicization The release from ordained status and return to laity standing. Also the process of laity taking on ministerial functions usually performed by clergy.

laity (From Gr. *laikos*, "belonging to the people") A term for those persons who are not ordained as clergy. Biblically, it refers to the whole people of God (Gr. *laos*, "people").

laity, ministry of the The recognition that Christian ministry is to be carried out by the whole people of God and not solely by those who are ordained clergy.

lake of fire A place of eternal torment for "anyone whose name was not found written in the book of life," as portrayed in the book of Revelation (Rev. 19:20; 20:10, 14, 15).

Lamb of God A reference to Jesus at his baptism by John the Baptist, who said that Jesus "takes away the sin of the world" (John 1:29; cf. 1:36). It became related to the picture in Isaiah (53:7; cf. Acts 8:32; 1 Peter 1:19) and shows Jesus as a sacrificial victim who takes away sin through his death.

Lambeth Articles (1595) A series of nine theological statements produced by Archbishop John Whitgift and the strong Calvinists of the Church of England on the doctrine of predestination. These asserted double predestination and were incorporated into the Irish Articles of Religion (1615).

Lambeth Quadrilateral (1888) Anglican statement of faith from the Lambeth Conference of Anglican bishops to supplement the Thirty-nine Articles on four points: Holy Scripture, the Apostles' and Nicene Creeds, Baptism and the Eucharist, and the historic episcopate.

lamentation A religious cry of sorrow or mourning (Gen. 50:10; 2 Sam. 1:17).

land, theology of the Biblically, the recognition of the importance of "the land" to the nation of Israel in defining its identity in relation to God's promises. Theologically, recognizing the importance of faithful stewardship of God's creation. The earth and all land is held as a sacred trust.

Landmarkism A Baptist view of the church deriving from J. M. Pendleton, *An Old Landmark Reset* (1854), which emphasizes an unbroken succession of true Baptist churches from the early church to the present as marked by the practice of baptism by immersion.

language, religious The language of a religious faith, in particular the terms associated with Christianity. In philosophical theology, the nature and function of religious language is considered as well as its validity.

language games A term used by the philosopher Ludwig Wittgenstein (1889–1951). He claimed that all words ("linguistic signifiers") are embedded in language games which define a system of rules governing the ways words are used in a context. This means these "games" affect the way we experience the world, for one must know the "games" to understand what is being said.

langue (Fr.) A term used by the Swiss linguistician Ferdinand de Saussure (1857–1913) for a formal, abstract language structure. It is distinguished from *parole*, which is a concrete act of speech. Some contemporary hermeneutic theories make use of this distinction.

lapsarian controversy A controversy among 17th- and 18th-century Calvinists about the order of the divine decrees and about whether the decree of predestination precedes or follows the fall into sin. This gave rise to the supralapsarian (before the fall) and infralapsarian (after the fall) views.

lapsi (Lat.) Those who "lapsed" or "fell" away from their faith during times of persecution, particularly at the time of the persecution (A.D. 250–51) by the Roman emperor Decius. A controversy ensued over whether they should be readmitted to church membership.

last days The days prior to the end of history or the return of Jesus Christ (Acts 2:17; 2 Tim. 3:1; James 5:3; 2 Peter 3:3).

last judgment/final judgment A nonbiblical term used in Christian theology for God's or Christ's ultimate judgment of nations and peoples at the end of history (Matt. 25:31–46; cf. the book of Revelation). Other biblical images such as the "day of the Lord" and the "day of judgment" point to the same reality. Reward or punishment follows.

last rites A term in the Roman Catholic Church for the prayers and sacramental rites administered to those about to die. They may include penance, anointing, and viaticum (Eucharist).

Last Supper *See* Lord's Supper

last things (Gr. *eschatologia*, "study of the last things") Those events which will mark the end of human history: the second coming of Christ, the resurrection of the dead, the last judgment, a "new heaven and new earth." Otherwise put, these include death, judgment, heaven, and hell.

last times *See* last days; last things

Lateran Councils Five ecumenical councils held at the Lateran Palace in Rome during the 12th to 16th centuries (1123; 1129; 1179; 1215; 1512–17). The Fourth Lateran Council was marked by significant papal legislation including a doctrine of transubstantiation. The Fifth Council condemned the conciliar decrees of the Councils of Constance (1414–18) and Basel (1431–49).

Latin church   The portion of the universal church which has been marked by its use of the Latin language and recognition of the pope as the head of the church. Also used as a synonym for the "Western" as opposed to the "Eastern" church (Eastern Orthodoxy).

Latin Rite   Most generally, the Christianity associated with the Roman Catholic Church as represented by the place of primacy for the bishop of Rome (the pope), the church's liturgy, canon law, and spirituality in distinction from Eastern or Eastern Orthodox churches and their rites.

Latitudinarianism   A tolerant theological view proposed by some 17th-century Anglican leaders ("broad churchmen") who sought a wide latitude in interpreting the church's doctrinal standards.

latria   (From Gr. *latreia*, "worship") In Roman Catholic theology, the adoration due to God alone in distinction from the "cult of dulia," which venerates saints.

Latrocinium (Robber Synod of Ephesus, 449)   (Lat. "Robber Council") Term for the Synod of Ephesus (449), which acquitted Eutyches of heresy and thus upheld Monophysitism. Its decisions were later reversed by the Council of Chalcedon (451).

latter days   A future time of judgment anticipated by Old Testament writers (Jer. 23:20; 49:39; Ezek. 38:16; Hos. 3:5).

Latter-day Saints   *See* Mormonism

lauds   (From Lat. *laudare*, "to praise") Morning prayers of praise offered at sunrise to begin the day. With vespers at the end of the day, one of the two principal times of daily prayer in Roman Catholicism and Anglicanism.

Lausanne Covenant (1974)   A document that emerged from the International Congress on World Evangelization (July 1974), attended by 2,700 participants from 150 countries and led by Billy Graham (b. 1918). The covenant expresses a deep commitment to evangelization and has been a framework for mutual cooperation.

law   That which is prescribed to regulate behavior. The Old Testament law includes the Ten Commandments (Ex. 20) and the various ritual prescriptions found in the Pentateuch or the books of the Law (Torah). Theologically, law expresses the will of God and is to be valued (Ps. 119).

law, ecclesiastical   The law that governs a church or ecclesiastical body.

law, natural   *See* natural law

law, revealed   *See* revealed law

law and gospel   A formulation emphasized by the Lutheran Formula of Concord (1577) to indicate two primary ways by which God relates to humanity: through the commands to be perfect by obedience to the law; and through the pardoning grace of love in the gospel of Jesus Christ.

law and grace   Two differing ways or forms of God's relating to humanity. A number of theological views as to the relation of the two terms have emerged (John 1:17; Rom. 4:16; 5:20; 6:14, 15).

law of Christ   (Lat. *lex Christi*) Term used by late-17th-century Arminian theologians to describe gospel precepts as encompassing the law of life, an equivalent to the natural law known to Adam and codified in the Decalogue.

law of God   God's will as expressed through positive and negative commandments. Often used to indicate the Ten Commandments (Ex. 20).

law of Moses   (Lat. *lex Mosaica*) The moral law given by God to Moses to regulate the conduct of the covenant people, as found throughout the Pentateuch (Josh. 8:31–32; 23:6; 2 Kings 23:25).

law of nature   (Lat. *lex naturae*) The universal moral law, believed by some theologians to be given by God to all persons or accessible to them through the use of their reason in relation to the order found in nature.

law-gospel dialectic   A characteristic method and sequence of Lutheran theology. The demands of the law, which cannot be met by human effort, are satisfied by God's grace in the gospel of Jesus Christ.

lawism The view that it is possible to state ethical requirements in the form of laws while avoiding attitudes of legalism.

lawless one The figure of antichrist (2 Thess. 2:8).

laxism In moral theology, the view that, in a case where there is doubt about whether a law exists or is applicable to a situation, and if there is the slightest hint of freedom, one may decide against the law. This view has been condemned by the Roman Catholic Church.

lay baptism A baptism administered by a person who is not ordained by an ecclesiastical body.

lay elders Church leaders who in presbyterian forms of church government make up, along with the pastor, the session of a local church and are equally represented in other governing bodies such as synods and general assemblies.

lay investiture *See* investiture controversy

lay ministries Those Christian ministries carried out by persons who are not ordained as clergy by an ecclesiastical body.

lay preacher One who preaches but is not ordained by an ecclesiastical body.

lay reader A layperson who is licensed to conduct religious services in the Church of England.

lay spirituality The spiritual insights, devotion, and practices that have emerged through the history of the church from nonordained, nonclergy or lay persons who live the Christian life.

lay theology The practice or doing of theology by laypersons who are not ordained by a church body or, in many cases, have not had formal theological education.

laying on of hands The ancient biblical practice of placing the hands on the head of another person or persons (Num.

27:18; Mark 5:23; Acts 6:6; 8:15–17). It is used in services for healing, confirmation, exorcism, and ordination.

layman/laywoman *See* layperson

layperson (From Gr. *laos*, "people") Any person who has not been ordained as clergy by an ecclesiastical body.

LB *See: Living Bible, The*

leap of faith The concept, emphasized by Søren Kierkegaard (1813–55), that faith is not produced by rational thought but that it is a decision in the face of a possibility, and thus is a "leap." The idea was also used by Rudolf Bultmann (1884–1976), Emil Brunner (1889–1966), and Karl Barth (1886–1968).

leaven (yeast) An agent of fermentation used as a symbol for human corruption (Matt. 16:6, 11; Luke 12:1) as well as, by Jesus, for the pervasive power of God's reign (Matt. 13:33; Luke 13:21).

lectern (From Lat. *legere*, "to read") A stand or desk that holds the Bible for public reading.

lectio continua (Lat. "continuous reading") The practice of reading Scriptures in worship services in a continuous manner, the next taking up where the previous one had ended. Also, preaching continuously through a portion of Scripture, usually a book, rather than on different selected passages.

lectio divina (Lat. "divine reading") Meditative reading of Scripture that leads to prayer. Medieval monastic codes assigned daily periods of reading (*lectio*). They eventually expanded to include the Bible, biblical commentaries, patristic theology, and spiritual writings.

lection (From Lat. *legere*, "to read") A reading of Scripture that has been prescribed for a certain service of worship in the church.

lectionary (From Lat. *legere*, "to read") A compilation of Scripture readings from the Old and New Testaments for each day of the year for personal use or for church worship services.

lector (Lat. "reader") One who reads a lesson or portion of Scripture in a worship service.

lectureships Annual gatherings for the Churches of Christ denomination that feature classes for instruction, sermons, and information to motivate church members to greater zeal and activity.

legalism A relationship or ethical system that is governed primarily by obedience to prescribed laws or rules.

legate, papal A representative of the pope to a particular church or an international council or conference. The legate promotes relations with governments and is also called an "apostolic delegate." A "nuncio" is a type of papal legate.

legend (From *legere*, "to read") A story that has religious importance but may be of questionable historical veracity.

legislative authority The right of an ecclesiastical body to regulate beliefs or practices.

Leibnitzian Pertaining to the philosophical views of the German philosopher and mathematician Gottfried Wilhelm Leibniz (1646–1716). He saw the soul as a monad of a higher grade that is over those of lower grades. He thus avoided a sharp dualism in metaphysics.

Leipzig, Disputation of (1519) An eighteen-day theological debate between Martin Luther (1483–1546) and Roman Catholic theologians Johann Eck (1486–1543) and Andreas Karlstadt (1480–1541) held in Leipzig and focusing on the differences between Luther's emerging Protestantism and Roman Catholicism.

leisure (From Lat. *licere*, "to be permitted") The cessation of work and freedom from obligation. An ethic of leisure in a Christian context would focus on responsible pleasure and the recognition that God has given good gifts for creatures to enjoy.

Lent (Middle English *lente*, "spring," from Old English *lengten*, "to lengthen [daylight]") The period of forty weekdays prior to Easter, beginning with Ash Wednesday. It was originally a time to prepare candidates for baptism and became a period of penitence for those who have been baptized.

lesbianism (From Gr. *Lesbios*, Lat. *Lesbius*, "of Lesbos") Emotional and sexual relationships between women or those identifying themselves as lesbians. Some feminist theologians have focused on the societal oppression experienced by those in these relationships.

lesson (From Lat. *lectio*, "a reading") A reading from Scripture during a worship service.

Levellers Seventeenth-century English religious and political group led by John Lilburne (1614–57) that opposed monarchy, sought the leveling of all ranks in the army and a more democratic government, and advocated full religious freedom.

Leviathan Biblical term for a sea monster, probably the crocodile (Job 41:1; Ps. 74:14); used as a symbol of powerful evil (Job 3:8; Isa. 27:1).

levirate marriage (Lat. *levir*, "husband's brother") The practice of a man marrying his brother's widow as prescribed in the laws of Moses (Deut. 25:5–10).

Levites The descendants of Levi, one of the 12 tribes of Israel, who were set apart to attend to the duties of religious sanctuaries.

Levitical system The system of Jewish religious regulations and laws found throughout the Old Testament. They are found in the book of Leviticus and were the norms for national life until the destruction of the Jerusalem Temple and the end of actual sacrifices (A.D. 70).

lex naturalis *See* natural law

Lex orandi lex credendi A phrase, usually attributed to Pope Coelestinus, or Celestine I (422–32), meaning: "The law of prayer is the law of belief." From this derived the view that the church's liturgy is a norm of faith.

lex talionis   Latin term for the law of retribution or punishment in kind associated with the Old Testament prescription of "an eye for an eye and a tooth for a tooth" (Ex. 21:24; Lev. 24:20; Deut. 19:21; cf. Matt. 5:38). In the Old Testament context, this law restrained retribution, rather than prescribing or permitting it.

liability   (Lat. *reatus*) The theological condition that results because of sin including the reality of guilt and punishment.

libation   (Lat. *libatio*, "pouring," "drink offering") In a Lord's Supper service, the action of pouring the wine from a flagon into a chalice or chalices.

libel   A defamation of a person or the person's reputation on the basis of false statements. Ethically, it is a forbidden action on the basis of the Ninth Commandment (Ex. 20:16), against "false witness." It is countered in the New Testament by positive commands to speak the truth (Eph. 4:15) and to show love (John 15:12).

Libellatici   (Lat.) Christians who during the persecution (250–51) by Decius purchased a required certificate (*libellus*) which indicated that the proper sacrifice had been offered. They did this to avoid martyrdom and sacrificing to pagan gods. They were readmitted to the church after penance.

liberal evangelicalism   A fluid description of those who have identified their faith with the church's evangelical and orthodox tradition but who have also stressed the need to accept a modern scientific worldview in order to effect a synthesis of the gospel with modern knowledge.

liberal theology/liberalism   A theological movement, stemming from F.D.E. Schleiermacher (1768–1834), that sought to reformulate Christian doctrine in contemporary terms. It emphasized the use of reason, science, freedom, and experience while focusing on human goodness, progress, and the continuities between the divine and human.

liberation   Release from a form of captivity into freedom. A theological image for Christian salvation as release from the captivity of sin into the freedom given in Jesus Christ (Gal. 5:1, 13; 1 Peter 2:16).

liberation theologies   Various 20th-century theological movements which see the gospel as liberation from all forms of oppression—economic, spiritual, political, and social. The emphasis is on "praxis," or the practical ways in which God's call for the liberation of the oppressed is accomplished.

libertarianism   An ethical approach that emphasizes liberty instead of action governed by the keeping of rules.

liberty, Christian   *See* freedom, Christian

liberty, religious   The right and freedom to hold and practice whatever religious beliefs one chooses instead of being restrained by a government.

liceity   (From Lat. *licere*, "to be permitted") A term in Roman Catholic canon law for the status of a sacrament in relation to church law. A sacrament is licit or legal if the law's regulatory provisions for it have been carried out.

license   (From Lat. *licere*, "to be permitted") A stage in ministerial ordination, with varied practices in different denominations. In some, there is a period of probation after licensure prior to ordination. In others, a licentiate may carry out nearly every ministerial function.

licentiate   (From Lat. *licentia*, "permission") One who is licensed and accorded certain ministerial privileges and responsibilities.

lie   The conveying of that which is not true. Such deception is condemned by God (Josh. 7; Prov. 12:22; Acts 5:1–11) and should not be part of the Christian life (Eph. 4:25; Col. 3:9; Rev. 21:8), since God is truth.

life   (Old English *lif*, related to Ger. *leib*, "body") The condition of being alive, used in Scripture both of physical life and of the quality of one's relationships with God and others (spiritual life).

life, book of   *See* book of life

Life and Work   Term for the branch of the ecumenical movement concerned with ways in which the church relates to the contemporary world. A part of the World Council of Churches since 1948.

life everlasting   *See* eternal life

life history   A record of one's life through letters, diaries, and autobiographies. Feminist theologians see life histories as ways for women to acknowledge the social origins of their experiences, make themselves the subjects of their histories, and practice consciousness raising.

life in the flesh   A way of describing a life lived in opposition to God and for the gratification of one's own desires, in contrast to "life in the Spirit" (Gal. 5:16–26).

life in the Spirit   The Christian life lived in obedience to God through the work of the Holy Spirit, in contrast to the "life in the flesh" that would seek self-gratification as primary (Gal. 5:16–26).

lifting of hands   A worship gesture during prayers, singing, or praise most often associated with charismatic and Pentecostal groups and based on biblical passages such as Pss. 63:4; 134:2; and 1 Tim. 2:8.

light   An ancient symbol of God and life everlasting. It was appropriated by Jesus (John 8:12) and remains a symbol of Christ in Christian art.

light, inner   *See* inner light

light of glory   (Lat. *lumen gloriae*) The heavenly life in which full knowledge of God is experienced.

light of God   (Lat. *lux Dei*) A theological expression for God's truth, holiness, purity, and wisdom. God is the ultimate source of all light, being an eternal and self-sufficient source (Ps. 118:27; 1 John 1:5; cf. Rev. 21:23; 22:5).

light of grace   (Lat. *lumen gratiae*) A term to describe the knowledge of God as God is known through the experience of divine grace.

light of nature   (Lat. *lumen naturae*) The knowledge of God that is obtained through God's revelation in nature.

light of the world   (Lat. *lux mundi*) An image of Jesus Christ (John 8:12; 9:5) used theologically and devotionally throughout Christian history. The image was also used by Jesus for his followers (Matt. 5:14).

likeness of God   A term, found in parallel with "image of God" (Gen. 1:26) and generally considered synonymous, to indicate the human-divine relationship (cf. Gen. 5:1; Eph. 4:24; James 3:9). Some theologians, including medieval Catholic scholars, distinguished "image" and "likeness."

limbo   (Lat. *limbus*, "border," "edge") In Roman Catholic theology, a place bordering on hell and purgatory to which souls that have not been redeemed by grace, but yet are not reprobates or pagan sinners, go at death. It plays no significant part in contemporary Catholic thought.

limbus infantium   (Also *limbus puerorum*) The "limbo of children" where, in Roman Catholic theology, the souls of children who died without having been baptized reside. The existence of limbo, however, has never been formally taught by the church.

limbus patrum   The "limbo of the fathers" where, according to Roman Catholic theology, the saints of the Old Testament awaited their final redemption through Jesus Christ in his "descent into hell." Also called "the bosom of Abraham" (cf. Luke 16:22).

liminality   (From Lat. *limen*, "threshold") Term used by theologians, in light of sociological and anthropological studies, to describe rites of passage in life as especially "sacred" or "religious." This provides a way to study the roles and places of religious experiences in social structures.

limited atonement   A theological concept, found in Calvinist theology, which maintains that Christ died only for the elect, who are the only recipients of salvation. Also called particular redemption. It was one of the five canons of the Calvinistic Synod of Dort and part of TULIP.

limited inerrancy   *See* inerrancy, limited

linguistic analysis   A 20th-century philosophical view that the truth or falsity of statements does not relate to any "objective" realities but to the meaning of the language used.

linguistics   The science of languages. It is of concern for theology since theology depends on conveying the meaning and truth of statements related to God's revelation and religious experience.

lion   Symbol of power and courage in the Christian tradition. In Christian art, a representation of the forces of good often in conflict with a dragon or the forces of evil when posed with a lamb or a human in its mouth or claws. A representation of the evangelist Mark.

litany   (Gr. *litaneia* from *litaneuein*, "to pray") A form of prayer used in public worship, often with petitions by the leader and responses by the people.

literal meaning   The meaning of a text when interpreted in a straightforward, nonsymbolic way. Also called "plain meaning" or "natural meaning."

literal sense of Scripture   (Lat. *sensus literalis*) The straightforward, nonsymbolic, grammatical meaning of a biblical text. Also called "plain," "natural," or "historical" sense. It is one of the classic "senses" of Scripture, along with the allegorical, anagogical, and tropological.

literalism   The practice of interpreting biblical texts in straightforward, concrete, and nonsymbolic ways. The term may imply that the interpreter is not open to the possibility of any validity arising from another means of interpretation.

literary criticism   The use of insights from studies of various kinds of literature to interpret biblical materials.

literary-framework theory   *See* pictorial-day theory

literary-source criticism   *See* criticism, literary-source

liturgical art   Art forms of various kinds used in worship to enhance the worship life or devotion of a Christian congregation.

liturgical books   Books containing the liturgical procedures for worship services of a denomination or church group. These books and prescribed services have varying degrees of authority for use in differing denominations.

liturgical commissions   Denominational and transdenominational groups that seek to foster education about liturgics and better liturgical practices within churches.

liturgical language   The components, both verbal and nonverbal, that make up the actions of worship as the liturgy is carried out. Liturgical language is considered to be communicative, performative, and metaphorical.

liturgical movement   A 20th-century movement in both Roman Catholicism and Protestantism, each of which, in its own ways, has sought to make the liturgies of divine worship more meaningful for participants and to give a more prominent place to liturgical forms.

liturgical reform   Attempts to change current liturgical forms or worship practices to make them more congruent with church tradition, more appealing to new and different groups, or for other reasons.

liturgical spirituality   The sense of spirituality that emerges from corporate actions of worship using liturgical forms, including those of the sacraments and ordinances of the church.

liturgical worship   Worship according to prescribed forms, in contrast to that which does not follow a formal structure (e.g., private prayer).

liturgical year *See* church year

liturgies (From Gr. *leitourgia*, "work of the people") The various services of worship used in churches during different occasions of the church year.

liturgiology The historical and theological study of liturgy.

liturgy (From Gr. *leitourgia*, "work of the people") The service of God offered by the people of God in divine worship.

liturgy of the hours *See* breviary

liturgy of the Word In the Roman Catholic tradition, the part of the Mass that extends from the first reading of Scripture until the prayer of the faithful. It includes the proclamation of the Word of God and precedes the sacraments.

living being A reference to the life that came to Adam when God breathed the breath of life into him (Gen. 2:7; 1 Cor. 15:45).

Living Bible, The (LB; 1967, 1971) A paraphrase English Bible translation made by Kenneth N. Taylor assisted by a committee. It was based on the American Standard Version, with its primary goal being communication. It became the most widely used English translation published by an individual.

living hope The expectation of future blessedness for those who believe on the basis of the resurrection of Jesus Christ from the dead (1 Peter 1:3).

living sacrifice The offering of one's life as a follower of Jesus Christ. The image points to committing life to Christ's purposes (Rom. 12:1).

local church *See* church, local

local preacher A term used in Methodism for one who is authorized or licensed to preach in a particular place.

loci (Lat. "places") A term for the various doctrines of theology or headings in a work of systematic theology.

loci communes (Lat. "common places") Collection of scriptural references and their interpretations that together constitute a consistent body of Christian doctrine. The term is also used for systems of doctrine and is used by Protestant theologians.

loci theologici (Lat. "fundamental theological truths") A book of theology. Also used by Lutheran theologians to designate the major "places" (Lat. *loci*) or headings of systematic theology.

locus classicus (Lat. "classical passage") A particular text, usually in Scripture, that is considered a primary place from which a doctrine or a biblical concept is derived.

Log College A small school begun by William Tennent (1673–1746) in Neshaminy, Pennsylvania, to provide education for the Presbyterian ministry. It operated in the 1730s and 1740s, prior to the establishment of formal seminaries.

logia (Gr. "sayings") A collection of sayings attributed to Jesus and used in the Gospels of Matthew and Luke, sometimes identified with the "Q" (Ger. *Quelle*) source for the Gospels. Examples are Mark 2:17, 27; Luke 19:10.

logic (Gr. *logikē*) The study of reasoning principles and argumentation. It is used in theological discourse as a means of establishing the validity of viewpoints.

logical empiricism *See* logical positivism

logical positivism A contemporary philosophical movement associated with the Vienna Circle (1920s), which sought to rid philosophy of all metaphysical statements and to restrict it to only those statements which can be verified by empirical evidence. Also called "logical empiricism."

logico-deductive method A method of reasoning which holds that the conclusions of an argument will follow logically and necessarily from the premises.

logocentrism A theory of language and reality which posits that there is an ultimate truth or absolute meaning in texts which is the foundation of all other meanings. This view is said by some critics, such as Jacques Derrida (b. 1930), to be characteristic of the whole Western metaphysical tradition.

Logos (Gr. "word," "reason") In Greek and Stoic philosophy, the universal power or mind that gave coherence to the universe. In Christian theology it refers to the second Person of the Trinity, Jesus Christ (John 1:1), who as the creative power of God embodied truth and was God incarnate.

Logos Christology Christological understanding of Jesus that begins with the divine, eternal Logos and sees Jesus as its concrete, historical expression.

Logos mysticism *See* Christ mysticism

logos spermatikos (Gr. "germinal word") A term used by Justin Martyr (c. 100–165) to express the view that each human being is united with God by means of the power of reason and thus may know God apart from special revelation or could have known God prior to the coming of Jesus Christ.

Lollards (From Dutch, "mumbler") Term for followers of John Wycliffe (c. 1330–84) who questioned a number of the doctrines and practices of the medieval Roman Catholic Church. Subsequently they merged with the developing Protestantism.

longsuffering (Lat. *longanimitas*) The spiritual experience of Christians who endure difficulties and sufferings over a long period of time with patience (Col. 1:11; 3:12).

longsuffering of God (Lat. *longanimitas Dei*) God's patience and forbearance in enduring sin and its consequences among humans rather than bringing humanity to immediate judgment (Micah 2:7; Rom. 2:4; 9:22; 2 Peter 3:15).

Lord (Heb. `adonay, Gr. kyrios) God. The supreme being to whom all allegiance, obedience, and worship is due. It is also used by Christians as a designation for Jesus Christ (Acts 11:17; Rom. 5:1, etc.) and as an expression of complete commitment to him.

Lord of hosts *See* hosts, Lord of

Lord's Day A designation for the first day of the week (Rev. 1:10), celebrated by Christians as the day of resurrection of Jesus Christ and thus the day of worship—Sunday.

Lord's Prayer The prayer taught by Jesus to his disciples and recognized by the Christian church as a model prayer (Matt. 6:9–13; Luke 11:2–4). It is also called the "Our Father" or Pater Noster and is used by the church in public worship and by Christians in private devotions.

Lord's Supper The sacrament of Communion, or the Eucharist. It celebrates the death of Christ, his presence with the church, and his future kingdom (reign). It was instituted by Jesus (1 Cor. 11: 23–26) at the Last Supper, the last meal which Jesus shared with his disciples before his crucifixion.

Lordship of Christ *See* Christ, Lordship of

love (Gr. *agapē,* as distinguished from *erōs* and *philia;* Lat. *amor*) Strong feeling of personal affection, care, and desire for the well-being of others. It is a primary characteristic of God's nature (1 John 4:8, 16) and the supreme expression of Christian faith and action (1 Cor. 13:13; Gal. 5:14; Eph. 5:2; 1 John 4:7–21).

love feast A worship service centering around a common meal reminiscent of the meals shared by early Christians ("agape [love] feasts") where the Lord's Supper was celebrated. Some denominations such as the Church of the Brethren may also include foot washing in their celebration.

love of God *See* God, love of

lovingkindness An English translation in the KJV and the American Standard Version of the Heb. *ḥesed* (Lat. *misericordia*). This rich term describes God's covenant loyalty, mercy, and steadfast love (Ex. 34:6; Deut. 7:12; Ps. 106:1).

Low Church A term used in Anglicanism, and more generally, to denote churches that do not emphasize ritual, liturgy, the sacraments, and historical traditions.

Low Mass (Lat. *missa lecta*) Traditional term in Roman Catholicism for a service of the Eucharist that is recited rather than sung by a priest and choir (High Mass).

Low Sunday A term used in the English church for the Sunday after Easter. It is also called Quasimodo Sunday (from the opening words of the Roman Catholic Mass). It is called "low" in contrast to the "high" feast of Easter. Since Vatican II (1962–65), it is called the Second Sunday of Easter.

lower criticism Textual criticism, a form of biblical research concerned with establishing the best and most accurate manuscript text of the Bible in the original languages.

Lucifer (Lat. "light bringer") A term which is used in Isa. 14:12–14 (KJV, NRSV: "Day Star") for the king of Babylon, but which has been used through Christian history to refer to Satan (cf. Rev. 12:7–9).

Lullism Followers of the philosophy of Ramón (Raymond) Lull (c. 1232–1316), a Franciscan missionary who worked among Muslims in North Africa. Lull was a philosopher who believed that all truth could be deduced from basic principles. He followed Augustine (354–430) while rejecting Averroism, and he studied cabalism. His profound mysticism presaged Teresa of Ávila (1515–82) and John of the Cross (1542–91).

lumen fidei (Lat. "light of faith") Revealed theological truth that is known only by God's special revelation and cannot be known from any other source. Examples include God as triune, the divinity of Christ, and creation *ex nihilo*. It was emphasized by Thomas Aquinas (1225–74).

lumen gloriae A term used in medieval Scholastic theology for the supernatural perfecting of the human power of knowing. The intellect gains an immediate vi-

sion of the divine essence (the beatific vision). It was used by Bonaventure (1221–74) and Aquinas (1225–74). See Ps. 36:9; Rev. 22:5.

lumen gratiae (Lat. "light of grace") God's direct gift of faith that cannot be attained by human reason.

lumen naturale rationis (Lat. "natural light of reason") The view that some knowledge of God may be attained by the use of human reason without the assistance of divine revelation.

luna/lunette (Lat. "moon") A circular receptacle within a monstrance that holds the consecrated Host in an upright position so it may be seen and venerated.

Lundensian school A 20th-century theological movement related to the University of Lund that emphasized love as the primary theological theme.

lust (Lat. *luxuria*) One of the "seven deadly sins" that relates to the mortal sin of improper sexual desire or indulgence.

Lutheran A member of the Lutheran communion, the Protestant denomination that emerged from the work of Martin Luther (1483–1546).

Lutheran scholastics Seventeenth-century Lutheran theologians who used "scholastic" methods, reminiscent of the methods of medieval theologians, to produce detailed and precise theological systems. Prominent were Martin Chemnitz (1522–86), John Gerhard (1582–1637), Abraham Calov (1612–86), and J. A. Quenstedt (1617–88).

Lutheranism The beliefs, practices, and churches that have been derived from the teachings and actions of Martin Luther (1483–1546). Its confessional standards are found in the *Book of Concord* (1580), particularly the Augsburg Confession (1530).

LXX A designation for the Septuagint version of the Old Testament, prepared during the 3d century B.C. It derives from the legend that the translation from Hebrew into Greek was made in seventy days by seventy scholars.

lying   Not conveying the truth. Biblically and ethically, lying is regarded as sinful (Col. 3:9) since God does not lie (Titus 1:2) and God forbids it (Ex. 20:16).

Lyons, Councils of   The 13th and 14th ecumenical church councils, held in Lyons, France. Lyons I (1245) considered immorality, the Greek schism, and Emperor Frederick II's break with the church. Lyons II (1274) defined the double procession of the Holy Spirit and gained a short union with the Greek Church.

Macedonianism   A sect deriving from Macedonius (d. 362), an Arian bishop of Constantinople, who denied that the Holy Spirit was divine. Also called the Pneumatomachi.

Madonna   (Ital. "my lady") The Virgin Mary, or a representation of Mary, usually with the child Jesus. The image appears in various forms of art such as painting, stained glass, sculpture, and medals.

Magi   (Gr. *magoi,* "sages," "wise persons") Name for the astrologers who followed the star to worship the infant Jesus (Matt. 2:1–12). Traditionally called the "wise men."

Magi, Adoration of the   The feast of Epiphany (January 6), which commemorates the homage of the Magi to the infant Jesus (Matt. 2:11) and represents God's self-revelation to the whole world.

magic   (Gr. *magikē*) The use of charms, spells, and rituals to control or influence events, in the belief that these elements may induce a supernatural being to act. The relation of magic to Christianity has a long history.

Magisterial Reformation   A term to refer to the pattern by which churches were established and supported by civil authority. It contrasts with the "Radical Reformation," in which church and state were completely separated.

magisterium   (Lat. *magister,* "master") The teaching authority of the church, especially as understood in Roman Catholic theology as resting in the pope and the bishops.

magistrate/magistracy   (From Lat. *magister,* "master") Those who are public officers and carry out governmental functions. Ethical issues about the duties of magistrates in relation to the law of God, to freedom of conscience, and other questions in pluralist societies lead to many significant concerns.

Magnificat   The first Latin word in the Vulgate (*Magnificat anima mea,* "My soul magnifies") of the song of Mary (Luke 1:46–55) at the greeting by her cousin Elizabeth, who says that Mary will be the mother of the Messiah.

mainline/mainstream churches   A term with varying meanings clustering around those Protestant denominations which have historically been major forces in American religious life. More generally it may include Roman Catholicism and Judaism. Emphasis on tradition and "standard brand religion" may also be meant.

major orders   In Roman Catholicism, the higher ranks of the ordained clergy, including the bishops, priests, deacons, and, formerly, subdeacons (abolished 1972).

Majoristic controversy   Sixteenth-century German Lutheran controversy over the relation of good works to salvation in which Georg Major (1502–74) taught the necessity for good works while also maintaining the doctrine of justification by faith.

maker A term used of God as creator, particularly in the opening of the Apostles' Creed: "I believe in God . . . , Maker of heaven and earth" (see Gen. 1:1).

malediction (Lat. "curse") A curse. The opposite of "benediction."

mammon (Aramaic "riches," Gr. *mamōnas*) Riches or possessions, which according to the Gospels can become dominant in human life and take God's rightful place. It is the term used in the KJV translation of Matt. 6:24 and Luke 16:13 and is now not commonly used in English.

man, doctrine of *See* humanity, doctrine of

man, natural Description of the human condition after the fall into sin (Gen. 3) and apart from salvation in Jesus Christ.

Man, Son of *See* Son of Man

Mandaeism A form of Gnosticism in the 1st and 2d centuries that combined elements of Persian dualism, astrology, Platonism, and Judaism.

mandorla (Ital. "almond") An oval halo in Christian art surrounding some representations of God, Christ, or the Virgin Mary and symbolizing divinity and holiness.

manducatio impiorum (indigna/indignorum) (Lat. *manducatio,* "eating") An issue of disagreement in 16th- and 17th-century Lutheran and Reformed theology as to whether those who are "impious" or "unworthy" receive Christ in the sacrament of the Lord's Supper. The Lutherans affirmed it; the Reformed denied it. Both agreed that the "unworthy" received judgment.

manducation (Lat. *manducatio,* "eating") In sacramental theology, the view that the body of Jesus Christ is actually eaten in the Lord's Supper.

Manichaeism A Persian religious movement founded by Mani (c. 216–76) that featured a dualism of good and evil expressed in a perpetual struggle between kingdoms of light and darkness. It exalted asceticism and advocated celibacy as means for salvation and became a major religious force.

manifestation (Translation of Lat. *patefactio,* "disclosure") A term for God's self-disclosure in Jesus Christ, nearly synonymous with "epiphany." Contrasts with "revelation," God's scriptural or verbal impartation of knowledge.

manna (Heb. *man,* Gr. *manna*) Food from heaven providentially provided by God for Israel in the wilderness (Ex. 16:4–36; Num. 11:4–9). It is used in the New Testament as a "type" or foreshadowing of Jesus Christ as the living bread from heaven (John 6:31–65) and in the Lord's Supper (1 Cor. 10:3).

manse (From Lat. *manere,* "to dwell") A house owned by a church to be used as the residence of the minister.

manuale (Lat. "something that can be held in the hand") A medieval term for a book used for administering the sacraments.

manuscripts of the Bible The early written texts of Scripture, copied by hand and varying in wording.

Maranatha An Aramaic expression meaning "Our Lord, come," transliterated into Greek (1 Cor. 16:22). It is understood either as an indicative or an exhortation (Rev. 22:20).

Marburg Articles (1529) The outcome of the Marburg Colloquy between German and Swiss Protestant reformers. Of 15 articles, Luther, Melanchthon, and Oecolampadius agreed with Zwingli and Bucer on 14 (or 14½), but not on the issue of whether or how Christ is present in the Eucharist.

Marcionism/Marcionites The teachings of Marcion (d. c. 160), which featured a sharp disjunction between the "God of wrath" of the Old Testament and the "God of love" of the New Testament and the view that Christ never became flesh. In Marcionism, Christianity replaces Judaism. Its canon was Luke's Gospel and ten Pauline letters.

Mardi Gras *See* Shrove Tuesday

marginality The social and material reality of those who cannot participate in the mainstream of society because they do not have adequate resources or opportunities.

Marian Referring to Mary, the mother of Jesus.

Marian devotion Devotional practices of individuals and groups that focus on honoring the Virgin Mary, particularly within the Roman Catholic tradition. Mary is viewed as the "mother of God" and as a "type" and "mother" of the church who exemplifies faith and hope.

Marian exile The exile of many English Protestants to the European continent at the accession of Mary Tudor ("Bloody Mary") to the English throne (1553). Leading centers were Bern, Zurich, and Frankfurt. Exiles in Geneva produced the Geneva Bible (1560). Many exiles returned when Elizabeth I became Queen in 1558.

Mariolatry The worship (Lat. *latria*) of Mary, the mother of Jesus. In the Roman Catholic tradition, Mary may receive *hyperdulia* (Lat., "special veneration") but worship (*latria*) is due only to God.

Mariology Theological teachings about Mary the mother of Jesus, found particularly within the Roman Catholic tradition.

mark of the beast A phrase in the book of Revelation (see 13:16–18; 14:11; 16:2; 19:20; 20:4), associated with the "number of the beast" (Rev. 13:18), and symbolizing the evil forces or persons who oppose God.

Markan hypothesis The theory held by many biblical scholars that the Gospel of Mark was the earliest of the four Gospels to be written.

marks of the church (Lat. *notae ecclesiae*) The "notes" of the church as found in the Nicene Creed are the church as "one, holy, catholic, and apostolic" (or unity, holiness, catholicity, and apostolicity). Protestant Reformers emphasized the marks as preaching the Word and right administration of the sacraments.

Maronites A term for (mainly) Lebanese Christians who originated from St. Maro (350–433). They became a separate ecclesiastical community in the 7th century under John Maron. They were Monothelite Christians, excommunicated by the Third Council of Constantinople (680). Now they are led by the Patriarch of Antioch and the East, who is approved by the pope.

marriage The joining of a man and a woman in a relationship of mutual love, fidelity, and commitment that may be sanctioned by the church (and state) and that in Christian contexts is a spiritual as well as physical union to be blessed by God.

marriage, spiritual A term for the highest aspect of contemplative prayer experienced by mystics. The marriage image points to the union of the soul with God.

marriage supper (feast) of the Lamb An image of the consummation of the reign of God (Rev. 19:7–9).

Marrow controversy An 18th-century controversy in the Church of Scotland over rival theological views of legalism and merit in contrast to God's grace in Jesus Christ.

martyr (Gr. "witness") One who witnesses to beliefs by dying for them. A long line of Christian martyrs begins with Stephen (Acts 7:59), and for some martyrdom represents the highest form of the imitation of Jesus Christ. It has been called the "baptism of blood."

martyrium A church built on top of the relics or tomb of a martyr.

martyrology The study of martyrs and their deaths. Also a record of martyrs and their lives. These are celebrated in the church by different feast days.

Marxism   The ideology that emerged from the works of the German social philosopher Karl Marx (1818–83). The teachings of G.W.F. Hegel (1770–1831) about the dialectical nature of history were interpreted in a materialistic, deterministic way to form dialectical materialism.

Mary, Assumption of the Blessed Virgin   The Roman Catholic dogma promulgated by Pope Pius XII (1950) which teaches that the Virgin Mary, the mother of Jesus, did not die but ascended in body and soul to heaven.

Mary, Virgin   The mother of Jesus (Matt. 1:18–25; Luke 1:43). In the Roman Catholic tradition, Mary is regarded as the most perfectly redeemed person and thus as a model of all those who are redeemed.

Mass   (Lat. *missa,* from *mittere,* "to send") The liturgy and worship service in which the Eucharist is celebrated and, more generally, the whole Roman Catholic service of worship. Traditionally, *Ite, missa est* ("Go, this is the dismissal") was said at the end of the service.

Mass, High   (Lat. *missa sollemnis,* "sung mass") The celebration of the Eucharist in the Roman Catholic Church with a deacon and subdeacon assisting the primary celebrant, accompanied by a choir, servers, and incense. The term is no longer used in the Roman Catholic Church.

Mass, Low   A term used in the Roman Catholic Church for a simplified Eucharist that was said and not sung (as was the "High Mass"). The term is no longer used.

mass evangelism   The practice of preaching the Christian gospel to large gatherings of people with the explicit purpose of seeking conversions to Jesus Christ. It is part of the larger "revivalism" tradition and is sometimes called "crusade evangelism."

material principle   That which is regarded as the church's central doctrine. The 16th-century Lutheran Reformers considered justification by faith to be the material principle of the Christian faith and the Scriptures to be the formal principle.

materialism   The philosophical view that matter is the ultimate reality from which all else emerges. It thus may be verified by the senses and investigated by scientific procedures. It is in opposition to idealism and all spiritual explanations of what is real.

matins   (Lat. *matutinus,* "of the morning") A service for the morning hours. In Anglicanism it is the service of morning prayer. In Roman Catholicism it is the first of the canonical hours that comprise the divine office, being divided into three psalms, three lessons, and three responses.

matrimony   (From Lat. *matrimonium,* "wedlock," "marriage") The act or state of marriage, regarded as a sacrament within the Roman Catholic tradition.

matter   That which is perceptible and physical. It has been contrasted to "form" in the history of philosophy and in theological discussions.

Matthew's Bible (1537)   An English translation of the Bible that was a revision of William Tyndale's work and included parts of Miles Coverdale's Old Testament translation along with interpretive notes drawn from Conrad Pellican (1478–1556).

matzo   The Hebrew term for unleavened bread. It is eaten by the Jews during the Passover celebration and represents their liberation and redemption by God.

Maundy Thursday   (From Lat. *mandatum,* "mandate," "commandment") Holy Thursday, before Good Friday, when Jesus commanded his disciples to follow his example of service in the washing of feet (John 13:5ff.). The term derives from the Latin *mandatum novum,* "I give you a new commandment, that you love one another" (John 13:34).

Mayflower Compact (1620)   Agreement signed by male passengers on the *Mayflower,* binding them to form "a civil body politic" and to obey laws enacted by that body after they landed at Plymouth Rock in Massachusetts.

Mazarin Bible   A Gutenberg Bible found in the library of Jules Mazarin (1602–61), a French statesman and cardinal. Since experts gave attention to it there, it is sometimes called the Mazarin Bible.

Mea culpa, mea maxima culpa   (Lat. "My sin, my great sin") An expression of contrition used particularly within the Roman Catholic tradition.

mean, doctrine of the   An ethical concept taught by Aristotle (384–322 B.C.) in his theory of moral virtue, according to which virtue is found as a "mean" or midpoint between vices of excess and deficiency. This approach has sometimes been adopted by Christian ethicists and theologians.

means of grace   *See* grace, means of

mechanistic   (From Gr. *mēchanē*, "machine") Term used to describe an understanding of the world as analogous to a machine, emphasizing the effects of causes. This viewpoint may try to explain all things without relation to a God.

Medellín Conference (1968)   The Second General Assembly of Latin American Bishops, convened by the Latin American Bishops' Conference at Medellín, Colombia (CELAM II), from which the theological meaning of "liberation" began to emerge into what became varying forms of liberation theologies.

mediating theology   A term used in various contexts to describe theologies that seek to find middle ground between competing theological ideas.

mediation   (Lat. *mediatio*, from *mediare*, "to divide in the middle") The bringing of parties together to try to effect a reconciliation. It is common to the various world religions in different forms. The principle is expressed throughout the Christian Scriptures.

mediator   (Lat. *medius*, "middle") One who stands between parties in order to

effect a reconciliation. The term is applied to Jesus Christ as the "one mediator between God and humankind" (1 Tim. 2:5), who has effected reconciliation by overcoming sin (cf. Heb. 8:6; 9:15; 12:24).

Mediatrix of All Graces   (From Lat. *medius*, "in the middle") In Roman Catholic theology, a title given to the Virgin Mary. Vatican Council II (1962) indicated that this title does not supplement or detract from the role of Jesus Christ as the sole Mediator of salvation.

medieval Scholasticism   *See* Scholastic theology; Scholasticism

medieval theology   The theology developed during the Middle Ages by theologians such as Anselm (c. 1033–1109), Abelard (1079–1142), Bonaventure (c. 1217–74), and Thomas Aquinas (1225–74) that provided a detailed basis for Roman Catholicism through the use of Scripture, reason, and church tradition.

meditation   (Lat. *meditatio*, "a thinking over") Reflection and thought upon a subject, often a scriptural passage, and often coupled with prayer, as an exercise in Christian devotion in order to gain spiritual insight.

meeting   Term used by some groups to denote a worship service. It is also used ecclesiastically to designate a gathering by a specific group to conduct official church business.

Megillah   (Heb. "scroll") A term for any of five biblical books (Esther, Ruth, Lamentations, Ecclesiastes, Song of Songs) recited from a scroll during the liturgy. Most commonly, it refers to the book of Esther read at Purim.

Melanchthonian   The line of Lutheran theology that follows the thought of Philip Melanchthon (1497–1560), a leading Lutheran theologian. The Augsburg Confession (1530), one of the major confessions of Lutheranism, was composed by Melanchthon and reflects his views.

Melchiorites   Those who followed the 16th-century Anabaptist leader and preacher Melchior Hoffmann (c. 1500–

1543) and became a distinct party within the Anabaptist movement.

Melchites (From Syrian "king") Syrian and Egyptian Christians who would not sanction Monophysitism but accepted the teachings of the Council of Chalcedon (A.D. 451). Their opponents called them "melchites" (royalists or imperialists), since this was also the view of the emperor in Constantinople.

meliorism (Lat. *meliorare,* "to make better") The view that humans must work cooperatively with God to create a universe with more good and less evil since God is omnibenevolent but not omnipotent, and thus needs human help. Humans cannot attain perfection but can indefinitely improve.

Melitian schisms Two separate 4th-century schisms in the Eastern church relating to two bishops named Melitius. Bishop Melitius of Lycopolis, Egypt, opposed an easy reentry to the church for those who had lapsed during persecutions. Bishop Melitius of Antioch was suspected of Arian viewpoints.

member One who is a formal and official part of a church or ecclesiastical body. The Christian church is composed of many members (Rom. 12:4–5; 1 Cor. 12:12–31).

memorial A common designation for something given to a church in memory of someone. The term is also used, in some forms of church government, for a formal petition or request made by one person or church body to another.

memorialism A view of the Lord's Supper often associated with the teachings of Huldrych Zwingli (1484–1531) in which the Supper is viewed as commemorative of Jesus Christ and that there is no "real presence" of Christ in any other than a symbolic sense.

memory (Lat. *memoria*) The capacity to bring to mind that which has gone before. "Remembering" is important in the Old Testament for recalling God's activities, especially in establishing covenants, liberating the people, and giving the law. Memory (anamnesis) is important for the New Testament for recalling God's gift of Jesus Christ and his saving acts (1 Cor. 11:24).

mendicant orders (From Lat. *mendicare,* "to beg") Predominantly, Roman Catholic religious orders that emphasize the vow of poverty. Also known as "friars."

Mennonites Followers of Menno Simons (1496–1561) and other Anabaptist leaders. They emphasize a radical separation from the world, community discipline, pacifism, independent local congregations, believers' baptism, and the life of holiness.

menology (Gr. *mēnologion,* Lat. *menologium*) A record or account of Christian saints arranged in calendar form. It is used liturgically.

mental prayer Prayer that is unspoken and silent and is primarily a focus of the mind or intellectual faculties upon God.

mental reservation (Lat. *reservatio mentalis*) An ethical term used to recognize limits that may be placed on what one confesses due to doubts or scruples.

Mercersburg theology A theological movement within American Calvinism developed at the German Reformed Seminary at Mercersburg, Pennsylvania. It was led by Philip Schaff (1819–93) and John Williamson Nevin (1803–86) and stressed the centrality of Christ and his presence in the Lord's Supper.

mercy (Lat. *misericordia*) Kind and compassionate treatment extending biblically to forgiveness and the gracious bestowal of that which is not deserved. It is an important descriptor of God's character and activities (Ps. 119:156; Jer. 31:20) and characteristic of the Christian (Luke 6:36).

mercy killing *See* euthanasia

mercy seat A piece of pure gold placed on top of the Ark of the Covenant (Ex. 25:17ff.), onto which the blood of the animal offered for atonement was sprinkled (Lev. 16:14–15), symbolizing God's gracious forgiveness of sin.

merit (Lat. *meritum,* from *mereri,* "to deserve") The worth or value of an act of obedience and, in an extended sense, that which a person who performs the act deserves. Theologically, the Protestant Reformers rejected the view that any human acts have merit before God.

merit, treasury of In Roman Catholic theology, the extra merit accumulated by Jesus Christ and the saints, upon which all who may need merit for eternal life may draw.

merit of Christ (Lat. *meritum Christi*) A theological term used to indicate the worthiness of Christ's death on the cross to be the satisfaction before God for human sin.

meritum de condigno (Lat. "merit of condignity," from *condignus,* "very worthy") Also "full merit." A term used in Scholastic theology for the merit gained by the work of the Holy Spirit within a regenerate person. It is "full merit" because the Spirit is good and the merit is based on God's justice standard.

meritum de congruo (Lat. "merit of congruity") Also "half merit." A term used in Scholastic theology for the merit gained by the work of the individual sinner in doing the best one can do. It is "half merit" because it is bestowed as a divine gift on the basis of God's generosity.

Messiah (Heb. *mashiah,* "anointed one," Gr. *Christos*) The promised deliverer of Israel who would establish God's rule. Christians see Jesus as the "Christ" and the one in whom God's promises are fulfilled (Acts 2:31–36) and who will ultimately rule the world and its new divine order (Phil. 2:5–11).

Messiah, Jesus as The Christian belief that Jesus was God's promised "anointed one" who fulfilled Old Testament prophecy and that he is the anticipated king and deliverer who brings salvation to the world (Acts 18:5, 28; Rom. 1:1, 7–8; 5:8).

messianic Pertaining to the Messiah; particularly used for biblical passages considered to be prophetic in anticipating a coming Messiah (Acts 9:1–7; Isa. 11:1–10, etc.).

messianic banquet *See* marriage supper (feast) of the Lamb

messianic consciousness A term used to describe an awareness Jesus might have had of his being the Messiah.

messianic hope The expectation throughout Judaism that a Messiah will arise in the nation. The hope evolved through the period of the Old Testament. It was especially strong prior to and during the time of Jesus' ministry, strengthened by the development of apocalyptic and eschatological writings.

messianic secret A term used to describe the phenomena found especially in the Gospel of Mark when Jesus instructs his followers not to proclaim him as the Messiah (Mark 8:30; 9:9). Other actions of his also point in this direction (Mark 1:25, 34, 43f.; 7:36, etc.).

messianism Belief in the coming of a Messiah. It is an important feature of Old Testament Judaism that developed through the centuries from the expectation of an ideal Davidic king to a Davidic figure who would appear at the end of the world.

metatheological Pertaining to discussion of theology in general, including its nature, bases, methods, and purposes.

metaethics A term used in the subtitle of Mary Daly's *Gyn/Ecology* (1978) to indicate a deeper, more "intuitive" type of ethics than male "ethics," which is said to be the study of ethical theories. Daly proposed the affirmation of deep dynamics of "female being."

metanarrative A term used by postmodern thinkers for the systems of myths that sustain social relationships in a society and form the basis for the society's legitimation. Postmodernists see metanarratives as being in demise because they no longer have credibility, since no myths can claim universality.

metanoia (Gr. "change of mind") A New Testament term for repentance that indicates sorrow for sin and turning (conversion) from sinfulness to righteousness through Jesus Christ (Mark 1:15; Acts 2:38).

metaphor   A figure of speech by which one thing is spoken of in terms of another (e.g., Job 8:16–17). Contemporary theological interest in metaphor relates to broader issues of religious language and specifically toward recognizing metaphor's open and tensive qualities.

metaphysical feminism   A feminist view which believes that one woman's experience can be all women's experience.

metaphysical gap   A term used to describe the completely different qualities of existence between God and humans, or humans and the rest of the created order.

metaphysical union   A term used in spiritual theology to indicate the idea that humans may become completely absorbed in God and thus experience the deepest possible union and "oneness."

metaphysics   (Gr. "beyond the physical") A philosophical term for "what is real" or questions of ultimate reality. This branch of philosophy is closest to religion, and thus metaphysicians have had significant influence on theology.

metaphysics, christological   Understanding all reality on the basis of Jesus Christ.

metaphysics, classical   The metaphysics of Plato, Aristotle, and their followers.

metaphysics, idealist   The metaphysics of the philosophers George Berkeley (1685–1753), René Descartes (1596–1650), Immanuel Kant (1724–1804), G.W.F. Hegel (1770–1831), and their followers.

metaxy   The "in-between" where the transcendent God touches the human realm.

metempsychosis   (From Gr. *meta-*, "change," and *empsychoun,* "to animate") The view held by some religious faiths that souls become continually reincarnated. It is rejected by Christianity.

method in theology   *See* theological method

Methodism   The teachings, organization, and church discipline that emerged from the work of John (1703–91) and Charles (1707–88) Wesley. Historically Methodism has been Arminian in theological orientation and episcopal in church government.

Methodist   A member of the Methodist communion, the Protestant denomination that emerged from the work of John Wesley (1703–91).

methodology   (Lat. *methodologia*) The means or process used in analyzing or presenting an issue.

metrical psalms   Biblical psalms paraphrased in meter so they may be sung in worship. They were used particularly in the Reformed tradition by Scottish Presbyterians, having gained a place in the liturgy with the Genevan Psalter of Calvin's Geneva.

metropolitan   (From Gr. *mētēr*, "mother," and *polis*, "city") A bishop with authority over a wider area such as a province instead of only over a diocese.

middle knowledge   (Lat. *scientia media*) A concept developed by the Jesuit Luis de Molina (1535–1600). It is God's conditioned and consequent knowledge of future events. God foreknows how each person will cooperate with grace. It was opposed by Thomists.

midrash   (Heb. "explanation," from *darash,* "to inquire into") Commentaries and explanatory notes on the Scriptures produced by Jewish rabbis from the period of the Babylonian exile until approximately A.D. 1200. Its two parts are halakah and haggadah.

midtribulationism   An interpretation of New Testament passages that speak of a "tribulation period" in the future and the view that the Christian church will endure the first half of the period before being "raptured" (Matt. 24:21–30).

Milan, Edict of (313)   An agreement between the emperors Constantine and

Licinius that established equal toleration for all religions within the Roman Empire. It thus made Christianity a legal religion.

militant, church *See* church militant

milk and honey A biblical image for peace and prosperity (Ex. 3:8; Lev. 20:24; Deut. 26:9). Newly baptized Christians during the early church period were given a taste of milk and honey.

millenarian movements Groups that have emphasized an (often) imminent return of Jesus Christ to earth and the establishment of a millennial rule on the earth by Christ and his saints that features righteousness and peace. Some groups are "premillennialists," others are "postmillennialists."

Millennial Dawnists *See* Jehovah's Witnesses

millennial kingdom The "thousand year" reign of Christ spoken of in Rev. 20:1–7.

millennialism (Lat. *mille,* "thousand" and *annus,* "year") Views about the "thousand year" reign of Christ (Rev. 20:1–7) on earth that ends the present age. The three chief positions have been premillennialism, postmillennialism, and amillennialism. Also "chiliasm" (Gr. *chilioi,* "thousand") and millenarianism.

millennialist One who holds to definite views about the "millennium" (Rev. 20:1–7).

millennium (Lat. *mille,* "thousand," and *annus,* "year") The thousand-year reign of Christ (Rev. 20:1–7).

millennium, views of the The differing views about the timing and interpretation of the "millennium" (the thousand-year reign of Christ) mentioned in Rev. 20:1–7. The major views are premillennialism, postmillennialism, and amillennialism.

Millerites Followers of William Miller (1782–1849), who founded the Adventist movement and prophesied that Jesus Christ would return to earth in 1843 or 1844.

mind (Lat. *mens*) Consciousness as an element in reality, in distinction from "matter." Theologically, when the mind is seen as the center for the power of "reason," questions arise about the ways mind and body relate; how the mind "knows" God; the mind's relation to "faith," etc.

mind-body Description of the spiritual and material dimensions of a human person. Used theologically in classic discussions of the doctrine of humanity. One aspect has been the question of whether or not there is a soul or mind that continues to exist after the death of the body.

minister (Lat. "a servant") One who serves God. The term is most often used for ordained clergy, though the biblical perspective is inclusive of all who seek to carry out God's will.

ministerial privilege Benefits or favors given to clergy by virtue of their status and sometimes as part of their remuneration.

ministry (Gr. *diakonia,* Lat. *ministerium,* "service") The service to God in Jesus Christ rendered by the church and by individuals through the power of the Holy Spirit.

ministry of the Word In Protestantism, a description for preaching that is biblically grounded. In Roman Catholicism, the first part of the Mass, including readings from Scripture, the creed, and the sermon. Also called "liturgy of the Word."

minjung theology (Korean, "people's theology") A theology developed by Korean Protestant theologians in which "minjung" is understood politically. Biblical, church history, and theological resources are interpreted from the perspective of "the people." It relates the gospel to Asian struggles for liberation.

minor orders In Roman Catholicism and Eastern Orthodoxy, those ministerial orders below the orders of bishops, priests, and deacons ("major orders"). These are lectors, cantors, and subdeacons in Orthodoxy, and, historically, lectors, acolytes, exorcists, and porters in Roman Catholicism. In the Roman Church since 1972, lectors and acolytes are no longer "orders" but "ministries," while the orders of exorcists and porters have been abolished.

minority group Those in a numerical minority. Often minorities lack political and social power. They may endure injustice and oppression from the majority. In other cases, a numerically smaller group may exercise major societal power, a condition pointed out by feminist writers about male dominance.

minster (Lat. *monasterium,* "monastery"; cf. Ger. *Münster*) A term for certain cathedrals and other larger church buildings in England stemming from its original meaning of the church attached to a monastery.

minutes *See* records

miracle (Lat. *miraculum,* from *mirari,* "to wonder") An event that is considered unusual or extraordinary in that it appears to be contrary to what is currently known of nature. Theologically, the emphasis is on what God has revealed through this event, as in the miracles of Jesus.

miracles of Jesus The various supernatural actions of Jesus as recorded in the Gospels. Theologically they are regarded as signs of his divinity and power over natural and cosmic forces and are revelatory of God's nature and purposes (see Matt. 8—9).

miraculous conception A term used most frequently to refer to the virgin birth of Jesus.

mirror of election (Lat. *speculum electionis*) A term used by John Calvin (1509–64) to indicate that it is in Jesus Christ that one's election is found and seen (*Institutes* 3.24.5). This means that assurance of salvation rests on the question, "Do I believe in Jesus Christ?" rather than various conjectures about election or predestination.

mishnah (Heb. "repetition" or "instruction") A method and practice of Jewish interpretation of Scripture. Collections of interpretations were made and drawn together in the Mishnah attributed to Rabbi Judah ha-Nasi (c. 135–c. 220). This comprehensive collection is second only to the Scriptures in authority for Jews.

misogyny (Gr. *misogynia*) The hatred of women, particularly by men. This is an ethical issue. It is also noted by feminist writers as a source of oppression for women.

missal/missalette (Lat. *missalis,* from *missa,* "mass") Book containing what is sung, chanted, or recited in the Roman Catholic Mass. The "Sunday Missal" provides materials for Sundays and holy days. The "Daily Missal" provides materials for every day of the year.

missiology The study of the mission of the Christian church.

mission (Lat. *missio,* from *mittere,* "to send") All that is done by the church and by Christians to serve God. More specifically, the term may be used to denote direct activities or tasks undertaken by the church for particular purposes.

missionary (From Lat. *mittere,* "to send") One who is sent on a mission, usually by the church, with a focus on sharing the gospel of Jesus Christ in some way.

missionary bishop A bishop who is called to serve in an area that has not as yet been formalized into a diocese.

missionary movement The expansion of the Christian church throughout the world according to its understanding of its mission as to proclaim the gospel of Jesus Christ in word and action.

missionization A zealous concern for missionary activity. It may also connote forms of oppression if standards and requirements are imposed which are unjust.

missions The term is often used to indicate those forms of ministries in which churches engage, either locally or globally, as a sharing of Jesus Christ.

miter (Gr. and Lat. *mitra,* "turban," "headband") The formal headdress worn by a bishop.

mixed chalice The practice in the early Christian church of mingling water and wine in the cup at the Eucharist. The practice was rejected by the 16th-century Protestant Reformers.

mixed marriage A marriage between Christians of differing religious bodies. The term has been particularly used for a marriage in which only one of the partners is Roman Catholic.

mixed motives In ethical theory, the recognition that an act may be performed from a primary motive while secondary motives may also be present.

modalism (Lat. *modus,* "form," "mode") A view of the Trinity considered by the early church as heretical. It was believed that the one God was revealed at different times in different ways and thus has three manners (modes) of appearance rather than being one God in three Persons.

Modalistic Monarchianism (Gr. *monarchia,* "absolute rule," "monarchy") A form of modalism that focused on the unity of God by seeing God as a divine monad with no distinctions within the divine Being. Thus God "appears" as Father, Son, and Holy Spirit.

model (From Lat. *modus,* "mode") An image or metaphor that presents a pattern for explanation. Some argue that "doctrines" are "models" in that they present a coherent way of explaining beliefs.

moderator (Lat. "manager," "director") One who leads a meeting. Used ecclesiastically within the Reformed tradition for the one who presides at meetings of church sessions or other governing bodies, including the General Assembly. Moderators have no special status over others.

modern theology A term to describe theology since the time of F.D.E.

Schleiermacher (1768–1834), recognizing that his theological approach began a new era.

modernism A theological movement of the late 19th and early 20th centuries among Protestants and Roman Catholics who sought to interpret Christianity in light of modern knowledge.

modernism, Catholic The movement among Roman Catholic theologians in the late 19th and early 20th centuries to interpret Christianity in light of modern knowledge. Leaders were Alfred Loisy (1857–1940) and George Tyrrell (1861–1909). It was condemned by Pope Pius X in 1907.

modernism, English A late 19th- and early 20th-century movement in English theology that sought to respond to modern thought by altering Christian doctrine, which was seen as evolving and in need of being reshaped by modern knowledge.

modernist An adherent of modernism.

modernist-fundamentalist controversy *See* fundamentalist-modernist controversy

modernity A term often used to designate the post-Enlightenment period in Europe and North America in which people turned to a scientific culture and its promises in order to fill a void left by a decline in religion. The values of the secular culture and rejection of religious authority are primary as well as a belief in knowledge as certain, objective, and good.

modes of being (Ger. *Seinsweisen*) A term used by Karl Barth (1886–1968) to describe the classical concept of the "Persons" of the Trinity.

Molinism *See* middle knowledge

moment A concept used in the writings of Søren Kierkegaard (1813–55) to describe the point where humans respond with faith to their encounter with God. It is the point where one passes from nonbeing into being. The formulation was also used by Rudolf Bultmann (1884–1976).

monarchial system of church government A form of church polity that is episcopal in nature and features a graded system of authority figures who exercise authority by virtue of their office.

Monarchianism, Dynamic A 2d- to 3d-century heresy teaching that Jesus was only God in the sense of having a power of influence (Gr. *dynamis*) resting on his human person.

monarchical (From Gr. *monarchia,* "one origin" or "one rule") In Trinitarian theology, the term refers to the Father as the source of the Son and Spirit and is sometimes heretically interpreted to mean that Jesus was not divine.

monastery (Gr. *monastērion,* from *monos,* "alone" or "hermit's cell") Building inhabited by men (monks) who have made religious vows and live out a form of monasticism.

monasticism/monachism (Gr. *monastēs,* "monk," "a solitary," from *monazein,* "to be alone") A form of the Christian life practiced by monks who take vows (usually of poverty, chastity, and obedience), practice asceticism and often live apart from the rest of the world in monasteries.

monenergism A christological heresy in the 7th century which taught that there was only one divine energy, or action, in Jesus Christ. It was developed by Sergius (d. 638), patriarch of Constantinople, in seeking reconciliation with Monophysitism. It was condemned with Monothelitism in 681.

monergism The view that the Holy Spirit is the only agent who effects regeneration of Christians. It is in contrast with synergism, the view that there is a cooperation between the divine and the human in the regeneration process.

monism (Gr.) The philosophical view that all reality is of one type or essence.

monk (Gr. *monachos,* Lat. *monachus,* "solitary") One who is removed from the rest of the world, usually living in a monastery, and who has taken vows of poverty, chastity, and obedience in order to live a life of deeper devotion to God.

monogamy (Lat. *monogamia*) The practice of being married only to one spouse at a time. It contrasts with polygamy (one man with several wives) and polyandry (one woman with several husbands). Monogamy has been the primary Christian norm for marriage.

monogenism The view that the total human race has its origins in a single couple of male and female.

monolatry (Gr. *monos,* "single," and *latreia,* "worship") The worship of one god though the existence of other gods may be acknowledged.

Monophysitism (From Gr. *monos,* "one," and *physis,* "nature") A christological view, regarded by the early church as heretical, which taught that Jesus Christ had only one nature rather than a divine and a human nature that were united in one person.

monotheism (From Gr. *monos,* "one," and *theos,* "God") Belief in one God.

Monothelitism (From Gr. *monos,* "one," and *thelein,* "to will") Monothelites held that Jesus Christ had only one will. This was rejected by the Third Council of Constantinople (680), which asserted that Christ had two wills, since he had two natures, but that they always acted in mutual accord.

monsignor (Ital. from Fr. "my lord") An honorary title used in the Roman Catholic Church, usually conferred by the pope.

monstrance (Lat. *monstrantia,* and *monstrare,* "to show") In the Roman Catholic Mass, the vessel with glass sides in which the eucharistic Host is shown to the people so that it may be venerated. It is also called an *ostensorium* (from Lat. *ostendere,* "to show").

Montanism The views, associated with Montanus in the 2d century, that stressed the outpouring of the Holy Spirit to Montanus through trances that led to his prophetic utterances about the return of Christ and the establishment of the new Jerusalem, together with an emphasis on asceticism. It was condemned by the church.

moral (Lat. *moralis*, from *mos, moris,* "custom") Relating to the principles of right and wrong behavior.

moral actions The deeds that can be considered to be either right or wrong according to some standard of morality.

moral agency/agents Humans as those who are capable of carrying out ethical actions.

moral argument for God An argument for the existence of God based on the view that there must be an ultimate explanation for why there are moral values and a concern for moral activity.

moral attributes of God Those characteristics of God that pertain to the ways God treats creatures as an expression of God's nature. These would include love (John 3:16), grace (Rom. 3:24), righteousness and justice (Ps. 89:14), and faithfulness (2 Tim. 2:13).

moral character One's basic disposition or nature with regard to questions of right and wrong (morality).

moral choice Decisions to be made that involve elements of right and wrong (morality) in contrast to those where that dimension is not present.

moral code A system or standard for right and wrong that indicates the nature of moral behavior.

moral competence The ability to make judgments on matters of morality or right and wrong behavior.

moral conduct One's behavior on issues of right and wrong (morality).

moral conscientiousness The sense of obligation one feels in regard to issues of right and wrong (morality).

moral corruption The status of humans who are so affected by sin that they are not able to make right ethical choices on moral matters.

moral decision A choice to be made that has moral significance.

moral development The evolution of the person through varying "stages," and the formation of character and habits that inform the means one uses for making choices of right and wrong.

moral education The communication and teaching of morals and values in relation to the expectations of culture and society.

moral evil Evil that emerges from the choices and actions of persons and affects other persons, in contrast to natural evil.

moral freedom One's capacity to make choices about right and wrong (morality).

moral inability *See* total inability

moral influence theory of the atonement The view that the death of Jesus Christ on the cross was the supreme example of God's love, and that by recognizing this, persons will respond to salvation and be influenced to live lives of love toward God and other people. It is associated with Peter Abelard (1079–1142).

moral judgment The ascertaining of what is right or wrong in an issue or a situation on the basis of some standard of morality.

moral law (Lat. *lex moralis*) A term for the Ten Commandments, or Decalogue, or for the law of Moses. Its purpose is to regulate conduct and ethical choices and it is distinct from Israel's ceremonial and civil laws.

moral matter An issue or situation that calls for a moral judgment. Also, that element of a human action which indicates what the action is; for example, that which distinguishes the act as a lie instead of a murder.

moral norms Those guides which influence moral actions or behavior.

moral perfection The fulfillment of the moral law, regarded in Christian theology as impossible because of the power of sin in human lives (Pss. 14:3; 53:3).

moral philosophy   An equivalent term for "ethics" and the examination of human behavior in terms of what is right and wrong, without using the perspectives of divine revelation.

moral preparation   A term used in Roman Catholic theology to indicate a person's preparation for receiving the Eucharist, including the renunciation of any sin or hindrance to the nature of the sacrament.

Moral Rearmament   *See* Oxford Group

moral responsibility   The status of being able to make choices about the rightness or wrongness of actions (morality), and thus being accountable for the choices that are made.

moral theology   A term used in Roman Catholic thought for the branch of theology that deals with the rightness and wrongness of human actions (morality) in relation to God. It is usually termed "Christian ethics" in Protestantism.

moral values   Those elements which are held to be right, important, and to be promoted both individually and in society, as ascertained by a standard for morality.

moral virtues   *See* cardinal virtues

moralist   One with a strong concern for issues of right and wrong (morality).

morality   (From Lat. *moralis,* "pertaining to manners") The rightness or wrongness of actions in relation to a standard or norm of conduct.

Moravian Brethren   Eighteenth-century refugees from Moravia, spiritual heirs of the Bohemian Brethren. Their theology blended Lutheranism and Pietism and they developed into the current Moravian Church, with an ordained ministry of bishops, presbyters, and deacons.

Mormonism   The movement that emerged from the teachings of Joseph Smith (1805–44), who in 1830 claimed to have received the Book of Mormon from an angel and to have received priestly powers. The Church of Jesus Christ of Latter-day Saints teaches premortal existence; it stresses morality, the millennium, and the evolution of humanity to eventual salvation.

morning prayer   *See* matins

mortal body   *See* body, mortal

mortal flesh   *See* body, mortal

mortal sin   *See* sin, mortal

mortalism, pure   *See* pure mortalism

mortality   (Lat. *mortalis,* "subject to death") The limitation of life by the inevitability of death.

mortification   (Lat. *mortificare,* "to mortify," from *mors,* "death," and *facere,* "to make") A theological term for the subduing or putting to death of the life of sin through repentance. In some traditions particular stress is on subduing sensual appetites and using ascetic practices.

Mosaic law   (Lat. *lex Mosaica*) The moral law given to Moses by special revelation at Mount Sinai and summarized in the Ten Commandments (Ex. 20:1–17).

motet   (Middle English from Old French *mot,* "a word, phrase") A choral composition for liturgical use, often drawn from biblical texts and performed without accompaniment.

Mother of God   (Gr. *theotokos,* Lat. *mater Dei*) A term sanctioned by the Council of Ephesus (431) for the Virgin Mary. It is used particularly in the Roman Catholic tradition to express Marian devotion.

motif research   A methodological approach to theology by several Swedish theologians who see the goal of theology as the discovery of the basic ideas that comprise the Christian faith. Through critical analysis and by "motif research" (*motivforskning*), fundamental ideas are discovered.

mourners' bench   The area at the front of a meeting place where those who responded to evangelistic preaching in American revival services gathered in response to the altar call. The unconverted could gather there to "mourn" over their sins. It was also called the anxious bench.

movable feasts The festivals of the Christian year that depend for their dating on the date of Easter. These include Ash Wednesday, Easter, Ascension Day, Pentecost Sunday, and Trinity Sunday, among others.

mover, prime *See* prime mover

Muggletonians 17th-century English sect derived from Lodowicke Muggleton (1609–98). He and his cousin John Reeve (1608–58) claimed to be the prophetic witnesses of Revelation 11:3 and taught that those who did not believe in them committed the unforgivable sin.

munus triplex (Lat. "threefold office") The mediatorial work of Jesus Christ expressed in his threefold office of prophet, priest, and king. These were used by John Calvin (1509–64) and later Reformed theologians as links between the work of Christ and the covenant history of Israel.

Muratorian Canon A list of biblical books considered authoritative by the late 2d-century church of Rome as determined from a manuscript fragment found by L. A. Muratori in 1740. Also called Muratorian fragment.

murder The intentional killing of another human being. It is condemned in the Mosaic law (Ex. 20:13), by Jesus (Mark 7:21), and for Christians (Rom. 1:29; James 4:2).

music, church Music used within the context of the church, particularly during a worship service that is devoted to the glory of God. It may be both instrumental and vocal.

music, sacred Both classical and popular music that have as their goal the worship and praise of God. The music is often performed within the context of Christian worship services.

mutual conversation and consolation Terms used in spirituality for processes such as counseling, Scripture study, and prayer, through which faith may be strengthened and Christian care and concern expressed.

mutuality A shared sense of responsibility and care for others in a relationship of equality. It is pointed to by feminist theologians as a more genuinely Christian and authentic way of relating to persons than the relationships based on authority and power that are prevalent.

mystagogy (Gr. *mystagōgia*, from *myein*, "to teach a doctrine," "to initiate into the mysteries") A term from the early church for a time of instruction on the Christian life after one's baptism and entrance into the church. *Mystagogia* were homilies on the sacraments by bishops.

mysteries (Gr. *mystēria*, "hidden things"; Lat. *mysteria*, "sacred rites") Truths not accessible by the power of human reason alone. The term is often used for the sacraments and biblically for God's hidden purposes (Eph. 1:9; 3:9).

mysterium tremendum A term associated with Rudolf Otto (1869–1937), designating a sense of the unfathomable mystery associated with the "numinous object," which induces awe or fascination (*mysterium fascinosum*) in the worshiper.

mystery (Gr. *mystērion*, Lat. *mysterium*, "secret") God's eternal purposes of redemption were hidden until the incarnation of Jesus Christ and the sending of the Holy Spirit to the church who reveals this mystery (Eph. 1:9; 3:3, 9). God's essential nature is mystery and must be revealed.

mystery religions Religions of the Greco-Roman world into which people were initiated and received special mysterious truths that they were to keep secret. The mystery religions sought to lift adherents from the mundane to divine harmony and immortality.

mystic (Gr. *mystikos*, "one initiated into mysteries") One who experiences direct apprehensions of the divine by immediate intuition, as well as a sense of spiritual ecstasy.

mystical body   An image of the church as the "body of Christ" (1 Cor. 12:27) and as a "mystery" through which God's purposes of redemption through Christ are being achieved through the work of the Holy Spirit. The church thus has a spiritual essence and, in some views, a sacramental character.

mystical experience   The religious experience of union with God, often associated with ecstasy and an overwhelming feeling of awe or blessedness.

mystical intuition   Another term for "mystical experience." Also the faculty of the mind through which a knowledge of God is revealed.

mystical sense of Scripture   (From Gr. *mystikos*) A form of the traditional allegorical sense of Scripture in which the hidden and deepest meaning of the text, which is available only to those who are progressing in their Christian devotion, leads to an encounter with Christ and a more profound sense of union with him.

mystical theology   A part of spiritual theology that deals with God's hidden and mysterious work of grace within a community and a person's life. A classic pattern for mystical theology is the "Threefold Way" of purgation, illumination, and union with God.

mystical union   (Lat. *unio mystica*) A direct communion with God (or Christ) that takes the believer to deeper levels of experiential awareness of God's presence and potentially to a beatific vision.

mystical vision   An element of mystical experience referring to apparitions of Jesus Christ or the saints as experienced by some mystics. In a more general sense it refers to the transformation that occurs within human consciousness toward a deeper awareness of the divine in mystical theology.

mysticism   (From Gr. *mystikos*, "belonging to secret rites") The direct apprehension of the divine or the numinous in an unmediated awareness.

mysticism, Christian   The experience of union with God by the bond of love that is beyond human power to attain and that brings a sense of direct knowledge and fellowship with God centered in Jesus Christ.

mysticism, extrovertive   The sense of the whole universe merging together harmoniously. Also the intense perception by the self of all events in ways that surpass ordinary experience.

mysticism, introvertive   The experience of the self in losing its awareness of its separate existence apart from all else and in being merged in union with God.

myth   (Gr. *mythos*, "tale," "fable") A story that is used to explain a belief, practice, or natural phenomenon and that has a religious or spiritual significance. The story can relate many truths that may seem potentially contradictory or unrelated. Mythology is the study of myths.

Nag Hammadi Library   A collection of ancient codices, written in Coptic, discovered at Nag Hammadi in Egypt (1945). These documents were 53 primary texts of Gnosticism that show the diversities among Gnostic views and have provided greater insight into the Gnostic phenomenon.

naming   Used by feminist writers for the task of redescribing reality through linguistic invention.

Nantes, Edict of (1598)   Agreement between the French King Henry IV and the Protestant Huguenots that gave them freedom of worship in certain geographical areas, granted civil liberties, and gave fortified cities of refuge. It was revoked by King Louis XIV (1685).

narrative passages   (Lat. *narrare*, "to tell") Those biblical passages which tell a story or form a plot line. This form is characteristic of large portions of the biblical materials.

narrative theology   A 20th-century theological movement that stresses the power of language and the essential narrative quality of Scripture and of human experience. The Bible provides stories that shape human life and consciousness as they are read and told.

narthex   (Gr. "an enclosure") A term for the entryway or vestibule of a church. Originally it referred to a deep porch at a church's entrance where people waited prior to the service and from where the "great entrance" began.

NASB   *See* New American Standard Bible

natalitia   (Lat. "birthdays") A term used in the early centuries of the Christian church to designate the death days of martyrs, marking their entrance into eternal life.

National Covenant (1638)   Scottish legal band of association that protested the attempt by King Charles I to establish episcopacy in Scotland. The Covenant defended the Reformed faith and was for all Scots to sign. Those who did were called Covenanters.

native religions   The religions of those who are indigenous to a particular geographical region.

Nativity, the   (Lat. *nativitas*, "birth") Ecclesiastical term for the birth of Jesus Christ, celebrated as Christmas (December 25).

Nativity of John the Baptist, Feast of the   Church festival celebrating the birth of John the Baptist (June 24), six

months prior to the birth of Jesus (Luke 1:26, 36).

Nativity of Our Lord, Feast of the   Church festival celebrating the birth of Jesus from the time of evening prayer on December 24, through the season of Christmas, until the Day of Epiphany (January 6). Most simply, another name for Christmas.

Nativity of the Blessed Virgin Mary, Feast of the   Church festival celebrating the birth of Mary, mother of Jesus, on September 8.

natural attributes of God   The attributes of God that describe God's relationship to the physical universe, such as God's knowledge, presence, and power (omniscience, omnipresence, omnipotence).

natural body   The body that humans have prior to their death and ultimate resurrection.

natural causation   The production of effects through other than supernatural factors.

natural condition   (Lat. *status naturalium*) The status of human beings without the grace of God.

natural contingency   A term used by Reinhold Niebuhr (1892–1971) to indicate the finite nature of humans who are, as a result, insecure and dependent.

natural ethic   A standard of behavior derived by observation of the world (nature) and strong in the Aristotelian and Stoic traditions. There is no appeal to special revelation. Also, naturalistic ethics.

natural evil   That which is considered evil and which emerges from the created order without the influence of humans, such as floods, earthquakes, and disease.

natural impulses   Those desires and inclinations which belong to humans in their theological condition of sinfulness.

natural law/law of nature   (Lat. *lex naturalis, lex naturae*) The moral law, universally imposed by God within all persons. Aristotelian and Stoic ethics led to a natural law theory to account for a natural moral awareness among persons. In Christian theology, Thomas Aquinas (1225–74) upheld it.

natural man   *See* man, natural

natural processes   Those actions and events which occur within the physical universe.

natural realm   A term used to designate the physical universe and its laws.

natural religion   A system of religious belief derived from observations of the physical world and discoverable by human reason without necessarily positing a supreme being or God.

natural revelation   (Lat. *revelatio naturalis*) The disclosure of God through nature or the natural order. Some have argued that this disclosure is accessible to all through reason; others that it is known only from the perspective of faith.

natural righteousness   *See* original righteousness

natural rights   A concept in ethics and legal theory that humans have certain inherent rights because of their status as human beings. These exist by virtue of natural law. In the Christian concept, humans as created in the "image of God" (Gen. 1:27) can be a starting point.

natural theology   (Lat. *theologia naturalis*) Knowledge of God attained through God's revelation in nature and available to human reason. The Roman Catholic tradition has emphasized it through Thomas Aquinas (1225–74). Some Protestants affirm it, while others, such as Karl Barth (1886–1968), reject it.

naturalism   The philosophical view that the universe exists as a self-contained whole and that it is self-directing. There is thus no supernatural element.

naturalistic ethics   Ethical structures and teachings derived from what one believes to be "natural" and "unnatural." Aristotelian and Stoic traditions developed concepts of natural law. Today the term "naturalistic ethics" is used for

ethical views that are based on a perception of nature or the senses without God.

nature   (Gr. *physis,* Lat. *natura*) Term for the aspect of reality in which changes can be perceived. Used theologically in the doctrines of the Trinity and Christology to indicate the being (Gr. *ousia*) or substance (Lat. *substantia*) of God and Jesus Christ.

nature, theology of   Theological perception of nature, and thus of its relation to God as creator and sustainer. It may be distinguished from "natural theology" in that a theology of nature does not seek to prove God's existence by unaided reason. Rather, it affirms God's activities in relation to nature.

nature and grace   The realities of existence in God's world. Used as a pair theologically to contrast human existence as sinful or the realm of the natural world (nature) in relation to God's redemptive activities and freely given salvation (grace).

nature of God   *See* God, nature of

nature worship   Worship of the physical world.

nave   (Gr. *naos,* Lat. *navis,* "ship") The main part of a church between the narthex and the chancel. The term derives from the image of the church as the ark ("ship") of salvation or the nave's shiplike appearance.

Nazarene, Church of the   American Protestant church of the Wesleyan tradition which originated in 1895. It stresses personal holiness and "entire sanctification," or Christian perfection through freedom from original sin, leading to a state of complete devotion to God. Divine healing is also affirmed.

Nazirite/Nazarite   (Heb. "dedicated" or "consecrated [one]") Member of a group of Israelites who vowed abstinence from eating or drinking the fruit of the vine, who let their hair grow long, and who sought to avoid contact with dead bodies (Num. 6), as a way of expressing their devotion to God.

NEB   *See* New English Bible

necessary being   A philosophical term for that which has its own power of existence within itself and therefore "must" necessarily exist. Theologically, this describes God.

necessitarianism   The view that all events happen by necessity, so that there is no free will. A synonym of "determinism."

necessity   (Lat. *necessitas,* from *necesse,* "needful") That which, philosophically, "must" occur by virtue of other conditions. This includes certain "laws" of reality.

necessity, relative/conditional   (Lat. *necessitas consequentiae*) A necessity that arises from a previous action or circumstance and is thus "conditional," as opposed to an "absolute" necessity.

necessity for salvation   The theological consideration which teaches that all persons, due to their sinful natures, have a necessary need for a saving relationship (salvation) with God.

necessity of compulsion   (Lat. *necessitas coactionis*) That which is necessarily imposed upon a person or event by a cause that is separate from it and not in accord with the will of that agent or thing.

necessity of nature   (Lat. *necessitas naturae*) The thought and action of a person that must occur by virtue of the person's nature, since no being can act in a way that is contrary to its nature.

necromancy   (Gr. *nekromanteia,* from *nekros,* "corpse" and *manteia,* "divination") Foretelling the future through communication with spirits of the dead. Related to sorcery and magic and condemned in the Mosaic law (Lev. 19:31; Deut. 18:10–12).

negation, method of   *See: via negativa*

negative theology   An approach to theology that emphasizes points of disagreement with other views and focuses on refuting these points rather than affirming its own theological points.

negligence, sins of   *See* sins of omission

neighbor   Biblically and ethically, the neighbor is one who is in need. The idea is extended by Jesus beyond the bounds of the covenant community. One "becomes" a neighbor when meeting that need (Lev. 19:18; Matt. 22:34–40; Luke 10:30–35).

Neo-Calvinism   Relating to a modern interpretation of Calvinism, sometimes used as a designation for the movement known as neo-orthodoxy.

neo-evangelicalism   *See* new evangelicalism

Neo-Kantianism   A philosophical movement from the 1860s until the end of World War I that followed the philosophy of Immanuel Kant (1724–1804), particularly in light of the prevailing idealism of the followers of G.W.F. Hegel (1770–1831).

neo-liberalism   A term that is used disparagingly by some to describe neo-orthodoxy which, it is claimed, is only a new form of the old liberal theology.

neology   (Gr. "new teaching") Term used by mid-19th-century British theologians in reference to German rationalistic theology, which was perceived as "new doctrine" and as contrary to Christian orthodoxy.

neo-orthodoxy   A theological movement including Karl Barth (1886–1968), Emil Brunner (1889–1966), and others. It opposed liberal theology and stressed the reinterpretation of Reformation themes such as God's transcendence, human sinfulness, and the centrality of Christ. It was dominant in Europe and America after World War II until the 1960s. Also called Neo-Calvinism, Neo-Protestantism, and Neo-Reformation theology.

Neo-Pentecostalism   Also called the charismatic movement, the term indicates the seeking of the "Pentecostal experience" (particularly speaking in tongues) by those outside Pentecostal churches.

neophyte   (Gr. *neophytos,* "newly born," "new convert") Term used in ancient liturgies for those who were newly baptized.

Neoplatonism   The work of Plotinus (A.D. 205–270) and others who reshaped the philosophy of Plato (428–348 B.C.). It competed with Christianity and taught that God relates to the world through various emanations.

Neo-Protestantism   *See* neo-orthodoxy

Neo-Reformation theology   *See* neo-orthodoxy

Neo-Scholasticism   A period (1860–1960) of revival of the philosophical tradition of medieval universities. It was led by Roman Catholic theologians in the wake of the Enlightenment as the best means to express historic, orthodox theological concepts. Thomas Aquinas (1225–74) was the prime philosopher.

Neo-Thomism   A Roman Catholic movement of the 19th and 20th centuries that revived the theology of Thomas Aquinas (1225–74) to make it the norm by which to judge all other theology and philosophy. Interpretations of Aquinas sought to assimilate into his philosophy the best of modern thought.

nepotism   (Ital. *nepotismo,* from *nepote,* "nephew") A practice of bestowing church offices or ecclesiastical preferments upon one's relatives.

Nestorianism   Followers of Nestorius (d. 451), who taught in effect that Jesus Christ was two separate persons as well as possessing two natures. This view was declared heretical by the Council of Ephesus (431).

New Age movements   Spiritualistic movements originating in the 1970s that have been a loose grouping of those who believe in reincarnation, the importance of dreams, astrology, psychic or holistic healing, and self-fulfillment, etc. Expanded human potentials and social and planetary renewal are advocated.

New American Bible (NAB, 1970)   The first officially sponsored translation of the Bible into English by the Roman Catholic Church. It replaced the Rheims-Douay version (1610). It was translated from the original languages by sixty scholars. In 1987 a new translation of the New Testament was produced.

New American Standard Bible (NASB; 1963, 1970)   An English translation of the Bible by fifty-eight translators who took a theologically conservative and literal approach to translation, seeking to follow the principles of translation used for the American Standard Version. The Old Testament was published in 1963; the New Testament in 1970.

New and Old School Presbyterians   Nineteenth-century division in American Presbyterianism between those upholding a strict Calvinism based on the Westminster Standards ("Old School") and those who wanted more latitude in confessional interpretation along with opposition to slavery and union with Congregationalists.

new being   In the theology of Paul Tillich (1886–1965), a prominent term for the authentic existence brought by Jesus as the Christ. It corresponds to traditional theological terms such as "new creation," "reconciliation," "regeneration," and "reunion with God."

new birth   *See* regeneration

new body   A term for the resurrection body received after death.

new commandment   Jesus' injunction to "love one another" (John 13:34).

new covenant   The anticipated action of God in establishing a personal relationship with people (Jer. 31:31–34), and seen in Christianity as fulfilled in Jesus Christ. The term is used by Jesus in relation to his death (Luke 22:20; 1 Cor. 11:25) and in the New Testament for the effects Jesus Christ brings (Heb. 8:8–13; 10:16–17; 12:24). Also, a term for the New Testament.

new creation   The new life of the Christian brought by God's regeneration in Jesus Christ through the power of the

Holy Spirit (2 Cor. 5:17; Gal. 6:15). More generally, the anticipated renewal of the created order by God in the "new heaven and new earth" (Rev. 21:1; cf. Rom. 8:18–21; 2 Peter 3:13).

New Divinity   *See* New England theology

new earth   *See* new creation

New England theology   A movement within 18th- and early 19th-century American Calvinism that brought together elements of Puritanism with other concerns such as the freedom of the will and divine justice. It stemmed from the works of Jonathan Edwards (1703–58) and his followers.

New England Way   A system of church government that developed in the Massachusetts Bay Colony in the 1630s that sought an outwardly "pure" church of genuine "saints" that would also be the predominant force in the civil government of New England towns. The Cambridge Platform (1648) solidified its foundations.

New English Bible (NEB; 1961, 1970)   English translation of the Bible officially commissioned by a majority of British churches and directed by C. H. Dodd (1884–1973). The New Testament appeared in 1961, the Old Testament and Apocrypha in 1970.

New Evangelicalism   A term for an American movement from the 1950s that sought to move beyond fundamentalism with a heightened social concern while also maintaining theologically conservative doctrine. It was transdenominational and has taken several expressions, particularly on biblical authority.

new fire, blessing of the   A ceremony at the beginning of the Easter Vigil in which new fire is struck as a symbol of creation and the resurrection.

New Hampshire Confession (1833)   A Baptist confessional statement espousing a moderate Calvinism that has served as a nonbinding document for numerous Baptist bodies.

New Haven theology   A theological movement originating at Yale University through Timothy Dwight (1752–1817) and Nathaniel W. Taylor (1786–1858) that opposed the current Calvinism, encouraged revivalism, and sought social reforms. Also called "Taylorism."

new heart   *See* regeneration

new heavens and new earth   *See* new creation

New Hermeneutic, the   A term associated with the interpretive approach of Rudolf Bultmann (1884–1976) and his followers, who adapted the work of the philosopher Martin Heidegger (1889–1976) and argued for the demythologization of the New Testament. They explored the relationship of language to meaning and events.

New International Version of the Bible (NIV, 1978)   An English translation made by a committee of more than one hundred evangelical scholars from more than a dozen evangelical seminaries. It was originated by the Christian Reformed Church, the National Association of Evangelicals, and the (now) International Bible Society.

new Israel   A theological term to denote the Christian church.

new Jerusalem   A futuristic image for the church (Rev. 3:12; 21:2).

New Jerusalem Bible (NJB, 1985)   A new edition of the Jerusalem Bible (1966), an English translation by Roman Catholic scholars that was based on the original languages, first published in 1966, following an earlier French edition. The general editor of the revision was Henry Wansbrough. It was inspired by a French revision (1973) and sought to avoid sexist renderings.

New King James Version (NKJV; 1979, 1982)   A revision of the King James Version of the Bible by over one hundred scholars to update the text but maintain it with as little change as possible. The New Testament appeared in 1979, the Old Testament in 1982. It has been used in theologically conservative churches.

new life   A theological designation of the Christian existence that comes through faith in Jesus Christ by the work of the Holy Spirit (Rom. 7:6).

New Light schism   Mid-18th-century divisions within American Congregationalism and Presbyterianism between those who emphasized correct, Calvinistic doctrine ("Old Lights") and those who supported the Great Awakening and revivalism ("New Lights"). Also called "Old Side" and "New Side" Presbyterians, who were reunited in 1758.

New Lights   A term from the Great Awakening in New England (1740–43). The New Lights were those who supported George Whitefield (1715–70) and his evangelistic efforts of mass revivals. Led by Jonathan Edwards (1703–58), they argued that the revivals were the work of God.

new measures   A term for the revivalist methods of Charles G. Finney (1792–1875) that emphasized the place of human efforts in obeying divine laws as a way of promoting religious awakenings.

new morality   A term associated with the view that new ethical standards were replacing traditional ethical values. It is often associated with the situation ethics approach that was prominent in the 1960s.

new people of God   A theological designation for the Christian church.

new quest of the historical Jesus   A movement begun by the German New Testament scholar Ernst Käsemann in 1953 that sought again to discover the historical personage of Jesus by maintaining that there is authentic history behind much of the text of the Synoptic Gospels. Study was made of the continuities between the historical Jesus and the Christ proclaimed in early Christianity.

New Revised Standard Version of the Bible (NRSV, 1989)   English translation of the Bible that was a revision of the Revised Standard Version (RSV; New Testament, 1946; Old Testament, 1952) based on newer manuscript evidence and contemporary translation practices.

New School theology (Presbyterianism)   The movement within 19th-century American Presbyterianism that supported revivalism and moral reform. Leaders included Albert Barnes (1798–1870) and Lyman Beecher (1775–1863). It was opposed by the "Old School," which stressed Calvinistic doctrine. A denominational split occurred (1837) that lasted until the 1869 reunion.

New Side Presbyterianism   In 18th-century American Presbyterianism, the side that promoted revivalism and particularly the work of George Whitefield (1715–70). A New Side synod of New York was formed that was reunited with the Old Side synods (1758), which had stressed confessional orthodoxy.

New Testament   (From Gr. *diathēkē*, "covenant," Lat. *testamentum*) The twenty-seven books accepted by the Christian church as Scripture and as God's revelation, centered in Jesus Christ. They constitute the norm for the church's life as expressions of the will of God.

New Testament theology   A term for the attempt to give historical descriptions and to synthesize the teachings of the New Testament as a whole on various themes.

new theology   A general title for the attempts of theologians to update theology and to adjust the Christian message to contemporary contexts.

New Thought   A philosophical point of view that emerged in the early 20th century that affirmed each individual's duty to be loyal to the truth as that person perceives it. God is basically perceived as universal love, life, truth, and joy; as one experiences these, one knows God.

New World Translation of the Bible (1961)   A translation of the Bible produced and used by the Jehovah's Witnesses.

New Yale school of theology   An approach to theology by theologians associated with Yale University, particularly George Lindbeck (b. 1923) and Hans Frei (1922–88). Theology is primarily concerned with "Christian self-description," since the Bible provides the sociolinguistic framework for Christian identity.

New Year's Day   The first day of a new year, celebrated in the church on January 1 as the Feast of Jesus' Circumcision.

Niagara Conferences   A series of 19th-century Bible conferences at Niagara-on-the-Lake, Ontario, Canada, to draw together evangelicals through Scripture studies. The conferences became increasingly focused on issues of biblical prophecy and spread Dispensationalism as a means of biblical interpretation.

Nicaea (Nicea), Council of (325)
The Christian church's first ecumenical council, called by the emperor Constantine to deal with Arianism. Its creed affirmed the divinity of Jesus Christ as of the "same substance" (Gr. *homoousios*) with God the Father.

Nicaea (Nicea), Second Council of (787)
The Christian church's seventh ecumenical council, called by the empress Irene to deal with the iconoclastic controversy. It decreed that those persons who are represented by images may be "venerated" but not "adored."

Nicene Creed   The Christian creed adopted at the Council of Nicaea (325). The creed in contemporary common use and called the "Nicene Creed" is the Niceno-Constantinopolitan Creed (381). The later creed modified the earlier one and affirmed a view of Jesus Christ to counter Arianism.

Niceno-Constantinopolitan Creed   The Christian creed adopted at the Council of Constantinople (381) and commonly referred to as the Nicene Creed. It is widely used liturgically. The creed is an expansion of the Nicene Creed (325) with a long section on the Holy Spirit. It

combated Arianism and affirmed the divinity of Jesus Christ.

Niebuhrian   The thought that derives from the American theologian Reinhold Niebuhr (1892–1971), who emphasized "Christian realism" as an ethical posture in relating love and justice. Pessimistic about human nature, Niebuhr saw the ambiguity and paradox in human decision-making.

Nihil obstat   (Lat. "Nothing obstructs") A phrase used within the Roman Catholic tradition to indicate that a book contains nothing contrary to official church dogma or that will harm the faith of its readers.

nihilianism   A christological view holding that Jesus Christ in his human nature was "nothing" and that his essential being contained his Godhead alone. It was condemned in 1170 and 1177.

nihilism   (From Lat. *nihil*, "nothing") A philosophical view that rejects all authority, tradition, and morality. As a 19th-century social and political philosophy it rejected religious and moral values.

Ninety-five Theses (1517)   The theological points traditionally believed to have been posted on the door of the Wittenberg church by Martin Luther (1483–1546) for debate within the Roman Catholic Church. They triggered the Protestant Reformation in Europe.

NIV   *See* New International Version

NJB   *See* New Jerusalem Bible

NKJV   *See* New King James Version

Noel   (Fr. from Lat. *natalis*, "birthday") Christmas or the Christmas season. Also, a Christmas song or carol.

noetic   (From Gr. *noētikos*, "intellectual," and *noein*, "to perceive") Relating to the mind or intellect. Pertaining to the view that understanding comes through rationality.

Noetics   (Gr. *noētikos*, "intellectual") Name for 19th-century professors of Oriel College, Oxford, who worked for greater intellectual freedom and theological understanding within Oxford University and the Church of England.

nominal Christian A term for one who, while officially affiliated with or a member of a church, does not appear to take the demands of Christian discipleship seriously.

nominalism (Lat. *nominalis,* "belonging to a name") A medieval philosophical view that universal ideas are only names. Only specific, individual things exist. Abstract ideas are merely labels used by the mind. It opposed "realism" and was taught by William of Occam (c. 1285–c. 1349).

nominalists Those who held to the philosophical view of nominalism.

nominating committee The group which presents persons' names for offices or positions to a church body in an election.

non posse non peccare/non posse peccare (Lat. "not able not to sin,"/"not able to sin") Theological formulations by Augustine (354–430) to indicate the condition of sinners on earth ("not able not to sin") and saints in heaven ("not able to sin").

nonbeing A term associated with the theology of Paul Tillich (1886–1965), describing the nothingness from which finite beings emerge and into which they pass. The nothingness is conquered by the ground of being (God) in Jesus Christ.

nonbiblical That which is not drawn directly from the Bible. Also used to indicate things that may be contradictory to biblical teachings.

non-Christian religions Those religious faiths which do not consider themselves Christian and do not consider Jesus Christ as fully God and fully human.

noncompatibilistic freedom The view that human freedom cannot be reconciled with God's determination of all that occurs.

Nonconformity The practice of not complying with a church body established by a government as an official religion. The term arose in English history when Puritans and Separatists would not adhere to the established Church of England from 1660 until the Toleration Act (1689).

nondenominational church A fellowship of Christians who meet for worship but who are not formally affiliated with an ecclesiastical denomination.

nonelect Those who have not been chosen by God for salvation, as compared to the "elect."

nonessentialism A philosophical view of truth which holds that the essential nature of a thing cannot be spoken of in isolation from, but only in relation with, other things. There are no intrinsic properties of an object in itself. Relational properties are qualities in relation to other things such as human interests and desires.

nonfundamental articles (Lat. *articuli nonfundamentales*) Those articles or doctrines of Christian faith, the denial of which does not endanger salvation. The existence of Christianity does not depend on these doctrines.

Nonjurors Church of England members who would not swear loyalty to William and Mary (1688) because of their contention that James II was the rightful king of England.

nonliturgical Christian groups Christian groups that do not adhere to a fixed form of liturgy for worship.

nontheistic religion A religion that does not teach a belief in God or gods.

norm (Lat. "rule," "pattern") In ethics, the rule, pattern, or model used to judge human action and behavior. Varying ethical theories and construction of norms from antinomianism to absolutism to situationism have developed.

norma normans (Lat. "the ruling rule") Designation for Holy Scripture by Protestants to indicate it is the authority by which all doctrine and teaching must be judged.

norma normans sed non normata (Lat.) The norm that rules other norms, as when Jesus Christ is seen as the final norm of theology.

norma normata (Lat. "the rule having been ruled") A designation for confessions of faith tested by Scripture and thus acceptable to churches.

Northfield Conferences   Nineteenth-century Bible conferences held at Northfield, Massachusetts, led by the American evangelist Dwight L. Moody (1837–99) that enlisted over 2,000 students for foreign missionary service and led to the founding of the Student Volunteer Movement.

notae ecclesiae   *See* marks of the church

notes of the church   *See* marks of the church

nothing/nothingness   (Gr. *mē on,* and *ouk on*) The Greeks distinguished between that which is not but has the potentiality to be (*mē on*) and "nothing" or "nonbeing" (*ouk on*). The Christian confession is that God created all "out of nothing" (*ex nihilo*) and was not limited in any way.

notitia   (Lat. "understanding") A classical component of faith that points to the intellectual dimension of the faith experience. The other components are *assensus* and *fiducia.*

noumena   Philosophical term for "things in themselves," which, according to Immanuel Kant (1724–1804) are not known other than by intellectual intuitions. Plato (428–348 B.C.) used the term to mean "the intelligible."

Nouvelle Théologie   (Fr. "new theology") A renewal of Roman Catholic theology in France through a return to the sources (Fr. *ressourcement*), particularly the work of Thomas Aquinas (1225–74). Also called "Neo-Scholasticism" or "Neo-Thomism."

Novatianism   A movement of the mid-3d to 6th centuries led by Novatian (c. 200–c. 258) that broke from the Christian church and took a "rigorist" stand toward "lapsed" Christians who had renounced their faith during persecutions in wanting them permanently excommunicated.

novena   (Lat. *novenus,* "ninefold") A devotional practice within Roman Catholicism of private and public prayer for nine consecutive days with the purpose of achieving a special grace. It emerges from biblical passages of prayer and waiting (Luke 24:49; Acts 1:13–14) and has its origins in medieval piety.

novice   (Lat. *novicius,* "new," "fresh") Name for those who enter the religious life as candidates or probationers prior to their profession of vows.

NRSV   *See* New Revised Standard Version

nullity   (From Lat. *nullum,* "nothing") A term in Roman Catholic canon law to indicate that an act or contract is not legal because some required aspect is not present. The principle has often been used in relation to declaring a marriage invalid.

number of the beast   The number "666" (variation in some manuscripts: 616) associated with an evil figure who is portrayed as opposing God (Rev. 13:18). Historically, various figures have been connected with the number through representations of their names by numbers, each letter being given a numerical value.

numerology, biblical   The study of the significance that certain numbers in Scripture may have.

numinous, the   (From Lat. *numen,* "deity") Elements in the experience of the holy that are fascinating, awe-inspiring, and mysterious.

nun   (Lat. *nonna,* fem. of *nonnus,* "monk") A female member of a religious order who has taken vows of poverty, chastity, and obedience. In the Roman Catholic tradition, nuns live a communal life.

Nunc Dimittis   (Lat. "Now you are dismissing [your servant]") The opening words in the Song of Simeon (Luke 2:29–32) in the Latin Vulgate.

nuncio, papal (From Lat. *nuntius,* "messenger") A type of papal legate who represents the pope to the religious and civil authorities of a country as well as to the particular churches in the nation or state. A nuncio is a papal legate holding the rank of ambassador.

nunnery (Middle English *nunnerie*) A convent for nuns.

nuptial(s) (From Lat. *nubere,* "to marry [a man]") Of or pertaining to marriage or a marriage ceremony.

nurturance Growth in nurturing is spoken of in feminist writings as needing the power of the nurturer to be healing and creative, while the relation should be mutual and reciprocal.

oath Formal affirmation calling upon God as a witness to the truthfulness of what is stated. It may be assertive in that it refers to the validity of a past or present fact. It may be promissory in that it refers to the reliability of a future commitment.

obedience (Lat. *obedire,* "to obey") The ethical response that inclines one to do what is lawful or required by one in authority. It describes the faith response of Christians to the will of God. More specifically, it is one of the three monastic vows of those entering religious orders.

obedience, vow of Promise by those who enter the religious life to obey God and their earthly superiors. Additional vows are of chastity and poverty.

obedience of Christ (Lat. *obedientia Christi*) The obedient work of Jesus Christ as the mediator between God and humanity who died to provide redemption. It is distinguished as his "active obedience," embracing his life and ministry and his "passive obedience" whereby he accepted suffering and death.

obediential potency (Lat. *potentia obedientialis*) In Roman Catholic theology, the intrinsic being of humans, which is open to God's self-communication (revelation) and thus for supernatural grace.

Human nature is thus open to God's radical self-expression in Jesus Christ.

Oberlin theology A 19th-century American Protestant theological movement emerging from Oberlin College in Ohio, led by Charles Finney (1792–1875) and others. It rejected traditional Calvinism and emphasized Christians seeking perfection, as well as revivalism.

obex (Lat. "hindrance") In Roman Catholic theology, a specific spiritual impediment to receiving sacramental grace.

object of election (Lat. *obiectum electionis*) Humans who are included in the elect of God and actually receive salvation. The term is used by both Lutheran and Reformed orthodox theologians.

object of faith (Lat. *obiectum fidei*) A term used by scholastic theologians for Scripture (the "formal object of faith") and Jesus Christ or God's whole revelation given in Christ (the "material object of faith").

object of theology (Lat. *obiectum theologiae*) Protestant scholastic theologians considered this to be God in God's revelation. The "material object" of theology is the substance of God's revelation and the "formal object" of theology is the method of knowing God's revelation or Scripture.

objectification   Treating persons as objects. Feminist writers see sexual objectification as the primary form of the subjection of women.

objective Christianity   A term found in the thought of Søren Kierkegaard (1813–55) to describe a detached and nongenuine Christianity, as if Christianity may be proved and tested and thus be "objective," rather than subjective in such a way as radically to affect one's being.

objective guilt   The guilt that is based on a genuine cause of doing something wrong rather than merely a feeling or perception of guilt.

objective knowledge   Knowledge that exists independently of a knower.

objective truth   Truth that exists independently of those who know it. In the thought of Søren Kierkegaard (1813–55), the "facts" that exist independently of a knower and do not affect that person in an existential manner.

objectivity   Insofar as possible, external detachment from what is perceived or affirmed so that "value free" judgments may be rendered.

oblates   (Lat. *oblatus,* "offered") A lay movement in the Roman Catholic Church for those who adhere to certain rules of life but do not live in a religious community setting.

oblation   (From Lat. *oblatio,* "an offering") A name for the Eucharist during the early church period. More specifically the term is used for the offerings of bread and wine in the Eucharist and also for the offering of the Christian's life in service to God through Christ (Rom. 12:1).

obligation   (Lat. *obligatio,* "a binding") In ethics, the claims upon one's conduct that transcend whatever one's own feelings about these claims may be. It is an unconditional requirement.

obsession   (Lat. *obsessus,* "being beseiged") A synonym for "possession" when referring to the belief that an evil spirit or demon is the motivating force for a person's behavior.

Occamism   The thought emerging from William of Occam (c. 1285–c. 1349), the medieval philosopher who sought to eliminate the concept of universals in favor of an extreme nominalism. He developed a *via moderna* ("new way") in contrast to the prevailing *via antiqua* ("old way").

Occam's razor   Philosophical maxim from William of Occam (c. 1285–c. 1349): "It is futile to do with more elements what can be done with fewer" (*Summa totius logicae*). It is sometimes called the "law of parsimony." This principle stresses simplicity.

occasional sermons   Sermons preached at other than normally scheduled Sunday worship services. These may be at special times in the life of the nation or community.

occasionalism   (From Lat. *occasio,* "event") A philosophical view denying causality in the natural realm and asserting that events are occasions through which God as sole causal agent effects change.

occult/occultism   (Lat. *occultus,* "concealed") Belief in and practice of astrology, magic, witchcraft, spiritualism, etc., in order to contact invisible powers and to use them for specific purposes. These have been condemned in Christianity.

Octateuch   (Gr. *okta-,* "eight," and *teuchos,* "book") A term for the first eight books of the Old Testament (the Pentateuch plus Joshua, Judges, and Ruth).

octave   (Lat. *octavus,* "eighth") The eighth day of a Christian festival or feast, or a period of eight days of observance beginning with the festival or feast. Presently only Christmas, Easter, and Pentecost have octaves in the Western church calendars.

odium theologicum   (Lat. "theological hatred") A colloquial expression that describes the feelings of malice that may arise from a theological controversy.

oecumenical   *See* ecumenical

offering (From Lat. *offerre,* "to carry up," "to offer") The presentation of one's self to God for service (see Rom. 12:1–2). Also used as a term for the Eucharist or the presentation of bread and wine in the Eucharist. In Protestantism, the presentation of gifts of money for mission.

offertory (From Lat. *offerre,* "to carry up," "to offer") The verses from the book of Psalms or other portions of Scripture that are sung while the offering is presented or the Communion elements are being prepared. In Protestant churches, an organ may play sacred music during the collection of the offering.

office A permanent and ongoing ministerial position within an ecclesiastical structure. Some offices are temporary in that they are to function for a certain time period or in relation to a specific church need. Others are believed to be established by divine law or Scripture.

office, daily (divine) Daily services of divine worship prescribed in Roman Catholic, Anglican, and to a lesser degree Lutheran churches. Also called "canonical hours," or "the hours."

office hymn A hymn to be used during the liturgy of the daily office.

officers, church Those who are selected to serve in official capacities in a church.

offices of Christ The work of Jesus Christ in relation to several aspects. These are usually that of "prophet," in which he reveals God's will (John 15:15); "priest," in mediating between God and humanity (Heb. 4:14–7:28); and "king," as proclaimer and embodiment of God's reign (Luke 17:21; 1 Cor. 15:25).

oikoumene *See* ecumenical

oil, anointing with *See* anointing

oil, holy Oil (usually olive oil) consecrated by a bishop on Holy Thursday for parish use throughout the year to anoint the sick, and in ceremonies of baptism, confirmation, and ordination.

Old Believers Russian Orthodox groups who resisted the reforms of Patriarch Nikon (1652–58) and who continue in two main groups reflective of traditional Russian piety.

Old Calvinists *See* New England theology

Old Catholics Three groups that rejected some of the decisions made at the Council of Trent (1545–63) and later, hold orthodox Christian doctrine, but are not in communion with the Church of Rome. They are also called "National Catholics."

old covenant A term for the Old Testament. The Greek *diathēkē* ("covenant") was translated *testamentum* ("testament") in the Latin Vulgate. Theologically from the Christian perspective, the old covenant, denoting God's covenantal relations with Israel as the people of God, contrasts with and prepares for God's new covenant in Jesus Christ (2 Cor. 3:14; Heb. 8:6–7).

old dispensation Another term for the Old Testament, or specifically the covenants that constituted God's relationship with humanity prior to the new covenant made in Jesus Christ.

old life A term for one's life prior to regeneration by God through the power of the Holy Spirit to bring faith in Jesus Christ.

Old Lights A term from the Great Awakening in New England (1740–43) for those who opposed the evangelistic preaching of George Whitefield (1715–70) on theological and social grounds. Led by Charles Chauncey (1705–87), they did not perceive the revivals as the work of God.

old nature A term for one's nature prior to regeneration by God through the power of the Holy Spirit to bring faith in Jesus Christ.

Old Roman Creed The primitive predecessor to the Apostles' Creed used by the church in Rome from the late 2d century. It was a short, interrogatory baptismal creed with three articles on God the Father, Jesus Christ the Son, and the Holy Spirit.

Old School theology (Presbyterianism)
The traditional Calvinism of 19th-century American Presbyterians upheld staunchly by professors from Princeton Seminary including Archibald Alexander (1772–1851) and Charles Hodge (1797–1878). They opposed the New School theology which supported revivalism. A denominational split occurred (1837) which lasted until the 1869 reunion.

Old Side Presbyterians   In 18th-century American Presbyterianism, the conservative side that stressed Calvinist, confessional orthodoxy. It was opposed to the pietism and emphasis on experience promulgated by William Tennent (1673–1746) and his Log College movement called "New Side" Presbyterians.

Old Testament   The biblical books considered by Christians to be canonical Scripture and the self-revelation of God and thus authoritative for Christian churches. The Roman Catholic canon numbers 46 books while the Protestant canon is composed of 39 books.

Old Testament believers   See Old Testament saints

Old Testament saints   A term for those prior to the coming of Jesus Christ who believed God's promises and were in a covenant relationship with the Lord. An example is Abraham (Gen. 15:6; Rom. 4:3). They are also called "Old Testament believers."

Old Testament theology   A term for the attempt to give historical descriptions and to synthesize the teachings of the Old Testament as a whole on various themes.

oligarchical system of church government   A Presbyterian form of church polity that gives representation to a select number of persons who exercise authority. These leaders are elected by church bodies.

omission, sins of   See sins of omission

omnibenevolent   (From Lat. *omnis,* "all," and *benevolentia,* "good will") A designation for God to indicate God's goodness and actions as a moral being in ways of love, mercy, and compassion.

omnipotence of God   See God, omnipotence of

omnipresence of God   See God, omnipresence of

omniscience of God   See God, omniscience of

omnitemporal   (From Lat. *omnis,* "all," and *temporalis,* "relating to time") Designation for God as existing at all times (eternal).

Oneida Community   A communal society originating in Putney, Vermont (1835), under the leadership of J. H. Noyes but associated with Oneida, New York. It taught a form of perfectionism, i.e., that the soul is freed from sin only when selfishness is eliminated. Strict discipline was imposed.

Oneness Pentecostalism   A form of Pentecostalism that began in 1914. It rejected the doctrine of the Trinity and insisted on rebaptism solely in the name of the Lord Jesus Christ. The United Pentecostal Church International or "Jesus Only" movement embraces this view.

only begotten   A term used in the KJV in John 3:16 that indicates the unique status of Jesus Christ as God's Son.

ontic   Pertaining to existing reality.

ontological argument   One of the classical arguments for the existence of God based on the powers of reason. As developed by Anselm (1033–1109), it considers God to be "that than which nothing greater can be conceived." As such, God must "exist" because to lack existence would be to be defective.

ontological deity of Jesus   A way of expressing the conviction that Jesus Christ in himself possessed all aspects of deity, as opposed to a "functional" view in which he would be considered "divine" because he acted or functioned in certain ways.

ontologism   A view condemned by the Roman Catholic Church (1861) that claims human knowledge is made possible solely through a direct, yet nonexplicit, vision of God's divine essence. It was taught by Malebranche (d. 1715), Giorbert (d. 1852), and A. Rosmini-Serbati (d. 1855).

ontology (From Gr. *on*, "being," and *logos*, "study") The philosophical study of being as being. It is thus the study of the underlying principles which are present in all things that exist solely by virtue of their existing.

open air meeting Services of worship held outside in open spaces, often as evangelistic or revival services and involving a community or region.

open Communion The practice of inviting all Christians present to participate in the sacrament of the Lord's Supper when it is celebrated in a worship service, as opposed to closed Communion, which restricts participation.

Ophites A Gnostic sect whose name derives from a Greek term meaning "followers of the serpent" and who regarded the serpent held up by Moses (Num. 21:8, 9; 2 Kings 18:4; John 3:14) as the supreme emanation of God.

oppression (From Lat. *oppressio*, "a pressing down") The condition of being treated unjustly and living without freedom. It is stressed by liberation theologians in describing the situations of the poor and marginalized who lack necessary freedom and rights due to the injustices of nations.

opus Dei (Lat. "work of God") Term used by Benedict (c. 480–547) and the Benedictines to indicate that the work of prayer and worship are humans' primary responsibilities, and thus the need to participate in fixed liturgical forms in religious communities.

opus operatum See: *ex opere operato*

oracles of God (Lat. *oracula Dei*) A term associated with the theology of John Calvin (1509–64) to indicate the various ways by which God speaks or is uniquely revealed: in the incarnation (Christ), Scripture, redemptive history, preaching, and the sacraments.

oral tradition Materials passed from one group to another through word of mouth instead of in written forms. Much of the biblical material was preserved this way prior to being written.

oral transmission The process of passing on oral traditions from one group to another.

Orange, Councils of (441, 529) Two church councils held in southern France. At the second council, the views of Augustine (354–430) on nature and grace were upheld against the view known as Semi-Pelagianism.

oratorio (Ital., from Lat. *oratorium*) A dramatic musical composition that features soloists, chorus, and orchestra.

oratory (Lat. *oratorium*, "place of prayer," from Lat. *orare*, "to pray") Roman Catholic term for a small chapel for private prayer.

ordain (Lat. *ordinare*, "to order") A designation for what God wills. Also, the conferring of a sacred office by a church body for the purposes of ministry.

order (Lat. *ordo*, "rank") Term for a church's organization or government.

order of created things (Lat. *ordo rerum creatarum*) The order by which God governs the course of all things in creation, in divine providence, in salvation, and in God's ultimate glorification. The term is typically used in Reformed scholastic theology.

order of decreed things (Lat. *ordo decretorum Dei*) The arrangement of the plan of salvation according to the decrees of God. It includes the question of infralapsarianism versus supralapsarianism in relation to God's decrees. It is an issue in Calvinistic theology.

order of salvation (Lat. *ordo salutis*) A term found particularly in Calvinistic theology to indicate the temporal order of the process of the salvation of the sinner according to the work of God. Elements include calling, regeneration, adoption, conversion, faith, justification, etc.

orders Religious institutes or communities.

orders, contemplative   Orders within the Roman Catholic tradition such as the Carthusian and Carmelite that are devoted to contemplation and prayer as means of glorifying God.

orders, major holy   *See* major orders

orders, ministerial   Most generally, the responsibilities, prerogatives, and privileges ministers receive when they are ordained by an ecclesiastical body.

orders, minor holy   *See* minor orders

orders, religious   Communities or societies that submit to a common rule or authority and rule of life.

orders, sacrament of holy   In Roman Catholicism, the sacrament that sets a person apart for the performance of sacred rituals. Also called ordination, it is performed through the laying on of hands (1 Tim. 4:14; 2 Tim. 1:6).

orders (ordinances) of creation   (Ger. *Ordnungen*) Term used by the 19th-century Erlangen school to describe its reading of 16th-century Lutheran theology as teaching certain established laws, prescriptions, imperatives, or positions in society that are known independently of the Word of God. These would include the state, marriage, and humanity in God's image.

ordinal   (From Lat. *ordo,* "order") Book containing the service for ordination of deacons, priests, or bishops. Also a book with occasional services requiring a bishop's leadership.

ordinance   (From Lat. *ordinans,* "arranging") A religious rite, similar to a "sacrament," engaged in as a memorial or act of obedience rather than as having sacramental efficacy. In nonsacramental Christian traditions, baptism and the Lord's Supper are considered ordinances.

ordinand   (From Lat. *ordinandus*) One who is ordained by an ecclesiastical body.

ordinary   (From Lat. *ordo,* "order") A fixed liturgical text, such as that used in the Eucharist. Also the components of a musical Mass including the Kyrie, Glo-

ria, Nicene Creed, Sanctus, and Agnus Dei. The term is further used for the bishop of a diocese.

ordinary language analysis   *See* philosophy, analytical

Ordinary Time   The periods of the liturgical year after Epiphany and Pentecost. This designation has been used in the Roman Catholic Church since 1969.

ordination   (Lat. *ordinatio,* "ordering") The act of setting a person apart for ministerial office either for the conferring of powers (sacramental view) or to recognize how God has acted in the person's life (nonsacramental view).

ordination of women   The practice of admitting women to ecclesiastical status as ordained persons. Some traditions have resisted opening the ministerial office to women and the issue has been widely debated.

ordo salutis   *See* order of salvation

organ   (Gr. *organon,* Lat. *organum,* "tool," "instrument") An instrument usually used in churches to provide sacred music for services of worship.

organ transplantation   The removal of an organ from one person who is dead or alive to be used in another person's body. A number of ethical issues surround this practice.

organic union/unity   The joining of two church bodies or denominations into one ecclesiastical unit. This official connection contrasts with the concept of a "spiritual unity" in which shared beliefs may be present without a formal official relationship.

organized church   A body of Christian believers joined in a formal organization with membership rolls so that an outward and visible expression of Christian commitment is present.

orientation   (From Lat. *oriens,* "east") The placement of a church structure so that its sanctuary points to the east. This emerged from the ancient Christian practice of facing east while praying. In

Judaism, prayer was offered facing east, toward the Jerusalem Temple.

Origenism The views emerging from the teachings of Origen (c. 185–c. 254) and his followers (Origenists) including the preexistence of human souls, the subordination of the Son to the Father, and the view of universal salvation (universalism). A number of these teachings were condemned by church councils.

original justice *See* original righteousness

original righteousness (Lat. *iustitia originalis*) A theological term for the perfect righteousness of Adam and Eve before God at their creation (Gen. 1), which was lost through the fall into sin (Gen. 3). Also called original justice or natural righteousness.

original sin (Lat. *peccatum originalis*) The condition of sinfulness which all persons share and which is caused by the sinful origins of the race (Adam and Eve) and the fall (Gen. 3). Theologically it consists of the loss of original righteousness and the distortion of the image of God.

orthodox (Gr. *orthodoxos*, from *orthos*, "right," and *doxa*, "belief," "praise") That which is considered to be correct or proper belief as defined by official ecclesiastical bodies.

Orthodox Church, the The churches that accept the primacy of the Patriarch of Constantinople and the teachings of the first seven ecumenical church councils. Also known as Eastern Orthodoxy, since most churches are in eastern Europe and the Middle East. A split from Western churches occurred in 1054.

Orthodox spirituality The religious and devotional practices found within Eastern Orthodox churches, stressing worship as adoration, a strong sense of the mystical presence of Christ, and emphasis on contemplation. Central as well are the liturgy and sacraments as well as observance of the church year.

Orthodox theology The theology of Eastern Orthodox churches. More gener-

ally, orthodox theology is theological belief that accords with an officially accepted ecclesiastical standard.

Orthodox tradition The tradition of Eastern Orthodox churches. More generally, basic Christian beliefs that are accepted by all Christian churches, often seen as expressed in the traditional Apostles' and Nicene Creeds.

orthodox view A view that accords with the standards considered to be correct belief by an ecclesiastical body.

Orthodoxy (Gr. *orthodoxia*, from *orthos*, "right" and *doxa*, "belief," "praise") That which is considered correct or proper belief, particularly the teachings of early ecumenical church councils from Nicaea (325) to Chalcedon (451). Also, the doctrine and practices of Eastern Orthodoxy.

Orthodoxy, Eastern *See* Eastern Orthodoxy

Orthodoxy, Feast of A festival observed by Eastern Orthodox churches on the first Sunday in Lent that celebrates the victory of right faith over all heresies. It originated to celebrate the defeat of the Iconoclasts and the restoration of icons in Orthodox churches (842).

orthopraxis/orthopraxy (From Gr. *orthos*, "right," and *praxis*, "practice") Right practice. Used in liberation theology to stress the importance of action concerned with the practical and political content of Christian faith.

orthros (Gr. "dawn") The morning office of prayers and worship in the Eastern church, corresponding to matins and lauds in the Western church.

Osiandrian controversy The controversy over the views of the Lutheran theologian Andreas Osiander (1498–1552). In 1550 he disagreed with Luther's understanding of justification by faith, teaching that in justification Christ infuses righteousness, or makes the believer righteous, rather than legally imputing righteousness to the believer. The Formula of Concord (1577) rejected Osiander's views (Art. 3).

ostensorium   *See* monstrance

other, wholly   *See* wholly other

otherworldliness   An attitude that focuses so strongly on life after death and issues of the spiritual life that the needs of the present world are unaddressed.

ousia   (Gr. "being," "substance"; Lat. *essentia, substantia*) A key philosophical and theological term used at the Council of Nicaea (325) to indicate that the Son, Jesus Christ, is of the same essence or substance as God the Father. Later the same was said of the Holy Spirit.

outer darkness   A term used by Jesus to describe being cast away from the presence of God (Matt. 8:12; 22:13; 25:30).

overture   A term used in a presbyterian form of church government for a formal communication from a presbytery to the General Assembly.

ox, winged   In Christian art, a symbol associated with the Gospel writer Luke.

Oxford Group   Nondenominational movement founded by F.N.D. Buchman (1928), who engaged in "life-changing" campaigns that stressed seeking God's guidance and obeying moral absolutes: purity, unselfishness, honesty, and love. In 1938 the movement became known as Moral Rearmament.

Oxford movement   A 19th-century movement for church renewal within the Church of England (1833–45) and within Anglicanism led by John Keble (1792–1866), E. B. Pusey (1800–82), and J. H. Newman (1801–90) that sought to recover the "catholic" elements in the church's doctrine and piety.

P

P   The "Priestly" source. A literary source of the Pentateuch identified because it is supposed to have been produced by priests. It is marked by more dignified language than some other Pentateuchal sources and consists of a combination of laws, editorial notes, and stories (e.g., Gen. 1).

pacifism   (Lat. *pacificus,* "peacemaking") The view that violence and war are morally wrong, and thus a strong dedication to the promotion of peace. This can lead pacifists to refuse to participate in war and to avoid violence at all costs.

paedobaptism   (From Gr. *pais,* "child," and *baptizein,* "to baptize") The practice of baptizing infants, or infant baptism. It is the practice of Roman Catholicism, Eastern Orthodoxy, and many denominations of Protestantism. Also pedobaptism.

pagan   (Lat. *paganus,* "peasant") One who is a non-Christian and thus does not worship the true and living God.

paganism   From the Christian point of view, religious and ethical views that are not Christian.

pain of God theology   A 20th-century theological movement associated with the Japanese Lutheran theologian Kazo Kitamori, who emphasized God's pain as the "heart of the Gospel." By serving God with human pain, our pain can be healed. This was indigenous Japanese theology in the post–World War II context.

Palamism   *See* Hesychasm

palimpsest   (From Gr. *palimpsēstos,* "rubbed again") A parchment from which writing has been erased so that another text may be entered. Many biblical manuscripts are of this type.

palingenesis (Gr. *palin*, "again," and *genesis*, "birth") The rebirth, new birth, or regeneration effected by the Holy Spirit in the work of salvation.

pall (From Lat. *pallium*, "cover") A covering used over the chalice during the service of the Eucharist. Also, the cloth draped over a coffin at funerals.

palm leaf (Gr. *palamē*, "palm of the hand") A Roman symbol of triumph. A crowd greeted Jesus' entry into Jerusalem on "Palm Sunday" with palms in the custom of Jewish pilgrims (John 12:13). In Christian art, the palm leaf became a symbol of martyrdom and triumph over death (Rev. 7:9–12).

Palm Sunday The Sunday prior to Easter, commemorating Jesus' entry into Jerusalem to the shouts of "Hosanna" and the waving of palms (John 12:13). It is the first day of Holy Week.

Panagia (Gr. "all holy") A title for the Virgin Mary in Eastern churches.

Pancake Tuesday *See* Shrove Tuesday

pancosmism A philosophical view which explains all things on the basis of cosmic forces. It removes all need for a divine being or God.

panentheism (Gr. *pan*, "all," *en*, "in," and *theos*, "God") Term coined by K.C.F. Krause (1781–1832) for the view that God is in all things. This view also sees the world and God as mutually dependent for their fulfillment. It differs from "pantheism," which views God as all and all as God.

panhenic feeling (From Gr. *pan*, "all," and *hen*, "one") The sense of oneness or unity with all things.

panlogism A term associated with the philosophy of G.W.F. Hegel (1770–1831) in which the nature of ultimate reality is perceived to be purely rational or a function of the mind.

Pannenberg Circle A 20th-century group of theological scholars who worked cooperatively and who shared the views of the German theologian Wolfhart Pannenberg (b. 1928). Emphasis is placed on eschatology, with a "theology of hope" as the starting point for theological reflection.

Pantocrator/Pantokrator (Gr. "ruler of all") Credal term for God the Father Almighty, denoting God's sovereignty over all created things. In Christian art, the image of Christ as the absolute ruler of the universe, particularly in domes of Byzantine churches.

panpsychism (From Gr. *pan*, "all," and *psychē*, "soul") The view that everything is essentially psychical and that God is fully immanent in the universe, being the psychic force present in every particle of matter.

pantheism (Gr. *pan*, "all," and *theos*, "God") A term coined by John Toland (1670–1722), literally meaning "everything God." The view is that God is all and all is God. It differs from "panentheism," which views God as in all.

papacy, the (Gr. *papas*, "father") The system of government in the Roman Catholic Church, in which the pope as bishop of Rome holds supreme authority as head of the church. Also the papal succession considered collectively, or simply the office of the pope.

papal blessing A benediction pronounced by a pope. It secures the privilege of a plenary indulgence. A priest who assists a dying person is also permitted to convey this blessing.

papal infallibility *See* infallibility, papal

Papal Mass A Roman Catholic Mass in which the pope sings and the Gospel and Epistle readings are sung in Latin and Greek.

Papal States Area of central Italy under control of the papacy from 756 until Italian unification in 1870. The pope is the secular head of the Vatican, Lateran, and Castel Gandolfo, which were declared papal territory in 1871.

papal supremacy The Roman Catholic view that the pope as successor to the apostle Peter as bishop of Rome is superior to all other bishops in the church (Matt. 16:18–19; John 21:15).

papist   A derogatory term for a Roman Catholic (who accepts the pope's authority).

parable   (Gr. *parabolē*, "a comparing") A short story based on common experiences that contains a meaning.

parables of Jesus   (Gr. *parabolē*, "a comparing") The stories told by Jesus throughout the Synoptic Gospels as a way of teaching. They convey meaning, particularly about the major subject of the reign ("kingdom") of God (see Matt. 13).

parachurch organizations   Groups that carry out specific missions, ministries, or social services outside established ecclesiastical structures or denominational boundaries. They are usually composed of persons from a varied group of representative churches.

Paraclete   (Gr. *paraklētos*, "one who is called to someone's aid," "helper," "advocate") A term used by Jesus for the Holy Spirit, who will be with Jesus' disciples after his death (John 14:16, 26; 15:26; 16:7). It is also used of Jesus himself (1 John 2:1; "advocate").

paradigm   (Gr. *paradeigma*, Lat. *paradigma*, "pattern") A model, pattern, or example. The term is used to indicate ways of thought in theology when materials are gathered and organized in specific patterns or ways, as in "doctrines."

paradigm shift   (From Gr. *paradeigma*, "pattern") The replacement of a model of interpreting reality or some particular issue ("paradigm") by a new one. Paradigms may also be called interpretive models, explanatory models, or models for understanding (Ger. *Verstehensmodelle*).

paradise   (Heb. *pardēs*, Gr. *paradeisos*, "a park," "garden") A description of the Garden of Eden and, in Judaism at the time of Jesus, the place where the righteous dead awaited a resurrection. In Christian theology, it is a synonym for

heaven (Luke 23:43; 2 Cor. 12:4; cf. Rev. 2:7).

paradox   (Gr. *paradoxon*, Lat. *paradoxus*, "contrary to all expectation") A true statement that appears to be contradictory. Some paradoxical Christian affirmations are: God as "one God in three Persons," Jesus as "fully divine and fully human," the believer as "righteous yet a sinner."

paradox, theology of   A term for various forms of existential theology and neo-orthodoxy, especially associated with Søren Kierkegaard (1813–55) and Karl Barth (1886–1968), that stressed the apparently contradictory nature of Christian teachings and saw in this a strong sign of their truth.

paraenesis   (Gr. "moral instruction," "exhortation") Term describing biblical passages such as Rom. 12; Col. 3:18ff.; and 1 Peter 2:1ff., where ethical prescriptions about Christian life and behavior are given.

parallelism, poetic   A characteristic of Hebrew poetry, found particularly in the book of Psalms, in which two sequential lines may exhibit synonymous (Ps. 61:1), antithetic (Prov. 17:22), or synthetic parallels of thought (Ps. 2:2).

paralogism   Reasoning contrary to the rules of logic.

paralogy   Postmodern approach to the analysis of discourse, stressing the differences and contradictions in language use. Its effect is to emphasize the pluralism, contingency, and particular character of discourse.

pardon   (Lat. *perdonare*, "to remit a debt") The forgiveness of a wrong or debt, used to indicate both God's action in forgiving those who repent (Isa. 55:7; Jer. 50:20) and the actions of persons toward others when wrongs have been done (see Matt. 18:21–35).

pardon, assurance of   *See* pardon, declaration of

pardon, declaration of   A scriptural or theological statement made in a worship service following a prayer of confession of sins, assuring the congregation of God's forgiveness. It is also called "assurance of pardon."

pardoner   In the Middle Ages, one who sold indulgences through which temporal punishments in purgatory could be remitted. This practice led to the initial complaints of Martin Luther (1483–1546) against the Roman Catholic Church. The Council of Trent (1545–63) ended the worst abuses.

parish   (Gr. *paroikia*, Lat. *paroecia*, "an ecclesiastical district") A geographical area served by a church as an area for ministry. The term is also used to designate the members of a church served by a pastor.

parish council   A term used with varying connotations in differing denominational groups. Most generally, it is an administrative board in a local congregation that has a form of oversight over the activities of the church community.

parity of ministers   A principle of government in some church polities, such as Presbyterianism, in which a governing body is composed of an equal number of ordained clergy and lay members.

parochial schools   (Gr. *paroikia*, "a parish") Schools operated by a church body (or parish), usually with the purpose of providing religious instruction in addition to other forms of education.

parole   (Fr.) A term used by the Swiss linguistician Ferdinand de Saussure (1857–1913) for a concrete act of speech. It is distinguished from the language system (*langue*) as a whole, which is the whole structure of a language. Some contemporary hermeneutic theories make use of this distinction.

Parousia   (Gr. *parousia*, "coming," "advent") A term used for the "coming of Christ," most usually focused on the "second coming" or future advent as indicated in the Nicene Creed: he . . . "will come again" (Matt. 24:27–39; Acts 1:11; etc.).

parson   (From Lat. *persona*, "person") A clergyperson in charge of a parish or, more generally, any member of the clergy.

parsonage   The residence of the clergyperson who serves a local congregation. It is usually owned by the church. Also called a "manse."

parthenogenesis   (From Gr. *parthenos*, "virgin," and *genesis*, "birth") "Birth from a virgin." Term denoting the virgin birth of Jesus Christ, by the power of the Holy Spirit, to his mother Mary (Matt. 1:23).

Parthenos   (Gr. "virgin") Designation of Mary the mother of Jesus (Matt. 1:23).

participation   A general term to describe how the nature of one being can have effects on another. An example is of interpersonal communication between two people and the communication between God and humanity.

Particular Baptists   A group of Baptists that began in England in the 17th century (1633) and that held to a Calvinistic instead of an Arminian view of theology.

particular judgment   A term used in Roman Catholic theology to indicate the judgment by God that each individual soul receives at the immediate point of its separation from the body.

particular redemption   *See* limited atonement

particularism   The view of salvation that considers salvation to be related to an individual's personal response to the Christian gospel, as contrasted to universalism, which teaches that God will save all persons regardless of their responses.

particularity   What is specific, definite, and distinctive. Often used to emphasize historical realities over generalized, abstract statements.

party spirit   A term for dissensions that divide a church body along varying lines (see 1 Cor. 3).

Pascal's Wager   A phrase associated with the philosopher Blaise Pascal (1623–62), who argued that in life persons bet their lives either that God exists or that God does not. If one bets there is a God and loses, nothing is lost. If there is a God, however, and one wagers on that, one gains infinitely.

Pasch/Pascha (Aram. and Gr. from Heb., "Passover") The Hebrew festival celebrated on the 14th of Nisan (Passover). The term came to be used by Christians for the Easter celebration due to the links between the date of Easter and Jewish Passover.

paschal (From Gr. *pascha*) Referring to the suffering and death of Jesus Christ (1 Cor. 5:7).

paschal candle A large candle used during Easter to indicate the presence of the risen Christ with the people of God. It is also used at baptisms and funerals to indicate dying and rising with Christ (Rom. 6:4) and the celebration of his victory over death (1 Cor. 15:51–58).

paschal controversy Disputes within the history of the church about the proper date for celebrating Easter (Gr. *pascha*).

paschal lamb Originally, the lamb eaten at Jewish Passovers after its sacrifice in the Temple (Ex. 12). The term is associated in the New Testament with Jesus Christ (John 1:29; 1 Cor. 5:7).

paschal mystery (From Heb. *pesah*, Gr. *pascha*, "Passover," and *mystērion*, "mystery") The full events of Christ's passion, death, resurrection, ascension, and the sending of the Holy Spirit, as these enact God's hidden plan of salvation which is now revealed.

paschal season/Paschaltide The period of the church year that is immediately after Easter and in which the victory of Jesus Christ over sin, death, and evil is celebrated. It is fifty days in length and culminates on Pentecost.

Paschal Vigil The celebration of the suffering, death, and resurrection of Jesus Christ through a service of worship held on the Saturday night before Easter. It is an ancient liturgical observance of the church and includes lighted candles, Scripture readings, preaching, the Eucharist, and the celebration or renewal of baptism.

Paschal Week *See* Holy Week

passibility (From Lat. *passibilis*, "suffering") Able to undergo suffering or pain; able to be changed by an external power. A theological question relates to whether God suffers or endures pain. Some contemporary theologians have favored this view which was rejected by the early church.

passion (From Lat. *passio*, "suffering") Inner emotional experiences. In the thought of Søren Kierkegaard (1813–1855), this forms the basis for ascertaining truth and genuine faith, rather than any outward objective "certainty."

Passion, instruments of the The tools or implements associated with the crucifixion of Jesus such as the cross, spear, sponge, vinegar, crown of thorns, cup.

passion of Christ (From Lat. *passio*, "suffering") A term for the sufferings of Jesus both spiritually and physically prior to and including his crucifixion (2 Cor. 1:5; 1 Peter 2:21; 3:18; 4:1; 5:1).

passion plays Dramatic presentations that portray the passion, suffering, and death of Jesus Christ.

Passion Sunday Formerly, the fifth Sunday in Lent, commemorating the Passion of Jesus Christ. Since the calendar reforms of 1969, it is observed on the sixth Sunday in Lent, which is also called Palm Sunday.

Passion Week *See* Holy Week

Passiontide Traditional commemoration of the sufferings of Jesus Christ during the two weeks prior to Easter in the church year. Currently, Palm Sunday is also designated Passion Sunday and thus the period is one week in duration. Since 1969 calendar reform, the term has not been used.

Passover (Heb. *pesah*, Gr. *pascha*) The Jewish commemoration of the "passing over" of the angel of death prior to the exodus from Egypt (Ex. 12:13, 23). The festival begins on the 14th day of Nisan and is eight days in duration.

Passover, Christian   A term for Easter and the celebration of Christ's victory over sin and death as the Jewish Passover had celebrated the exodus and liberation of Israel from slavery (see 1 Cor. 5:6–8).

Passover lamb   The lamb sacrificed at Jewish Passover celebrations (Ex. 12:21; 2 Chron. 30:15, 17; cf. Mark 14:12; Luke 22:7). The term is used by the apostle Paul as a designation for Jesus Christ (1 Cor. 5:7).

Passover meal   The commemorative Jewish meal remembering the deliverance of the nation of Israel from slavery in Egypt through the exodus event (see Ex. 12:1–28).

pastor   (From Lat. *pascere*, "to pasture," "to feed") A shepherd of a flock. The term denotes one who has spiritual oversight over a congregation of Christian believers in a church or Christian community (Eph. 4:11).

pastoral   (Lat. *pastoralis*) Having the relationship of a pastor to people, or referring to elements relating to a pastor. More generally it refers to the care and nurture of Christian faith.

pastoral associate   A term with a variety of meanings in differing ecclesiastical bodies. It basically refers to a person who assists a pastor in carrying out duties in a parish. Generally the person is not ordained by an ecclesiastical body.

pastoral care   The practical expression of the church's ministry of love for the needs of the community, the people of God, and individuals. It is enacted in a wide variety of ways and through many forms of ministry.

pastoral epistles   The New Testament letters to Timothy and Titus, which deal particularly with "pastoral" elements. They are written to individuals rather than churches. Also called the Pastorals.

pastoral letter   In liturgical traditions, a letter from a bishop to a diocese, or from a house of bishops to all within its jurisdiction. In nonliturgical traditions, a letter from a minister to a congregation.

pastoral ministry   The exercise of care and oversight of a group of Christian believers. The term is used for the ministry of the universal church as a whole and, in specific contexts, of church congregations served by a pastor.

pastoral office   The ecclesiastical status of pastor.

pastoral prayer   An extended prayer offered by the pastor during worship in many Protestant churches, including elements of praise, thanksgiving, confession, and intercession.

pastoral staff   Those who serve in the capacity of pastor in a church or other institution. Also, literally, a staff (crozier) similar to a shepherd's crook, used by a church official as an emblem.

pastoral theology   A branch of practical theology dealing with the relationships between the Word of God and the Christian lives of God's people.

pastoral visitation   The practice of those in pastoral ministry of calling on their parishioners in their homes, in hospitals, or in any situation. It is a form of interpersonal ministry and emerges from the practice of the apostles (Acts 5:42). It has been stressed in Protestantism as a means for spiritual counseling and an expression of care and love.

pastorale   (Ital.) A cantata or musical composition focused on the life and work of ministry.

pastoralia   A segment of theological study concerned with the life and conduct of pastors.

pastorate   (Lat. *pastoratus*) A term to indicate a pastor's ministry with a certain church in terms of its place, duration, or nature.

paten   (Gr. *patanē*, Lat. *patina*, "dish") A plate, often of gold or silver, used to hold the bread in Holy Communion. It often covers the top of the chalice that holds the wine.

Pater Noster (Lat. "Our Father") Designation for the Lord's Prayer from its first two words in Latin (Matt. 6:9–13; Luke 11:2–4).

paternalism (From Lat. *pater,* "father") Attitudes or actions in dealing with others in the way of a father with children and thus with an exercise of power. Feminist theologians have recognized the frequency with which this is practiced by males in society and in the church in relation to women.

paternity, divine Designation of God in relation to Jesus Christ in the Trinity. It is also a designation for the adoption of believers into the family of God and their relationship to God (Rom. 8:15–16).

pathos (Gr. "suffering") Deep compassion for others. The term is used for the sharing of sufferings that Christians are called upon to enter into with others. Some also speak of the "pathos of God" in relation to God's compassion for the world and suffering in Jesus Christ.

patriarch (Gr. *patriarchēs,* from *patria,* "family," "clan," and *archēs,* "ruler") In Roman Catholicism and Eastern Orthodoxy, a term for bishops who are of high status. Historically, the term was for bishops of five important bishoprics.

patriarchal Term used for an attitude of men and a way of acting toward women that is oppressive in its use of power throughout a culture. It is male domination over every aspect of women's existence: political, economic, social, sexual, religious, etc.

patriarchal period The ancient period of significant Old Testament figures, from Abraham, Isaac, and Jacob, extending through Joseph.

patriarchates, the five ancient Five jurisdictions of Christian patriarchs in the period of the ancient church: Rome, Antioch, Alexandria, Jerusalem, and Constantinople.

patriarchs Significant ancient biblical leaders including Abraham, Isaac, Jacob, and his twelve sons who headed the twelve tribes. These are perceived by New Testament writers as establishing the line through which the Messiah (Jesus) came (Acts 7:8, 9; Rom. 9:5; 15:8; Heb. 7:4).

patriarchy Male authority system that oppresses and subordinates women through social, political, and economic institutions and practices.

Patrimony of St. Peter Lands in Italy that were ruled directly by the papacy until 1870. They were also known as the Papal States.

patripassianism (From Lat. *pater,* "father," and *passus,* "having suffered") A 3d-century view that the Son (Jesus Christ) is a form of the Father and that therefore the Father actively suffered on the cross in the death of Jesus. It was considered heretical by the church as a form of modalism. Also called "theopassianism."

patristic theology *See* patristics

patristics The study of the theological work of the early Christian church fathers.

patrology The study of the life and works of the early Christian Fathers or early church theologians ending in approximately 636 in the Western church with the death of Isidore and in 749 in the Eastern church with the death of John of Damascus.

patron saint A saint associated with a particular land, church, institution, or profession. In the Roman Catholic tradition the saint is venerated as an intercessor and special protector.

Paulicians A sect from the 5th century in the Byzantine Empire, perhaps taking its name from Paul of Samosata (3d century), who maintained a Manichaean dualism and taught that the man Jesus became "Christ" through merit, while rejecting the Old Testament, baptism, and the Lord's Supper.

Pauline theology The theological perspectives developed from the New Testament writings of the apostle Paul.

Paulinism A theological viewpoint drawn exclusively from the writings of the apostle Paul and the neglect of other portions of the New Testament.

pax *See* kiss of peace

Pax vobiscum (Lat. "peace be with you") An ecclesiastical greeting stressing God's presence and peace.

peace (Heb. *shalom*, Gr. *eirēnē*) Fullness, well-being. A Hebrew term used both for greeting and farewell with great richness of meaning. It is much more than lack of war and points to full societal and personal well-being, coupled with righteousness and possible only as a gift of God.

peace, theology of A theological perspective that sees all Christian theology from the viewpoint of the peace that God establishes with the world in Jesus Christ (Acts 10:36; Rom. 5:1; Eph. 2:15) and that God desires as the primary mode for human relationships (Matt. 5:9; Rom. 12:18; 2 Cor. 13:11).

peace churches A term coined in 1935 to describe Mennonites, Friends (Quakers), and Brethren church bodies that share views of nonresistance and oppose war. In contemporary times, these groups have sought ways of reconciliation between East and West through cooperative programs and educational activities.

peace offering A Jewish sacrificial offering in which the blood was poured as a libation, the fat burned on the altar, and the meat eaten by the offerer and friends. It was a voluntary offering (Lev. 3; 7:11–38; "offering of well-being" [NRSV]).

peacemaking A view of the task of Christian churches that pursues the biblical vision of peace as eschatological, as linked with justice, as communal and personal, as divine gift and human task, and as requiring witnesses and agents (Matt. 5:9).

peacock, the A symbol of immortality in Christian art because of the belief that a peacock's flesh never decayed.

Peasants' Revolt (1524–26) An uprising by German peasants due to economic difficulties that Martin Luther (1483–1546) bitterly opposed. Thomas Müntzer (c. 1490–1525) took a leading role and grievances were issued at Memmingen in 12 Articles (March 1525). Lutheran princes forcefully suppressed the revolt.

pedilavium *See* foot washing

pedobaptism *See* paedobaptism

Pelagianism The theological views associated with the British monk Pelagius (c. 354–c. 420), who in theological debate with Augustine (354–430) argued for a totally free human will to do the good and held that divine grace was bestowed in relation to human merit. These views were condemned at the Council of Ephesus (431).

pelican, the A Christian symbol of the sacrifice of Jesus Christ to redeem humanity. In Christian art, the pelican is portrayed as piercing its breast with its beak to feed its young with its blood, thus symbolizing Christ's sacrifice of himself.

penal law The law that regulates penalties for violations of church laws in the Roman Catholic tradition.

penal-substitutionary theory of the atonement A view of the atonement that stresses Christ's death as a perfect payment for the penalty of human sin that is accepted by God, whose wrath and judgment are satisfied by this work of Christ, the sinner's substitute. It has been influential in Protestantism and evangelicalism.

penance (Lat. *paenitentia*, "penitence") The action of showing sorrow and remorse for sin. It is one of the seven sacraments of the Roman Catholic Church (also called "sacrament of reconciliation"), and the prescribed way for post-baptismal sins to be forgiven. Its elements are contrition, confession of sin, and "doing" of penance.

penitence (Lat. *paenitere*, "to repent") The condition of being sorrowful and remorseful for sins one has committed.

penitential books Books used in the Roman Catholic tradition that prescribe how priests should hear confessions of sin and assign various kinds of penance.

penitential psalms Seven psalms stressing the confession of sins and repentance: Pss. 6, 32, 38, 51, 102, 130, and 143.

penitential rite A part of the opening rite of the eucharistic celebration in the Roman Catholic Mass. It consists of a prayer of confession of sinfulness with responses.

penitential tradition The tradition that shows concern for repentance and forgiveness of sins committed after Christian baptism. This is seen in the Roman Catholic sacrament of penance as well as, more generally, in classic prayers, acts of contrition, manuals, and other spiritual exercises.

penitential works Actions carried out as a sign of repentance and the desire to amend one's life.

penitents (From Lat. *paenitere*, "to repent") Those who repent of their sins and seek restoration in the church.

Pentateuch (From Gr. *pentē*, "five," and *teuchos*, "book") A term for the first five books of the Old Testament: Genesis, Exodus, Leviticus, Numbers, and Deuteronomy. They are known in Judaism as the Torah or books of the Law.

Pentecost/Day of Pentecost (Gr. *pentēkostē*, "fiftieth") The Jewish Festival of Weeks (Ex. 23:14–17) that began when the first fruits of the harvest were presented to God 50 days after Passover. On this day, 50 days after the resurrection of Christ, the Holy Spirit came to the church (Acts 2). It has also been called Whitsunday.

Pentecostal movement, modern An early 20th-century movement that saw itself as recapturing the renewal experienced by 1st-century Christians who had received the Holy Spirit.

Pentecostalism Movements that experience the gifts of the Holy Spirit, most often prominently including *glossolalia*,

or "speaking in tongues" (Acts 2). Also, the several denominations arising from early 20th-century revivals that stress a special baptism of the Holy Spirit after conversion.

penultimate Next to last or next to the ultimate. In the theology of Dietrich Bonhoeffer (1906–45), it refers to everything prior to God's action of justification.

people of God A theological term to designate those people with whom God has established a covenant relationship. The people of Israel in the Old Testament experienced this (Judg. 20:2). The Christian church also understands itself in this way (Heb. 4:9; 11:25; cf. 1 Peter 2:9–10).

people's theology *See* minjung theology

per capita apportionment An amount of money required to be paid to a church governing body based on the number of members in a particular congregation.

perdition (Lat. *perdere*, "to destroy") A term for the condemnation received at the last judgment by those who have not been obedient to God (see Matt. 3:12; 8:12; Mark 9:43).

perennialism (Lat. *philosophia perennis*, "perennial philosophy") The view, popularized (but not originated) by Aldous Huxley (1894–1963) in *The Perennial Philosophy* (1944), that a universal core of religious and philosophical truths are common to all the world's great religious traditions. These are chiefly meditative, mystical, and ethical in nature.

perfect contrition A technical term, associated with Peter Abelard (1079–1142), for a form of contrition in which the sinner's love for God leads one to repent of sin, seek forgiveness, and promise not to sin in the future. The Council of Trent (1545–63) considered it part of the sacrament of penance.

perfect state A theological description of the condition of humans before the fall into sin (Gen. 1–2) as well as of the future heavenly condition of experiencing perfect fellowship with God.

perfection   (Lat. *perfectio*) The highest or most complete condition to be experienced. The "perfection of God" is God's absolute excellence. The ultimate human perfection is only to be found in the heavenly state. In Wesleyan thought, Jesus' injunction (Matt. 5:48) is seen as a call to perfect love.

perfection, counsels of   *See* counsels of perfection

perfectionism   The view that human perfection is possible whereby Christian believers no longer sin. In feminist theology, some argue that women set perfectionist standards for themselves or have them imposed upon them and that this is detrimental to self-image and self-realization.

perfectionist denominations   Church bodies, usually of the Wesleyan tradition, that teach an "entire sanctification" or the possibility of believers attaining a state of not sinning in the present life.

perichoresis   (Gr. *perichōrēsis*, "penetration"; Lat. *circumincessio*, "coinherence") A term used in the theology of the Trinity to indicate the intimate union, mutual indwelling, or mutual interpenetration of the three members of the Trinity with each other. Also used for the relation of the two natures of Christ.

pericope   (Gr. "a section") Technical term for a particular segment of the biblical text usually defined by containing one story, event, or parable in the synoptic Gospels. An example is Mark 3:1–6.

perishable body   A term used by the apostle Paul to indicate the physical nature that is subject to death and that is transient. It will give way to the resurrection body, which is imperishable (1 Cor. 15:53, 54).

permanent deacon   An order of ministry, within several church bodies, in which one is ordained as a deacon and can carry out various ministerial functions but not move on toward church ordination.

permission (permissive will of God)   (Lat. *permissio*) As distinct from an active willing, the term is used in relation to the will of God. John Calvin (1509–64) denied the distinction between God's active willing and God's permitting an action. Later Reformed theologians made the distinction.

permissive will of God   *See* permission

perpetual virginity of Mary   A Roman Catholic belief that Mary the mother of Jesus was a virgin at the time of Jesus' birth and continued to be a virgin throughout her life.

persecution   The many forms of difficulties that come to the Christian church and to individual Christians because of their discipleship and commitment to Jesus Christ (Matt. 10:16–25; Mark 10:39).

perseverance of the saints   (Lat. *perseverantia sanctorum*) The belief that God's elect who believe in Jesus Christ are held secure by God's power, despite temptation and sin. Their salvation will not be lost (see John 10:28). It was one of the five canons of the Calvinistic Synod of Dort (1618–19) and part of TULIP.

person   (Gr. *prosōpon*, Lat. *persona*) Boethius (c. 480–524) defined person as "an individual substance of a rational nature." Contemporary theologians emphasize the relational nature of personhood. The three "Persons" of the Trinity relate freely, equally, and in full love with each other.

person, God as   *See* God, personality of

person of Christ   *See* Christ, person of

personal ethics   The standards and norms by which individuals make ethical decisions.

personal evangelism   The sharing of the gospel message of Jesus Christ by one person with another.

"personal is political"   Carol Hanisch, in *Notes from the Second Year* (1970), states that "The personal is political," indicating that distinctions between personal and public realms do not exist.

Feminist theologians have pointed to the importance of recognizing this perspective.

personal relation   (Lat. *relatio personalis*) In the doctrine of the Trinity, the property of each member that identifies the Persons of the Godhead in relation to each other. The term indicates the internal dynamics of the three Persons among themselves.

personal rule of life   *See* rule of life

personal salvation   The personal relationship of an individual to God on the basis of faith in Jesus Christ that brings salvation.

personal union   (Lat. *unio personalis*) The union of the divine and human natures in Jesus Christ.

personalism   A philosophical approach concerned with persons and self-conscious experience as basic to reality. Liberation theology criticizes this approach as not paying sufficient attention to historical context.

personality   (Lat. *personalitas*) The visible aspects of a person's character as it is expressed and impresses others. The total configuration of responsive tendencies ("traits"). Each personality is unique, an expression in the Christian view of the diversities of the image of God in humans.

personhood   That which expresses one's self as a person. Feminist theologians have shown the ways in which the personhood of women is often oppressed and made subservient to the desires of males. Liberation or salvation may entail the full expression of the woman's self in new ways.

Perth, Articles of (1618)   Five articles forced on the Church of Scotland by King James I. They required confirmation, kneeling at the Lord's Supper, and other practices that were not in the Presbyterian tradition.

Peter, primacy of   The view that Peter was the leader of the apostles. In the Roman Catholic tradition, Peter is believed to have been the first pope on the basis of receiving the "power of the keys" from Jesus (Matt. 16:18).

Peter's Pence   Money contributed annually by Roman Catholics throughout the world to support the papacy. It began in England in the 8th century as a one penny tax per family.

petition   (From Lat. *petere,* "to seek," "to ask") A portion of a prayer that is composed of supplications and intercessions when requests are made known to God (see 1 Sam. 1:27; Ps. 20:5; Phil. 4:6).

Petrine   Relating to the apostle Peter. Also, a type of church authority in the Roman Catholic tradition that traces the origin of the papacy to Peter.

Petrine succession   In the Roman Catholic tradition, the process by which popes continue in the succession of the apostle Peter as vicars of Jesus Christ and head of the universal church.

Petrine theology   The theological perspectives developed by the New Testament writings attributed to the apostle Peter: 1 and 2 Peter.

pew rents   The practice of charging an annual fee for the use of church pews. In colonial America social hierarchies were reflected by the location of the family pew as determined by the amount paid in the pew rents, which were also used for ministerial salaries.

pews   (From Lat. *podia,* pl. of *podium,* "raised place," "balcony") Straight-backed wooden benches arranged in rows for seating in churches.

Pharisees   (Heb. "separated ones") Jewish party during Jesus' time that obeyed the written law of Moses and its unwritten interpretations, known as the tradition of the elders (Mark 7:3). They focused on holiness (Lev. 19:2). Some were hostile (John 7:32), others were helpful to Jesus (Luke 13:31).

phenomenal   (Gr. "appearance") Relating to appearance, what is perceived by a human observer. A number of philosophical and theological questions relate to the issue of what humans may perceive.

phenomenalism   A philosophical view that physical objects have no independent existence apart from how they are experienced by humans as "sense data."

phenomenological analysis   An examination of elements as they appear to human sense experience.

phenomenology   (Gr. *phainomenon,* "what appears") A philosophical viewpoint associated with the work of Edmund Husserl (1859–1938) and others. It focuses on the basic character of subjective processes. The material world is seen as the bearer of the sacred, a key insight for sacramental theology.

phenomenology of religion   The study of the ways human consciousness or self-awareness about God-concepts develops within the evolution of cultures. The term can refer to the philosophical movement emerging from the work of Edmund Husserl (1859–1938), or to those who apply descriptive methods to religion study.

philanthropy, Christian   (Gr. *philanthrōpia,* from *philein,* "to love," and *anthrōpos,* "humanity") The love, care, help, and giving to others done from the motive of Christian love.

Philippists   Followers of the Lutheran reformer Philip Melanchthon (1497–1560), who were accused by rigorous Lutherans ("Gnesio-Lutherans") of being "crypto-Calvinists" or holding Calvinistic opinions and of being too ready to compromise with Roman Catholicism.

philosophical ethics   The moral theories derived from basic philosophical commitments. Prominent are deontological ethics which stress rules; teleological ethics emphasizing consequences; and character (virtue) ethics which make the character of the agent a determinative factor for ethical values.

philosophical theology   The approach to theology that employs the methods, terms, and resources of philosophy for theological work.

philosophy   (From Gr. *philia,* "love," and *sophia,* "wisdom") Love of wisdom. The study of ultimate reality by the use of human reason, logic, ethics, etc., to answer such questions as: What is real? How do we know? What are we to do?

philosophy, analytical   A 20th-century philosophical movement that shifts from philosophy's traditional focus on metaphysics and epistemology to the analysis of language and the structures of sentences. Also called "ordinary language analysis."

philosophy of Christ   (Lat. *philosophia Christi*) A phrase used by Desiderius Erasmus (1467–1536) for his moderate approach to the reform of the Roman Catholic Church. He urged moral improvements, education, the imitation of Christ, and a downplaying of the externals in religion.

philosophy of religion   The investigation through philosophical means of the phenomena regarded as "religion" and "religious experience" by examining their truth claims, language, and belief structures.

Phos Hilaron   (Gr. "joyous light") An ancient and beloved hymn to Christ as the Light of the world that was sung in Greek when lamps were lit at the time of evening prayer.

Photian schism   The 9th-century controversy between the Western and Eastern churches over issues of clerical celibacy, fasting, anointing with oil, and the double procession of the Holy Spirit. The Greek theologian Photius (c. 820–91) and Pope Nicholas I excommunicated each other.

phylactery   (Gr. *phylaktērion,* Heb. *tephillin*) A small leather boxlike case containing four strips on which are inscribed four biblical passages (Ex. 13:1–10, 11–16; Deut. 6:4–9; 11:13–21). They are worn by Jews to remind them of religious obligations (cf. Matt. 23:5).

physis (Gr. "nature"; Lat. *natura*) Term used during early church Trinitarian and christological controversies to indicate the intrinsic principle of a reality. The Godhead is three Persons who exist in one "nature." Jesus Christ is one person who has two "natures"—divine and human.

pictorial-day theory   A way of reading the creation account in Gen. 1 as being written according to logic and not according to chronology. Thus it would not need to correspond with geological evidence.

Pietà   (Ital. "pity," Lat. *pietas,* "piety") A statue of the Virgin Mary holding the dead body of Jesus. The form was often used during the Renaissance period.

pietism   An approach to Christianity that emphasizes personal religious experience. In a derogatory sense it connotes an excessive concern for personal religious devotion and the leading of the Holy Spirit with not enough stress on reason and the intellectual dimensions of Christian faith.

Pietism, German   A Christian renewal movement in 17th-century Germany through Philipp Jacob Spener (1635–1705) and A. H. Francke (1663–1727) that stressed the need for personal communion with God and the devotional life.

Pietists   The adherents of 17th-century German Pietism. More generally, pietists are those who stress religious faithfulness and the practices of Christian devotion.

piety   (Lat. *pietas,* "duty to God") Devotion and commitment to God expressed in the Christian life through a variety of actions. Different expressions and emphases for piety are found throughout Christian history. The term is sometimes used synonymously with "spirituality."

pilgrim church   A description of the Christian church that emphasizes its earthly, historical existence as well as its transitory and changeable nature as it moves toward the ultimate reign of God.

pilgrimages   Journeys made by devoted religious adherents to places regarded as particularly holy.

Pilgrims/Pilgrim Fathers   Separatists from the established English church who sailed to Massachusetts on the *Mayflower* in search of religious freedom (1620). They became famous in American religious history for the establishment of the Massachusetts Bay Colony.

Pisa, Council of (1409)   Church council that sought to end the Great Schism of the Western church but that left the church with three popes (Gregory XII, Benedict XIII, and Alexander V).

pistology   (Gr. *pistis,* "faith," and *logos,* "study") The study of faith or of theological belief.

plain meaning   *See* literal meaning

plainsong/plain chant   (Lat. *cantus planus,* "unaccompanied song") An unmeasured, unaccompanied unison vocal melody sung in church during worship. It is often considered to be synonymous with the Gregorian chant and may be called "plain chant."

Platonism   The views emerging from the Greek philosopher Plato (428–348 B.C.) that took many forms and that have influenced Christian theologians. Plato stressed the ideal over empirical reality and encouraged the use of the mind.

play   *See* leisure

pleasure   (From Lat. *placere,* "to please") That which gives joy, satisfaction, or gratification. In ethics, the sensation may be morally neutral or positive when it accompanies virtuous activities.

plenary indulgence   In Roman Catholic theology, an indulgence that may remit all temporal punishment for an individual's sins.

plenary inspiration   *See* inspiration, plenary

plenary sense   *See* sensus plenior

plenitude, principle of   The philosophical principle that the universe is most fully actualized and perfected when God allows the divine nature to enter into things.

plentitude of power   (Lat. *plenitudo potestatis*) A term designating the pope's fullness of power in religious matters as compared to the partial power exercised by other bishops of the church.

plērōma / plērōsis   Fullness or completeness. The term is used of the nature of God or Jesus Christ (Col. 2:9). Theologians such as Origen (c. 185–c. 254) and Tertullian (c. 160– c. 220) used it for the fullness of divine revelation that is experienced by the Christian faith.

pluralism   (Lat. *pluralis*) A philosophical view holding that reality is composed of various things or states in contrast to monism, which holds that there is only one underlying reality.

pluralism, religious   Diversities of thought, cultures, values, religions, etc., in a society.

Plymouth Brethren   A Protestant body that formed its first congregation in Plymouth, England, as a reaction against the Church of England. John Nelson Darby (1800–1882) became its leader. There are no ordained clergy and stress is laid on leadership by the Holy Spirit, Bible study, evangelism, prophecy, and premillennialism.

pneuma   *See* spirit

pneumatic ecclesiology   Recognition of the Holy Spirit as the one by whom the church is created and sustained.

pneumatology   (From Gr. *pneuma*, "spirit," and *logos*, "study") Theological doctrine of the Holy Spirit. In the early church, the doctrine of the Spirit began in the 4th century with controversies about the Spirit's divinity.

Pneumatomachians   (Macedonians)   Literally "spirit-fighters." A 4th-century group of followers of Macedonius, bishop of Constantinople, who did not believe in the full divinity of the Holy Spir-

it but that the Spirit was subordinate to God the Father and God the Son. Their teaching was condemned by Pope Damasus in 374.

poena damni   (Lat. "the punishment of the damned") A phrase in scholastic theology often now interpreted figuratively to indicate a state of estrangement from God.

poena sensus   (Lat. "the pains of sensation") A phrase in scholastic theology to describe the means by which the unrighteous would be tortured in hell.

point of contact   (Ger. *Anknüpfungspunkt*) An issue in 20th-century theology as to whether or not there is within the sinner anything that may be appealed to as a means of preparing one for the gospel from within one's self. Emil Brunner (1889–1966) affirmed it; Karl Barth (1886–1968) denied it.

polemic   (Gr. *polemikos*, from *polemos*, "a war") Confrontational argument challenging a particular position.

political theology   Theological views stressing the political implications of the Christian faith. In the 20th century it has been associated with a Roman Catholic, J. B. Metz (b. 1928), and a Protestant, Jürgen Moltmann (b. 1926). It was a precursor of liberation theologies.

political theory   The theory of forms of government and methods of social organization. Theological and ethical perspectives may help shape one's political theory.

politicization   The making political of actions or policies. Liberation theologians use the term for the process by which poor people can become critically aware of their situations. Their political environments can be changed as they enact their awareness in just ways.

politics   (From Gr. *politikos*, "civic") The art or science of government. It may also refer to the organized conduct of relationships in any form of human community. Many theological and ethical issues are inherent in this concept including church-state relations and human freedom.

politics of identity Feminist practices which assume there is something shared universally or held in common by all women. Examples would be a nature or an essence. This would allow for a claim of commonality in oppression.

polity (From Gr. *politeia*, Lat. *politia*, "administration of a commonwealth") A form of church government adopted by an ecclesiastical body.

polyandry (Gr. *polyandria*) Having more than one husband at one time. This practice, as polygamy, has traditionally been rejected as an appropriate marriage pattern for Christians.

polydaemonism (From Gr. *poly*, "many," and *daimōn*, "demon") The belief in and worship of many spirits.

polygamy (Gr. *poly*, "many," and *gamos*, "marriage") Marriage of one man to more than one wife at the same time. It has usually been rejected as being contrary to God's will by Christians.

polygenism The view that human evolution from the animal kingdom took place in the same species in a plurality of cases. Opposed to "monogenism," which is the view that all living humanity is biologically descended from a single human couple.

polyglot Bibles (Gr. *poly*, "many," and *glōtta*, "tongue") A Bible that contains the Hebrew and Greek texts with translations in various languages. The first was the Complutensian Polyglot (1521–22). Others were published in Antwerp (1569–72), Paris (1629–45), and London (1654–57).

polytheism (Gr. *polytheos*, "of many gods") Belief in many gods.

Pontifex Maximus/Pontifex Summus (Lat. "supreme pontiff") A title for the pope ever since the pontificate of Leo the Great (440–461).

Pontiff, the Holy (Lat. *pontifex*, "high priest") A term for the pope in the Roman Catholic tradition.

pontifical (Lat. *pontificalis*, "belonging to a pope") Referring or having to do with a pope or the papacy.

pontificate (Lat. *pontificatus*, "the office of a pope") Period during which a person is pope.

pool, baptismal A pool of standing water used for baptisms; a baptistery.

poor, the Those who are economically or spiritually without sufficient resources. God has special concern for the poor (Deut. 23:24–25; Isa. 1:23; 10:2) and they are blessed (Matt. 5:3; Luke 6:20). Contemporary liberation theology emphasizes reading Scripture from the perspective of the poor.

poor of Yahweh, the (From Lat. *pauper*) Those in Israel who lack sufficient resources to support life. They are the needy, without power, and abused by those with greater power. God is specially concerned with them (Ps. 12:5) and commands care for them (Deut. 15:11).

pope, primacy of the *See* primacy of the pope

pope, the (Gr. *pappas*, Lat. *papa*, "father") Title of the bishop of Rome in the Roman Catholic tradition in his capacity as the Vicar of Christ and earthly head of the universal church established by Christ.

popery Pertaining to the pope or to Roman Catholicism, often used in a derogatory manner.

popular culture The spontaneous amusements and mass entertainments of a cultural group.

popular movement (From Lat. *populus*, "people") Those activities of people in a society which form an identifiable cause. Liberation theology indicates the importance of such movements, which may stand in opposition to official political groups or the institutional church.

popular religion Religious expressions or patterns of behavior that exist apart from more "established" forms of religion as found in church bodies and their organized structures.

popular theology   A term associated with liberation theology which emphasizes theology that is done by people in base communities in solidarity with one another rather than solely by academic or church theologians. Laypersons, the poor, and the oppressed think about and articulate Christian faith.

pornography   (Gr. *pornographos,* "writing about prostitutes") Sexual material that depicts and encourages violent and coercive sexual degradation.

positive theology   A term used in the Roman Catholic tradition to denote theology derived from historical facts and concrete data. Its method is inductive as contrasted to the deductive methods of systematic theology. Historical theology is one form of positive theology.

positive thinking   A variety of Christian thought associated with Norman Vincent Peale (1898–1993) which stresses that optimistic thought processes in facing problems can bring beneficial results, since God wants what is best for people.

positivism   Philosophical view that facts alone are certain and only what is personally experienced can be true. Associated with Auguste Comte (1798–1857), the term broadly means relying on the methods used in the natural sciences.

positivism, logical   A 20th-century philosophical movement, associated with the Vienna Circle (1920s), that sought to eliminate metaphysical elements and restrict meaningful statements to those that can be verified by sense data or empirical evidence. Also called logical empiricism.

positivism, theological   Any theological system that does not claim to be constructed on metaphysical or philosophical foundations but instead on religious or theological foundations.

posse peccare, posse non peccare   (Lat. "able to sin," "able not to sin") Theological descriptions of humanity in the works of Augustine (354–430) that describe the sinful condition of humanity

("able to sin") and then the condition of those who have received the grace of God in Jesus Christ ("able not to sin").

possession, demon   *See* demon possession

possibility thinking   An approach to Christianity associated with Robert H. Schuller (b. 1926) that stresses a focus on the positive "possibilities" in every situation, which can be realized with God's help.

possibles   A philosophical term for conceiving of objects that can exist but are not eternal in themselves. The concept is seen as important as a background for views of the freedom of God and of creatures, prayers of petition, and human responsibility.

postapostolic age   Period of church history after the death of Jesus' apostles.

post-Christian era   Term used by some to indicate that by the late 20th century, Christian beliefs and values had become obsolete and thus Christianity's influence was diminished.

postcommunion   (Lat. *post,* "after") In Roman Catholic liturgy, the concluding section of the Eucharist after Holy Communion has been received. Also used for the prayer following the reception of the Eucharist, which asks that the Sacrament may benefit the particular day or season.

postconversion experience   Term often used to designate the view that some Christians receive a special "baptism of the Holy Spirit" after their conversion to Jesus Christ.

postcritical   A term used to describe the stage of consciousness that emerges after one first accepts something, then questions or doubts it, and then comes back to it with new questions and experiences. Its meanings may then emerge in new ways. The term may apply to one's appropriation of biblical symbols.

postcritical naïveté   *See* second naïveté

postcritical reconstruction   According to some, the need for contemporary theologians to reconstruct modes of meaningfulness that emerge from the ancient symbols of the Christian faith and have been perceived to convey God's revelatory truths. This is done in a modern culture where meaning is purely subjective.

postexilic The experience of the Jewish people after their return from exile (587–538 B.C.) in Babylon by Cyrus' edict in 538 (2 Chron. 36:22–23; Ezra 1:1–4).

postil (Lat. *postilla,* "marginal gloss," "book of sermons") A collection of sermons on portions of Scripture. Important theologians during the Reformation period popularized such collections. The term may be derived from the words: *post illa verba scripturae,* "after those words of Scripture."

postlapsarianism *See* infralapsarianism

postliberal theology/postliberalism A theological perspective espoused by George Lindbeck (b. 1923) who claimed that religious doctrines function as "rules" for appropriate communal ways of speaking. The Bible's language and narratives should define the world so Christians can make sense of life in biblical terms.

postlude (Lat. *post,* "after," and *ludere,* "to play") Music after the ending of a worship service.

postmillennialism Eschatological view that teaches Jesus Christ will return following the millennium or thousand-year reign mentioned in Rev. 20:1–7.

postmodern theology Contemporary theology done in the context of postmodernism which, many see, has the task of reconstructing Christian symbols to speak meaningfully in a culture that is marked by a quest for holism and in which all claims to universality are rejected.

postmodernism Description of a contemporary intellectual and cultural climate as a stage beyond the "modernism" introduced by the Enlightenment. It is marked by a rejection of "objective truth," the powers of reason, and claims of universality. Texts and symbols are emphasized together with a corporate under-

standing of truth that is relative to each community in which one participates.

postmortem evangelism The view that persons may have an opportunity to respond to the gospel of Jesus Christ or receive salvation after their death. Also called "second probation."

postresurrection appearances Biblical appearances of Jesus Christ after his resurrection from the dead (Matt. 28:16–20; Luke 24:13–35; John 20:19–29).

postresurrection community The group of believers who existed after the resurrection of Jesus Christ from the dead and who formed the basis for the early Christian church.

poststructuralism A movement beyond structuralism, also called deconstructionism. Meaning is not seen as inherent in a written (biblical) text but emerges only as an interpreter enters into dialogue with a text. It affirms the assumptions of postmodernism.

posttribulationism The eschatological belief that the church will endure a time of suffering during the tribulation period, until the return of Jesus Christ at the end of that period.

postulant (Lat. *postulans,* from *postulare,* "to demand") A candidate for a religious order who spends a period seeking admission and becoming a novice (novitiate).

postulates, theological The theological method of inferring an unknown truth from truths that are already known and seem to require its existence.

potency (Lat. *potentia*) The opposite of "act." The capacity of an object to remain the same and yet be further determined by a being that is distinct from it. Or, basically, the power to accomplish change or to come into being.

potentiality (Lat. *potentialitas,* "capacity") A philosophical term for the powers a thing possesses inherently by virtue of its being what it is.

poverty (From Lat. *pauper,* "poor") The condition of those who lack sufficient resources for life. Poverty is an important ethical concern for Christians.

poverty, vow of   The renunciation of the right of ownership. Along with vows of chastity and obedience, it is one of the vows taken by monks and nuns in the Roman Catholic tradition.

power   (Gr. *dynamis,* Lat. *potentia*) The ability to become or effect something. Also (Lat. *potestas*), rule or dominion in terms of law or legal jurisdiction. Liberation theologies focus on the ways power is used, particularly for oppression of people.

power, absolute   (*potentia absoluta*) God's omnipotence or power to effect all possibilities, limited only by God's own character or nature. God is thus beyond all laws that are divinely ordained for the functioning of the universe.

power, ordained   (Lat. *potentia ordinata*) A term for the power by which the world was created and is sustained by God. This power is limited, being exercised in order to guarantee the world's ongoing existence. The term is in contrast to God's omnipotence (Lat. *potentia absoluta*), which is the fullness of God's power.

power of being   The capacity or ability to exist. Paul Tillich (1886–1965) used the term as a synonym for "ground of being" (God).

power of the church   (Lat. *potestas ecclesiae*) The power of the church's ministry in terms of teaching, governing, forgiveness, and benevolence. Lutheran and Reformed theologians of the scholastic period recognized that the church's power derives from Christ and depends on Christ.

practical divinity   *See* practical theology

practical reason   A term used to describe the process of applying thought to action. It contrasts with theoretic reason, which is concerned with producing knowledge. In the Christian context, one's practical reason may be shaped by God's law and the teachings of Scripture as the framework for ethical actions.

practical syllogism   (Lat. *syllogismus practicus,* "the practical syllogism") A way of understanding the certainty of election ("assurance") for an individual, as advocated by Reformed theologians, particularly Puritans. It basically states: "Whoever believes is elect; I believe, therefore I am elect." Some also focused on "good works" as a sign indicating one's election.

practical theology   (Lat. *theologia practica*) Critical reflection on the church's life in both corporate and individual expressions. Often included are disciplines such as Christian education, homiletics, liturgics, and pastoral care. More broadly it relates to sanctification and living the Christian life. It has also been called practical divinity.

pragmaticism   *See* pragmatism

pragmatics   (From Gr. *pragmatikos,* Lat. *pragmaticus,* "skilled in business") Practical concern for the usefulness and effectiveness of, for example, Christian doctrines. In semiotics, the study of the relationships of signs and symbols to their users.

pragmatism   (From Gr. *pragmatikos,* Lat. *pragmaticus,* "skilled in business") A philosophical movement stressing knowledge derived from experience and experimentation concerned to solve practical problems so that truth is tested by its utility and consequences.

praise   (From Lat. *pretium,* "worth") Honor and adoration given to God as a celebration of God's being and worth. It is a constant biblical ascription and injunction that creatures should praise God as the Lord (Pss. 106:1; 117:1; 135:1; 147:1).

praise service   A service of worship which emphasizes the praise of God. It usually includes songs and hymns of praise as well as other expressions of thanksgiving. In some traditions, Christian testimonies as to what God has done in one's life are shared.

Praise the Lord   *See* hallelujah

praxis (Gr. "action," "practice") A term used in liberation theologies for a combination of action and reflection which seeks the transformation of oppressive situations and the social order. It marks the beginning place for theological reflection and focuses on the dialectic of theory and practice.

prayer (From Lat. *precari,* "to entreat") Human approach to God and addressing God in praise and adoration, confession, thanksgiving, supplication, and intercession. A consciousness of God's presence, love, direction, and grace may be experienced.

Prayer, Lord's *See* Lord's Prayer

prayer, prophetic The prayer by a prophet. More generally, a prayer recognized as being particularly expressive of God's will and prayed on behalf of an issue or situation that is of great importance for the church, particularly as the church is called to make a decision or move into a new direction in Christian mission and ministry.

prayer books Books containing official services for church worship. The term may also be used for collections of prayers for public or private worship use.

prayer breakfast A popular practice of Christians gathering for breakfast and spending extended time in group and personal prayer.

prayer cloth Especially among charismatics and Pentecostals a cloth brought to a healing meeting, where an evangelist prays and lays hands on it so that the person may take it to a sick friend to transmit God's healing powers (see Acts 19:11–12).

prayer meetings Meetings of Christians for the purpose of offering prayers to God. They were popularized in America in connection with 19th-century evangelistic campaigns and have been continued in numerous churches.

prayers for the dead A practice in Roman Catholicism and Eastern Orthodoxy of offering prayers on behalf of those who have died. It is believed that those in purgatory are assisted in reaching heaven.

pre-existentianism *See* preexistence of souls

pre-Pentecost period The period prior to the Pentecost event (Acts 2) including the Old Testament period and the time described in the New Testament before the coming of the Holy Spirit at Pentecost.

pretribulational rapture The view that true Christian believers (the "church") will be "raptured" or taken in the air to be with Christ at his return, which will be prior to a period of great tribulation. Thus the church will escape the tribulation.

pretribulationism A view of the future which teaches that the Christian church will escape the coming period of great tribulation by virtue of being removed from the earth ("raptured") at the return of Jesus Christ.

preacher (Middle English *prechur,* from Lat. *praedicare,* "to proclaim") One who preaches. The person is usually an ordained clergyperson.

preaching (Lat. *praedicatio,* "a public proclaiming") The act of proclaiming, and in the Christian context, the proclamation of the Gospel of Jesus Christ or the Word of God.

preaching, theology of (From Lat. *praedicare,* "to proclaim") The understanding that there is a theological basis for the proclamation which occurs in preaching and that preaching is a means God uses to convey a knowledge of God and to communicate with people. Included are understandings of God's Word, the Holy Spirit, the power of language, etc.

preambles of faith (Lat. *praeambula fidei*) A term used in Roman Catholic theology prior to Vatican II (1962–65) for the introductory premises or presuppositions that precede an act of faith. These are things known through reason and historical knowledge as a prelude to faith.

prebend   A cathedral benefice intended to "supply" (Lat. *prebere*) its holder with benefits. "Prebendary" is now an honorary title in the Church of England.

precentor   (Lat. "one who sings before") The person responsible for the singing of choirs and congregations in churches.

preceptive will of God   (Lat. *voluntas Dei praecepti*) The revealed will of God, the will of the precept, or that which God directly commands to be done.

precepts   (From Lat. *praeceptum*) Matters of obligation established by God or by a superior for those in religious communities who have taken a vow of obedience.

Precious Blood   The human blood of Jesus indicating his true humanity. Symbolically, it refers to Jesus' atoning death on behalf of sinners who regard this action as of utmost value. In the Roman Catholic tradition the blood is venerated as symbolizing Christ's self-giving life (1 Peter 1:18–19).

Precisian/Precisianist   (From Lat. *praecidere,* "to be brief") A term applied to 16th- and 17th-century English Puritans because of their scrupulous regard for various religious doctrines and practices.

precritical   A description of biblical interpretation that does not use the methods of biblical criticism to examine biblical materials.

predefinition   A term used particularly in the Roman Catholic tradition to describe predestination in relation to a creature's individual free actions. It also has a role in the doctrines of God's providence, the inspiration of Scripture, etc., affirming the interplay of God's will and human freedom.

predestinarianism   Pertaining to the doctrine of predestination. This term is often used to describe an extreme form of the doctrine that would deny all forms of human freedom.

predestination   (Lat. *praedestinatio*) God's actions in willing something to a specific result. It is also called foreordination. Some Christian theologians, particularly in the Reformed tradition, have seen it as indicating God's eternal decree by which all creatures are foreordained to eternal life or death. It may also be used synonymously with "election" and indicates God's gracious initiation of salvation for those who believe in Jesus Christ.

predestination, double   A term for the view that God both predestines or elects some to salvation and condemns others to damnation, both by eternal decrees. This view is associated with supralapsarianism and sees election and reprobation as positive and coordinate decrees.

predestination, single   A term for the view that God predestines or elects some to salvation by means of a positive decree while those who are not saved condemn themselves because of their sin. This view is associated with infralapsarianism. The unsaved are "passed over" in that they remain in their sin. Thus there is only a single positive decree of election or predestination.

predetermination   A term used in the work of Thomas Aquinas (1225–74) for God's free decision to allow humans to perform actions while infallibly determining beforehand what the humans will do.

predictive prophecy   A term for those utterances of the biblical prophets which declare future events that will come to pass.

preevangelization   Term used by those who seek to prepare a locality for evangelization by carrying out a variety of activities in anticipation of the preaching of the gospel.

preexistence   (From Lat. *praeexistere,* "to exist beforehand") A term used for Jesus Christ as the eternal Logos of God, the second Person of the Trinity, who existed prior to the incarnation, i.e., prior to becoming a human person, Jesus of Nazareth.

preexistence of Christ   The theological affirmation that Jesus Christ as the second Person of the Trinity has existed eternally and thus prior to his incarnate state as Jesus of Nazareth. It is affirmed in the Nicene Creed (325) and biblically in passages such as John 1:14; 1 Cor. 8:6; Col. 1:15–17; Heb. 1:1–2.

preexistence of souls   The view that human souls exist prior to their bodily existence. It has been condemned as heretical by the Christian church. Also called preexistentism.

preface   (From Lat. *praefatio,* "a saying beforehand") In the central part of the eucharistic service, the introduction to the eucharistic prayer, or great thanksgiving. The preface begins with the Sursum Corda ("Lift up your hearts") and ends with the Sanctus.

preferential option for the poor   A term used in liberation theology to describe God's special concern for those in poverty and their advantage in being able to know God. It was first used at the Medellín Conference (1968) with the understanding that the church should support the cause of the poor in the face of injustice and oppression.

preincarnate humanity   A belief that Jesus Christ was human before he was born as Jesus of Nazareth. The effect of the view is that Jesus brought his human nature with him to the incarnation.

prelate   (Lat. *praelatus,* from *praeferre,* "to place before") A high church official, such as a bishop or archbishop, who has authority to govern in a public forum. The term "prelacy" pertains to the office.

prelude   (From Lat. *praeludere,* "to play beforehand") Music played before a service of worship.

premillennialism   The belief that Jesus Christ will return to earth prior to a period of one thousand years during which he will reign ("millennium"; Rev. 20:1–5).

premillennialist   One who holds to premillennialism.

premoral evil   A term used in Roman Catholic moral theology for the disvalue of a human action which affects, but does not always determine, whether or not an act is moral. It becomes a moral evil when it takes effect without a sufficient reason.

premundane fall   *See* fall, premundane

Preparation, day of   (Gr. *paraskeuē*) Friday, the day prior to the Sabbath and thus the day for which preparations for the Sabbath were made. The Gospels record the crucifixion of Jesus as taking place on this day (Matt. 27:62; Mark 15:42; Luke 23:54; John 19:14, 31, 42).

preparation for conversion   (Lat. *praeparatio ad conversionem*) A sense of sin and remorse, or other feelings that can be seen as preceding and preparing the way for the work of the Holy Spirit in conversion. The preparation is a work of grace. Martin Luther (1483–1546) referred to the "terrors of conscience" (Lat. *terrores conscientiae*).

preparation for the gospel   (Lat. *praeparatio evangelica*) A term used to describe the work of God in preparing the world for the coming of Jesus Christ. Early church theologians considered the work of the "Logos" in human reason, pagan philosophy, etc., prior to Christ's coming as elements of preparation.

presbyter   (Gr. *presbyteros,* "elder") A term used in presbyterian forms of church government for elders who govern local congregations. It is derived from the functions of the New Testament leaders (Acts 14:23; 15:4; 1 Tim. 4:14; James 5:14). Also used for "bishops" (Titus 1:7), priests, and ministers.

presbyterate   (Lat. *presbyteratus*) The office of a presbyter. Or, a body of presbyters. In the Roman Catholic tradition, the union of all priests (presbyters) with their diocesan bishop upon their ordination.

presbyterial   (From Gr. *presbyteros,* "elder") A form of church government where authority for decision making is in presbyteries, composed of clergy and lay elders from local churches. Presbyteries are linked to similarly structured larger bodies called "synods" and then to a general assembly.

Presbyterian One who adheres to a presbyterial form of church government. Also, a theological tradition stemming from the work of John Calvin (1509–64) and other Protestant Reformers known as the Reformed tradition. A number of Presbyterian church bodies are found throughout the world.

presbyterian form of church government *See* presbyterial

Presbyterianism The stream of Christianity that follows a presbyterial form of church government and holds Presbyterian theological beliefs, which are part of the Reformed theological tradition.

presbyterium (Lat. "body of presbyters") A term for the area of a church building reserved for the seating of clergy.

presbytery The grouping of Presbyterian churches in a particular area that assumes governmental oversight over the individual churches through representative elders and clergy. Also, the jurisdiction of a presbytery. The term is sometimes used to designate a priest's residence.

prescience, divine (Lat. *praescientia,* "foreknowledge") God's foreknowledge of all that happens (e.g., Ps. 139:4). It is a function of divine omniscience.

presence, bodily The view in the theology of the Lord's Supper that the body and blood of Jesus Christ are present in the Lord's Supper in the bread and wine.

presence, divine God's being with the creation and with God's people. The term is also used to designate God in heaven. It is synonymous with the "immanence of God."

presence, real (Lat. *praesentia realis*) A theological term used particularly in orthodox Lutheran theology to indicate that the true body and blood of Jesus Christ are genuinely and illocally present in the Lord's Supper, in, with, and under the elements of the bread and wine.

presence of Christ (Lat. *praesentia Christi*) The ongoing relationship of Jesus Christ to the Christian church as he promised (Matt. 28:20; John 14:23; 15:4–7). The church has debated the way in which Christ is present in the sacrament of the Lord's Supper in a theological sense.

Presentation of Christ in the Temple Feast commemorating Jesus' presentation to God in the Jerusalem Temple by his parents (Luke 2:22–39), forty days after his birth (Ex. 13:2; Lev. 12:2–8). It is celebrated on February 2. Formerly called Candlemas, it is the Purification of the Blessed Virgin Mary in Roman Catholicism.

Presentation of the Blessed Virgin Mary Feast celebrated on November 21 in Eastern Orthodoxy and Roman Catholicism commemorating the presentation of Mary the mother of Jesus in the Temple when she was three years old (based on the apocryphal Protevangelium of James, written around A.D. 150).

Presentation of the Lord Contemporary designation for Candlemas or the Purification of the Blessed Virgin Mary in the Roman Catholic tradition.

preservation (From Lat. *pre,* "before," and *servare,* "to watch over") An aspect of the Christian doctrine of providence which indicates that God sustains or continues to maintain the creation.

presider (From Lat. *praesidere,* "to preside") A term for anyone who oversees an act of public worship.

presuppositionalism A philosophical approach to theology which claims that all systems of knowledge are constructed on assumptions that cannot be proved about God, humanity, and reality. Thus no claims of objectivity can exist.

presuppositions Those first principles or assumptions to which one is committed that go before an argument or a viewpoint and from which the view is derived. Philosophically and theologically, presuppositions about a number of issues are very important in guiding the development of thought.

preterist view   (From Lat. *praeteritus,* "past") An interpretive view of the book of Revelation that maintains all its prophecies have already been fulfilled and are past or were being fulfilled when the book was being written.

preterition   (From Lat. *praeteritio,* "a passing by") A term used by infralapsarian Calvinists to indicate that not all persons are elected by God for salvation and thus some are "passed over" and allowed to face the consequences of their own sin. Contrasted to reprobation.

preunderstanding   (Ger. *Vorverständnis*) The view that in biblical interpretation there are inevitable presuppositions that come with the interpreter from theological and life sources that become part of the interpretive process itself. These need to be identified and their importance recognized.

prevenient grace   *See* grace, prevenient

pride   (Lat. *superbia*) One of the medieval "seven deadly sins" that is the opposite of humility. Augustine (354–430) considered it the most basic sin, which stood at the root of the fall (Gen. 3). It is the exaggerated valuing of one's self or too much love of the self (Lat. *amor sui*).

prie-dieu   (Fr. "pray-God") A kneeling bench used in the Roman Catholic Mass and in weddings in various churches. It has a padded cushion for kneeling and a small bookrest.

priest   (Gr. *hiereus,* from *presbyteros,* "elder"; Lat. *sacerdos*) Term for clergy below the office of bishop in some churches. The term is used only in the plural in the New Testament to describe Christians (Rev. 1:6; 5:10; 20:6; cf. 1 Peter 2:9). A priest is the people's representative with God.

priest, Christ as   Designation used in the letter to the Hebrews for the unique sacrificial work of Jesus Christ in offering himself to God to remove the sin of humanity (Heb. 9:11–28) and to establish a new covenant with God (Matt. 26:62–68; Mark 14:58ff.).

priest, high   *See* high priest

priestess   A woman who carries out religious duties and functions as a people's representative to God. Counterpart to "priest."

priesthood   Those who serve in the capacities of priests or priestesses.

priesthood, the holy   In the Roman Catholic tradition, priests as ordained clergy are considered as Christ's representatives in the world. The priesthood is seen as the highest spiritual state of power and sacredness.

priesthood of all believers   A theological view emphasized by Martin Luther (1483–1546) to emphasize that Christian believers have direct access to God and do not need to go through an intermediary priest, except for Jesus Christ (Heb. 3:1; 4:14).

primacy   *See* primate

primacy of the pope   The Roman Catholic view that the pope is the highest spiritual authority for the church and the primary bishop among all other bishops in the church.

primary actuality   (Lat. *actus primus*) A thing's existence as distinct from what it does or its operations.

primate   (From Lat. *primas,* "of the first") Title for the chief bishop or archbishop of a country or region's oldest diocese. The title is usually honorary.

primatial   Referring to the role of a leader or primate among bishops in the government of a church or group of churches.

prime matter   (Lat. *materia prima*) A theological term for the earth in its unformed state as the first creative act of God (Gen. 1:2).

prime mover   Also "first mover" or "unmoved mover." A Greek philosophical view that there is an ultimate cause or "mover" (God) who initially set the universe in motion. The degree to which this "mover" is consistent or congruent with the Christian view of God has been much debated.

primitive church   The period of church history during which Jesus' apostles were alive, usually seen as extending from 30 to 100 A.D.

primitive revelation   The view that a minimum of divine revelation existed for humanity from the beginning of its existence.

primordial being   A term used in the death of God theology of Thomas J. J. Altizer (b. 1927) for the transcendent God as God existed prior to becoming increasingly incarnate in the world.

primordial nature of God   A term used in the process philosophy of Alfred North Whitehead (1861–1947) for the "mental pole" in God or God's grasp of all possibilities. This includes evaluating all possibilities and results in a harmony or "primordial vision."

primordial sacrament   A designation in Roman Catholic theology for Jesus Christ as the first and most basic sacrament, from which other sacraments derive through his church.

primus   (Lat. "first") The presiding bishop of the Episcopal Church in Scotland.

primus inter pares   (Lat. "first among equals") Term used of a bishop, and also for the pope by those who would seek church union and who are willing to designate the bishop of Rome in this way.

Prince of Peace   A theological designation for Jesus Christ (cf. Isa. 9:6) as one who brings peace and who is himself God's peace (Eph. 2:14–17).

Princeton theology, Old   The Calvinistic theology taught by Presbyterian theologians at Princeton Seminary from 1812 until 1921. Major figures include Archibald Alexander (1772–1851), Charles Hodge (1797–1878), A. A. Hodge (1823–86), B. B. Warfield (1851–1921), and J. Gresham Machen (1881–1937).

principalities and powers   A term for the forces of evil in the cosmos that seek to exercise power in the present age (Rom. 8:38; Eph. 6:12) but which are ultimately defeated through the death and resurrection of Jesus Christ (Eph. 1:20–21).

principia theologiae   (Lat. "fundamental principles" or "foundations of theology") A term used by Protestant scholastic theologians to indicate Scripture and God as the two fundamental principles of theology. These embrace both the divine revelation and the one who does the revealing. In scholastic systems, a definition of theology is often given, followed by a *locus* on Scripture and one on God.

principle   (Lat. *principium*) In the thought of Thomas Aquinas (1225–74), "everything from which anything proceeds in any manner." To indicate philosophical or theological principles is to identify significant basic convictions, which then have emerging implications.

prior   (Lat. "superior") The elected head or "superior" of a priory or religious house who leads various religious orders of monks, mendicants, and canons regular.

prioress   (Lat. *priorissa*) A female head of a priory of nuns who is next to the abbess in authority.

priory   (Lat. "the first") A residence for a religious community. It is under the direction of a prior ("the first" of the community).

Priscillianism   Ancient church heresy connected with Priscillian, bishop of Ávila (380–81), who denied the Trinity and Christ's deity and taught modalism. It was condemned by several church councils during the 4th to 6th centuries.

prison epistles   The name given to books of the New Testament attributed to the apostle Paul while he was imprisoned in Rome. These include Ephesians, Colossians, Philippians, and Philemon.

private judgment The recognition that individual Christians may choose how they wish to interpret the Scriptures and that they are personally responsible to God for their choices.

private revelation In the Roman Catholic tradition, a self-communication by God to an individual that does not require faith to receive and is not to be preserved and passed on by the church.

privatio boni (Lat. "privation of the good") The theological view that God created all things good and that evil must be defined as nonexistence or a negation or limitation of that which does exist. This view is associated with Augustine (354–430).

privatization of sin *See* sin, privatization of

procathedral Church used temporarily by a bishop as a cathedral until a permanent cathedral is available.

probabiliorism (Lat. *probabilior,* "more likely," "more credible") A term used in Roman Catholic moral theology in opposition to "probabilism." It teaches that it should be assumed that a particular way of action is subject to the law unless it is more "probable" that it is not.

probabilism (Lat. *probabilis,* "likely," "credible") A moral system in the Roman Catholic tradition that opposes "probabiliorism." It teaches that one may follow a "probable" path when there is moral doubt about the application of a moral law.

probation (Lat. *probatio,* from *probare,* "to prove") A view that human life on earth is only a preparation period for eternal existence.

probationer (From Lat. *probare,* "to prove") One who has completed ministerial training but has not yet received a specific call or entered a vocation. In some churches, one may preach the gospel but not yet be ordained.

process of regeneration The view that the transformation of a Christian believer's life by God is a gradual process and not an instantaneous event.

process philosophy A system of thought associated with Alfred North Whitehead (1861–1947) and Charles Hartshorne (b. 1897) that sees "becoming" as the basic reality of the universe which is evolving. God is also changing and developing through God's interaction with the natural world and humanity.

process theism An understanding of God according to process theology emphasizing God's dipolarity, God's ability to be affected by creation, and God's luring and persuasive power.

process theology Theological movement emerging from the work of the philosophers Alfred North Whitehead (1861–1947) and Charles Hartshorne (b. 1897). It emphasizes "becoming" over "being" or "substance" and affirms divine participation in the evolving world process.

procession of the Spirit, Trinitarian (Gr. *ekporeusis,* Lat. *processio,* "to emanate from another") In the theology of the Trinity, the order of relationships among Father, Son, and Holy Spirit in which the Son "proceeds from the Father" and the Holy Spirit "proceeds from the Father and the Son" (Lat. *filioque,* Western church). In the Eastern church a "single procession" of the Spirit from the Father alone is taught.

processional (Lat. *processionale*) A book that contains the texts of hymns, litanies, and prayers that are used during church liturgical processions. Also a hymn or musical composition played during a procession.

processions, liturgical (From Lat. *procedere,* "to proceed") Movement by people from place to place as religious actions within a worship service.

proclamation (Gr. *kērygma,* Lat. *praedicatio, proclamatio*) A term used for Christian preaching as the announcement of the news of the gospel of Jesus Christ (Rom. 16:25; 1 Cor. 15:14; 2 Thess. 2:14).

procreation (From Lat. *procreare,* "to procreate") The bearing of children. Issues surrounding choices made in relation to procreation are ethical in nature.

procurator   (Lat. "manager," "administrator") The official in charge of the physical aspects of a monastery or religious community. In the Church of Scotland, a legal officer who offers advice to church courts in judicial matters.

profane   (Lat. *profanus,* from *pro,* "before," and *fanum,* "temple") That which is not holy or sacred. More strongly, that which is blasphemous and treats the sacred with contempt.

profanity   (From Lat. *pro,* "before," and *fanus,* "temple") That which does not belong to the sacred. More commonly, that which pollutes or shows contempt for the sacred. Ethically, it is an act or attitude or speech that treats the sacred as nonsacred. This is the effect of profane speech.

professing Christians   Those who publicly confess their Christian faith and consider themselves Christians.

profession   (Lat. *professus,* from *profiteri,* "to confess openly") That which one confesses or believes as a religious faith. Also the act of taking vows upon entrance into a religious order.

profession, religious   The taking of vows of poverty, chastity, and obedience and thus entering into the "religious life" of special devotion.

proglossolalia position   The view that the gift of speaking in tongues (glossolalia) is a spiritual gift that is and may be operative in the contemporary church.

progressive creationism   *See* creationism, progressive

progressive revelation   *See* revelation, progressive

prohibited degrees   Relationships that exist by blood or marriage that prohibit persons from marrying each other, e.g., mother and son. In some traditions these are made explicit in church law.

projectionism   Transferral of a need or attribute of a person or group to another

object. In the view of Ludwig Feuerbach (1804–72), "God" is an imaginary being onto which an ideal human nature has been projected.

prolegomena   (From Gr. *prolegein,* "to say beforehand") Those things which come before the main body of a work. In theology, certain issues and questions that prepare the way for treating other major topics.

prolepsis   (Gr. *prolēpsis,* "an anticipating") That which anticipates a future event. The resurrection of Jesus Christ may be seen as anticipating the final consummation and future resurrection of humans, and thus as proleptic. This theme is stressed in the writings of Wolfhart Pannenberg (b. 1928).

promise   (From Lat. *promittere,* "to send before") A commitment to an obligation to do or not to do something. Ethically, promises relate to commitments and truthfulness. A promise is morally binding in terms of justice and mutual fidelity. It binds actions to words.

Promised Land   The land of Canaan or Palestine promised by God to Abraham (Gen. 12; 17:8) and his posterity and regarded by the Jewish people as God's special gift to the nation of Israel.

promises of God   (Lat. *promissiones Dei*) That which God intends to provide, most specifically the provision for salvation to humankind.

proof text   The citation of a single biblical verse as a justification for a theological argument or position.

proofs for the existence of God   *See* theistic proofs

propaedeutics   (Gr. *propaideuein,* "to teach beforehand") Introductory principles and ideas needed for the proper study of a subject. Some elements for the study of theology, such as sources of authority and theological method, are dealt with prior to formal doctrinal study.

propaganda   (From Lat. *propagare,* "to spread, extend") Used in the Roman

Catholic tradition for various church bodies that seek to change the beliefs of others and spread the teachings of the church.

propassions of Christ Christ's physical and psychological passions which he possessed and used in perfect ways according to his sinless divine nature. This term distinguishes such passions from those that exist within sinful human beings.

proper qualities (Lat. *idiomata*) The attributes or properties that identify the particular individuality of a certain thing and are thus "proper" to it.

propers, liturgical (From Lat. *proprius,* "own," "belonging to") Liturgical texts used in worship services that change according to the day or season of the church year.

properties, Trinitarian Traditional designations for the personal properties of the Godhead: the paternity of the Father, the filiation of the Son, and the spiration of the Holy Spirit.

property (Lat. *proprietas*) An incommunicable attribute of something. The term is used in relation to the doctrine of the Trinity and the incommunicable attributes of the Father, Son, and Holy Spirit.

property, personal (Lat. *proprius,* "one's own") That which one possesses as one's own and about the use of which one must make ethical decisions.

prophecy (Gr. *prophēteia,* Lat. *prophetia*) Speaking on behalf of God to communicate God's will for a situation. In the New Testament it is a gift of the Spirit (Rom. 12:6; 1 Cor. 12:10; 14:22). It is also used for the prediction or declaration of what will come to pass in the future.

prophesyings/prophecy A practice of 16th- and 17th-century English Puritans in which clergy would gather to interpret Scripture and preach sermons as a means of education and edification. The practice had begun during the Protestant Reformation in Zurich (1525).

prophet (Heb. *nabi',* Gr. *prophētēs,* "one who announces") One who speaks on behalf of God to God's people, most prominently the Hebrew prophets whose writings are found in the Old Testament.

prophet, Christ as A description of the role of Jesus Christ as declarer of God's Word and will during his earthly existence (John 15:15). "Prophet" is also one of the classic "offices" of Christ along with "priest" and "king."

prophetic conferences A number of gatherings in 19th-century America, notably in Niagara, New York, where leading dispensational and premillennial teachers and preachers expounded their understandings of biblical prophecy. They played a formative role in the rise of fundamentalism.

Prophets, Former In the Hebrew canon, the books of Joshua, Judges, Samuel, and Kings.

Prophets, Latter In the Hebrew canon, the books of Isaiah, Jeremiah, Ezekiel, and the Book of the Twelve, or Hosea, Joel, Amos, Obadiah, Jonah, Micah, Nahum, Habakkuk, Zephaniah, Haggai, Zechariah, and Malachi.

Prophets, Major A term for the longer Old Testament prophetic books: Isaiah, Jeremiah, Lamentations, Ezekiel, and Daniel.

Prophets, Minor A term for the shorter Old Testament prophetic books: Hosea, Joel, Amos, Obadiah, Jonah, Micah, Nahum, Habakkuk, Zephaniah, Haggai, Zechariah, and Malachi.

propitiation (Lat. *propitius,* "favorable") A theological term for making atonement for sin by making an acceptable sacrifice. Some English translations use the term (Rom. 3:25; Heb. 2:17; 1 John 2:2; 4:10) to describe the death of Christ. Some theories of the atonement relate this to God's wrath.

proportionalism In ethics, a teaching suggesting that determining the rightness or wrongness of an action may be done by a relative "weighing" of the positive results of the action with the negative results. Thus good and evil reside in results of an action and not in the action itself.

propositional view of revelation   *See* revelation, propositional view of

propositionalism   Means of stating ideas in such a way that they can be judged either true or false.

proselyte   (Gr. *prosēlytos,* Lat. *proselytus,* "one who has come to a place," "a convert")   One who has come into a new religious faith. Used biblically to indicate one who has converted to Judaism (Acts 2:10; 6:5).

proselytism   (From Gr. *prosēlytos,* Lat. *proselytus,* "one who has come to a place," "a convert")   The practice of seeking others to become adherents of one's religious faith.

proskynesis   (Gr. "adoration," "obeisance")   The veneration offered to icons and other sacred objects. In the Eastern Orthodox tradition, the practice of making the sign of the cross as an act of devotion.

prosōpon   (Gr. "person")   A term used in Trinitarian and christological controversies in the early church to designate the Godhead as three distinct "Persons" and Jesus Christ as one "Person." It did not have the metaphysical precision needed for technical distinctions.

prosphora   (Gr. "that which is offered," "gift")   Designation for the consecrated bread used in the Eucharist in Eastern churches. The remainder of the bread (Gr. antidoron) is distributed at the end of the service as blessed but not consecrated food.

Protestant   (From Lat. *protestari,* "to bear witness," "to testify")   One who adheres to the theological views that emerged from the 16th-century Reformation in Europe. It is also used for those churches which separated from the Roman Catholic Church at that time and the groups continuing their traditions.

Protestant ethic   The moral values associated with the developing Anglo-Saxon Protestantism of 17th-century England. Some, such as the German sociologist Max Weber (1864–1920), have argued that capitalism emerged from these emphases on hard work, the profit motive, and religious and personal freedom.

Protestant liberalism   The theologies stemming from Friedrich Schleiermacher (1768–1834), Albrecht Ritschl (1822–89), and Adolf von Harnack (1851–1930). They sought a spirit of inquiry that was critical and scientific, and they stressed human autonomy, the principle of dynamism, and the evolving of good toward the kingdom of God.

Protestant orthodoxy   A term for the highly technical theological systems developed by 17th-century Lutheran and Reformed theologians that became the standard theological understandings of many Lutheran and Reformed churches.

Protestant principle   A designation for "justification by faith alone" as taught by Martin Luther (1483–1546) to be the key to salvation. Paul Tillich (1886–1965) used the term to indicate that there is always a lack of perfect identity between the symbols of faith and their infinite object.

Protestant Reformation   The 16th-century European movement led by figures such as Martin Luther (1483–1546), Huldrych Zwingli (1484–1531), and John Calvin (1509–64) that developed Protestant theology and Protestant churches in the context of the predominant Roman Catholicism.

Protestant scholasticism   The highly developed, technical theology written by 17th-century Lutheran and Reformed theologians that in form resembled the Scholasticism of medieval theologians. Also called Protestant orthodoxy.

Protestant-Catholic relations   The ecumenical relations between various Protestant churches and the Roman Catholic Church, enhanced by the opportunities opened by the Roman Catholic Vatican Council II (1962–65).

Protestantism The understandings of Christian faith and theology that emerged from the 16th-century Protestant Reformation and that led to the formation of numerous church bodies.

prothesis (Gr. "preparation") In the Byzantine Rite, the rite of preparation for the eucharistic elements that takes place before the beginning of the liturgy. Also, a table on which the eucharistic bread and wine are prepared.

proto-evangelium The "first gospel" as a reference to the statement in Gen. 3:15, which has been taken by some biblical interpreters as predicting the defeat of evil by the victory of Jesus Christ and thus as the first promise or "gospel" of a coming Redeemer.

protology A term for the revealed doctrine of "first things," or the beginning of the world, in contrast to "eschatology," or the doctrine of the "last things."

Proto-Luke Term for a supposed draft of Luke's Gospel believed by some biblical scholars to have been written before Luke as it is now composed and drawn from sources unique to Luke as well as from other source materials.

prototype (From Gr. *protos,* "first," and *typos,* "a figure," "model") A term for describing Jesus Christ and his work of salvation in that he is the one who draws others into relationship with God. In this way Christ is the model or the one from whom the whole group of believers is formed.

proverb (Lat. *proverbium,* "maxim," "adage") A short saying in common use that conveys wisdom. The book of Proverbs in the Old Testament is considered part of the wisdom literature.

providence, divine (Gr. *pronoia,* Lat. *providentia,* "beforehand," from *providere,* "to provide") God's maintenance, guidance, and continuing involvement with creation and humans as means of carrying out divine purposes in history (Acts 4:28; Rom. 8:29–30; Eph. 1:5, 11).

providence, doctrine of The Christian understanding of God's continuing action by which all creation is preserved, supported, and governed by God's purposes and plans for human history and for human lives.

province (Lat. *provincia*) The territory presided over by an archbishop or metropolitan. Some regional leaders of Roman Catholic religious orders are designated "provincials."

provincial (Lat. *provincialis,* "belonging to a province") An official in a religious order who is responsible to the superior general.

provolution A term from the work of Jürgen Moltmann (b. 1926) which looks to the eschatological future centered in God's ultimate kingdom and then seeks to derive an action program for the present that will move the church and history toward that future.

provost (Lat. *praepositus,* "head," "chief," "overseer"; Ger. *Probst*) Title for certain ecclesiastical and academic officers with administrative duties.

prudence (Lat. *prudentia*) A form of knowledge that directs practical judgments and decisions associated with care, due deliberation, and caution. It is one of the four cardinal virtues and has been called the rudder virtue since it "steers" all other virtues.

psalm (Gr. *psalmos,* "song sung to a harp") A hymn, sacred song, or poem. The book of Psalms (the Psalter) is composed of 150 religious poems, prayers, and praises of ancient Israel, arranged in five books (Pss. 1–41, 42–72, 73–89, 90–106, 107–150).

psalm tones Melodic formulas (melodies) used in singing the psalms. Each tone consists of two phrases that balance each other. In Gregorian chant, there is a psalm tone for each church mode. Medieval music theory recognized eight church modes or musical scales.

psalmody (Gr. *psalmōdia,* Lat. *psalmodia*) The use of the book of Psalms during

Christian worship. Psalms may be used antiphonally, responsorially, in congregational singing, and by chanting.

psalter (Gr. *psaltērion,* "stringed instrument") Ancient stringed instrument used in Jewish worship. The Psalter is also a term for the book of Psalms, which has been prominently used through the centuries in Christian liturgies and for psalm singing, as well as for personal devotions.

Pseudepigrapha (Gr. *pseudepigraphos,* "with false title") Writings attributed to those who were not the actual authors. Used for Jewish writings not included in the Septuagint version of the Old Testament, such as the *Assumption of Moses* and the *Psalms of Solomon.*

psilanthropism (Gr. *psilanthrōpos,* "merely human") The view that Jesus Christ was only human and nothing more.

psychiatry The medical treatment of mental illnesses. Numerous ethical issues are raised in questions relating to psychiatric care.

psychoanalysis A term invented by Sigmund Freud (1856–1939) to describe his theory of the psyche and his methods and techniques for understanding and treating it. The insights derived from psychoanalysis may supplement or challenge certain theological perspectives.

psychological analogy The use of human analogies from the mind or soul to provide a way of describing the Trinity. Associated with Augustine's (354–430) analogy of "being," "knowledge," and "love" for the Father, Son, and Holy Spirit.

psychology of religion The use of insights and methods from the discipline of psychology to various forms of religious activity, behavior, and experience. Early practitioners of this study were William James (1842–1910) and Pierre Janet (1859–1947).

psychosomatic unity (From Gr. *psychē,* "soul," and *sōma,* "body") The view that the human is a whole person and that

while "body," "soul," and "spirit" may be helpful designations, the person should be viewed as a total unity.

psychotherapy Method of treatment used in psychoanalysis or psychiatry.

public-private dualism A way of perceiving reality and living so that one set of standards or actions is appealed to in public situations or contexts while another is used in private relations. This approach encounters numerous Christian ethical problems and is not usually regarded as justifiable.

Puebla Conference (1979) The Third General Assembly of Latin American Bishops, convened by the Latin American Bishops' Conference at Puebla, Mexico (CELAM III), from which emerged a document that showed liberation to be an "integral part" of the church's mission. A chapter was devoted to the "preferential option for the poor."

pulpit (Lat. *pulpitum,* "platform") The elevated place in which the preacher stands to deliver a sermon.

pulpit, central (center) A pulpit placed in the center of the chancel area in a church sanctuary. It is a typical form in many Protestant churches where an emphasis is placed on the "centrality" of the Word of God in Scripture and preaching.

pulpit exchange The practice of two clergypersons switching "pulpits" either to preach at a single service or services or to perform ministerial duties in each other's churches for a period of time.

pulpit supply A minister who provides preaching for a certain church for a specific worship service or over a period of time.

punishment (Lat. *poena*) The penalty paid for certain actions. In Protestant theology, the punishment due to human sin has been removed by the obedience of Jesus Christ unto death. Punishment may be enacted by humans in society against those who break laws.

punishment, eternal The expression of God's judgment whereby the wicked are eternally separated from God and receive the consequences of their sinfulness (Matt. 25:46; 2 Thess. 1:9; Jude 1:7).

pure act *See: actus purus*

pure mortalism A view that the death of the body means the cessation of life, since life is so closely identified with the organism itself. It is a form of annihilationism.

purgative way (Lat. *via purgativa*) In mystical theology, the first of three stages of mystical experience in which one seeks cleansing from all sin and every element that hinders the ability to receive a vision of God.

purgatory (Lat. *purgatio*, "cleansing") A doctrine prominent in medieval Catholicism and taught in the Roman Catholic tradition. Purgatory is a place where the souls of the faithful dead endure a period of purification and cleansing for sin prior to their entrance into heaven. It completes sanctification.

purification (Lat. *purificatio*) The act of cleansing, carried out particularly in the Old Testament through various Jewish rituals (Num. 8:7; 19:9, 17). Its purpose is to restore one to life in the religious community or to a relationship with God.

Purification of the Blessed Virgin Mary *See* Presentation of Christ in the Temple

purificator (From Lat. *purificare*, "to make pure") Small white linen cloth used to wipe the paten and dry the chalice during the Eucharist.

Purim A Jewish festival celebrated each spring remembering the deliverance of the Jews from the massacre of the armies of the Persian Empire (Esth. 9:26ff.).

Puritan ethic A designation for attitudes and values associated with 17th-century English Puritanism such as industriousness, discipline, honesty, moderation, humility before God, thrift, and self-sufficiency.

Puritan piety (spirituality) The devotional orientation of Puritans that focuses on such elements as the study of Scripture, the importance of preaching, God's providential ordering of life, and Christian obedience.

Puritan theology The theological views articulated by various 16th- and 17th-century English and American Puritan theologians such as William Perkins (1558–1602), William Ames (1576–1633), John Owen (1616–83), Jonathan Edwards (1703–58), and others who were Calvinistic in orientation.

Puritanism, American Seventeenth-century American religious movement that continued church reform impulses from English Puritanism and was expressed through Presbyterian and Congregationalist streams. It was Calvinistic in theology, and strongest in New England where it was a major cultural force.

Puritanism, English Sixteenth- and seventeenth-century Protestant religious movement that sought to "purify" the Church of England in more Reformed Protestant directions. It designates differing groups. The movement was Calvinistic in theology and presbyterian or congregational in church government.

Puritans Sixteenth- and seventeenth-century English (and later American) Protestants who sought reform of the Church of England based on their understandings of Scripture. They generally adhered to the thought of John Calvin (1509–64) and stressed theology as leading to ethical action while ethics is grounded in true theology.

purity, ritual Cleanness and uncleanness according to the Jewish law, as ascertained through certain practices or the avoidance of other practices (see Lev. 11–17). In the Christian perspective, Jesus Christ abolished prescriptions for ritual purity and demanded purity of heart (Matt. 15:1–20).

purity of the church *See* church, purity of the

purpose That toward which something or someone tends, or which one intends to do. The aim or intentionality of an act may be a factor in determining its ethical goodness.

Puseyism A term for Tractarianism and the Anglo-Catholicism associated with Edward B. Pusey (1800–1882), who stressed the doctrine of the real presence of Christ in the Eucharist, the need for confession of sin, and other elements from the Roman Catholic heritage of Anglicanism.

putative marriage (From Lat. *putativus*, and *putare*, "to suppose," "to reckon") A marriage that is declared invalid for some reason though it was initiated in good faith by at least one of the parties involved.

Pyrrhonism A skeptical philosophical system associated with Pyrrho (c.

360–c. 275 B.C.), who argued that it is not possible to attain any absolute knowledge or certain truth. Now used for any skeptical thought system.

Pythagoreanism The thought emerging from the Greek teacher Pythagoras (c. 580–500 B.C.), who founded a philosophical school (or religious society) at Croton around 531 B.C. Tenets were the immortality of the soul imprisoned in a cycle of reincarnations. Through study one could break the cycle and attain salvation. Followers maintained high moral standards.

Pyx (From Gr. *pyxis*, "wooden container," Lat. *pyxis*, "little box") A receptacle for holding the consecrated bread of Holy Communion that can be carried to the sick.

Q (Quelle) The German term *Quelle* ("source"), used by biblical scholars to indicate a presumed source for portions of the Gospels of Matthew and Luke that are similar to each other but are unlike anything in the Gospel of Mark.

Quadragesima (Lat. "forty") The forty-day season of Lent, extending from Ash Wednesday to Holy Saturday.

quadriga (Lat. *quadrigae*, "a set of four") The term for the four senses of Scripture recognized by medieval biblical interpreters: literal, moral, allegorical, and anagogical.

quadrilateral, Wesleyan A 20th-century description of sources of authority in the thought of John Wesley (1703–91): Scripture, tradition, the Holy Spirit, and reason.

Quakers/Quakerism (Society of Friends) Founded in England in the mid-17th century by George Fox (1624–91), Quakers emphasized a doctrine of the "inner

light" (illumination by the Holy Spirit) and rejected clergy, sacraments, oath taking, military service, and war. Members of the Society were called "Friends." The name "Quakers" came from their trembling at the Word of God.

qualitative distinction *See* infinite qualitative distinction

qualities, absolute The characteristics or attributes of God that are independent of God's relationship with persons or created objects.

quality of life A consideration in contemporary discussions about the use of life-support systems to prolong biological life as well as debates about euthanasia. How it is measured and how much weight it should have are much debated.

Quartodecimanism (*quartusdecimus*, "fourteenth") Practice of some early Christians in Asia Minor of observing Easter on the 14th day of the Jewish month of Nisan, regardless of what day of the week it fell on, rather than celebrating it on the following Sunday.

Queen of Heaven   A term for the Virgin Mary in the Roman Catholic tradition. It comes from the belief that after her assumption into heaven, Mary was crowned Queen of Heaven. The feast of Mary the Queen is celebrated on May 31 and the queenship of Mary is observed on August 22.

Quesnellianism   Followers of the Jansenist Pasquier Quesnel (1634–1719), who taught a rigid doctrine of the irresistibility of grace, and held that grace is not to be found outside the Roman Catholic Church. His views were condemned by Pope Clement XI (1713).

quest of the historical Jesus   A term associated with the work of Albert Schweitzer (1875–1965) and attempts to write a "life of Jesus" with attention to subjecting the figure of Jesus to the forms of historical inquiry used in the study of other historical characters.

Quicunque Vult   (Lat. "Whosoever will") The first words of the Athanasian Creed: "Whosoever wills to be saved . . ." The Latin term is often used as a designation for it.

quietism   Any system of spirituality that emphasizes waiting on God. Also,

Quietism was a 17th-century Roman Catholic school of spirituality, associated with Miguel de Molinos (c. 1627–96), Madame Guyon (1648–1717), and François Fénelon (1651–1715), which taught that one may pass beyond sin to union with God.

Quinquagesima   (Lat. "fiftieth") The fiftieth day prior to Easter. Used to designate the Sunday before Ash Wednesday.

quinque viae   *See* Five Ways, the

Qumran   Site at the northwest end of the Dead Sea where the Dead Sea Scrolls were found (1947). A Jewish group of (probably) Essenes lived at Qumran during biblical times (c. 150 B.C.–A.D. 70).

Quo vadis?   (Lat. "Where are you going?") Legendary question of Peter to Christ in the apocryphal *Acts of Peter* (c. A.D. 200) that caused Peter to return to persecution and martyrdom in Rome when Christ responded, "To Rome to be crucified again."

quod ubique, quod semper, quod ab omnibus creditum est   (Lat. "that which has been believed everywhere, always, and by all") Criteria of Vincent of Lerins in his *Commonitorium* (A.D. 434) to designate what constitutes the beliefs of Christian faith.

rabbi   (Heb. *rabbi,* "my master," Gr. *kyrios*) A teacher of Jewish law. Jesus was recognized as a rabbi (Matt. 26:49; Mark 9:5; 14:45). Also, an ordained Jew who is usually the spiritual leader of a congregation.

rabbinic   Pertaining to the rabbis as teachers and practitioners of Jewish law.

race   François Bernier's term (1684) to categorize persons in regard to various

genetic characteristics. Theologically and ethically, all races are equal in God's sight and human solidarity rooted in creation in the image of God transcends racial lines. Racial discrimination is evil.

racism   Incidental as well as systematic practices of discrimination, oppression, and domination on the basis of race. It is considered within Christian ethics to be sinful and evil behavior.

Racovian Catechism (1605) A catechism by the followers of Faustus Socinus (1539–1604) that deviates from orthodox Christianity by not espousing the Trinity or the incarnation of Jesus Christ as the eternal Son of God.

Radical Reformation The "left" or "third" wing of the Protestant Reformation that describes those who sought a radical approach, a return to early Christian precedents for the nature and government of the church, rejecting national or state churches. Among others it included Anabaptists such as the Mennonites and the Amish.

radical theology Attempts to explain the Christian faith in terms drawn from scientific assumptions, and the consequent rejection of traditional ideas that do not match these assumptions.

raised with Christ Pauline expression of the union of believers with Jesus Christ in his death and resurrection to eternal life (Rom. 6:1–11).

Rally Day A term used in American Sunday schools for a Sunday on which students are promoted to the next class or department. It has often been marked by a special Sunday school service featuring recitations of Bible verses.

ransom theory of the atonement The view that Jesus Christ procured salvation by shedding his blood as a ransom to Satan to deliver humanity from bondage to evil. It is associated with the thought of Origen (c. 185–c. 254).

Ranters A 17th-century English group, often confused with Quakers, that denied the authority of the Bible, the creeds, and the church's ministry while appealing to the inward authority of the Holy Spirit in an attempt to recover the vitality of the early Christian church.

rape Violent coercion of sexual intercourse. Feminist writers frequently define rape as an act and a social institution based on violence that perpetuates patriarchal domination.

rapture (From Lat. *raptus,* "carried off") An expression of intense religious experience. Also, the rapture, a view found in premillennialism, which teaches that when Christ returns to the earth, believers will be raptured, or raised from the earth to meet him in the air (1 Thess. 4:17).

rapture, midtribulational view of the View that the church will endure half a tribulation period predicted in Scripture (Matt. 24:21–30) before being raptured at the return of Jesus Christ to earth.

rapture, partial The view that some persons will be raptured sooner and others later depending on their state of spiritual readiness.

rapture, posttribulational view of the View that the church will not be raptured at the return of Christ until after the end of a tribulation period predicted in Scripture (Matt. 24:21–30).

rapture, pretribulational view of the The view that the church will be raptured at the return of Christ prior to a period of tribulation predicted in Scripture (Matt. 24:21–30).

rationalism The philosophical view that truth is known through human reason. Some forms of rationalism accept that the existence of God can be proved through reason, others do not. As an approach to religion, it assumes religion to be a cognitive rather than a psychological, sociological, or economic phenomenon.

rationalist One who espouses rationalism and believes that truth is known through human reason.

rationality Conformity to reason and such elements as intelligibility, consistency, coherency, order, logical structure, completeness, testability, and simplicity.

Ratisbon (Regensburg), Conference of (1541) An attempt by Charles V in Ratisbon (Regensburg), Germany, to reconcile Roman Catholicism and Lutheranism. The issues of church authority and the Eucharist proved to be barriers. Both the pope and Luther later rejected the agreement made there.

reader A nonordained person who assists in the liturgy by reading or preaching in a worship service.

reader-response criticism   A method of biblical interpretation that arose in the 1960s. It maintains that the meanings of a text come solely from the individual reader and not from the text or its author's intention.

reading, spiritual   A classic means by which one experiences an awareness of God through writings that focus on aspects of Christian faith and experience. Traditionally, spending time each day in this type of reading has been a means of Christian devotion.

real presence of Christ   The view that Jesus Christ is truly present in the celebration of the Lord's Supper. Theologians and church bodies have differed on the exact way that this real presence—as opposed to a figurative or symbolic presence—is to be understood.

realism   (From Lat. *res*, "thing") The view that objects of knowledge truly exist apart from our knowledge of them, in contrast to idealism and phenomenalism. In medieval philosophy, the view that universals have an independence apart from the mind that perceives them. It contrasts with nominalism.

realism, biblical   *See* biblical realism

realism, ethical   A term associated with Reinhold Niebuhr (1892–1971) to describe an ethical approach to moral and political concerns that seeks to take into account all factors in a situation that offer resistance to established norms, especially the factors of self-interest and power.

realism, political   An ethical and political view stressing the world's imperfection and the limits on humans' abilities to improve it.

Realism, Scottish   *See* Common Sense philosophy

realism, sociological   An approach focusing on the ways people in groups behave and how social structures actually function.

realism, theological   A 20th-century view contrasting with theological idealism or liberalism stressing God's initiative in revelation.

realistic-headship view of the imputation of sin   A belief associated with Augustine (354–430), who taught that all humanity was present in Adam and that Adam acted in a way representative of all people when he sinned. Thus all humans were present and participants in the original sin of Adam (1 Cor. 15:22).

reality   (Lat. *actus*) That which exists—as opposed to that which can exist or has the potential to exist (Lat. *potentia*).

realized eschatology   *See* eschatology, realized

reason   (Lat. *ratio*) The mental capacity or power to use the human mind in reaching and establishing truth. Also, the premise or ground of an argument. A theory or structure of knowledge.

reasoning   Traditionally, the use of the power of thought and laws of logic to make judgments. Some feminist writers argue on the basis of psychological and social development that there are distinctive "female" forms of reasoning while "neutral" standards of rationality are male biased.

REB   *See* Revised English Bible

rebaptism   Participation in baptism after one has already been baptized. Some churches that do not recognize the validity of infant baptism baptize when one becomes a convert. Some churches rebaptize using a different means or mode of baptism such as immersion.

rebellion   (Lat. *rebellio*, "a revolt") A biblical concept for sin in which humans are seen as acting against God's will and thus refusing to live obediently to God.

rebirth   (Also "new birth," "born again," "born from above," or regeneration) The complete transformation of existence by the Holy Spirit and thus entrance into the family of God (see John 3:3).

recapitulation   (Lat. *recapitulatio*, Gr. *anakephalaiōsis*, "summing up") A view of early Christian theologians, particularly Irenaeus (c. 130–c. 200). God "sums up all things in Christ" (Eph. 1:10) as the Second Adam who restores the sinful creation by redeeming all the sin done in Adam.

received text (Lat. *textus receptus,* "received text") The Greek text of the New Testament as published by Erasmus (1516). It was considered thereafter to be the standard or most authentic text.

recension (From Lat. *recensio,* "a reviewing") A revision of an earlier (biblical) text by an editor. More generally, the term is used to indicate the existence of one or more text "families" of an ancient document.

receptionism A view of the real presence of Christ in the Lord's Supper held by many Anglicans and Methodists. The bread and wine are believed to remain unchanged after their consecration, while the believing communicant receives Christ's spiritual body and blood with them.

rechte Lehre (Ger. "right teaching or doctrine") A Lutheran expression used during the period of scholastic theology in the 17th century to indicate what was true doctrine according to Scripture.

recidivism (Lat. *recidivus,* "relapsing") The yielding to temptation that causes Christians to fall back into certain sins. It may be a pattern of behavior that leads to repeated relapses into the same kind of sin without any attempts to avoid it.

recluse (From Lat. *recludere,* "to shut off") A person who chooses to live apart from the world for the purposes of religious devotion. A hermit.

recollection (Lat. *recollectio*) The concentration of the whole person in seeking to experience the presence of God by eliminating distractions.

recompense *See* reward

reconciliation (Gr. *katallagē,* Lat. *reconciliatio,* "a bringing together again") Bringing together parties who are estranged. It is a key image of the salvation accomplished by Jesus Christ in his death and resurrection (2 Cor. 5:16–21). Christians are to be reconciled with God and with others (Matt. 5:23–24).

reconciliation, liturgy of A contemporary name for the Roman Catholic sacrament of penance that gives ritual expression to contrition for sin. It consists of four parts expressed in each of three ritual forms. The parts are contrition, confession, act of penance or satisfaction, and absolution.

reconstituted body The resurrection body (1 Cor. 15) that will presumably exhibit some continuities with the present body but also important differences.

reconstructionism, Christian A movement begun in the 1960s, associated with Rousas John Rushdoony and others, that seeks to restructure American society in ways that explicitly express Old Testament laws.

records (minutes) The official proceedings of a church meeting or governing body which constitute the normative account of what transpired.

rector (Lat. "ruler," "leader") In the Protestant Episcopal and Roman Catholic traditions, the clergyperson who serves a parish. Generally, the supervising officer of a religious institution.

rectory (Lat. *rectoria*) The house in which a rector lives.

recusant (From Lat. *recusare,* "to refuse") One who refuses to obey an established authority. The term applied to those in England who refused to obey the Act of Uniformity (1559) and attend Church of England services. In the 16th and 17th centuries they faced penalties. The law was repealed in 1791.

redaction (Lat. *redactus,* from *redigere,* "to bring back") Editorial ordering of textual materials.

redaction criticism (Ger. *Redaktionsgeschichte*) The scholarly study of the editorial methods used by New Testament writers—particularly in the Synoptic Gospels—to order and shape the materials they took from other sources.

redactor (From Fr. *rédacteur*, "one who brings back") One who edits textual materials.

redeemed (From Lat. *redimere*, "to buy back") A designation for Christians who have received salvation through Jesus Christ and are thus brought back into the relationship with God that they are intended to have (Gal. 3:13; Rev. 14:3, 4).

Redeemer (Lat. *redimere*, "buy back") God as the rescuer and recoverer of Israel (Isa. 41:14; 44:24; Jer. 50:34). A designation for Jesus Christ, who brings salvation and the redemptive relationship God intends to have with those who believe (Rom. 3:24; Eph. 1:7, 14; Col. 1:14).

redemption (Lat. *redemptio*, from *redimere*, "to redeem") A financial metaphor that literally means "buying back." Used theologically to indicate atonement, reconciliation, or salvation wherein liberation from forms of bondage such as sin, death, law, or evil takes place through Christ.

redemption, covenant of *See* covenant of redemption

redemption, particular *See* atonement, limited

redemptive history *See: Heilsgeschichte*

Redemptrix *See* Coredemptrix

reductionism Explanation of complex ideas in terms not appropriate to their complexity. Often refers to attempts to explain beliefs in ways that do not assume God's reality, such as sociologically, psychologically, or philosophically.

reference In matters of church government, the point in a constitution, official manual, or book of church order that is applicable in a particular instance or in relation to a particular question.

reform movements Movements that focus on a spiritual renewal of the church and its mission.

Reformation, Counter *See* Counter-Reformation

Reformation, Protestant The movement that sought initially to reform the Roman Catholic Church but that led to the establishment of separate branches of Christianity collectively called Protestantism. It is connected particularly with the work of Martin Luther (1483–1546) and later John Calvin (1509–64), among others.

Reformation Day The recognition in Protestant churches of October 31, the eve of All Saints' Day when in 1517 Martin Luther (1483–1546) is said to have nailed his 95 theses to the door of the castle church in Wittenberg. This event initiated the Protestant Reformation.

Reformation theology The theology emerging from the 16th-century Protestant Reformation, particularly the theologies of Martin Luther (1483–1546) and John Calvin (1509–64). Key emphases include the Scriptures as authority, Christ as the sole agent of salvation, and faith as the means of justification.

Reformed A term for churches and the theological tradition that emerged from the work of John Calvin (1509–64) and other reformers such as Huldrych Zwingli (1484–1531) and Heinrich Bullinger (1504–75), in contrast to the Lutheran Reformation and to Anabaptism.

Reformed churches Those churches which have emerged from the theological work of John Calvin (1509–64), Huldrych Zwingli (1484–1531), John Knox (c. 1513–72), and other Reformers, marked by theological understandings consistent with Calvin and usually a presbyterian form of church government.

Reformed theology The theological tradition that emerged from the work of John Calvin (1509–64) and other reformers such as Huldrych Zwingli (1484–1531) and Heinrich Bullinger (1504–75), in contrast to Lutheran theology. Key aspects include God's initiative in salvation, and election, and union with Christ.

Reformed tradition The theological tradition that emerged from the work of John Calvin (1509–64) and other reformers such as Huldrych Zwingli (1484–1531) and Heinrich Bullinger (1504–75) in contrast to Lutheranism and Anabaptism in the 16th century.

reformers Leaders who seek to reform the church, its theology or practices. The term is most often used for the major Protestant leaders Martin Luther (1483–1546), Huldrych Zwingli (1484–1531), and John Calvin (1509–64), who sought reform of the Roman Catholic Church during the 16th-century Reformation.

Refreshment Sunday The fourth Sunday in Lent, also called Laetare. Its name comes from the lessening of the Lenten discipline on that Sunday (Lat. *laetare*, "to lessen"). It is parallel to Gaudete Sunday, the third Sunday in Lent.

regenerate (From Lat. *regeneratio*, "rebirth") Those who have experienced regeneration or the new birth by the power of the Holy Spirit and have become Christian.

regeneration (Gr. *palingenesia*, Lat. *regeneratio*, "new birth," "new life") The action of the Holy Spirit, who transforms the lives of those given the gift of faith so they experience a "new birth" and salvation through Jesus Christ (Titus 3:5).

regeneration, baptismal *See* baptismal regeneration

Regensburg, Conference of *See* Ratisbon, Conference of

registers Record books containing official church documents or lists, such as of those baptized, confirmed, or admitted to church membership.

regula fidei *See* rule of faith

regular clergy A term used in the Roman Catholic tradition for those priests who belong to orders or congregations, in distinction from the "secular" priests (clergy), who have a vocation in the world. Regular clergy live under a "rule" for ordering life and devotion.

reification (From Lat. *res*, "thing") The fallacy noted in philosophy of treating a psychological or mental entity as though it were a thing. Also called hypostatization.

reign of God *See* kingdom of God

reincarnation (Lat. *re-*, "again," and *incarnare*, "to incarnate") The belief that a soul is reborn in another body after death. It was held by Origen (c. 185–c. 254) but rejected by mainstream Christianity. Also called transmigration of souls or metempsychosis.

relational theology A term that embraces a variety of expressions of emphasis on interpersonal relationships as central to one's theological outlook. Largely an American movement, prime examples have been Harry Emerson Fosdick, Samuel Shoemaker, Norman Vincent Peale, and Eugenia Price.

relative qualities A term for the characteristics or attributes of God that describe God in relationship to God's creation.

relativism Most generally, a philosophical term for the belief that no absolutes exist. It is also used for the view that all knowledge is relative to the knower. In ethics the term indicates the view that no criteria for ethical judgments can be claimed and that morality varies with the culture.

relics (Lat. *reliquiae*, "remains") The remains of a special, sacred person or object that are venerated.

religion (Lat. *religio*) A term with a variety of definitions. Religion includes ritual, social, and ethical elements combined with belief in an unseen world and often a deity. Beliefs may be expressed through myths or doctrines.

religion, anthropology of *See* anthropology of religion

religion, comparative *See* comparative study of religion

religion, natural Religion based on the belief that humans are capable of creating a system of religious thought by the use of reason and without the need for divine revelation.

religion, phenomenology of *See* phenomenology of religion

religion, philosophy of *See* philosophy of religion

religion, psychology of   *See* psychology of religion

religion, revealed   Religion based on the view that humans are not capable of coming to a knowledge of God by their own reason but are in need of divine revelation.

religion, sociology of   *See* sociology of religion

religionless Christianity   A phrase associated with Dietrich Bonhoeffer (1906–45), who believed that a religion that needs a God to solve problems or explain its mysteries is obsolete, since persons have been learning to live without God. Now God must be found in the middle of life, in human strengths and weaknesses.

Religionsgeschichtliche Schule   (Ger.) "history of religion school." An approach and method of studying religion associated with 19th- and early 20th-century German scholars using data drawn from the study of all religions as a means of interpreting the nature and meaning of Christianity.

religiosity   (From Lat. *religiosus*) An excessive or affected religious zeal. It connotes an outward display of actions without a correspondingly genuine valuing of religion.

religious   (Lat. *religiosus*, "reverencing the gods") A member of a religious congregation or order in the Roman Catholic tradition (a religious). Also, generally, having to do with religion. More specifically, practicing piety or godliness.

religious a priori   A term in philosophical theology since the time of F.D.E. Schleiermacher (1768–1834), who argued that there is an innate capacity within humans for religion that can be the presupposition for all particular religions.

religious education   *See* Christian education

religious epistemology   The study of the basis and apprehension of religious knowledge.

religious experience   A special sense of the presence of the divine or of one's relationship to the holy. It is an experience or aspect of experience that one believes possesses religious significance or meaning.

religious freedom   *See* religious liberty

religious institute   In the Roman Catholic tradition, a group authorized by a church authority to live together in community and whose members have taken vows of poverty, chastity, and obedience.

religious language   *See* language, religious

religious leader   One who guides or directs others in religious matters. Concerns may be with intellectual, emotional, spiritual, or activist directions.

religious liberty   The freedom to practice one's own form of religion according to the dictates of conscience without coercion or interference from an outside force such as a government.

religious orders   A term used in the Roman Catholic tradition for groups of men and women who have committed themselves to a specific form of religious life. Vows include poverty, chastity, and obedience.

religious socialism   A 20th-century European movement seeking to unite socialism with Christianity and its expectation of the kingdom of God.

Religious Society of Friends   *See* Quakers/Quakerism

reliquary   (Lat. *reliquiae*, "remains") Receptacles that hold the relics of saints.

remarriage   Being married again after a marriage annulment, a divorce, or the death of a spouse.

remission of sins   (Lat. *remissio peccatorum*) The forgiveness of that which separates humans from God (sin) and its penalties through faith in Jesus Christ.

remnant   (From Lat. *remanere*, "to stay behind") A portion of an original group. In Israel's history, that portion of the nation which remained faithful to God.

Remonstrance (1610)   (From Lat. *remonstrare*, "to point out") A statement of views drawn up at Gouda, the Netherlands, by 46 pastors who favored the views of James Arminius (1560–1609) and rejected orthodox Calvinism. Response was made at the Calvinistic Synod of Dort (1618–19). Those who signed the Arminian doctrinal statement were called Remonstrants.

remunerative justice *See* distributive justice

Renaissance (From Fr. *renaître*, "to be born anew") A period in European history (c. 1300-c. 1600) that marked a cultural transition from medieval to modern times. The rebirth of learning and other cultural elements set the stage for the Protestant Reformation.

renewal movements Groups within both Roman Catholicism and Protestantism that seek to deepen their church's spiritual mission or theology to bring about a return to, or renewal of, faithfulness to Jesus Christ.

renewal, church An increased degree of devotion and faithfulness to the gospel of Jesus Christ experienced by Christian congregations through a variety of means and actions. The term is also used for efforts to bring about this condition.

renouncing the discipline *See* renunciation of jurisdiction

renunciation (From Lat. *re-*, "back," and *nuntiare*, "to tell") Renouncing or turning away from the ways of the world or the works of evil to be a Christian disciple and follow Jesus. Also the act of disavowing, abandoning, or rejecting something, as when one renounces the teachings or discipline of a church.

renunciation of jurisdiction A formal way of disassociating oneself from a church by asserting that one is no longer bound by the church's order, discipline, or jurisdiction. This also means the loss of one's ministerial ordination.

renunciation of the devil A portion of the baptismal service from the early Christian centuries in which those to be

baptized are asked if they "renounce the devil and all his works." Its intention is to indicate a willingness to forsake all evil ways of life.

reordination The practice of reordaining to the priesthood those who had been ordained by heretical sects. It was gradually rejected in light of the views of Augustine (354–430) and others that a sacrament may be valid even if it is administered by heretical priests.

reparation (Lat. *reparatio*, "a renewal") The action of making amends for past offenses. It describes Christ's death in that it restored the divine-human relationship. In some Roman Catholic communities, the term describes good works or acts of penitence for sins against another person.

repentance (Heb. *shub*, Gr. *metanoia*, Lat. *poenitentia*) The act of expressing contrition, penitence, and contrition for sin. Its linguistic roots point to its theological meaning of a change of mind and life direction as a beginning step of expressing Christian faith (Acts 26:20).

representative, Christ as The view that Jesus Christ represents all humanity through his becoming human and is thus a "second Adam." The term is also used to indicate that Christ represents humanity in his death to gain salvation for the world.

reprobates (Lat. *reprobi*) Those who are passed over in their sinfulness by God and do not receive salvation. In medieval theology they are those of whom it is foreknown that they will not accept divine grace and will therefore die in a state of sin.

reprobation (Lat. *reprobatio*, "rejection") God's action of leaving some persons in the state of their own sinfulness so that they do not receive salvation but eternal punishment. In some theological views it is considered a decree of God for damnation.

reproduction The process of the continuation of the human species. Many feminist writers see lack of reproductive freedom for women as a main form of women's oppression.

reproductive rights/freedom   Many feminist writers see these rights and freedoms as including the right and freedom to become a mother, to practice contraception, and to choose abortion.

Requiem Mass   In the Roman Catholic tradition, a Mass (Eucharist) offered on behalf of someone who has died. The service begins: *Requiem aeternam dona eis, Domine* ("Give them eternal rest, O Lord"). It is now called the mass for the dead or the mass of Christian burial.

reredos   (From Lat. *retro-,* "backward," and *dorsum,* "back") A screen or ornamented wall of stone or wood behind an altar in the eastward position. It may be decorated with carved figures.

res sacramenti   (Lat. "the thing of the sacrament") The thing toward which the visible sign of a sacrament points. Theologically, the visible signs in baptism (water) and the Lord's Supper (bread and wine) point to the person of Jesus Christ, who is known in the sacraments with his merits and benefits for those who believe in him. Also *res signata* ("the thing signified").

reservation of the Eucharist (Sacrament)   (From Lat. *reservare,* "to keep back) Maintaining the consecrated bread from the Eucharist for use at a later time for those in need of the Sacrament between celebrations of the Eucharist or at the time of death.

reserve   A term used by mid-19th-century Tractarians to describe the withholding of deep doctrinal teachings of Christianity from those recently converted to the faith.

resistible grace   A theological term used against the Reformed view of "irresistible grace" by Lutheran and Arminian theologians who teach that God's saving grace is universally offered and may be refused by anyone by an action of their free will.

response   *See* versicle

responsibility   The ethical recognition of obligation and accountability for attitudes and actions. Also, that for which one is responsible.

responsorial psalmody   The practice of a congregation singing a brief response to verses of a psalm sung by a cantor or leader in public worship. The response may be as simple as the word "Alleluia" or "Amen."

responsory   (From Lat. *responsorium*) The repetition of a whole or part of a chant after a soloist has sung the chant.

ressourcement   French term for a return to the original sources to inform contemporary understanding. It has been used to describe the recovery of the teachings of Thomas Aquinas (1225–74) and the *Nouvelle Théologie* of "Neo-Scholasticism."

restitution   (From Lat. *restituere,* "to restore") In ethics, the principle of "commutative justice" whereby there is reparation made for an action of injury or injustice to another.

Restoration movement   A 19th-century American religious movement that sought church reform according to New Testament patterns. It was committed to biblical authority and church unity. The Christian Church (Disciples of Christ) emerged from the movement.

restoration of Israel   The view that the Jewish people will return to the biblical land of Palestine and also come to acknowledge Jesus as the Messiah prior to the end of the world.

restorationism   The view that the creation and humans will return to their initial state of well-being either when God acts to redeem the whole creation (Rom. 8:21–22) or, as in Origen (c. 185–c. 254), through universal salvation. In Roman Catholicism, the desire to return to pre-Vatican II Catholicism.

resurrection   (Lat. *resurrectio,* "a rising again from the dead") God's raising of Jesus Christ from the dead (Acts 2:32; 4:10; Gal. 1:1). Also the future rising of all persons prior to the final judgment (John 5:25–29; 1 Cor. 15; Rev. 20:4–15).

resurrection, first   A term associated with interpretations of Rev. 20:5. The premillennialist interpretation is that this refers to a physical resurrection of only Christian believers. A second resurrection is of unbelievers. The amillennialist view is that the verse refers to a spiritual resurrection or new birth.

resurrection body   The body received by those who will be raised from the dead by the power of God (1 Cor. 15:35–54). It is a complete transformation of the physical into a spiritual body. The identity and continuity of human personality is maintained in an eternal state.

resurrection life   The new existence given to those who know the power of Jesus Christ's resurrection (Phil. 3:10) and who live in light of this reality. It is also the future life in glory which is eternal and which comes through Jesus Christ (John 11:25).

resurrection of Jesus Christ   God's raising of Jesus Christ from death to life on the third day (Sunday) after his crucifixion (Acts 4:10; 5:30; Rom. 10:9). Christ is thus alive and worshiped as the risen Lord (Phil. 2:6–11) who rules the world and is present in the world and with the church (Matt. 28:20).

resurrection of judgment   The action of God in raising persons from the dead who will be judged and face condemnation (John 5:29; Rev. 20:4–15).

resurrection of life   The action of God in raising persons from the dead who will be judged and receive life (Matt. 25:46; John 5:29).

resurrection of the body   The theological belief that those who will be raised from the dead by the power of God will receive a resurrection body that will exist eternally (1 Cor. 15). The resurrection body is not a resuscitation of the former physical body but a new form of existence.

resurrection of the dead   A general resurrection of all those who have died

prior to an ultimate or last judgment (John 5:28–29; Acts 24:15).

retaliation   (From Lat. *re-*, "back," and *talio,* "punishment in kind") To return an action in response to an action. Often in ethics, the returning of evil for evil, an act warned against by the New Testament (Rom. 12:17; 1 Thess. 5:15; 1 Peter 3:9).

retreat   A time set aside, often at a special place, for renewal of the spiritual life, often through the use of religious exercises such as silence, meditation, and reflection. It is both a place and a spiritual experience of groups and/or individuals.

retribution   (Lat. *retributio,* "repayment") Ethically, retaliation for a wrong that is done (Jer. 5:9; 9:9).

retributive justice   The view that God's justice intends to give sinners that which their sins deserve (Jer. 5:29; 20:12).

reunion   The uniting of church bodies that have been separated over a period of time.

revealed law   A term for the moral law as revealed to Moses by God on Mount Sinai (Ex. 20ff.). It contrasts with a natural law that may be known from nature. The Mosaic law as a divine revelation indicates God's clear, complete, and perfect law for the lives of God's covenant people.

revealed theology   The theological understandings that emerge from Scripture as compared to "natural theology," which seeks a knowledge of God from the natural world and by human reason.

revelation   (Lat. *revelatio,* "an uncovering") An act of self-disclosure and self-communication.

revelation, accommodated   *See* accommodation

revelation, anthropic   God's revelation as given in human forms or in forms with which humans are familiar.

revelation, biblical   The self-disclosure of God through the biblical writings.

revelation, divine (Lat. *revelatio,* "an uncovering," from *revelare,* "to unveil") The self-disclosure and self-communication of God by which God conveys a knowledge of God to humans. It is important since it makes known that which is inaccessible to human reason alone.

revelation, general God's self-disclosure and self-communication in the universe and created world (Ps. 19; Rom. 1:19ff.). Theologians have debated whether faith is necessary to perceive this revelation and in what ways it is accessible to those who are sinners.

revelation, indirect The view of some theologians, such as Emil Brunner (1889–1966) and Karl Barth (1886–1968), that God's revelation in Scripture is not directly and unequivocally identical with the Scriptures, but that the revelation occurs indirectly, because the Bible is a human book that points or witnesses to God's revelation.

revelation, models of A way of indicating theological views about the nature of God's revelation and how it is perceived by constructing schematic prototypes or organizing images that provide differing responses to various aspects of the issue of revelation.

revelation, natural God's revelation through the created universe and in nature (Ps. 19; Rom. 1:19ff.).

revelation, nonpropositional view of The view that God's revelation is a revelation of the divine self and is not to be equated with statements or propositions about God.

revelation, progressive The view that God's revelation, as known through Scripture, is a continuing process in which later revelation is built on earlier, so that new aspects of revelation may occur.

revelation, propositional view of The view that God's revelation in Scripture may be conceptualized through statements or propositions that convey truths about God and are thus God's revelation.

revelation, signs of A term associated with the work of Karl Barth (1886–1968) and others who see God's revelation as an event in which humans encounter God. Signs of revelation are the means or instruments God uses to signify and occasion revelation, the primary sign being the Holy Scriptures.

revelation, special God's particular self-revelation at specific times and places and to particular people, as in the events of Israel's history and, for Christians, fully in Jesus Christ. The Bible as the record of God's word and action is also considered a special revelation.

revenge *See* vengeance

reverence for God (Lat. *reverentia,* from *re-,* "again," "in response," and *vereri,* "to fear," "to respect") Respect and honor due to a person as well as the worship that is due to God.

reverend (Lat. *reverendus,* "worthy of being honored," "reverence") A formal title for clergy used since the 15th century.

reversal, law of *See* law of reversal

Revised English Bible (REB, 1989) A revision of the New English Bible (1961, 1970) by a multidenominational group of Protestant British scholars. The translation seeks a fluent style of English with appropriate dignity for liturgical use and intelligibility for worshipers.

Revised Standard Version of the Bible (RSV; 1946, 1952) A revision of the American Standard Version (1901) by 32 scholars. The goal was to modernize language, using the most reliable biblical manuscripts. The New Testament appeared in 1946, the Old Testament in 1952. Both were revised in 1962. It was the most popular mid-century Protestant-sponsored version.

Revised Version of the Bible (RV, 1881–85) A revision of the Authorized (King James) Version of the Bible carried out by British and American scholars. The British revisers published the New Testament in 1881 and the Old Testament in 1885. Also called the "English Revised Version."

re-visioning In feminist writings, the historical, cultural, and psychic examination of women's cultural past to create a woman's history.

revisionism (From Lat. *revidere*, "to look back at") Questioning and reconceiving the central tenets of a tradition.

revitalization movements An identification used by anthropologists and sociologists for religions that seek to retrieve or revive all or parts of their traditional beliefs and practices in the face of important economic, political, and religious changes that endanger the community's self-identity.

revival (From Lat. *revivere*, "to live again") A term to designate a sense of the work of the Holy Spirit among persons or in churches that brings a new sense of vitality and devotion. The term also refers to a short period when evangelistic meetings are held to increase religious zeal.

revival, theology of The recognition of God's work through the Holy Spirit at various times and places to bring a renewed sense of God's presence and work among people and in churches. Historically, differing theological emphases and practices have been associated with the revival phenomenon.

revival movements The patterns or trends through periods of church history when a sense of spiritual renewal and revitalization attributed to the work of God has been experienced. Emphasis may be placed on conversion to Christ. English Methodism and the Great Awakening in the American colonies of the mid-18th century featured such movements.

revivals/revivalism Periodic attempts, often through mass meetings, of promoting spiritual fervor and commitment, accompanied by calls for personal decisions of faith in Jesus Christ and a concern to rouse people to greater spiri-

tual vitality. Various techniques are employed to reach these goals.

reviviscence (From Lat. *reviviscere*, "to live") A term used in Roman Catholic sacramental theology to signify that a sacrament administered once (such as baptism, which cannot be repeated), but that was not effective due to the resistance of the recipient, may take effect later when the resistance is removed.

revolution (Lat. *revolutio*, "a revolving") A radical change, often used in a political sense when an established government is overthrown. At various historical points, Christians have engaged in revolutionary activities and have justified their actions theologically and ethically.

revolution, theology of A theology associated with the "theology of hope," which sees the coming future reign (kingdom) of God as secured by the crucifixion and resurrection of Jesus Christ as imposing an inclusive and unending revolution for the Christian believer and the church.

reward In Roman Catholic moral theology, the final attainment of blessedness and eternal life in heaven as a result of the cooperation of faithful Christians with God's grace, for which they gain merit.

Rheims-Douay Version of the Bible (1582, 1609) First Roman Catholic translation of the Bible from the Latin Vulgate into English. The New Testament was published in Rheims (1582) and the Old Testament in Douay (1609). It was revised several times and was the approved version for English-speaking Roman Catholics for three centuries.

right hand of God (the Father) A term used to indicate the power and authority of God. In the Apostles' Creed it describes the place of the ascended Christ (Acts 7:55–56; Rom. 8:34; Eph. 1:20).

right-to-life/pro-life movement A movement begun in America in 1966 that opposes attempts to take innocent human lives from the time of conception. The group has been especially adamant in opposing abortion.

righteous indignation   An anger that is justified on the basis of ethical concerns over wrongs that have been done.

righteousness   (Heb. *ṣedaqah*, Gr. *dikaiosynē*, Lat. *iustitia*) Biblically the term embraces a number of dimensions relating to God's actions in establishing and maintaining right relationships. Ethically it is a state of moral purity or doing that which is right (Pss. 96:13; 97:6; 106:3).

righteousness, civil   The doing of actions that may be considered as good or the possession of personal virtues that may be commendable in a cultural context but that are not regarded as earning favor or merit before God.

righteousness, human   Virtues or ethical human activities that may emerge in any human life but that do not earn favor or merit with God.

righteousness, original   *See* original righteousness

righteousness of faith   (Lat. *iustitia fidei*) The right relationship with God granted to those to whom the gift of faith in Jesus Christ is given (Rom. 4:13). Faith is the divinely appointed means by which the right relationship with God through Christ is attained.

righteousness of God   (Gr. *dikaiosynē theou*, Lat. *iustitia Dei*) God's doing what is right. God's acts are right by virtue of their being done by God, the source of all goodness and right. God's holy will and God's holy law thus coincide. God grants salvation through Christ's cross as an act of righteousness (Rom. 3:21–31).

rights, human   A legal or moral right that is or should be possessed by all human beings. Various theological and ethical justifications for the concept have been proposed in support of the concept. Yet numerous difficulties are encountered in trying to give it specificity.

rights of labor   In ethical theory, powers or privileges believed to be held by employees or those who are workers. Church ethical pronouncements condemn situations where the rights of laborers are violated. Labor is seen as a good gift of God to be used for the common good.

rigorism   (From Lat. *rigor*, "inflexibility") A dimension of moral theology where insistence is made that a law or rule be adhered to even if it is doubtful that it is any longer valid or in force. More generally it refers to the opposite of laxity on moral issues.

risk   A term associated with Søren Kierkegaard (1813–55), who said that genuine faith involves not intellectual certainty but risk or a leap of faith by which one commits one's whole being without certainties. Thus true faith will be a risk to the intellect.

rite   (Lat. *ritus*, "religious custom," "religious usage") An order for worship. Also, a collection of liturgical services used by an identifiable segment of the church or originating in a specific geographic area.

rites, last   *See* last rites

Ritschlianism   A type of theology, emerging from the work of Albrecht Ritschl (1822–89), that is concerned particularly with justification, ethics, and the Christian community while deemphasizing metaphysics and religious experience.

ritual   (Lat. *ritualis*) A set or form of religious observances that are enacted to represent a religious experience or set of beliefs.

ritual of purification   The Old Testament rite of cleansing after the birth of an infant (Lev. 12; Luke 2:22–39).

ritualism   The use of ritual, usually in worship, which may be construed by some to be excessive. In the 19th century, English Anglo-Catholic priests who sought to introduce new worship ceremonies into the church were accused of ritualism.

Robber Synod of Ephesus   *See* Ephesus, Robber Synod of

rogation days (From Lat. *rogare,* "to ask") Days set aside for prayer and fasting in supplication to God for fruitful fields. Earlier, they were on April 25 and the three days preceding Ascension Day. Currently, some liturgies provide liturgical texts for the stewardship of creation.

rolls Lists maintained by church bodies to indicate various kinds of status such as those who are baptized, active or inactive members, those who have died.

Roman Catholic A member of the Roman Catholic Church. Also used to indicate the teachings and practices of Roman Catholicism.

Roman Catholic Church The church body that recognizes the bishop of Rome as the vicar of Christ and supreme head of the universal church.

Roman Catholic theology The theological understandings developed by the Roman Catholic Church. Official dogmas are developed through the church's teaching office (the magisterium), by the pope, and by church councils. The teachings of church theologians may thus be given official sanction.

Roman Catholicism A term used since the time of the Protestant Reformation to describe the beliefs and practices of Christians who recognize the pope, as the bishop of Rome, to be the head of the church and Christ's representative on earth.

Roman Creed, Old A baptismal creed from the second half of the second century that was a precursor of the Apostles' Creed.

Roman Rite The liturgy of the Roman Catholic Church, the most widely-used Christian rite in the world.

romanticism A literary, artistic, philosophical, and theological movement rejecting Enlightenment rationalism in favor of an emphasis on feeling, artistic sensitivity, and community. It is a German theological movement associated with F.D.E. Schleiermacher (1768–1834).

Rome, bishop of According to Roman Catholic tradition, the apostle Peter was the first bishop of Rome. His successors are now designated to be pope, the vicar of Christ on earth and authoritative head of the Roman Catholic Church.

Rosary (Lat. *rosarium,* "rose garden," "string of beads") Roman Catholic devotional prayer. It includes multiple recitations of the Hail Mary ("Ave Maria") preceded by the Lord's Prayer ("Pater Noster") and followed by a doxology ("Gloria Patri"). The string of 55 (or 165) beads assists the memory.

Rosary, mysteries of the Elements of the Christian faith that are to be meditated upon while reciting the Rosary. The three classes of mysteries are joyful, sorrowful, and glorious—all relating to Jesus and the Virgin Mary.

Rose without Thorns, the Designation of the Virgin Mary. Roses symbolize Mary's love, compassion, and charity in Christian art.

Rosicrucians (From Lat. *rosa,* "rose," and *crux,* "cross") Members of a 17th- and 18th-century secret society that honored the rose and the cross as symbols of Christ's resurrection and redemption.

rostrum (Lat. "ship's prow") A platform in a place of worship from which speaking or preaching is done and on which usually stands a pulpit.

Roundheads A term used for 17th-century Puritans during the English Civil War, when their hair was cut short in contrast to the longer hair of the Cavaliers, who supported King Charles I.

RSV *See* Revised Standard Version

ruaḥ *See* spirit

rubricism (From Lat. *ruber,* "red") The view that worship must be carried out by strict attention to carefully defined rules or rubrics.

rubrics (From Lat. *ruber,* "red") The directions for conducting church services, liturgical actions, and gestures. They have often been printed in red to distinguish them from the texts of the service.

rule A document, often written by the founder of a monastery or order, that indicates the purposes, foundations, means, norms, and regulations that will guide the lives and experiences of those who submit themselves to the rule. Four major rules are those of Saints Basil, Augustine, Benedict, and Francis.

rule of faith (Lat. *regula fidei*) In the early church, the developing baptismal formula which defined the teachings of the apostles and which then became more formal. During the Protestant Reformation the term denoted the Scriptures as the source of authority which conveyed Christ.

rule of life A pattern of devotion for each day to assist in one's spiritual discipline. The rule may include prayer, work, recreation, and rest as means of glorifying God.

rural dean In the Church of England, a clergyperson whom a bishop appoints to be head of a group of parishes and who serves as a liaision between the bishop and the clergy.

Russian Orthodox theology The theology developed by Russian Orthodox churches and theologians with distinctively Russian emphases. It has preserved the Greek thought of patristic theologians, been influenced by Protestant scholasticism and Pietism, and claimed a special place and destiny for the Russian people.

RV *See* Revised Version

S

Sabaoth Hebew term for "of hosts," which is used in the frequent title for God as the Lord of hosts (Heb. *Yahweh seba'ot*, Ps. 46, etc.). It points to God's sovereignty over all creation and history.

Sabbatarianism (Lat. *sabbatarius,* "belonging to the Sabbath") An emphasis developed in 17th-century England and by later Puritans and others that stressed the strict observance of the Fourth Commandment to keep the Sabbath Day holy (Ex. 20:8). The Sabbath was kept on Sunday as the Christian day of worship.

Sabbath (Heb. *shabbat,* "rest") The seventh day of the week, set apart for worship and rest (Ex. 20:8; cf. 31:13–17; Deut. 5:14). It is a holy day in Judaism. Christian practice has been to observe Sunday for worship in celebration of Christ's resurrection.

sabbatical year A designated period of one year in seven years in which the Jews were to let their ground be idle, release debtors, and let the poor gather from the fields (Ex. 21:2–6; 23:10–11; Lev. 25; Deut. 15:1–3). It was to remind the nation that all it possessed belonged to God.

Sabellianism Also modalism, Modalistic Monarchianism. Teaching of Sabellius (early 3d century), who taught that God is one nature and person who has three names: Father, Son, and Holy Spirit. This view of the Trinity was considered heretical by the church, which taught that God is one and that the Godhead consists of three persons.

sacerdotalism (From Lat. *sacerdos,* "priest") The view that with ordination a person receives the ability to administer the sacraments and thus to convey God's grace in a priestly manner. Also used to indicate an excessive domination or reliance on clergy in the life of a church.

sacral (Lat. *sacrum,* "sacred") Pertaining to the sacred or that which is set apart for religious usage.

sacrament (Gr. *mystērion,* "mystery"; Lat. *sacramentum,* "oath") An outward sign instituted by God to convey an inward or spiritual grace. Sacraments are liturgical practices of churches. Roman Catholicism recognizes seven sacraments; Protestants two.

Sacrament, the Blessed A term used in the Roman Catholic tradition for the Eucharist.

sacrament of baptism The recognition that baptism has a sacramental character as a sign or means of God's grace.

sacrament of the Lord's Supper The recognition that the Lord's Supper has a sacramental character as a sign or means of God's grace.

sacramental action (Lat. *actio sacramentalis*) The full activities associated with the administration of a sacrament by all the participants. Protestant theologians have maintained that there is no continuation of the sacrament after the sacramental actions have been completed. In the Roman Catholic view of transubstantiation, in which the elements of the Lord's Supper become the body and blood of Christ, for example, the view is that the elements continue to remain thus after the sacrament is celebrated.

sacramental healing The use of outward signs or symbols in the context of prayers for healing. Historically, these have included the laying on of hands (Acts 9:17), anointing with oil (James 5:14), and Holy Communion.

sacramental sign In Roman Catholic theology, the outward or visible element in a sacrament (matter) accompanied by a proper word or declaration by the priest (form). Both elements are necessary for a valid sacrament.

sacramental systems The forms of ritual associated with sacraments through which God's grace is conveyed.

sacramental theology Theological beliefs about the sacraments of the Christian church.

sacramental union (Lat. *unio sacramentalis*) A term associated with Lutheran theology and the view that in the Lord's Supper there is a union between the body and blood of Jesus Christ and the outward elements (bread and wine) of the sacrament.

sacramentalism The theological conviction that God's grace is conveyed through religious rites designated as sacraments.

sacramentalists Those who hold to the efficacy of the sacraments and their necessity for salvation.

sacramentality, principle of A theological characteristic of Roman Catholicism which sees all reality (animate and inanimate) potentially or in actual fact as bearing God's presence and being instruments for God's saving activities on behalf of humanity.

sacramentals Religious activities similar to sacraments which are considered within Roman Catholicism and Eastern Orthodoxy to bestow benefits indirectly to those who use them. Examples include making the sign of the cross, saying the Rosary, and keeping the stations of the cross.

sacramentarians Term used by Martin Luther (1483–1546) to describe theologians, particularly Huldrych Zwingli (1484–1531), who took the view that the body and blood of Jesus Christ were only symbolically (sacramentally) present in the Lord's Supper.

sacramentary (From Lat. *sacramentum,* "oath," "sacrament") In Roman Catholicism, the liturgical book containing the texts for the Eucharist and propers, but not those parts of the Mass sung by the choir. The missal replaced this book in the 10th century.

sacraments, dominical (Lat. *dominicalis, dominicus,* "of a master or lord") Those sacraments instituted and participated in by Jesus Christ. Protestants consider these to be baptism and the Lord's Supper. In the Roman Catholic tradition, seven sacraments are recognized.

sacraments, justifying In Roman Catholic theology the sacraments of baptism and reconciliation (penance), which are considered to bring justification or salvation.

sacraments, the seven The sacraments recognized in the Roman Catholic tradition and in Eastern Orthodoxy: baptism, confirmation, Eucharist, reconciliation (penance), anointing of the sick (extreme unction), marriage (matrimony), and holy orders (ordination).

sacramentum *See* sacrament

sacred, the (From Lat. *sacer,* "holy") That which is regarded and revered as holy or able to induce an experience of the divine.

Sacred Heart of Jesus Devotion within the Roman Catholic tradition to the humanity of Jesus Christ expressed through the image of the physical heart as the center of life and symbol of love.

sacred history The history recorded in the Scriptures as God's work within the totality of world history.

sacrifice (Lat. *sacrificium,* from *sacer,* "sacred," and *facere,* "to make") Something of value offered as an act of worship or devotion to God. Sacrifices were offered throughout the Old Testament (Gen. 4:3–5; 8:20–22), accompanied covenant making (Ex. 24:3–8), and were of various types.

sacrificial offering The various things presented in worship to God as an act of devotion. The Old Testament describes different types of animal sacrifices. The New Testament sees the death of Jesus Christ on the cross as a sacrificial offering for the sin of the world (Eph. 5:2; Heb. 5:3; 10:12).

sacrificial system A form of religious practice in which something such as an animal, crops, or precious objects are offered in worship to a deity as an act of

devotion. This was characteristic of the religion of Israel in the Old Testament, where burnt, cereal, and peace offerings were made.

sacrilege (Lat. *sacrilegium,* "profanation of sacred things") The violation or desecration of a sacred place or thing.

sacristan (From Lat. *sacer,* "sacred") A term for a sexton or one who has charge of the materials in a church that are used for worship.

sacristy (From Lat. *sacristia,* "holy things") A room in a church in which vestments and other things necessary for a worship service are kept and where those participating in worship may robe.

Sadducees (Heb. *ṣadduqim,* Gr. *saddoukaioi,* Lat. *sadducaei*) A priestly party in Judaism who were priests in the Jerusalem Temple and who sought to preserve the identity, religion, and culture of the Jews. During Jesus' time they conflicted with the Pharisees and were criticized by Jesus (Matt. 22:23–33).

saga A term used by some scholars, particularly Karl Barth (1886–1968), to describe the stories in Genesis 1–11, which he considered imaginative and poetic reconstructions of primal history. They are believed not on the basis of history or science but by the faith given through the Holy Spirit.

saint (Gr. *hagios,* Lat. *sanctus,* "holy one") Popularly, one who is considered particularly holy or devoted to God. The term is used in the New Testament only in its plural form. There it refers to all members of churches who are Christians consecrated to God through Jesus Christ (2 Cor. 8:4).

sainthood The status bestowed by the Roman Catholic Church on particularly holy persons through a process of beatification and canonization.

saints, communion of *See* communion of saints

saints, devotion to the Honoring and venerating saints of special significance by various means, including prayers, offerings, pilgrimages, veneration of relics, and dedication of churches. These practices are part of the Roman Catholic tradition.

saints, invocation of The practice in Roman Catholicism of calling on departed saints for help or intercession.

saints, perseverance of the *See* perseverance of the saints

saints, veneration of *See* saints, devotion to the

saints' days Days throughout the church year on which particular Christians (saints) are recognized and remembered.

salt Used in Old Testament ceremonies and rituals (Num. 18:19; Lev. 2:13) and as a metaphor by Jesus for his disciples (Matt. 5:13). In the Roman Catholic tradition it has been used in the sacrament of baptism, when it was placed on the candidate's tongue with the words, "Receive the salt of wisdom."

salutary act In Roman Catholic theology, a human action that leads toward justification or, in the case of those who are justified, an action that contributes to attaining the beatific vision. The act comes from the grace of God.

salvation (Lat. *salvatio*, from *salvare*, "to save") God's activities in bringing humans into a right relationship with God and with one another through Jesus Christ. They are saved from the consequences of their sin and given eternal life. Biblical images for salvation vary widely.

salvation, doctrine of The theological study of how salvation is accomplished, including concepts such as regeneration, faith, justification, conversion, union with Christ, adoption, sanctification, perseverance, and glorification. Also called "soteriology."

Salvation Army A Christian organization founded by William Booth (1829–1912) in London (1865) to fight against poverty and human sin. Its worship services are informal, there are no sacraments, and its theology is Arminian in nature. Members wear military uniforms and are active in social ministries.

salvation by grace The theological view, emphasized in Protestantism, that Christian salvation comes through God's free mercy and love for sinners. It is given as God's free gift of grace—without any merit or worthiness on the part of the individual who receives it.

salvation by works The view that Christian salvation may be obtained by doing certain moral or meritorious actions that gain favor from God. It is associated with the heresy of Pelagianism from the early church period.

salvation history (Ger. *Heilsgeschichte*) Biblical events narrated from the perspective of faith and indicating God's redemptive purposes for the world.

Salve Regina (Lat. *Salve Regina, mater misericordiae*, "Hail, queen, mother of mercy") A widely used prayer to the Virgin Mary dating from the 12th century. Its invocation is: "Hail, holy queen, mother of mercy, our life, our sweetness, and our hope . . . "

salvific will of God God's will that all persons come to know and love God and thus receive salvation (1 Tim. 2:4).

Samosatenes Followers of Paul of Samosata, the 3d-century bishop of Antioch, who taught a form of Dynamic Monarchianism. The Godhead was composed of the Father, Wisdom, and Logos. Jesus was a human, specially endowed with the Spirit, who through the merit of his Passion became the Savior of the world.

sanctification (Gr. *hagiasmos*, Lat. *sanctificatio*) The process or result of God's continuing work in Christian believers through the power of the Holy Spirit. In Protestant theology this occurs after justification and is growth in grace and holiness of life marked by good works.

sanctification, entire *See* entire sanctification

sanctify (Lat. *sanctificare*, from *sanctus*, "holy," and *ficare*, from *facere*, "to make") To make holy by purifying from sin.

sanctifying grace A term used in Roman Catholic theology to describe the grace that is received through the sacraments. The term combines what Protestantism refers to as justification and sanctification.

sanctity (From Lat. *sanctus,* "holy") That which is regarded as being holy, sacred, or having divine qualities.

sanctorum communio *See* communion of saints

sanctuary (From Lat. *sanctuarium,* "holy place") The area in a church where worship takes place—immediately around an altar, Communion table, or pulpit.

sanctuary, right of The recognition by Roman law from the 4th century that criminals may claim protection in a sacred place or house of worship. The right is rooted in a regard for the sacredness of places of worship and the desire not to violate sacred space.

sanctuary movement An American movement committed to the illegal transporting of refugees from Central America into the United States and helping them to become established. Support for their actions is rooted in the biblical example of providing a place of refuge (Num. 35:6–34).

Sanctus (Lat. "holy") The angelic hymn "Holy, Holy, Holy" (or "Holy, Holy, Holy Lord"), derived from Isa. 6:3 and Matt. 21:9 and used in the eucharistic service in the Roman Catholic Church and other churches. It is sung as the hymn "Holy, Holy, Holy" in many churches.

Sandemanians An 18th-century American religious group that followed the teachings of Robert Sandeman (1718–71). He emphasized that the state has no authority over the church and revived practices of early Christianity in regard to church order, foot washing, and the holy kiss.

Sardica, Council of (343) A church council that was called by emperors Constantius II and Constans I to settle the Arian controversy but that only increased tensions between portions of the church in the East and West. It restored Athanasius to his see and formally recognized the Roman see as a court of appeal.

sarx (Gr. "flesh") A term used, particularly in Paul's writings, for sinful human nature as it exists apart from a relationship with God (Gal. 5:17, 19; Eph. 2:3).

Satan (Heb. "accuser," "adversary") The devil, who represents the most diabolical evil in opposition to God and God's purposes (Matt. 4:10; Luke 10:18; 2 Cor. 2:11). Originally an "accuser" (Job 2:1–7; Zech. 3:1–2), Satan is seen by some as personal. Cf. Rev. 12:7–12. Satan is doomed (Rev. 20:2, 7, 10).

Satan, fall of The view that Satan was originally an angel who disobeyed God and fell into sin prior to the creation of the human race. The view rests on the Latin translation of Isa. 14:12, which identifies the Day Star (NRSV; the planet Venus) as Lucifer ("light bearing"), a name for Satan (cf. Rev. 12:7–12).

satanic forces The view that forces of evil, such as demons, assist in the work of Satan to counter the will of God in the world.

Satanism The practice of worshiping Satan.

satisfaction (Lat. *satisfactio,* "making amends," "reparation") The reestablishment of one's relationship with God through some means of making amends or repayment. In Roman Catholic theology, the sacrament of reconciliation allows sinners to make satisfaction for sin through contrition, confession, and absolution.

satisfaction theory of the atonement A view of the atonement of the death of Christ that sees Christ's death as providing the means by which amends are made for human sin. Jesus Christ satisfies the requirements of God for providing forgiveness. In Protestant theology, his obedience pays for human guilt and punishment.

Savior (From Gr. *sōtēr*, Lat. *salvator*, "one who saves," "savior") A biblical term for God as deliverer and protector (2 Sam. 22:3; Isa. 49:26; 1 Tim. 1:1; Titus 1:3), as well as for Jesus Christ, emphasizing his work as the one who brings salvation (Acts 13:23; 2 Tim. 1:10).

Savoy Conference (1661) A meeting between Church of England bishops and Puritan representatives after the restoration of the monarchy under Charles II in order to review the *Book of Common Prayer* and worship practices.

Savoy Declaration (1658) A statement composed by English Congregationalists (Independents) that set forth theological beliefs and views of church government. Theologically it presented views close to the Westminster Confession (1646) and maintained that church power is vested in local congregations.

sawdust trail A term used in 19th-century American revivalism for the practice of would-be converts coming forward at the close of a service to indicate their conversion to Jesus Christ.

Saxon (Reine) Confession (1551) A Protestant confessional statement written by Philip Melanchthon (1497–1560) at the request of the emperor Charles V for the Council of Trent (1545–63).

Saybrook Platform (1708) A document of American Congregational churches that met in Saybrook, Connecticut, to draft a statement on church discipline.

sayings of Jesus Those New Testament verses which portray the utterances of Jesus. Scholars have various views of whether the verses were actually spoken by Jesus or added later by redactors.

scandal (Gr. *skandalon*, Lat. *scandalum*, "a snare," "stumbling block") That which causes one to stumble or is an offense. The apostle Paul describes the crucifixion of Jesus Christ in this way (1 Cor. 1:23).

scapegoat A goat that symbolically received the sins of the people of Israel and was then driven into the wilderness to carry the sins away on the Day of Atonement (Lev. 16:10).

schism (Gr. *schisma*, from *schizein*, "to split") A formal break or division within a religious group, often arising from long-standing disagreements.

Schism, Great (1054; also 1378–1417) The major division between Eastern (Eastern and Greek Orthodox) and Western (Roman Catholic) Christian churches over the Western use of *filioque* ("and the Son") in the Nicene Creed. The Western church's division (1378–1417) under rival claimants to be pope at Avignon and Rome is also referred to by this term.

Schleiermacherian Those who followed the theological understandings of F.D.E. Schleiermacher (1768–1834), sometimes called the father of modern theology. He claimed religion was founded on intuition and feeling and he located authority in religious experience, a sense of "absolute dependence" on God.

Schleitheim, Seven Articles of (1527) A confession of faith adopted by Anabaptist theologians at Schleitheim, near Schaffhausen, in Germany on February 24, 1527. It included a rejection of infant baptism and the use of oaths, and the religious detachment from government.

Schmalkaldic Articles (1537) A confession of faith written by Martin Luther (1483–1546) to be presented to the council summoned by the pope at Mantua (1537). The articles were later included in the Lutheran *Book of Concord* (1580).

Schmalkaldic League An alliance among Protestant groups in Germany (1531–47) that united Lutherans, Zwinglians, and German Protestant princes against Charles V.

Scholastic theology A term for the theology "of the schools" used to designate the formal theology of the medieval period marked by a heavy use of logic, reliance upon philosophical concepts, and linguistic precision. Its goal is to present a systematic ordering and investigation of Christian truths.

Scholasticism (From Lat. "place of learning") The system and method of learning for philosophy and theology during the medieval period as developed in European university contexts. It relied on philosophical methods and the use of reason to make clear divisions and distinctions within a body of knowledge.

scholasticism, Protestant The heavy use of logic, philosophical concepts, and linguistic precision characteristic of medieval theology as adapted by 17th-century Lutheran and Reformed theologians during the period of Protestant Orthodoxy. It featured detailed systems that provided intricate discussions of many theological issues.

scholia (Gr. pl. of *scholion*) Explanatory notes placed in the margins of ancient manuscripts, particularly in manuscripts of biblical materials and early Christian texts.

Schoolmen A term for the teachers of philosophy and theology in medieval universities. Prominent examples are Thomas Aquinas (1225–74) and John Duns Scotus (c. 1265–1308).

schools of theology An expression for the development of theological thought that occurs from one theologian or group of theologians and becomes an identifiable movement such as Alexandrian and Antiochene schools, Augustinianism, Thomism, Lutheranism, Calvinism, Wesleyanism, and Barthianism.

Schwabach, Articles of (1529) A Lutheran confession of faith of 17 Articles composed by Martin Luther (1483–1546) that was intended to unite Lutherans against Roman Catholics, Anabaptists, and Zwinglians.

Schwärmer (Ger. "fanatic") A term denoting the swarming of bees around a beehive. It was used by Martin Luther (1483–1546) as a term for those who spiritualized the gospel or stressed personal experience over the Word and sacraments. He applied it to Zwingli and the Anabaptists.

Schwenckfeldians Followers of Kaspar Schwenkfeld (c. 1489–1561), an early follower of Martin Luther (1483–1546) who broke with him over views of the sacraments. They later resisted German Lutheranism, particularly the union of church and state.

science of religion A field within religious studies that seeks to provide a scientific explanation of religion. Emphasis is on the description rather than the explanation of religion. The term is used interchangeably with "phenomenology of religion."

scientia media (Lat. "middle knowledge") A term coined by the Spanish Jesuit theologian Luis de Molina (1535–1600), who attempted to reconcile divine foreknowledge with human freedom. "Middle knowledge" is God's knowledge of things that are not now but will be if certain conditions are met.

scientific method The procedures used in various sciences to arrive at conclusions. Though definitions vary, it refers to the process of systematic inquiry and evidence testing. Theologians may or may not define their own theological methods as following the pattern of scientific method.

scientism A term usually used in a derogatory sense for those who consider scientific knowledge to be the only true or valid knowledge. It is often used synonymously with positivism.

Scientology A form of psychotherapy promulgated by L. Ron Hubbard (1911–76), a science fiction writer, who maintained that humans can solve all their problems by freeing their inner spiritual beings.

Scofield Reference Bible **(1909)** A highly influential study Bible produced by the American Bible conference speaker Cyrus I. Scofield (1843–1921) that conveyed in its annotations a premillennial, dispensational interpretation of Scripture.

Scopes ("Monkey") Trial   A famous trial in Dayton, Tennessee (1925), in which a high school biology teacher, John Scopes, was indicted for teaching evolution. Though Scopes was found guilty (the verdict was later overturned), the trial damaged the image of fundamentalists, who were antievolution on the basis of a literal reading of Genesis 1.

Scotism   The philosophical system expounded by John Duns Scotus (c. 1265–1308) that gave primacy to love and will in both God and humans. It contrasted with the Thomism of Thomas Aquinas (1225–74) that emphasized knowledge and reason.

Scots Confession (1560)   (Lat. *Confessio Scotica*) A confession of faith written by leading Scottish Reformers, chiefly John Knox (c. 1513–72), as the first confession of the Scottish Reformed Kirk (Church). It was the sole confessional standard until replaced by the Westminster Confession (1647).

Scottish Realism   *See* Common Sense philosophy

screen   (Middle English from Middle Dutch *scherm*, "a shield") The division between the choir and the nave, often elaborately carved wooden or stone structures in English churches.

scriptural holiness   A phrase used by John Wesley (1703–91) for sanctification. Wesley saw the spread of scriptural holiness to be a major reason for God's having raised up the Methodist Church.

scriptural proof   Citations of scriptural passages or verses used to justify or warrant a theological position.

Scripture   (Lat. *scriptura*, from *scribere*, "to write") Writings regarded as sacred. In the Christian tradition, the Old and New Testaments are considered Holy Scripture in that they are, or convey, the self-revelation of God. The term may refer to a single verse or the whole Bible.

Scripture, authority of   In the Christian view, the conviction that the writings of the Old and New Testaments have a unique status in being and/or conveying God's self-revelation. They are thus to be recognized as such and obeyed as reliable guides for Christian living.

Scripture, doctrine of   The teachings of churches about the nature of the Bible and ways in which it is to be understood. Elements of the doctrine include issues of authority, inspiration, the function and use of Scripture, and perspectives for interpretation (hermeneutics).

Scripture, phenomena of   The characteristics of Scripture as found in the biblical texts themselves.

Scripture alone   *See: sola Scriptura*

Scripture principle   *See: sola Scriptura*

scrupulosity   (Lat. *scrupulus*, "uneasiness") Technical term in moral theology in which a mental or spiritual reservation (scruple) about the rightness of an action is expressed. "Scrupulosity" may also denote the condition of a person who sees and fears sin where none exists.

seal   (Middle English *seel*, from Old French, from Lat. *sigillum*, "a little image." Related to *signum*, "mark," "sign") An identifying mark to signify authenticity, authority, or the confirmation of a relationship. John Calvin (1509–64) saw the sacraments as "signs and seals" of grace.

seal of confession   The absolute obligation of Roman Catholic priests not to reveal the contents of anything said by a penitent in the confessional during the sacrament of penance.

séance   (From Fr. *seoir*, Lat. *sedere*, "to sit") A meeting at which a medium or spiritualist attempts to communicate with the dead. This form of activity has been rejected by the Christian church (see 1 Sam. 28:7ff.).

secession   (Lat. *secessio*, "a going aside") The withdrawal of a body of people from a congregation or a group from a church denomination. A new church body is usually formed.

second Adam/last Adam An image of Jesus Christ drawn from the writings of the apostle Paul (Rom. 5:14; 1 Cor. 15:45), in which Christ as the bringer of redemption is contrasted with the "first Adam," through whom sin entered the world. The image is developed by Irenaeus (c. 130–c. 200) in his writings on salvation.

second blessing A term used in Holiness churches to denote a separate, special action of the Holy Spirit to deliver believers from the power of sin and evil habits after the work of regeneration and the new birth.

second causes/secondary causes (Lat. *causae secundae*) A philosophical distinction used in scholastic theology to designate the way God acts in the universe: not by direct interventions, but in and through the finite order of the universe. There is a concurrence of the divine (primary) and human (secondary) causality.

second chance The theological view that persons who have not previously accepted Jesus Christ as their Lord and Savior may have the opportunity to do so after their death. It is also called second or future probation.

second coming (advent) of Christ (Gr. *parousia*, "coming") The view that Jesus Christ will return again to the earth in power and glory at the end of the world (Matt. 24:29ff.; 1 Thess. 1:10; 4:16).

Second Council of Nicaea (787) The seventh ecumenical council of the Christian church, which was called by the empress Irene to deal with the iconoclastic controversy and which authorized the veneration but not the adoration of images of Christ, Mary, angels, and saints.

second death An image found in the book of Revelation that represents an eternal and spiritual death (Rev. 2:11; 20:6, 14; 21:8).

Second Great Awakening *See* Great Awakenings, the

Second Helvetic Confession *See* Helvetic Confessions

second naïveté A term associated with the interpretive theory of Paul Ricoeur (b. 1913) in which symbols must be approached at a point with a critical exposure to the symbol. One begins with the symbol in order to establish meaning. The "first naïveté" is simply immediate exposure to the symbol. It is also called "postcritical naïveté."

Second Person of the Trinity In Christian Trinitarian theology, a term for the eternal Son or Logos, Jesus Christ, as a member of the Godhead.

second probation/future probation The view that even after death persons will have an opportunity to hear the Word of God, respond to the gospel of Jesus Christ, and receive salvation (1 Peter 3:19–20; 4:6). It contends that there is a divine perseverance toward salvation. Also called "postmortem evangelism."

second resurrection A term inferred by some from Rev. 20:5 pertaining to the resurrection of those who are not raised from death until the end of a millennial period. Premillennialists consider it a resurrection of unbelievers. Amillennialists interpret it as a physical resurrection of all believers.

Second Vatican Council *See* Vatican Council II

second-Adam Christology A christological approach that emphasizes the image of Jesus Christ as the "second Adam" who through his work has reversed the curse and destruction to the human race that came through the sin of the "first Adam" (Rom. 5:12–21). It was used by Irenaeus (c. 130–c. 200).

sect (From Lat. *secta*, "party," "faction") A sociological term, often set in opposition to "church." A sect is a group with voluntary membership, exclusive in its views, and emphasizing separation from the world and prevailing institutions.

sectarianism (From Lat. *secta*, "party," "faction") An extreme form of devotion to a particular point of view, often quite narrowly defined and at variance from more widely held perspectives.

sectary (Lat. *sectarius,* from *secta,* "faction") A term, often used derogatorily, to denote those who break away or secede from an established church. Used by Anglicans to denote Nonconformity in 17th-century England.

secular (Lat. *saecularis,* from *saeculum,* "age," "generation") In common usage, that which is worldly, earthly, and temporal and thus not religious or spiritual. Also used to describe those who are not bound by monastic rules, vows, or church authority.

secular Christianity A 20th-century designation for the attempt to adapt Christianity to contemporary culture in ways consistent with the secular world.

secular clergy In the Roman Catholic tradition, those clergy who are not formally associated with a specific religious order or community. These are in contrast to "regular clergy."

secular humanism A term, often used pejoratively, to indicate the view that humans themselves determine all ultimate values and that there is no divine origin or grounding for human beliefs.

secular theology A term that emerged from the thought of Dietrich Bonhoeffer (1906–45), in which the emphasis is on a theology of Christian involvement with the world rather than a retreat from the world into a privatized faith.

secularism (Lat. *saecularis,* from *saeculum,* "age," "generation," "the world") A term that relates human viewpoints, beliefs, values, actions or institutions to the world in contrast to relating them to religious dimensions beyond the natural order.

secularity (Lat. *saecularis,* from *saeculum,* "age," "generation," "the world") A method of thought and way of perceiving reality that disregards religious claims and proceeds purely on the basis of the perceived (natural) world.

secularization (From Lat. *saecularis,* from *saeculum,* "age," "generation," "the world") The process of moving from an orientation that includes a religious dimension for thought and action to one that is focused on the world itself as the only perceived reality.

security, eternal *See* perseverance of the saints

Seder (Heb. "order") A term used for the Jewish Passover, particularly the order of service used at the table on Passover night.

see (Lat. *sedes,* "a seat") The center of authority of a bishop, archbishop, or pope, usually a geographical location. Denotes a diocese or an archdiocese.

See, the Holy Designation for the pope as well as sometimes the papal court or the immediate area over which the pope holds jurisdiction.

seed of faith (Lat. *semen fidei*) The initial beginning of faith in a person by the work of the Holy Spirit in the process of regeneration.

Seekers Those in 17th-century England who were not affiliated with any church but were searching and wandering to find a church fellowship. Many became Quakers. The term "seekers" is used today for those who may attend a church seeking something, and thus not having made a commitment to Jesus Christ.

Seelenabgrund (Ger. "the ground of the soul") Related terms are (Lat.) *scintilla animae,* "the spark of the soul," and (Gr.) *syntērēsis,* "the conscience." In mystical theology, the concept of an innate spark of the divine within each individual. It is a point of contact for union with God.

sees, the four ancient The traditional significant centers of Christianity at Constantinople, Alexandria, Antioch, and Jerusalem in the Eastern Orthodox Church.

segregation (From Lat. *segregare,* "to set apart") The social separation of groups of people, often on the basis of race or gender. The practice is sinful insofar as it negates the unity of all persons in Jesus Christ (Gal. 3:28) and when it oppresses groups through denial of their human dignity.

self One's beliefs about who one is and perceptions of this identity in relation to other members of a community.

self-actualization Autonomy or the realization of one's full potential and freedom. The term is used by some feminist theologians to indicate that for many women, "sin" is not "pride" but the failure to assume full responsibility for their lives, make free decisions, and thus not to be self-actualized.

self-consciousness The explicit perception of the self. Used by feminist writers to describe the critical method of feminism, which includes reading, speaking, and listening to oneself and other women as a means of apprehending the self politically in society.

self-deceit/self-deception The inability or failure to admit the truth about oneself, often in relation to the morality of certain actions.

self-denial Biblical requirement for those who would be followers of Jesus Christ (Matt. 16:24ff.; Mark 8:34; cf. Titus 2:12). It entails the submission of the human will to the divine. The term is also used for the disciplinary practice of giving up bodily pleasures for spiritual purposes.

self-determination The ability to make one's own choices freely without external influences. Also the ability of a nation to make its own political choices.

self-emptying *See* kenosis

self-esteem One's belief in oneself and self-respect.

self-examination Critical reflection on one's conduct and motives in relation to one's standards. The practice is enjoined by Scripture in relation to participation in the Lord's Supper (1 Cor. 11:28) and more generally as part of one's ongoing Christian experience (2 Cor. 13:5).

self-existence of God *See* God, aseity of

selfhood, social nature of The recognition that humans are social beings and that a sense of an individual self is impossible without others with whom one is in relationships.

selfishness An inordinate concern to satisfy one's own desires and fulfill one's own needs. From the Christian perspective this attitude violates the command of Christ to love others (Matt. 19:19; 22:39) and to live with the needs of others as foremost (cf. 2 Cor. 12:20; Phil. 2:3; James 3:14,16).

self-justification The attempt to gain a right standing before God on the basis of one's own actions or works (Luke 10:29).

self-love Esteem and care for oneself as commanded in Scripture (Lev. 19:18; Matt. 19:19; 22:39; Gal. 5:14). In the Christian tradition it is also recognized that excessive self-love can be sinful and that discipleship may call for a willingness not to value the self too highly (Luke 14:26).

self-revelation One's openness and willingness to be known as a human being to other people. Theologically, the term can refer to God's action in making the divine self known through specific actions, in the Scriptures, or supremely in Jesus Christ.

self-righteousness An attitude in which one justifies one's own actions as being virtuous. This attitude may take on the characteristic of feeling oneself to be morally superior to others.

self-understanding A term, found in some 20th-century theologians influenced by existentialism, for the perceptions humans have of themselves and their relationships with others. In theology, these writers have said that theology's task is to articulate and understand these human perceptions.

semantics (From Fr. *sémantique*) The branch of linguistics that deals with the nature, structure, and changes of meaning in speech forms. This discipline may be applied to the study of biblical texts.

Semi-Arianism   A view from the Arian controversy in the early church in which those who did not fully support Arius or the view of the Council of Nicaea (325) proposed that Jesus Christ is *homoiousios* ("of like essence") to God the Father. Thus he is similar, but not identical in being with God the Father.

Semi-Augustinianism   A term used in connection with the Council of Orange (529), in which the views of Augustine (354–430) on the nature of grace were upheld against Pelagianism, yet without endorsement of the Augustinian views of election and predestination.

seminary   (Lat. *seminarium,* "seedbed," "nursery") A school which educates and prepares persons for the Christian ministry through instruction in theological disciplines. Also, the building housing the school.

semiology/semiotics   (From Gr. *sēmeion,* "a sign") Study of how all sign systems (literature, the media, social codes and ideologies) function like languages to establish meanings for their recipients.

Semi-Pelagianism   A mediating view of human nature between that of Augustine (354–430) and that of Pelagius (d. c. 420). John Cassian (c. 360–435) taught that the initial step of faith was taken by a person's own will and that divine grace came later. This view was condemned by the Council of Orange (529).

Semites   Ancient people who spoke languages such as Akkadian, Hebrew, Phoenician, Aramaic, and Arabic and lived in Assyria, Babylonia, Aramaea, Canaan, or Phoenicia. Jews and Arabs are the contemporary representatives.

Sens, Council of (1140)   A church council in which Bernard of Clairvaux (1090–1153) prosecuted the case of heresy against Peter Abelard (1079–1142), who was found guilty of deficient views of the Trinity and the grace of God in the process of salvation.

sense, allegorical   *See* allegorical sense of Scripture

sense, anagogical   *See* anagogical sense of Scripture

sense, literal   *See* literal sense of Scripture

sense, mystical   *See* mystical sense of Scripture

sense, tropological   *See* tropological sense of Scripture

sense of divinity   (Lat. *sensus divinitatis*) An innate, intuitive perception in all people of the existence of the divine, which forms a basis for all religion and a natural theology. John Calvin (1509–64) recognized that sin distorted this knowledge and thus it cannot bring salvation. It leaves humans inexcusable before God. Also called "sense of deity" (Lat. *sensus deitatis*).

senses of Scripture   The various ways in which Scripture passages and verses may be understood. Traditionally these have been the literal or plain, allegorical or typological, tropological or moral, and anagogical or eschatological. The literal or plain sense has been recognized as primary.

sensuality   (Lat. *sensualitas,* "capacity for sensation") The dimension of human consciousness relating to the body. Also, indulgence in bodily pleasures. Some elements in the Christian tradition have diminished the importance of the body, leading some to call for a new appreciation of the positive nature of sensuality.

sensus deitatis   *See* sense of divinity

sensus divinitatis   *See* sense of divinity

sensus plenior   (Lat. "fuller sense") A term used in biblical interpretation for the view that there is meaning to Scripture passages beyond what was originally intended by the biblical writers and that this meaning emerges through the life and experience of readers.

sentences   A form of theological writing prominent in the Middle Ages. It provided a systematic presentation of

Christian doctrine through the method of question; scriptural, credal, and patristic citations; and arguments in favor of the orthodox view. This form was replaced by the summa.

separation of church and state   The view that there should be distinct and separate spheres of activities for ecclesiastical bodies (church) and political entities (state), each maintaining a legal independence from the other. The question of the relation between the two has been perennial in Christian ethics.

separatism   The view of some feminist writers that the only way for women to develop their own strengths is to be separated from male-dominated institutions. The term also refers to the "Separatists," those 16th- and 17th-century English church bodies that withdrew from the Church of England.

separatism, ecclesiastical   A withdrawal or advocacy of withdrawal from a church body by a person or groups of persons. The reasons given may vary widely.

Separatists   (From Lat. *separatio*, "a severing") A term for the English Puritan Robert Browne (c. 1550–1633) and his followers, who separated from the Church of England. It was later applied to English Congregationalists and others who formed their own churches. Also called Separatism.

Septuagesima   (Lat. "seventieth") The third Sunday before Lent (ninth Sunday before Easter), which is approximately seventy days before Easter.

Septuagint (LXX)   (Lat. *septuaginta*, "seventy") The translation of the Hebrew Scriptures into Greek completed approximately a century before Christ. Its name derives from the tradition that it was the work of seventy (or seventy-two) men. It was the Bible of the early church and included the Apocrypha.

sepulchre   (Lat. *sepulcrum*, "a burying place") A term used in the KJV for graves or tombs. Most prominently it denotes that of Joseph of Arimathea

(Matt. 27:57–60), in which the body of Jesus was placed after the crucifixion and which was empty on Easter morning (Matt. 28:1; Mark 16:2).

seraphim   Six-winged creatures portrayed in Isaiah's Temple vision as glorifying and praising God, perhaps as a high class of angels (Isa. 6:2, 6, 7). The term "seraphim" may mean "burning ones."

sermon   (Lat. *sermo*, "conversation," "discourse") A proclamation, based on Scripture, in public worship for the purpose of conveying God's Word in a specific congregational context.

Sermon on the Mount   The teachings of Jesus recorded in Matt. 5–7 (parallel in Luke 6:20–49), including the Beatitudes, the Lord's Prayer, and ethical injunctions. They indicate attitudes and actions of Christian discipleship.

Sermon on the Plain   A shorter version of the Sermon on the Mount, recorded in Luke's Gospel (6:20–49). It contains the Beatitudes, the Lord's Prayer, and ethical injunctions.

servant   (Heb. *'ebed*, Gr. *doulos*) One who serves another. In the biblical context, the term often means a slave, one without rights. Jesus used it to express a relationship between humans and God (Matt. 6:24; 10:24; 24:45). Christians are servants of Christ (1 Cor. 4:1; Phil. 1:1).

servant of the Lord   One who is fully devoted to God (Deut. 34:5; Luke 1:38). The term also emerges from the picture in Isaiah of one who is completely dedicated to the Lord and suffers on behalf of the people (Isa. 42:1–4; 49:1–6; 50:4–9; 52:13–53:12). These passages have been variously interpreted.

Servant Songs   Four biblical passages (Isa. 42:1–4; 49:1–6; 50:4–9; 52:13–53:12) describing the "servant of the Lord," whom some have identified with historical individuals or the nation of Israel itself. From the Christian perspective, the servant has been identified as prophesying Jesus Christ.

service (From Lat. *servire*, "to serve") Biblically, service is the work usually done by slaves. In the Christian context, the work of slaves for masters is now offered on behalf of Christ to others (Gal. 5:13; 1 Cor. 9:19; 2 Cor. 4:5).

servus servorum Dei (Lat. "servant of the servants of God") Image used by Pope Gregory the Great (c. 590–604) for the Christian's role, and since the time of Pope Gregory VII (1073–85) as a title for the pope.

session, church In churches with presbyterian forms of church government, the governing body of a local congregation, composed of elders. Its moderator is usually the pastor. Its size varies and it is charged with maintaining spiritual oversight of the congregation.

session of Christ (From Lat. *sessio,* "a sitting") The ongoing work of Christ, who is seated at the right hand of God (Mark 16:19; Acts 2:33; Rom. 8:34; Col. 3:1; Eph.1:20–23).

seven churches of Asia, the The churches to which the writer of the book of Revelation addresses comments: Ephesus, Smyrna, Pergamum, Thyatira, Sardis, Philadelphia, and Laodicea (Rev. 1:11).

Seven Councils, the The seven ecumenical councils of the early church from 325 to 787 A.D., in which theological forms of major elements of Christian doctrine were established.

seven deadly sins *See* sins, seven deadly

seven gifts of the Holy Spirit From the Latin text of Isa. 11:2, these have been said to be: wisdom, understanding, counsel, fortitude, knowledge, piety, and the fear of the Lord.

seven last words of Jesus A compilation of phrases recorded in the Gospels as uttered by Jesus during his last hours on the cross before his death (Matt. 27:46; Luke 23:34, 43, 46; John 19:26–27, 28, 30).

seven sacraments *See* sacraments, the seven

seven virtues Traditionally these consist of faith, hope, and charity ("theological virtues"); prudence, justice, temperance, and fortitude ("natural virtues").

seven words from the cross *See* seven last words of Jesus

Seventh-day Adventism A Protestant group originating in the United States (1863) with a focus on keeping the Jewish Sabbath (Saturday) as the day of worship, believers' baptism, the imminence of the second coming of Christ and the millennium, soul sleep, and abstinence from alcohol, tobacco, and certain foods.

seventy weeks A term in the book of Daniel (9:20–27) in which an "anointed one" ("Messiah") is portrayed as arising and then being cut off for a period of "seventy weeks," after which Jerusalem and the Temple will be destroyed. It is taken as a prophetic reinterpretation of Jer. 25:11f.

sex The biology of a person in terms of anatomy as male or female. Gender may then refer to culturally conditioned sex roles. Issues regarding sexuality are ethical in nature.

sex difference The differences between the sexes on a wide variety of attitudes and abilities.

sex roles A societal role associated with men or women based on their biological sex.

Sexagesima (Lat. "sixtieth") The second Sunday before Lent, which is approximately sixty days before Easter.

sexism A social relationship in which one sex is denigrated by the other or denied rights or privileges on the basis of their sex. Feminist theologians have pointed to its pervasiveness in church and culture, urging its recognition as sinful and its opposition as a matter of justice.

sext (Lat. "sixth") The office celebrated at noon in the liturgy of the hours, or "the hours." It was prayed at the sixth hour of the Roman day (12 noon).

sexton (From Lat. *sacristanus,* "one in charge of sacred vessels") One who is given charge over the physical maintenance of a church.

sexual ethics/morality Standards of behavior and the assessment of moral rights and wrongs in relation to sexual matters and relationships.

sexual harassment Unwanted sexual advances by one person toward another. Feminist writers have indicated its cultural prevalence and unjustness.

sexual identity A sense of one's own human sexuality as a dimension of constituting a sense of self.

sexuality Sexual character. Recognition of expressions of and influences on the relationships of embodied persons. Sexuality issues are ethical issues and relate to a range of attitudes and activities.

Shakers The United Society of Believers in Christ's Second Appearing, founded by Jane and James Wardley in England (1747). A millennialist offshoot of the Quakers, initially called "shaking Quakers," the group migrated to the United States and established socialist communities. They were pacifists who shouted and danced at worship and believed in Christ's second coming in female form.

shalom *See* peace

shame The feeling arising from a sense that one has failed to live up to ideals or expectations or has done something disgraceful or dishonorable. Biblically, it is related to the failure to obey God's law or do God's truth and may be a step toward forgiveness and repentance (Ps. 44:15).

sharing A term used particularly in American evangelicalism for the verbal expression of experiences and ideas related to a dimension of the Christian life. It often centers on what God has done and is doing, or what the believer hopes God will do in the future.

Shekinah (Heb. "dwelling") A term that in the writings of the rabbis came to mean the presence of God. It occurs as a manifestation (revelation) of God.

Though not found in the Old Testament, the term may be used in reference to God's glory filling the Temple (1 Kings 8:11; 2 Chron. 7:1) or God's presence in the cloud (Ex. 14:19), etc.

Shema, the (Heb. "hear") The central theological and liturgical affirmation of Judaism. It is recited in home and synagogue worship and affirms a monotheistic faith in God as the sovereign Lord (Deut. 6:4–9; 11:13–21; Num. 15:37–41). The term is the Hebrew word that begins Deut. 6:4.

Sheol Biblical term for the underworld destination of the souls of those who die (1 Kings 2:6; Prov. 9:18). It is often translated "grave," "pit," or "hell" (Job 17:13–16; Lat. *infernus*). It became associated with the Greek "Hades" and the notion of judgment.

shepherd (Gr. *poimēn*) One who tends sheep. Sheepherding was a common, humble vocation, and the image is used figuratively to describe God's activities (Ps. 23; Isa. 40:11; Ezek. 34), and for Jesus (John 10:11, 14). It is also used equivalently with "pastor" (Eph. 4:11; cf. 1 Peter 5:1–4).

Shepherd, the Good A title of Jesus based on the images of Luke 15:3–7 and John 10:1–18.

shepherding movement A movement associated with various charismatic and house church groups and seeking to stimulate a greater degree of Christian discipleship. Each church member is responsible for "shepherding," or encouraging others' spiritual growth. Group leaders are responsible to church elders.

shibboleth (Heb. "a stream") A code word used as a test by Jephthah to distinguish Gileadites from Ephraimites, who were unable to pronounce it correctly (Judg. 12:4ff.). Used to indicate a practice or custom distinctive to a certain religious faction. Also, any password.

ship An emblem used by early Christians to represent the church of Christ sailing in life's troubled seas and carrying the faithful to salvation. In Roman Catholicism, Peter is often portrayed at the helm. The main area of a Christian church is called the "nave," Latin (*navis*) for "ship."

showbread (shewbread) (Heb. *leḥem panim,* "bread of the Presence") The 12 loaves of unleavened bread placed on a special table in the holy place of the Tabernacle and Temple in Old Testament times (Ex. 25:30; 1 Kings 7:48). They represented the twelve tribes of Israel (Ex. 28:10) and God's presence.

shrine (From Lat. *scrinium* "a chest") A holy place to which Christians may make a pilgrimage. Originally a box-shaped receptacle that held the relics of a saint.

Shroud, Holy (Shroud of Turin) A linen cloth found in the Turin Cathedral in Italy that has been traditionally said to be Jesus' burial grave cloth. It bears a stained image that in a photographic negative shows the outlines of a man. The Shroud has been scientifically tested and determined to be no older than the medieval period. But it continues to be a source of fascination.

Shrove Tuesday (From Old English *scrifan,* "to write," "prescribe" [penance]) The day prior to Ash Wednesday, also known as Mardi Gras (Fr. "fat Tuesday"). Its name derives from "shrive," meaning to hear or make confession. It is a day on which confession and feasting are done.

sign (Lat. *signum*) A thing, such as an object or a word, that points beyond itself toward another thing. Since everything in the universe may be considered a "sign," the human mind must judge or interpret each time a thing is encountered. Augustine (354–430) considered sacraments "visible signs of divine things."

sign, visible *See* visible sign

sign gifts A term used by some who view certain extraordinary gifts of God's Spirit, such as the gift of tongues or healing, as special evidence of the Spirit's work.

sign of peace A liturgical greeting used in worship services among Christians as a reminder of unity in Christ's love. Practices vary from greetings, to embraces, to handshakes.

sign of the cross A sign of devotion prominent within the Roman Catholic and Episcopal traditions. The movement of the right hand from head to breast to left shoulder to right shoulder to outline the shape of a cross. In the Eastern church the last movement is from right to left across the shoulders.

significance Term used by Julia Kristeva in *Desire in Language* (1980) to describe the work of language, which enables a text to signify what communicative speech does not say, and which represents a disruption of patriarchal order.

signs Biblically, important events or actions that point to God's intentions or presence. They may appear miraculous (Ex. 4:1–9; 7—11) or as natural phenomena (Gen. 9:13). They may be identifiable marks (Gen. 17:11) or eschatological ones (Mark 13:4). Jesus performed signs (John 2:11).

silence (Lat. *silens,* "silent") The time of stillness used for private and corporate meditation in worship and devotion. It is part of some monastic codes and has as its purpose a deeper perception of God.

silence, argument from (Lat. *argumentum e silentio*) A deduction made from the lack of reference to a subject in any known sources, often considered weak in its effect.

silent prayer The practice of praying inaudibly. In addition to praying this way for private devotion, churches often include such a period in their worship services.

simul iustus et peccator (Lat. "both righteous and a sinner") A phrase used by Martin Luther (1483–1546) to describe the condition of the Christian who is justified by faith alone and declared righteous in God's sight, yet who still experiences sin and unrighteousness in the Christian life.

similitudo Dei   (Lat. "likeness of God") A parallel to the "image of God" (*imago Dei*) found in Gen. 1:26, where humans are said to be made in the "image and likeness of God," denoting a fundamental, basic relationship between humans and their Creator. Some have sought to distinguish "image" from "likeness" of God in this verse.

simony   (Lat. *simonia*) Term derived from the story of Simon Magus (Acts 8:18–24) and denoting the attempt to make a profit through buying or selling spiritual things. Historically it has been associated with the buying or selling of church offices.

simplicity   *See* God, simplicity of

simultaneity with Christ   A concept in the thought of Søren Kierkegaard (1813–55), who described the sense in which the Christian is with Jesus Christ when the believer is present to Christ, and Christ to the believer, in the fullness of salvation. Christ is thus an eternal contemporary with the believer.

sin   Various Hebrew and Greek words are translated "sin" with many shades of meaning. Theologically, sin is the human condition of separation from God that arises from opposition to God's purposes. It may be breaking God's law, failing to do what God wills, or rebellion. It needs forgiveness by God.

sin, actual   Thoughts, words, or deeds that constitute a deliberate violation of God's will and law and are thus sinful.

sin, Adam's   The sin portrayed in the story of the Garden of Eden (Gen. 3) as attributed to Adam's disobedience to God's will (cf. Rom. 5:12–21).

sin, bondage to   The theological view that the power of sin is such as to enslave a person. One's whole orientation, outlook, and actions express a sinful nature (John 8:34; Rom. 7:25).

sin, consequences of   The theological as well as practical results of sinfulness,

both temporally and eternally (Rom. 6:23).

sin, conviction of   *See* conviction of sin

sin, corporate effects of   The results of sin in groups beyond an individual's life. In the Old Testament, the whole community could experience the consequences of one person's sin (Josh. 7:1). The apostle Paul indicated these consequences in relation to the sin of Adam (Rom. 5:12–21).

sin, deliberate   Actions done willingly that are against God's will and thus sinful.

sin, deliverance from   The theological view that salvation in Jesus Christ frees or liberates one from the binding power of sin in one's life. Christ thus delivers one from the consequences of sin's power of death and frees one for new life (Rom. 5–8).

sin, imputation of   (Lat. *imputatio peccati*) The ascribing of the sin of Adam and Eve (Gen. 3) to their posterity because of their representation of the whole human race. All humans are thus sinners (Ps. 51:1–5; Rom. 5:12; Eph. 2:1–3).

sin, individual   The sin of a particular person in contrast to the corporate sin of a group of persons.

sin, mortal   In Roman Catholic theology, sin that can cause eternal, spiritual death, in contrast to venial (slight) sin. Mortal sin causes a complete rupture of one's relationship with God.

sin, nature of   That which is common to all sin in representing what sin is. Sin may be described theologically as being that which is "against" (*contra*) God and God's will (Ps. 51:4).

sin, original   *See* original sin

sin, power of   The ongoing ways in which sin exercises a controlling force in the lives of sinners (Rom. 3:9; Gal. 3:22).

sin, privatization of   The view of sin that limits its power and effects, recognizing only what it does within an individual and that person's relationship with God. There is no sense of the corporateness of sin or its social effects.

sin, propagation of   (Lat. *propagatio peccati*) The continuing effects of sin as spread throughout the human race as a result of the fall of Adam into sin (Gen. 3; Rom. 5:12–21).

sin, remission of   *See* remission of sins

sin, slavery to   *See* sin, bondage to

sin, social   The recognition that the power and effects of sin extend throughout the social fabric of a culture and have far-reaching consequences.

sin, structural   The recognition that the power of human sin affects institutions and structures of a society in pervasive ways so that the processes and actions of these entities will be influenced.

sin, unforgivable (unpardonable)   *See* sin against the Holy Spirit

sin, universality of   The view that sin affects all human beings (Pss. 14:3; 53:3; Rom. 3:9, 23; 5:12).

sin, venial   In Roman Catholic theology, a slight sin in the sense of being sin that does not rupture one's relationship with God. It is in contrast to "mortal sin." Venial sin is evil and inclines one away from God but is less severe in its effects than a mortal sin would be.

sin, wages of   *See* sin, consequences of

sin against the Holy Spirit   (Lat. *peccatum in Spiritum Sanctum*) The blasphemy against the Holy Spirit about which Jesus spoke (Matt. 12:31–32; Mark 3:28–29; Luke 12:10) is also called the "unforgivable sin" and has been understood as an ultimate rejection of the truth of salvation which the Spirit conveys.

sin bearing   The concept that Jesus Christ has carried the sin of the world (Heb. 9:28), in a way similar to that of the scapegoat which carried away Israel's sin into the wilderness (Lev. 16: 8–22).

sin offering   A ritual offering made in ancient Israel as a means of expiation and forgiveness of sins. Bulls, goats, lambs, doves, and pigeons were used (Lev. 4:4, 23, 28, 32; 5:7). Sin offerings served for ritual cleansing and for forgiveness for unintentional sins, and were made at each of the Hebrew festivals.

single procession of the Holy Spirit The view of Eastern Orthodoxy that in the Godhead the Holy Spirit proceeds only from the Father and not from the Father and the Son (Lat. *filioque,* "and the Son"), as taught by Western churches. This was a main point that caused the Eastern and Western churches to split in 1054 after the *filioque* was added by the Western church to the Niceno-Constantinopolitan Creed (381).

sinlessness   The state or condition of being without sin.

sinlessness of Christ   (Gr. *anamartēsia,* Lat. *impeccabilitas*) The view that Jesus Christ was sinless and without sin (Gr. *anamartētos*) in his unfallen human nature. He thus maintained perfect communion with God (2 Cor. 5:21; Heb. 4:15; 1 John 3:5). It was affirmed by the Council of Chalcedon (451).

sins, seven deadly   In Roman Catholic theology, seven sins or faults of particular seriousness in regard to their moral tendencies: pride, covetousness, lust, envy, gluttony (greed), anger, and sloth.

sins of commission   Those sins which are carried out by actions, as opposed to sins of omission.

sins of ignorance   Sins committed out of unawareness of a law or condition. In the Old Testament, cities of refuge were established for those who committed such sins (Num. 35:9–34; Josh. 20).

sins of omission   Sins that result from a failure to act, as opposed to sins of commission (Matt. 25:41–46).

sister, religious   A woman who takes vows (poverty, chastity, and obedience) and becomes part of a religious community of women. The term is used as a synonym for "nun."

sisterhood   In feminist experience, the female bonding and self-affirmation and identity found in a woman-centered vision and definition of womanhood.

situation ethics The view that the rightness or wrongness of an action must be judged in relation to the particular situation or context in which it occurs. The stress is on relationships and character rather than universal rules. Love is primary. Also called contextual ethics or the new morality.

situational theology *See* contextual theology

Sitz im Leben (Ger. "setting in life") A term used in biblical interpretation that seeks to ascertain the particular context or circumstances in which a certain passage originated.

Six Articles, the (1539) Regulations promulgated in the Church of England under King Henry VIII to maintain the church's unity after the time when the church broke from Roman Catholicism and prior to its becoming an officially Protestant body. They were more oriented to Catholicism than the Ten Articles (1536).

skepticism (From Gr. *skeptikos,* Lat. *scepticus,* "thoughtful," "inquiring") A term used in philosophy for the view that true and reliable knowledge cannot be attained in some areas of investigation, such as morality, metaphysics, or theology.

slander (From Lat. *scandalum,* "cause of offense") The defamation of another's reputation by false accusation (Ps. 15:3; Matt. 15:19). Ethically it involves the sin of lying and injustice caused in seeking to do harm. Restitution and forgiveness are necessary. Also called "calumny."

slavery A condition of involuntary servitude. While slavery was practiced during biblical times, the emergence of biblical principles and eventually Christian ethical views that recognized the evils of slavery as a social phenomenon have led to its condemnation in many countries.

Small Catechism, Luther's (1529) A simple textbook of Christian doctrine written by Martin Luther (1483–1546) to provide adults and children with an introduction to the Christian faith. Together with the Large Catechism (also 1529), it became part of the Lutheran *Book of Concord* (1580).

small group movement A transdenominational movement of groups of persons who meet together for specific purposes, often for prayer, Bible study, or faith sharing as a means of renewal and strengthening for their Christian lives.

sobornost An untranslatable term used in the Russian Orthodox Church, approximately meaning "fellowship" or "group consciousness." It refers to the worshiping community's feeling of oneness and the communion of one with another in the liturgy. It embodies a conciliar and collegial ideal.

social action Corporate activity that seeks to effect social change. Individuals and churches often engage in social action in attempts to secure justice, peace, or what are considered to be other implications of the Christian gospel.

social conditioning The recognition of the role and impact that social environments and contexts play in shaping significant aspects of behavior, including religious beliefs and practices.

social consciousness The perceptions of reality shared by a group. Feminist writers argue that there are differences between the social consciousness of men and that of women, as, for example, in differing perceptions of the world.

social ethics Ethical reflection that focuses on social structures, processes, or communities of persons. The term also describes the patterns of moral judgments and behavior engaged in by groups of persons. The church's concerns for the ethical life as they take shape in society are also social-ethical.

Social Gospel A 19th- and early 20th-century American movement, primarily in Protestantism. It applied the Christian faith to contemporary social conditions in an industrialized society and focused on impoverished urban workers. It stressed justice and the establishment of the kingdom (reign) of God.

social ministry Service offered in ministry by churches and individuals to relieve human suffering and provide for the needs of the community. It often focuses on issues of justice in society as well as being concerned with the basic necessities of life for those without resources.

social principles The designation for official statements of the United Methodist Church on social issues. It derives from the Methodist "Social Creed" (1908) and may be revised only by the General Conference.

Socialism, Christian A mid-19th-century English movement led by F. D. Maurice (1805–72) and others that opposed capitalism. European Christian Socialism has united principles of socialism with emphases of Christian faith to effect political and social reforms. The kingdom (reign) of God is a key visionary symbol.

society (Lat. *societas*, "community") A group of people who form a distinct community. In the Christian context, the issue of society focuses on how human communities and institutions relate to God and to the Christian faith.

Society of Friends *See* Quakers/Quakerism

Society of Jesus *See* Jesuits

Socinianism/Socinians The views and followers of the thought of Faustus Socinus (1539–1604). It was a rationalistic theology that denied the orthodox views of the person and work of Jesus Christ and other Christian doctrines. In America the movement was absorbed in Unitarianism.

sociological determinism The view that certain behavior patterns and outcomes are conditioned and determined by sociological factors.

sociology of knowledge A concept that originated with Karl Marx (1818–83) and was developed through the Frank-

furt school by Karl Mannheim and Louis Althusser. It contends that all thinking, consciousness, or knowledge is socially constructed. It can either legitimate or subvert the prevailing material relations, depending on whose social construction it is.

sociology of religion The study of religion from the perspectives of sociological theory and in its sociocultural context.

Socratic Pertaining to the thought or philosophical method of the Greek philosopher Socrates (c. 470–399 B.C.), who is considered in many ways to be the founder of philosophy. The question-answer method employed in philosophy and theology is often called the "Socratic method."

Soissons, Councils of (1092, 1121) Two church councils that dealt with a charge of tritheism against Roscellinus (1092) and the censuring of a work by Peter Abelard (1079–1142) on the Trinity (1121). Abelard's work was condemned for Sabellianism and burned.

sola fide (Lat. "by faith alone") A slogan of the Protestant Reformation used by Martin Luther (1483–1546) on the basis of Rom. 3:28 to indicate that justification of the sinner (salvation) comes only to those who have faith and is not achieved through any "good works."

sola gratia (Lat. "by grace alone") A slogan of the Protestant Reformation indicating that the basis for Christian salvation is solely the grace of God and not any human achievement. It is God's initiative and action which is the agent of salvation.

sola Scriptura (Lat. "Scripture alone") A slogan of the Protestant Reformation indicating that the church's authority is only the Holy Scriptures and not ecclesiastical traditions or human opinions. This was called the "formal principle" of the Reformation, or the "Scripture principle."

Solemn League and Covenant (1643) The pact which pledged Scotland to support the parliamentary forces in the English Civil War and in which England promised to reform church worship, doctrine, discipline, and government according to "the Word of God and the example of the best Reformed churches."

solidarity of the human race   The view that the actions of the biblical Adam in regard to sin (Gen. 3) have continuing effects for the entire human race (Rom. 5:12).

solifidianism (solafidianism)   A term used at points to caricature the doctrine of justification by faith alone (*sola fide*) as taught by the Protestant Reformers, particularly Martin Luther (1483–1546). He translated the term *pistei* ("by faith") in Rom. 3:28 as (Ger.) *allein durch den Glauben* ("only by faith").

solipsism   (Lat. *solus,* "alone," and *ipse,* "self") The philosophical view that the self with its perceptions is the only reality that exists and that all else depends on the self and has no independent existence.

solitary Christianity   The view that the Christian life can be lived apart from the lives of other persons because what is primary is one's own personal relationship with God and not a communal experience of faith.

solo Christo (solus Christus)   (Lat. "by Christ alone"; "Christ alone") A slogan of the Protestant Reformation which emphasized that it is only Jesus Christ who brings salvation and that there is no other way to come to salvation except through him.

sōma   *See* body

Son of David   A term Christians see fulfilled in Jesus of Nazareth as part of the Davidic dynasty, which, as promised, would rule Israel (2 Sam. 7:14–17) as God's "anointed" (Gr. *Christos*). Jesus' Davidic lineage is mentioned at points (Matt. 1:2–17; Mark 10:47; Luke 1:32; Acts 2:29–30; Rev. 5:5; 22:16).

son of God   An individual who stands in a special relationship with God is a son or child of God (Gal. 4:6–7). The concept is used in the Old Testament for Israel as a nation (Ex. 4:22–23), David (2 Sam.

7:14), and kings (Ps. 2:7). In the New Testament, Jesus Christ is God's unique Son (Mark 1:11; John 11:27; 2 Cor. 1:19).

Son of Man   A Hebrew or Aramaic expression that may be a synonym for humankind (Ezek. 2:1; "mortal" in NRSV) or refer to an apocalyptic figure who will judge the righteous and unrighteous at the end time (Dan. 7:13–14, KJV). It is also used as a title for Jesus (Mark 2:10; 8:38) in each sense.

song leader   One who leads congregational singing in a church service or special service such as a revival service.

soothsaying   The practice of making predictions about the future, associated in ancient Israel with sorcery and condemned (Deut. 18:10, 14; 2 Kings 21:6; Jer. 27:9).

sophia   (Gr.; Heb. *ḥokmah,* "wisdom") In the Old Testament, a (grammatically feminine) personification of God who is an agent of creation and a guide for the world (Job 28:20–28; Prov. 8:22–32). Jesus Christ is referred to as the "*sophia* of God" (1 Cor. 1:24; cf. Col. 1:15–20).

sophiology   Study of wisdom (Gr. *sophia*). A philosophy or theology centered on the concept of wisdom.

sophism   (Gr. *sophisma,* Lat. *sophisma,* "fallacy") A term for the use of arguments that appear to be correct but that are actually fallacious.

sorcery   (Old Fr. *sorcerie,* "casting of lots") The use of magical or supernatural powers to produce an effect on objects or people. The practice is condemned in the Scriptures (2 Chron. 33:6; Gal. 5:20).

sorrowful mysteries, the five   In Roman Catholic theology, the second part of the Rosary recalling Jesus' agony in the Garden, scourging at the pillar, crowning with thorns, carrying of the cross, and crucifixion.

sorrows of Mary, the seven   In the Roman Catholic tradition, seven sorrows experienced by the Virgin Mary for her suffering Son during his life. Also used to describe the sorrows Mary endured at the stations of the cross during Jesus' passion and crucifixion.

soteriological (From Gr. *sōtēria,* "salvation") Pertaining to the doctrine of salvation.

soteriology (From Gr. *sōtēria,* "salvation") The doctrine of salvation.

soul (Heb. *nephesh,* Gr. *psychē,* Lat. *anima*) Primarily, "soul" is the life principle (Gen. 2:7). For Hebrews it indicated the unity of the persons who were living bodies. The New Testament term also refers to one's life (Matt. 2:20) or existence after death (Luke 21:19).

soul, creationist view of the The view that God directly creates a new "soul" at the instant of one's conception. This would mean that the soul is not transmitted naturally by parents.

soul, origin of the The issue of when the soul begins in or as a human body.

soul, traducianist view of the *See* traducianism

soul, transmigration of the The belief in some religions that a soul may be reincarnated a number of times in different beings. This view is common in Eastern religions but is rejected by Christianity. Also "metempsychosis."

soul friend In spirituality, a special friend who knows another in very personal ways and may serve as a spiritual director or mentor.

soul sleep (Gr. *psychopannychia*) The view that there is a period between one's death and the final resurrection in which one's self ("soul") is in an unconscious state.

soul winning A term from American revivalism and evangelicalism referring to the process of gaining converts to Christianity.

soul-body dualism A way of describing a person that distinguishes between the physical body and the immaterial soul. This leads to the view that the body is mortal and the soul immortal, a prominent view in Greek philosophy

and in the Western intellectual tradition.

soul-extinction The view that no soul exists without a body, so that after death a person becomes nonexistent.

source criticism *See* criticism, source

sovereign will A term for the will of God, which is not conditioned or bound by any other power and thus exists as the supreme and sovereign reality over all else.

sovereignty of God *See* God, sovereignty of

sparking A term used by Mary Daly in *Gyn/Ecology* (1978) for women's language to describe women's experience and realities.

speaking in tongues *See* glossolalia

special calling *See* calling, special

special revelation *See* revelation, special

species (Lat. "a seeing") A group of individual entities that are considered as a group because of a certain element they have in common. Also, the empirical ("accidental") reality of a being that can be directly perceived by sensory experience (in distinction from the "substantial" reality, or "substance").

spectator (Lat. "a looker-on") A term used by theologians such as Søren Kierkegaard (1813–55), Karl Barth (1886–1968), and others to indicate that the reality of Christianity is only known by those who participate in it by faith and not by those who are merely "onlookers" without obedience to God.

speculative (Lat. *speculativus*) Projecting an overall understanding of a truth through rational thought.

Speyer (Spires), Diets of (1526, 1529, 1542, 1544) Sixteenth-century legislative gatherings at the port of Speyer (Germany). The emperor Charles V granted princes the right to determine the religion of their areas (1526). In 1529, Roman Catholics voted to end toleration for Lutherans. The minority who made a protest" (Lat. *protestatio*) were called Protestants.

spinning   Metaphor used by Mary Daly in *Gyn/Ecology* (1978) for the destructive/constructive creation of women's knowledge, which is always changing and forming new threads between unlinked sections of reality.

spiration   (Lat. *spiratio,* "a breathing") A term emphasized by some in relation to 2 Tim. 3:16, which speaks of the Scriptures as "God-breathed." It emphasizes the divine origination of the Scriptures.

spirit   (Heb. *ruah,* Gr. *pneuma,* Lat. *spiritus,* "breath," "spirit") A being that does not have a material substance. This includes God (John 4:24), the Holy Spirit as the third Person of the Trinity, and the dimension of human life that enables a relationship with God.

Spirit, fruit of the   The listing of the results of the Holy Spirit's activities in Christian lives according to the apostle Paul: love, joy, peace, patience, kindness, generosity, faithfulness, gentleness, and self-control (Gal. 5:22–23). These contrast with the "works of the flesh" (Gal. 5:19–21).

Spirit, Holy   *See* Holy Spirit

Spirit, outpouring of the   A term for the special manifestation of the Spirit of God or Holy Spirit, particularly on the Day of Pentecost (Acts 2; cf. Joel 2:28).

Spirit, personality of the   The Holy Spirit of the Godhead as a person who is fully and wholly God and not an impersonal force or power or a lesser being. The Niceno-Constantinopolitan Creed (381) affirmed that the Holy Spirit shared the same divine status (coeternal) with God the Father and God the Son.

Spirit, procession of the   *See* procession of the Spirit, Trinitarian

Spirit, sealed with the   God's gift of the Holy Spirit to those who believe in Jesus Christ as a means of the continuing divine presence in their lives and to mark them as belonging to the family of God (2 Cor. 1:22; Eph. 1:13; 4:30).

Spirit, witness of the   *See* internal testimony (witness) of the Spirit

Spirit, work of the   The many actions of God's Holy Spirit in creation and the world, in the church, and in the lives of Christian believers. The Spirit inspires Scripture, illumines believers, guides biblical interpretation, and works to incorporate the creation into the life of God (Rom. 8:9–30).

spirit of adoption   The work of the Holy Spirit in adopting believers into the family of God through faith in Jesus Christ, thereby giving them an intimate relationship with God (Rom. 8:15, 23; cf. Gal. 4:6; Eph. 1:5).

Spirit of God   God's mysterious power and presence within the created order, in communities, and within individuals. The divine Spirit was active in creation, in inspiring persons, and as present in the covenantal community. Called the Holy Spirit in the New Testament, the Spirit dwells with the church and with Christians, and is active in the world (Rom. 8:1–25; 1 Cor. 12:4–13).

spirit of the world   Earthly wisdom and concerns that stand in contrast to the wisdom and gifts given by God through the Holy Spirit (1 Cor. 2:12).

Spirit of truth   A designation for the Holy Spirit, who comes to lead the disciples of Jesus into all truth (John 14:17; 15:26; 16:13; cf. 1 John 4:6).

spirit of wisdom   A gift of God given to assist God's people in knowing and doing God's will (Deut. 34:9; Isa. 11:2; Eph. 1:17).

Spirit-filled   Groups that emphasize the indwelling of the Holy Spirit in believers use this term to describe that experience (Eph. 5:18).

spiritism   The belief in spirits that affect the present world and humanity, as well as the belief that humans can come in contact with these spirits and receive their powers. Also spiritualism.

spirits, discernment of   A gift of the Holy Spirit to believers that enables them to know and identify which spirits are from God (1 Cor. 12:10).

spirits in prison, proclamation to the A phrase found in 1 Peter 3:19 that has been variously interpreted. Some contend it refers to preaching during the time of Noah; others believe that Jesus preached to those in Sheol between his death and resurrection. Another view is that it refers to Jesus' earthly preaching ministry.

spiritual (Lat. *spiritualis*) Pertaining to the spirit or nonmaterial.

spiritual blindness A term for the condition of those who do not and will not recognize the work of God (Rom. 1:21; 2 Cor. 4:4).

spiritual body The imperishable body possessed by believers at the resurrection (1 Cor. 15:42–49).

spiritual combat *See* spiritual warfare

spiritual coming The view that the second coming of Jesus Christ (Gr. *parousia*, "coming") is not a visible or bodily return to earth, so that it may have already occurred, for example, at Pentecost.

spiritual condition A term used to describe the status of one's relationship with God. Typically it is used by those who draw a sharp distinction between the "saved" and "unsaved."

spiritual death A theological term for ultimate separation from God.

spiritual development The sense of the growth and maturing of one's Christian life and experience.

spiritual direction The conscious orientation of one's Christian life toward a deeper communion with God and toward ways of living that God desires. These are discerned through the help of others or another, often called a "spiritual director" or "spiritual mentor."

spiritual director One who acts as a guide, confidant, and often confessor for another in order to enhance the experience of Christian faith. Classically, a spiritual director is one who has attained a firm knowledge of Christian belief and can deal with persons in sensitive and helpful ways.

spiritual fellowship An association or group that maintains a relationship without an outward or visible expression. The Christian church is sometimes considered in this way, in that there is a spiritual unity of believers in Christ that does not depend on an outward manifestation.

spiritual feminism The construction of cultural archetypes of power used by women to articulate desire through symbols and rituals.

spiritual formation The evolving growth of one's Christian spiritual life in conformity with Jesus Christ. It is marked in various ways, including the sense of one's obedience to Christ and union with him (Gal. 2:20).

spiritual friend One who establishes a special relationship of love and care for another, often becoming one who helps another discern the will of God for life or who assists another in attaining a deeper spiritual communion with God. Also called "soul friend."

spiritual gifts *See* gifts, spiritual

spiritual growth *See* spiritual development

spiritual healing The curing of diseases or physical illnesses by nonphysical means, as with the miracles of Jesus. Also called "faith healing," the term refers to this same type of healing in the present time through the power of faith or prayer. It may also refer to the healing of one's inner self.

spiritual kingdom A term to indicate the rule of Jesus Christ in the lives of those who believe. This is thus not an outward, political, or social expression.

spiritual life One's openness and sensitivity to the nonphysical and thus the transcendent dimensions of human existence.

spiritual poverty A term defined by some liberation theologians as a total availability to the Lord and the recognition that one has no other sustenance than the will of God. This rejects the interpretation of Matt. 5:3 that defines it only as detachment from material goods.

spiritual presence (Lat. *praesentia spiritualis*) The means by which a spiritual or immaterial being is present—as opposed to a physical presence. Reformed theology uses the term for the mode of Christ's presence in the Lord's Supper. Faith, by the work of the Spirit, perceives Christ's presence.

spiritual qualities Those aspects of the work of God's Holy Spirit that become apparent in persons' lives.

spiritual realm The place where spiritual beings such as God, angels, or demons dwell (Eph. 6:12). The term may also be used by those who divide reality into an outward or physical realm and an inward or spiritual realm.

spiritual resurrection A term that may designate one's coming to new life in Jesus Christ by the work of the Holy Spirit.

spiritual sins Attitudes or motivations that are not in accord with the will of God and thus are sinful (Jer. 17:9; Matt. 15:19; Mark 7:21). These contrast with physical actions that are sinful.

spiritual strength The power and endurance given by God's Holy Spirit to withstand temptations, sufferings, and evil and to live the Christian life.

spiritual theology A way of viewing theology from the perspectives of spiritual formation or living the Christian life through personal devotion and with discipleship in the community of faith. In the Roman Catholic tradition it has included foundational, mystical, moral, and ascetical theology.

spiritual truths Knowledge that may be attained only through God's direct revelation or illumination by the Holy Spirit and that is not accessible by human rationality alone.

spiritual union The relationship and fellowship that Christian believers have with Jesus Christ and with one another in the universal church.

spiritual unity The sense of the common union of Christian believers with each other in the church universal that exists despite the differences of church bodies or denominations.

spiritual warfare A New Testament theme expressed in images of combat and athletics to indicate the cosmic struggles of those in the Christian life against the powers of evil, and specifically the struggles between the "flesh" and the "spirit" (Rom. 8:38–39; Gal. 5:13–26; Eph. 6:10–17; Heb. 12:1).

spiritualism The belief that the only realities are spirit. Term for a variety of religious movements that seek communication with the spirits of those who are dead. Also spiritism.

spirituality The quality of being spiritual. Historically, varieties of spiritualities have emerged relating to different religious traditions. They take shape through rituals and practices.

spirituality, Christian Most generally, the living of the Christian life. The term indicates the work of the Holy Spirit in Christian experience. Christian spirituality has many dimensions that are expressed through rituals and practices to enhance the sense of God's presence and reality.

spirituality of God God as immaterial and nonphysical.

spiritually dead A term for those who do not have a relationship of faith with God through Jesus Christ and are living in the power of sin (Eph. 2:5).

spirituals Religious songs developed among African-American slaves in the United States. Spirituals testified to authentic Christian experience as well as, by the use of coded lyrics, signifying escape times and routes, etc.

sponsor (Lat. "answerable person") One who stands with a child during infant baptism and often pledges to be concerned with the child's nurture and growth in the Christian faith. In some traditions called a "godparent." In other traditions, the church congregation fulfills this role.

spooking   A term used by Mary Daly in *Gyn/Ecology* (1978) to describe the recalling and remembering of witches' power that casts spells on those who terrorize women.

spoon, liturgical   A special utensil for removing foreign particles that might fall into the wine during Holy Communion or for administering the wine to those unable to drink from a cup. In Eastern churches it is the means of administering the mixture of wine and bread to the laity.

sprinkling   A method of administering baptism in which a small amount of water is sprinkled on the person's head. The action may be seen as representing the cleansing action of God's grace. It is also a mode for infant baptism.

Spy Wednesday   The Wednesday of Holy Week so named from its being the day on which Judas Iscariot betrayed Jesus (Matt. 26:14–16).

stain of sin   (Lat. *macula,* "stain") The spiritual results of sin as it affects human nature and renders one impure in God's sight.

standards, confessional   Those documents or elements of belief which are officially adopted by a denomination or church body.

standing   One's ecclesiastical status. A minister, for example, may be in "good standing," indicating that all requirements and responsibilities are met.

staretz   (Russian, "an elder, spiritual father") In the Russian Orthodox Church, a person (usually a monk) who gives spiritual instruction and guidance to individual Christians.

state   The source of a nation's government and the institution in which is lodged social authority and power. It functions to maintain order and to provide services. Christian views of the state have recognized its institution by God (Rom. 13), but also its potential to be demonic (Rev. 13).

state church   A church established by law as the official church of a nation.

state of exaltation   *See* exaltation of Jesus Christ

state of humiliation   *See* humiliation of Jesus Christ

stated clerk   In presbyterian forms of church polity, the person who is elected to maintain official records of a church session, presbytery, synod, general assembly or classis.

stated meeting   A gathering of an official ecclesiastical group at a set time for the purposes of conducting church business.

states of Jesus Christ   A theological description of Jesus Christ in his humiliation, or earthly life and sufferings, and his exaltation, his ascension to heaven and reign at the right hand of God.

Stations of the Cross   A form of devotion (pictures, points, images) in fourteen parts that represent the way of Jesus Christ to Calvary and his crucifixion. This devotional exercise is usually performed during Holy Week and has been associated primarily with the Roman Catholic tradition.

statue   (Lat. from *stare,* "to stand") A three-dimensional representation of Christ, the Virgin Mary, or a saint that is used for veneration in the Roman Catholic tradition. The veneration is directed toward the person represented and not the statue itself.

stealing   The procurement of something that is not rightfully one's own. It is an action forbidden in God's law expressed in the Ten Commandments (Ex. 20:15).

stereotypes   Preconceived ideas of individuals, groups, or objects which may cause them not to be treated with understanding or justice. They thus pose ethical issues.

steward   (Gr. *oikonomos*) In biblical times, the overseer responsible for planning and administering the household

(Gr. *oikos*). Theologically, a designation for those who manage the resources God has given, in the world and in the church (1 Cor. 4:1–2; Titus 1:7; 1 Peter 4:10).

stewardship (Gr. *oikonomia*) The responsibility given to humans in creation for managing the resources of the earth (Gen. 1:26). In the church, Christian stewardship involves the whole of life since all life comes from God and is to be lived for God's glory (1 Cor. 4:1–2; 9:17; 1 Peter 4:10).

stigmata (Gr. "pricks of a pointed instrument," Lat. "marks") In Christian history, the phenomenon of marks appearing on the body in the places corresponding to Christ's Passion wounds—hands, feet, side. A prominent stigmatic was Francis of Assisi (1181/82–1226). Cf. Gal. 6:17.

Stoicism A school of Greek philosophy emerging from the "porch" (Gr. *stoa*) where philosophers taught. It was popular in the Roman Empire (Acts 17:18) and emphasized ethics, harmony with nature, the suppression of emotions, and divine law. Its vocabulary influenced some New Testament writings of Paul.

stole (From Gr. *stolē*, Lat. *stola*, "robe") A vestment in a liturgical color worn over the shoulders of ordained ministers.

stoup (Middle English *stowp*, "a vessel") A container for holy water found at the entrance of churches. Those who enter may dip their fingers of their right hand into the vessel and bless themselves by making the sign of the cross.

structural violence *See* institutionalized violence

structuralism A method of analyzing that seeks to identify and describe the deep structures or systems in all people that underlie phenomena such as language, texts, societies, or the human mind. The hidden structures give rise to the text as it is encountered and help in the interpretation of its meaning.

structuralist exegesis A form of biblical analysis or interpretation that seeks to go beyond the outward plot sequences of a narrative to ascertain the deep structures that underlie it. These deep structures are recurring patterns expressed in sign-codes that must be deciphered.

stylites (Gr. *stylitēs*, "dwelling on a pillar") Solitary ascetic monks ("pillar saints") who lived on top of a pillar. The practice was begun by Simeon Stylites (c. 390–459) on a 12-foot-square platform on top of a 55-foot pillar in Syria. Stylites flourished in Egypt during the 5th to 10th centuries.

sub specie aeternitatis (Lat. "under the form of eternity") A phrase that captures the perspective of viewing an event or idea from the perspective of God and God's will for the world.

subdeacon (Lat. *subdiaconus*) An assistant to a deacon from the 3d century. The highest of the minor orders in the medieval church, abolished as an order by the Roman Catholic Church in 1972.

subjective experience An experience that happens only to a particular person and is not verifiable by others.

subjective knowledge A way of describing a knowledge that is not detached ("objective") but that involves the knower fully in it.

subjective truth The determining of truth in terms of its effect on the person or knower rather than by whether or not it corresponds to an external standard.

subjectivism An approach to knowledge emphasizing the knowing subject rather than the object to be known. The effect is to make knowledge relative. Ethically this leads to the view that one's personal attitudes or actions determine what is morally right or wrong.

subjectivity Personal involvement by which one's perceptions and understandings are derived from one's own characteristics or experiences.

sublapsarianism *See* infralapsarianism

submersion *See* immersion

subordination (From Lat. *subordinare*, "to order") The subjugation of one group or person to another. Feminist writers have traced the subordination of women to men through various phases to the present day.

subordinationism   A theological term for the view that the nature and status of Jesus Christ is less than that of God the Father, or that the Holy Spirit is inferior to the Father and the Son. These positions were rejected by the Council of Constantinople (381). Subordinationist views appeared in Arianism and in writers such as Origen (c. 185–c. 254).

subsidiary, principle of the   (From Lat. *subsidium*, "support") A principle expressed by Pope Pius XI (1931), namely, that the best institution to respond to a social task is the one closest or most proximate to it. Thus a state should not try to do for a community or family what those groups can do for themselves.

subsistence   (Lat. *subsistentia*, "self-contained existence") The term that came to be used to describe the existence of the one God as a Godhead of Father, Son, and Holy Spirit.

subsistence theory   A theological explanation for the hypostatic union in Jesus Christ. According to this theory, Jesus' human nature, which was substantially complete in itself, did not have an independent existence. It existed ("subsisted") from its union with the divine Logos. This preserves the unity of the two natures.

subsistent relations   In Trinitarian theology, the view that the divine Persons of the Godhead are identical to the divine substance. This means that since to be a divine Person is to be in relation to the other Persons, all that is in God is identical for each of the Persons.

substance   (Lat. *substantia*, "that which stands under") Translation of the Greek terms *hypostasis* and *ousios*. It was used in the Nicene Creed and early Christian writings to refer to God in God's eternal being as Father, Son, and Holy Spirit.

substance criticism   (Ger. *Sachkritik*) A practice of biblical criticism in which a

critic after determining the meaning or "substance" of a passage through scholarship may go on to criticize and affirm or reject this meaning.

substitutionary death of Christ   The view that Jesus Christ in his death was the substitute for sinners who, because of their sin, rightly deserve to die and to face God's judgment. Also called the "vicarious atonement" (Mark 10:45; 2 Cor. 5:21; 1 Peter 2:24). The benefits of Christ's death are received by faith.

succentor   (Lat. "accompanier") Assistant to the precentor of a cathedral. The function of the succentor is to lead the choir in singing.

suffering   (From Lat. *sufferre*, "to undergo") To bear pain, distress, or injury. Theologically, suffering is seen in the context of God's redemptive and sustaining love and in the overall framework of God's will. Some suffering is attributable to evil; undeserved suffering is endured by faith.

Suffering Servant   An image from the Servant Songs of Isaiah (particularly Isa. 52:13–53:12) indicating that the servant of the Lord is one who suffers on behalf of the people. Judaism sees this as prophetic of Israel, Christians as a prophecy of the sufferings of Jesus Christ for the sin of the world (Mark 10:45).

suffering with Christ   A term used in the writings of Paul to indicate the believer's union with Jesus Christ to the degree that one enters into Christ's sufferings or undergoes affliction and suffering because of love for him (Rom. 8:17; Phil. 3:10; cf. Phil. 1:29).

sufficient grace   God's gracious help to endure a situation or perform an action (2 Cor. 12:9). In Roman Catholic controversies, sufficient grace was one kind of "actual grace" (the other was "efficacious grace"). God's grace was seen as "sufficient" for salvation. It became efficacious when accepted by a person.

suffragan bishop   (Lat. *suffragium*, "a ballot," from *suffragari*, "to vote for," "to support") The term in the Church of

England for an assistant bishop who helps the bishop of a diocese.

suffrages (Lat. *suffragia,* "prayers seeking favor") A part of liturgies in the Western church in which petitionary and intercessory prayers are offered.

sui generis (Lat. "alone of its kind") Philosophical description of God as unique and the only living and true God.

suicide (Lat. *suicidium,* "killing of oneself") The direct and deliberate taking of one's own life. It has traditionally been regarded by the church as a sinful act.

summa (Lat. "the main point") A comprehensive system of theology. Particular examples of summas are those written by medieval Christian theologians such as Peter Abelard (1079–1142), Peter Lombard (1100–1160), and Thomas Aquinas (1225–74). The summa functioned to synthesize the main issues of theology.

summum bonum (Lat. "supreme good," "highest good") Designation for God as the one who is intrinsically good in the divine self, and as the ultimate end toward whom all human endeavor is directed.

Sunday (From Gr. *hēmera hēliou,* "day of the sun"; Ger. *Sonntag*) The first day of the week, marked by worship among Christians in celebration of the resurrection of Jesus Christ (Mark 16:9; Luke 24:1). It was called the "Lord's Day" by the early church (Rev. 1:10).

Sunday observance The recognition of Sunday as a day of worship. Churches and cultures have varied in the ways by which Sunday is observed in terms of activities, commerce, and religious life.

Sunday school movement The movement that initially established schools on Sundays for instructing children, which have evolved into the Sunday school as a period for religious instruction, usually held in relation to times of Sunday worship. It was begun by Robert Raikes (1735–1811) in Gloucester, England (1780).

super oblata The "prayer over the offering," found in the liturgy of the Roman Catholic Church, in which prayer is made for the acceptance of that which has been offered within the context of the Eucharist that is to be celebrated.

supererogation, works of (Lat. *supererogare,* "to pay out over and above") In the Roman Catholic tradition, the view that good works may be freely done that exceed the basic commands of God or morality. These acquire "merit" for the common benefit of the church.

superintendent (From Lat. *superintendere,* "to have oversight of") A church office that evolved after the Protestant Reformation but now has been abolished in most churches, except for Methodism. There it is an officer with limited powers for oversight of a district. Also "district superintendent."

superior (Lat. "upper," "greater") In the Roman Catholic tradition, the head of a religious order, house, or congregation who exercises authority.

supernatural, the (Lat. *supernaturalis*) That which is beyond the natural order. A realm of being or name for "God" that is beyond and superior to the universe.

supernatural endowment *See: donum superadditum*

supernatural existential A term in the theology of Karl Rahner (1904–84) to indicate the view that the potential for knowing God is in every human being and that this potential functions throughout life. Thus there is always an operative grace at work and no one is totally apart from grace.

supernatural illumination A term for the work of the Holy Spirit in giving knowledge and perception beyond what could be attained by human reason or rationality, particularly in regard to recognizing Jesus Christ as Lord and Savior and the Scriptures as the Word of God.

supernatural qualities   Those attributes or qualities that are associated with a supernatural being, or God. They are thus not possessed in the same way by humans.

supernatural realm   A description for that which is beyond the universe or outside the natural forces in the world.

supernatural religion   A term contrasted to "natural religion" and conveying the conviction that a religion is based on a divine revelation as an expression of a supernatural force or being.

supernatural work   Action that comes from God and is beyond all human capacities to perform.

supernaturalism   The philosophical belief that there is reality to a supernatural dimension to existence and that this must be taken into account for issues of metaphysics, epistemology, ethics, etc.

supersensual sphere   A term denoting whatever lies beyond the capacities of the human senses to perceive.

supersessionism   The belief that on the basis of the coming of Jesus as the Messiah (Christ), the Christian church has superseded Israel as the chosen, covenant people of God.

superstition   (Lat. *superstitio*, "excessive fear of the gods") A term often used pejoratively to describe a belief or practice that the speaker believes is irrational or false.

Supper, Last   *See* Lord's Supper

Supper, Lord's   *See* Lord's Supper

supplication   (From *supplicare*, "to kneel down," "to pray") The act of praying for someone or something (Pss. 6:9; 30:8; Eph. 6:18; Phil. 4:6).

supralapsarianism   (From Lat. *supra lapsum*, "above the fall," "prior to the fall") A technical term used in Calvinist theology for the view that the election and reprobation of individual persons occurs in the decrees of God as logically prior to the decrees for creation and the fall. It differs from infralapsarianism.

Supremacy, Acts of (1534, 1559)   Acts of the English Parliament (1534) designating King Henry VIII and his successors as head of the Church of England, removing the power of the pope. It was repealed under Mary Tudor but subsequently Queen Elizabeth I was declared "supreme governor" of the realm and all spiritual things (1559).

surd evil   In the philosophical thought of Edgar Sheffield Brightman (1884–1953), a term for the kind of evil that has no possibility of being used for a good purpose, no matter what occurs around it.

surety, Christ as   Jesus Christ as taking upon himself the means of securing salvation for humankind by offering himself as the pledge, guaranty, and assurance by which salvation is accomplished. Understandings of how this was accomplished vary with differing views of his atoning death on the cross.

surplice   (From Lat. *super*, "over," and *pellicum*, "fur coat") A white liturgical garment of knee or ankle length worn over a cassock by ministers during a worship service.

Sursum Corda   (Lat. "Lift up your hearts") Ancient liturgical response that precedes the preface in a celebration of the Eucharist or in the Mass. Later the salutation "The Lord be with you" and the congregational response "And also with you" were added.

swearing   *See* oath

Swedenborgianism   The views emerging from the thought of Emanuel Swedenborg (1688–1772), a Swedish scientist and religious thinker. His spiritual visions led to allegorical interpretations of Scripture and to a pantheistic religious system. His followers founded the Church of the New Jerusalem.

Syllabus of Errors (1864)   The 80 propositions Pope Pius IX issued against theological liberalism. Their major themes were against pantheism and naturalism, rationalism, and political liberalism as it affected church prerogatives.

syllogism (Gr. *syllogismos*, "a reckoning together") A form used in logical discourse by which if the first two of a set of three propositions are true, then logically, so is the third. The conclusion is drawn from the major and minor premises. It has been used in theological reasoning as well.

symbol (Gr. *symbolon*, "token," "pledge") That which represents or stands for something else. It is considered to express the reality it symbolizes but is not literally equivalent to it. The term is also used for creeds, as representations of Christian faith.

symbol, theological A representation that stands for a theological reality, as, for example, the cross stands for the death of Jesus Christ or more generally, for the Christian faith itself.

symbolics (From Gr. *symbolon*, "token," "pledge") The theological study of Christian creeds or confessions of faith.

synagogue (Gr. *synagōgē*, "assembly") The assembly for worship (congregation) or the place of worship or worship center in Judaism. Both Jesus and Paul taught and preached in Jewish synagogues (Matt. 4:23; Mark 1:21; Acts 13:5; 17:1).

synapheia (Gr. *synapheia*, "union," "conjunction") A term for the combination of the two natures (divine and human) in Jesus Christ. Contrasted with Greek *henōsis*, the "union" of the two natures.

synaxis (Gr. "assembly," "congregation") Any assembly that gathers for worship. The term was used in the early church. In the Western church it became the term for a noneucharistic service of readings and prayers.

syncretism (Gr. *synkrētismos*, Lat. *syncretismus*, "union of two parties against a third") In ancient philosophy, a blending together of views from different philosophical or religious perspectives. It is now often used pejoratively for a collection of views without coherence or unity.

syncretistic controversy A 17th-century debate over the proposal by the Lutheran theologian George Calixtus (1586–1656) that Roman Catholics, Lutherans, and Reformed groups unite on the basis of commonly held beliefs, as for example in the Apostles' Creed. All groups rejected his efforts.

syncretistic theology A theology that incorporates elements from a variety of major religious faiths.

synderesis A term used technically by Thomas Aquinas (1225–74) to indicate the moral and religious condition that is basic to all persons and through which they appropriate fundamental principles of moral responsibility. May be distinguished from (Gr.) *syneidēsis* ("consciousness," "conscience") or Lat. *conscientia*, the conscience acting as a guide to conduct.

synergism (Gr. *synergos*, Lat. *synergismus*, "a working together") Working together in the gospel (Rom. 16:3, 9, 21). Theologically the term is used for views of salvation, particularly Semi-Pelagianism and Arminianism where the human will cooperates with the divine will in achieving salvation.

synod (Gr. *synodos*, "a meeting") A formal meeting of church leaders to deal with ecclesiastical matters. In presbyterian forms of church polity, a governing body for a geographical region between the session of the local church and a general assembly.

Synoptic Gospels (Gr. *synoptikos*, "a seeing together") A term for the first three Gospels of the New Testament: Matthew, Mark, and Luke, because they present the life of Jesus in a similar fashion, drawing from some common sources, in contrast to the presentation in the Gospel of John.

Synoptic problem A question in New Testament studies about the literary similarities and differences among the Synoptic Gospels (Matthew, Mark, and Luke). The issues relate to what sources they had in common and what is unique to the particular writings.

syntactics The particular branch of semiotics (the theory of signs) that deals with the formal relationships between signs and symbols in a system.

synthetic statement   In logic, a statement in which the predicate adds to the information given in the subject. In contrast, an analytic statement is one in which the predicate is self-contained within the subject.

system   (Gr. *systēma,* from *synistanai,* "to place together"; Lat. *systema*) An attempt to arrange elements in an order or relationship to form a whole or a unity, as in various philosophical or theological "systems" of thought.

systematic theology   The branch of Christian theology that attempts to present theological thinking and practice in an orderly and coherent way. It may be based on Scripture and expressed through doctrines. It implies an underlying philosophical frame of reference and a method to be followed.

syzygy   (Gr. *syzygia,* "pair") A term used by early Gnostics to indicate a pair of cosmological opposites, such as female and male. It was believed that the interaction of "pairs" brought the universe into being.

Tabernacle   (Heb. *'ohel mo'ed,* "tent of meeting"; Lat. *tabernaculum*) The portable tent in which the Hebrews worshiped during the wilderness period of wandering (Ex. 25—27; 36—38). The Jerusalem Temple replaced it. In the Roman Catholic tradition, the "tabernacle" is the boxlike receptacle for the eucharistic elements.

Tabernacles, Feast of   (Heb. *Sukkot*) Also called the Festival of Booths and Festival of Ingathering. Along with Passover and the Festival of Weeks, one of the three major Jewish feasts. It was Israel's autumn harvest festival, when worshipers lived in "booths" remembering God's protection (Lev. 23:39–43).

taboo   (Polynesian *tapu,* "forbidden") Persons, objects, or acts of behavior that are forbidden by religious teachings or practices.

Taborites   A 15th-century movement within the Hussites in Bohemia that took an extreme and revolutionary view of church and state. It resisted established powers and demanded the abolition of law courts. Its name came from Tabor, a

city in which John Huss (c. 1372–1415) once preached.

Taizé Community   An ecumenical and monastic community in Taizé, France, founded by Roger Schutz (b. 1915) in 1940 to revive monasticism within Protestantism. It has become famous for its efforts in strengthening Christian unity.

Talmud   (Heb. "study," "teaching") Fifth-century A.D. comprehensive commentary on Mishnah (teachings of earlier rabbis) that is rabbinic Judaism's principal text. Of the two Talmuds, the Palestinian and the Babylonian, the latter is normative for Judaism.

Tanakh   The traditional Jewish name for the Hebrew Bible. It is formed from the initial letters of the Bible's three main divisions: *Torah* (Pentateuch), *Nebi'im* (Prophets), and *Ketubim* (Writings).

targum   (Heb. "translation," "interpretation") An Aramaic translation or paraphrase of the Hebrew Scriptures, with interpretive additions, used in public readings in synagogues for the benefit of Jews who could not understand Hebrew after it was no longer used as their colloquial language.

tautological statement   A term in logic for a statement that is "analytical," meaning that subject and predicate are logically identical.

Taverner's Bible (1539)   An English translation of the Bible edited by Richard Taverner, a Greek scholar. The text was of Matthew's Bible with some changes in the Old Testament based on the Vulgate. The Bible follows Tyndale's New Testament with changes from the Greek. It introduced "parable" (for "similitude") and "passover."

Taylorism   The thought emerging from Nathaniel W. Taylor (1786–1858), an American Congregational minister and theologian. Also called the "New Haven" or "New England" theology. Taylor taught at Yale College and sought to synthesize traditional Calvinism with revivalism.

Te Deum Laudamus   (Lat. "We praise you, O God") The opening words of a 5th-century hymn of praise to the Father and the Son, often set to music.

teaching   Biblically, that which the Lord teaches is to be remembered (Ex. 13:9) and obeyed (Deut. 4:1; Ps. 78:1), as are the teachings of parents and the wise (Prov. 1:8; 13:14). Jesus taught (Matt. 4:23; John 6:59), and so did the apostles (Acts 2:42; 2 Tim. 1:13).

teaching office   Biblically, a designated "spiritual gift" (Rom. 12:7; 1 Cor. 12:28–29). The recognition of this ability to guide learning is recognized in some churches with an office of teacher. In the Reformed tradition from the time of John Calvin (1509–64), teachers have been seen as a permanent office in the church (*Institutes* 4.3.4) and pastors have been designated as teaching elders.

technology   (Gr. *technologia*, "systematic treatment") Invention of techniques and processes, methods and procedures to transform the natural world into a human world to provide for human needs and desires. The moral and ethical implications of highly technological societies are far-reaching.

teleological argument   (From Gr. *telos*, "end," "purpose") One of the five arguments for the existence of God formulated by Thomas Aquinas (1225–74). The order of the universe is said to imply a designer who has shaped the universe to fulfill divine purposes as a final goal.

teleology   (From Gr. *telos*, "end," "purpose") Study of the end or final purposes of the universe. It can refer to a philosophical or theological system which holds that the universe has purpose or design. Ethically, it is assessing right or wrong in relation to the ends to which actions lead.

televangelism   In 20th-century America, the televised evangelistic and religious services of independent evangelists and preachers. These often also include a solicitation for funds to sustain the ministries.

temperance   (Lat. *temperantia*, "self-control") One of the traditional cardinal virtues, considered the foundation of them all. It refers to the practice of moderation in all things and the control of mind and body by the reason. It has also become associated with alcohol consumption, as moderation or abstinence.

temperance movement   Organized efforts in 19th- and 20th-century America to encourage abstinence, as well as moderation, in the consumption of alcoholic beverages.

Temple   The structure in Jerusalem that was the center of worship and the national life of Israel from the 10th century B.C. when it was built by Solomon until its destruction by Rome in A.D. 70. It was rebuilt twice and had three periods, during which the temples of Solomon, Zerubbabel, and Herod stood.

temptation   (From Heb. *nasah*, Gr. *peirazein*, Lat. *temptare*, "to test") Enticement to evil and sin. Biblically it is "proving by testing" to show someone's commitment to God (Job 1—2), as well as the inducement to sin. God does not tempt (James 1:12–15). Jesus was tempted but did not sin (Heb. 4:15).

temptations of Jesus   The experience of Jesus in the wilderness after his baptism. He was tempted to turn away from the will of God through his encounter with Satan, who tempted him to turn stones into bread, throw himself down from the pinnacle of the Temple, and worship the devil (Matt. 4:1–11).

tempter   One who tries to lead another into sinfulness. The term is particularly associated with Satan (Mark 1:13; 1 Cor. 7:5).

Ten Articles (1536), the   A confessional statement ordered by King Henry VIII for the Church of England after his break from Roman Catholicism. It was a compromise document with mixtures of Roman Catholic and Protestant theology and was replaced the following year.

Ten Commandments   God's law, given to the people of Israel through Moses, representing the enduring will of God for the lives of those who would live in relationship with God. Also called the Decalogue (Gr. "ten words"), they are found twice in the Old Testament (Ex. 20:1–17; Deut. 5:6–21).

Ten Tribes of Israel   The ten northern tribes of Israel: Asher, Dan, Ephraim, Gad, Issachar, Manasseh, Naphtali, Reuben, Zebulun, and part of the tribe of Benjamin. They separated from the two southern tribes, i.e., Judah and part of Benjamin, after Solomon's reign.

Tenebrae   (Lat. "darkness") A service held during Holy Week during which lights are gradually extinguished and the service ends with worshipers departing in darkness.

tenets, theological   Theological beliefs held as being true.

tent meetings   A term for the religious camp meetings of 19th-century America where participants would live in tents, eat, and worship together for several days.

terce   (From Lat. *tertia,* "third") The daily prayer service held about 9 A.M., the third hour (Lat. *hora tertia*) of the Ro-

man day. It has traditionally been associated with the crucifixion (Mark 15:25).

terminism   (From Lat. *terminus,* "boundary," "end") The view that God has imposed a time limit for each person's opportunity to receive salvation.

territorialism   A 16th- and 17th-century European view that in a territory where a state church exists, the civil authority has the right to specify what doctrine is to be adopted.

tertium quid   A term found in medieval logic for the search for a "third something" when two opposites had been explored and neither was found to provide a satisfactory answer. More generally, it refers to a middle course as an alternative to extremes in an ethical dilemma.

testament   (Gr. *diathēkē,* Lat. *testamentum*) A person's last will to dispose of property. Also, a covenant—as at Sinai (Ex. 31:18; 34:29; cf. Heb. 9:1, 4). Both senses are found in Gal. 3:15–18. The term is also used for the division of the Bible into Old and New Testaments (covenants).

testes veritatis   (Lat. "witnesses to the truth") Term used by the 16th-century Protestant Reformers to refer to the early church fathers.

testimonium internum Spiritus Sancti *See* internal testimony (witness) of the Holy Spirit

testimony   An account of one's personal religious experience often shared either one to one with another person or in the context of a "testimony meeting" or revival.

Tetragrammaton   (Gr. "four letters") The designation for the four Hebrew consonants that refer to the God of Israel: YHWH or JHWH (Ex. 3:15; 7:1). It is now rendered "Yahweh." The name was considered too holy to speak, so the term "Lord" (Heb. *Adonai*) was used. The ASV rendered it "Jehovah."

Tetrapolitan Confession (1530)   A Protestant confession of faith written by

Martin Bucer (1491–1551) and two others to present to the emperor Charles V. It sought to reconcile Lutheran and Reformed views and is the oldest German Reformed confession. Also called the Strasbourg or Swabian Confession.

Tetrateuch (Gr. *tetra*, "four," and *teuchos*, "book") Term for the first four books of the Old Testament, which scholars believe emerged from the same three sources: J (Yahwist), E (Elohist), and P (Priestly).

TEV *See* Today's English Version

textual criticism *See* criticism, textual

textus receptus (Lat. "received text") Term for the published edition of the Greek New Testament text that was used from the 16th to the 19th century as the primary text, and that on which the King James Version (KJV) is based. It has now been superseded as the most reliable Greek text.

thanatology (From Gr. *thanatos*, "death," and *logos*, "study") The study of death and dying in all their aspects.

thanatopsis (From Gr. *thanatos*, "death," and *opsis*, "sight") A belief about death. Also, a meditation or writing on death.

thank offering An offering made to God in thanksgiving for blessings (Lev. 7:12; cf. Ps. 107).

thanksgiving An expression of gratitude. A type of prayer in which, both publicly and privately, believers offer their gratitude to God for all blessings and goodness received.

thanksgiving, great prayer of A prayer in eucharistic liturgies that celebrates the work of the Father, Son, and Holy Spirit as an expression of thanksgiving prior to the reception of the elements of the Communion.

thaumaturgus (Lat. "miracle worker") Designation for saints who were considered to have performed miracles either during their lives or after they were canonized in response to prayers made to them.

theandric acts A way of designating that the actions of Jesus Christ performed as a human being may also be said to have been performed by him as God, since he was one person with two natures.

theism (From Gr. *theos*, "God") Belief in a god. Also belief in one God (monotheism) in contrast to belief in many gods (polytheism). It sees the universe as emerging from a single source and not by its own principle. It contrasts with monism, which would assume a self-principle.

theism, dipolar A term in process philosophy and theology for the view that God has two poles or aspects. One is God's abstract essence, which is absolute, eternal, and unchangeable. The other is God's concrete actuality, which is temporal, relative, dependent, and changing constantly.

theistic evolution *See* evolution, theistic

theistic finitism Belief in a personal God who is limited. It was promoted by the philosopher Edgar Sheffield Brightman (1884–1953). Also called "finitistic theism."

theistic naturalism The view that God is a tendency or process within the natural order that is evolving toward expressing creative values. It is a basic concept of process philosophy.

theistic philosophy Any philosophical system that includes belief in a god.

theistic proofs Philosophical arguments to prove the existence of God. Five theistic arguments are found in the theology of Thomas Aquinas (1225–74).

theocentric (Gr. *theos*, "God," and *kentron*, "center") God-centered. Revolving around the reality of belief in God.

theocracy (Gr. *theokratia*, "God-rule") A view of government in which God is acknowledged to be the supreme ruler. The will of God, as interpreted by those who are considered to represent God, becomes the law. The term was coined by the 1st-century historian Josephus for the Mosaic law.

theodicy (From Gr. *theos*, "God," and *dikē*, "justice," "right") The justification of a deity's justice and goodness in light of suffering and evil. The term was coined by the philosopher Gottfried Leibniz (1646–1716), though the issue has long been explored religiously.

theologia crucis *See* theology of the cross

theologia gloriae *See* theology of glory

theologian One who does theology or makes theological statements.

theological determinism Any theological system that views human actions and activities as caused by God.

theological education The process of educating persons in the theological disciplines. It is carried out in a professional context through seminaries or divinity schools, as well as through various settings in local churches with laity.

theological encyclopedia (From Gr. *en kyklō*, or *enkyklios paideia, enkyklopaideia*, "instruction in a circle" or "circle of instruction") A description of the complete circle of theological knowledge as it is presented for instruction. The presentation is arranged according to the interrelationships of the different areas of theology. Since the 18th century, the four traditional divisions have been: biblical, historical, systematic, and practical theology.

theological exegesis A term stressing a focus on the theological messages or emphases in biblical texts. This is in contrast to a focus on biblical criticism and other forms of biblical interpretation.

theological framework An overall theological viewpoint that provides a basis or structure for life and thought.

theological language The language used for theological discussion or discourse. Philosophical problems of theological language relate to its validity, verification, and character or nature.

theological method The way by which theology is done. Historically, a number of methods for doing Christian theology have emerged. Each rests upon and enacts a number of assumptions such as the nature of humanity, of language, of the world, of God and God's revelation, as well as ways of knowing.

theological positivism *See* positivism, theological

theological prolegomena (From Gr. *prolegomenon* "that which goes before") Material that is dealt with prior to the exposition of a formal theological system. This may include discussion of the theological task, the nature of theology, sources of authority, method to be used, etc. Synonymous with theological propaedeutic.

theological propaedeutic (From Gr. *propaideia*, "preparatory education of a boy") A general introduction to the study of Christian theology. It functions as a type of map for orientation to the theological disciplines.

theological seminaries (From Lat. *seminarium*, "seed plot") Educational institutions where the theological disciplines are taught and which educate persons for a variety of forms of service, including as pastoral ministries and teachers. They are often founded and supported by specific church denominations.

theological tradition A framework or particular set of doctrinal teachings that is adhered to and perpetuated.

theological virtues *See* virtues, theological

theologoumenon (theologumenon) (Gr. and Lat. "speculation on divine things") A theological statement made by a theologian as a theologian rather than as representing an official teaching of a church. It also refers to theological statements derived from Christian doctrines and not based on historical evidence.

theology (Gr. *theologia*, from *theos*, "God," and *logos*, "speech"; Lat. *theologia*) Language or discourse about God.

It can be a scientific, methodical attempt to understand God's divine revelation. It has classically been seen as "faith seeking understanding."

theology, apophatic　*See* apophatic theology

theology, archetypal　(Lat. *theologia archetypa*) God's infinite knowledge of the divine self that is known only to God. Scholastic theologians perceived this as the pattern or "archetype" for all true theology that is attempted by humans.

theology, ascetical　*See* ascetical theology

theology, biblical　*See* biblical theology

theology, cataphatic　*See* cataphatic theology

theology, catechetical　(Lat. *theologia catechetica*) A term for basic theological knowledge that is important for all Christian believers. It may include such elements as the teachings of the Apostles' and Nicene Creeds, the meaning of the sacraments, the Ten Commandments, and the Lord's Prayer.

theology, Christian　*See* Christian theology

theology, conservative　*See* conservative theology

theology, contextualization of　*See* contextual theology

theology, dialectical　*See* dialectical theology

theology, doctrinal　*See* doctrinal theology

theology, dogmatic　*See* dogmatic theology

theology, ectypal　(Lat. "ectypal theology") The knowledge of God that is available to human beings as that is expressed in theological systems. In scholastic theology, it is a reflection of the knowledge of God available only to God ("archetypal theology"). Ectypal reflects archetypal theology.

theology, feminist　*See* feminist theologies

theology, higher　(Lat. *theologia acroamatica*) A term used by 17th-century Lutheran theologians for the detailed theology taught in universities for clergy and theologians to acquaint them thoroughly with the intricacies of Christian theology. It contrasts with catechetical theology.

theology, liberal　*See* liberal theology/ liberalism

theology, liberation　*See* liberation theologies

theology, liturgical　Theological understandings related to the church's liturgies and liturgical traditions.

theology, monastic　The theological understandings developed among those who serve in monastic communities.

theology, mystical　*See* mystical theology

theology, natural　*See* natural theology

theology, negative　*See* negative theology

theology, norm of　The principle or concept around which theology is organized. Some argue that the gospel of Jesus Christ is the material norm and the Bible is the formal norm of theology. Roman Catholicism sees a conjunction of Scripture and tradition as what is normative. Others consider human experience a norm.

theology, pastoral　*See* pastoral theology

theology, positive　*See* positive theology

theology, process　*See* process theology

theology, revealed　*See* revealed theology

theology, sources of　The places or capacities from which theological reflection and construction emerge. Prominent have been Scripture, church tradition, human experience, and reason. Some have emphasized various combinations of these as the place where theological reflection begins.

theology in itself　(Lat. *theologia in se*) A term used in medieval philosophy

(Scotism) for the theology which is known only in the divine mind. It was used by 17th-century Protestant scholastic theologians for an ideal form of theology that transcends its occurrence in any individual mind.

theology of angels (Lat. *theologia angelorum*) A term used to denote the kind of theology known by angels as superior spiritual beings, and thus as a higher form of the knowledge of God than can be attained by humans.

theology of Christians (Lat. *theologia viatorum*, "theology of the pilgrims") A term for the limited and imperfect theology of Christian believers on earth compared to the theology of those who have attained heaven ("theology of the blessed").

theology of crisis *See* crisis theology

theology of culture An understanding of human culture that embraces all the creative achievements of people in light of theological convictions. Important issues include views about the nature of different theological topics, as well as the nature of a culture in terms of its ideals, goals, and values.

theology of feeling A term associated with the theology of F.D.E. Schleiermacher (1768–1834), which stresses the place of emotion and intuition. Religious language is seen as the means of religious self-consciousness. Humans feel a sense of "absolute dependence" on God.

theology of glory (Lat. *theologia gloriae*) A term used by Martin Luther (1483–1546) for the current speculative, scholastic theology that emphasized God's glorious attributes rather than the divine self-revelation in the sufferings and cross of Jesus Christ (Lat. *theologia crucis*).

theology of grace *See* grace

theology of hope A term associated with the work of Jürgen Moltmann (b. 1926), which emphasizes the place of eschatology as a beginning point for theology. It is grounded in the resurrection of Jesus Christ as the culmination of all God's promises and as the guarantee of the future reign of God.

theology of liberation A comprehensive term for a number of theological streams that seek liberation or freedom for those who are oppressed. Movements for liberation begin with action, and as Christian theologies they bring faith to reflect on praxis. Basic is the view that genuine faith includes liberation.

theology of paradox *See* paradox, theology of

theology of revivalism The theology frequently undergirding the efforts of revivalism. It stresses the sinfulness of human beings and their need for the grace of God and salvation, calling forth a "decision for Christ" that will lead to conversion. Historically, there has often been a link with emotionalism.

theology of the blessed (Lat. *theologia beatorum*) The theology of those who have attained heaven. It is fuller and more complete than the theology of those on earth (*theologia viatorum*). It is sometimes called the "vision of God" (Lat. *visio Dei*).

theology of the cross (Lat. *theologia crucis*) A term of Martin Luther's (1483–1546) that he contrasted with a "theology of glory," pointing out that God's revelation is known in the weakness and scandal of the cross of Jesus Christ and not through speculative reason and human reason.

theology of the unregenerate A term for the view that a person may know and understand a fully orthodox theological system but yet not have experienced God's grace in a personal way and responded in faith

theology proper The theological study of the doctrine of God.

theomachy (Gr. *theomachia*, from *theos*, "God," and *machē*, "battle") The opposition between God and Satan or, more generally, any opposition to God's will.

theomorphic (From Gr. *theos*, "God," and *morphē*, "form") Possessing a divine form or quality.

theonomism (From Gr. *theos*, "God," and *nomos*, "law") The view that God's will is totally free to choose and whatever is chosen by the will of God is ultimately right and good. There is no other standard to be sought than God's will.

theonomy (Gr. *theos*, "God," and *nomos*, "law") Ruled or controlled by God. In the thought of Paul Tillich (1886–1965), it is the fulfillment of the law of one's own being as it is united with the source and ground of being (God).

Theopaschites (From Gr. *theopaschitēs*, "God suffering") A 6th-century A.D. Monophysite group which believed that the divine nature of Jesus Christ suffered on the cross.

theopassianism *See* patripassianism

theopathy (From Gr. *theos*, "God," and *pathos*, "feeling") A direct experience of God. Also an intense absorption in religious experiences.

theophany (From Gr. *theos*, "God," and *phainesthai*, "to appear") An appearance of God that is perceptible to human sight (e.g., Ex. 33:17–23).

theophoroi ("God-bearing," from Gr. *theos*, "God," and *pherein*, "to bear") A term used by early Christians to indicate their belief that Jesus Christ or his Spirit dwelt within them.

theopneustos (Gr. "God-breathed," "inspired by God") A term that designates the "inspiration," or "God-breathed" character, of the Jewish Scriptures (2 Tim. 3:16). The Christian church has also applied this concept to the New Testament Scriptures as a way of indicating that Scripture originates with God.

theopoiesis (Gr. *theopoiēsis*) The view that human beings become a god. Eastern theologians distinguished this from their view of *theosis.*

theory (Gr. *theōria*, "a looking at") A particular attitude or way of approaching the world and, by extension, a statement of principles involved rather than the practice of a science. The relation of "theory" and "practice" is an ongoing question of theological method.

theory of knowledge One's commitment to a certain way in which one comes to know something. Major philosophical movements include rationalism, empiricism, idealism, existentialism, positivism, etc. These philosophical views also bring theological implications.

theos (Gr. "god") The supreme being or deity. In the Christian tradition, God is the creator of all things who redeems a sinful world through Jesus Christ and who continues to incorporate the world into the divine life of God by the Holy Spirit. God is a trinity, one God in three persons.

theosis (Gr. *theōsis*, "deification," "divinization," "making divine") The view held by Eastern Orthodox theologians that salvation from sin consists of the process of "deification," through which believers become united with Christ's divine nature and thus with God.

Theosophy (Gr. "wisdom of God") A philosophical system that seeks meaning in human existence through combinations of insights from world religions, philosophy, science, and the occult. The Theosophical Society (founded 1875) promotes these views and stresses the spiritual evolution of humanity.

Theotokos (Gr. "God-bearer") A term used in the ancient church for Mary as the "mother of God." It was used at the Councils of Ephesus (431) and Chalcedon (451) to affirm the deity of Jesus Christ. Because Jesus had two natures, it was permissible to speak of Mary as "God-bearer," since the human Jesus was also the divine Jesus.

Third Person of the Trinity A designation for the Holy Spirit, who is fully divine and shares the same "substance" or "Godness" as God the Father and God the Son. The Spirit is referred to in the Nicene Creed (381) as "the Lord and giver of life."

Third Reformation   *See* Radical Reformation

third use of the law   (Lat. *tertius usus legis*) A term of John Calvin's (1509–64), who taught that the law of God not only reveals human sin and promotes political and civil order. Its third and most important use is as a norm and guide for Christian believers, as it reveals the will of God for their lives.

third-eye theology   A term used by the Asian theologian Choan-Seng Song (b. 1929) for the need of Christians to train themselves to see Jesus Christ through the "eyes" of persons in China, Japan, Asia, Africa, and Latin America.

third-world theologies   Theologies that have emerged from areas sometimes designated as the "third world" (a term that some find pejorative): Latin America, Africa, and most parts of Asia. These include various theologies of liberation.

Thirteen Articles (1538)   A Latin manuscript found in the papers of Thomas Cranmer (1489–1556) that contained theological statements from a conference of German Lutheran and English theologians. They were never adopted by English authorities and were dependent on the Augsburg Confession (1530).

Thirty Years' War (1618–48)   The last European war of religion, which devastated central Europe. It involved German Protestants and Roman Catholics, later including France, Sweden, and Denmark opposing the Holy Roman Empire and Spain. It ended with the Peace of Westphalia. Secularized international relations took shape after this time.

Thirty-nine Articles (1563)   The doctrinal standards of the Church of England and of Episcopal churches throughout the world. They emerged from earlier doctrinal formulations and were adopted as a middle course between Reformation and Roman Catholic views, though with some Calvinistic emphases.

thnetopsychism   (From *thnētos,* "liable to death," "mortal," and *psychē,* "soul") The belief that the soul dies when the physical body dies but that it may be raised again in the future resurrection.

Thomism   Philosophical and theological views from the work of Thomas Aquinas (1225–74), highly influential in the Roman Catholic Church. Four phases include periods of defense (13th–15th centuries), commentaries (1450–1630), disputations, systems (1500–1720), and revival (1860–1960).

Thomist   One who is committed to Thomism and the system of thought produced by Thomas Aquinas (1225–74).

threefold office of Christ   *See: munus triplex*

Threefold Way   A classical description of stages of mystical theology or religious experience moving from purgation, to illumination, to union with God.

three-hour devotion   The ancient practice of observing a service of worship on Good Friday from noon to 3 P.M. (Matt. 27:45, "the sixth to the ninth hour") in commemoration of Jesus' passion on the cross. The contemporary practice exists among Christian churches in local communities.

thurible   (From Lat. *thus,* "incense") A container, often called a censer, which is a metal pan containing hot coals and suspended on a short chain. It burns incense for a service of worship and is swung gently to create smoke.

thurifer   (Lat. "incense carrier") One who carries a censer or thurible during a liturgical procession.

Thursday, Holy   *See* Holy Thursday

tiara, papal   (Gr. *tiara,* "a form of headdress") Papal crown which the bishop of Rome wears at ceremonies, except when conducting services of worship.

Tillichian   Referring to the theological system of Paul Tillich (1886–1965). He defined religion as one's "ultimate concern" and saw theology as relating to existential questions. "God" is the "ground of being," sin is "estrangement." The "Christ" brings a reunion or salvation, creating a "new being."

time   The period between the creation of the universe and its ultimate consummation. Time contrasts with eternity. Biblically and theologically, God transcends time, but humans are time-bound creatures until they enter into life after death and exist eternally.

tithe/tithing   (Gr. *apodekatoun*, "to give one-tenth"; Anglo-Saxon *teotha*, "tenth") The practice of giving one-tenth of one's property or resources to support a religious institution as response to God for God's blessings. It was done in Israel (Deut. 14:22ff.) and at the time of Jesus (Matt. 23:23).

Today's English Version (TEV, 1976)   A dynamic-equivalent translation of the Bible produced by the American Bible Society. It is also known as the Good News Bible (GNB). It aimed at making the Scriptures accessible in as simple a vocabulary as possible. The New Testament appeared in 1966.

tokenism   A small formal concession to a principle or a demand, perhaps intended to fulfill a requirement but without a genuine commitment to the issue being addressed. Ethically the term has been used in a number of contexts, particularly in regard to race and gender issues.

Toledo, Councils of   Sixteen councils called by Visigoth kings in Toledo, Spain, from c. 589 to 702. Two earlier councils (c. 397 and 527) were of minor importance. The councils combined elements of church and state, issuing professions of faith, rules for church discipline, law codes, and legislation.

tolerance, religious   (Lat. *tolerantia*, "a bearing," "supporting," "endurance") To permit, allow, and respect the beliefs and practices of others with regard to religious faith and practices.

Toleration Act (1689)   Legislation by the English Parliament at the beginning of the reign of William III that provided permission for Nonconformists—those who would not participate in the Church of England—to preach, teach, and have houses of worship.

tongues, speaking in   *See* glossolalia

tonsure   (Lat. *tonsura*, from *tondere*, "to shear") The act of clipping the hair or shaving the head as a sign of entrance into a monastic order in the Roman Catholic Church. Also, the part of the head left bare when such shaving is done. It is no longer practiced as an initiatory rite.

Torah   (Heb. "instruction," "law") God's revelation to Moses at Mount Sinai was of God's torah ("instruction" or "law") as the expression of God's will for the nation of Israel. The Pentateuch is known as the Torah. By extension, in Judaism, torah is any expression of God's will.

Torgau Articles, the (1530, 1574, 1576)   Lutheran confessional documents that dealt with Roman Catholicism, the Lord's Supper, and internal Lutheran disagreements.

total depravity   The view, characteristic in Reformed theology, that sinfulness pervades all areas of life or the totality of human existence. This belief was one of the five canons of the Calvinistic Synod of Dort (1618–19) and part of TULIP.

total inability   A concept found in Reformed theology to stress the view that because of their sinfulness, humans are not able to perform any action that will lead to their salvation. God must take the initiative to give the gift of faith and repentance.

totalistic relativism   The view that there are no absolutes and that all things, including knowledge, are relative to the knower.

totem   (Ojibwa *ototeman*, "he is a relative of mine") A nonhuman entity, often an animal, symbolizing a first ancestor of a group. Also, the image of such an entity. Totems inspire strong emotions.

The concept is significant in understanding structures of human cognition.

tract (Lat. *tractus,* "a drawing out") A short writing with a religious or evangelistic message.

Tractarianism The early stages of the Oxford or Anglo-Catholic movement in 19th-century England, marked by the production of a number of tracts that sought to return the Church of England to its Roman Catholic, rather than Protestant, roots.

tradition (Gr. *paradosis,* Lat. *traditio,* from *tradere,* "to deliver," "to hand over") The transmission of received teaching or practice. In Christianity, the church's tradition centers in God's revelation in Jesus Christ. The term has come to mean the genuine preservation of the apostles' faith.

traditional theology A general name for a theology that is accepted without a detailed examination. It may also refer to general, Christian orthodox theology, in contrast to unorthodox views on certain issues.

traditionalism Appeal to past forms of a religion, culture, or pattern of belief or behavior. Also a reaction to modernity, holding that faith in divine revelation communicated through tradition is the only source of religious knowledge.

traditor (Lat. "traitor," from *tradere,* "to deliver") Term for one of those who "turned over" copies of the Christian Scriptures during a period of intense persecution in North Africa in the reign of Diocletian (284–305), when it was illegal to possess the Scriptures. Whether such persons should be readmitted to the church was debated in the Donatist controversies.

traducianism (From Lat. *tradux,* "vine-branch," "shoot") A theological view according to which the human soul is propagated by parents to children. Also called "generationism." It contrasts with "creationism," the view that God creates each new soul at conception.

tragedy (Gr. *tragōidia,* Lat. *tragoedia*) The primary literary genre for conveying questions about suffering and the meaning of evil.

transcendence of God *See* God, transcendence of

transcendency (From Lat. *transcendere,* "to climb over," "to surpass") Description of God as being over and beyond the created order in all aspects.

transcendent (From Lat. *transcendere,* "to climb over," "to surpass") Philosophically, that which stands beyond all limits of human experience. In the philosophy of Immanuel Kant (1724–1804), that which is beyond human knowledge. Typically, in Christian theology, God is described as transcendent.

transcendental philosophy A description of the philosophy of Immanuel Kant (1724–1804) and his followers. Kant argued that there are transcendental structures to human reason which make it possible for sense perceptions to become knowledge. This readiness to affirm being is a precondition for all knowledge.

transcendental theology Theology oriented to exploring the fundamental conditions for theological knowledge.

Transcendental Thomism A 20th-century Roman Catholic theological movement to join the philosophy of Thomas Aquinas (1225–74) with the philosophy of Immanuel Kant (1724–1804) and his followers. It is associated with Karl Rahner (1904–84) and Bernard Lonergan (1904–85).

Transcendentalism A 19th-century movement, associated with Ralph Waldo Emerson (1803–82), Samuel Taylor Coleridge (1772–1834), and others, that emphasized the intuitive over the scientific, the inspiration of the individual soul, and an ideal and spiritual reality beyond the world of space and time.

transcendentalism, Kant's A characteristic of the philosophy of Immanuel Kant (1724–1804) and other philosophers who by the "transcendental method" seek to show the necessary conditions for the truth of a proposition, experience, or body of knowledge. The focus is on the objects of thought, not sense experience.

Transcendentalists Nineteenth-century New England religious thinkers such as William Ellery Channing (1780–1842), Ralph Waldo Emerson (1803–82) and Henry David Thoreau (1817–62), who stressed that the truth of the universe could be attained through subjective intuitions and inspiration.

transcendentals (Lat. *transcendentalia*) A philosophical term for those properties which are common to all objects of whatever nature, such as reality, being, truth, goodness, being something, and unity, according to Aquinas (1225–74).

transdenominational That which goes beyond denominational lines.

transept (Lat. "transverse enclosure") An extension of a church at right angles to the nave, often added to provide more space on the sides of the altar.

transferral (From Lat. *transferre*, "to bear across") That which is passed on from one to another. Used theologically to speak of human sin as passed on to Jesus Christ in his death on the cross. Also used to indicate the passing on of the righteousness of Jesus Christ to those who believe.

transfiguration of Christ Jesus' appearing in a glorious form on a mountain with Elijah and Moses (Matt. 17:1–13; Mark 9:2–13; Luke 9:28–36). The incident was a preview of his glory after the resurrection. It is celebrated as a church festival in Eastern and Western churches on August 6, or, more recently in some Western churches, on the Sunday before Lent.

transfinalization A Roman Catholic view of the Eucharist in which it is believed that the formula of consecration spoken over the elements changes their purpose or finality so that they serve a new function. Their finality is changed from food to be eaten to nourishment for Christians.

transformation of life *See* regeneration

transforming grace A theological term for the effects of God's grace in lives as changes are effected on the basis of receiving the benefits of God's actions in Jesus Christ.

transgression (From Gr. *parabainein*, Lat. *transgredi*, "to step over") A biblical image for sin as overstepping the boundaries set by God, and thus as the breaking of God's law (Ex. 34:7; Ps. 32:1; Rom. 5:14; Gal. 6:1).

transignification A view of Christ's presence in the Eucharist according to which the formula of consecration spoken over the bread and wine changes their meaning or significance, although in actual substance the elements remain the same. They now carry a more important value or significance.

translation of persons Being taken to heaven while still alive and thus bypassing the experience of death. This is portrayed in the biblical accounts of Enoch (Gen. 5:24; Heb. 11:5) and Elijah (2 Kings 2:11).

translations, biblical The rendering of the Scriptures into another language from their original texts in Hebrew (Old Testament) and Greek (New Testament).

transmigration of souls *See* soul, transmigration of the

transubstantiation (Lat. *transubstantiatio*, "essential change") In Roman Catholic theology at the consecration in the Mass, the changing of the substance of bread and wine, by God's power, into the substance of Jesus Christ's body and blood, which become present while the "species" (bread and wine) remain.

transvaluation The process carried out by feminist theologians to reorient a Christian doctrine and its value in light of women's experience. It is a replacing of doctrines dislocated by patriarchal Christianity.

Treacle Bible (1539) (Gr. *thēriakē*, Lat. *theriaca*, "antidote against the bite of a serpent," "antidote against poison") A name for the Great Bible of Miles Coverdale (1488–1568) because of its translation, "There is no more treacle [balm] in Gilead" (Jer. 8:22).

treasury of merit In the Roman Catholic tradition, the view that the good works done by some saints, or holy persons, including Jesus Christ, can benefit others. In the Middle Ages it led to the concept of indulgences. Contemporary Roman Catholic theologians see it as a metaphor for ways in which the faith of Christ and the saints helps others. Also called treasury of the church.

treasury of the church *See* treasury of merit

tree of the knowledge of good and evil In the story of Adam and Eve in the Garden of Eden, the tree from which the couple was forbidden to eat and from which, when they did eat, sin and the breaking of their relationship with God resulted (Gen. 2:17; 3:1–24).

Trent, Council of (1545–63) A Roman Catholic Council called by Pope Paul III for church reform in light of the Protestant Reformation and for clarification of church teachings. Its canons and decrees provided official church dogma that was comprehensive in scope. Its work remained intact until Vatican II (1962–65).

trespass (Gr. *paraptōma*, "false step"; Lat. *delictum*, "transgression") A biblical image for sin as a deviation from the right way that God prescribes (Rom. 5:15–20; Eph. 1:7; Col. 2:13).

trial (Gr. *dokimasia*, Lat. *tentatio* or *temptatio*, "testing," "examination") Theologically, the testing from Satan or the power of evil, trying to draw one into sin (Lat. *tentatio seductionis*). Also, God's purposes to test and strengthen believers' faith (*tentatio probationis* [Heb. 12:7; James 1:2]).

trials for ordination The prescribed examinations or work required of a person by a denomination in the process of moving toward ordination as a clergyperson.

Tribulation period (Great Tribulation) A term often used in Dispensationalism to indicate a seven-year period of suffering prior to the second coming of Jesus Christ and the beginning of the millennium (Matt. 24:21–30). Various views of the church's relation to the Tribulation period have been proposed.

tribulational views Differing views on the relation of the Christian church to the Great Tribulation period (Matt. 24:21–30). They are pre-, mid-, and post-tribulationism, depending on whether the church endures none, some, or all of the Tribulation. The debates are found in fundamentalism.

tribunal (Lat. "judgment seat") An ecclesiastical court. The term is used in the Roman Catholic tradition, in which every diocese has a tribunal. It deals most often with issues concerning the validity of marriages.

trichotomism (From Gr. *trichotomia*, "division into three") A theological view of anthropology in which humans are seen as consisting of body, soul, and spirit (1 Thess. 5:23). It contrasts with dichotomism, which distinguishes body and soul (Matt. 10:28).

Tridentine (Lat. *tridentinus*, "of Trent") Referring to the Council of Trent (1545–63). More broadly, the term is used for the theological, disciplinary, liturgical, and cultural features of the Roman Catholic Church that resulted from the Council of Trent.

Triduum Sacrum (Lat. "the sacred three days") The final three days of Holy Week that commemorate the Lord's Supper (Maundy Thursday), the Passion of Jesus (Good Friday), and the Death of Christ (Holy Saturday).

Trinitarian (From Lat. *trinitas*, "a triad") Relating to the Trinity and the Christian view that God is one God in three Persons.

Trinitarian formula The Christian church's traditional use of the phrase: "Father, Son, and Holy Spirit," particularly upon the occasion of baptism.

Trinitarian functions The differing works of the three Persons of the Trinity: Father, Son, and Holy Spirit. In classical theology, the work of one member of the Trinity is also considered to be the work of the whole Trinity. The term is similar to the term "economic Trinity."

Trinitarian mysticism A term in mystical theology to indicate the direct experience of relationship with the three Persons of the Trinity.

Trinitarian properties The characteristics that are common to all three members of the Trinity, in distinction from those that are unique. For example, "humanity" is unique to the Second Person (Jesus Christ), but not to the Father or the Holy Spirit.

Trinitarianism A reference to the Trinity as understood in Christian theology. The term may be seen in contrast to Unitarianism.

Trinity, doctrine of the (From Lat. *trinitas,* "triad") The Christian church's belief that Father, Son, and Holy Spirit are three Persons in one Godhead. They share the same essence or substance (Gr. *homoousios*). Yet they are three "persons" (Lat. *personae*). God is this way within the Godhead and as known in Christian experience.

Trinity, economic *See* economic Trinity

Trinity, essential The church's doctrine of the Trinity, that God is a trinity in unity and a unity in trinity. God as three in one is experienced by humans as Father, Son, and Holy Spirit. The three Persons of the Trinity share the same essence and relate to each other in love.

Trinity, immanent *See* immanent Trinity

Trinity, psychological analogies of the Ways of seeking understandings of the "oneness" and "threeness" of the divine Trinity. The analogy is drawn with a human person as subject who has faculties of memory, understanding, and will. The person is "one," yet functions psychologically in three ways. Used by Western theologians.

Trinity, social analogies of the Ways of drawing analogies from human social experience to portray the relationships of Father, Son, and Holy Spirit as the Trinity. There may be a lover, the beloved, and their mutual love. The image was used by Cappadocian theologians.

Trinity Sunday The first Sunday after Pentecost, when the church celebrates the Holy Trinity.

Trisagion (Gr. "thrice holy") A liturgical response, "Holy God, holy mighty, holy immortal, have mercy on us," used in ancient liturgies, particularly in Eastern churches. It is seen as a blend of the Sanctus ("Holy, Holy, Holy," Isa. 6:3) and part of Ps. 41:3 LXX (42:2).

tritheism (Lat. "three gods") Belief in three separate and individual gods. Some early formulations by Christian theologians were considered to move in this direction. Early Christian apologists sought to defend the faith from charges of belief in three gods.

Trito-Isaiah (Third Isaiah) Name for the last 11 chapters (chaps. 56–66) of the book of Isaiah, considered as a literary unit.

triumphalism A view that stresses the victories or triumphs of the Christian life or the Christian church. It may be viewed negatively if it does not give a true picture of situations or is used as an excuse to cover up injustices or instances of oppression.

triune (Lat. *tri,* "three," and *unus,* "one") Being three in one.

triune God (From Lat. *tri,* "three," and *unus,* "one") Christian view of God existing as the Trinity of Father, Son, and Holy Spirit; one God in three Persons.

Triunity of God The ultimate unity of the three Persons in the Godhead as one God. In Christian usage, the term "Trinity" points to the three Persons; "Triunity" points to their oneness as one God.

Tropici A 4th-century group that considered the Spirit to be an angel of the highest rank and thus not fully divine.

They were opposed by Athanasius (c. 293–373).

tropological sense (Gr. *tropologia,* "figurative speech") One of the traditional four senses of Scripture. Focused on the spiritual or moral, and thus figurative, meaning of biblical passages or texts.

truce of God (Lat. *pax, treuga Dei*) Term used in the medieval period for those days or seasons when the church ordered warring parties to cease fighting. At points these included from Saturday evening until Monday morning and the seasons of Advent and Lent.

true church The genuine church of those who truly believe in Jesus Christ and have received salvation. The marks or signs of the true church have been variously understood.

Trullan Synod (692) A synod that met in a domed room (Lat. *trullus*) of the emperor Justinian II's palace in Constantinople to complete the work of the Fifth (553) and Sixth (680) General Councils.

trust (Lat. *fiducia;* Old Norse *traust,* "firmness") Confidence in something or someone, often used as a primary description for faith (Lat. *fides,* Pss. 31:14; 115:9). Trust is to be placed in God (Ps. 4:5) who justifies (Rom. 4:5) and is ultimately trustworthy (2 Tim. 1:12).

trustee One who serves as an accountable party for a church's (or other organization's) legal and financial obligations.

truth (Gr. *alētheia,* Lat. *veritas*) That which accords with reality or is genuine. The Hebrew Old Testament emphasis is on trustworthiness and reliability, supremely God's (Deut. 32:4). In the New Testament, Jesus is truth (John 14:6). The church seeks to understand the truth of God's revelation in Scripture.

truth claim The claim that there is sufficient evidence for a proposition that it can be warranted as true. The concept is important in philosophical analyses of Christian and other religious thought.

truthfulness (Lat. *veracitas*) That which conveys the truth. Ethically, it is the virtue of conveying one's thoughts accurately and in ways appropriate to one's circumstances.

Tübingen school A 19th-century movement connected with the University of Tübingen that applied the developing historical-critical approaches to the Bible. It was founded by F. C. Baur (1792–1860) and applied the methods of G.W.F. Hegel (1770–1831) to biblical and historical studies.

TULIP An acronym and memory tool for the traditional five points of Calvinism that emerged from the Synod of Dort (1618–19). The theological points are Total depravity, Unconditional election, Limited atonement, Irresistible grace, and the Perseverance of the saints.

tutiorism (Lat. *tutior,* "safer") A form of moral theology which teaches that one must always abide by the principle or law in any case of moral doubt. It is the "safer" way. This view is sometimes called extreme rigorism.

Twelfth Night The evening of the 12th day after Christmas. It is also referred to as Epiphany, commemorating the coming of the Magi to Jesus (January 6).

Twelve, the *See* twelve disciples

twelve disciples (apostles) The original followers of Jesus according to the Gospels: Peter, Andrew, James, John, Philip, Bartholomew, Thomas, Matthew, James, Thaddaeus, Simon the Zealot, and Judas Iscariot (Matt. 10:1–4). Sometimes called the Twelve.

Twelve Great Feasts The twelve feasts of Eastern churches: Nativity of Mary, Exaltation of the Cross, Entrance of Mary into the Temple, Nativity of Jesus, Theophany, Hypapante, Annunciation, Entrance into Jerusalem, Ascension, Pentecost, Transfiguration, and Dormition.

twofold knowledge of God A description of the themes used by John Calvin (1509–64) to provide a structure for his definitive edition of the *Institutes* (1559). Human knowledge of God is the knowledge of God the Creator and the knowledge of God the Redeemer.

twofold nature of faith   Faith considered as both belief in propositions and trust in the person of Jesus Christ.

twofold nature of Jesus   The Christian church's view that Jesus Christ had both a divine and a human nature united in his one person.

twofold state of Jesus   A concept that structures Christology. It is based on Christ's state of humiliation (Lat. *status humiliationis*), including his incarnation and crucifixion, and his state of exaltation (Lat. *status exaltationis*), including his resurrection, ascension, and exaltation (Phil. 2:5–11).

two-source hypothesis   A scholarly explanation for the relationships among the Synoptic Gospels (Matt., Mark, Luke). In this view Mark's Gospel was written first. Matthew and Luke used his framework for their Gospels plus materials from "Q" (Ger. *Quelle*, "source"). Thus Mark and Q are the two Gospel sources.

two-swords theory   A view stated by Pope Gelasius I (494) which claimed that the state and the church are the two earthly realms of power. How they relate to each other has been the subject of much debate.

Tyndale's New Testament (1525)   The first printed English Scripture. It was translated by William Tyndale (c. 1494–1536) at Worms and was highly influential on subsequent translations, particularly the King James Version. Tyndale completed a partial translation of the Old Testament before being burned at the stake.

type   (Gr. *typos*, Lat. *typus*) An example or figure. In biblical interpretation, a type is a person or event that foreshadows or symbolizes another (Rom. 5:14). For example, the book of Hebrews shows Melchizedek as a type of Christ (Heb. 6:19–7:28). Cf. 1 Peter 3:21.

typicon   (Gr. "model," "rule") Term for a liturgical manual in the Eastern church that prescribes rules for conducting services. The term may be more generally used for a handbook of liturgical procedures.

typological interpretation of Scripture   A means of interpreting Scripture which views Old Testament persons and events as symbolically anticipating or foreshadowing New Testament occurrences (Rom. 5:14; 1 Cor. 10:2; Heb. 6:19–7:28; 1 Peter 3:21).

typology   (From Gr. *typos*, "a figure," and *logos*, "study") The study of Old Testament types as anticipating New Testament persons or occurrences (Rom. 5:14; 1 Cor. 10:2; Heb. 6:19–7:28; 1 Peter 3:21).

tyrannicide   (Lat. *tyrannicidium*, "killing of a tyrant") The killing of a tyrant by a private individual or group. Ethical justifications for such an action have been sought in various ways. Where legal means of removing officials are found, the issue has been less critical.

ubiquitarianism   (Lat. *ubique*, "everywhere") A Lutheran view about the presence of Christ in the Lord's Supper. It holds that Christ in his glorified human nature is present everywhere and by the power of the Holy Spirit can be present in all celebrations of the Lord's Supper. This is possible through the union of the human nature with the divine person of the Word (Logos).

ubiquity (Lat. *ubique*, "everywhere") Omnipresence. Applied to God's (or Christ's) presence in every place at every time. Lutheran understandings of the Eucharist support ubiquitarianism.

ultimate concern A term used in the theology of Paul Tillich (1886–1965) in various ways. One use is to define religion as the human quest for ultimacy and thus as the phenomenon of ultimate concern (faith) seeking fulfillment (salvation). This indicates its fundamental importance to human existence.

Ultradispensationalism An extreme form of Dispensationalism in which the Christian church is seen as beginning in Acts 13 or Acts 28 rather than in Acts 2 at Pentecost.

ultramontanism (Lat. "beyond the mountains," referring beyond the Alps to Rome, as viewed from France) Papal supremacy over regional churches. Also a 19th-century Roman Catholic movement that sought to centralize church authority in the papacy so that the church might be renewed.

unbaptized infants Those who have not received the sacrament of baptism as infants. More specifically, those infants who die without having been baptized.

unbelief From the Christian perspective, the rejection of the message of Christianity.

unbeliever From the Christian perspective, one who does not believe in the message of Christianity.

unchurched Those who do not belong to or participate in the life of a Christian church.

uncircumcised Those who are not circumcised. The term was used by Jews in biblical times for Gentiles.

unclean In biblical usage, a person or object that violates a ritual law of Israel.

unconditional covenant of God A covenant made with persons by God which will be fulfilled solely on the basis of God's promises and not because of any requirements fulfilled by humans.

unconditional election A view associated with Augustine and Calvinism that God elects to save some solely on the basis of God's freedom and love and not on the basis of any merit or efforts on the part of humans. It was one of the five canons of the Calvinistic Synod of Dort (1618–19) and part of TULIP. Also called unconditional predestination.

unconditional predestination *See* unconditional election

unconscious, the That which is repressed from consciousness.

unconscious faith The view that Christian faith and belief can exist apart from conscious reasoning power and self-awareness, as in the view that baptized infants may have unconscious faith.

unconscious sin Sin committed unwittingly or without an awareness of the wrong involved. A sin of ignorance (Ezek. 45:20).

uncritical Referring to a view that accepts something as true at face value without concern for seeking evidence. An uncritical faith is a faith that does not question or emphasize intellectual aspects of Christian faith.

unction (Lat. *unctio,* from *ungere,* "to anoint") Anointing with oil as a symbolic part of a religious ceremony.

unction, extreme *See* anointing of the sick

unction, holy (Lat. *unctio,* from *ungere,* "to anoint") In the Roman Catholic tradition, the anointing that takes place at various points such as at the consecration of an altar, at confirmation, and at ordination. Also, the anointing of the sick and dying or dead.

underground churches Churches that are forced to meet secretly because of illegality or threats of persecution.

understanding (Old English *understandan,* "to stand under") That which one comprehends or knows at a level beyond simple acquaintanceship. Christian belief has been seen to involve one in faith which seeks further understanding of God and all theological dimensions of God's revelation.

unfaithfulness Failure to keep one's obligations. Theologically, an aspect of sin in which humans do not maintain the relationship of obedience and service to God they were created to have (2 Chron. 29:6; Rom. 3:3).

unforgivable sin *See* sin against the Holy Spirit

unforgiven sin Sin that is not pardoned, perhaps because it has not been confessed to God or to others and is not forgiven.

unfree An action that is caused or determined by an external force and is thus not attributed to a person.

unfrock *See* defrock

ungodliness Attitudes or actions that are not in conformity with the will of God.

Uniate churches (From Russian *uniyat*, "a union") Term for those Eastern churches that have the same doctrines as the Roman Catholic Church but use an Eastern (rather than Western) liturgy and also permit their priests to marry. These include Armenian and Maronite churches.

Unification Church A religious organization founded by Rev. Sun Myung Moon (b. 1920) in 1954 and named The Holy Spirit Association for the Unification of World Christianity. Moon's followers regard him as the Messiah. He claims to have laid the foundations for the kingdom of God (1960).

Uniformity, Acts of (1549, 1559, 1662) English legislative actions to secure conformity to the Church of England.

unigenitus (Lat. "only begotten") A term used in the ancient creeds to indicate the unique relationship of Jesus Christ to God the Father as God's eternal Son.

unio mystica *See* mystical union

union, essential (Lat. *unio essentialis*) Union of two different essences, such as God's union with all things.

union, hypostatic *See* hypostatic union

union, mystical *See* mystical union

union, personal *See* personal union

union, sacramental *See* sacramental union

union by adoption (Lat. *unio per adoptionem*) Term for the christological heresy of adoptionism, which views Christ's union with God as beginning and occurring at Jesus' baptism as symbolized by the descent of a dove (Luke 3:21–22).

union churches A church building jointly used by ecclesiastical bodies of different denominations. More generally, community churches in America that are nondenominational.

union of believers The bond of Christian love which unites Christian believers on the basis of their common faith in Jesus Christ.

union with Christ (Lat. *unio cum Christo*) Believers' unity with Jesus Christ on the basis of faith by the power of the Holy Spirit (Gal. 2:20).

union with God The relationship of believers with God on the basis of the salvation they receive through Jesus Christ.

unipersonality of God The view that God is one person, and thus a denial of the doctrine of the Trinity.

Unitarianism The belief that God is one. It contrasts with Trinitarianism, which holds that God is one God in three persons. The modern religious movement arose from the liberal theologies of Faustus Socinus (1539–1604) and others and grew to formation of the Unitarian Universalist Association (1961).

Unitarians Those who believe that God is only one person and who thus reject the doctrine of the Trinity and the divinity of Jesus Christ.

unitary view of human nature The view that humans should be regarded as a holistic unity rather than perceived as having components such as body, soul, and spirit.

Unitas Fratrum *See* Bohemian Brethren

unitive way In classical mysticism, the final goal of union with God. It brings a sense of "walking with God" and the habitual practicing of Christian virtues as well as contemplative prayer.

unity (Lat. *unitas*, "oneness") Used theologically to describe the oneness between the members of the Godhead, the relationship between God and believers through Jesus Christ, and the relationship of believers in Christ with one another. Also, a religious movement stressing positive thought and prayer.

unity of believers The oneness of believers in Jesus Christ with each other, for which Jesus prayed (John 17:21) and which is found now in the Christian church (1 Cor. 12:12–31; Gal. 3:28; Eph. 4:1–6).

unity of the church The essential oneness of the Christian church on the basis of its theological unity with God through Jesus Christ, maintained by the power of the Holy Spirit (1 Cor. 12:12–31; Eph. 4:1–6).

Unity School of Christianity A New Thought religious movement that was founded in Kansas City, Missouri, by Myrtle and Charles Fillmore (1889). They stressed the practical aspects of Christianity and were clearly influenced by the teachings of Christian Science.

universal availability of salvation The view that salvation in Jesus Christ is free and offered to all persons.

universal church *See* church universal

universal conversion The view that all persons will eventually repent of their sins, be converted to Jesus Christ, and ultimately receive salvation.

universal death The recognition that all persons ultimately die (Heb. 9:27).

universal depravity The recognition that all persons are sinners (Rom. 3:23).

universal explicit opportunity The view that every person will at some point have the explicit chance to believe in Jesus Christ, even if that occurs after

death (1 Peter 3:19). Also called "second probation."

universal grace *See* universality of God's grace

universal history All the events of human history. Some theologians (e.g., Wolfhart Pannenberg) believe God's revelation occurs in all of history, not only in the "holy history" or history of salvation derived from the biblical materials.

universal priesthood *See* priesthood of all believers

universal reconciliation The view that all persons have been reconciled to God through the work of Jesus Christ, whether or not they have responded to him in faith or are aware that this reconciliation has taken place. It may be used as a synonym for Universalism or universal salvation.

universal response *See* universal conversion

universal restoration The view initially taught by Origen (c. 185–c. 254) that all things in the universe will ultimately be returned to the state in which they were created by God.

universal salvation *See* universalism

universal tendency Description of that which is found in all persons, such as the proclivity to sin.

Universalism (From Lat. *universalis*, "belonging to the whole") The view that all persons will ultimately receive salvation from God.

universalism, hypothetical *See* hypothetical universalism

Universalist One who holds to universalism as a theological view.

universality of God's grace The view that God's grace for salvation has been extended to all people.

universals (Lat. *universalis*, "that which pertains to all") The philosophical attempt to describe that which is common to all, for example, human nature as common to all humans. In medieval philosophy, controversies over universals was part of the nominalist-realist discussions.

universe, origin of the   The question of what is the source of all that exists. In Christian thought, God is the originator (creator) of the universe and all within it.

univocity   A view of language in which names are seen as being univocal, i.e., having the same meaning throughout their various uses. Or, the exact application of a name or term to two different things.

unknown God   An inscription on an altar in Athens referred to by the apostle Paul (Acts 17:23). Some theologians use the concept to explain that this is who is being sought when non-Christians perform religious duties and offer worship. The religious person is seeking the one, living God.

unleavened bread   Bread baked without yeast. It is used in Jewish Passover meals (Ex. 12:8, 17–20) and often in Christian eucharistic services.

unlimited atonement   *See* atonement, universal

unmoved mover   A term used by Aristotle (384–322 B.C.) for the nature of God. God must be the only reality that does not move, since everything else changes, being moved by something other than itself. God does not move, change, or decay.

unorthodox   That which does not accord with accepted or orthodox views. Often used to denote a nontraditional theological position.

unpardonable sin   *See* sin against the Holy Spirit

unquenchable fire   An image for the eternal punishment spoken of in Scripture in relation to God's judgment of the unrighteous (Matt. 18:8; 25:41; Luke 3:17; Jude 1:7).

unregenerate   Those who have not experienced regeneration by God's Holy Spirit and thus do not have faith in Jesus Christ.

unrighteous   Those who are not righteous. In the Christian context it means those who are sinful and have not experienced forgiveness or salvation in Jesus Christ (Acts 24:15; 2 Peter 2:9).

unrighteousness   The condition of not being righteous and thus not rightly related to God through Jesus Christ.

unsaved   Those who have not experienced the salvation given by God in Jesus Christ.

Urgeschichte   (Ger. "prehistory") A term from dialectical theology to describe historical events that have a significance beyond themselves in that they are used as a means of God's self-revelation (e.g., the resurrection of Jesus Christ).

Urim and Thummin   (Heb. literally, "lights" and "perfections") Objects used by high priests in the Old Testament to seek the divine will in doubtful situations (Ex. 28:30; Num. 27:21; 1 Sam. 28:6).

Urmarkus   (Ger. "primitive Mark") A supposed oral or written source standing behind the Gospel of Mark.

use of the law   (Lat. *usus legis*) Protestant theologians identify three basic uses of the moral law: the political or civil use, the pedagogical use, and the didactic use. The "third use" (Lat. *tertius usus legis*) was key in Calvin's thought for the believer's use of the law as a norm for conduct.

usury   (From Lat. *uti*, "to use") The practice of lending money in order to gain interest. The practice was forbidden in the Old Testament (Ex. 22:25; Lev. 25:35–37). It was gradually accepted by Christian churches after the rise of capitalism.

Utilitarianism   A 19th-century ethical theory that decisions and actions should be judged on utility, or attaining "the greatest happiness for the greatest number." It is associated with the Oxford philosopher Jeremy Bentham (1748–1832).

utopianism   Term derived from Thomas More's (1478–1535) name "Utopia" (Gr. "not a place") for an ideal society. Utopianism is the view that this society may be attained on earth. Some have equated the "kingdom of God" with a type of utopianism.

utraquism   (From Lat. *uterque*, "both") The view that the clergy and laity should receive both the bread and the wine in Holy Communion. This was argued by John Huss (c. 1372–1415) against the view of the medieval church. It was condemned at several church councils (1415, 1532, 1551).

Utraquists   Followers of John Huss (c. 1372–1415) who sought to reform the church through preaching the gospel in Bohemian, permitting laity to receive both the bread and wine at Communion, reform of clerical abuses, and banning clergy from owning secular property. They were also called Hussites.

Utrecht, Declaration of (1889)   A doctrinal statement that provided the basis for the Old Catholic Church. It expressed adherence to the faith of Roman Catholicism but rejected its dogmas of papal infallibility and the immaculate conception of Mary.

vacancy   An official term for a church office, pastorate, or other situation in which no one is presently serving.

vacation Bible school/vacation church school   A term used in American Protestant churches for a period, usually one or two weeks, in which children are brought together during their (summer) school vacation for the purposes of Christian education and fellowship.

Vaison, Councils of (442, 529)   Two church councils at Vaison (southeastern France). One dealt with issues of church order and specified regulations for those who were penitent (442); the other concerned the liturgy (529).

Valence, Councils of (374, 529, 855)   Three of the most important church councils at Valence (in Dauphiné, southeastern France) dealt with church discipline (374), Pelagianism and Semi-Pelagianism (529), and predestination (855).

Valentinians   Gnostic followers of the 2d-century theologian Valentinus of Alexandria (d. 165).

validation   In Roman Catholic canon law, the making right of an action not previously considered to be legal. The act may be repeated in the correct manner, under particular conditions, or declared valid by an authority who or which can rectify the act. More generally, an official ratification as when an ecclesiastical governing body recognizes and sanctions the legitimacy of a person's call to serve a church or form of ministry.

validity   (From Lat. *validus*) In Roman Catholic theology, that which is correct according to canon law and which produces the intended results. Thus the sacraments have validity when correctly administered. Canon law assumes that all acts are valid and legal unless proven otherwise.

validity of sacraments   Sacraments are valid when considered to be correctly administered. In baptism, for example, most churches require the Trinitarian formula to be pronounced and water (the correct "matter") to be used.

value/value judgments   (Lat. *valere*, "to be worth") That which is considered to have worth and importance. In ethics, choices and actions are carried out in relation to that which is considered to have value. They are thus value judgments.

Van Tilian   A system of Christian apologetics based on the views of Cornelius Van Til (1895–1987), a Calvinist philosopher and theologian who asserted that all truth is based on God's revelation. Humans cannot truly know themselves unless they first know God's revelation. He emphasized apologetics.

Vatican   The pope's residence as well as the territory surrounding his palace and St. Peter's Church in Rome, Italy.

Vatican City   The territory surrounding the Vatican Palace in Rome. It is itself a sovereign state. Surrounded by the city of Rome, it is the smallest sovereign state in the world (108.7 acres). Also called State of Vatican City.

Vatican Council I (1869–70)   The 20th council of the Roman Catholic Church, convened by Pope Pius IX. It intended to define the church's beliefs in light of contemporary theological liberalism and secular philosophical movements. It approved documents on faith and reason, and on papal primacy and infallibility.

Vatican Council II (1962–65)   The 21st council of the Roman Catholic Church, convened by Pope John XXIII. It enacted extensive church reforms and cast traditional Catholic doctrines such as revelation, salvation, and the church in new theological frameworks. Its actions have had far-reaching effects worldwide.

veil, religious   (From Lat. *velum*, "curtain") A headdress women wear to express their specific vocation, status, or role in the Roman Catholic Church. Traditionally, novices have worn white, while professed sisters wear black veils.

venerable   (Lat. *venerabilis*, "worthy of respect") In the process of beatification in the Roman Catholic Church, the title given to a person who has reached a specific stage in that process. In the Church of England, the way of addressing an archdeacon.

veneration of images   The act of showing deep respect and reverence for a symbol such as the cross or icons.

veneration of relics   Giving honor and respect through various means, such as genuflection to objects believed to be associated with Christ or with Christian saints.

veneration of saints   *See* saints, devotion to the

veneration of the cross   *See* adoration of the cross

vengeance   (From Lat. *vindicare*, "to avenge") Carrying out retribution for a wrong done or believed to have been done by someone. In the Judeo-Christian tradition, vengeance is to give way to love (Lev. 19:18). Ultimate vengeance belongs only to God (Deut. 32:35; Rom. 12:19; Heb. 10:30).

Veni Creator Spiritus   (Lat. "Come, Creator Spirit") A 9th-century hymn to the Holy Spirit attributed to Rabanus Maurus (c. 780–856). It is often used in worship at ordinations, dedications of churches, and the openings of synods as well as on Pentecost Sunday.

venial sin   *See* sin, venial

venturum   (Lat.) The future in the sense of the invasion of the present by a future power that is yet to come.

veracious authority   The right to command beliefs or actions on the basis of special knowledge.

verba institutionis   *See* words of institution

verbal inspiration   *See* inspiration, verbal theory of

verbum visibile   (Lat. "visible word [of God]") The definition of a sacrament used by Augustine (354–430) and others which emphasizes its direct relationship to the Word of God.

verificational analysis   A form of contemporary analytic philosophy which claims that a synthetic statement cannot be true unless it can be verified by sense data. An equivalent term for logical positivism.

verissime et maxime esse   (Lat. "in the truest and most ultimate [maximum, greatest] way") Phrase used to designate God as the supreme good in the universe and as a fully perfect being.

Vermittlungstheologie   *See* mediating theology

vernacular   (Lat. *vernaculus*, "native") The native language of a country, region, or culture. Christians have been concerned that the Scriptures be translated into the vernacular language of every culture. Also, it is important for Christian worship and liturgy to be in the vernacular so understanding among participants may take place.

versicle   (Lat. *versiculus*, "little verse") A short sentence followed by a brief response, used in worship.

vespers   (From Lat. "evening star") Evening prayer as the liturgy of the church celebrated in early evening within the Roman Catholic, Anglican, and Lutheran traditions. Also called evensong. The orders of worship and liturgies vary.

vessels, sacred   Receptacles and utensils used in the eucharistic service. In the Roman Catholic Church these include chalice, paten, ciborium, pyx, capsula, lunette, and monstrance.

Vestiarian (Vestments) Controversy   Controversy due to the requirement by English bishops sanctioned by Queen Elizabeth I (1588). Clergy were required to wear a cope and surplice as vestments in worship. Many Puritan ministers lost their positions since they considered these as remnants of Romanism.

vestigia Trinitatis   (Lat. "marks of the Trinity") Analogies for the Trinity taken from daily life and experience, an approach rejected by some theologians (such as Karl Barth) as being inadequate and theologically inappropriate.

vestigium Dei   (Lat. "vestige of God") Used to describe the traces of God found in all creatures (except humans), as contrasted to the image of God ("imago Dei") in which humanity was created.

vestments   (Lat. *vestimenta*, from *vestis*, "garment") Garments worn by worship leaders as they lead worship.

vestry   (Lat. *vestiarium*, "a wardrobe," from *vestire*, "to clothe") The place where worship leaders put on their vestments. Also the place where parish business is conducted (Church of England), as well as a name for the collective gathering of church leaders who meet as a council.

Vetus Latina   (Lat. "Old Latin") The Latin translation of the Bible used in the church prior to the Vulgate translation by Jerome (4th century). Early evidence of its existence dates from the 3d century from Tertullian (d. c. 220) and Cyprian (d. 258). A number of manuscripts exist.

via affirmativa   *See: via positiva*

via analogiae   *See* analogy, way of

via antiqua   (Lat. "the old way") A term used for a school of thought in late medieval scholastic theology. Those loyal to the "old way" stressed the older theologians of the High Middle Ages such as Thomas Aquinas (1225–74) and Duns Scotus (c. 1265–1308). It contrasted with the *via moderna.*

via crucis   (Lat. "the way of the cross") Description of the way to the cross that Jesus traveled on his way to be crucified.

via dialectica   (Lat. "the dialectic way") A method of question and answer used to try to establish God's existence.

Via Dolorosa   (Lat. "sorrowful way") The path Jesus walked through Jerusalem from his trial by Pilate to his crucifixion on Golgotha. It now features 14 stations of the cross and is followed as a means of devotion, particularly during Holy Week.

via eminentiae   (Lat. "the way of eminence") A way of speaking about God. It uses analogy to suggest that since humans are made in the image of God it is possible to describe God as possessing, perfectly, qualities found in humans such as love, goodness, and faithfulness. It is also called the *via positiva* ("positive way").

via illuminativa   *See* illuminative way

via media (Lat. "the middle way") Term used to describe the identity of Anglicanism as a middle way between Roman Catholicism and Protestantism. It was coined by John Henry Newman (1801–90) during the Oxford movement.

via moderna (Lat. "the modern way") A term used for a school of thought in late medieval scholastic theology. Those who emphasized the "modern way" followed theologians such as William of Occam (c. 1285–1347) and Gabriel Biel (c. 1420–95). This contrasted with the *via antiqua*.

via negativa (Lat. "the negative way") A way of speaking about God that takes human characteristics and describes God in terms of their opposite, such as: humans are finite; God is infinite.

via positiva (Lat. "the positive way") A way of speaking of God that legitimates the use of human qualities in describing God since humans and God are in relationship through humanity's creation in God's image. Also called the *via eminentiae*.

via purgativa   See purgative way

via unitiva   See unitive way

viaticum (Gr. *ephodion*, Lat. "food for the journey") Term used for the Holy Communion and other rites administered to one near death in preparation for the journey into the next world and eternal life. It is the last sacrament in the Roman Catholic Church. Formerly called last rites.

viator (Lat. "wayfarer," "sojourner") Image for Christians on the journey of life as spiritual wayfarers or pilgrims. While they live in the world they anticipate the future life to come (Heb. 13:14).

vicar (Lat. *vicarius*, "a substitute") One who has authority to act in the place of another. In the Church of England the term is used for a clergyperson who serves a parish as its minister.

vicar, apostolic A Roman Catholic term for a bishop sent to a diocese without a bishop. The term was also used for bishops or archbishops to whom the pope designated part of his jurisdiction.

vicar general A pope's or bishop's ecclesiastical representative who is the chief administrative officer of a diocese. In the Church of England, an appointed lay legal officer who is a deputy for the Archbishop of Canterbury (or York).

Vicar of Christ Roman Catholic term for the pope as the representative of Christ on earth. It has also been used of other bishops in the Roman Catholic tradition.

Vicar of Peter An ancient traditional title for the bishop of Rome (the pope), who functions as the head of the visible church in the apostolic succession originating with the apostle Peter.

vicarage The residence or status of a vicar.

vicarious atonement See atonement, vicarious

vicarious death of Christ See Christ, vicarious death of

vicarious faith (From Lat. *vicarius*, "a substitute") The belief that one might have faith on behalf of another, as for example, parents for children.

vicarious satisfaction See Christ, vicarious death of

vicarship The status, rights, and privileges of a vicar.

vice (Lat. *vitium*, "fault") A self-chosen desire to do that which is wrong, bad, or sinful. The opposite of virtue.

viceregent, Christ as Theological description of the ascended Christ who "sits on the right hand of the Father" and who rules and acts on God's behalf.

vices, the seven See sins, seven deadly

victorious Christian life An evangelical spiritual movement that grew from the Wesleyan/Holiness tradition and teaches the possibility and ways by which one might attain freedom from every known sin.

Vienne, Council of (1311–12) The 15th ecumenical council, called by Pope Clement V (1308), which dealt with questions of heresy, support for the Holy Land, and church reform as well as the theological issues of the passibility of Christ, a definition of the soul, and a defense of infant baptism.

vigil (Lat. *vigilia,* "night spent in watching") Night before a feast day, during which the church would "watch" through the night by prayer and self-examination in preparation for the dawn of the coming day.

Vincentian Canon The prescription of Vincent of Lerins (d. 445) that Christian orthodoxy may be understood as *quod ubique, quod semper, quod ab omnibus creditum est* ("that which has been believed everywhere, always, and by all").

vincible ignorance A term used in Roman Catholic moral theology for an ignorance that results from the failure to acquire information that is important to enable one to avoid sin. It should be able to be removed through ordinary care. It contrasts with "invincible ignorance."

vinculum amoris (Lat. "binding or uniting love") A term from Augustine (354–430) which refers to the Holy Spirit as the bond of love that unites the Father to the Son and the Son to the Father in the Trinity.

Vinegar Bible (1716–17) A Bible printed at Oxford by John Baskett (d. 1742) in which the heading of Luke 20 read: "The Parable of the Vinegar" instead of "The Parable of the Vineyard."

violence (Lat. *violentia*) The use of various kinds of force that inflict harm on individuals or groups. This is a social-ethical issue and raises questions of whether or not the use of violence can ever be morally justifiable from a Christian perspective.

Virgin, assumption of the *See* Mary, Assumption of the Blessed Virgin

virgin birth, the Reference to Jesus as born of the "Virgin Mary" (Matt. 1; Luke 1–2). The virgin birth as a church teaching is found in the Apostles' and Nicene Creeds. Its theological significance has been variously understood. Some have interpreted it literally, others symbolically.

virginal conception of Jesus The belief that Jesus was conceived by the Virgin Mary by the power of the Holy Spirit without a human father involved in conception (Matt. 1 and 2). The term is often used synonymously with the "virgin birth of Jesus."

virginity, perpetual *See* perpetual virginity of Mary

virtual intention A Roman Catholic belief that a sacrament is valid if a priest intends to administer it, even if he is distracted and not focused on the event throughout its administration.

virtualism A view of the Lord's Supper, associated with John Calvin (1509–64), which emphasizes that Jesus Christ is truly present in the Supper and that the virtue or benefits of his death are communicated as those who have faith partake of the elements, which remain as actually bread and wine.

virtue (Gr. *aretē,* "excellence," Lat. *virtus,* "worth") A disposition that creates passions or habits (Lat. *habitus,* "character") which dispose one ethically to do the right thing. The opposite of vice.

virtue, infused In Roman Catholic moral theology, a virtue given directly by God rather than acquired by natural means. Traditionally, the theological virtues (faith, hope, and love) have been considered to be infused directly by God.

virtues (Gr. *aretē,* "excellence"; Lat. *virtus,* "worth") Habits or qualities that are considered to be good according to a moral or religious standard.

virtues, cardinal (From Lat. *virtus,* "strength," and *cardo,* "hinge") The virtues that are the hinges of the Christian moral life: faith, hope, love, prudence, justice, temperance, and fortitude.

virtues, Christian *See* virtues, theological

virtues, the seven *See* virtues, cardinal

virtues, theological Those good habits of thought or will approved by God and characteristic only of those who have received grace. Medieval theologians used the term to describe faith, hope, and love (1 Cor. 13) in contrast with the four natural virtues known by natural law. Collectively these are referred to as the seven virtues.

visible church   The outward, organized church on earth. It was contrasted in the thought of Augustine (354–430) with the "invisible church," the genuine believers in Christ on earth and in heaven.

visible sign   In Augustine's (354–430) view, sacraments are "visible signs of divine things," or "a visible sign of an invisible grace." A sacrament must have both a form of matter ("visible sign"), such as water in baptism or bread and wine in the Lord's Supper, as well as a word of promise or pronouncement that elucidates the divine meaning which is conveyed by the visible sign.

visio Dei   *See* beatific vision

vision, beatific   *See* beatific vision

vision of God   *See* beatific vision

visions   *See* apparitions

Visitation of Mary   The visit of Mary to her cousin Elizabeth when Elizabeth was six months pregnant with John the Baptist (Luke 1:39–56). In the Roman Catholic tradition the Feast of the Visitation is celebrated on May 31.

visitation of the sick   An expectation for followers of Christ (Matt. 25:31ff.). It also refers to a service in the *Book of Common Prayer* used when a clergyperson visits those who are sick.

vita venturi saeculi   (Lat. "the life of the world to come") A way of referring to the future kingdom of God or heaven.

vocabulary   (From Lat. *vocabulum*, "a word") The use of terms to define realities. Feminist writers seek to redefine vocabularies relating to women. This helps shape feminist consciousness.

vocation   (Lat. "a calling"; from *vocare*, "to call") God's calling of persons to be Christians. More specific is the view that God calls persons to certain professions

or ways of life as avenues of Christian service and devotion. No specific vocation is considered superior to others.

vocations   Roman Catholic designations for specific religious callings such as priest, monk, or nun.

voice   (From Lat. *vox*, "a voice") The "speaking" or presentation of thought or feeling. It is used theologically to designate the expressing of views by previously marginalized persons such as the poor or women, who now can make their perspectives known for a fuller life participation.

voluntarism   (Lat. *voluntarius*, "at one's pleasure") Philosophical term coined by Ferdinand Tönnies (1885–1936) to describe the historic view that the will has precedence over the intellect. It is also the theological view that the will of God has primacy over all else and is necessarily good.

voluntary   (Lat. *voluntarius*) A musical piece played by an organist to begin or end a service of worship. In theology and ethics, an act is voluntary if it is free and uncoerced, made on the basis of intellectual knowledge, and proceeds from the will. One is thus responsible for the act.

voluntaryism   (Lat. *voluntarius*, "at one's pleasure") A view of the church and its membership, government, and practice that emphasizes free choice and decision so that churches should be self-supporting and free from state support and control.

votive   (Lat. *votum*, "vow") Originally, referring to a private vow to honor God. In the Roman Catholic tradition it denotes doing something to honor God, a saint, or an aspect of the faith such as lighting votive candles, attending a votive Mass, or making a votive offering.

votive Mass   (From Lat. *votum*, "vow") A Roman Catholic Mass that is provided for a special occasion.

votum   (Lat. "a vow") In Roman Catholic theology, the intention (explicit or implicit) to use the church's sacraments even though one does not have the opportunity to do so. Also, an opinion rendered before action is taken in a cause, usually by a bishop or superior.

vow(s) (Lat. *vovere*, "to vow") That which one has promised, particularly to God or to other persons, that binds one to them. In the Roman Catholic tradition, the entrance to the religious life is marked by vows. Other vows may be made for undertaking specific actions.

vowel points The marking symbols placed under consonants in the Hebrew language indicating distinctive vowel sounds.

Vulgate (Lat. *vulgatus,* "common," "popular") The Latin translation of the Bible produced by Jerome (347–420), made during the years 382–87. It was the common version for the Western church from the 5th to the 16th century and was the basis for the official version in the Roman Catholic Church from the 16th to the 20th century.

wafer (Old Fr. *waufre*) Unleavened bread or cake that is used in the Eucharist in the Roman Catholic Church and that becomes the body of Christ at its consecration by the priest (transubstantiation).

wake (From Lat. *vigilia*, "a keeping awake") A vigil or holiday and today, a parish festival. The term is also used for a period of gathering prior to or after a funeral and before a burial. In the Roman Catholic tradition the service is called the vigil for the deceased.

Waldensians A 12th-century French religious movement of the followers of Peter Waldo (Valdes of Lyons) who preached in Lyons (1170–76) and whose "poor men" lived lives of poverty, simplicity, and evangelism. They were persecuted as heretics by the Roman Catholic Church from 1184.

Walloon Confession *See* Belgic Confession

war Armed conflict between nations. Christians have viewed war in a variety of ways, from pacifism, to the just war, to the crusade.

watch-night service A service introduced by Methodist churches. It is held on New Year's Eve as a preparation for the coming year and as an alternative to the excesses often associated with secular celebrations.

water, holy *See* holy water

waterbuffalo theology Term used by Japanese theologian Kosuke Koyama (b. 1929) to indicate that the Christian faith must be conveyed in terms that are understandable in local cultures. The image of the waterbuffalo is significant for working persons in Asian cultures.

wave offering A prescribed offering of the Jewish religion in biblical times in which bread and boiled meat were waved before the Lord and eaten by priests (Lev. 7:28–34; 23:10–20).

Way, the (Heb. *derek*, Gr. *hodos*) A term for the Christian faith used during the apostolic age (Acts 9:2; 19:9, 23; 22:4; 24:14, 22). It is used biblically to indicate the course of life or choices one makes, as in wisdom literature and in Jesus' teaching (Matt. 7:13–14).

Way International, The A religious group formed in the mid-1950s which denies the divinity of Jesus Christ and believes that speaking in tongues is the genuine worship of God.

ways of the spiritual life   *See* Threefold Way

WCC   *See* World Council of Churches

wealth   Accumulation of things of value. Various views of wealth are found in the Christian tradition ranging from qualified approval to complete rejection. Wealth may be used widely for the good of others (1 Tim. 6:8–9, 17–18) or become an idol (Matt. 6:24; Mark 10:23).

wealth, gospel of   A term derived from the title of an essay by the philanthropist Andrew Carnegie in which he maintained that moral and strong persons grew wealthy while those who are poor are deservedly so. The view, an expression of social Darwinism, helped shape 19th-century American capitalism.

wedding   The ceremony that marks the beginning of a marriage. It is often done in a religious context and, theologically, takes place in the presence of God.

Wee Frees   A popular name for a small number of persons who broke away from the Church of Scotland during the Disruption (1843) and formed the Free Church of Scotland.

Weeks, Feast of   One of the three required annual feasts for male Israelites and one of the first of the two agricultural festivals (Ex. 34:22–23). Its date was seven complete weeks after the harvest season was consecrated.

Weltanschauung   *See* worldview

Wesleyan tradition   The tradition emerging from the teachings of John Wesley (1703–91) emphasizing prevenient grace, freedom of the will, and the possibilities of total sanctification. It is used to characterize Methodism and also aspects of the Church of the Nazarene.

Wesleyanism   The theology based on the views of John Wesley (1703–91), founder of Methodism. Wesley followed the theological views of James Arminius

(1560–1609). Wesleyanism as a distinct theological movement is found within the Methodist, Nazarene, and Wesleyan Church traditions.

Western church   A term for Christianity in the Western world. Also designates Roman Catholicism in distinction from Eastern Orthodoxy, after the division of 1054.

Western Schism   *See* Schism, Great

Western Text   The name for a family of early manuscripts of the Greek New Testament, so designated by the 19th-century biblical scholars B. F. Westcott (1825–1901) and F.J.A. Hort (1828–92). They found these to be of Western origin.

Western theology   Designation for the theological views that have emerged in the Latin (Western) as compared to the Greek (Eastern) churches.

Westminster Assembly (1643–49)   The gathering of Reformed theologians at Westminster Abbey in England at the order of the Long Parliament. 151 members (30 laity) during 1,163 sessions produced the Westminster Standards, which have served as significant doctrinal and governing standards in Calvinistic churches.

Westminster Catechisms   The Larger and Shorter Catechisms as part of the Westminster Standards produced by the Westminster Assembly (1643–49). They served as theological resources for clergy as well as a guide to Reformed understandings of the Christian faith for generations of adults and children.

Westminster Confession of Faith (1646)   An important theological statement written by Calvinists during the English Civil War that became a primary church confession for the Church of Scotland and American Presbyterianism. It was presented to Parliament in December 1646. It is a comprehensive statement that also influenced Congregationalism and some Baptists.

Westminster Standards, the   The documents produced by the Westminster

Assembly (1643–49) including the Westminster Confession of Faith (1646), Larger and Shorter Catechisms (1647), Directory for the Public Worship of God (1644), and Form of Presbyterial Church Government (1645).

Westphalia, Peace of (1648)   The peace accord that marked the end of the political and religious conflicts of the Thirty Years' War in Central Europe (1618–48). It reconfirmed the religious settlement of the Peace of Augsburg (1555), extended legal recognition to Calvinists, and widened freedom of worship.

Whitby, Synod of (663–64)   Church assembly held in Northumbria to discuss differences between the Roman and Celtic groups of English Christians.

Whiteheadian   Views derived from the philosophy of Alfred North Whitehead (1861–1947), associated with process philosophy and theology. His major emphasis was on the evolving nature of reality—its "becoming" as opposed to traditional emphases on its ontological "being." God is also "becoming."

Whitsunday   (Anglo-Saxon *hwita sunnandaeg,* "white Sunday") The seventh Sunday and 50th day after Easter, on which the descent of the Holy Spirit upon the early church (Acts 2) is celebrated as a church festival. It is most commonly called Pentecost Sunday.

Whitsuntide   A period of weeks beginning with Pentecost Sunday (Whitsunday) in the church year.

wholly other   A term derived from Søren Kierkegaard (1813–55), who in his view of divine transcendence spoke of God as "absolutely different" from human reason. In the writings of Karl Barth (1886–1968) and Emil Brunner (1889–1966), God who is so completely different from humans is "wholly other."

wickedness   That which is evil and contrary to the will of God (Gen. 13:13; Isa. 26:10; Mark 7:22; Rom. 2:8).

widows   Women who remained unmarried after the death of their husbands were of special concern in ancient Israel as powerless persons (Ex. 22:22). They were recipients of Christian care by churches (Acts 6:1–3; 1 Tim. 5:3–16).

will   (Lat. *voluntas*) The interior source of power through which choices are made. It is distinct from the intellect.

will, bondage of the   *See* bondage of the will

will, freedom of the   *See* free choice

will of God   (Lat. *voluntas Dei*) The expression of God's desire or intention. It may be considered the "highest good" (Lat. *summum bonum*) of all things and is operative to defeat evil within the universe. Theologians have distinguished different elements for describing the will of God.

willful sin   Those acts or intentions chosen as deliberate expressions of rebellion against the will of God.

wine   (Lat. *vinum*) Fermented juice of grapes used for many purposes. These include as part of life (Ps. 104:14–15), medicinally (Luke 10:34), and as festive drink (John 2:3). Drunkenness was sinful (Isa. 5:11–17; Rom. 13:13). Jesus used wine as a symbol for his blood (Luke 22:20).

wine, eucharistic   Wine that is used in celebrations of the Eucharist or Lord's Supper. A eucharistic prayer of consecration is often offered, Christ's words of institution of the Supper are remembered (1 Cor. 11:23–26), and the wine is distributed to the worshiping congregation.

wisdom   (Gr. *sophia,* Lat. *sapientia*) Knowledge of what is good and true and thus the basis for what is true or false. The term has a long philosophical history, since "philosophy" means "love of wisdom." It is an attribute of God and a gift of the Spirit (Isa. 11:2; Eph. 1:17).

wisdom literature   Old Testament writings that contain practical wisdom for living life in accord with the will of God. These include: Job, Proverbs, Ecclesiastes in the Jewish and Protestant canons of Scripture. The Roman Catholic canon includes in addition Ecclesiasticus and Wisdom of Solomon.

wisdom of God   *See* God, wisdom of

witch   (Old English *wicce,* "wise woman") Witches were traditionally seen as women who conveyed evil. Witches were prosecuted and persecuted by Christians who accused them of heresy. The term is used by some feminist writers in a positive sense in speaking of women goddesses and women's spiritual powers.

witchcraft   The practice of using human powers in concert with demonic forces. Biblically it is condemned (Ex. 22:18; Deut. 18:9–14; Gal. 5:20) as being contrary to the worship of the true God.

witness   (Gr. *martyria*) One who testifies of what is known to be true, especially in relation to the Christian gospel. The image is an important one for those who are "witnesses" to Jesus Christ (John 1:7) and the Christian faith (Acts 1:8; 2:32).

witness of the Holy Spirit   *See* internal testimony (witness) of the Holy Spirit

Wittenberg, Concord of (1536)   An agreement between Lutherans and Zwinglians on the doctrine of the Lord's Supper. It was primarily Lutheran in orientation and did not endure because the Swiss Zwinglians could not ultimately accept it.

Wittgensteinian   Philosophical views of Ludwig Wittgenstein (1889–1951), who engaged in linguistic analysis. He compared the many functions of language to games with their own rules on what is permitted and not permitted to be said and how people actually use language. Usage determines meaning.

womanist theology   Theology as articulated by women of color. It is a way for women to claim their roots, define themselves, embrace and consciously affirm their cultural and religious traditions as well as their own embodiment. A primary concern is for liberation from all forms of oppression.

***Woman's Bible, The* (1895, 1898)**   A Bible produced by Elizabeth Cady Stanton (1815–1902) that followed selections from the King James Version with commentaries. The work highlighted passages concerning women with the intent of overcoming prevailing antiwomen interpretations.

womanspirit   A feminist spiritual philosophy weaving together strands of women's history and mythology, based on belief in the Great Goddess, and advocating studies of astrology, dreams, Yoga, etc.

women in the church, issue of   The question of the roles women may carry out in the church, particularly relating to their ordination as Christian ministers and leaders.

women-church   Term used by feminist writers for the bonds of association and intimacy established by women with each other as alternatives to traditional "churches." It is both a movement and a concept.

women's liberation   An early designation for the movement that sought freedom and equality in all areas of life for women. More generally, the concern for justice for women and women's full participation in society. Women's concerns are the focus for a variety of persons and coalitions.

women's reality   A term for women's experience and ways of perception. Feminist theologians do theology from this reality.

women's rights   Those rights in a society which belong to women. In cases of oppression, women have historically not been accorded the same rights and privileges within a society as men. Women's rights movements have emphasized this. Feminists, both male and female, have maintained the focus.

women's studies   Examination of disciplines from women's perspectives or those subjects focused directly on women's experience. While these exist as discrete forms of studies, a number of intellectual and religious disciplines now have a concern to incorporate women's insights throughout their work.

wonders   A term for miracles that emphasizes their capacity to induce astonishment. A contemporary "Signs and Wonders" movement in various evangelical bodies emphasizes the unexpected and extraordinary workings of God in individual lives.

Word, the   (Gr. *logos*) A designation for Jesus Christ (John 1:1) as the revelation of God. It is also used as a term for Holy Scripture, as well as to describe what is proclaimed in Christian preaching. The power of the Word (Heb. 4:12) to accomplish God's purposes and transform life is clear.

Word and Sacrament, office (ministry) of   A ministerial office in which one is authorized to preach and administer the sacraments in churches. The term is used predominantly in Presbyterian churches.

Word of God   (Heb. *dabar,* "word," "event") God's self-revelation as the incarnate Word (Jesus Christ; John 1:1–14), the written Word (Holy Scripture; Matt. 15:6), and living Word (preaching). The term was virtually synonymous with early Christian proclamation (Acts 4:31; 2 Cor. 2:17; Col. 1:25).

word of pronouncement   In Roman Catholic theology, the formal proclamation that must be made to ensure the efficacy of sacraments.

word of the Lord   A term used especially by Old Testament prophets to indicate that the message they were proclaiming originated from God and was thus God's self-communication for the situation. It is often used liturgically after the reading of the Scripture: "This is the Word of the Lord."

Word-flesh Christology   A theological framework that emerged in the early church for Christology, which began with Jesus Christ as the divine Word who became flesh (human) and took on a human physical nature, but not a human soul.

Word-(hu)man Christology   A theological framework that emerged in the early church for Christology. It taught that Jesus Christ as the second Person of the Trinity took on a full human nature.

words of administration   The words used to accompany the giving of the elements in the Eucharist.

words of institution   (Lat. *verba institutionis,* also *verbum consecratorium,* "word of consecration") The words associated with the establishment of the Lord's Supper in the Scriptures and now uttered when the Eucharist is observed (1 Cor. 11:23–26; cf. Matt. 26:26–29; Mark 14:22–25; Luke 22:14–20).

work   (Gr. *ergon*) In Christian perspective, a means of glorifying and serving God by providing for the needs of others and of society. The Christian understanding of vocation includes God's call to persons to perform labor. In this way they live out their Christian commitments.

work, theology of   The view that daily work can have meaning and significance as a means of glorifying God and fulfilling God's vocational call to service. This has been emphasized in Protestantism and was the subject of the encyclical *Laborem Exercens* ("On Human Work," 1981) by Pope John Paul II.

work of Christ   That which Jesus Christ did during his earthly life and ministry. Theologically the term refers to his death and resurrection, which bring salvation.

work of God, alien   (Lat. *opus alienum*) The work of God that does not seem proper or rightly considered to be God's work in light of divine attributes such as goodness and mercy. An example is the work of God's will in and through the sinner. God's alien work is penultimate to God's "proper work."

work of God, proper   (Lat. *opus proprium*) God's work, such as creation, providence, and grace, that seems consistent with divine attributes such as God's goodness, justice, and mercy. God's proper work is ultimate over God's "alien work." These distinctions were made by medieval and other theologians.

worker priests   A group of over 100 French and Belgian Roman Catholic priests who sought to evangelize alienated Roman Catholic workers by joining the workforce. This experiment was carried out between 1944 and 1954 until it was suppressed by the church as compromising the nature of the priesthood.

works   Theological term referring to actions, whether God's or humans. Theological controversies have centered on the place of works in the process of salvation.

works, covenant of   The view that God established a covenant with Adam through which obedience would lead to eternal life and disobedience to judgment. The view was developed by 17th-century Reformed covenant theology and is found in the Westminster Confession of Faith (1646; chap. 7).

works, good   *See* good works

works of God   (Lat. *opera Dei*) A designation for God's creation and providential preservation of the created order. More generally, the term refers to all God's activities.

works of mercy, the seven   *See* corporeal acts, the seven

works of supererogation   (Lat. *opera supererogationis*) Works beyond those necessary for salvation. In traditional Roman Catholic theology, the view that saints had performed works full of merit that were beyond those required in God's law.

works righteousness   The view that human works can have a status before God and can contribute either fully or partially toward the granting of salvation.

world   In scriptural usage, God's earthly creation, the entire cosmos; or theologically, those powers and forces that oppose God (1 John 2:15–17; 5:4). Yet the

world is where God's work and will are accomplished. It is the arena in which the church's mission and Christian service are enacted.

world come of age   A phrase associated with Dietrich Bonhoeffer (1906–45), who spoke of his contemporary world as one that no longer naturally turned to religion or faith to find answers to questions. Humans operate autonomously and do not require God as a working hypothesis for life.

World Council of Churches (WCC)   Ecumenical body formed in Amsterdam (1948) that brought together worldwide those churches confessing "the Lord Jesus as God and Savior according to the Scriptures." The churches "seek to fulfill together their common calling to the glory of one God, Father, Son, and Holy Spirit."

world evangelism/evangelization   The efforts of Christian churches, groups, and individuals to proclaim the Christian gospel throughout the entire world. It takes many forms, most prominently the mass evangelism of evangelistic crusades, in which thousands of people are brought together for preaching services.

world missions   The efforts of Christian churches, groups, and individuals to carry out the mission given by Jesus Christ throughout the whole world. In Europe, the 19th century was the era in which world missions became an important church focus as well as the purpose for independent missionary societies.

world religions   A 19th-century term for religions that transcend national borders and focus on views of salvation. They include: Judaism, Christianity, Islam, Hinduism, Buddhism, Shinto, and Confucianism/Taoism. Christian attitudes toward the religious pluralism of many faiths vary.

worldliness   A concern for things of "this world." It is used by some to indicate social conditions and culture. Others use it in a negative sense for a too-great concern or identification with the contemporary culture and a too-small concern for seeking the will of God.

worldly holiness   A term used to describe Christian discipleship as marked by a full participation in the world and all its structures and opportunities while maintaining a lifestyle which conveys a vital and vigorous "holiness" or dedication to God and obedience to Jesus Christ.

worldview   (Ger. *Weltanschauung*) One's conceptual way of perceiving reality. The term is sometimes used as the equivalent of philosophy of life, world outlook, ideology, or creed.

Worldwide Church of God   A movement founded by Herbert W. Armstrong (1892–1986) in 1933 as a breakaway from the Seventh-day Adventist Church. The movement accepts Adventism, believes in British Israelitism, stresses tithing and prophecy. It pioneered in mass communication through radio, television, and magazines.

Worms, Colloquy/Disputation of (1540–41)   A brief meeting held at Worms, with Johann Eck (1486–1543) representing Roman Catholicism and Philip Melanchthon (1497–1560) representing Protestantism. Their purpose was to find common theological ground, which they did in their conclusions about original sin.

Worms, Concordat of (1122)   An agreement that ended the investiture controversy. Pope Callistus II and King Henry V agreed that elections for bishops and abbots in Germany would take place in the king's presence and that he would present their scepters.

Worms, Diet of (1521)   Meeting of the German Diet in the city of Worms, in which Martin Luther (1483–1546) was confronted with his writings and ordered to denounce them. He responded: "Here I stand, I can do no other. God help me." Luther was declared an outlaw and hid for ten months in Wartburg castle.

Worms, Synod of (1076)   A synod convened by the emperor Henry IV to defend his claims in the investiture controversy. It condemned Pope Gregory VII and called for his deposition for various crimes. The pope excommunicated the emperor in response.

worship   (From Old English *weorthscipe*, "worth-ship") The service of praise, adoration, thanksgiving, and petition directed toward God through actions and attitudes. Christian worship is Trinitarian in form as praise is offered to God through Jesus Christ by the power of the Holy Spirit.

worship, order of   The sequence of liturgical actions in a service of worship. It is often printed in a "bulletin."

worship, public   The open worship and praise of God by an assembly of Christian believers.

worship, theology of   The theological understandings of worship as the praise and service of God. Worship is central to the Christian life and involves a total response of devotion from believers. It is guided by Scripture and is enabled by the work of the triune God, who alone is to be glorified.

worship service   *See* worship, public

wounds of Christ, the five sacred   The wounds suffered by Christ during his crucifixion. They were in his hands, feet, and side (John 19:34). In the Roman Catholic tradition, devotion to the wounds has centered on a graphic emphasis on Christ's suffering and pains. Reappearing wounds are called "stigmata."

wrath of God   *See* God, wrath of

Writings   *See* Hagiographa

Württemberg Confession (1552)   A 35-article confession of faith drafted by Johann Brenz (1499–1570) to present a Protestant position to the Council of Trent. The articles were Lutheran in orientation and influential in the drafting of the Thirty-nine Articles (1563).

Wycliffe Bible (c. 1384)   The first complete Bible in English was translated under the influence of John Wycliffe (c. 1330–84) by his followers Nicholas of Hereford and (possibly) John Purvey. It circulated in manuscript form and was a translation from the Latin Vulgate.

Wycliffites   *See* Lollards

Yahweh Transliteration of a major Old Testament name for God composed of the Hebrew consonants YHWH and which is usually translated "Lord" in contemporary English versions. The term has also been transliterated as JHVH yielding "Jehovah."

Yahwist The writer of the "Yahwist" (or J) source of traditions in the Pentateuch that are distinguished by the designation "Yahweh" for God.

Yale school of theology *See* New Yale school of theology

year, Christian *See* church year

Yew Sunday A medieval designation for Palm Sunday arising from the practice of carrying yew branches, instead of palms, in liturgical processions.

Yom Kippur *See* Atonement, Day of

Yule A term for Christmas and the festivities surrounding it.

Zealot (Gr. *zēlōtēs*) One who is enthusiastic and determined for a cause. Particularly used of a Jewish nationalistic group which sought revolution in Palestine (A.D. 66–70). Some were disciples of Jesus (Mark 3:18; Luke 6:15). More generally, Jews who rigorously kept the law.

Zion (Heb. "fortress") Used in the Old Testament for all or part of Jerusalem. In both Old and New Testaments it refers to God's heavenly city (Isa. 60:14; Heb. 12:22; Rev.14:1). In the Christian church it is an image for heaven.

Zionism A contemporary movement that seeks to restore the Jewish people to the land of Israel as their historic homeland since biblical times.

Zionism, Christian A Christian movement so designated because of its way of interpreting the Bible, which says that the Jews will be gathered together prior to the return of Jesus Christ (premillennialism). Those who hold this belief have been supportive of the attempts of

Zionism to restore the Jewish people to Israel.

Zurich Agreement (1549) (Lat. *Consensus Tigurinus*) An agreement between John Calvin (1509–64) and Heinrich Bullinger (1504–75) that affirmed a spiritual presence of Christ in the Lord's Supper by the power of the Holy Spirit. It brought Swiss Reformed churches closer together.

Zwickau prophets Anabaptists expelled from Zwickau who came to Wittenberg (1521). They emphasized eschatology, and they rejected infant baptism and the professional ministry. They were forced to leave Wittenberg in 1522.

Zwinglianism The theological views derived from Huldrych Zwingli (1484–1531). In particular, a view of the Lord's Supper which stressed the Supper as a sign of Christian commitment and thus a memorial representation of Christ's death. It does not specifically convey the grace of God.

Works Consulted

Achtemeier, Paul J., ed. *Harper's Bible Dictionary*. New York: Harper & Row, 1985.

Angeles, Peter A. *Dictionary of Christian Theology*. San Francisco: Harper & Row, 1985.

Atkinson, David J., David F. Field, Arthur Holmes, Oliver O'Donovan, eds. *New Dictionary of Christian Ethics and Pastoral Theology*. Downers Grove, Ill.: InterVarsity Press, 1994.

Bowden, John, *Who's Who in Theology*. New York: Crossroad, 1991.

Brauer, Jerald C., ed. *The Westminster Dictionary of Church History*. Philadelphia: Westminster Press, 1971.

Buttrick, George A., ed. *Interpreter's Dictionary of the Bible*. 4 vols. Nashville: Abingdon Press, 1962.

Childress, James F., and John Macquarrie, eds. *The Westminster Dictionary of Christian Ethics*. Rev. ed. Philadelphia: Westminster Press, 1986.

Coggins, R. J., and J. L. Houlden, eds. *A Dictionary of Biblical Interpretation*. Philadelphia: Trinity Press International, 1990.

Crim, Keith, ed. *Interpreter's Dictionary of the Bible, Supplement*. Nashville: Abingdon Press, 1976.

Cross, Frank L., and E. A. Livingstone, eds. *Oxford Dictionary of the Christian Church*. 2d ed. Oxford: Oxford University Press, 1974.

Davies, J. G., ed. *The New Westminster Dictionary of Liturgy and Worship*. Philadelphia: Westminster Press, 1986.

Douglas, J. D., ed. *The New International Dictionary of the Christian Church*. Rev. ed. Grand Rapids: Zondervan Publishing House, 1974.

————. *New 20th-Century Encyclopedia of Religious Knowledge*. 2d ed. Grand Rapids: Baker Book House, 1991.

Douglas, J. D., Walter A. Elwell, and Peter Toon, eds. *Concise Dictionary of the Christian Tradition*. Grand Rapids: Zondervan Publishing House, 1989.

Edwards, Paul, ed. *The Encyclopedia of Philosophy*. 4 vols. New York: Free Press, 1973.

Elwell, Walter A., ed. *Evangelical Dictionary of Theology*. Grand Rapids: Baker Book House, 1984.

Erickson, Millard J. *Concise Dictionary of Christian Theology*. Grand Rapids: Baker Book House, 1986.

Ferguson, Sinclair, David F. Wright, and J. I. Packer, eds. *New Dictionary of Theology*. Downers Grove, Ill.: InterVarsity Press, 1988.

Freedman, David Noel, et al., eds. *The Anchor Bible Dictionary*. 6 vols. Garden City, N.Y.: Doubleday & Co., 1992.

Gehman, Henry Snyder, ed. *The New Westminster Dictionary of the Bible*. Philadelphia: Westminster Press, 1970.

Harvey, Van A. *A Handbook of Theological Terms*. New York: Macmillan Co., 1964.

Hauck, F., and G. Schwinge. *Theologisches Fach- und Fremdwörterbuch*. Göttingen: Vandenhoeck & Ruprecht, 1987.

Hexham, Irving. *Concise Dictionary of Religion*. Downers Grove, Ill.: InterVarsity Press, 1993.

Kauffman, Donald T. *The Dictionary of Religious Terms*. Westwood, N.J.: Fleming H. Revell Co., 1967.

Kelly, Joseph F. *The Concise Dictionary of Early Christianity*. Collegeville, Minn.: Liturgical Press, 1992.

Komonchak, Joseph, et al., eds. *The New Dictionary of Theology*. Collegeville, Minn.: Liturgical Press, 1990.

Lewis, Charlton T., and Charles A. Short. *A Latin Dictionary*. Oxford: Clarendon Press, 1879.

MacGregor, Geddes. *Dictionary of Religion and Philosophy*. New York: Paragon House, 1989.

McBrien, Richard P. *Catholicism*. Rev. ed. San Francisco: HarperSanFrancisco, 1995.

McKim, Donald K., ed. *Encyclopedia of the Reformed Faith*. Louisville, Ky.: Westminster/John Knox Press, 1992.

Muller, Richard A. *Dictionary of Latin and Greek Theological Terms*. Grand Rapids: Baker Book House, 1985.

Musser, Donald W., and Joseph L. Price, eds. *A New Handbook of Christian Theology*. Nashville: Abingdon Press, 1992.

Pfatteicher, Philip H. *A Dictionary of Liturgical Terms*. Philadelphia: Trinity Press International, 1991.

Rahner, Karl, ed. *Encyclopedia of Theology: The Concise Sacramentum Mundi*. Rev. abr. ed. New York: Crossroad, 1975.

Ramm, Bernard. *Handbook of Contemporary Theology*. Grand Rapids: Wm. B. Eerdmans Publishing Co., 1966.

Reid, Daniel G., et al., eds. *Dictionary of Christianity in America: A Comprehensive Resource on the Religious Impulse That Shaped a Continent*. Downers Grove, Ill.: InterVarsity Press, 1990.

Richardson, Alan. *Theological Word Book of the Bible*. New York: Macmillan Co., 1951.

Richardson, Alan, and John Bowden, eds. *The Westminster Dictionary of Christian Theology*. Philadelphia: Westminster Press, 1983.

Russell, Letty M., and J. Shannon Clarkson, eds. *Dictionary of Feminist Theologies*. Louisville, Ky.: Westminster John Knox Press, 1996.

Smith, Jonathan Z., and William Scott Green, eds. *The HarperCollins Dictionary of Religion*. San Francisco: HarperSanFrancisco, 1995.

Wakefield, Gordon S., ed. *The Westminster Dictionary of Christian Spirituality*. Philadelphia: Westminster Press, 1983.

Ziefle, Helmut W. *Dictionary of Modern Theological German*. 2d ed. Grand Rapids: Baker Book House, 1992.